Politics in the United Nations System

Edited by Lawrence S. Finkelstein

Duke University Press

Durham and London   1988

Library of Congress Cataloging-in-Publication Data

Politics in the United Nations system
Includes bibliographies and index.
1. United Nations. I. Finkelstein, Lawrence S.
JX 1977P59   1988   341.23   87-27240
ISBN 0-8223-0804-5
ISBN 0-8223-0820-7 (pbk.)

The important thing in thinking about international affairs
is not to make moral judgments or apportion blame
but to understand the nature of the forces at work
as the foundation for thinking about what, if anything,
can be done.

George F. Kennan

Contents

●

Foreword

●

It was Socrates, when speaking about individuals, who told his judges that the unexamined life was not worth living. That same principle might be applied to public institutions. A transnational or intergovernmental organization that does not examine its viability will not be able to adjust to the flow of history and will not be worthwhile.

At the age of forty-two, the United Nations is undergoing serious self-examination. Individuals, governments, high-level experts, and, importantly, scholars are assessing the purpose, direction, and the role of the World Organization. Its harshest critics seem outraged that the United Nations is imperfect. Its most vocal supporters ask for it to change faster. This volume is a part of the Socratic examination of the life of the United Nations system, and, as such, it makes a valuable contribution.

Existence, Aquinas argued, precedes essence. The existence of the United Nations system cannot be questioned; what is at issue is its essence. The history of international organizations over the last two hundred years—from the Concert of Europe, to the Hague Conferences, to the League of Nations, to the United Nations—has convinced the world's leaders of the need for an international organization of the scope of the United Nations. As has often been said, if the United Nations did not exist, it would have to be created. What must concern us is the essence of the World Organization, its role and purposes.

One role that the United Nations has always had, and which it continues to have, is what one essayist in this volume refers to as "value allocation." Through debates, international treaties, and international conferences, the Organization has been able to bring to prominence—that is, to allocate high value to—the most critical ideas that must be of concern to governments. That role needs to grow even stronger as the Organization remains ready to provide international machinery that can deal effectively with global concerns.

The United Nations has, for example, done much to enable nations to address such issues as conflict resolution, human rights, and disarmament, to name only a few. If we look at the conflict in the Middle East, a situation that has concerned the World Organization almost since its inception, Security Council Resolutions 242 (1967) and 338 (1973) remain the soundest basis for fruitful negotiations on a durable solution to the problems of that region. Similarly, Security Council Resolution 598 1987 has established the basis agreed to by all members of the Security Council to end the tragic conflict between Iran and Iraq. The Universal Declaration of Human Rights, together with the other human rights Conventions adopted by the United Nations, set enduring standards for the world community that are universally accepted.

In conjunction with the decolonization process, in which the United Nations has played a crucial role, development has been accorded high importance since most of the newly independent nations were economically underdeveloped. More recently, it has become evident that there is a triangular relationship among disarmament, economic development, and international security, so that the need for disarmament has assumed a new dimension. Only last year, in fact, the United Nations held an international conference on the relationship between disarmament and development, in which international security was also given major attention.

The fact that major disarmament negotiations are now taking place outside the United Nations, on a bilateral basis between the Soviet Union and the United States—a process wholeheartedly endorsed by the United Nations—does not mean the Organization played no role in bringing about those negotiations. As one essayist in this volume states, one must distinguish between "output" and immediate "effects." The output of United Nations decisions can be significant even if they do not produce effects that are immediately evident. On disarmament issues the Organization has certainly helped to mobilize public opinion in favor of disarmament. But it has also had consequent "effects," since almost all the arms limitation agreements that have been reached in the postwar period have emerged from the disarmament negotiating forum of the United Nations.

Much attention in recent years has been focused on administrative and budgetary matters in the Organization. Measures are now being implemented to increase efficiency and effectiveness. This process is necessary to ensure that the United Nations can meet the needs of the governments and peoples of the world whose confidence and support are essential for the achievement of United Nations objectives.

The United Nations must be sensitive to the wisest ideas and counsel that the intellectual community of the world has to offer. It must become a vehicle through which intellectual resources and practical experience can be integrated for the benefit of all humanity. It must provide, through its various agencies, an accessible arena for dynamic concepts—for dialogues with practitioners and academicians in the many fields relevant to United Nations endeavors. The authors of this volume have made a valuable contribution to that dialogue, one which merits wide attention.

Javier Pérez de Cuéllar
Secretary-General of the United Nations

Preface

●

As it entered its fifth decade the United Nations' attainment of middle age was widely acknowledged, but not as widely celebrated. The General Assembly's fortieth anniversary proceedings evoked what has been termed "the largest gathering of world leaders in history."[1] Yet while some came to praise, many came to doubt. There were even grounds for wondering whether some may have come to bury this institutional Caesar.

To say that the United Nations in its forties has been having a midlife crisis is not too extreme. Yet there is more reason than not to expect that the organization will continue. The Reagan administration, which had been among the doubters and which some had thought a potential gravedigger, showed signs of revived commitment to support of the UN after the 41st Session of the General Assembly in 1986 adopted reforms favored by the United States and other Western members. Even earlier the United States, while making no bones about its very public role as a vigorous critic of the UN, asserted its commitment "to stick with it"[2] in a statement designed to counter uncertainty on that point generated by the U.S. withdrawal from UNESCO at the end of 1984 and the then-virulent congressional campaign to escape distasteful obligations imposed by UN decisions.[3]

Besides, the UN has survived major crises in the past, including the memorable session of the General Assembly in 1964 when no votes could be taken about issues on the agenda for fear that doing so would blow the organization apart. It has already existed more than twice as long as its predecessor and model, the League of Nations. In its forties the UN confronts no present or foreseeable world crisis to undermine its foundations, as Nazi and Japanese aggression did to the League in the 1930s. This is true even though the UN's Secretary-General, Javier Pérez de Cuéllar, discerns in the world "new phenomena alien to the relatively orderly world of sovereign governments about which the United Nations Charter was written."[4]

The crisis of the United Nations is a crisis of confidence. Secretary-General Pérez de Cuéllar has recently said that "between the massive weaponry of the nuclear powers on the one hand, and the desperation of the underprivileged on the other, there lies a great vacuum of legitimate and respected international authority."[5] He implied that the central issues of the United Nations concern its place in filling that vacuum. In saying that "the United Nations simply must be made to succeed," he directed attention to the question of the United Nations' utility as a source of "legitimate and respected international authority."

The UN's role as a "legitimate and respected authority" has very much concerned the foreign policy leaders of the United States and of other countries—Israel notably among them—which have seen their interests jeopardized by UN decisions taken under the majority procedures of the organization. U.S. Ambassador Jeane Kirkpatrick had that role in view when she testified that: "To an extent greater than often realized, what occurs at the United Nations involves central issues of world politics and frequently touches upon vital U.S. national goals and interests."[6] In acknowledging the importance of the United Nations as a political institution Ambassador Kirkpatrick was not expressing satisfaction with the organization, which was then approaching its fortieth anniversary. On the contrary her remarks were more a cry of anguish over the strain in relations between the United States and the organization it had done so much, with such high hopes, to bring into being after World War II. Anguish showed in the extraordinarily candid admission of Secretary of State Shultz to an American audience that the United States had in the past "failed to take the United Nations seriously," that "disillusionment . . . had led us, in a sense, to withdraw," and that, as a result, the United States had failed "to take part in the 'party system' that was developing inside the United Nations."[7] He went on to say that the United Nations "has a unique influence on global perceptions. The United Nations defines, for much of the world, what issues are and are not important and of global concern."

That the relationship between the United States and the UN is in a parlous state is further attested by:

various U.S. actions to withhold fund payments called for by decisions of the General Assembly;
congressional insistence that financial assessments be linked to voting power;
widespread frictions over "politicization" of supposedly technical agencies;
a variety of congressional initiatives to restrict U.S. participation;
withholdings of dues payments to UNESCO and the International Labor Organization (ILO);
temporary withdrawal from the ILO, capped by the definitive termination of membership in UNESCO at the end of 1984.

The malaise does not affect only the United States. Britain withdrew from UNESCO at the end of 1985. So did Singapore.[8] There are persistent indicators that other Western countries—the Federal Republic of Germany, Japan, Belgium, Denmark, and the Netherlands among them—might also move toward withdrawing from UNESCO.[9] The less-developed countries (LDCs) and the members of the Non-aligned Movement (NAM), which comprise a large voting majority in UN agencies, have also been frustrated by their inability to convert votes into new rules of equity.

There is friction in the gears that connect members to the UN and other agencies in the UN system. This volume assumes that disagreement over the legitimacy to be accorded the authority of the UN and other agencies comprising the UN system is a main source of the friction. Empirically there undoubtedly is struggle over this issue. It centers particularly on efforts to exert and extend such authority and on how it is exercised. In other words the friction results from the nature and conduct of politics in the UN system. The politics represents the predominant discord and occasional convergence among the member states, which view the international problems of our times through the lenses of geographic, historical, ideological, religious, and ethnic diversity.

Except for the introduction and conclusion the chapters that follow are case studies. They ask how politics in the UN have changed over the forty years of the system's existence. They take account of institutional differences among the agencies in the system, the functions they perform, and the roles of the relevant actors. Shedding further light on the evolving nature of politics in the UN system may be helpful in the difficult adjustments that are required if the frictions are not to burn out the gears of national interactions with international bodies.

Notes

1. Elaine Sciolino, "Taking Sides, Not Transcending Them, at the U.N.," *New York Times Week in Review*, October 20, 1985, 4E.

2. Secretary George Shultz, "The United Nations after Forty Years: Idealism and Realism," address before the United Nations Association of San Francisco, the San Francisco Chamber of Commerce, and the World Affairs Council of Northern California, June 26, 1985. *State Department Bulletin* 85, 2101 (August 1985): 20.

3. This has been termed "nullification," a reference to John C. Calhoun's doctrine before the U.S. Civil War, asserting that South Carolina had a constitutional right not to be bound by—that is, to nullify—national decisions of which it did not approve. See Lawrence S. Finkelstein, "Forty Years of the United Nations: From the Multilateral Diplomacy of Sovereign Equality toward the Politics of Value Allocation," paper presented to the workshop on the UN at forty during the annual meeting of the International Studies Association, Atlanta, Georgia, March 1984, 6–7; and Ronnie W. Faulkner and Michael M. Gunter, "The New Relevancy of an Old Philosophy: Ambassador Moynihan's 'Calhounian' Strategy at the United Nations," paper prepared for delivery at the 1986 annual meeting of the American Political Science Association, the Washington Hilton, August 28–31, 1986.

4. Javier Pérez de Cuéllar, "The UN Simply Must Be Made To Succeed," *New York Times Week in Review*, October 20, 1985, 21E.

5. Ibid.

6. Ambassador Jeane J. Kirkpatrick, "U.S. Participation in the United Nations," statement before the Subcommittee on Foreign Relations of the Senate Appropriations Committee, March 2, 1984, in *State Department Bulletin* 84, 2085 (April 1984): 68–69.

7. Shultz, "The United Nations after Forty Years," 3–4. The UN has been termed "a dangerous place" in two recent books about the UN. See Daniel Patrick Moynihan, *A Dangerous Place* (New York: Berkley Books, 1980), and Abraham Yeselson and Anthony Gaglione, *A Dangerous Place: The United Nations as a Weapon in World Politics* (New York: Grossman, 1974). See also the article by Assistant Secretary of State for International Organization Affairs Alan L. Keyes, "Fixing the UN," *The National Interest* (Summer 1986): 12–23; and Burton Y. Pines, "Introduction," in *A World without a U.N.*, ed. Burton Y. Pines (Washington, D.C.: The Heritage Foundation, 1984), xvi.

8. Singapore distinguished the grounds for its withdrawal from those given by the United States and the United Kingdom. It said that membership in UNESCO did not produce benefits for Singapore commensurate with the costs of belonging.

9. See, for example, Barthold C. Witte, "UNESCO—Crisis and Reform," *Aussen Politik* 35, 3 (Autumn 1984): 262–71; and Chester E. Finn, Jr., "The Rationale for American Withdrawal," *Comparative Education Review* 30, 1 (February 1986): 146.

Acknowledgments

●

This is evidently a collaborative work and it is with sincere pleasure and gratitude that the editor acknowledges the helpful and effective collaboration of the authors represented within these covers. Without it, there could have been no book.

All but two of the chapters were first given as papers in a series of panels organized by the editor at national and regional meetings of the International Studies Association, under the auspices of its International Organization Section. Robert S. Jordan was chair of the section then, and his help was as generous as it was indispensable.

The quality of the work has benefited no little bit from the comments of the two reviewers for Duke University Press. To Professor Jack Donnelly of the University of North Carolina, as well as the reviewer who remains anonymous, sincere thanks are owed and hereby tendered.

The Department of Political Science at Northern Illinois University has been helpful in more ways than it knows, unless it is more careful than I believe in monitoring its telephone and materials budgets. Above all, however, it made available the services of helpful graduate assistants, Graham Shephard and Zhu Liang. To the two of them I proffer thanks which cannot suffice. Zhu Liang, particularly, labored beyond the call of duty in preparing the indexes. His primary reward has to be the satisfaction of a job well done.

Working with an old friend has been a satisfaction of the relationship with the publisher, Duke University Press. My thanks are given to Dick Rowson, Director of the Press, for having greased the ways to ease and facilitate the launching of our joint product. Bob

Mirandon has been a compassionate and efficient editor and he has managed the services of a helpful crew of copy editors, designers, and others whose work behind the scenes enabled the book to emerge on schedule. Thanks go to all.

Most important, Non's patience in abiding the perversities of a distracted and beleaguered author and editor and in providing the psychological and logistic support on which the enterprise has depended can only be insufficiently acknowledged here.

Lawrence S. Finkelstein
LaGrange, Illinois
November 1987

1

The Politics of Value Allocation

in the UN System

Lawrence S. Finkelstein

●

The Concept of Politics in the UN System

This chapter sets the stage for the examination of UN politics in the chapters that follow. It adopts a modified version of David Easton's now-axiomatic definition of politics as the authoritative allocation of values for the society. Easton's definition could be understood to require that, to be considered political, an activity has to succeed in allocating values definitively. But this requirement would be an absurdity. To define politics in this way would exclude conflict or struggle over values when definitive allocative consequences do not occur. Politics, however, evidently involves attempts to allocate values when the attempts fail as well as when they succeed. This principle holds true for decisionmaking bodies in the UN system as much as for domestic governing organs. Therefore this study considers UN politics as an activity that is concerned with the authoritative allocation of values in the UN system.[1] "Authority"[2] for this purpose is legitimate—that is, it is accepted by those to whom it applies.

If politics is thus about struggle over authoritative outcomes, then a great deal of what goes on in the UN system is well described as political. The relevant actors in UN bodies—diplomats representing their governments, representatives of international nongovernmental organizations, members of the international agencies' staffs and the executive heads—devote considerable effort, energy, time, and ingenuity to shaping what the agencies decide and do.

Easton's definition of politics emphasizes allocation of "values." This term is often understood to mean the higher aspirations of society. Certainly struggle over such values goes on in the UN system. To prove this statement it is necessary only to refer to the major, often lengthy, imbroglios that have occurred in UN bodies over such principles as self-determination, economic equity, human rights, freedom of information, security, and territorial integrity. Yet to confine the notion of politics to struggle over such issues seems too limiting, because a great deal of obvious politics in the UN system has to do with allocation of other disputed outcomes, such as material costs and benefits, specific rules, and—as has already been suggested—allocative authority itself, or power in the system. Since its purpose is to gain a better understanding of politics in the UN system, this book will extend the concept of politics beyond Easton's so that it covers whatever ends the actors pursue in UN bodies. This book will thus be concerned with understanding the allocation of whatever is sought by the relevant actors in the UN system.

The objectives sought by the actors may be material—for example, money, raw materials, or territory—or not—for example, principle, status, power, or legitimacy. Such objectives are not limited to what has been called "high politics."[3] The objectives may be ultimate— the ends sought by the actors—or intermediate, or instrumental— the means seen as relevant to the attainment of desired ends. In some cases what actors struggle over is both an end and a means, as is true of elections to prestigious positions, which give status but which also convey influence in the struggle over ends. In this broad sense politics is to be found in all the decision categories of the typology presented in the important study by Cox and Jacobson, *The Anatomy of Influence:* representational, symbolic, boundary, programmatic, rule-creating, rule-supervisory, and operational.[4] It deserves emphasizing that extending Easton's definition to cover any objective of the actors in the UN leads to a very broad definition of politics. Doing so seems warranted, however, because the actors in the UN system struggle over many kinds of outcomes that the system allocates. Beginning to understand what is going on may thus require casting a very wide net.

Including the instrumental objectives of the actors in the UN system is especially important because it calls attention to differences over the legitimation of symbols, norms, or principles as means to be employed in the continuing struggle over material or higher ends and in the effort to achieve rules that definitively allocate values. Conceiving of politics in this way helps to explain the intensity of struggles over verbal formulas, such as the question of whether "self-determination" is a rule or merely a "principle," the standards of the New International Economic Order (NIEO) and of the New World Information and Communication Order (NWICO), and the content of the Universal Declaration of Human Rights and other nonbinding international resolutions, recommendations, or declarations. In this perspective symbolic formulations and declaratory assertions are not mere "verbiage" to be dismissed as insignificant because they are not immediately effective, but are rather instrumental objectives that are significant because of their employment in continuing political campaigns over ends. Secretary Shultz and Ambassador Kirkpatrick were right in believing that UN agency decisions affect important national interests of members.[5] The "legitimacy" of majority endorsement is employed as an instrument of influence.

The UN system, like other international organizations, poses issues about the nature of politics that differ from those of centralized governments. UN agencies exist in the international system, in which there is presumed to be no hierarchy of decision. The "horizontally organized" system of sovereign states endows each sovereign member with the ability to block a decision that requires its agreement by withholding its consent. Such a system resembles what Morton Kaplan, in a different context, termed a "unit veto" system.[6] The League of Nations Covenant mirrored this understanding of the nature of the international order by requiring unanimity for decisions by the Assembly and the Council. In the contemporary UN system the understanding is represented by the general rule that what UN bodies decide cannot bind members unless they consent to be bound, with constitutionally specified exceptions to which the members have given their consent by accepting membership in the first place.

Thus the norm of the international system is that authoritative allocation of what states value—the "politics" of this book—requires the consent of the states affected by the allocative decision. This norm is synonymous with what we have traditionally known as diplomacy, or the conduct of relations among sovereign states. Diplomacy is unit veto international politics. According to this norm international organizations ought to be artifacts of diplomacy. In this view intergovernmental organizations (IGOs) are means to enable states to have diplomatic relations that otherwise would be too complicated, or even impossible, to manage in the traditional modes of diplomacy. IGOs in this sense are conveniences of diplomacy.

Yet it is striking that in the UN system many decisions are constitutionally taken by voting. On the face of it voting to reach decisions is inconsistent with the systemic norm associated with sovereignty described in the preceding paragraphs. Unmistakably, many conflicts among states over their objectives are decided by votes, following majority rules. Valued consequences are allocated this way. Many, perhaps most, UN agency decisions derive their authority from majority votes. Even when voting does not occur, when decisions are arrived at by consensus, for example, they emerge in a constitutional context that makes voting available as the means of decision. Thus politics in UN agencies assumes a form that resembles the methods of politics we are accustomed to in domestic, hierarchically organized political systems, as well as the diplomatic kind of politics the systemic norm leads us to expect to prevail. Obviously these two kinds of politics differ greatly from each other in their effects on the interests of member states and in their implications for the nature of the international system. As to the latter it may not be too far-fetched to speculate that the widespread rule that decisions should be made by majority votes might in the long run deal a mortal blow to sovereignty as the basis of the international order.

The difference between the two modes of politics is unquestionably important. For one thing, a great deal of bitter dispute occurs in UN agencies over the binding effect to be given majority decisions. Majorities—such as, in recent years, the large group of less-developed countries (LDCs) comprising the Group of 77 (G-77)—seek to employ the voting rules as instruments of real power. These groups want majority decisions to be binding. Minorities, such as the industrially developed countries led in recent years by the United States, emphasize the norms of traditional sovereignty. Such disputes can accurately be termed struggles over the nature of effective power in international organizations, or over what comprises authoritative allocation. One form this struggle has taken in recent years has been reliance on consensus procedures as a means of assuaging the concerns of minorities that their sovereign rights will be trampled by "tyrannical" majorities. Resort to consensus is a barrier erected in the struggle over allocative authority. It is a pragmatic device to protect the sovereign interests of states in the minority and also to buffer the system of sovereignty against the pressures of majority processes. It seeks to emphasize bargaining in the traditional diplomatic mode over voting in the political mode. The ultimate outcome of the struggle over allocative authority is not now predictable.

Politics in the UN system may thus be depicted as falling along a spectrum from decisions that depend for their authority on the consent of member states to those that do not—usually because authority stems from majority votes. In between the extremes lies the interesting zone of struggle over whether decisions can be taken by majorities or whether every member's consent is required. Because decision power is dispersed among numerous individual actors in the consent, or unit veto, system, it is termed "decentralized" to distinguish it from the more "centralized" system of decision by majorities.[7] At the far centralized end of the spectrum are decisions by executive heads and staffs of agencies when they allocate objectives contested by members without any votes being taken.

The spectrum of the politics of value allocation in the UN system is shown in the following diagram:

| Decentralized unit veto | ⟷ | Intermediate zone of struggle over author- itative allocation | ⟷ | Centralized decisions |

The diagram deliberately does not delimit the zones. Their boundaries are not determinate. The processes involved are not static; instead, as will be shown, they are dynamic. Examining these processes is a primary purpose of this volume.

At the outset of the UN era the UN system was seen as preeminently a system of multilateral diplomacy lacking centralized authority and rooted in inherited and traditional concepts of states as sovereign, immune to the effects of decisions to which they did not consent.[8] Even so, some centralized authority existed from the beginning, such as the compulsory assessment powers given to the General Assembly in Article 17 of the UN Charter and the plenary organs of specialized agencies in comparable constitutional provisions. The powers given to the UN Security Council to take enforcement measures under Chapter VII of the UN Charter, coupled with the requirement of Article 25 that members carry out Security Council decisions, seemed an unusually great centralization of power. But, as is well known, such Security Council decisions depend on the "concurring votes of the permanent members,"[9] the so-called veto power. Thus the Security Council arrangement was a hybrid—a unit veto for the Big Five countries, whose consent was deemed essential to the working of the security system, but a high degree of centralization from the perspective of all other members. Selection of the executive heads of UN agencies was to be by majority decisions, except that the UN arrangement was again hybrid because of the requirement that a Security Council recommendation, subject to Great Power veto, precede majority decision by the General Assembly.[10] Admission of new members is ordinarily by two-thirds majorities, but the UN again is hybridized.[11] Election of judges to the International Court of Justice requires majorities in both the UN General Assembly and the Security Council, but with no veto operating in the latter.[12] Elections to subordinate bodies were to be by majority votes, although in the case of the UN elections to the Security Council, Economic and Social Council, and Trusteeship Council were to be by two-thirds majorities of those present and voting.[13] Internal matters involved no vetos.

With the passage of time there has been movement in both directions along the spectrum. Some powers found in the original constitutional instruments have atrophied. For example, the binding authority given to the Security Council has vanished in practice. The hypothesis of this book, however, is that the predominant movement on the spectrum has been from required consent toward majority procedures. In part this shift has resulted from the exploitation of constitutional authority and from the discovery and use of implicit powers, such as the power to decide on programs and to create new organizations by majority votes.[14] The hypothesis does not imply that the evolution is completed. Recent struggle in the intermediate zone provides cogent evidence that such movement is not necessarily irreversible. The hypothesis does imply that there is a new mix between the original decentralized system, with authority found in the consent of each member state, and the later centralizing tendencies to find authority in majority conclusions.

The idea that there is a dynamic mix between the two types of political processes implies that they may be unevenly distributed throughout the system. Not only may different agencies follow different patterns in reaching decisions but such differences may exist between organs within the same agency, as was obviously intended to be the case between the UN Security Council and General Assembly, for example. Even the same organ may behave differently depending on the issues on the agenda. The rest of this chapter outlines only some of the questions that are relevant to making such comparisons of the political modes followed in the UN system.

Political Objectives in the UN System

The objectives of politics in the UN system encompass both ends and means. The ends sought span the range of subject matter that the agencies deal with; they also span all the kinds of things that the agencies do. The latter are usefully delineated in the Cox-Jacobson typology of functions that international agencies perform, referred to previously.

Members want outcomes that serve their interests in: security against external threat; disputes over territorial limits; affirmations of the legality of their behavior and condemnations of the behavior of adversaries; promulgation of norms and rules; funds; technical assistance; autonomy from external intervention in their affairs, changes in the domestic practices of others that adversely affect their interests, or conflict with the principles they espouse; recognition; status; and international positions for their nationals. The list is virtually endless and infinitely varied. The politics of international organizations thus coincides in scope and complexity with the ends of the member states. Moreover, as has already been suggested, the actors conflict over means to their ends. Some means double as ends, such as status, legitimacy, and access to the international processes.

The complexity does not end there, however. So far this section has assumed that the actors are the states that comprise the memberships of the UN agencies. Other actors are important too—nongovernmental organizations, international organizations, their executive heads and staffs, and, notably for this purpose, parts of governments interacting with each other and with sectors of the international organizations in what has been called "transgovernmental relations."[15] Insofar as the latter involves parts of national organizations, whether governmental or nongovernmental, their ends may relate as much to objectives being contested at home as to ends directly at issue in the international system. The international objectives sought in such cases may be instrumental to the desired domestic consequences. The boundary between international and domestic politics becomes very permeable.[16]

Calling attention to the diversity of objectives contested in UN agencies points to questions about whether differences among them lead to differences in political processes and to different kinds of outcomes. Only some of the more important questions can be dealt with in this chapter. One question, however, is how the salience of what is at stake to the actors affects the politics.

Salience

The more salient issues are to governments,[17] the more important they feel it is that they do not lose control over decisions affecting what they have at stake. Such governments resist decisions by majority rule. They also are uncomfortable with decisions by agency executive heads or staffs, an advanced form of centralization of decision in the system at the outermost end of the spectrum shown in the preceding diagram.

Special voting arrangements are intended to provide assurance to members with especially high stakes in the issues that they cannot lose control of decisions about them. The veto in the UN Security Council is such an arrangement,[18] as are the weighted voting provisions that prevail in the World Bank and the International Monetary Fund.[19] A more recent case is the formula of the International Maritime Satellite Organization (INMARSAT), which weights voting by financial contributions.[20] Special voting arrangements like these have been devised to protect the interests of the states that believe they have the most at stake, because they are the richest, technologically most advanced, or militarily the strongest, and thus have the greatest interest in the decisions that the organizations make, the most to risk, and the heaviest responsibilities in the system.

However, the salience of issues on UN agendas has been growing for the G-77 countries as well. They attach salience not only to issues affecting their international economic benefits but also their autonomy, power, and status in the UN system. One result has been the introduction of special voting arrangements in some agencies since the weight of G-77 numbers has come to be felt in the system. In recent cases the voting rules have been designed to ensure at least blocking control to the LDCs as well as to other groups in the organization. An example is the scheme of weighting by groups in the International Fund for Agricultural Development (IFAD).[21] A comparable result is obtained in the United Nations Industrial Development Organization (UNIDO) through the allocation of seats in the Program and Budget Committee, an arrangement that in effect gives a disguised veto over program and budget decisions to the less-developed countries when they have voting cohesion.[22]

Thus, increasingly, salience has come to cut both ways in North-South relations in the UN system. Struggle in the intermediate zone has resulted. In one form it has led to the kind of rules to share control referred to in the preceding paragraph. Another form has been emphasis on what appear to be "diplomatic" modes of decision, such as the "conciliation procedure" of the United Nations Conference on Trade and Development (UNCTAD)[23] and consensus procedures that have assumed increasing importance widely throughout the system,[24] including UNCTAD.[25] A third form has been effort to revise particular decision rules to protect the states that claim to have most at stake in the decision categories against domination by voting majorities. For the United States under the Reagan administration, for example, agency expenditures became an issue of high salience. One result was the reduction of U.S. financial contributions to the UN mandated by the Kassebaum Amendment. Such pressure from the U.S. led the UN General Assembly in 1986 to strengthen the budget-controlling function of the Committee on Program and Coordination (CPC) and, by providing that decisions should be by consensus, the control of the main contributors within the committee. Another case involved UNESCO. There the United States failed in its effort in 1984 to alter the voting rules in the Executive Board with respect to budget and other important decisions.[26] In 1987 the United States was moving in the same direction outside the UN system. It was, for example, seeking to restructure the voting procedures in the Inter-American Development Bank (IDB) "so that representatives of member countries which provide the vast bulk of the Bank's usable resources can exercise more authority over loan quality."[27]

The salience of activities in the UN system thus seems to have been growing for a broadening circle of member states and has been intensifying for key members, including the United States. Judging by the decision procedures that emphasize control by members, the movement has been from centralized toward more decentralized decision procedures.

This movement is not the whole story, however. Cox and Jacobson have pointed out that the actors' self-serving interests in an issue on the agenda—their "stakes"—may be countered by the importance they attach to finding an international solution.[28] Resolving a dispute or crisis or assuring that a problem is dealt with may prove more important to states in the end than persistence in defending their positions against the demands of others with interests at stake. Agreement reached this way involves what has been called "policy coordination,"[29] which, as Keohane has shown, can be a form of self-interest pursued by states in the "self-help" international system.[30] In such cases agreement is often reached diplomatically— that is, with the consent or at least acquiescence of all those whose collaboration is required. Sometimes, however, the decision processes are centralized, or have components of centralization. And the international solution to the problem may involve centralized authority to act subsequently.

Components of centralization in both the process and the solution characterized the creation of the United Nations Emergency Force (UNEF) as the instrument for dealing with the Suez Canal crisis of 1956. What was at stake in that crisis was surely of very highest salience for the principal actors. Yet the history of the crisis does not altogether support the hypothesis that only a unit veto process is compatible with high salience of the issues.

For one thing, although the solution that was reached had to have the consent of all the main actors, a central component of the agreement to create UNEF was Egypt's very reluctant consent to allow UNEF to be stationed on its territory. Egypt had a veto, but was persuaded not to cast it. Its consent, in the final analysis, although not coerced can hardly be described as "voluntary"; it was induced. Egyptian President Gamal Abdel Nasser was persuaded to agree to what he had strongly resisted at the outset. This agreement occurred in a marathon negotiating session with UN Secretary-General (Syg) Dag Hammarskjöld, who wielded the authority of the United Nations and represented the desire of its members that a solution be found for the crisis.[31] In this crucial negotiation Egypt negotiated with the executive head of the United Nations rather than with other vitally interested states alone, as the hypothesis about salience would lead us to expect.

Moreover, throughout the affair it was apparent that Hammarskjöld exercised extraordinary authority in shaping the solution, particularly as it involved the United Nations force. Finally, in this instance, the member states delegated extraordinary authority to the Secretary-General to direct UNEF throughout its life. Virtually unilaterally Hammarskjöld set the ground rules for the design and conduct of UNEF, which became the model for subsequent UN peace-keeping operations. The Secretary-General was the commanding general of UNEF, its political guide, and the UN's primary diplomatic agent in managing the affairs of UNEF for the eleven years that it helped stabilize the Egyptian-Israeli border. When the time came the decision to withdraw UNEF was taken by Secretary-General U Thant on his own authority.

Thus centralized authority of a far-reaching character was compatible in the Suez-UNEF case with the high salience of the issues. To be sure, Hammarskjöld's authority was always confined within the broad limits of what the interested parties would accept. Yet he was not without leverage in moving those limits. Basically the Secretary-General's latitude derived from the fact that the states with power to obstruct could agree only that the threat to the peace in the Middle East and in the world had to be contained and could not agree on much more than that. The source of his latitude was to be found in the relatively wide interstices of agreement among the powers. At least, this was a blurred outcome for the salience hypothesis.

Later, in the Congo case, another UN force was set up. ONUC (from the French, *Opération des Nations Unies aux Congo*) involved comparable leadership and latitude for the Secretary-General. In this case the Syg commanded an army that actually engaged in substantial combat operations. Again authority was found in the interstices of agreement among the main actors after the original convergence of purpose among the relevant powers gave way to disagreement. At one critical juncture the Soviet Union lacked the resources to obstruct by intervening in the field or by commanding dominant political influence in New York. It could not wield a veto in the UN General Assembly because its support was not indispensable. The sequel, the "financing crisis" of 1964–65, demonstrated that Soviet powerlessness was not a permanent feature of UN peace-keeping decisions. Yet later Secretaries-General and key Secretariat members have exercised considerable authority in the management of peace-keeping operations in the persistent interstices of governmental agreement.[32]

Moreover, many peace-seeking roles that would have been conducted by committees of states in the early days of the UN have come to be handled over the years by executive heads of international agencies—especially the UN Secretary-General—or under their authority. Recent examples include the go-between function of Secretary-General Pérez de Cuéllar's representative in the Afghanistan war and the direct involvement of the Syg himself in the dispute between France and New Zealand over the *Rainbow Warrior* affair in the form of a "ruling" he handed down in July 1986.[33]

The subsequent chapters in this book present examples of comparable developments with respect to other issues of high salience to states, cases in which states seeking solutions to urgent and/or important problems have resorted to centralized means of getting the job done. Often the centralized mechanism is the executive head of a UN agency, as in the case of the initiative exercised by the UN High Commissioner for Refugees.[34]

The salience of collective solutions, these examples suggest, interacts with and may reduce the salience of competitive national interests. Thus the high salience of a value to an actor does not necessarily correctly predict the acceptability of a centralized versus a decentralized decision procedure or outcome. Moreover, it is important not to regard salience as necessarily static. Change of government may produce a change in a state's view of the salience of an issue. Factors bearing on an issue may change to alter its salience to a government. For example, the UN political record on an issue may alter a government's view of the balance between the political and other costs and benefits of continuing to protect its autonomy.

Can the lesson be that the obvious hypothesis about salience, set forth at the beginning of this section, may be wrong? An alternative might be as follows. States turn to international organizations to do things that they cannot do, or cannot do as well, themselves. When such tasks have very high salience to governments, their need is greatest. Avoiding cataclysm in the Middle East in 1956 is one example. In such cases states will try to control the behavior of the international agencies to protect or serve their interests. Finally, however, they have to agree that the task must be performed, even if the result is not optimal, or even when it is harmful to their partisan interests in the stakes. In such circumstances high issue salience may correlate with high centralization of agency decisionmaking and action, including autonomous authority for the executive head as necessary. States, obviously, do not always act in their own best interests. They do not always follow the logic of this paragraph. But they sometimes do. When that happens, the salience-autonomy relationship may be U-curved rather than a straight line.

Ends and Means:
Legitimacy, Principles, and Rules

Another important question has to do with the interaction of ends and means as objectives in the politics of the UN system. International actors, it has been said above, pursue objectives as ends in themselves and as means to other ends.

Legitimacy is an important case in point. In calling attention to the UN's role in providing "collective legitimization" I. L. Claude shrewdly observed that the "obverse of the legitimacy of power is the power of legitimacy."[35] States seek legitimacy as an end in UN organizations when, for example, their statehood is acknowledged through membership. National liberation organizations seek observer status. For both the legitimacy also provides access to the organization's platform and to its programs and resources. Namibia is a recent, perhaps extreme, example. The UN Council for Namibia was admitted to full membership in the Food and Agriculture Organization (FAO) in 1977 and in the International Labor Organization (ILO) and UNESCO in 1978, even though the country itself was not a state and thus did not meet the membership requirement.[36] The legitimization of Namibia's status in this way was seen by its supporters as a means toward achieving the end objective—Namibia's independence from South African rule. The other side of that coin is the effort to delegitimize "pariahs"—for example, Israel, South Africa, Chile under Pinochet, and Portugal under Salazar—through the mobilization of majority opprobrium and attempts to cut off access and rights of participation.[37]

Legitimacy thus applies to particular cases as both ends and means. It also applies to attempts to introduce new principles and rules to guide or govern international behavior, or to change old ones. Rules and principles are ends in themselves. They are also instruments for allocating the end values they are intended to regulate. When there is wide agreement on the rules and principles—unanimity or consensus—they can achieve legitimacy either under a unit veto or a centralized majority decision rule. When states disagree on these issues there is struggle over the claim to legitimacy and over the power to assert it, as efforts are made to achieve legitimacy for contested objectives by majority voting. The legitimacy of majority endorsement is sought because it is believed to be an asset in the continuing effort to change the rules definitively and operatively.

Minorities have been willing to concede a legitimacy to adoption of principles by majorities that they have adamantly denied to imposition of rules the same way. Thus, in some cases, principles have been moved by majority action from the intermediate zone of uncertainty and struggle over authority into the zone of centralized authority, while struggle over rules on the same issues has remained in the middle zone. Acceptance of legitimacy in the one case and rejection in the other has produced "a curious amalgam of what appears to be authoritative power to establish principles and the sovereign right not to be bound by them."[38] The legitimacy of the former is employed in the continuing campaign to undermine the latter, as in the international mobilization to overturn apartheid. Recent recognition that this has been so—as in Secretary Shultz's San Francisco address referred to previously—may activate greater minority resistance to the legitimization of principles by majorities.

Allocative Processes

Some centralized decisions are constitutionally mandated. Financial assessments are an example. Another interesting one is the authority in Article 22 of the UN Charter to create self-contained "second tier" international organizations by resolutions adopted under majority procedures. Some such organizations have far-reaching powers, which in some cases even resemble governing powers. The list of important agencies created in this way includes the UN High Commissioner for Refugees (UNHCR), the UN Council for Namibia, the UN Relief and Works Agency for Palestine Refugees (UNWRA), the UN Tribunal for Libya, and the UN Temporary Executive Agency for West New Guinea/Irian (UNTEA).[39] The UN Development Program (UNDP) was created this way, as were the UN Industrial Development Organization (UNIDO) and the UN Capital Development Fund (UNCDF).

There are also mixed cases, in which decisions involve processes from both ends of the spectrum, centralized and unit veto processes. This has been called "mingling."[40] Some international organizations have been created this way. Although they are treaty-based—that is, they rest on consent of the signatories—they nevertheless came about in response to the exertion of majority pressures through the governing bodies in the UN system. The International Fund for Agricultural Development (IFAD) is an example.

Mingling describes UNDP decisions. Program decisions are made by centralized procedures, usually involving pro forma approval by the Governing Council of programs advanced by the administrator. The programs themselves, however, are worked out to meet the preferences of the recipient countries, normally in conformity with their national development plans. They are thus designed in the unit veto mode. Moreover, the funds UNDP dispenses are voluntarily provided.

Another example of mingling is the role of the organizations in the international treaty process. Majorities can shape the treaties and decide their content. They become formally effective, however, only through the acquiescence of states that retain the freedom not to become bound. In these and other examples of mingling majority pressures may narrow the freedom of resistant states to exploit the leverage inherent in the right not to participate.

Another category involves the employment of implied or inferred majority decision powers when the constitutions are silent. Agencies create and run programs this way. While most of the funds to support such activities are raised through voluntary pledging, considerable sums from the regular agency budgets are appropriated by majority procedures and spent for programs throughout the UN system.[41] Moreover, the funds are allocated and spent by centralized processes. Programmatic decisions evoke subsequent fiscal obligations in many cases. By and large, members accept the decisions and pay the bills even when they have opposed the particular program or objected to the budget totals.[42]

Priorities are established and substantial resources allocated throughout the system. The conditions attached and the consequences can be great. An example is the role of the International Monetary Fund (IMF) in providing monetary assistance to countries with balance of payments difficulties. It often exercises a power to impose "conditionality" on recipients, a power that was not in the original Articles of Agreement.[43] Such actions have led to domestic disorder in countries thus forced to tighten their fiscal belts.

Such assertions of decision power by UN agencies were often not anticipated when the original constitutional instruments were drawn up. The development of such programmatic authority represents a considerable growth of function and assertion of power by the international agencies. In many ways they now behave as governments.

Unmistakably there has been a growth in majority voting as the means of decision. The underlying reality, of course, is more complex. Even when votes are taken they come ordinarily at the end of a process of bargaining among the interested states or groups of states that seek to arrive at agreements or at least to narrow differences. Much of this bargaining occurs outside the formal meetings, in the "corridors" and frequently in the normal channels of state-to-state diplomacy. In this sense UN agency decisions represent mingling even when they take the form of majority votes. Particularly, great diplomatic effort is ordinarily invested in trying to secure the compliance of all states whose agreement, or at least non-obstruction, is necessary for the success of the measure being acted upon. There is not much point in adopting a resolution setting up a program that requires access to the territory of a state (Egypt for example in the UNEF case referred to above) or asylum for refugees from across the border, if the state refuses to comply. The same principle applies to the other state-controlled resources that are needed if decisions are to be carried out—money, technological cooperation, the enactment of domestic laws, and so on.

At the same time it is important to recognize that such diplomacy occurs in a setting in which voting is available as the means for adopting decisions. Compliance of states can be induced by the awareness that, in the end, resistance cannot prevent the adoption of a measure a majority supports. Especially for small states it can be uncomfortable to be exposed as holdouts against the will of the majority or as out of step with the norms of the groups or blocs to which they belong. And it must be emphasized that, finally, there are many instances of majorities taking decisions against the resistance of powerful states. Often, as was said in the preceding section of this chapter, such decisions are intended to gain the advantage that attaches to legitimization of contested policies by majorities.

Controversial majority decisions may provoke the resentment of the minorities whose program preferences are overridden by the majorities. The frictions over such issues certainly contributed to the disaffection with UNESCO that led to the withdrawal of the United States and Britain. Such frictions contribute also to initiatives to reduce agency budgets. Advocates see smaller budgets as desirable in themselves and as instrumental in gaining leverage over program choices. They lead also to efforts to "restructure" agencies, both to strengthen and to control majority processes and to link financial contributions to voting strength. Refusal to pay for "objectionable" expenses is a means of protest as well as a way the losers have to avoid the burdens the majorities wish them to carry.

Legislation: Principles, Norms, and Rules

As is to be expected in a nonhierarchical international order constitutionally legitimized legislative authority in the UN system is rare, limited, and specific. For the most part the expectation is that rules will be established by the treaty method—that is, in a decentralized mode in which the consent of states is necessary before rules can take effect and the consent of each state is necessary if it is to be bound.[44] The ability to withhold consent is the minimum resource of every state whose participation is relevant to the desired outcome. Where the result sought by the desired treaty calls for assets controlled by states—resources, access, participation in a variety of ways, including but not limited to control over force and its use—the states that command such resources have greater bargaining power over the outcomes than do others.

Constitutionally the role of the UN agencies and their organs is to provide forums in which agreement can be sought in the first instance as to agendas for rule formulation. There is general agreement among those who have studied international processes in recent years that being able to determine such agendas carries with it important influence. Majority processes are generally followed in setting agendas.

Then, after bargaining among members, rules are recommended for authoritative adoption by members' ratifications. This pattern has been employed frequently and it would be pointless, and might not be possible, to list the instruments establishing new rules that have been adopted in this manner. They cover the full range of subjects with which international organizations deal. It deserves emphasizing, however, that the tension between the role of majorities in setting agendas and recommending rules and the sovereign ability of states not to accept them shows up in the fairly large number of instruments that have been adopted but have not commanded enough acceptance to take effect or, even though in legal effect, to be effective. A recent important example is the UN Law of the Sea Treaty, which has not gained enough ratifications to take effect since its promulgation in 1982 (by a vote of 130 to 4, with 17 abstaining), seems unlikely to do so soon, and, even if it does, may not command the support of countries essential to its effective fruition.[45] All together, however, the overall record is probably captured well in the recent characterization of "the volume, density and complexity of the newly created bodies of law" as "impressive evidence of the extent to which the present decentralized legal order has found it necessary to develop particular legal regimes to serve felt needs." The author of that observation finds the development of this body of law, which the late Wolfgang Friedman termed a "law of international cooperation,"[46] to be "the product of negotiation and pressure which reflects the power and capabilities of the participating states."[47]

A permutation of the theme is the mobilization of pressure to insert in treaties standards that were not intended to be binding when they were incorporated by majority vote in prior instruments, however named. The presumed legitimacy of provisions incorporated in nonbinding resolutions, declarations, or recommendations is employed as an instrument to induce enlarged acceptance of such provisions in binding instruments. The history of the drafting of the two Covenants on Human Rights following the adoption of the Universal Declaration of Human Rights is an outstanding example. Another is the similar use to which the UN General Assembly's resolution in 1971 declaring the seabed "the common heritage of mankind" has been put.[48]

Rule formation by the treaty method is but one dimension of the effort to alter or create rules in the UN system. It may perhaps even comprise only a small portion of the total effort. Most of the time, attempts to create rules, or at least what has been called "public policy,"[49] go forward without benefit of treaty.

One technique is reiteration. Standards enunciated by majorities that control decisions are referred to as sources of legitimacy in sequential reiteration in instruments adopted by other organs of the UN system and by other bodies, such as the Assembly and Council of Ministers of the Organization of African Unity (OAU), the Islamic Assembly and Conference of Heads of State of the Nonaligned Movement (NAM). Principles or norms are bounced from sounding board to sounding board with accelerating momentum in the effort to establish their legitimacy. Frequently the sounding board of choice is the preambular language of a new resolution intended to build on the precedents. The phenomenon is well understood by the professionals who have invested endless tedious hours in the struggle to insert or exclude such preambular references.

Reiteration may occur in the same body, especially the UN General Assembly. The intent is the same—to build up a cumulative record of norm or standard assertion to be read as evidence of the existence of customary law or international public policy. This is not the place to probe the depths of the argument over "instant custom."[50] What matters is whether, and in what respects, this way of attempting to create rules is effective. Does reiteration of norms in individual organs in the UN system, or among them, lead to acceptance and application of the norms? The evidence is fragmentary. There are the conclusions of legal scholars that law does develop this way.[51] Recently, there has also been evidence that instruments adopted by international organizations that do not directly bind the affected states nevertheless enter into the reasoning of domestic courts, which, minimally, seem reluctant to find them invalid or inapplicable and which sometimes feel bound to apply them.[52] There are glimmerings of an emergent international human rights law based on the widespread and reiterated assertion of standards in instruments that, even when they do not bind states directly, may nevertheless be found applicable by domestic courts.

The practice of developing norms in this way is widespread and varied. It includes efforts to alter: the general rules of the international system, as in the NIEO and the Charter of Economic Rights and Duties of States;[53] particular rules of broad application, such as the General System of Preferences (GSP); and particular rules affecting individual issues, such as the status of Jerusalem, the legitimacy of apartheid, independence for Namibia, and the legitimacy of Israel. One perhaps surprising development has been the extent to which the UN Security Council has become implicated in the rule-making process, particularly with respect to issues of colonialism and racial policies in southern Africa.[54]

There are also reasons to believe that this "legislative" process may have constraining effects on states, even when what is involved has nothing to do with rule formation. When Ambassador Kirkpatrick referred to the legislative role of the UN organs[55] she probably did not intend to imply a law-making role in the strict sense, but meant, rather, the cumulative effect of UN actions on beliefs about what is moral and what is acceptable behavior[56]—in short, about legitimacy.

Authority as an End

Much of the politics of North-South relations has had to do with efforts to establish the authority of majority actions in the international agencies. The disagreements about authority have been a by-product of struggles over legitimacy, norms, rules, and principles. Authority has also to some extent been a direct objective of the parties.

One form the politics has taken has been the issue of "restructuring" the UN's machinery in the fields of economic and social affairs.[57] Although one purpose of the restructuring effort was simply to rationalize a system that had grown and dispersed badly and too much, a parallel purpose was the G-77's desire "to make the system more responsive." The G-77 thus "sought to strengthen those forums and institutions that were amenable to their interests."[58] One dimension of this thrust has been the wish of the G-77 to alter in their favor the voting arrangements that have given special influence— amounting to a veto power for the United States in some cases—in the World Bank and the IMF. It is notable that the voting strength of the LDCs has shown considerable relative growth in the IMF, partly because of what might be termed natural causes—that is, the growth in their relative numbers and the increase in exports by some LDCs that influenced quota increases. Overall the proportions of quotas have shifted in the IMF as follows:[59]

	Industrial Members	All Nonindustrial Members
1966	72%	28%
1983	63%	37%

One recent study concludes that the LDCs have had an influence over the distribution of voting power in the IMF, especially with respect to the system of special majorities required for specified categories of decisions.[60]

The LDCs also sought, with considerable success, to gain power by ensuring that they are well represented in elected organs and other bodies. They have organized effectively to achieve elected offices in the plenary and executive bodies and in the plethora of commissions, committees, and working parties to be found in the UN system. They have gained increased numbers and ratios of placements in the international civil service and, particularly, in leadership positions in the secretariats.

That the issue of authority in the system is not one-sided is shown by the recent pressures from the developed countries, led by the United States, to introduce new means of control to protect their interests.[61]

Blocs and Group Representation

Decisionmaking in the UN system is strongly influenced, if not determined, by convergence of groups of members to accumulate voting power. The practice has become so well entrenched, and is of such significance, that both scholars and practitioners have referred to some such groupings as political parties.[62] The groupings are regional or subregional as well as interest or ideology-based. The Nonaligned Movement has been described as based on an "activist ideology" in pursuit of national independence and full equality for new states.[63] Cohesion is maintained by focusing on issues on which there is agreement, for example, Middle Eastern, southern African, and disarmament resolutions in the case of NAM.[64] The G-77 membership, now more than 120 states, overlaps that of the NAM. The G-77 is the instrument for concerting objectives, policies, and tactics among the LDCs with respect to the rules and structure of international economic relations.[65]

The strength of the Third World coalition has depended on the members' ability to coalesce in order to concentrate their voting strength. Considering the diversity and range of countries comprising the coalition, this has been no mean feat. As Rothstein has shown, however, maintaining cohesion has required the group to avoid contentious issues in its ranks and to come to rest on lowest common denominators—often at the level of aspiration, principle, and rhetoric—rather than grapple with the hard issues that might have divided them. Another consequence has been rigidity in the bloc's bargaining position. Flexibility would incur the difficulties of renegotiating the consensus so painfully arrived at within the bloc.[66]

Even the high degree of cohesion the G-77 has maintained in negotiations with other groups, however, has not "offset the greater power of the defenders of the status quo."[67] The movement achieved some successes, but has fallen short of its stated goal of reforming the rules and structure of the international economic system.[68] Indeed, the movement has of late met what may prove a setback— the determined effort by developed countries to strengthen their means of institutional control in the system.

Regionalization has been an important trend in the organization of participation in the UN system. Originally regional caucuses were formed primarily to help regional groupings to compete for and obtain seats in the agencies' elected boards, councils, commissions, and other subordinate bodies and to elect individuals of their choice to offices of prestige and influence. Now the demands of conflicting regional blocs are often accommodated by adherence to conventions under which the groups alternate in the nomination of candidates whose election is normally assured.[69] Such conventions now govern the election of the President of the UN General Assembly, for ex-

ample, as well as thè choice of candidates for places in elected organs throughout the system. In some agencies, UNESCO for example,
regionalization has been incorporated in the formal rules for elections and other decisions.[70]

There are thus emergent methods of organizing decision and action that do not conform either with the unit veto mode as it existed
in the League of Nations Covenant or with one-nation–one-vote
majority decisionmaking. In a seminal article Gidon Gottlieb has
called attention to the precariously effective operation of a new dynamic he termed "parity." "Parity" represents "the organization of
states into global political parties and alignments which do not follow the big power bloc politics of the first years of the UN." Parity
requires that "agreement be reached between the main parties or
groups of states on the basis of the equality of groups of states rather
than on the basis of the equality of individual states."[71] Regional
groups clearly have such status in the major interregional blocs and
also directly for many purposes in the decision processes of UN
agencies. The United States seemed to give explicit endorsement
to this principle when it unsuccessfully sought voting procedures
in UNESCO "to assure that, in major matters, UNESCO decisions and
programs enjoy the support of all geographic groups."[72] The United
States did so again in applauding the emphasis on group representation and consensus in the Committee on Program and Coordination, which was the essence of the improvements accepted by
the UN General Assembly during its 41st Session in 1986.

What is not clear, as Gottlieb emphasizes, is whether this elevation
of the status of groups so that they exercise what amounts to group
vetoes will withstand the temptations to override such vetoes in
order to claim the stamp of legitimacy believed to inhere in majority
approval of instruments adopted in international organs.[73] If the
"parity principle" gains in acceptance, that would enhance the efficacy of groups and inject a real focus of resistance to efforts to
reach decisions by majorities.

A corollary development has been the practice of representation—
as distinguished from direct participation of all member states—in
negotiations, the preliminaries, and sometimes even the formalities
of decisionmaking. Representation was built into the quota voting
arrangements of the IMF and the World Bank from the beginning.
Sydney Bailey has referred to the development of a practice in the
UN Security Council whereby "members were not only selected by
the regional group but were, in a more formal sense, representative
of and responsible to it."[74]

The difficulty of conducting complex negotiations among large numbers of states, grouped increasingly in large caucuses, blocs, and coalitions, has led to fairly widespread resort to representative practices. Committees by whatever name are composed on the basis of formal criteria of representation. The states chosen are unevenly caught up in the interactive development of policies and tactics with the groups they represent. The practice has been apparent in the functioning of the G-77 and NAM with respect to the issues falling under the rubric of the NIEO.[75]

Richard Cooper has placed this development in an evocative perspective, referring to the linkage between what he described as the effective performance of the IMF and "the beginning of representative government at the global level, with constituents being nations rather than individuals."[76]

Minority Responses:
Opting In and Opting Out

Minority resistance to majority procedures has been growing in the UN system. Uneasiness over the one-nation–one-vote arrangement of many decision bodies has had a long history.[77] Previous sections of this chapter have already referred to some measures that minorities have resorted to in countering the weight of majority votes. However, the widespread resort to consensus instead of the counting of votes as a means of reaching decisions deserves a few more words. Consensus generally helps minorities because it permits any state to prevent a decision. It thus universalizes the veto and, in effect, returns to the constitutional principle of the League of Nations.

Consensus procedures do not always work that way, however, as Robert Gregg has observed.[78] When consensus becomes a totem of agency procedure, majorities can employ it as a means to intimidate those who might otherwise dissent. Disrupting consensus can come to be viewed as "antisocial" behavior. While minority states can in the end disrupt consensus and force a vote count, the disincentives to doing so can become very powerful, to the point where dissent is expressed only over issues of utmost importance by powerful member states. On lesser matters disagreement may be suppressed or, to put it another way, the threshold for disagreeing may be raised. When consensus works this way it may be more obstructive to serious search for compromise solutions than when the expectation is that differences will be settled by voting.[79]

Another way that minority states resist majority decisions is to refuse to pay assessments for expenditures of which they disapprove. By and large, states have done reasonably well in paying agency assessments, even when the budgets have included items that the states have opposed.[80] All the same, refusal to pay the costs of unacceptable decisions has a long history in the UN. The United States may have been the first to do this when it refused, in 1954, to pay its assessed share of compensation awarded to Americans fired from the Secretariat under McCarthyite pressures by the United States on the Secretary-General.[81] The Russians and other members of the Soviet bloc refused to pay assessed costs of UN peace-keeping forces—especially UNEF and ONUC—and other costs resulting from UN security actions that they had opposed. The Soviet bloc was joined by France in the case of ONUC. The resulting constitutional crisis in 1964–65 led the United States to declare that it would reserve the right to do the same. In recent years the practice has become chronic, with UN agencies finding themselves among the objects of the invigorated congressional practice of imposing restraints on foreign policy expenditures. In two cases—against the ILO in 1970 because of the appointment of a Soviet national as an Assistant Director-General,[82] and against UNESCO in 1975–76 because of action against Israel—the U.S. actions were clearly retaliatory. In both cases there was a carrot as well as a stick and the funding was renewed relatively soon.

Members' refusal to pay for costs of which they disapprove may be thought a form of "opting out" of majority actions. When the assessments result from constitutionally validated decisions, this form of opting out is evidently not legal. When the funding mechanism is voluntary pledging, refusal to participate is legitimate and may be thought the converse of "opting in," whereby those states that choose to undertake an activity are free to do so. States are, for example, free to respond or not to the appeals of the UN High Commissioner for Refugees for funds to support new activities.[83]

Management of voluntary contributions may also be a form of influence. A study on the United Nations Relief and Works Agency for Palestine Refugees has shown how voluntary donors can shape what is done by the conditions they attach to their contributions.[84] The United Nations Fund for Drug Abuse Control (UNFDAC) provides one among other examples of a donor, in this instance the United States, deriving positive influence from its control over its voluntary contributions.[85]

The institution of "trust funds" scattered throughout the UN system is another example of a device whereby donors, usually individual states, can choose to support particular designated activities of international agencies. This might be described as "buying" or "buying into" international agency programs or services. It has recently been described as an "a la carte" approach to the provision of international service.[86] The phenomenon has been growing in scope and, presumably, in importance, although it has been little studied.

Broadly, opting out and opting in constitute a way to advance purpose and conduct activities when either general agreement and/or general capacity to act is lacking. When this practice enables those wishing to do so to perform a humane service, it is a form of benevolent decentralization to avoid the hazards of centralized decisionmaking. This principle holds true for many of the Funds in Trust established by Scandinavian countries, in UNESCO, for example.[87] When politically contentious activities are involved the schismatic possibilities are evident.[88]

Opting out is not limited to financial involvement. It applies also to policy guidelines, rule formulation, and rule observance. Recent analysis of the General Agreement for Tariffs and Trade (GATT), for example, suggests that the international trade regime is a partial one, with various states remaining free not to agree to or carry out rules that are adopted and obeyed by others.[89] In a way the practice of Great Power abstention in the UN Security Council is another form of opting out, as is the practice of introducing reservations to consensus decisions rather than obstructing them by insisting on a split vote.

The threat to withhold funding, and actually doing so, has been supplemented by threats to withdraw from participation—in the International Atomic Energy Agency and elsewhere—over the possible denial of a seat to Israel. After giving the required two years' notice the United States withdrew from the ILO in 1977 over a series of charges about politicization and bias, including the grant of observer status to the Palestine Liberation Organization; it returned in 1980.[90] After the required one year's notice the United States withdrew from UNESCO on December 31, 1984, claiming that its demands for reforms had been insufficiently met. This act gave rise to strong official hints that it involved a strategy to enhance American leverage over reforms elsewhere in the system, including the UN itself.[91]

The practice in its several variants deserves more attention than it has received. Overall it enables states or groups of them to pursue their purposes without obstruction by others. The latter protect themselves against being implicated unwillingly. In its respect for the preferences of states in the system, opting in or out is predominantly a form of the old diplomacy.[92] In the scheme of this chapter it also represents struggle over allocative authority in the intermediate zone.

Political Roles of Actors in the UN System

At the outset of the UN era the predominant expectation was that states would be the only significant actors in the system of multilateral diplomacy of sovereign equality. Yet from the beginning there were provisions for other actors to perform significant roles. Since then their roles have grown in scale and importance.

Among the other actors are the regional and other interstate formations whose importance has been emphasized earlier in the chapter. No further attention need be given to them here, except to note that they have come to play roles comparable to those of political parties in pluralist political systems. Like the political parties in the United States, they were not anticipated in the beginning. Executive heads of the agencies and nongovernmental organizations are two other categories of actors that deserve a few words.

Executive Heads

Starting from constitutional bases that gave them greater prominence and larger roles than had been allotted their prewar predecessors, executive heads have in various ways become significant political actors in the UN system. This accretion of political influence has sometimes been controversial. One proof is the intense struggle that sometimes accompanies their nomination and election to office. Another is the aura of controversiality that attaches to the names and records of some who have held the office of executive head, for example: Dag Hammarskjöld, C. Wilfred Jenks,[93] Robert S. McNamara,[94] and Amadou Mahtar M'Bow.[95] The point deserves emphasis. Executive heads of UN agencies have unmistakably become major political actors and major issues of international political controversy, beyond the political struggle that accompanies their selection.

One measure of the importance of the executive heads is that there are so many more of them now than when the UN began. The proliferation of new agencies in the UN system has created as many more executive posts.

As principal administrative officers of their agencies, the executive heads are inescapably involved in allocative roles that are political as that term is used in this study. This political involvement has become the more inescapable as the agencies have assumed major operational functions, ordinarily by the majority decision procedures outlined above.

Their functions of preparing and recommending budgets, appointing staffs, and shaping and administering the program decisions made by the governmental bodies are political in the sense that they allocate what members seek. As the programs and operations have grown the executive heads have become, simply, indispensable. A great deal of what governments collectively want agencies to do can only be accomplished by executive action. They negotiate, or supervise negotiation, with governments and with other agencies about the design and implementation of programs—that is, about the allocation of resources. Given the difficulties that governments have in allocating values among themselves, the executive heads are thrust willy-nilly into the allocative processes.

Sometimes executive authority is thought to result from the indifference or apathy of governments. This has been said of UNESCO. The charge may be accurate as history, but it is far from certain that more attentive governments could have done much better in resolving their differences over agency priorities, or that they will be able to do so in the future. Executive initiative and the authority that accompanies it may be the only alternative to agency deadlock.

Much of the exercise of allocative authority by executive heads and their staffs proceeds without controversy. Much of the actual allocation of the extensive resources of the UNDP, for example, including its relations with other agencies in the system, is reciprocally conducted essentially by the agency staffs.[96] The key may be in the mingling process. Although the agency decisions are centralized and autonomous, voluntary funding and home government participation in program design ensure that principal actors in the programs have control over what matters to them. What is salient to them cannot be threatened, although both donors and recipients sometimes have to put up with less than optimal outcomes. Severe neuralgia seems to set in when the principal sources of funds, especially the United States, discover that they are asked to fund activities of which they do not approve that affect their salient interests.

In addition to their indispensability executive heads have other

resources available to them on which members depend: their presumed impartiality and their roles as custodians of the organizational
ideologies that identify and give character to their institutions.[97]
Especially when the agencies are complex, they derive great power
from their control of the institutional apparatus and their unique
command of indispensable knowledge and intelligence. They have
the material assets of the agencies to bargain with.[98] They also play
a role in establishing by their own actions the norms by which
they are judged.[99] Not only have executive heads become permanent
features of the UN system, but they have irreversibly become powerful actors.

Nongovernmental Organizations

International nongovernmental organizations (INGOs) have had a
place in the UN system from its early days. Article 71 of the UN
Charter authorizes the association of nongovernmental organizations
with the activities of the UN and gives them status and rights in the
organization. That article itself reflected NGO (nongovernmental organization) involvement at the San Francisco Conference that
adopted the UN Charter in 1945. The U.S. delegation arranged for
consultation with a group of forty-two national organizations[100] that
played a very active role, especially with respect to economic, social,
and human rights matters. Article XI(4) of the UNESCO Constitution
also authorizes the association of NGOs with the organization. Tri-
partism in the ILO goes back to that organization's origin after World
War I and ensures a direct decision role in the ILO for national trade
unions and business organizations.

All the same, the pervasive and significant role INGOs have come
to play in the system is surprising. Their active participation, especially in social and human rights matters, is more than significant—it is indispensable. Their role is not, moreover, limited to
issues of relatively low salience to governments, as is evidenced
by the prominence and effectiveness of such agencies as Amnesty
International. INGOs have grown in numbers even more rapidly than
have IGOs. The presence of NGOs throughout the UN system, and
the active roles they play, are eloquent testimony to the fact that
the international system, and the UN system within it, is more than
a system of sovereign states.[101] Only a few comments on NGOs can
be accommodated in the scope of this chapter, although succeeding
chapters will give further evidence of their significance.

Working with delegates of governments, INGOs are responsible for getting issues on the agendas of organs throughout the UN system. INGOs have been especially active and important in focusing spotlights on human rights abuses and in pressing for adoption of rules to regulate international treatment of human rights.[102] They have also provided significant stimulus to the development of international policy on environmental and ecological matters during the 1970s,[103] among other issues on which they have been active. They supply relevant information and ideas. They lobby intensively and employ their national connections to bring influence to bear on bureaucracies and legislatures in support of international positions they favor.

They have been especially important in monitoring performance under the human rights instruments that they have helped to bring about. Their role in this respect is controversial, particularly as it steps on the corns of countries that are not eager to expose their national human rights practices to probing international inquiries. The result often is controversy over the accreditation of NGOs and about their status before international bodies.[104]

INGOs and NGOs participate in networks of communication and influence with like-minded government bureaus and personnel and with segments of international secretariats.[105] They supply expertise, experience, and resources that bear both on policymaking and on implementation in the field. INGOs carry a great share of the load in the administration of refugee programs in Africa and Asia.[106] They similarly are deeply implicated in many aspects of international technical assistance in Third World settings. Their indispensability gives them important access to and leverage over decisions as to how the relevant international standards should be carried out in the field.

Overall it seems likely that INGOs work to support international action and centralized decisions and, hence, to reduce the control and vetoes of member states. By their very nature INGOs, which predominantly represent the world of democratic pluralism, are no great respecters of the rigidities of sovereign statehood. Even so, some NGOs may reinforce the salience of stakes to their governments and stimulate government intervention to control decisionmaking and action by the international agencies, and thus strengthen unit veto powers. An example is the role of the Heritage Foundation in accentuating the salience of UNESCO's alleged "statism" and other perceived faults to the U.S. government. Similarly the AFL-CIO imposed its views of the perceived inadequacies of the ILO on the U.S. government when George Meany was its president.[107]

Whatever the direction of NGO influence, one thing is clear. NGOs directly and INGOs through their national affiliates bridge the boundaries between the international and the domestic spheres. They are well described by the term "transnational," and their near omnipresent influence in the UN system means that the latter is inescapably infused with important transnational components interacting with the international character usually attributed to it. A flow chart of many decisions in the UN system would look like this: NGOs ⟷ INGOs ⟷ member states ⟷ IGO processes ⟷ IGO results (decisions, programs, etc.) ⟷ members ⟷ NGOs. The essential point is that there is an unbroken continuity between the domestic and international dimensions of decisionmaking on many issues dealt with by UN agencies. Nongovernmental organizations help to make this so.

Summing Up

This chapter has sought to lay the basis for the case studies of UN system politics that follow by identifying some of the main aspects of the conduct of politics in the system in light of a broad definition of the term "politics." The central theme has been that there is significant tension in the system between the diplomatic and the political approaches, the latter emphasizing voting as the means of decision, whereas the former emphasizes the autonomy of sovereign states.

What difference does the distinction make? In one perspective it is another way of asking the question put by many, most recently by Jacobson in *Networks of Interdependence*: "whether or not the territorial state is the ultimate form of political organization."[108] This chapter hypothesizes that, although the picture is blurred and in many places hard to decipher, there has been movement away from the decentralized system of respect for sovereignty and toward a more centralized system of decision that in some respects approaches being international governance. That speculation, however, is rendered very uncertain by the fact that, if it makes sense to describe that movement as an incipient reform of the international system, we are now witnessing a vigorous counterreform that may still be in its early stages. The tension alluded to previously is particularly acute as this is being written.

A different perspective leads to concern about which way works best. Which approach—the diplomatic or the political—works better in meeting the needs of humanity? Here, we are handicapped by the inadequacy of our instruments for assessing the impacts of what international organizations do. We are not able to evaluate the performance of international organizations very well. It is even more difficult to relate results that we cannot measure to political processes that are complex and often not unidimensional in terms of our central question.

All we can do is theorize. Here the starting point is the nature of the international system to which the chapter alluded early—rooted in sovereignty, without hierarchy or systemic means of compulsion. From that it follows that international organizations will be most effective when their decisions reflect the willing acceptance of the states that are the main actors in the system. When all agree, there is no great problem. Then the decision modes do not matter. Agreement can be expressed either in a form that acknowledges the sovereignty of the states or in a form that nominally follows majority procedures. What, however, of the situation when there is not such agreement? The nature of the international system leads to the speculation that decisions taken by majorities against the resistance of minorities, or that involve struggle over the authority to adopt them in what this chapter has called the intermediate zone, will not be effective. Much evidence supports this speculation.

This theory, however, is a static view of how governments behave. What governments agree to and what they will do are far from static. There are many examples of original resistance giving way to final, if grudging, acceptance. Much of the growth of the UN system—the creation, for example, of the International Development Association (IDA), UNDP, and UNCDF—results from the effect of majority pressures in eroding the resistance of the minority whose participation was essential if the new agencies were to perform their roles. Nowadays developed countries are showing a degree of affirmative interest in UNIDO, which they opposed at the outset. Does it matter that in some of these cases—IDA and UNIDO for example—the acceptance was tactical, designed to avert even less desired alternatives, rather than wholehearted and enthusiastic?

Colonialism, apartheid, and racism have all been established as legitimate objects of concern by agencies in the system, struggled over, and ultimately effectively delegitimized as a result of political processes that transited the middle zone of the decision spectrum set out earlier in this chapter. By general agreement the NIEO has failed of adoption. Certainly the developed countries have by and large resisted the transformations pressed upon them by the coalition of the less developed. Yet even here there have been some positive movements. The General System of Preferences, the Integrated Program of Commodities, debt relief for LDCs, and several special facilities of the IMF all emerged from struggles between North and South over NIEO-related issues in what this chapter has called the intermediate zone. Whatever else is true of these examples, they represent movement by developed countries over time. from their original positions of obduracy.

The central concern, the bottom line in the contemporary jargon, may well be the one emphasized recently by Robert Keohane, who urged that greater attention be given to "changes in societies' definition of their own interests."[109] Do pressures exerted by majority processes in the UN system over time alter the views of the minorities as to their interests in what the majorities seek? More fundamentally, will resistant states learn over time to accommodate to the requirements of a system dominated by majority processes?

Notes

This chapter is a revised version of a paper presented at the annual meeting of the International Studies Association, Washington, D.C., March 6, 1985. It also draws on an earlier version, "Forty Years of the United Nations: From the Multilateral Diplomacy of Sovereign Equality Toward the Politics of Value Allocation," presented to the workshop on the UN at forty during the annual meeting of the International Studies Association, Atlanta, Georgia, March 1984; and on the paper "International Organizations as Political Systems," delivered at the 1986 annual meeting of the American Political Science Association, Washington, D.C., August 28–31, 1986.

Helpful criticisms by two anonymous reviewers for the Duke University Press, Inis L. Claude, Martin David Dubin, Daniel Fendrick, Margaret P. Karns, M. J. Peterson, John Ruggie, Oscar Schachter, and Michael G. Schechter are gratefully acknowledged.

1. See Lawrence S. Finkelstein, "The Politics of National Governments and of International Intergovernmental Organizations: Are They Comparable?" paper presented at the annual meeting of the International Studies Association, Mexico City, April 1983; Richard M. Mansbach and John A. Vasquez, *In Search of Theory: A New Paradigm for Global Politics* (New York: Columbia University Press, 1981), 30; Roger A. Coate, *Global Issue Regimes* (New York: Praeger, 1982), 28–48; and Robert Gregg, "The Apportioning of Political Power," in *The Changing United Nations*, ed. David Kay (New York: *Proceedings* of the Academy of Political Science, 1977), 70–73.

2. See Robert L. Peabody, "Authority," *International Encyclopedia of the Social Sciences*, vol. 1 (Macmillan and Free Press, 1968), 474.

3. There is argument over the usefulness of the traditional dichotomy between "high" and "low" politics, especially in thinking about international relations. For an affirmative view, see Charles Pentland, "International Organizations," in *World Politics: An Introduction*, ed. James N. Rosenau, Kenneth W. Thompson, and Gavin Boyd (New York: The Free Press, 1976), 628–29.

4. Robert W. Cox, Harold K. Jacobson, et al., *The Anatomy of Influence* (New Haven, Conn.: Yale University Press, 1973), 9.

5. See George Shultz, "The United Nations after Forty Years: Idealism and Realism," address before the United Nations Association of San Francisco, the San Francisco Chamber of Commerce, and the World Affairs Council of Northern California, June 26, 1985. *Department Bulletin* 85,2101 (August 1985): 20. See also Jeane J. Kirkpatrick, "U.S. Participation in the United Nations," statement before the Subcommittee on Foreign Relations of the Senate Appropriations Committee, March 2, 1984. *State Department Bulletin* 84,2085 (April 1984): 68–69. She stated: "The decisions of the United Nations are widely interpreted as reflecting 'world opinion' and are endowed with substantial moral and intellectual force. The cumulative impact of decisions of UN bodies influences opinions all over the world about what is legitimate, what is acceptable, who is lawless and who is repressive."

6. Morton A. Kaplan, *System and Process in International Politics* (New York: John Wiley and Sons, 1957), 50–51.

7. This usage borrows from Inis L. Claude's concept that collective security as the UN Charter intended it to be administered by the UN Security Council represented a centralization of power and authority as compared with the classical balance of power. See Inis L. Claude, *Power and International Politics* (New York: John Wiley and Sons, 1957), 21. This notion of centralization and decentralization should not be confused with the fact that functions and authority are dispersed among agencies in the UN system and outside it.

8. UN Charter, Article 2,1. See also the comment by Richard Bissell in "US Participation in the UN System," in *The US, the UN, and the Management of Global Change*, ed. Toby Trister Gati (New York: New York University Press, 1983), 100.

9. UN Charter, Article 27,3.

10. Ibid., Article 97.

11. Ibid., Article 4,2.

12. ICJ Statute, Articles 4, 8, 10, and 12. See also Thomas M. Franck, *Judging the World Court* (New York: Priority Press, 1986), 6, 7.

13. UN Charter, Article 18,2.

14. Article 22 of the UN Charter specifically authorized the General Assembly to create "subsidiary organs."

15. Robert O. Keohane and Joseph S. Nye, Jr., "Transnational Relations and World Politics," *International Organization* 25, 3 (Summer 1971): 733.

16. On "impermeability" as a characteristic of the modern state, see John H. Herz, "Rise and Demise of the Territorial State," reprinted in *The Nation-State and the Crisis of World Politics*, ed. John H. Herz (New York: David McKay, 1976), 101.

17. On salience, see Mansbach and Vasquez, *In Search of Theory*, 102–13.

18. The original rationale for the veto was that, since the Great Powers would be the ones ultimately called on to preserve peace and suppress threats or acts of aggression under Chapter VII, they had to be protected against loss of control over the "chain of events" that might lead to such enforcement decisions in the Security

Council, as well as over such decisions themselves. See Ruth B. Russell, assisted by Jeannette E. Muther, *A History of the United Nations Charter: The Role of the United States 1940–1945* (Washington, D.C.: Brookings, 1958), 721–24.

19. See the treatment of this subject in Frederick K. Lister, *Decision-Making Strategies for International Organizations: The IMF Model* (Denver: University of Denver Graduate School of International Studies, Monograph Series in World Affairs, vol. 20, book 4, 1984).

20. Ibid., 121–22.

21. Ibid., 120–21.

22. Ibid., 124.

23. See, for example, Javed Ansari, *The Political Economy of International Economic Organization* (Boulder, Colo.: Rienner, 1986), 262. Ansari says that UNCTAD has never used this procedure.

24. For discussions of the nature and role of consensus, see M. J. Peterson, *The General Assembly in World Politics* (Boston: Allen & Unwin, 1986), 81–89; Ansari, *The Political Economy*, 125; and F. Y. Chai, *Consultation and Consensus in the Security Council* (New York: United Nations Institute for Training and Research, 1971), especially 11, 41–43.

25. Ansari, *The Political Economy*, 262.

26. First the United States proposed that Executive Board decisions about budget and programs require approval of members contributing fifty-one percent of the budget. When this failed to gain support it requested that approval be necessary by eighty-five percent of the fifty-one-member body. *Assessment of U.S.-UNESCO Relations, 1984*, report of a Staff Study Mission to Paris-UNESCO to the Committee on Foreign Affairs, House of Representatives, January 1985, 19–20.

27. "Baker Expresses Disappointment over IDB Negotiations," *Washington Weekly Report* 12, 7 (February 20, 1987): 2.

28. Cox, Jacobson, et al., *The Anatomy of Influence*, 420–23.

29. Charles Lindblom, cited in Robert O. Keohane, *After Hegemony: Cooperation and Discord in the World Political Economy* (Princeton, N.J.: Princeton University Press, 1984), 51.

30. Ibid., 49–64.

31. One account is Brian Urquhart, *Hammarskjöld* (New York: Knopf, 1973), 184–94. It may be relevant that the consent Egypt gave in 1956 was withdrawn, disastrously, in 1967. The veto was withheld initially, but not abandoned.

32. See Brian Urquhart, "The International Civil Servant," in *The International Executive: Papers from a Princeton University Conference*, ed. Leon Gordenker (Princeton, N.J.: Princeton University Center of International Studies, 1978), 43–45; Thomas M. Franck, "Filling the Void: Action by the Secretary-General in the Face of Inaction by Everyone Else," in Franck, *Nation against Nation: What Happened to the U.N. Dream and What the U.S. Can Do About It* (New York: Oxford University Press, 1984), 134–60; Alan M. James, "Kurt Waldheim: Diplomat's Diplomat," *Yearbook of World Affairs, 1983*, 81–96; and Javier Pérez de Cuéllar, "The UN Simply Must Be Made To Succeed," *New York Times Week in Review*, October 20, 1985, 21E.

33. "Ruling Pertaining to the Differences between France and New Zealand Arising from the Rainbow Warrior Affair," *American Journal of International Law*, 81, 1 (January 1987): 325–28.

34. See Chapter 9 by Leon Gordenker in this volume.

35. See Inis L. Claude, Jr., "Collective Legitimization as a Political Function of the United Nations," in *International Organization: Politics and Process*, ed. Leland M. Goodrich and David A. Kay, Jr. (Madison: University of Wisconsin Press, 1973), 210.

36. Isaak I. Dore, *The International Mandate System and Namibia* (Boulder, Colo.: Westview Press, 1985), 215–16.

37. In some ways these delegitimizing activities of recent years are the mirror image of U.S. efforts in the early days to deny admission to East European states in the Soviet bloc and, until 1971, to deny a seat to the People's Republic of China.

38. Finkelstein, "Some Aspects of Power Sharing in International Organizations," in *Shared Power: What Is It? How Does It Work? How Can We Make It Work Better?* ed. John M. Bryson and Robert C. Einsweiler (Lanham, Md.: University Press of America, forthcoming).

39. The preceding draws from Edward H. Buehrig, "The Resolution-Based International Agency," *Political Studies* 29, 2 (1981): 217–31.

40. Finkelstein, "Some Aspects of Power Sharing."

41. The World Bank is an interesting case. It raises most of the money it lends by borrowing autonomously in the world's money markets. It also reinvests substantial sums of its own profits, more than $2 billion since 1964. See *World Bank Annual Report 1984*, 181.

42. This generalization is correct even though the cumulative arrearages to the agencies are significant. For example at the end of calendar year 1983, arrearages to the UN totaled $171 million. Some of this represented tardiness in payment by countries that had foreign exchange difficulties in meeting the obligation or, as in the case of the United States, a deliberate policy of delay. (Early in 1984 the United States paid some $22 million of the $27 million that had been outstanding at the end of 1983.) It also reflects what may be a growing tendency toward "politically motivated nonpayment,"—for example, the policy followed by the Soviet Union and others in the Soviet bloc and the United States as a means of protesting decisions of which they do not approve. At the end of 1983, for example, the USSR was at the top of the list, with an arrearage of $41 million, and other members of the Soviet bloc owed a further $36 million. By the beginning of 1987, however, the United States was the leading nonpayer as a result of a combination of executive and congressional decisions to refuse or delay payment to the UN. The issue will be considered further later in this section in the context of minority techniques of resisting majoritarian tendencies.

43. See Benjamin J. Cohen, "Balance-of-Payments Financing: Evolution of a Regime," *International Organization* 36, 2 (Spring 1982): 462–63.

44. For a discussion of the difference between these two types of consent, see chapter 15 of this volume.

45. For a tentative projection to the contrary based on an imaginative examination of the relevant capacities of signatories, see Clifton E. Wilson, "Treaty Law: Measuring Rules of the Game," paper prepared for delivery to the 1984 International Studies Association convention in Atlanta, Georgia, 25–29.

46. Wolfgang Friedman, The *Changing Structure of International Law* (New York: Columbia University Press, 1964), 64ff.

47. Oscar Schachter, "The Nature and Process of Legal Development in International Society," in *The Structure and Process of International Law*, ed. R. St. J. McDonald and D. H. Johnston (The Hague: Martinus Nijhoff, 1983), 754.

48. UN General Assembly Resolution 2749(XXV), December 17, 1971.

49. See Ralph Zacklin, "The Challenge of Rhodesia: Toward an International Public Policy," *International Conciliation* 575 (November 1969). See also chapter 7 by Donald Puchala in this volume.

50. Bleicher is among those who have argued that reiteration may have legislative effect. See Samuel A. Bleicher, "The Legal Significance of Re-Citation of General Assembly Resolutions," *American Journal of International Law* 63, 3 (July 1969):444–76. On the other side see, for example, Alice B. Haemmerli, "International Law and Majority Rule: The Case for Conservatism," in *U.S. Policy in International Institutions: Defining Reasonable Options in an Unreasonable World*, ed. Seymour Maxwell Finger and Joseph A. Harbert (Boulder, Colo.: Westview Press, 1978), 338–62; and Leo Gross, "The Development of International Law through the United Nations," in *The United Nations: Past, Present, Future*, ed. James Barros (New York: Free Press, 1972), 171–217.

51. Among recent examples, see Schachter, "The Nature and Process," 788–95. See also Edward McWhinney's conclusion: "The General Assembly resolution begins to take on a declaratory, hortatory quality under the impetus of Third World drafting and direction; and in spite of the denials by Western jurists and publicists of any present law-making character, such resolutions to an increasing extent in recent years come to acquire a sense of prophecy and of law-in-the-making . . . as 'soft' law they have a habit of turning out to be the 'hard' law of tomorrow or the day after tomorrow," in Edward McWhinney, Q. C., *United Nations Law Making: Cultural and Ideological Relativism and International Law Making for an Era of Transition*, (New York: Holmes & Meier, 1984), 46. For an argument that these processes do not create rules, although they may be involved in binding rules being created, see chapter 2 by Robert Riggs in this volume.

52. See Christopher H. Schreuer, "The Relevance of United Nations Decisions in Domestic Litigation," *International and Comparative Law Quarterly* 27 (January 1978): 1–17. This article deals with cases from the United States, France, the United Kingdom, Australia, Italy, the Federal Republic of Germany, Israel, Spain, Egypt, and Rhodesia. Two recent cases in the United States are relevant: *Filartiga v. Peña-Irala*, 630 F.2d 876 (2d Cir. 1980); and *Rodriguez-Fernandez v. Wilkinson*, 506 F. Supp. 787 (D. Kan. 1980). For a somewhat skeptical reading of the significance of these cases, see Richard B. Bilder, "Integrating International Human Rights Law into Domestic Law—U.S. Experience," *Houston Journal of International Law* 4, 1 (Autumn 1981): 1–13. See the other articles on these cases in the same issue of the *Houston Journal of International Law* for less skeptical readings. See also Friedrich Kratochwil, "The Role of Domestic Courts as Agencies of the International Legal Order," in *International Law: A Contemporary Perspective*, ed. Richard Falk, Friedrich Kratochwil, and Saul H. Mendlovitz (Boulder, Colo.: Westview Press, 1985), 236–63.

53. On this subject, see chapter 4 by Robert Gregg in this volume.

54. Davidson Nicol, *The United Nations Security Council: Toward Greater Effectiveness* (New York: UNITAR [United Nations Institute for Training and Research], 1982), 13; and Ivor Richard, "The Council President as a Politician," in *Paths to Peace: The UN Security Council and Its Presidency*, ed. Davidson Nicol (New York: Pergamon Press, 1981), 252.

55. "[T]he United Nations resembles the legislature in the parliamentary system." See Ambassador Jeane J. Kirkpatrick, address given at Arizona State University,

Tempe, Arizona, October 23, 1981, reprinted in Jeane J. Kirkpatrick, *The Reagan Phenomenon—And Other Speeches on Foreign Policy* (Washington, D.C.: American Enterprise Institute for Public Policy Research, 1983), 82.

56. See Ambassador Kirkpatrick's remarks quoted in note 5 above. See also Friedrich Kratochwil, "The Force of Prescriptions," *International Organization* 38, 4 (Autumn 1984): 685–708.

57. See Ronald I. Meltzer, "UN Structural Reform: Institutional Development in International Economic and Social Affairs," in *The US, the UN, and the Management of Global Change*, ed. Toby Trister Gati (New York: New York University Press, 1983), 38–62. Meltzer, "Restructuring the United Nations System: Institutional Reform Efforts in the Context of North-South Relations," *International Organization* 32, 4 (Autumn 1978): 993–1018; and John P. Renninger, "Restructuring the UN System," in *The Emerging International Economic Order: Dynamic Processes, Constraints, and Opportunities*, ed. Harold K. Jacobson and Dusan Sidjanski (Beverly Hills, Calif.: Sage, 1982): 257–77.

58. Renninger, "Restructuring the UN System," 259.

59. The figures are from Lister, *Decision-Making Strategies*, 68–71. The quotas are not synonymous with votes because each member has 250 "basic votes" in addition to those associated with the quota.

60. Ibid., 94–95.

61. See pp. ix, 9 above.

62. See Robert Gregg, "The Apportioning of Political Power"; Robert Rothstein, *Global Bargaining: UNCTAD and the Quest for a New International Order* (Princeton, N.J.: Princeton University Press, 1979), 179; and Jeane J. Kirkpatrick, "The U.N. and the U.S.," in *The U.N. under Scrutiny*, ed. Midge Dector, et al. (The Heritage Foundation, 1982), 25; Kirkpatrick, *The Reagan Phenomenon*, 82; and Shultz, "The United Nations after Forty Years."

63. Peter Willetts, *The Non-Aligned Movement* (New York: Nichols, 1978), 22, 29. Jackson takes a different view, that the bond is "psychological reassurance and a sense of common identity," in Richard L. Jackson, *The Non-Aligned, the UN and the Superpowers* (New York: Praeger, 1983), 236.

64. Ibid., p. 142.

65. See, for example, Robert A. Mortimer, *The Third World Coalition in International Politics* (Boulder, Colo.: Westview Press, 2nd ed., 1984).

66. See Robert L. Rothstein, "Regime Creation by a Coalition of the Weak: Lessons from the NIEO and the Integrated Program for Commodities," *International Studies Quarterly* 28, 3 (September, 1984): 326; and, in general, Rothstein, *Global Bargaining*. For an argument that consensus in interbloc negotiations concealed divergence within the bloc, see Harold K. Jacobson, et al., "Revolutionaries or Bargainers? Negotiators for a New International Economic Order," *World Politics* 35 (March 1983).

67. Mortimer, *The Third World Coalition*, 173, and Rothstein, "Regime Creation," 307. See also chapters 4 and 6 in this volume, by Robert Gregg and Robert Friedheim, respectively.

68. Recent scholarship concludes that the LDCs sought to effect reform within the existing international economic system rather than to overturn it, despite some "radical" pressures from within their ranks. See Mortimer, *The Third World Coalition*; Rothstein, "Regime Creation," 311–12; and Jacobson, et al., "Revolutionaries or Bargainers?" 367. Jacobson, et al. approvingly note Helmudt Schmidt's characterization of the NIEO negotiations as "a struggle for the world product."

69. See, for example, Richard Bernstein, "Divers African Nations Find Unanimity at U.N.," *New York Times,* January 25, 1984, 3.

70. UNESCO, *Manual of the General Conference: 1977 Edition,* 61–62, 65–67.

71. Gidon Gottlieb, "Global Bargaining: The Legal and Diplomatic Framework," in *Law-Making in the Global Community,* ed. Nicholas G. Onuf (Durham, N.C.: Carolina Academic Press, 1982), 110.

72. United States Permanent Representative to the United Nations Educational, Scientific and Cultural Organization (UNESCO), letter to the Director-General for Ambassador Jean Broward Shevlin Gerard, July 13, 1984 (xerox), 2–3. See also *Assessment of U.S.-UNESCO Relations, 1984,* 49.

73. Gottlieb, "Global Bargaining," 114, 117.

74. Sydney Bailey, "Evolution of the Practice of the Security Council," in *Paths to Peace: The UN Security Council and Its Presidency* (New York: Pergamon Press, 1981), 45. This interpretation is not, however, supported by Ivor Richard, "The Council President," 247.

75. See Mortimer, *The Third World Coalition;* Jackson, *The Non-Aligned;* Willetts, *The Non-Aligned Movement;* and Rothstein, "Regime Creation." For a different example, see Chadwick P. Alger, "Negotiation, Regionale [sic] Groups, Interaction and Public Debate in the Development of Consensus in the United Nations General Assembly," *Transactions of the Sixth World Congress of Sociology* (1966), 323–33. See also chapter 6 on UNCLOS by Robert Friedheim in this volume.

76. Richard Cooper, "Prolegomena to the Choice of an International Monetary System," in *World Politics and International Economics,* ed. C. Fred Bergsten and Lawrence Krause (Washington, D.C.: Brookings, 1975), 94.

77. See, for example, Richard N. Gardner, "United Nations Procedures and Power Realities: The International Apportionment Problem," Department of State *Bulletin* (May 10, 1965). In this article, Gardner, who was Deputy Assistant Secretary of State for International Organization Affairs at the time, referred to a State Department study conducted in 1962 that concluded that the interest of the United States would not be served by substituting a weighted voting arrangement for the one-member–one-vote system that prevailed.

78. Gregg, "The Apportioning of Political Power," 72.

79. This view of consensus was expressed, for example, by the U.S. Permanent Representative to UNESCO during the Spring 1984 meeting of the Executive Board. Consensus, she said, was not agreement but no more than "agreement not to disagree." See also Barthold C. Witte, "UNESCO—Crisis and Reform," *Aussen Politik* 35, 3 (Autumn 1984): 226.

80. See note 42, above.

81. Ruth B. Russell, "United Nations Financing and the 'Law of the Charter,' " *Columbia Journal of International Law* 5, 1 (1966): 75; John G. Stoessinger, *The United Nations and the Superpowers* (New York: Random House, 1965), 46; and Thomas M. Franck, *Nation against Nation,* 100–02.

82. Gregory T. Kruglak, *The Politics of United States Decision-Making in United Nations Specialized Agencies: The Case of the International Labor Organization* (Washington, D.C.: University Press of America, 1980), 149–64.

83. See chapter 9 by Leon Gordenker in this volume.

84. Edward H. Buehrig, *The UN and Palestinian Refugees: A Study in Nonterritorial Administration* (Bloomington, Ind.: Indiana University Press, 1971), 177–78.

85. *The United States Participation in the* UN: *Report by the President to the Congress for the Year 1982*, 158.

86. Americans for the Universality of UNESCO, *Newsletter* 1, 4 (October 1985): 12.

87. Edward Poultney, "UNESCO's Development Aid 'Matchmakers,'" UNESCO *Features* 807 (1985): 11–14.

88. Buehrig, *The* UN *and Palestinian Refugees*, 54–58.

89. See chapter 5 by Ronald I. Meltzer in this volume; Raymond Vernon, "Old Rules and New Players: GATT in the World Trading System," draft, May 11, 1983, Harvard CFIA (Center for International Affairs) 25th Anniversary; Charles Lipson, "The Transformation of Trade: The Sources and Effects of Regime Change," *International Organization* 36, 2 (Spring 1982).

90. Walter Galenson, *The International Labor Organization: An American View* (Madison, Wisc.: University of Wisconsin Press, 1981), especially 252–69.

91. See Alan L. Keyes, "Fixing the UN," *The National Interest* 4 (Summer 1986): 12–23.

92. See chapter 15 of this volume for further discussion of "opting out."

93. For evidence of the controversiality of Jenks' tenure as Director-General of the ILO, see Kruglak, *The Politics of United States Decision-Making*, 152–55.

94. See chapter 12 by Michael Schechter in this volume.

95. For an examination of M'Bow's controversiality, see chapter 13 on "The Political Role of the Director-General of UNESCO" in this volume.

96. On such interagency relations, see Lawrence S. Finkelstein, "The IR of IGOs (A Preliminary Excursion into the Significance of What International Intergovernmental Organizations Do with Each Other)," paper delivered before the annual meeting of the International Studies Association, 1980. On the predominant role of the staff in the International Bank for Reconstruction and Development, see William Ascher, "New Development Approaches and the Adaptability of International Agencies: The Case of the World Bank," *International Organization* 37, 3 (Summer 1983): 415–39. See also Kendall Stiles, "A Glimpse Inside the IMF: Some Observations on Staffing, Power and Debt Negotiations in the International Monetary Fund," prepared for delivery at the 1985 annual convention of the International Studies Association, Washington, D.C., March 5–9, 1985.

97. See Oscar Schachter, "The International Civil Service," in *Dag Hammarskjöld Revisited: The* UN *Secretary-General as a Force in World Politics*, ed. Robert S. Jordan (Durham, N.C.: Carolina Academic Press, 1983), 59–61.

98. Kruglak records the belief that Jenks' control of patronage when he was Deputy Director-General of the ILO may have helped him to be chosen Director-General. See Kruglak, *The Politics of United States Decision-Making*, 152–53.

99. Schachter, "The International Civil Service," and Finkelstein, "Some Aspects of Power Sharing."

100. *Charter of the United Nations. Report to the President on the Results of the San Francisco Conference*, by the Chairman of the United States Delegation, the Secretary of State, June 26, 1945, 27–28, 262–66.

101. For a description of the activities of selected INGOs and NGOs, see Peter Willetts, ed., *Pressure Groups in the Global System* (London: Frances Pinter, 1982). The title of the volume is itself revealing about an important aspect of the international role of NGOs and INGOs.

102. See chapter 8 by David Forsythe in this volume.

103. See chapter 7 by Donald Puchala in this volume.

104. "Rights Groups in Losing Battle for U.N. Role," *New York Times*, March 9, 1987, 5. See also Chiang Pei-heng, *Non-Governmental Organizations at the United Nations: Identity, Role, and Function* (New York: Praeger, 1981).

105. For an interesting case study of an influential network in the field of civil aviation, see Christer Jönsson, "Interorganization Theory and International Organization: An Analytical Framework and a Case Study," *International Studies Quarterly* 30, 1 (March 1986). This case study of a network centered on the International Air Transport Association (IATA) showed how influence could be effectively exerted to change a policy of the U.S. government.

106. See chapter 9 on UNHCR by Leon Gordenker in this volume.

107. Kruglak's is a good account; see *The Politics of United States Decision-Making.*

108. Jacobson, *Networks* p. 14.

109. Robert O. Keohane, "The Study of International Regimes and the Classical Tradition in International Relations," prepared for delivery at the 1986 annual meeting of the American Political Science Association, the Washington Hilton, August 28–31, 1986.

2

The United Nations and the Politics of Law

Robert E. Riggs

●

Distinguishing Law and Politics

International law has traditionally been regarded as a "body of rules and principles binding upon . . . states in their relations with one another."[1] In contrast a more recent definition by Weston, Falk, and D'Amato holds that international law should be viewed not as a set of rules applicable to states, but rather as "a configurative *process* of authoritative *and* controlling decision which, through an inter-penetrating medley of command and enforcement structures, both internal and external to nation-states, effects value gains and losses across national and other equivalent political boundaries."[2]

The first definition has the advantage of simplicity. The second, though weighed down by a heavy load of professional jargon, is more attuned to the growing complexity of contacts within the global system and the normative structures that have developed to regulate those contacts. States are still the principal subjects of international law, but they are not the only subjects. Intergovernmental organizations, as well as states, are juridical persons with rights and duties under international law. So also, for some purposes, are individuals and nongovernmental organizations. The International Centre for the Settlement of Investment Disputes (ICSID), for example, was established precisely because of the need for judicial settlement procedures not subject to the control of any government and applying equally to governments and private entities.

This chapter adopts a concept of international law that, like the Weston definition, presumes the application of a variety of prin-

ciples, rules, and cross-national decision processes to a variety of
subjects ranging from states to individuals. Use of the term "law,"
however, will differ in one important respect from that of Weston
and his colleagues. They treat law as a *process* of effecting "value
gains and losses," whereas I will retain the more common notion
of law as a body of *principles, rules,* and *decisions* having some
obligatory or binding character. Law is obviously related to the process of distributing rewards and benefits. But treating law as process
obliterates the distinction between law and politics and can only
lead to analytical confusion in a study concerned with the relationships between them.

Although law and politics are not identical, the Weston focus on
law as process draws attention to their close interconnection.[3] As a
product of the political process law is the medium by which certain
value allocations are defined and legitimized. Once enunciated, law
affects subsequent allocations by inhibiting some political actors
and extending the reach of others in their efforts to influence decision outcomes. Law, moreover, is virtually meaningless without
reference to its origin and application within the political process.
Principles and rules standing alone are mere abstractions. They gain
meaning and specificity by application to concrete situations.

Knowledge of process is also essential to the evaluation of claims
that particular principles, rules, or decisions have the status of law.
Political actors frequently invoke "law" in support of their positions
because law has an authoritative quality lacking in other rules. Law
is law because it has legitimacy—those to whom it is addressed
recognize an obligation to comply. If a rule can be characterized as
law it becomes a more effective resource for those who have an
interest in its acceptance and application. In this dialogue the origin
of the rule is crucial because the credibility of the claim generally
depends on the process from which the rule emerges. This is true
in national legal systems, where rules are regarded as law when
they have been produced by accepted procedures, most commonly
by judicial or legislative action in accordance with constitutional
norms. It is also true of international law.

The United Nations and
the Global Law-Making Process

UN agencies affect the development of international law in a variety
of ways. Treaty and custom have traditionally been the primary

means for creating binding international obligations, and the United Nations has contributed to both. Article 38(1) of the Statute of the International Court of Justice includes "general principles of law recognized by civilized nations," judicial decisions, and "the teachings of the most highly qualified publicists" along with treaty and custom as sources of international law. Each of these sources undoubtedly has contributed to the development of new international law through iteration by domestic and international tribunals or by governments groping for an applicable rule of law. Such rules do not become general international law, however, until they achieve general acceptance by states, presumably through the operation of custom or inclusion in international conventions. Obviously no judge or legal writer, however highly qualified, has authority to legislate for the international community.

In addition to their role in treaty making and the development of customary law, UN agencies and other intergovernmental organizations have added something distinctive to the norm-creating process by adopting various modes of majority rule for amendment of their constitutive documents as well as for ordinary decisionmaking. This chapter briefly examines UN contributions to international law through custom and treaty, and then considers at greater length the legal effects of other forms of rule making by UN agencies.[4]

The United Nations and Traditional Modes of Norm Creation

The UN role in producing multilateral treaties is easy to document. Its contribution to international customary law is probably of equal significance, though less obvious because the solidification of state practice into a customary legal norm is always beset with uncertainties. Frequently the two processes are interrelated. A treaty creates legal obligations among the parties to the instrument but does not of itself establish rules of general international law. It is applicable to all states only if all states are parties. Even a widely ratified multilateral convention does not create legal obligation for the minority of states that fail to ratify it. Nonratification need not be conclusive, however. Over a period of time third-party observance of the rules embodied in the treaty can give those rules the status of customary international law. The point at which this transformation occurs may not be readily identifiable. But when it does occur states that previously were not obligated to comply with the treaty are now bound by the rule as embodied in customary international law. The interrelationship also runs in the opposite direction. If a treaty embodies existing rules of customary law, nonsignatories are still not obligated by the treaty but may nevertheless be subject to the same or a similar obligation under the customary international norm.

As sources of international law, treaty and custom share a common respect for the principle of consent, although their modes of consent differ. With treaties the act of consenting is formal ratification. With customary law the consent is manifest by conforming to the general practice in the *belief* that conformity is a matter of legal obligation or, in the case of a newly developing norm, a *claim* that a state has acted as a matter of legal right. The psychological belief-claim element of consent is commonly referred to by the Latin term *opinio juris*. Reliance upon state behavior, which is sometimes ambiguous, and the need to discover "beliefs," obviously makes consent to customary law more difficult to ascertain.[5] It also raises the question of how much consent is required and who is bound by the rule. A treaty is binding upon the parties, however few or numerous, as soon as all or a specified number have ratified. Custom, by contrast, does not ripen into a binding legal norm until it has achieved acceptance among most (but not necessarily all) states.[6]

As forums where the vast majority of states interact regularly, the UN and its related agencies have performed a catalytic function in the development of both treaty law and customary law. The customary law includes rules defining the role of international organizations within the international system, as well as general international law governing the conduct of states. The actions of states within the UN system and in activities fostered by the United Nations may be legal acts that serve as evidence of emerging international custom. UN resolutions, for example, which have only recommendatory force in themselves, are sometimes cited by domestic courts as evidence of customary international law.[7] The United Nations is also continuously engaged in law making through the drafting of multilateral treaties, some of which may be ratified by a substantial majority of UN members and thus provide a uniform rule of law for many states. Some treaties achieve still wider application through the operation of custom.

In drafting, or encouraging the drafting, of law-making treaties, the United Nations has used a variety of forums. The Sixth Committee of the UN General Assembly, a sessional committee on legal matters, drafted the widely ratified Convention on Genocide. The

United Nation Committee on the Peaceful Uses of Outer Space has done the spade work on a number of treaties relating to outer space.[8] The Commission on Human Rights of the UN Economic and Social Council has served as the primary drafting agency for numerous human rights treaties, including the comprehensive International Covenant on Civil and Political Rights and the International Covenant on Economic, Social and Cultural Rights. Other treaties have been drafted by special conferences convened by the UN General Assembly, perhaps most notably the UN Convention on the Law of the Sea approved and signed in 1982 by a UN conference that had met periodically for nearly a decade. Since 1966 a United Nations Commission on International Trade Law has been drafting rules for international commercial transactions, and a UN Commission on Transnational Corporations has labored for more than a decade on a draft code on multinational corporations. The International Labor Organization, UNESCO, the International Maritime Organization, and virtually every intergovernmental organization within the UN system have also produced treaties within their respective fields of competence.

While activities bearing on law making are thus widely dispersed within the UN system, the UN International Law Commission (ILC) was established for the specific purpose of assisting the Assembly in discharging its Charter responsibility for "encouraging the progressive development of international law and its codification."[9] Originally a collegial body of fifteen members, the commission presently consists of thirty-four legal specialists elected by the General Assembly for five-year terms. Each is supposed to be a person "of recognized competence in international law." In recent years foreign office lawyers have become more numerous than the university professors who once dominated the commission. Seats are distributed by agreed formula among the political-geographic regions of the world, and by tacit agreement there is always one national of each permanent member of the Security Council on the commission. The commission thus combines the expert with the political. Legal expertise is essential to effective performance, but the commission's work must also be politically acceptable if it is to win the consent of states necessary to convert its draft proposals into binding obligations.

The commission has drafted a number of multilateral treaties designed to codify, clarify, and in some instances modify specific areas of international law. Several have been ratified and are currently

in force, including treaties dealing with ocean law, the immunities
of diplomats, the reduction of statelessness, consular relations, and
the law of treaties, among other subjects. A convention on the law
of treaties between states and international organizations was
opened for ratification in 1986. When the International Law Commission completes its work on a draft treaty, the normal procedure
is submission to the General Assembly for approval and convening
of a conference of plenipotentiaries to negotiate the final document.
The commission is currently working on drafts relating to jurisdictional immunities of states and their property, state responsibility,
international liability for injurious consequences of acts not prohibited by international law, the status of the diplomatic courier
and diplomatic bag, the nonnavigational uses of international wa-
tercourses, relations between states and international organizations,
and a code of "offences against the peace and security of mankind."
The last mentioned code, an attempt to specify in greater detail the
principles of international law set forth in the Nuremberg Charter,
has been on the ILC agenda since its first session in 1949. So also
has the question of state responsibility for internationally wrongful
acts. Viewed as a whole the ILC has a record of solid but unspec-
tacular achievement in the development of international law. It
represents a "low-profile, technical-legal approach"[10] that concen-
trates on matters of little urgency and secondary political importance.
The larger, highly charged issues of global law making find their
way to other arenas more universal in membership and less conservative in outlook.

Other UN Rule Making: Law without Consent?

UN agencies engage in much rule making outside the treaty process.
While most of the rules are not generally applicable international
law, many are legally binding upon some or all of their respective
member states. The latter include rules governing the internal operations of international organizations and, in some instance, rules
of external application.

Internal Rules of International Organizations

Internal rules govern the structure and process of an international
organization, while rules of external application set standards for
state conduct outside that organizational setting. The requirement

of a two-thirds majority for the adoption of "important" resolutions in the UN General Assembly is an example of an internal rule. A resolution calling for the creation of a subsidiary UN body, such as a special commission on Namibia, is another. The subsequent functioning of the commission may have some impact on the world outside, just as a resolution adopted by a two-thirds majority may have an external application, but its creation is an internal matter. In contrast a resolution urging termination of hostilities between Iran and Iraq is clearly external in its application. Although closer to the borderline between the two, a UN rule fixing member contributions to the organization is best classified as an external rule, since state decisions about resource allocation involve national, not international, decisionmaking. The principal types of internal rules are rules of procedure for assemblies, councils, committees, and other deliberative bodies; rules for budgeting, program planning, and expenditure of funds; regulations governing staff and UN property; rules for the internal operations of field missions; and decisions on organizational matters such as the creation of subsidiary organs, election of officers, designation of members of UN organs, and admitting or expelling members.[11]

Internal rules, as a class, have the attributes of law. States and other persons subject to the rules recognize their legitimacy and usually comply with them. In theory and in common practice they are binding on their subjects. More than three decades ago Philip Jessup called attention to the legal character of procedural rules, asserting that within the scope of their operation they were in fact binding rules of law. "It is submitted," he said, "that the rules of procedure, or what we may call the 'parliamentary law' of an international organization, may properly be considered as part of international law of the same general binding character as treaty law and therefore legally binding upon the states members of the organization."[12] That judgment is widely accepted today, and is supported by the general practice of international organizations.

The legal quality of procedural rules can be explained by reference to the political circumstances of their origin. Some rules are authoritative because they appear in an organization's constitution, which has been approved through the treaty process. Ready examples are voting procedures, which typically are specified in the basic document. Such rules of procedure are binding upon the parties because states are bound in good faith to comply with the treaties they ratify or accede to.[13]

Consent by each participating state is the central feature of the treaty-making process and a principal reason for according legitimacy to the treaty. Significantly, however, the UN Charter and the constitutional documents of most other international organizations permit amendment by less than unanimous consent. Amendments to the UN Charter may be proposed by a two-thirds vote of the General Assembly and ratified by a similar proportion of the total membership, acting through their respective constitutional processes, provided each permanent member of the Security Council concurs (Article 108). Such new "constitutional law" of the organization is no longer legitimized by unanimous consent, but becomes law by virtue of compliance with Charter provisions previously consented to. Sovereign autonomy and independence are no doubt preserved by an objecting state's option to withdraw from the organization, but that possibility takes nothing away from the binding quality of the amendment for those choosing to remain.

In addition to specifying a number of procedural rules organization charters generally vest authority to make other procedural rules in the various deliberative organs that may be established. Thus the UN Charter empowers the General Assembly (Article 22), the Security Council (Article 30), the Economic and Social Council (Article 72), and the Trusteeship Council (Article 90) each to "adopt its own rules of procedure." The General Assembly is also authorized to establish regulations governing the appointment of UN staff. Nothing in the Charter expressly specifies that such rules and regulations constitute "law" binding upon members and UN employees. Yet no one doubts the obligation to comply or, in the case of staff at least, the right of the organization to apply sanctions for noncompliance. The practice of states within the organization clearly vindicates these expectations.

Consent remains the rationale for treating procedural rules as law, even though unanimous consent is not required to adopt them. As with the amendment process, member states, by approving the Charter, consented to the procedures by which rules would be made. The rule is legitimized by the process, ultimately traceable to the underlying consent. A prior question, of course, is why states would consent to such a process, given the prospect that each might at some time find itself in the minority? The simple answer lies in expediting the business of the organization. If unanimous consent is required for every decision, including those of a procedural nature, the wheels of the organization will turn very slowly, if at all.

The purposes that justify establishment of the organization in the first place are certain to be frustrated if the organization cannot act; and required unanimity is frequently a formula for inaction.

States thus accept and observe procedural rules as binding for the same reasons of practicality that underlie their initial consent to a charter placing such rule-making authority in the hands of a majority. Observance is further encouraged by the practical ability of the majority to enforce its will in procedural matters. If the majority wishes to consider a resolution adopted according to a particular rule of procedure, it is for all practical purposes adopted. There is little the dissenters can do about it besides protest. Procedural rules can be enforced as long as a majority is willing to abide by them and accept the consequences.

The preceding discussion of the legal quality of procedural rules has direct application to the United Nations and its specialized agencies because each of them has a basic constitutional document adopted through the treaty process. For the many international agencies owing their inception to a resolution adopted by an existing international organization, rather than to a multilateral treaty, the chain of legal authority linking procedural rules to the consensual act of treaty ratification is a little longer.[14] The links in the chain seem sturdy enough, however, and the authority ultimately traceable to a treaty creating the parent organization is reinforced by the practical need for agreed rules permitting the new organization to function and the ability of majorities to enforce them.

Most other types of internal law are authoritative for the same reasons as procedural rules. They have their initial basis in organizational charters, and they can ordinarily be enforced despite the objections of a minority. The UN Charter, for example, expressly authorizes the creation of subsidiary organs (Articles 22, 29, 68), the election of members of the various organs (Articles 23, 61), admission and expulsion of members (Articles 3, 4, 5, 6), the approval of a budget (Article 17), and the adoption of rules governing UN staff (Article 101). Authority to make rules for the internal governance of field missions can be reasonably implied from the power to create subsidiary organs and to regulate staff. As to enforcement by the majority, if a subsidiary organ is created over the objection of some members, those objections cannot prevent it from coming into being as long as the states that voted for it are willing to have their representatives serve on it. Dissenters may refuse to participate and— judging by a growing UN practice—refuse to contribute financially to its support; but this need not prevent the organ from functioning. Elections, admissions, and expulsions are similarly self-enforcing, and the United Nations as a corporate entity can enforce its regulations against individual staff as long as it has the support of a majority of members. Expenditures, of course, are well within the power of the organization to control. Once title to funds has passed from the donor to the recipient organization, the organization can manage them just as other property or corporate assets.

Rules and Decisions Having External Application

The multilateral treaty process is essentially the same, whatever organization may happen to initiate it. Internal rules also are similar from one intergovernmental agency to another. Organizations differ substantially, however, in the nature and legal status of their rules and decisions intended to have external application. For that reason the practice of a number of specialized agencies will be briefly noted, in addition to the United Nations itself.

The UN Charter. The UN Charter lays down a number of rules applicable to the conduct of member states. Article 2, paragraph 2, a catch-all provision, requires all members to "fulfill in good faith the obligations assumed by them in accordance with the present Charter." This merely reiterates existing law, since good faith observance of treaties was a preexisting international norm and would have applied to the UN Charter the same as to all other treaties, whether or not restated here.

Other paragraphs of Article 2 impose upon members a far-reaching obligation to "settle their international disputes by peaceful means" (paragraph 3) and to "refrain . . . from the threat or use of force against the territorial integrity or political independence of any state" (paragraph 4).[15] The nonuse of force for aggressive purposes may also have been a preexisting principle of international law. The Nuremberg Court acted on that premise, although the claim was not undisputed.[16] Whatever the historical status of the rule, it is the law of the United Nations, with its near universal membership. Unfortunately the application of the rule remains far from clear in theory and far from uniform in practice;[17] and self-defense, enshrined in Article 51, has been widely used by states as a justification for military activities directed against other states.[18]

The Charter also commits members, jointly and individually, to "promote" solutions to the world's social and economic problems

(Articles 55, 56). The commitment is so expansive, however, that it can scarcely constitute a rule of law demanding any particular conduct from a state. Arguably it might of its own force prohibit gross violations of human rights,[19] but even there the commitment is too amorphous to be very constraining. Such Charter provisions have their greatest impact upon international law by providing the basis for the drafting of treaties and the adoption of resolutions giving more specific content to the obligations. *Treaties*, of course, become law between the parties. The impact of *resolutions* purporting to expand or specify Charter obligations will be discussed below.

Other legal obligations flowing from the Charter, most of them governing member relations with the organization, are quite specific. Article 73e requires states administering non-self-governing territories to report regularly on their administration. The general observance of this rule has been marred somewhat by frequent controversy as to the self-governing status of particular territories. Article 94 restates a rule of general international law that parties to a dispute submitted to an international tribunal for judicial settlement (in this case the International Court of Justice) must comply with the decision of the court. Article 104 obligates members, within their respective territories, to grant the United Nations "such legal capacity as may be necessary for the exercise of its functions and the fulfillment of its purposes." Similarly, Article 105 guarantees to the organization and its officials "such privileges and immunities as are necessary" for the fulfillment of their functions.[20]

Article 17 also is regarded as making the General Assembly's budgetary assessments legally binding upon member states.[21] Over the years, however, the force of the obligation has weakened. As a practical matter if a state refuses to pay its assessments, no prior or subsequent majority vote can force it to do so. This was demonstrated in the peace-keeping finance crisis of 1964–65 and has since been repeatedly reaffirmed. Currently more than twenty-five countries refuse to support certain UN activities and, in consequence, have withheld a portion of their assessed contributions. The Soviet Union has often rejected assessments for peace-keeping operations. The United States has also treated some of its UN assessments as less than obligatory. For several years the United States has refused to pay costs associated with the Law of the Sea Conference, the Palestine Liberation Organization, and the South West Africa People's Organization. More recently, congressionally mandated cost cutting has forced much larger defaults. Especially significant has

been the Kassebaum Amendment, which limited the U.S. contribution to no more than twenty percent of the assessed UN budget,
beginning with the 1987 UN fiscal year, until such time as voting
on budgetary matters is made proportional to each state's contribution. Unless the United Nations changes its voting procedures
(highly unlikely) or reduces the U.S. assessment below the present
twenty-five percent (slightly less unlikely), or Congress changes its
mind about this and other UN funding cuts (unpredictable), the
United States will soon become the UN's largest defaulter.[22]

The tension between legal obligation, on the one hand, and lack
of practical capacity to enforce payment of contributions, on the
other, has dictated caution by the Assembly majority in using its
assessment power. Where major donors have balked at coerced
support of special programs and projects, the Assembly has normally
created "voluntary" funds to which members are urged but not required to contribute. Most development assistance programs, such
as the UN Development Program, fall in this category. The UN regular
budget, supported by assessment, includes some funding for technical assistance, but the amounts are relatively meager. For peace-
keeping the problem has been alleviated but not wholly resolved
by financing some operations through voluntary contributions.

In recent years big donors have raised serious objections to the
size of the regular budgets of the United Nations and its related
agencies. Vehement protest by the United States, the Soviet bloc,
and most Western industrialized countries persuaded the UN majority to limit budgetary growth for the 1984–85 biennium, and again
for the 1986–87 budget period, to about one percent (after adjustment for inflation). The United States had pressed for no growth
and no adjustment for inflation. At UNESCO, by contrast, the majority
voted a 3 to 4 percent real increase for its 1984–85 biennium, which
led some Western members to call for new procedures giving large
donors more control over budgetary matters. The 1986–87 biennium
did see drastic budgetary reductions, but not as the result of procedural reform. Rather, the withdrawal of three countries that had
accounted for nearly thirty percent of assessed contributions to
UNESCO—the United States in 1984, and the United Kingdom and
Singapore in 1985—created a deficit that could only be met by substantially reduced expenditures.

Since international law is in part a creature of custom, the behavior
of states has implications for the legal status of rules governing the
financing of UN operations. The principle of binding budgetary assessments, as embodied in Article 17, probably remains intact for

the ordinary expenses of the organization. Members continue to recognize the obligation and generally to observe it. Even the United States, with its current budgetary delinquency, does not deny the obligatory character of the assessment. The experience with peace-keeping finance, however, as well as other program-specific withholding of contributions by states, suggests that the obligation may become attenuated where a state has a strong objection to a particular program within the regular UN budget. This phenomenon could be equated to a situation not uncommon in other areas of international law where lack of adequate enforcement machinery permits violations of law to go effectively unchallenged. In many such instances, however, the precise nature of the rule and of the alleged violation are sufficiently ambiguous to leave room for a plausible argument that no violation has occurred. Not so with payment of budgetary assessments. No doubt exists when a contribution is due and unpaid. And when delinquency equals or exceeds a state's assessed contributions for two years, a sanction is available— the deprivation of a vote in the Assembly. If the Assembly fails to apply this sanction, it has acquiesced to the delinquency, and a transformation in the rule, or its obligatory character, may well be under way.[23]

Beyond the few obligations arising directly from the Charter, do UN organs have authority to bind member states without their consent? The answer, generally speaking, is only to a very limited extent. Except for internal rules, the Assembly's power is limited to recommendation. The same is true of every other UN organ except the Security Council and the International Court of Justice. The Charter appears to confer upon the Security Council substantial power to issue commands in matters relating to international peace and security, but the power has seldom been used and in practice has not been very significant. Decisions of the International Court of Justice are, by general international law and the express terms of the Charter, binding upon parties to the case.[24] The Court has no authority to decide a case, however, unless the affected parties have consented to its jurisdiction, either by agreement to refer the particular case to the Court or by prior agreement to accept the Court's jurisdiction in a specified class of cases.[25] This preserves the principle of consent and therefore adds little to the capacity of the UN to bind states against their will.[26]

The Force of General Assembly Resolutions. The legal effect of General Assembly resolutions has been a subject of continuing interest to scholars, as well as to UN members.[27] A general legislative power for the Assembly was specifically rejected at the San Francisco Conference,[28] but that has not prevented persistent claims that particular Assembly resolutions, including some of external application, have legal effects. Four broad types of legal effects have been claimed:

(1) resolutions have binding effect as internal rules, a category previously discussed;

(2) resolutions may contribute to the formation of new international law by crystallizing international opinion, redefining old rules in an authoritative way, influencing state practice, or serving as a step in the treaty process;

(3) by purporting to state rules of law, Assembly resolutions are evidence that such rules exist;

(4) some resolutions amount to legislation, creating new international law for member states and possibly for the whole international community.[29]

The binding effect of internal rules, as noted above, is generally conceded, and no one denies that Assembly resolutions sometimes influence the formation of new international law. The proposition that resolutions may be evidence of existing law is not in principle contested either, although the credibility of the evidence in particular cases is frequently disputed. On the other hand the claim that resolutions can ever of their own force "legislate" rules of external application is much harder to sustain. The few occasions when Assembly resolutions have imposed binding obligations upon states or have passed directly into general international law can be explained on grounds other than the force of the resolution itself. For example Assembly action on the former Italian colonies of Libya, Eritrea, and Italian Somaliland, taken in 1949 and 1950, was accepted as binding by all the states concerned. But this was because France, the Soviet Union, the United Kingdom, and the United States had agreed in the treaty of peace with Italy to let the Assembly dispose of the territories if the powers were unable to agree among themselves by September 1948. On this subject Assembly action was the practical equivalent of legislation, but only by virtue of the prior treaty, not through anything inherent in the Assembly process.

Resolution 95 of the first General Assembly, endorsing the legal principles contained in the Nuremberg Charter, illustrates another type of Assembly "law making." The Nuremberg Charter and Resolution 95 defined three types of international offenses: traditional war crimes, crimes against peace, and crimes against humanity. The rules relating to war crimes were based on laws and customs of warfare then generally accepted; but the right to punish individual political leaders for acts of international aggression (crimes against peace), and maltreatment by a government of its own populace (included within crimes against humanity), was by no means clearly established as international law before 1945. Since their adoption by the Assembly in 1946, however, all three categories of offenses have been regarded as part of general international law.

This case, more than the former Italian colonies, might suggest some inherent power in the Assembly to legislate in appropriate circumstances, or at least to make an authoritative restatement of the law. Resolution 95 did, apparently, perform a catalytic function in transforming specific claims into rules of law. And if it happened once, might not this "Resolution 95" phenomenon be repeated for other statements of legal principle adopted by the Assembly with little or no opposition? In theory, perhaps, it could, but in practice the essential corroborating elements are almost never present with Assembly resolutions. Resolution 95 was in many respects unique, evoked as it was by unspeakable atrocities and devastating armed conflict still fresh in the minds of government leaders. Repeated statements by the victorious allies both in and out of the UN provided the requisite evidence of *opinio juris*, and the ongoing war crimes trials were there to put the seal of practice upon the spoken commitment.[30]

Despite the singularity of those circumstances, proponents of the General Assembly's legislative competence see law making by declaration as a repeatable process.[31] Oliver Lissitzyn has insisted that UN declarations of legal principle adopted by a large majority of states may sometimes be an adequate substitute for widespread state conformance to a practice. Customary law arises from common expectations that states will act in a particular way as a matter of legal right or duty, and such "expectations may rest not only on actual conduct, but also on other forms of communication, including the verbal."[32] Treaties obviously create such expectations, and so—in his view—may UN declarations: "If such statements or declarations emanate from a large number of States and purport to deal with a legal matter, they may be regarded in some circumstances as indications of a general consensus amounting to a norm of international law."[33] Louis B. Sohn has more recently voiced a similar conviction that Assembly declarations may amount to "consensus decisions"

that governments "are willing to accept as new international law,
or a new interpretation of a previously accepted, more general principle."[34] If that is true, the Resolution 95 phenomenon undoubtedly
is repeatable. But if it is true, the development of customary law is
reduced to a claiming procedure without the need for validation by
other confirming state conduct.

A somewhat more tentative jurisprudential basis for ascribing
"limited legislative competence" to Assembly resolutions "supported by a consensus of the membership" has been elaborated by
Richard Falk.[35] The Assembly's lack of formal legislative authority
is not decisive because "in other legal contexts the characterization
of a norm as *formally binding* is not very significantly connected
with its *functional operation* as law."[36] Thus courts, national and
international, cite treaties and nonbinding declarations almost in-
terchangeably in support of their decisions, while states frequently
honor nonbinding understandings (for example the 1958 moratorium
on nuclear testing) and ignore opinions of the International Court
of Justice (for example the advisory opinion on peace-keeping finance). With such an indefinite line separating "*binding* from *nonbinding* norms governing international behavior, . . . the formal
limitations of status, often stressed by international lawyers, may
not prevent resolutions of the General Assembly, or certain of them,
from acquiring a normative status in international life."[37]

Falk is most persuasive in his discussion of the impact of Assembly
resolutions upon subsequent political behavior, although the thrust
of the argument is to emphasize the legitimating effects of subsequent events and of contextual factors that fuel the traditional process of creating customary law. His comments merit quotation at
length:

> In a social system without effective central institutions of gov-
> ernment, it is almost always difficult, in the absence of formal
> agreement, to determine that a rule of law *exists*. Normativity is
> a matter of degree, expressive of expectations by national gov-
> ernments toward what is permissible and impermissible. Certainly
> norm-declaring resolutions are legal data that will be taken into
> account in legal argument among and within states. A main func-
> tion of international law is to establish an agreed system for the
> communication of claims and counterclaims between international
> actors and thereby to structure argument in diplomatic settings.
> Diplomats in search of grounds for justification or of objection
> readily invoke resolutions of the Assembly. These efforts at per-

suasion do not seem to be influenced by whether resolutions are capable of generating binding legal rules or merely of embodying recommendations. The degree of authoritativeness that a *particular* resolution will acquire depends upon a number of contextual factors, including the expectations governing the extent of permissible behavior, the extent and quality of the consensus, and the degree to which effective power is mobilized to implement the claims posited in a resolution.[38]

Thus the limits on the Assembly's "quasi-legislative" competence spring less from lack of formal competence than from political constraints imposed by the need to mobilize "effective community power in support of legislative claims."[39]

Falk's analysis has intuitive appeal to students of politics, since it reflects quite accurately the way states use Assembly resolutions in the political-diplomatic bargaining process. Implicitly, however, it undermines the concept of law by blurring the distinction between law and nonlaw. Law no longer describes a discrete category of rules distinguished from other rules and principles by their obligatory quality. Instead all rules fit along a continuum and all are law, to a greater or lesser extent, depending on their placement on the continuum. The practical problem of ascertaining whether and when a particular rule has become law is thus transmuted into a denial of any theoretically meaningful threshold between law and nonlaw. Should this view be widely accepted, the ultimate consequence would be less to heighten respect for Assembly resolutions than to reduce the normative power of the law itself.

Absent some such relativistic theory of the law, the arguments against attributing legislative force to General Assembly resolutions are convincing. Julius Stone has argued that Assembly resolutions simply do not deserve such status because, "even when purporting to be 'declaring' or 'interpreting' law," they are likely to be "operations of power politics rather than explorations of truth."[40] Worse still, conferring the status of law upon "whatever precepts serve the interests of States positioned to stack votes in the General Assembly" would divorce law from its moorings in "existing constellations of power" and thus threaten "the survival of both the United Nations and the general international legal order."[41] This point of view is not necessarily confined to persons sharing Professor Stone's obvious contempt for the behavior of Assembly majorities. Nicholas Onuf, who is much more sympathetic to the concept of law making by declaration, nevertheless concludes that "the unwillingness of

Western states to accept" this new source of law is "an insurmountable obstacle to its actually existing."[42]

A contrary case, indeed, is hard to sustain.[43] The UN Charter, taken together with deliberations of the San Francisco Conference, establishes beyond doubt that Assembly resolutions were intended to be only hortatory in nature, with clearly specified exceptions relating primarily to internal organizational matters. Since then this understanding has been repeatedly confirmed in statements by member states, and it has been implicitly affirmed by the practice of following up certain declarations with a treaty-drafting process when legally binding effects are intended.[44]

The law of the Charter may be supplemented by customary law, but no serious argument can be made that states have by custom come to accept Assembly resolutions as law. The evidence is all to the contrary: states do not recognize any such general legislative power in the Assembly. Nor is there any basis for asserting a rule of customary law that Assembly resolutions constitute law in particular instances. Many resolutions command huge majorities; many even are adopted by consensus. But such majorities often include states that voted for the resolution, or failed to object, in order to avoid tarnishing their image by voicing opposition. This is not the stuff of which legal rules are made. Quite the reverse; such behavior is possible precisely because states know the resolution will have no legally binding effect.[45]

Denying the legislative competence of the Assembly still leaves a place for Assembly declarations within the existing law-making processes of the international system. Besides the Assembly's role in the drafting of multilateral treaties, discussed above, weight may be given to Assembly resolutions as part of the "practice of states" that contributes to the development of customary international law. UN debates, votes, amendments, and even nonadopted resolutions may also be regarded as facts of legal significance to the extent they bear on international law. But these "facts," standing alone, are not sufficient to constitute new customary law. They must be considered with other elements of state practice in determining whether a new customary norm has developed. An Assembly declaration may be a catalyst for state conduct that hastens the development of customary law.[46] Or it may be a declarative statement of existing international law. But in either case the status of the rule as law depends on the totality of state practice, of which the declaration itself is only one element.

Frequently the re-citation of Assembly resolutions by the Assembly or by other international bodies is offered as evidence of a continuing practice that constitutes international custom.[47] Each re-citation is undoubtedly an additional legal fact to be taken into account, but in totality all such reiterations constitute conclusive proof only of a custom of re-citing resolutions, not of the obligatory nature of the rules they contain. The same considerations that leave the original declaration devoid of legislative effect are present in each re-citation and all of them. The principles still require validation through confirming state conduct in other contexts.

The sensible controversy is not whether Assembly resolutions have the force of law in their external applications: most assuredly they do not. The real issue is whether a given rule enunciated by the Assembly has been adequately validated as customary law by other indexes of state acceptance. This is frequently a question on which reasonable people can disagree. Thus an advocate of a new international order can plausibly argue that "the largely hortatory propositions of yesterday contained in such resolutions as those on decolonization, national ownership of natural resources, and the like have really represented law-in-the-making in their execution and development, and now number among the accepted principles of the 'new' international law."[48] This may or may not be correct, depending on the particular proposition being discussed. But stating the argument in that fashion makes reasoned discussion possible by focusing on state acceptance rather than Assembly authority as the central issue.

Legislation by UN Specialized Agencies

Within the UN system a number of specialized agencies and other intergovernmental organizations cooperate with the Assembly and its subordinate organs but are legally independent, subject to their own charters and responsive to their own governing bodies. Like the United Nations, the specialized agencies "legislate" with respect to their own internal practice, and all have provisions for amendment of their constituent conventions by less than unanimous consent. Some, in limited substantive areas, have authority to adopt rules that create various kinds of legal obligations for their members.[49]

The nature and status of internal law enacted by these agencies is not essentially different from the internal rules of the United Nations. Their procedures for "constitutional" amendment, despite variations in detail, are also broadly similar.[50] In most of them an amendment may be proposed by a two-thirds vote of the organization's assembly, conference, or congress. The World Bank, the International Development Association, and the International Monetary Fund are exceptions, requiring only a majority of votes cast by their Boards of Governors. The International Finance Corporation (IFC), another financial institution connected with the World Bank, demands a larger majority, but the amendment process is complete when action by the IFC Board of Governors is taken. Despite the IFC exception, subsequent ratification of proposed amendments by members acting individually through their respective governmental processes is the general rule, and acceptance by two-thirds of member states is the most common requirement for entry into force.[51]

As is true of treaties, the process of ratifying amendments to the constitutive conventions of international organizations ensures that each ratifying state is genuinely committed to the acceptance of a binding legal obligation. Unlike the usual treaty process, however, the ratification requirements of most agencies leave the possibility that as many as one-third of the members may be bound without their consent. The dissenters might still vindicate their sovereignty by withdrawal from the organization, but such a drastic action could only be justified by interests strong enough to outweigh the values of cooperation that initially prompted membership in the organization.

In addition to internal rules and constitutional amendments several agencies have limited authority within specified substantive areas to impose other legal obligations upon their members without the consent of each affected state. These agencies include the International Telecommunication Union (ITU), the Universal Postal Union (UPU), the International Civil Aviation Organization (ICAO), the World Meteorological Organization (WMO), and the World Health Organization (WHO).

Fundamental ITU rules governing telecommunications can be legislated through the revision of its convention, which requires majority approval in the ITU Plenipotentiary Conference and ratification by individual states. The ratification requirement suggests the absence of any legislative effect, but in practice many states are bound without ratification because new amendments are treated as provisionally in force for all states at a specified date regardless of the number of ratifications.[52] UPU legislation of rules for international

letter post is similar—a majority in the UPU Congress, followed by
individual ratification, but with entry into force at a date specified
in the amendment regardless of the number of ratifications. Compliance is obligatory for every state unless it chooses to withdraw
from the UPU, but this is ordinarily not a feasible or desirable option.[53]

The ICAO[54] and the WMO[55] by majority vote have the authority in
certain subject areas to adopt technical regulations with which
members are legally bound to comply unless the member gives
written notice of inability to do so. The "notice" loophole undoubtedly dilutes the binding quality of the rule, but good faith is assumed
and the practice of states suggests that lack of economic and technical resources, not willful disregard, is at the root of most noncompliance. The WHO is also empowered to adopt regulations on specified technical matters that bind all members not objecting within
a given time period.[56] This preserves the right of individual consent
but leaves the possibility that the legal obligation may be accepted
through inadvertent failure to give notice of rejection. In all of these
agencies the deliberations are pointed toward accommodation and
consensus in the formulation of binding rules, with majority vote
the last resort.

The World Bank group of agencies (the International Bank for
Reconstruction and Development, , the International Development
Association, and the International Finance Corporation) and the International Monetary Fund (IMF)[57] present another approach to authoritative rule making. They have no formal authority to legislate
for their members, but their governing bodies have the power to
make authoritative interpretations of their respective constitutive
documents, which in some instances may amount to legislation. In
addition their daily activities employ contractual techniques intended to create legal obligations. Their business is lending money,
and borrowers obtain money only upon conditions specified in
binding legal instruments. Some loan agreements take treaty form;
others do not. But the lending agencies are careful to ensure that
the obligation is there. Almost invariably the obligation extends beyond timely repayment. The agreement is likely to cover the objects
for which the money may be spent and frequently imposes other
economic conditions. Conditions attached to IMF credits, in particular, often demand fiscal and economic discipline that countries
would not adopt on their own. Proceeding on a case by case basis,
the World Bank and the IMF may impose much broader limitations

upon a state's freedom of action than other intergovernmental organizations with ostensibly broader powers of legislation could ever hope to do.

Legislation by Majorities: Why It Exists Anywhere

Increasing interdependence has caused international organizations to proliferate, but states remain reluctant to entrust legislative authority to majority decision. International law is still a product mainly of treaty and custom. International organizations have made the treaty process more effective, and they also contribute to the development of customary law. This is particularly true of the UN system, whose agencies claim near universal membership. But neither function constitutes legislation in the sense of a majority enacting law in disregard of minority objections.

Some such legislative power does exist within the UN system, however, and this needs to be accounted for. The most pervasive form of legislation is internal law—the rules governing each agency's organization, procedure, and program decisions. As noted earlier this kind of legislative authority is not hard to explain. If procedure and program decisions depended on unanimous consent, large membership organizations would be virtually immobilized. An organization that cannot act is useless. If the organization is to function effectively, all must follow the same rules. Majority rule in internal matters is the price paid for a viable organization.

The price might be too high for some states if the same majorities consistently outvoted the same minorities. But UN deliberations are often marked by a genuine search for consensus, and when disputes arise the alignments differ enough from one group of issues to another that every state votes sometimes with the majority.[58] Moreover, majority rule is everywhere mitigated by political realities. In a few organizations, such as the World Bank or the UN Security Council, differences in power are recognized by giving greater weight to the votes of some states. Even where each state has an ostensibly equal vote, some states are inevitably more equal than others.

Every intergovernmental organization within the UN system also has some authority to legislate external rules through amendment of its constitutive document. Many constitutional amendments concern matters of internal structure and procedure, but some deal with rules applicable to the external conduct of states. Permitting amendment by majority action probably reflects an implicit assumption that basic principles should not be forever frozen in a mold that seemed desirable or expedient to the founders. Requiring unanimous consent could have that effect. Since constitutional amendment is an extraordinary process, fundamental change would not be anticipated often in most agencies. Oppressive amendments might conceivably be adopted, but each state has recourse to the ultimate safety valve—withdrawal from the organization if its interests are too seriously threatened. Although no state may individually thwart the collective will of the others, its own sovereign right to escape the obligation is preserved.

The rationale for constitutional amendment by majority decision is obviously persuasive, since every UN-related agency has it. The more interesting question is why some organizations, but not others, have provision for enactment of legally binding rules as part of the regular order of business. The ITU and UPU do it through amendment of their basic conventions; the ICAO, WMO, and WHO do it through prescribed legislative processes. The UN Security Council has authority, largely unused, to order mandatory enforcement action against states that threaten the peace. Most other UN agencies do not purport to make binding enactments at all, relying upon recommendation to induce the necessary cooperation.

The Security Council's paper enforcement powers were the product of especially compelling historical circumstances. The exigencies of war, still raging in Europe and the Far East, account for the founders' readiness to entrust such important security decisions to an eleven-member body dominated by the five permanent members. The prevention of future world war was an overriding objective at the San Francisco Conference, and unified action by the Great Powers within the framework of a universal security system was the logical way to achieve it. Those assumptions about the desirability of peace and the need for Great Power unity are still valid, but one may justifiably doubt that any such power would be given to the Security Council if the United Nations were being created today.

The specialized agencies that regularly exercise significant legislative or quasi-legislative authority are a more fruitful subject for generalization. They have common features that suggest that some conditions may be regularly associated with authoritative rule making by majorities. Perhaps significantly, each relevant characteristic relates to the function of the organization[59] and not to its structure, decisionmaking processes, or leadership patterns. The common features may be described as follows:

(1) The organization's function is highly technical in nature and thus dependent upon the advice of trained experts in the relevant scientific fields.

(2) The function is specific in the sense of being limited to a narrow area of public policy. Indeed, within each organization that exercises such authority, legal obligation is attached to rules only in specialized areas of the agency's field of operation.

(3) Technological change makes periodic revision of the rules a requisite to effective performance. Cumbersome, protracted methods of rule change may delay or preclude reaping the benefits of technological advances.

(4) Effective performance requires universal application of uniform rules among states affected by the function. Some rules are undoubtedly better than others but, within the range of options that might win support from bona fide technical specialists, uniformity is generally more important than the technical differences between viable options. Where uniformity is desirable but not necessary, rules generally take the form of recommendations rather than requirements, even within organizations that have legislative or quasi-legislative powers.

(5) The function may be important but the issues it raises are ordinarily low in controversiality. There is general agreement on the broad purposes to be achieved; hence disagreement, though sometimes severe, is likely to center more on technical considerations than on vital national interests.

The World Bank and the IMF illustrate one additional variable associated with the capacity to make authoritative decisions: money. Although both institutions required initial infusions of capital from member states, and capital subscriptions by members have been increased over the years, neither is heavily dependent on members for replenishment of funds. Both are lending institutions that demand and receive repayment with interest. They are, so to speak, independently wealthy. The World Bank obtains most of its lending capital through borrowing on world capital markets, just as a commercial bank might do. The IMF has been more dependent on periodic increases in member capital subscriptions, not as replenishment but as an addition to total capital in order to supply increased liquidity demanded by a rising volume of world trade. Since 1969 the Fund also has found a way to augment its resources without cost to members, which has eased if not eliminated the need for periodic increases in capital subscriptions. It has done this by creating a paper asset called Special Drawing Rights, which increase the usable reserves of hard currency available to its members without increased member subscriptions. This ready access to and control of massive amounts of funds does not give either agency general power to legislate for member states, but it does augment their capacity to drive hard bargains and impose upon individual states a contractual obligation to fulfill those bargains.

Conclusion

The United Nations and its specialized agencies have played an important role in the development of international law since 1945, primarily through the traditional norm-creating processes of treaty and custom that rely upon consent. True legislative power, in the sense of majorities binding minorities against their will, exists primarily with respect to internal rules and constitutional amendment.

A few agencies within the UN system have limited powers to legislate binding rules of external application without unanimous consent. These grants of power are usually limited to specific, technical activities of low controversiality, where effective international cooperation depends on application of uniform rules, and technological change makes periodic revision necessary. Most permit lawful noncompliance upon timely notification that compliance is not practicable. In all such agencies rule making relies heavily on input from technical experts, and the decisionmaking style is to achieve consensus whenever possible rather than exercise the majority's power to override minority objections.

These facts suggest that technological change has been a moving force behind most innovations in law making at the international level. International organizations are themselves a response to technologically induced opportunities for improving the lot of mankind that in previous centuries were nonexistent. Where limited legislative powers have been conferred, it has usually been done to secure the benefits of technical advances.

But the pressures of technology upon international rule making do not all point in the direction of binding legal obligations legislated by majorities. Slouka, for example, has argued that technological change is steering "the international normative process . . . towards the production of an endless multiplicity and diversity of norms distinguished more by their temporariness and flexibility than durability and firmness."[60] The effect is not so much to encourage the growth of legislation by majorities as to encourage consensus on practical ways of dealing with problems. This same idea is reflected in Buergenthal's comment that "the real genius" of the ICAO's regulatory system "lies in its noncompulsory character," and that its "complex and sophisticated aviation code," developed over the years "with almost no opposition from the Contracting States, would not be in existence today without this built-in flexibility."[61] It is also reflected in Leive's conclusion—based on detailed study of the WMO, the WHO, and the Joint FAO/WHO Codex Alimentarius Commission—that mandatory rules are generally less acceptable to states and often no better observed than nonbinding recommendations.[62]

Four decades of the United Nations have produced only modest, incremental growth in the legislative powers of international organizations. *Claims* to legislative effects have escalated more markedly, especially on behalf of General Assembly resolutions. But such claims cannot and do not give recommendations the force of law. The General Assembly is not the authoritative voice of a world community. It is only one of many group voices speaking for interests that some or all share. The decentralization of decisionmaking among a multitude of sovereign states within the international system is matched by proliferation of collective decisionmaking among a multitude of international agencies. The complexity of this decentralized system is further heightened by transnational interactions among bureaucratic subsystems of state and organizational actors, where interests are not exclusively bounded by national lines. The workability of the system depends on accommodation, not enforced conformity to binding rules. Successful accommodation of interests may promote greater willingness to accept binding rules. But forty years' experience with the politics of UN law making has demonstrated that accommodation must come first.

Notes

1. J. L. Brierly, *The Law of Nations*, ed. Humphrey Waldock (New York: Oxford University Press, 1963), 1.

2. Burns H. Weston, Richard A. Falk, and Anthony A. D'Amato, *International Law and World Order* (St. Paul, Minn.: West Publishing, 1980), 14. The definition has much in common with concepts and terminology found in the work of Myres

McDougal and David Easton. See, for example, McDougal, "The Impact of International Law upon National Law: A Policy-Oriented Perspective," *South Dakota Law Review* 4 (1959): 34–35; Easton, *A Framework for Political Analysis* (Englewood Cliffs, N.J.: Prentice-Hall, 1965), 50; Easton, *The Political System* (New York: Alfred A. Knopf, 1953), 129 and passim. But see, for example, Gaetano Arangio-Ruiz, *The United Nations Declaration on Friendly Relations and the System of the Sources of International Law* (Alphen aan den Rijn: Sijthoff & Noordhoff, 1979), 34–35, and H. L. A. Hart, *The Concept of Law* (Oxford, England: The Clarendon Press, 1961), 78; both defend the more traditional concept of law as a body of rules or norms.

3. Perhaps this is what Weston and colleagues had in mind, since their formulation relied heavily upon McDougal, "The Impact of International Law," who stressed the importance of both "rules" and "operations" to an understanding of international law. See also Christoph C. Schreuer, *Decisions of International Institutions before Domestic Courts* (New York: Oceana Publications, 1981), 1–2.

4. For a similar classification of "law making" processes see Charles Henry Alexandrowicz, *The Law-Making Function of the Specialized Agencies of the United Nations* (Sydney, Australia: Angus & Robertson, 1973).

5. The practice of states is often observable, and much can be learned from official records of states as they are made available. But how is a state's belief in the existence of legal obligation expressed? This presents no problem if an official statement accompanies the act. D'Amato suggests that the "simplest objective view of *opinio juris* is a requirement that an objective claim of international legality be *articulated* in advance of, or concurrently with," the act that constitutes conformity to the practice. Anthony A. D'Amato, *The Concept of Custom in International Law* (Ithaca, N.Y.: Cornell University Press, 1971), 74. Articulation under such circumstances would undoubtedly be good evidence. More often the sense of obligation is deduced from the practice itself, which seems justifiable as long as the state actor is aware of the claimed legal consequences of the act and no disavowal of those consequences is made. See Nicholas G. Onuf, "Global Law-Making and Legal Thought," in *Law-Making in the Global Community*, ed. Nicholas G. Onuf (Durham, N.C.: Carolina Academic Press, 1982), 18.

6. Or at least among states to whom the custom might apply, such as members of an international organization or states within a region having distinctive regional norms. See, for example, Edward McWhinney, *United Nations Law Making* (New York: Holmes & Meier, 1984), 8–20, which discusses "the spatial dimension of international law." And see Prosper Weil, "Towards Relative Normativity in International Law?" *American Journal of International Law* 77, 3 (July 1983): 433–34, commenting on the opportunity for individual states to "opt out" of a rule of customary law. For more extensive treatment see D'Amato, *The Concept of Custom;* and Michael Akehurst, "Custom as a Source of International Law," *British Yearbook of International Law* 48 (1974–75): 1–53.

7. Notable illustrations in the United States are *Filartiga* v. *Peña-Irala*, 630 F.2d 876 (2d Cir. 1980), which found torture committed by an official of a foreign state against a national of that state to be a violation of international law; and *Rodriguez-Fernandez* v. *Wilkinson*, 505 F. Supp. 787 (D. Kan. 1980), aff'd, 654 F.2d 1382 (10th Cir. 1981), which reached a similar conclusion with respect to arbitrary prolonged detention of an alien by the United States government. In each instance the court cited the Universal Declaration of Human Rights, although the Appeals Court in *Wilkinson* affirmed the lower court decision on the basis of domestic rather than

international law. On the general subject see Gregory J. Kerwin, "The Role of the United Nations General Assembly Resolutions in Determining Principles of International Law in United States Courts," *Duke Law Journal* (September, 1983): 876–99; Richard B. Lillich, "Invoking International Human Rights Law in Domestic Courts," *University of Cincinnati Law Review* 54, 2 (Spring 1985): 367–415; Christoph H. Schreuer, "The Relevance of United Nations Decisions in Domestic Litigation," *International and Comparative Law Quarterly* 27 (January 1978): 1–17; Krzyztof Skubiszewski, "Recommendations of the United Nations and Municipal Courts," *British Yearbook of International Law* 46 (1972–73):353–64.

8. These include the 1967 Outer Space Treaty, the 1968 Treaty on the Rescue and Return of Astronauts, a Convention on International Liability for Damage Caused by Space Objects (1971), a Convention on Registration of Objects Launched into Outer Space (1975), and an Agreement Governing the Activities of States on the Moon and Other Celestial Bodies (1979).

9. UN Charter, Article 13(1)(a). For detailed discussions of the commission and its work see B. G. Ramcharan, *The International Law Commission* (The Hague: Martinus Nijhoff, 1977); Herbert W. Briggs, *The International Law Commission* (Ithaca, N.Y.: Cornell University Press, 1965); and Mohamed El Baradei, T. M. Franck, and R. Trachtenberg, *The International Law Commission: The Need for a New Direction* (New York: UNITAR [United Nations Institute for Training and Research], 1981). An annual report on the work of the commission is published by the United Nations as a supplement to the Official Records of the General Assembiy. A summary of each annual session, from the perspective of the American participant, is published in the *American Journal of International Law*. See, for example, Stephen C. McCaffrey, "The Thirty-Seventh Session of the International Law Commission," *American Journal of International Law* 80, 1 (January 1986): 185–96.

10. McWhinney, *United Nations Law Making*, 104.

11. This list leans heavily on Henry G. Schermers, *International Institutional Law*, vol. 1 (Leiden: A. W. Sijthoff, 1972), 483–84.

12. Philip C. Jessup, *Parliamentary Diplomacy: An Examination of the Legal Quality of the Rules of Procedure of Organs of the United Nations* (Leiden: A. W. Sijthoff, 1956), 204.

13. The meaning of the treaty obligations may, however, change over time. Article 31 of the Vienna Convention on the Law of Treaties provides that a treaty is to be interpreted "in accordance with the ordinary meaning to be given to the terms of the treaty" but that the parties shall also take into account "(a) any subsequent agreement between the parties regarding the interpretation of the treaty or the application of its provisions; [and] (b) any subsequent practice in the application of the treaty which establishes the agreement of the parties regarding its interpretation." U.N. Doc. A/CONF. 39/27, p. 289.

14. Data presented in Harold K. Jacobson, William M. Reisinger, and Todd Mathers, "National Entanglements in International Governmental Organizations," *American Political Science Review* 80, 1 (March 1986): 141–59, indicate that most organizations established in recent years are offshoots of existing organizations. A majority vote in favor of a resolution is substituted for the more cumbersome process of treaty drafting, signature, and ratification.

15. See also Article 33, which urges recourse to specified modes of pacific settlement or to other peaceful means of the parties' choice.

16. See, for example, George A. Finch, "The Nuremberg Trial and International Law," *American Journal of International Law* 41, 1 (January 1947): 20–37, esp. 25–26.

17. The General Assembly's definition of aggression, Resolution 3314(XXIX), December 14, 1974, leaves much unclarified and specifically exempts force in aid of the right to self-determination, which itself is a highly flexible concept. John F. Murphy, *The United Nations and the Control of International Violence: A Legal and Political Analysis* (Totowa, N.J.: Allanheld, Osmun, 1982), 126, observes: "Even if they are often honored in the breach, the prohibitions of Article 2(4) against the threat or use of force . . . have served the world community well," at least as applied to "traditional violence." They have had less relevance, however, for internal wars and other nontraditional violence. Ibid., 135.

18. The United States, for example, sought to justify its mining of Nicaraguan harbors and other acts in support of the Contras as self-defense. In upholding Nicaragua's legal claim against the United States, the International Court of Justice reaffirmed the validity of the principle of self-defense under Article 51 of the Charter, but held that hostile acts by the United States against the Sandinista government did not fall within it. "Military and Paramilitary Activities in and Against Nicaragua" *(Nicaragua v. United States of America)*, Merits, Judgment, ICJ *Reports* (1986): 14.

19. Judge Stephen M. Schwebel has argued, as indeed have many others in and outside the United Nations, that South African apartheid is unlawful by virtue of Articles 1, 55, and 56 of the Charter, all of which refer to the promotion of human rights. See "Contemporary Views on the Sources of International Law: The Effect of U.N. Resolutions on Emerging Legal Norms," *Proceedings, American Society of International Law* (1979): 330. The practice of states since 1945, however, supports an interpretation that Articles 1, 55, and 56 are aspirational and not intended to impose specific legal obligations upon states.

20. Details of these obligations have been specified in international instruments. See, for example, Convention on the Privileges and Immunities of the United Nations of February 13, 1946, 1 United Nations Treaty Series (U.N.T.S.) 15, 21 United States Treaty Series (U.S.T.) 1428; Agreement Between the United Nations and the United States of America Regarding the Headquarters of the United Nations of June 26, 1947, 11 U.N.T.S. 11, United States Treaties and International Agreements Series (T.I.A.S.) 1676.

21. See, for example, Leland M. Goodrich, Edvard Hambro, and Anne Patricia Simons, *Charter of the United Nations: Commentary and Documents*, 3rd ed. (New York: Columbia University Press, 1969), 154, which states that Article 17 "gives the General Assembly power to apportion expenses of the United Nations among members and places upon them the obligation to pay the amounts thus determined." The International Court of Justice has also reached the same conclusion. See "Certain Expenses of the United Nations" (Article 17, paragraph 2, of the Charter), Advisory Opinion of July 20, 1962, ICJ *Reports* (1962): 193. And see also "Separate Opinion of Hersh Lauterpacht in Voting Procedure on Questions Relating to Reports and Petitions Concerning the Territory of South-West Africa," ICJ *Reports* (1955): 115. When the peace-keeping finance question was submitted to the International Court of Justice for an advisory opinion, rendered in 1962, the issue was not whether the Assembly had any authority to make obligatory assessments upon members, but whether the costs of peace-keeping could properly be treated as "expenses of the

Organization" and thus within the obligatory assessment power derived from Article 17. The Court concluded that they were. International Court of Justice, "Certain Expenses."

22. Near the end of its 1986 session the General Assembly moved part way toward the U.S. position by agreeing that its twenty-one-member Committee for Program and Coordination (CPC) should by consensus fix an overall ceiling on each biennial budget submitted to the General Assembly, which the General Assembly is not to exceed. In practice this gives each member of the CPC, including the United States, the opportunity to veto a proposed ceiling that is excessive. The CPC, along with the Advisory Committee on Administrative and Budgetary Questions, screens the UN budget prior to deliberation by the Assembly. See UN Document A/41/L.49/Rev. 1, December 19, 1986. The U.S. ambassador to the United Nations, Vernon A. Walters, claimed that the new arrangements largely satisfy U.S. concerns and said he would ask Congress to restore funds previously withheld. *The New York Times* (December 21, 1986): sec. 1, p. 5.

23. See note 13 supra regarding the effect of subsequent practice on Charter interpretation.

24. Advisory opinions, rendered at the request of authorized UN organs, are binding on no one, although they may have weight as authoritative restatements of international law.

25. As of July 31, 1986, forty-seven states, with varying reservations, had declarations on file pursuant to Article 36 of the Statute of the International Court of Justice (the "Optional Clause") accepting the Court's jurisdiction "in relation to any other state accepting the same obligation." See *Report of the International Court of Justice*, UN Document A/41/4 (1986). The texts of the declarations are reproduced in the *International Court of Justice Yearbook*, published annually at the Hague.

26. Not infrequently the Court may claim jurisdiction through a previous commitment of one of the parties, over the objection of that party. In such instances the objecting state has sometimes continued to deny jurisdiction and refused to participate further in the proceedings. India refused to participate in the "Trial of Pakistani Prisoners of War Case" *(Pakistan v. India)*, ICJ *Reports* (1973): 328; Iceland did the same in the "Fisheries Jurisdiction Case" *(United Kingdom v. Iceland, Federal Republic of Germany v. Iceland)*, ICJ *Reports* (1974): 3, 175; so did Turkey in the "Aegean Sea Continental Shelf Case" *(Greece v. Turkey)*, ICJ *Reports* (1978): 1; and Iran in the "Case Concerning United States Diplomatic and Consular Staff in Teheran" *(United States v. Iran)*, ICJ *Reports* (1980): 3. More recently, the United States rejected the Court's finding of jurisdiction in "Military and Paramilitary Activities in and against Nicaragua" *(Nicaragua v. United States of America)*, ICJ *Reports* (1984): 392. The U.S. response is discussed in *The New York Times* (January 19, 1985):p. 1, col. 6.

27. See, for example, Arangio-Ruiz, *The United Nations Declaration;* Obed Y. Asamoah, *The Legal Significance of the Declarations of the General Assembly of the United Nations* (The Hague: Martinus Nijhoff, 1966); Samuel A. Bleicher, "The Legal Significance of Re-Citation of General Assembly Resolutions," *American Journal of International Law* 63, 3 (July 1969): 444–78; Jorge Castaneda, *Legal Effects of United Nations Resolutions* (New York: Columbia University Press, 1969); Richard A. Falk, "On the Quasi-Legislative Competence of the General Assembly," *American Journal of International Law* 60,4 (October 1966): 782–91; Rosalyn Higgins, *The*

Development of International Law through the Political Organs of the United Nations (London: Oxford University Press, 1963); Rosalyn Higgins, "The United Nations and Law-Making: The Political Organs," *Proceedings, American Society of International Law* (1970): 37–48; D. H. N. Johnson, "The Effect of Resolutions of the General Assembly of the United Nations," *British Yearbook of International Law* 32 (1955–56): 97–122; Christopher C. Joyner, "U.N. General Assembly Resolutions and International Law: Rethinking the Contemporary Dynamics of Norm-Creation," *California Western International Law Journal* 11 (1981): 445–78; McWhinney, *United Nations Law Making*, 45–46, 55–58; Oscar Schachter, "The Nature and Process of Legal Development in International Society," *The Structure and Process of International Law: Essays in Legal Philosophy, Doctrine and Theory* in ed. R. St. J. Macdonald and Douglas M. Johnston (The Hague: Martinus Nijhoff, 1983), 745–808, esp. 787–95; Schreuer, "The Relevance of United Nations Decisions," 45–64; Stephen M. Schwebel, "The Effect of Resolutions of the U.N. General Assembly on Customary International Law," *Proceedings, American Society of International Law* (1979): 301–09; F. Blaine Sloan, "The Binding Force of a 'Recommendation' of the General Assembly of the United Nations," *British Yearbook of International Law* 25 (1948): 1–33; Julius Stone, "Conscience, Law, Force and the General Assembly," in *Jus Et Societas: Essays in Tribute to Wolfgang Friedman*, ed. Gabriel M. Wilner (The Hague: Martinus Nijhoff, 1979), 297–337.

28. A Philippine proposal to vest authority in the Assembly to make rules of international law, subject to a majority vote in the Security Council, was defeated by a vote of 26–1. *Documents of the United Nations Conference on International Organization*, vol. 9 (1945), 70.

29. The categories are adapted from Hermann Mosler, *The International Society as a Legal Community* (Alphen aan den Rijn: Sijthoff & Noordhoff, 1980), 88.

30. Louis Henkin, *How Nations Behave* (New York: Columbia University Press, 1979), 182, views the Assembly action somewhat more cynically as illustrating the adoption of "resolutions of legislative import which appear idealistic and which no nation sees as directed at its own behavior." If Henkin is right, the proscription of crimes against peace and crimes against humanity may be applicable only to political and military leaders of a defeated enemy state.

31. The kinds of resolutions most likely to contain statements of legal principles are commonly called "declarations," but they are and will be treated here simply as a species of resolution. For a more extensive discussion of declarations see Aranzio-Ruiz, *The United Nations Declaration*, and Asamoah, *The Legal Significance*.

32. Oliver Lissitzyn, *International Law Today and Tomorrow* (Dobbs Ferry, N.Y.: Oceana, 1965), 35. See Schwebel, "The Effect of Resolutions," 302–03, for a discussion of contrasting points of view on this issue.

33. Lissitzyn, *International Law*, 35–36. Jorge Castaneda, *Legal Effects*, 172, calls Assembly declarations of principles "persuasive evidence of the existence of the rule of law they enumerate," which create a "presumption that such a rule or principle is a part of positive international law."

34. Louis B. Sohn, "The International Law of Human Rights: A Reply to Recent Criticisms," *Hofstra Law Review* 9, 2 (Winter 1981): 352. The opinion of the International Court of Justice in the case of *Nicaragua* v. *United States of America* also takes the position that General Assembly declarations relating to the use of force in international relations have embodied legal commitments: "The effect of consent

to the text of such resolutions cannot be understood as merely that of a 'reiteration or elucidation' of the treaty commitment undertaken in the Charter. On the contrary, it may be understood as an acceptance of the validity of the rule or set of rules declared by the resolution by themselves." "Military and Paramilitary Activities in and against Nicaragua" *(Nicaragua v. United States of America)*, Merits, Judgment, ICJ *Reports* (1986): 100.

35. Richard A. Falk, *The Status of Law in International Society* (Princeton, N.J.: Princeton University Press, 1970), 175. This essay was first published as an article entitled, "On the Quasi-Legislative Competence of the General Assembly." Falk describes his view as "a middle position between a formally difficult affirmation of true legislative status and a formalistic denial of law-creating role and impact." Ibid., 174. Although not at the extreme, Falk seems clearly oriented toward the law-making pole.

36. Ibid., 175.

37. Ibid., 176.

38. Ibid., 178.

39. Ibid., 181. Falk suggests that a voting majority of two-thirds might satisfy this requirement if both the United States and the Soviet Union were included. Ibid.

40. Stone, "Conscience, Law, Force," 334.

41. Ibid., 334–35.

42. Onuf, "Global Law-Making," 27.

43. The following analysis relies heavily on Arangio-Ruiz, *The United Nations Declaration*.

44. Ibid., 18–20.

45. For an elaboration of these ideas see ibid., 22–30. See also Schwebel, "The Effect of Resolutions," 302, who, in summarizing this view of the law, observes, "states often don't meaningfully support what a resolution says and they almost always do not mean that the resolution is law. This may be as true or truer in the case of unanimously adopted resolutions as in the case of majority-adopted resolutions. It may be truer still of resolutions adopted by 'consensus.' " He then adds (while acknowledging that "the other pole of this problem also has much to be said for it"), "I confess to much sympathy for the foregoing line of analysis, for my personal experience so fully bears it out."

46. A strong case can be made that the Assembly has hastened norm creation in such areas as human rights, the use of international force, and outer space. See Joyner, "U.N. General Assembly Resolutions," 464–69; and chapter 8 by David Forsythe on human rights in this volume.

47. See discussion in Bleicher, "The Legal Significance."

48. McWhinney, *United Nations Law Making*, 58. "In strictly juridical terms, the General Assembly resolutions on such key subjects as decolonization and independence, on national ownership and control over natural resources, and on a New International Economic Order may not be, in their immediate origins 'hard' law; but as 'soft' law they have a habit of turning out to be the international law-in-action of today and the 'hard' law of tomorrow or the day after tomorrow." Ibid., 46. For further discussion of hard versus soft law, see R. R. Baxter, "International Law in 'Her Infinite Variety,' " *International and Comparative Law Quarterly* 29 (October 1980): 549–66; Michael Bothe, "Legal and Non-Legal Norms—A Meaningful Distinction in International Relations?" *Netherlands Yearbook of International Law* 11

(1980): 65–95; Ignaz Seidl-Hohenveldern, "International Economic Soft Law," *Recuil des Cours* (1979-II): 165–246; and Weil, "Towards Relative Normativity."

49. Alexandrowicz, *The Law-Making Function,* and Evan Luard, *International Agencies: The Emerging Framework of Interdependence* (Dobbs Ferry, N.Y.: Oceana, 1977), discuss the legislative competence of numerous international agencies.

50. For a careful, factual comparison of amendment procedures and grants of formal legislative competence, see Edward Yemin, *Legislative Powers in the United Nations and Specialized Agencies* (Leiden: A. W. Sijthoff, 1969). A somewhat more recent discussion of these and other agencies, focusing more on functions than on legal competence, is Luard, *International Agencies.*

51. Amendments to the constitutive conventions of the FAO, UNESCO, and WMO need not be ratified unless they impose new obligations upon member states.

52. For discussion of the organization and functioning of the ITU see chapter 11 by George Codding in this volume, and George A. Codding, Jr., and Anthony M. Rutkowski, *The International Telecommunications Union in a Changing World* (Dedham, Mass.: Artech House, 1982); and David M. Leive, *International Telecommunications and International Law: The Regulation of the Radiospectrum* (Dobbs Ferry, N.Y.: Oceana, 1970).

53. The most complete treatment of the Universal Postal Union is still George A. Codding, *The Universal Postal Union* (New York: New York University Press, 1964).

54. For discussion of ICAO rule making, see Thomas Buergenthal, *Law-Making in the International Civil Aviation Organization* (Syracuse, N.Y.: Syracuse University Press, 1969). For a more politically oriented study, see Young W. Kihl, *Conflict Issues and International Civil Aviation Decisions: Three Case Studies* (Denver, Colo.: University of Denver Press, 1971).

55. An excellent survey of WMO history, structure, and functions is found in David M. Leive, "The Regulatory Regime for Meteorology," *International Regulatory Regimes,* vol. 1 (Lexington, Mass.: Lexington Books, 1976), 153–329.

56. Extended treatments of the WHO as an institution include Robert Berkov, *The World Health Organization: A Study in Decentralized International Administration* (Geneva: Librairie E. Droz, 1957); Peter Corrigan, *The World Health Organization* (Hove, England: Wayland Publishers, 1979); David M. Leive, "The International Health Regime," *International Regulatory Regimes,* vol. 1 (Lexington, Mass.: Lexington Books, 1976), 1–152.

57. Some recent book-length analyses of the World Bank agencies include Edward S. Mason and Robert E. Asher, *The World Bank since Bretton Woods* (Washington, D.C.: Brookings Institution, 1973); Bettina Hurni, *The Lending Policy of the World Bank in the 1970's* (Boulder, Colo.: Westview Press, 1980); Hassan M. Selim, *Development Assistance Policies and the Performance of Aid Agencies* (London: Macmillan, 1983). For studies of the establishment and early performance of the IDA and the IFC, see James H. Weaver, *The International Development Association* (New York: Praeger, 1965); and James C. Baker, *The International Finance Corporation* (New York: Praeger, 1968). Literature on the IMF and the international monetary system is vast. See, for example, Benjamin J. Cohen, *Organizing the World's Money* (New York: Basic Books, 1977); Frederick K. Lister, *Decision-Making Strategies for International Organizations: The IMF Model* (Denver, Colo.: Graduate School of International Studies, University of Denver, 1984); Andreas F. Lowenfeld, *The International Monetary Fund* (New York: Matthew Bender, 1977); Tony Killick, ed.,

The IMF *and Stabilization: Developing Country Experiences* (London: St. Martins Press, 1984); John Williamson, ed., IMF *Conditionality* (Washington, D.C.: Institute for International Economics, 1983).

58. Chadwick F. Alger was one of the first to note the unifying effect of "cross-cutting cleavages" in international organization. See his "Non-Resolution Consequences of the United Nations and Their Effects on International Conflict," *Journal of Conflict Resolution* 5 (1961): 128–45. An organization suffers stress when alignments become solidified for a wide range of issues. The East-West cleavage imposed strains upon the United Nations during its early years, as the North-South cleavage does now.

59. The emergence of "function" as the central variable inevitably calls to mind the theory of functionalism elaborated by David Mitrany in a number of writings, most notably *A Working Peace System: An Argument for the Functional Development of International Organization* (London: Royal Institute of International Affairs, 1943), and in a neofunctionalist variant associated with Ernst B. Haas, *Beyond the Nation State: Functionalism and International Organization* (Stanford, Calif.: Stanford University Press, 1964). The theory will not be examined here, but a recent discussion of the subject is found in Robert E. Riggs and I. Jostein Mykletun, *Beyond Functionalism* (Minneapolis, Minn.: University of Minnesota Press, 1979).

60. Zdenek J. Slouka, "International Law-Making: A View from Technology," in *Law-Making in the Global Community*, ed. Nicholas G. Onuf (Durham, N.C.: Carolina Academic Press, 1982), 132.

61. Buergenthal, *Law-Making*, 121.

62. Leive, *International Regulatory Regimes*, vol. 2, 584.

3

Unit Veto Dominance

in United Nations Peace-Keeping

Alan M. James

●

In the parlance of the United Nations the phrase "international peace" now encompasses a great deal more than it did when the organization was founded.[1] Then it had a narrow and precise connotation, the essential physical feature of which was the absence of armed hostilities between sovereign states. Accordingly, peace could be said to be threatened only when such a conflict was imminent or likely. It was on this conceptual basis that the UN Charter set out a number of things that the organization might do to check any threats to the peace and to counter any aggressive acts that actually took place. Now, however, the ambit of the phrase has been considerably extended in resolutions emanating from the UN, so that a number of situations that are deemed by the majority to be both unpleasant and aggravating are also deemed to represent a threat to international peace. In consequence the organization regards itself as entitled to say and even do far-reaching things in relation to these matters. In this chapter, however, the focus will be the UN's response to threats to or breaches of peace in the narrower sense of the term.

The Charter Provisions

The UN Charter points in two very different directions when it deals with the organization's role regarding interstate conflict that is potentially or actually physical in nature. On the one hand it speaks in the language of authoritative decisions—and, moreover, decisions that are both drastic and highly centralized. Thus, although it has a limited membership, the Security Council is to act on behalf of the whole organization, and all the member states undertake to accept and carry out the Council's decisions. Furthermore, under Chapter VII of the Charter (Articles 39–51), the Council is authorized to take all manner of action to maintain the peace. It may call on members to implement a partial or complete severance of economic relations and communications with a misbehaving state, and may also require a breach of diplomatic relations. If these measures prove insufficient, it may, in the impressive language of Article 42, "take such action by air, sea, or land forces as may be necessary to maintain or restore international peace and security." Thus, in respect of the most sensitive and costly area of international activity, the Charter provides for the taking of authoritative decisions not even by a simple majority of the whole membership, but just by a qualified majority (seven out of eleven until the end of 1965; nine out of fifteen since 1966) of the Security Council. On paper the Council takes on the appearance of an extremely powerful executive committee. It is depicted as a kind of politburo of an incipient world state.

On the other hand, however, the same document also speaks in the language of unit veto diplomacy. That is to say it relies, in certain crucial respects, on the consent of the UN's members for decisions and action in support of peace. All the units making up the system have a veto as far as their own involvement in enforcement action is concerned. Some can prevent the system from taking any action at all. The first of these negative aspects is seen in the Charter requirement that the Council may demand military assistance only from those member states that have specifically agreed in advance to provide it. In addition members specify what military assistance they may be called upon to provide. (No such agreements have yet been signed.) The absence of such agreements does not, of course, prevent the possibility of the Council being supplied with armed force voluntarily at a time of crisis. But this draws attention to the second negative aspect of the Charter scheme; namely, that any Council decision of a substantial kind requires the concurring votes of all five permanent members—quickly amended in practice to the requirement that none of them should vote against the proposal. Accordingly, this class of members—Britain, China, France, the Soviet Union, and the United States—are in a particularly privileged position because any one of them can stop the Council doing or saying anything that is not liked. It is, however, these Great Powers that might be expected to present the gravest threats to international peace and that will assuredly have a significant range of friends on behalf of whose interests they may be expected to act.

Giving a veto to the permanent Council members (and also a veto on any proposal that it be taken away) therefore meant that there would be many occasions on which peace might be threatened or broken, but in respect of which the Council would be unable to act. Putting it another way, with regard to peace and security the Security Council would only be in a position to take action, or even to express a point of view, if all five permanent members were in agreement, or if none of them took their lack of agreement beyond an abstention when the matter came to a vote. This is the unit veto system with a vengeance, given that certain key states are not only themselves able to opt out of any proposed action, but are also able to stand in the way of the Council making any kind of move. And inasmuch as the UN Charter provides that in matters of peace and security the Security Council has prime responsibility for action, the UN as a whole can be seen as largely emasculated in respect of the achievement of its main purpose.

For two rather different reasons, however, this is to paint a somewhat inadequate picture of the UN as it existed at the moment of its birth. In the first place there was a good deal to be said for the principle that the Security Council should not be in a position to take action against, or against the wishes of, any of its putative leading members. If the Security Council were to be seriously divided against itself, no general good would be accomplished by one group putting on the mantle of the whole organization in the action that it was taking against the other. Far better that the reality of a divided UN be recognized and the warring groups confront each other outside the organization.

Second, although the Council was meant to play the leading UN role in respect of the maintenance of peace, it was not given sole organizational responsibility. The General Assembly, where all member states are represented, was given the power to discuss these matters and make recommendations regarding any such issues that were not being considered by the Council. As the veto does not apply to any proposal in the Council that a matter be removed from its agenda (this being a procedural and not a substantive proposal), the way has always been clear for the consideration of a threatening situation to be, in effect, transferred from the Council to the Assembly, with a view to the latter making some positive recommendation. Moreover, if the Assembly were not already meeting, a special session could be summoned either by the Security Council (this, too, being a procedural question and therefore not subject to the veto) or by a majority of the member states.[2]

Of course, any action that resulted from an Assembly recommendation would reflect the unit veto pattern of international activity. All member states would, in law, be able to do as they pleased. Even those that voted in favor of the Assembly resolution would not, just by virtue of their vote, be legally bound to do anything about it. The remarks made in the last two paragraphs do not, therefore, detract from the basic point that—notwithstanding the tenor of the Charter with regard to the powers and responsibilities of the Security Council—the organization that was founded in 1945 appeared to rely almost wholly on the traditional unit veto method of operation so far as the maintenance of international peace and security was concerned. Authoritative decisions taken by a few on behalf of the many and binding all to take action at least of a nonforceful kind were in theory possible but in practice not very likely.

In fact, in practice the UN has never responded in exactly this way to an armed conflict or situation in which fighting appeared imminent. The furthest it has gone—and to put it this way is not to underestimate the strength or novelty of the action that was taken— is, on one occasion, to recommend that UN members give armed assistance to a state that had been invaded. This decision was taken by the Security Council immediately after the attack by North Korea on South Korea in June 1950. Moreover, all those resisting North Korean aggression were put under a single UN military command. Formally speaking, therefore, it was the UN that fought in Korea during the three subsequent years.[3] However, the institutional situation that produced this result was very unusual in that the Soviet Union was absenting itself from the Security Council at this time. Thus the Soviet Union was not in a position to cast a veto—which it assuredly would have done had it been present. Furthermore, there were many who saw what happened in Korea as a case of the organization being, as it were, captured by the United States and its allies and used as a front for U.S. anticommunist foreign policy. Partly for this reason the steam soon went out of the idea that, on future occasions when the Security Council was blocked by a veto, the General Assembly might make the kind of recommendation that the Council had made in June 1950. The United States also lost its initial enthusiasm for this scheme. Thus, in effect, the UN abandoned any expectation that it would respond to armed hostilities in the manner set out in the Charter. However, one should not assume that circumstances will never arise in which an appropriate coalition of members might want to act in accordance with Chapter VII.

Alternatives to Enforcement

The failure to operationalize Chapter VII of the Charter has not, however, meant that the UN has closed its eyes to armed hostilities. What the UN often has done is to respond to them in one or both of two main ways. The first is verbal and the second physical.[4]

The UN's verbal response is, in the name of either the Security Council or the General Assembly, to denounce aggressive behavior. It may be described as creed-protecting activity in that the impropriety of using armed force against the territorial integrity or political independence of a state has now become a fundamental international tenet. Of course the very fact that creed-protecting statements are sometimes found to be necessary means that the injunction against the use of aggressive force is not always observed—a not uncommon situation regarding even the most basic of normative principles. Nevertheless, the fact that this particular principle receives what appears to be universal international acceptance has given it a special significance, enabling it to be pictured as an essential—arguably the most essential—element in the credal system of the international society. And by regularly pointing its finger at many of those who offend the principle the UN may be depicted as its guardian.

The organization's physical response is to engage in what has become known as peace-keeping activity.[5] This involves the establishment on the ground, in areas that have been the scene of considerable tension if not of full-scale hostilities, of military forces or observer groups. However, although military in composition and, in the case of the forces, equipped with arms, it is not the mission of peace-keeping forces or observer groups to impose themselves on one or both of the parties. Instead the essence of peace-keeping activity as it has been developed by the UN is that it is squarely based on the principle of consent. This applies both to its composition, in that no UN member state is legally or physically obliged to supply contingents or members, and to its relations with the disputants. Thus a peace-keeping force or observer group can only proceed to and remain in the area in question with the permission

of the host state or states, and the effectiveness of the operation
depends on the cooperation of the parties. The arms of such a force
are for self-defense only, as this kind of operation is very definitely
not of the enforcing sort envisaged in Chapter VII of the Charter.[6]

The UN's peace-keeping activity may be divided into two chief
categories. The first may be described as face saving, in that it involves the despatch of a UN mission to help disputing but pacifically
minded states to get out of a diplomatic or military predicament. It
may be conducted with a view either to sorting out just part of a
longer-term problem or to patching up an entire dispute. The second
type of UN peace-keeping activity will be called fire watching,
meaning that an operation has been established to assist in the
maintenance of calm along a tense line or region of confrontation.
The mission watches out for small incidents with a view to preventing their spread, both by direct local action on the mission's
part and by calling on the relevant national authorities to take appropriate dampening measures. Additionally the purpose of fire
watching may be advanced by agreed preventive measures, such
as the institution of a buffer zone between the armed forces of the
two sides, analogous to the creation of a firebreak in highly flam-
mable areas.

In the ensuing analysis of these responses to international hostilities the UN will frequently be referred to as an actor in relation
to or on the scene of tension.[7] This is an almost unavoidable form
of shorthand. However, the analysis is based on the assumption that
in understanding UN action prime attention must be given not to
the organization as an independent entity, nor to its individual
servants—the members of its Secretariat—but to the various member
states. They are seen as dominant within the UN, so that anything
that the UN says or does is a consequence of a successful coalition
of interested parties. The other side of this assumption is that a
particular resolution or operation is not going to be supported by
any state that sees it as directly contrary to its interests. Thus UN
resolutions and operations may be depicted to some degree as a
reflection of the foreign policies of those in favor of them. Furthermore, if a state seeks or permits the deployment of UN military
personnel on its territory, it is assumed that some very direct foreign
policy interest is being served. After all, states do not lightly agree
to the presence of foreign soldiers on their soil, or on ground that
they control, no matter how exalted the auspices under which they

serve or how innocuous their mandate. It is also assumed that those
states supplying military personnel for the UN are at the very least
not opposed to the purposes of the operation in question, and may
very well be actively in favor of it.

None of these remarks denies that, in respect of their attitude to
international hostilities, member states may be subject to influences
that flow from the existence of the UN as a distinct organization.
States may sometimes feel a sense of duty arising out of their conception of the UN's general ethos, or out of their understanding of
the specific legal obligations they are under in their capacity as
members. More likely is the possibility of their changing their position somewhat as a result of pressures from other member states
in relation to an issue or activity that would not have presented
itself were it not for the existence of the UN—or at least would not
have presented itself in so sharp and immediate a form. The point
here is that being a member of the UN requires one to take a stand
on all sorts of issues that hardly would have arisen otherwise. Resolutions regarding international hostilities have to be voted on;
views have to be expressed regarding the UN's activities in the field;
requests for help for UN peace-keeping missions have to be decided
upon. All these matters may offer opportunities for states to advance
their interests and persuade others to move in their direction. But
membership in the UN inevitably makes international life more
complicated, often without the likelihood of immediate profit, and
almost always with plenty of opportunity for offending others. Yet
another influence to which member states of the UN may be subject
flows from the role and activities of the Secretary-General and his
senior officials. Such pressure on member states is unlikely to be
frequent and is only rarely of much weight. However, very occasionally it may have impact that is awkward to resist.

All told, therefore, the member states of the UN are far from being
in watertight compartments, merely doing within the organization
what they are already doing outside it. This point deserves particular
emphasis because the focus of this chapter is not on politics within
the UN, but on the UN in international politics. Attention is primarily
paid to outcomes and effects rather than to the processes within the
organization. However, while member states may modify their
stance as a result of their participation within the UN, it must not
be assumed that on matters as important as those relating to international hostilities they are often going to be substantially moved

away from positions adopted outside the organization. It is the national interest, nationally reckoned, that will usually determine a nation's course.

Creed Protecting

Another way of putting this last point is to say that, on questions relating to international hostilities, the principle of majority rule finds no significant place in international relations and hence in the UN. A state usually will not be willing to follow a particular course just because a majority of states favor it. It is in this sense that authoritative decisionmaking has no bearing on the matters under discussion. However, if a large number of states are in agreement on a particular issue and use the UN to express their agreement, this diplomatic consensus may be regarded as having some extra weight, of a legitimizing kind, by virtue of the fact that it is presented in the name of the UN. In some circumstances the voice of the universal organization is more than the sum of its individual vocal cords. This occurs when the issue in question is one on which there is some consistency of approach across different issues of the same kind so that it does not just evoke a fortuitous combination of individual interests. In these circumstances the UN may be seen as speaking in a quasi-authoritative manner. But not fully authoritative, for two reasons. Firstly because its voice is not going to be automatically heeded by the state that is being addressed. And secondly because those making up the majority are not going to accept the principle of majority rule when very consequential matters are concerned, such as the interpretation of their common decision and the imposition of sanctions on the malefactor. These are large qualifications, undoubtedly justifying the prefix "quasi" before the term authoritative. Yet, seen from a different angle, the more interesting point perhaps is not the limited effect of such decisions, but the fact that this sort of consistent decisionmaking is taking place and is of some diplomatic consequence.

This kind of creed-protecting activity is most notable with regard to certain types of armed hostilities. Indeed, it is arguable that it only appears on this issue. One might argue, for example, that matters relating to colonialism and racism compose a separate category having to do with campaigning against a minority rather than the defense of a universally accepted creed. Be that as it may, the international creed can certainly be said to include a prohibition on the use of armed force to undermine a state's territorial integrity or political independence and also on the associated activity of armed intervention. Flowing from this position, the annexation of any part of another's territory is necessarily forbidden and any measures that encourage part of another state's territory to secede (other than in a colonial situation) are also universally frowned upon. The common thread here, of course, is not so much an aversion to armed force (after all, it is universally regarded as legitimate in self-defense and in support of certain causes), as respect for the territorial integrity of the existing members of international society. The UN is not willing to take up arms simply in support of this principle—although it is interesting to note that when a UN peace-keeping force was in the Congo (now Zaire) in the early 1960s it was eventually used to end the secession of Congo's Katanga province.[8] Nevertheless, at the verbal level the UN's performance has been impressive.

UN targets have been wide ranging. Names, it is true, have not always been named for good diplomatic reasons, including the desirability of maximizing the amount of support for this creed-protecting activity. But there has never been any doubt about who was being referred to. In very recent years, for example, the Soviet Union has been condemned for its invasion of Afghanistan,[9] U.S. intervention in Grenada has been deplored,[10] Vietnam has been severely criticized for its occupation of Kampuchea,[11] the Security Council has declared Israel's decision to annex the Golan Heights to be invalid,[12] Indonesia has been taken to task for its invasion of East Timor,[13] Iraq has been strongly condemned for its use of chemical weapons against Iran,[14] and the unilateral declaration of independence by the Turkish state in northern Cyprus has been declared null and void by the Security Council.[15] This is quite a collection, and is a testimony to the way in which the UN is overseeing, in a relatively impartial way, the standards of the international society. Of course, making such declarations is not the same as taking action over breaches of international standards. Acting against such violations would involve a fundamental change in the working of the international system. But at the quasi-authoritative level the UN can be seen as a promising guardian of the international creed.

Face Saving

Peace-keeping activity, like that of creed protection, requires decisions on the part of UN organs. But there is little that is authoritative about these decisions, except in the narrow technical sense that they are necessary for the UN to act at all. The reason for this is the absence of any consistency of approach to the issue of UN peace-keeping; the response is not regarded as always appropriate when international hostilities occur. In other words it is very much a matter of ad hoc calculation, on the part of both the disputants and by-standers, as to whether resort might be had to the UN. Of course, some unofficial observers purport to see any decision of the UN as superior in quality to a similar decision by an individual state or a less than universal organization. But there is no evidence either in the practice of states or at the level of theory for this approach. For this reason peace-keeping activity must be categorized as unit veto in character. This is not to play down its importance, either in in-dividual cases or as a general phenomenon, but it can hardly be seen as an indication that the UN—and thus the international so-ciety—is moving in the direction of centralized authority as far as activity on the ground to control international hostilities is con-cerned. Decisions on this matter sometimes are now made centrally, in the sense that the UN can be seen as a central institution, but this is chiefly a matter of convenience, not because the center carries any particular authority.

Reference has been made to the two-fold distinction that may be made regarding the roles of peace-keeping activity. The first of these roles, face saving, is designed to help disputing states out of a dif-ficulty. It is, therefore, far removed from the forceful and authori-tative action that is outlined in the Charter as appropriate for dealing with threats to and breaches of the peace. The peace will have been in danger and perhaps even broken. But there is no question of an aggressor being physically admonished and hauled away from its victim or of the UN engaging in an independent act of pacification. Face saving involves putting aside the issue of who is in the right and who is in the wrong and suppressing any inclination simply to bang the disputants' heads together. Instead face saving offers one or both parties a way out of the conflict on which they have em-barked, or are about to embark, without causing them too great a loss of public dignity. Of course everyone who is awake will know what is really happening: that one or both sides are climbing down or even in a full-scale retreat. But how things are formally done is a matter of great importance to states and to many groups and in-dividuals. Thus, if the UN is manifestly not wielding a big stick, it is vastly easier for an embarrassed disputant to comply with its call and make use of its facilities.

The key factor here is that, at least on the surface, the discomfited disputant(s) are acting voluntarily. A choice has been made. The UN is operating in the mode of counselor and not of judge and advantage is being taken of it. It is, however, not only the consent of the state most deeply in trouble that is necessary for such a face-saving scheme to get under way. It may be, of course, that both disputants are glad to seize on a nonviolent and honorable way out of the situation in which they find themselves. But even if only one of them is seriously inconvenienced the cooperation of the other is necessary. The crucial element is not just the absence of immediate duress from the UN—which in the conditions that have prevailed since 1945 is in any event extremely unlikely—but simply the absence of duress. If, therefore, one party is in the ascendant, it must be willing to stay its hand so that the other can disengage itself in a manner that can be given the appearance of not being forced upon it. Face saving, in other words, is not a unilateral act but requires agreement with and perhaps forbearance from the other party. The way out has to be engineered jointly by all those directly involved, even if only one of them is in urgent need of the exit, because otherwise face would not be convincingly maintained.

The UN's role in this procedure will be to facilitate the disputants' disengagement and withdrawal by despatching a body of nonfighting troops or an observer group to the point of confrontation. For this to be done the express consent of the state or states on whose territory the UN mission is to operate will be required. There should not be a major problem in this regard, as the host(s) will probably be one or both of the parties to the conflict, and the UN is most unlikely to make any firm face-saving proposition unless they have already agreed on such a formula. Alternatively, if two states should fight on the territory of a third and innocent party, that state will presumably be only too willing to admit a small nonfighting unit from the UN so that it can get rid of a couple of unwelcome belligerents.

Exactly what the UN peace-keepers (as personnel of this type have come to be called) will do will be dependent on the nature of the situation. It may be that they will need to arrange and watch over the disentangling of the armies of two sides so that each party can be sure that the other is not going to gain a temporary advantage from this process. It could be that initially they just have to interpose themselves along a new cease-fire line so that the combatants now have a reasonable excuse for not shooting at each other. The peace-keepers may in some more substantial way be cast in a role to which their name points, thus providing one state with some superficially plausible ground for abandoning a military initiative. Or they may be asked to arrange for the transfer of territory from one state to another in a way that minimizes the indignity to the departing state.

For any peace-keeping initiatives to occur, however, it is not just the consent of the parties that is necessary, but also the consent of the UN. The operation has to be authorized. For this the Security Council is the most obvious body, but it is also something that might be done by the General Assembly. In either case the issue will be considered by the relevant member states in the light of their interests. Positive votes are not going to be elicited just by the argument that the proposed operation will make some contribution toward peace. Certainly the agreement of the contestants on such a scheme will generate a good deal of voting support, for many would then regard it as churlish to refuse a moderate helping hand. But this is another way of saying that the interests of these states will not be set back by the UN giving this kind of assistance. Sometimes states may have very pressing reasons for refusing to countenance a UN face-saving operation, either because they would themselves be directly offended by it or because they have friends they are anxious to please that take an unaccommodating line. Accordingly, a veto may be cast in the Security Council, and if the matter is considered by the Assembly it may be that even in that veto-free environment the necessary two-thirds majority will not be forthcoming.

However, even if there is no difficulty in eliciting the support of member states, the matter is still not finally settled because there is the question of resources to attend to. The question of finance, while it may eventually prove very awkward, is unlikely to cause any delay. It will either be anticipated, perhaps with some optimism, that all members will in due course meet the extra assessments that may be levied in respect of the operation. Or even if the authorizing resolution has specified voluntary financing it will certainly be assumed, in the pressure of the moment, that appropriate monies will eventually be provided. The question of personnel for the operation cannot, however, be postponed. There may be real difficulty here. For example, putting together an acceptable mix of contingents in a UN force—one that is right both operationally and politically, taking account of the views of the membership at large and, especially, the host state—may not be the most straight-forward of tasks. But there are usually a number of countries that are, in principle and for more than one reason, willing to let their troops serve in a UN force or to let some of their officers act as UN observers. So personnel of a sufficiently satisfactory kind are likely to be made available with reasonable despatch.

What all these observations about the nature of a UN face-saving operation underline, however, is that the whole enterprise bears the unmistakable and unambiguous stamp of unit veto diplomacy. In order for the UN to be effective certain states have to provide the necessary personnel on an entirely voluntary basis. The fi-nancing of the operation may be formally presented in an author-itative framework but in practice the consent of the member states, and especially of the richer ones, is a key element. But above all the agreement of the disputants is essential if a face-saving operation is to be of any help to them. And although there is no question of the UN imposing itself on the parties by physical force, there is also no question of disputants accepting a face-saving mission just be-cause an organ of the UN has suggested it. The UN may propose, but the parties very definitely dispose. Their consent and cooper-ation are vital ingredients, without which the UN can do nothing in the field, no matter how imposing the number and identity of those in favor of the idea or the strength of the words that are addressed to the parties.

Of course, the parties may be influenced by what the UN says, perhaps to a considerable and crucial degree. And it is likely that at a time of international crisis it will be the UN that is discussing the need for a modification of the parties' stance and perhaps sug-gesting the availability of a face-saving arrangement, rather than the parties urging the UN to throw them some kind of lifeline. How-ever, even if the parties are influenced by the UN's expressed wishes it may be confidently assumed that the influence will stem much less from the mere fact that it is the UN speaking than from the degree of diplomatic weight that the UN's view represents. The rel-evant resolution will, as it were, be a proxy for a number of states whose opinion is important for one or both of the states being ad-dressed. Furthermore, it remains that the consent of the parties is essential if a UN plan for a face-saving operation is to go forward. Accordingly, such a scheme is, in political terms, more realistically seen as the disputants making use of the organization than as the organization, as such, persuading the disputants to make use of its peace-keeping facilities. There will generally be some predisposition in the UN to look favorably on this kind of scheme. States in trouble, however, usually accept such an arrangement only reluctantly, as the least of the available evils in the circumstances. This disparity of attitudes underlines still further the point that the UN's despatch of a face-saving mission is not at all a case of the organization making authoritative decisions. Instead, UN face saving is very much an instance of one working of the unit veto system.

Illustrations of Face Saving

The very first major instance of what was soon to be called peace-keeping activity is a good illustration of this argument. At the end of October 1956 Israel, Britain, and France launched an attack on Egypt that was a considerable military success but a diplomatic disaster.[16] Thus the advancing belligerents decided to call off their assault, even though the Anglo-French strategic objective—physical control of the Suez Canal—had not yet been achieved. However, the withdrawal was done as part of an arrangement that involved the despatch to Egypt by the UN of an Emergency Force to "secure and supervise the cessation of hostilities."[17] In one sense of the word the UN force was not intended to "secure" a cease-fire. Rather, it was hoped that the UN force would increase the stability of one that had already been agreed. But the significance of this wording related to the fact that ostensibly Britain and France had gone into Egypt to separate the forces of Israel and the host state, and more particularly to ensure that the Suez Canal continued to function smoothly. In consequence the arrival of the UN force provided the Anglo-French aggressors with some spurious ground for arguing that the honorable but burdensome task in which they had been engaged was now being conducted by the UN, thus enabling them to leave. Indeed, before long this reasoning was extended to include the suggestion that the English and French had always hoped to galvanize the UN into just this sort of activity. No one was fooled. But face was sufficiently saved and before the end of the year the British and French departed.

In a similar way the final departure of Israel from Egyptian territory was considerably eased by the face-saving facilities offered by the UN force. Israel was reluctant to leave both the Gaza Strip—

from which a number of guerrilla-type raids had been mounted into adjacent Israeli territory—and the area of Sharm al-Sheikh, from which Egypt had blockaded the Israeli port of Elath at the head of the Gulf of Aqaba. Eventually, in March 1957, and in response to strong U.S. pressure, Israel left. But there was an understanding that the UN force would be stationed in both these areas, enabling Israel to present the final evacuation as no great threat to its security. As it happened Israel went a bit too far in this respect, announcing its belief that not only would freedom of navigation be maintained through the Gulf of Aqaba but also that the UN would exercise exclusive military and civilian control in the Gaza Strip. The last point had been far from agreed, and Egypt made it plain that it would not allow its hand to be forced in this way, immediately sending Egyptian civilian administrators back into the Strip. But the main purpose of the exercise had been served in that Israel had been induced to withdraw. In some probably substantial measure this was because a UN force following in its footsteps enabled Israel to go without too much loss of face.

The acceptance at the height of this crisis of the proposal that a UN force be sent to Egypt, linked as it was with an agreement on a cease-fire and an implication that the invaders would withdraw, was also of considerable face-saving value to the United States. For the whole affair was extremely embarrassing to the leading Western power. Its two main NATO allies were embarked upon a venture that it strongly opposed and that was also receiving almost universal condemnation. Naturally, the Soviet Union made the most of the crisis and even talked, in a vague way, about intervention. Accordingly, the idea of a UN force was very warmly received in Washington, and provided much diplomatic and psychological assistance to the American policy makers. (Indeed, they may even have originated the idea.)

Seventeen years later, in another Arab-Israeli war, the establishment of a UN peace-keeping force played a very similar role, except that now it was both superpowers that gladly grasped the opportunity to save face—and possibly much else. After about two weeks of fighting in the war of October 1973 both the Soviet Union and the United States judged that a cease-fire was imperative, especially on the Egyptian front. They therefore steamrollered such a call through the Security Council on October 22 but proved to have insufficient control over the combatants. In response to the renewed fighting the Soviet Union took measures that suggested it was preparing for large-scale intervention. This resulted in the United States putting its forces worldwide on a high state of alert, and a full-scale superpower crisis appeared imminent. However, on October 23 a further call for a cease-fire was backed with a decision to send UN observers to supervise its maintenance. And on October 25 the Security Council agreed to a proposal—instigated by the United States—from eight nonaligned states that a new UN Emergency Force (a nonfighting force) be set up for despatch to the area. The Soviet Union also supported the idea, and in this way the threat of superpower confrontation immediately receded.[18]

Egypt, too, had enormous cause to be grateful to the UN for this further peace-keeping activity. At the start and during the first part of the war Egypt had no interest in a cease-fire because it was enjoying unaccustomed military success. But then Israel broke across to the western bank of the Suez Canal and surrounded the Egyptian Third Army on the southeast bank of the canal and also the town of Suez. Faced with imminent danger of the annihilation or capture of a large part of its forces Egypt had no real alternative but to accept the October 22 call for a cease-fire. However, although Israel formally did the same, the Israeli forces on the spot continued to fight with a view to improving their position. This led to Egypt's urgent, if not abject, endorsement of, first, the idea that UN observers should be sent to the area and, second, that they should be replaced by a UN force. The first elements of the force arrived in Cairo late on October 26 and with their appearance on the 27th at the most intense line of confrontation the fighting died down and what proved to be a final cease-fire came into effect. Egypt had not come out of it too well in bare military terms, but at least had not been completely humiliated. For that Egypt owed a lot to the UN force.

There was one other matter on which the UN Emergency force helped Egypt to save some face. It concerned the transport of non-military supplies to the Egyptian Third Army following the final cease-fire and prior to the implementation of the Disengagement Agreement reached in January 1974, and also the supply of food, water, and medicine to the town of Suez during the same period. The position of the surrounded soldiers and civilians had rapidly become very grave because they lacked the bare essentials of life. It might be that the disputants would themselves have worked out some humanitarian scheme. But undoubtedly the presence of the UN force as a neutral intermediary greatly assisted both the reaching and the execution of a solution to this problem.

Finally, Israel too was to some extent assisted by the establishment of the second UN Emergency Force. Even at the military level a supervised cease-fire was not wholly contrary to Israel's interests. It had done well, but had some problems with control of the large area of the west bank of the canal that it had succeeded in overrunning. And although part of the Egyptian Army was surrounded, and much of the rest had established an essentially defensive posture in Sinai, its morale was still relatively good and the possibility of its resupply by the Soviet Union could not be excluded. More important, however, was the growing political dissatisfaction with the war in Israel. The way Israel had been taken by surprise and the early reverses it suffered (on the Golan Heights as well as in Sinai) led to a general lack of confidence in the defense apparatus. Moreover, Israel's loss of life in battle had been relatively high— about 2,500—and several hundred soldiers had been taken prisoner: both of these issues are always sensitive in Israel. Accordingly, there was quite a bit to be said for putting an end to the battle and adding to the security of the cease-fire by the establishment of a UN peace-keeping force.

It is also plausible to argue that the establishment of another peace-keeping force in the same general area, southern Lebanon in 1978, made some contribution to the saving of Israel's face.[19] In a retaliatory move Israel sent troops into southern Lebanon in mid-March and soon controlled a six-mile-deep zone along the entire length of the Israeli-Lebanese border. Israel's detailed motives and intentions were, and remain, somewhat obscure. But what became immediately clear was that a number of states, including the United States, were extremely cross about Israel's action. U.S. anger largely related to its desire that the preliminary discussions about a peace treaty, which were then going on between Israel and Egypt, should not be jeopardized. Accordingly, and contrary to Israel's wishes, the United States pressed hard and successfully in the Security Council for a resolution calling both for a withdrawal and for the establishment of a UN force to supervise it. Israel's response was to press much further into Lebanon, chiefly, it seems, so that a bigger section of the country would be handed over to the UN and made into the area of operation of the supposedly "interim" force that was being set up. This done, Israel withdrew within three months, although it handed over the southernmost section of Lebanon not to the UN but to a puppet regime of its own. Israel may not have wished to leave so soon, but the fact that a UN force would be op-

erating in southern Lebanon produced some ground for claiming
that the threat to Israel from Lebanese-based Palestinian guerrillas
had been reduced. In consequence it was not unreasonable for Israel
to withdraw. In a confused situation, but one in which strong U.S.
pressure was evident, some Israeli face had been saved through the
mounting of a UN force.

Three other UN peace-keeping operations with a face-saving element may be mentioned. Following a revolution in Yemen in 1962
the new republican regime immediately received substantial military support from Egypt (then called the United Arab Republic)
and the deposed royalists were assisted from neighboring Saudi
Arabia. In April 1963 both states were persuaded, through the combined efforts of the UN Secretary-General and an emissary of the
United States, to end their involvement in Yemen's internal affairs.
An important part of the agreement was the establishment of a UN
Observation Mission intended to give each intervener an impartial
assurance that the other was honoring its word.[20] This arrangement
was designed to enable both of them to disengage with some honor
because they would have a public guarantee that neither of them
was being tricked. Each could explain that it was reasonable to depart since the other intervener was manifestly doing so. In the event
this plan came unstuck. Egypt changed its mind about the merits
of the agreement and stayed on, in strength, for another four years.
Thus the UN mission was itself, within a year or so of its establishment, making a somewhat inglorious departure. But the discredit
really lay with the interveners, and especially with the Egyptians,
because the success of the UN mission was premised upon their
cooperation.

Another operation was set up in 1965 to supervise both the cease-
fire that had been agreed in a war between India and Pakistan and
the withdrawal of the armed forces of each belligerent to their home
country. Here too it was highly desirable that each side should have
some assurance that the disengagement operation was being conducted in a balanced way so that neither party would feel at a temporary military disadvantage and worry about the situation being
capitalized upon by the other side. To achieve this the introduction
of an impartial intermediary was called for to assist both sides to
reach a detailed withdrawal agreement and watch over and report
on its execution. This, therefore, was a large part of the intended
task of the UN Observer Mission.[21] Again, however, things did not
work out exactly according to plan. For most of its nearly six months

of life the mission was involved in trying to maintain the cease-fire. Eventually, however, a disengagement agreement was reached and successfully executed, with the useful assistance of the UN's observers and with no loss of face felt by either side.

The clearest case of the UN saving face, however, occurred in respect of the former Netherlands territory of West New Guinea.[22] In 1949 it had been impossible to agree on whether West New Guinea should be transferred to Indonesia along with the rest of the Netherlands East Indies when Indonesia became independent. Consequently, the matter was put on one side with a view to reaching a settlement within the next year. In fact more than a decade passed without an agreement. In the early 1960s the Indonesians began to land infiltrators in the territory and threatened to step up their military pressure. The prospect of a physical conflict between a NATO member and a large Asian state was most unwelcome in the Western world and the UN Secretary-General asked a leading American diplomat to mediate. He was successful, and the agreement was signed in August 1962. It provided that the Netherlands should hand the territory over to the UN, which would administer it for an unspecified period of not less than seven months. Then the UN would hand it over to Indonesia, with the qualification that before the end of 1969 the inhabitants should be asked whether they wished to remain with their new masters. The necessary arrangements for this "act of free choice" were to be made by the Indonesian government with the advice and assistance of the UN Secretary-General.

In these ways Dutch face was triply saved. In the first place they would not actually have to hand the territory over to those who had been so stridently demanding it, which also removed the risk of any unhappy incidents taking place during, and perhaps upsetting, the transfer. Secondly, the open-ended length of the UN administration enabled the Dutch to envisage a longer rather than a shorter term of UN control, which meant that the Dutch could depart with a relatively easy mind. And thirdly, the projected act of free choice permitted the Dutch to reconcile their departure with their professed concern about the right of the inhabitants to self-determination. In fact, of course, the crucial step was the actual Dutch departure. Once they were gone the UN handed the territory over to Indonesia seven months to the day after its own arrival. And the so-called act of free choice could never realistically be seen as anything other than a formality (and for some time there was actually some doubt as to whether it would even be held). But the essential thing with regard to the maintenance of peace and security was that the UN was able to assist the saving of the Netherlands' face, thus allowing it to make a voluntary departure.

Fire Watching

The second way in which the UN has made a direct contribution to the maintenance of international peace and security has been through fire watching. This phrase refers to the presence of UN military personnel at points or along lines of actual or anticipated tension. They may be individual observers of officer rank drawn from a variety of countries and constituted into a UN-run group. Or they may consist of battalions and specialist groups from the armies of a number of member states brought together under a UN commander and associated military staff to form an international force. But in either event their purpose is *not* to engage in the activity that is typical of military personnel: fighting. Indeed, with one exception (the forces that operated in Yemen), UN military observer groups have never carried any arms. And UN forces have been equipped only with light arms for individual and positional self-defense.

The reason for this policy is that UN forces are definitely not in the business of imposing themselves on disputing parties. There is no question of authoritative decisionmaking, of the parties being physically held apart by the UN. Instead, the UN is called in simply to keep an eye on the situation, to watch out for local fires so that something may be done about quenching them at the earliest possible moment. In other words this aspect of UN activity is in the nature of an early-warning system, alerting either the parties or interested outsiders to the need for firm action to maintain peace. Of course there has to be a disposition on the part of outsiders and, above all, the disputants to keep the situation in check, because there is no way the UN can force them to be restrained if they are not of a basically pacific or nonwarlike mind. But if there is a disposition in favor of peace the presence of a UN mission will facilitate, and indeed encourage, calming action at a stage when the situation might still be relatively easy to control. That stage could soon pass, which underlines the importance of on-the-spot fire watchers.

Furthermore, a fire-watching mission may be able to persuade the parties to take preventive measures with a view to making the outbreak of accidental conflagration less likely. An observer group, for example, may reach agreement with one or both parties to reduce the incidence of provocative activities. A UN force may do likewise, but will also, by its very nature, have additional preventive potential. Its size will almost certainly entail that it be physically interposed between the armed forces of the two sides, thus creating something in the nature of a buffer zone. This step will have three prophylactic consequences. First, it will reduce the possibility of incidents between the two sides arising out of civilian activity at or near the cease-fire line because the UN force will be on hand to control civilian movement. Second, a buffer zone will discourage guerrilla-type raids across the line, whether these are genuinely the product of free enterprise or the officially unofficial type. This effect also arises from the fact that the dividing line will be under international surveillance, which will to all intents and purposes be constant, together with the associated fact that the parties will at least formally be committed to the maintenance of calm. Third, the presence of a UN force along one or both sides of the border will also mean that the armed forces of the disputants are at a certain distance from each other. This distance will prevent the sort of incident that can so easily arise when opposed and perhaps edgy soldiers are in view of each other. Avoiding such incidents is particularly important because firing that begins in these circumstances can spread very quickly and be hard to extinguish.

It will be clear from these remarks, however, that peace-keeping groups of a fire-watching kind are only able to assist in the maintenance of peace if the parties cooperate toward that end. The UN missions may make a positive contribution through their vigilance and their suggestions. But ultimately peace depends on the disputants. And if one or both of them decide to resume or precipitate battle the presence of a UN mission, even of a UN force between the two sides, will be no more than a minor inconvenience. In this sense the UN is operating in the context of a unit veto diplomacy in that it plays an essentially secondary part, the primary role being reserved for the relevant member states.

As in the case of face-saving activity, fire watching is seen most basically in the fact that the host state must give specific permission for the fire watchers to operate on its soil. Ideally such personnel would be based on the territory of both disputants, but it may be sufficient for them to work on just one side of the relevant demarcation line. It would also, in theory, be possible for UN forces to be located in one state even if the other disputant is hostile to their appearance in the area. But as a practical matter at least the passive assent of both parties will probably be required for a fire-watching operation to get under way. There are two reasons for this.

The first reason is political and refers to the assumption that, if there is strong opposition to the idea of a fire-watching mission from one of the parties, the UN Security Council (and also the General Assembly) may be very hesitant about establishing it. And if a positive decision is taken, there may be some problem with getting contributors because the dissatisfied party will see the whole operation as a diplomatically hostile act. This difficulty points to the second reason, which is conceptual. It relates to the fact that the idea of fire watching is premised upon the impartiality of the fire watchers.

Fire watchers are looking out for—and concerned about—fire, no matter who is responsible for it. Their job is simply to locate a danger and to do what they can to eliminate it—chiefly by calling on well-placed parties with fire extinguishers to use. If, however, one of the parties does not see a need for this kind of activity, but the UN nonetheless goes ahead with it, it is highly likely that the operation will assume the quite different character of finger pointing rather than fire watching. What the UN will in effect be doing is expressing doubt about the pacific intentions of one party to the dispute and establishing a mechanism that can, if the situation changes for the worse, readily identify the wrongdoer and provide chapter and verse in respect of the iniquity. Politically, as well as literally, the UN will be performing a one-sided rather than an impartial activity. For this reason there is doubt about the peace-keeping credentials of the UN Special Commission on the Balkans, which was operating in the late 1940s,[23] and also, possibly, of the UN Observation Group in Lebanon, which spent a few months in that country in 1958.[24]

Fire watching, therefore, is based upon some measure of cooperation from both sides. Both must, at least for the time being, have an interest in the maintenance of calm. It may be that, as with face saving, the discovery of this interest is partly the result of pressure from the political organs of the UN. But in the case of fire watching— as with face saving—the messages that will have the greater effect will be those from significant member states, even if only expressed in their individual votes, rather than the collective view of the whole organization. And again the crucial stage will be the response of one or both parties to such pressures, since the key decisions lie with them. This fact just emphasizes the unit veto character of the

activity of fire watching, as does the fact that fire watching also depends upon the relevant political organs of the UN taking a decision
in its favor and on some member states providing the required personnel and money. The necessary actions cannot be required by
some of others, in the manner of authoritative decisionmaking. And
if members are not immediately forthcoming on a voluntary basis,
the most that can be done is a careful effort to elicit their support.
Even then positive responses will probably reflect not so much the
persuasive powers of others as national calculations of interest.

At this point, however, it is necessary to make a distinction between the decisions to establish, maintain, and continue a fire-
watching operation and the actual activity of the UN mission on the
ground. Whereas the former certainly reflects the unit veto nature
of the international system, the latter does so only to a certain extent.
That extent is admittedly large, but nonetheless at the margin a UN
fire-watching operation moves away a little from the unit veto end
of the spectrum in that the UN as a whole becomes linked, through
its operation in the field, with the assertion of the value of peace.
That value is hardly "allocated" because no authoritative action is
involved. But the UN does become identified with peace in the dispute in question, and may be able to make some very small contribution to its maintenance.

It was suggested previously that a fire-watching operation depends, at bottom, on the cooperation of the parties for its success
and that if one or both of the parties are bent on war they will not
be materially held up by the presence of some UN peace-keepers.
Life, however, does not always slot smoothly into one or other of
these extremes and sometimes the presence of a UN mission may
have some deterrent bearing on the attitudes and activities of one
or both parties. This influence is a consequence of the fact that the
fires a UN group will be despatched to watch are by no means always
accidental. The disputants may well have some tendency to commit
arson and if they are determined to do so a UN peace-keeping mission will be unable to stop them. But on occasion they may be less
than fully committed to this course. It may represent a temptation
that may or may not be resisted. And it is possible that the decision
in favor of, as it were, water rather than fire, may be attributable to
the presence on the spot of a UN observer group or international
force. Its deterrent effect may be of two associated kinds.

First, the thought that detailed and impartial evidence of responsibility for a fire will be instantly available to a wide audience

may give pause to the would-be arsonist. Such evidence is likely
to lead to a good deal of criticism of the state in question, with the
identity of the informant perhaps making the amount and strength
of the criticism rather greater than might otherwise have been the
case. No state would welcome this. Second, there is the consideration that the UN as a whole will be widely seen as having been
gratuitously bruised by the aggressor state. The organization was
doing its part for peace and got not thanks but stones. The UN will
be seen as having been brushed or even thrust aside, perhaps as a
victim of international hooliganism. In itself this critical response
is not likely to have any very dramatic consequences. It is what the
member states do that counts, not the feelings and dignity of the
organization. But the perceived affront to the latter may cause some
member states to have second thoughts about the incident. And that
is something that an intending aggressor might not lightly disregard.

It must be emphasized that it would be a grave mistake to make
too much of such deterrent influences. Anxiety about the consequences of riding roughshod over the UN's peace-keepers, or about
the effect of what they will say, is not likely to weigh as heavily
with disputing states as a number of other considerations. And in
any event firm evidence about the effects of such susceptibilities,
or even of their existence, is not at hand. But on a priori grounds
it is reasonable to suppose that sometimes, at a rather flexible margin, these considerations could have an impact on the attitudes and
policies of states. By raising the flag of peace in a tense area, the
representatives of the world organization may perhaps have made
it a little less likely that the peace will be broken. Not, certainly,
when one side has decided to throw down the gauntlet. But in less
clear-cut situations the possibility should be borne in mind that a
UN peace-keeping operation may have an influence that is not entirely a reflection of the pleasure of states.

Illustrations of Fire Watching

Most of the UN's peace-keeping activity, in terms of the operation's
size, length, and salience, has consisted of fire watching. All of these
operations have been of value, in that they have helped disputing
states to implement their—at least temporary—pacific dispositions.
On occasion the UN has provided essential help, in cases in which
it is hard to see how the parties might have avoided war without
the aid of the peace-keepers. And in each case it is possible that

now and then the balance may have been tipped against bravado and in favor of restraint on account of the presence of a peace-keeping mission.

The work of the UN Truce Supervision Organization along most Israeli-Arab borders from 1949 to 1967, for example, was often effectively sedative.[25] Similarly, the existence of the Military Observer Group on the cease-fire line in Kashmir from 1949 to 1971 helped India and Pakistan to maintain calm in that area for much of the period.[26] Wars did break out in both regions, underlining the point that the mere presence of UN observers is certainly no guarantee of peace. But between times the UN groups made it easier for the parties to avoid war.

After the UN Emergency Force sent to Suez in 1956 had assisted the departure of the invaders, it took up a position along the Egyptian side of that country's border with Israel, and watched over it for ten years. It was a time of notable calm in the area, all the more remarkable on account of its previously troubled condition. Undoubtedly this was not the direct result of the presence of a UN force, but it seems clear that the force helped both parties to keep things quiet—which was what they wanted for the decade in question.[27]

Then, however, came the controversial events of 1967. The UN Secretary-General withdrew the force, at the firm request of the Egyptian President, and war between Israel and Egypt (and also Syria and Jordan) broke out a couple of weeks later, with catastrophic consequences for the Arabs. A heap of scorn and abuse fell on the head of U Thant for his allegedly submissive response to President Nasser and the outbreak of the Six Day War was widely seen as the direct consequence of Thant's action.[28] There are huge shortcomings in both these suggestions. But the interesting thing is that they imply a much more authoritative and influential role for the UN than it actually possessed. In part the ascription of these characteristics to the UN by states was, of course, a way of trying to evade their own responsibility for the happenings of that year. But presumably it may also in some measure have reflected a none-too-closely examined feeling that it was proper for the UN to have some authority in relation to peace and war.

Meanwhile, two other fire-watching forces had been set up. That in the Congo was based on a false premise in that there was never too much danger of the Cold War spreading in a significant way to Central Africa. Every geopolitical consideration was clearly against the despatch and supply of a Soviet expeditionary force to the Congo. And attempts to exert leverage in a less heavy-handed way would have run up against huge political, cultural, and racial obstacles. But at the time there was considerable apprehension on this score. As it happened the UN's Congo force was chiefly valuable for what it was able to do in getting the new African state on its feet, including some activity that went far beyond what was anticipated when the force was set up.[29]

In Cyprus, however, some genuine and extremely important fire watching took place. From 1964 to 1974 the UN force operated throughout the island, watching over local dividing lines and points of tension between the Greek-Cypriots and the Turkish-Cypriots. Had the UN peace-keepers not been on hand international peace might easily have been broken through the escalation of small incidents.[30] After Turkey's 1974 invasion and occupation of the northern third of the island state the UN force engaged in fire watching of a more conventional kind along the buffer zone between the Turkish forces and those of the (Greek) Cypriot government. It does so still.[31]

Early in the 1970s two further fire-watching forces were established. The one sent to Egypt in 1973 has already been mentioned in a face-saving context. Once the immediate crisis died down the force watched over the cease-fire line in the by now usual fire-watching manner and progressed eastward across Sinai in 1974 and 1975 to occupy the buffer zones that were established by the Disengagement Agreements of those years.[32] The 1979 peace treaty between Egypt and Israel made provision for the force's continuation in this type of role. However, the threat of a Soviet veto (the Soviets acting chiefly at the instigation of their extremist Arab friends) meant that the force came to a peaceful end in 1979.[33]

The Disengagement Observer Force established in 1974 on the revised cease-fire line between Syria and Israel, however, continues to exist. It watches over a buffer zone between the armed forces of the two erstwhile belligerents and checks on their observance of agreements regarding the limitation of forces and armaments in bands of territory to the rear of their front lines.[34]

The last UN force to be mentioned in this connection is again one that has been referred to earlier: the Interim Force in Lebanon.[35] Once the Israelis had formally withdrawn from that country in 1978 the force watched over as much of its area of operation as it could gain effective access to and played a useful role in limiting the anti-

Israeli activities of Palestinian guerrillas in southern Lebanon. However, Israel invaded again in 1982, and for the next three years the UN force was behind Israel's front lines, and was largely reduced to humanitarian work. Since Israel's withdrawal in 1985 the UN force has again been trying to maintain calm in the complex political situation that obtains in southern Lebanon. The force has not always been successful in this enterprise, for reasons usually well beyond its control. But neither has it been without success. And if the force were to be withdrawn the situation would almost certainly be much more hazardous—in both political and humanitarian terms. Then there would be much vigorous jockeying for control of the vacated area by the local armed groups and their international backers.

As this brief survey makes plain the activity of fire watching is very much a reflection of unit veto diplomacy. Such forces and observer groups operate by leave of their hosts and their success depends on the cooperation of the disputants. If that cooperation is forthcoming UN forces can play a very useful pacificatory role. Moreover, the establishment of a UN peace-keeping body along a tense dividing line gives the UN as a whole some stake in the maintenance of peace. There is not much that the UN as such can do about putting any weight behind this commitment, however. And the various member states are not going to go far out of their way to back up the organization unless they perceive that such a course is also in their own individual interests, as individually conceived. But although it is lightweight and elusive, the UN's assertion of the value of peace through its establishment of fire-watching patrols should not be disregarded. It is unlikely that the disputants regard the presence of the UN's representatives between them as never of any restraining significance whatsoever. Accordingly, the analyst must also note that fire watching is not wholly and exclusively confined to the unit veto end of the spectrum of possibilities that is theoretically open to the world organization.

Summation

Overall, however, most of the UN's responses to international hostilities are firmly at the unit veto end of the spectrum. Not only is the bulk of its fire-watching activity of this nature but also all of its face-saving work. It is only when one looks at the UN's efforts at creed protection that one can see what might be called quasi-authoritative decisionmaking. This development is impressive testimony to how the UN has managed to create something of an independent role for itself in the world of sovereign states. But in terms of its impact on armed hostilities it is exceedingly marginal, if indeed it should count as having any effect at all. And this should cause no surprise. The international society continues, understandably, to deal with interstate hostilities firmly on a unit veto basis. However, within this approach room has been found for some very useful pacifying contributions from the now-universal organization. The UN's peace-keeping work does not make a primary contribution to the prevention of war because the states concerned are still clearly in control of their own destinies. But at the secondary level the UN can, on the basis of the cooperation of the parties, make a very useful—and perhaps even an essential—contribution to the maintenance of peace. This may not be much, but in a dangerous world it should be nurtured. As the old saying goes, every little bit helps.

Notes

1. This chapter is a revised version of a paper presented to the International Organization section of the annual convention of the International Studies Association, held in Washington, D.C., in March 1985, under the title "Politics in the UN System: The Issue of Peace and Security." I am very grateful to Lawrence Finkelstein for his detailed advice on the reshaping of the paper.

2. UN Charter, Article 20.

3. On the UN operation in Korea see: L. M. Goodrich, *Korea: A Study of US Policy in the United Nations.* (New York: Council on Foreign Relations, 1956); L. M. Goodrich, "Korea: Collective Measures against Aggression," *International Conciliation* 494 (October 1953); and E. Luard, *A History of the United Nations, Vol 1. The Years of Western Domination 1945–1955.* (London: Macmillan, 1982), ch. 13.

4. This essay does not examine the UN's efforts to settle disputes by way of investigation, mediation, conciliation, and good offices. Chapter VI of the Charter sets out the UN's competence in this area, and the UN has had a good deal of experience in the matter. For an analysis of its earlier activities see, A. James, *The Politics of Peace-Keeping.* (London: Chatto and Windus, 1969), chs. 2 and 3. Nor does the essay examine the role of the International Court of Justice—a principal organ of the UN— in the pacific settlement of disputes.

5. Historically viewed, the concept of peace-keeping is one that was developed in connection with the practice of the UN. But it is not an activity exclusive to the UN, either in principle or in practice. And recently there have been several non-UN peace-keeping operations. For these, and a discussion of the arguments regarding the relative desirability of UN and non-UN peace-keeping operations, see A. James, "Options for Peace-Keeping," in J. O'C. Howe, ed., *Armed Peace: The Search for World Security* (London: Macmillan, 1984). See also M. Tabory, *The Multinational Force and Observers in Sinai* (Boulder, Colo., and London: Westview Press, 1986);

and N. A. Pelcovits, *Peacekeeping on Arab-Israeli Fronts* (Boulder, Colo., and London: Westview Press, 1984).

6. On the general nature of peace-keeping, see D. Hammarskjöld, "The UNEF Experience Report," in A. W. Cordier and W. Foote, *The Public Papers of the Secretaries-General of the United Nations. Vol IV: Dag Hammarskjöld 1958–1960*. (New York: Columbia University Press, 1974). See also D. W. Bowett, *United Nations Forces: A Legal Study* (London: Stevens, 1964; New York: Praeger, 1965); A. M. Cox, *Prospects for Peacekeeping* (Washington, D.C.: Brookings Institution, 1967); P. Frydenberg, ed., *Peacekeeping: Experience and Evaluation* (Oslo: Norwegian Institute of International Affairs, 1964); James, *The Politics of Peace-Keeping*, ch. 1; A. James, "The UN: Brother, Big Brother, or Buffer?" in *The United Nations and the Quest for Peace* (Cardiff: Welsh Centre for International Affairs, 1986); and R. B. Russell, *United Nations Experience with Military Forces* (Washington, D.C.: Brookings Institution, 1964).

7. For a discussion of the UN as an independent actor, see A. James, "International Institutions: Independent Actors?" in A. Shlaim, ed., *The Year Book of International Organization* (London: Croom Helm, 1976). For a discussion of the independent possibilities open to the UN Secretary-General, see A. James, "The Secretary-General. A Comparative Analysis," in *The United Nations and Diplomacy*, ed. G. R. Berridge and A. Jennings (London: Macmillan, 1985).

8. For a discussion of the UN's role in Katanga, see D. N. Chatterji, *Storm over the Congo* (New Delhi: Vikas, 1980); James, *The Politics of Peace-Keeping*, ch. 11; E. Luard, "The Civil War in the Congo," in *The International Regulation of Civil Wars*, ed. E. Luard (London: Thames and Hudson, 1972); C. C. O'Brien, *To Katanga and Back* (London: Hutchinson, 1962); and K. P. Saksena, *The United Nations and Collective Security* (Delhi: D K Publishing House, 1974).

9. UN General Assembly Resolutions ES-6/2 (1980), 36/34 (1981), 37/37 (1982), 38/29 (1983), 39/13 (1984), and 40/12 (1985).

10. UN General Assembly Resolution 38/7 (1983).

11. UN General Assembly Resolutions 34/22 (1979), 35/6 (1980), 36/5 (1981), 37/6 (1982), 38/3 (1983), 39/5 (1984), and 40/7 (1985).

12. UN Security Council Resolution 497 (1981).

13. Recent UN General Assembly Resolutions are 37/30 (1982), 38/402 (1983), and 39/402 (1984).

14. UN Security Council declaration of March 30, 1984.

15. UN Security Council Resolution 550 (1984).

16. On the role of the UN Emergency Force in Egypt during the first six months of its life, see E. L. M. Burns, *Between Arab and Israeli* (London: Harrap, 1962); L. M. Goodrich and G. L. Rosner, "The United Nations Emergency Force," *International Organization* 9, 3 (Summer 1957); A. James, "UN Action for Peace: 1. Barrier Forces," *The World Today* 18, 11 (November 1962) and B. Urquhart, *Hammarskjöld* (London: Bodley Head, 1972), ch. 8.

17. General Assembly Resolution 998 (ES-1).

18. The creation of the second UN Emergency Force is discussed in N. Bar-Yaacov, "Keeping the Peace between Egypt and Israel 1973–1980," *Israel Law Review* 15, (April 1980); A. James, "Recent Developments in UN Peace-Keeping," *Year Book of World Affairs 1977* (London: Stevens, 1977); and J. C. Jonah, "Peace-Keeping in the Middle East," *International Journal* 31, 2 (Winter 1975–76).

19. See further, M. Boerma, "The UN Interim Force in the Lebanon: Peacekeeping in a Domestic Conflict," *Millennium: Journal of International Studies* 8, 1 (Spring 1979); A. James, "Painful Peacekeeping: The UN in Lebanon 1978–1982," *International Journal* 38, 4 (Autumn 1983); and R. Thakur, "UN Peacekeeping: The UN Interim Force in Lebanon," *Australian Outlook* 35, 2 (August 1981).

20. The UN Yemen Observation Mission is discussed in C. V. Horn, *Soldiering for Peace* (London: Cassell, 1966); James, *The Politics of Peace-Keeping*, ch. 4; and D. W. Wainhouse, et al., *International Peacekeeping at the Crossroads* (Baltimore: Johns Hopkins University Press, 1973), ch. VI.

21. See further, S. Chauhdry, *The UN India-Pakistan Observer Mission 1965–66* (unpublished Ph.D. thesis, University of Keele, England, 1979); James, *The Politics of Peace-Keeping*, ch. 4; and R. W. Reford, "Unipom: Success of a Mission," *International Journal* 27, 2 (Summer 1972).

22. See further, J. Citrin, *United States Peace-Keeping Activities* (Denver, Colo.: University of Denver Press, 1965), Ch. IV; W. Henderson, *West New Guinea: the Dispute and Its Settlement* (South Orange, N.J.: Seton Hall University Press, 1973); James, *The Politices of Peace-Keeping*, ch. 5; J. M. van der Kroef, "The West New Guinea Settlement," *Orbis* 7, 1 (Spring 1963); and P. M. van der Veur, "The UN in West Irian: a Critique," *International Organization* 18, 1 (Winter 1964).

23. See further, James, *The Politics of Peace-Keeping*, ch. 6.

24. The Westerners on the Security Council fairly clearly hoped that the despatch of the UN Observation Group in Lebanon would provide evidence of an attempt by left-wing Syria to undermine a controversially pro-Western regime. See H. Trevelyan, *Public and Private* (London: Hamish Hamilton, 1980), p. 39. In the event, however, the reports of the group—appointed by the Secretary-General and made up of an Indian, a Norwegian, and an Ecuadorean—gave little satisfaction to the West and, in particular, to the United States. When the Lebanese regime appeared to be in greater danger, therefore, the United States intervened unilaterally. See further Citrin, *United Nations Peace-Keeping Activities;* G. L. Curtis, "The UN Observation Group in Lebanon," *International Organization* 17, 4 (Autumn 1964); James, *The Politics of Peace-Keeping*, ch. 6; and Urquhart, *Hammarskjöld.*

25. See further, O. Bull, *War and Peace in the Middle East.* (London: Cooper, 1976); Burns, *Between Arab and Israeli;* Horn, *Soldiering for Peace;* and James, *The Politics of Peace-Keeping*, ch. 7.

26. See further James, *The Politics of Peace-Keeping*, ch. 7, and "Recent Developments"; S. Lourie, "The UN Military Observer Group in India and Pakistan," *International Organization* 9, 1 (February 1955); and Wainhouse et al., *International Peacekeeping*, ch. III.

27. See the works quoted in note 16 above; and A. Eban, *An Autobiography.* (London: Weidenfeld and Nicolson, 1978), ch. 8; James, *The Politics of Peace-Keeping*, ch. 8; and G. Rosner, *The United Nations Emergency Force* (New York: Columbia University Press, 1963).

28. See further, E. L. M. Burns, "The Withdrawal of Unef and the Future of Peacekeeping," *International Journal* 33, 1 (Winter 1967–68); M. Cohen, "The Demise of Unef," ibid.; *The Public Papers of the Secretaries-General of the United Nations: Vol. 7. U Thant 1965–1967.* eds. A. W. Cordier and M. Harrelson, (New York: Columbia University Press, 1976); R. Higgins, *UN Peace-Keeping: Documents and Commentary 1946–1967: Vol. 1. The Middle East* (London: Oxford University

Press, 1969), pt. 2, sect. 9; A. James, "U Thant and his Critics," *The Year Book of World Affairs 1972* (London: Stevens, 1972); and I. J. Rikhye, *The Sinai Blunder* (New Delhi: Oxford University Press and I B H, 1978).

29. See further, G. Abi-Saab, *The United Nations Operation in the Congo 1960–1964* (London: Oxford University Press, 1978). R. Dayal, *Mission for Hammarskjöld: The Congo Crisis* (London: Oxford University Press, 1976), C. Hoskyns, *The Congo since Independence January 1960–December 1961* (London: Oxford University Press, 1965); James, *The Politics of Peace-Keeping*, ch. 9; E. W. Lefever, *Uncertain Mandate: Politics of the UN Congo Operation.* (Baltimore, Md.: Johns Hopkins University Press, 1967); B. Urquhart, *Hammarskjöld*, ch. 15, 16, 17, and 18; and S. R. Weissman, *American Foreign Policy in the Congo, 1960–1964* (Ithaca, N.Y.: Cornell University Press, 1974).

30. See further, J. Boyd, "Cyprus: Episode in Peacekeeping," *International Organization* 20, 1 (Winter 1966); M. Harbottle, *The Impartial Soldier* (London: Oxford University Press, 1970); James, *The Politics of Peace-Keeping*, ch. 8; and J. A. Stegenga, *The United Nations Force in Cyprus* (Athens: Ohio State University Press, 1968).

31. See further, W. W. Dobell, "Policy or Law for Cyprus?" *International Journal* 31, 1 (Winter 1975–76); James, *The Politics of Peace-Keeping;* and A. James "Kurt Waldheim: Diplomats' Diplomat," *Year Book of World Affairs 1983* (London: Stevens, 1983).

32. See works cited in note 18 above, and P. C. Harvey, "The Operational Effectiveness of UN Peace-Keeping Operations with Particular Reference to UNEF II, October 1973–September 1975" (unpublished M.A. thesis, University of Keele, England, 1976–1977); and B. Urquhart, "UN Peacekeeping in the Middle East," *The World Today* 36, 3 (March 1980).

33. For subsequent events involving the establishment of a non-UN peacekeeping force, see A. James, "Symbol in Sinai: The Multinational Force and Observers," *Millenium: Journal of International Studies* 14, 3 (Winter 1985).

34. See further, James, "Recent Developments"; and A. James, *The UN on Golan: Peacekeeping Paradox?* (Oslo: Norwegian Institute of International Affairs, 1986).

35. See works cited in note 19, above.

4

The Politics of International Economic
Cooperation and Development

Robert W. Gregg

●

Although the verb may be ill-chosen, the United Nations celebrated
its fortieth birthday in 1985. In some periods of history forty years
would be an inconsequential moment; but the years since 1945 have
been characterized by such far-reaching changes that today the
founding of the UN seems to belong to another, by now quite remote,
age. Since the San Francisco Conference nuclear weapons have
transformed the calculus of war. One barrier after another has been
breached under the onslaught of revolutions in technology and
communications. Two states of continental proportions have acquired superpower status, but subsequently discovered that their
ideologies do not travel well and that in their quest for dominance
their military and economic might is not always fungible. Colonial
empires have crumbled and the map of the world now shows three
times as many sovereign states as assembled at San Francisco, most
of them small, poorly endowed, and conspicuously non-Caucasian
in population. The state itself is, in Harlan Cleveland's metaphor,
leaking power,[1] and whether sovereignty is in fact at bay or not,
transnational corporations and other actors are increasingly challenging the authority of governments in the conduct of foreign policy.

The impact of these changes has, inevitably, been felt at the
United Nations, and it does not take a mass of documentary evidence
to convince us that the UN has had difficulties adapting to these

changes. The conventional wisdom is that the global institution has been in declining health for some years. In retrospect the UN's golden age came relatively early, lasted for only a brief time, and has been succeeded by a long twilight of frustrated expectations.[2] Whether this obviously troubled institution, created in the waning days of World War II, still has relevance for the much changed and rapidly changing world of the 1980s is a question about which diplomats and scholars may disagree. Of one thing we may be certain, however: substantial efforts have been made over the years to modify the UN and its rules and procedures, and those efforts have been led in the main by states that believe that many of the bargains struck "at the creation" are today inapposite and dysfunctional.

A principal objective of most of these efforts has been the extension of the UN's authority, at least in some areas of its mandate. That objective would be accomplished by substituting a centralized system of decision by majorities for the Charter system, which Lawrence Finkelstein has characterized as one of "multilateral diplomacy, lacking centralized authority, and rooted in inherited and traditional concepts of states as sovereign, immune to the effects of decisions to which they do not consent."[3] This campaign for centralization of authority via majoritarian decisionmaking has, of course, been vigorously resisted by advocates of the view that authority resides in the consent of member states. Although the Charter seems to support the latter position, it has proved to be a remarkably elastic document, affording revisionist majorities with numerous opportunities to challenge the strict constructionists, by action as well as by rhetoric. Thus while UN politics has been about apartheid in South Africa, the rights of Palestinians, trade and development, disarmament, and a host of other matters, it has also been about the authority of the UN to allocate values.

It is the thesis of this chapter that this struggle over UN authority to allocate values has been the most important feature of UN politics in the global organization's first forty years; that the most important focus of this struggle has been in the area of international economic cooperation and development; that the original bias of a decentralized, unit veto system has been eroded in this area under mounting pressure from a coalition of developing Third World countries; but that efforts to centralize authority and invest majority decisions with more weight than the Charter seems to confer have reached a plateau from which further movement is increasingly problematic, at least in the near term.

These are parlous times for the United Nations. Those who support a decentralized, unit veto system, most notably the United States, are highly critical of the relentless pressure for a more authoritative UN and its intended consequence, a shift in control of the world economy. They have been able to contain this pressure, but the effort has taken its toll in confidence in and support for the organization. On the other hand those who want the UN to have more authority to allocate values that are unobtainable or extremely difficult to obtain by other means are increasingly frustrated by their inability to transform the UN. They may win symbolic victories and claim that overwhelming majorities confer legitimacy upon the principles and norms they espouse, but rarely have they been able to turn these "victories" into rules that authoritatively allocate values and they do not appear to possess the leverage to do so. The result is a standoff—an ongoing conflict between an irresistible force and an immovable object, two rocks between which the United Nations is slowly being ground down.

This chapter is about the measures that have been taken to accommodate the large and frustrated UN majority and the conflict that has marked adoption of those measures and that still surrounds other proposals to reform the United Nations. As Lawrence Finkelstein has observed, the measures taken have produced "a new mix between the inherited assumption that the system was decentralized in the sense that authority was to be found in the consent of each member state and the newer centralizing tendencies to find, or assert, authority in majority conclusions."[4] That new mix is nowhere more in evidence—nor is it anywhere more important—than in the economic sector. It is in this area that the struggle over the apportionment of political power in the United Nations has been most acute.

The Ascendancy of the Economic Development Agenda

The decision to focus on the economic sector in this assessment of the politics of value allocation in the United Nations is attributable to a number of interrelated trends, none of them new, but all of them gaining momentum as the UN enters its fifth decade. The most obvious of these trends is the increased importance that the great majority of UN members has assigned to its mandate in the field of economic cooperation and development. The ascendancy of this set of issues has been so pronounced that it is fair to say that it now enjoys a preeminent place among the UN's several purposes. A second and parallel trend has been the relative decline in the salience of other issues that formerly occupied more prominent places on the UN's agenda. The ascendant economic issues have generated much of the pressure for treating majority decisions as binding.

A third trend is the increasing interconnectedness of issues, as perceived by the majority of United Nations members. The preoccupations of the majority have created what might be termed a superpurpose that subsumes the seemingly diverse goals of the organization. Everything is now related to everything else, so that emphasis on economic issues is not necessarily achieved at the expense of other issues, but is conceptually linked to them and they to it. These trends require further brief comment, for they give shape to the politics of value allocation in the United Nations in its fifth decade.

Let us first consider maintenance of peace and security and promotion of equal rights and self-determination of peoples, two of the UN's primary purposes as adumbrated in Article 1 of the Charter. There can be no question but that the United Nations is still very much concerned with these Charter purposes; but they are no longer the UN's most important business. One reason the maintenance of peace and security is of lesser importance at the United Nations today is not just that the UN has failed to resolve or even ameliorate many conflicts, but that the UN's members seem to be more tolerant of violent conflict than they once were.[5] The persistence of certain disputes and "crises" tends to produce a weary acceptance, especially when the historical record shows that systemic stability can withstand a rather substantial amount of violent conflict and that the superpowers have become quite adept at managing conflict, learning from experience and acquiring confidence in their ability to contain both their rivalry and their clients within safe and permissible bounds. The Cold War may once again have turned more bitter in the 1980s, but this unwelcome trend has not led to demands that the UN play a more active role in damping down conflicts.

The end—or the virtual end—of the process of decolonization has also contributed to the decline of the peace and security issue. Many of the conflicts with which the UN grappled for many years were associated with decolonization and the liberation movements that spurred it on. The new generation of postcolonial conflicts within and between Third World states has not stimulated a comparable demand for UN intervention, largely because such conflicts, unlike those associated with decolonization, tend to divide the Third World at the United Nations. These divisions not only produce cautious UN responses, they also militate against demands for centralizing authority in the UN to deal with such conflicts. In this most sensitive of issue areas those who would benefit most from the decisions of an authoritative UN in one conflict are quite likely to be part of a minority resisting such authority in the next; thus in this field there is an understandable cautiousness about investing the General Assembly with authority to allocate values.

The decline of the self-determination issue is also a function of the virtual end of colonialism. Those territories that have not yet achieved independence are relatively few and almost invariably small and of doubtful viability; it is widely perceived that these territories pose special problems, and were it not for the frustrating cases of the Namibians and the Palestinians, the issue of self-determination would all but disappear from the UN's agenda. There is little enthusiasm for making an issue of self-determination for peoples seeking autonomy at the expense of postcolonial regimes. The existing nation-state is being challenged by disaffected minorities in several places, including some where the state is an artificial legacy of the colonial era. But these claims do not, as a rule, command great sympathy and there is certainly no movement within the UN to broaden the meaning of self-determination and thus to reinvigorate that particular issue.

Then there is the problem of apartheid, an issue that is partly one of self-determination and partly one of equal rights; it is likely to be a major item on the UN's agenda for as long as that abominable practice continues. But this is a special case, a grievance against a particular state; no matter how galling the failures to effect change in Pretoria's policies, or how many the meetings and resolutions devoted to apartheid, the issue of which it is the most visible symbol is in decline at the UN, sustained by a few hard, residual cases and the conviction that neocolonialism and racism are still with us.

These issues—apartheid, Namibia, the Palestinians—are among those that generate demands for a more authoritative UN. Majorities in favor of UN action as opposed to mere rhetoric are overwhelming in all three cases, as they have been throughout most of the push for decolonization. Large and persistent majorities have contributed significantly to the delegitimization of colonialism, of apartheid, and of South Africa's occupation of Namibia, and, somewhat less clearly, to the legitimization of Palestinian demands for a nation-state. Any inquiry into the politics of value allocation in the United Nations would have to consider the struggle attending these issues. But while the promotion of self-determination continues to occupy a significant portion of the UN's time, the center of gravity of UN attention has shifted. Important as the maintenance of peace and security and the realization of self-determination of peoples are, these purposes have been eclipsed in importance by the pursuit of international economic and social cooperation.

The Charter speaks initially of achieving "international cooperation in solving international problems of an economic, social, cultural or humanitarian character,"[6] and subsequently states that the UN "shall promote higher standards of living, full employment, and conditions of economic and social progress and development" and "solutions of international economic, social, health, and related problems."[7] These are very general and inclusive statements of purpose, and very poor guides to the thrust of UN activity in the economic and social spheres today. The broad and eclectic mandate has been narrowed and given more focus, to the point where it is essentially a mandate for the economic development of Third World countries. In the beginning there were relatively few such countries and UN corridors and chambers did not ring with talk of development. Although the United Nations was, as the founders had intended, much more active in economic matters than the League of Nations had been, its role was modest, with the major responsibility for international economic and social cooperation vested in other institutions, each with its own sectoral mandate.

As new states from the Third World joined the United Nations and ultimately became the overwhelming majority of the membership the priorities that had characterized the organization's early years were modified. "Gradually," one observer writes, "the new nations have taken over the UN, imbuing it with their values and cutting it to their cloth."[8] This "takeover" of the UN, this revision of priorities, could only have occurred if the Third World states were more or less of one mind as to what they wanted the UN to be and to do. Inevitably the new majority sought and found issues that united them rather than those that were divisive. They did not have far to look: virtually all of these states were, in the parlance of the day, underdeveloped or developing. Whatever other purposes the UN pursued, it was clear that it would be a development institution.

The economic and social mandate received a boost and in the process the diffuse and vague objectives of the Charter were transformed into an urgent commitment to speed development.

The evidence of the ascendancy of this purpose is to be found at every hand. There is the proliferation of UN organizations and programs and funds, which together constitute a major effort to involve the United Nations more fully and forcefully in issues of development. Some of these bodies, such as the United Nations Development Program (UNDP) and the United Nations Conference on Trade and Development (UNCTAD), are among the most important in the UN complex based on the size of their budgets and the attention paid to them by scholars and practitioners alike.

The United Nations has also demonstrated the high priority it attaches to development with a series of special sessions of the General Assembly, major ad hoc global conferences, specially designated years and decades, and resolutions rendered more dramatic by calling them declarations and charters. It is not only in the realm of economic cooperation and development that the UN has resorted to such strategies, but it is in this area that it has expended the most effort by far. Three times between 1974 and 1980 the UN held a special session of the General Assembly with a development focus. The 1970s saw the beginning of almost yearly global conferences on themes directly or closely related to development, including environment, population, food, human settlements, technical cooperation, science and technology for development, and new and reusable sources of energy. Nor has this highly visible form of consciousness-raising and political pressure yet run its course. The United Nations is now well into its Third Development Decade; no other UN objective has been accorded such sustained prominence. This whirlwind of activity was to have culminated in the establishment of a New International Economic Order, the subject of several landmark General Assembly resolutions.[9]

We also gain insights into UN priorities by noting trends in the allocation of resources and staffing patterns. In the final analysis what is important is what the members are prepared to fund and to staff. In the aggregate UN activities in the field of international economic cooperation and development receive the lion's share of the assessed budget, and of course virtually all of the voluntarily subscribed budgets, such as that of the UNDP, are targeted for development. Although it is difficult to be precise about such matters because of definitional problems and the need to allocate large administrative and support costs, it would appear that the United Nations spends more than six times as much of its assessed budget on its economic activities as on peace and security.[10] The budgetary emphasis on the economic is an inevitable consequence of the programmatic activities, conferences, and subsidiary bodies that have mushroomed in that sector. Inasmuch as there is a direct correlation between the size of a unit's budget and the size of its staff, it follows that the great majority of UN personnel are working on economic issues or are providing support services for those who are.[11]

All of this programmatic activity, together with the budget and staff to support it, reflects not only shifting priorities but also an intensifying conflict over the allocation of values by the United Nations. In no area have the pressures to centralize authority within the UN been more vigorous or more prolonged. The values at stake have, of course, included money, with persistent Third World efforts to increase the flow of resources to those countries through the UN and to change the rules governing distribution of global wealth. Other values have also been contested, including status, power, and legitimacy. And while the results have fallen far short of what the Group of 77 wants, they have not been negligible.

Leaving aside for the moment the question of whether there has been movement toward centralized majority decisionmaking in this sector, the UN community itself would seem to have dispelled any doubt about the reversal of priorities among UN purposes. When interviewed in a recent study some 125 high-ranking officials in the UN Secretariat and high-level members of permanent delegations to the UN made clear that they value economic welfare and social justice more highly as United Nations objectives than they do peace and security.[12] Such a view is obviously at variance with the expectations of the founders and the dominant concerns of the members during the UN's early years. It is not only a reflection of the changed composition of the UN's majority, but of the changes in the needs and expectations of the majority resulting from changes in the global context within which the United Nations functions.

Important as the growing emphasis on economic issues has been, it would be less significant if it were not for the fact that economic issues have been politicized and linked to other issues in ways that give the UN's economic mandate a very different character from that of other international organizations. This is the third and in some respects most important trend justifying the focus on the UN's role in achieving international economic and social cooperation in our study of the politics of value allocation in the United Nations. Economic issues have become the stuff of high politics, not only in the sense that they have risen to the top of the agenda and now command high-level attention, but also in the sense that they have been demystified and become acceptable fare for debate and action by the generalists at the UN as well as by the specialists in other international forums. As economic issues became more prominent at the UN they were addressed not by a different set of actors but by the same people who argued the indisputably political issues of peace and security and self-determination, and in the same supercharged atmosphere in which states confronted each other on those other issues.

Moreover, the Third World majority discovered that these several issues meshed, that their grievances reinforced each other. Instead of crosscutting lines of cleavage developing within the UN membership, opposing coalitions on one issue have tended to reappear again and again on other issues. Thus the Third World countries that constitute the majority and provide momentum for action on economic development are also the movers and shakers within the United Nations on other emotional and volatile issues, including support for the Palestinians and Namibians, opposition to the policies of Israel and South Africa, demands for the end of all residual colonialism, and charges of racism, neocolonialism, cultural imperialism, and other forms of intervention, almost always by Western states, in the Third World. Although there are, of course, exceptions—that is, issues that divide the Third World and produce different voting patterns—it is fair to say that these countries generally control the agenda and function more or less as a bloc, suppressing intramural conflicts at the UN in the interest of preserving group solidarity.[13]

A pattern has emerged over the years wherein the many grievances and demands of the Third World are repeatedly linked in rhetoric and resolution. Thus the several issues that most trouble member states from the Third World are perceived to be related, somewhat in the manner of a syndrome, and responsibility for all of these problems is ultimately laid at the doors of the same handful of Western states and their practices. Economic development may be the UN's primary purpose today, but it is simply another stage in the long-term struggle for self-determination. The United Nations was instrumental in bringing about political self-determination through decolonization; but the process is far from complete, for the legacies of colonialism and new forms of the supposedly ex-orcized practice live on. Mohammed Bedjaoui puts it this way: "a developing country tries to become a grown-up state, but the ways leading to this may be difficult or temporarily impracticable because of the imperialist grip. It is then reduced to the condition, to a greater or lesser extent, of a probationary state, travelling along paths forced upon it by various circumstances."[14] The campaign for a New International Economic Order is, in effect, as much about self-determination as it is about economic cooperation between developed and developing countries.

Similarly, the UN objective of maintaining international peace and security may not so much have lost its salience as been transmuted in the eyes of the majority into an aspect of its larger quest for a new order. In its original formulation the UN mandate to maintain peace and security carried a conserving rather than a transforming connotation. But the Third World majority now tends to find the old order itself a threat to peace and security because it perpetuates hegemony and dependence, justifies intervention, sanctions racism, frustrates development, and fosters the conditions that breed disorder and violence. It is no accident that UN resolutions dealing with economic matters frequently contain preambular paragraphs that recite the full litany of Third World grievances and place blame for all manner of problems—economic, social, and political—on "the system" and the Western states that have created it and that benefit from it.[15]

This linking up of issues is more than mere scapegoating. It has contributed to a breaking down of issue compartmentalization and the gradual emergence of economic development as a superissue that both subsumes and affects other issues. The United Nations, by placing so much emphasis on its economic mandate and by defining that mandate as it has, has made its performance in that area a primary focus for those seeking to evaluate the global body. This emphasis, coupled with the fact that this is the area that has witnessed the broadest and most sustained campaign for a more authoritative UN, makes economic development a natural focal point for analysis of the politics of value allocation in the United Nations.

The Charter Mandate and U.S. Hegemony

There was no question about it in 1945: the UN's central task, its principal raison d'être, was the maintenance of peace and security.

The United Nations was, of course, designed to be a multipurpose institution, as the League of Nations before it had been. Although the founders of the UN were anxious to distance themselves from the failed League, they could not help but be influenced by the League model and experience. Rather than abandon the Covenant's emphasis on economic and social affairs, they chose to incorporate into the UN's Charter the essence of the recommendations to strengthen that mandate that had been made by the Bruce Committee in 1939, too late for the ill-fated League.[16] But purposes other than peace and security were nonetheless ancillary and instrumental within the framework of the Charter. The major powers wanted (or were willing to accept) a security organization; there was never any question of their supporting a United Nations in which purposes other than peace and security were paramount.

The role assigned to the United Nations by the Charter in economic and social affairs reflected the prevailing circumstances of the time, and the prevailing circumstances included, most importantly, the dominant position of the United States and the relative strength of Western views and assumptions. The seeds that would mature into the two major postwar challenges to Western ideas and American hegemony had been planted much earlier, but neither the challenge of Soviet-based communism nor the revolt of the South against Western political, economic, and cultural control and influence figured prominently in the shaping of the UN system.

Although the United Nations Charter is obviously not a Soviet, much less a communist, blueprint for world order, the USSR did play an important role in the design of the UN, opposing centralized majority decisionmaking as adamantly as the staunchest supporter of free market principles. Distrustful of international organizations, but aware of their value for relationships with noncommunist states, the Soviets were tenacious (and on the whole successful) in their efforts to make sure that UN authority would be severely circumscribed. The Soviets were more concerned with hobbling the UN than in turning it into an important instrumentality for global problem solving. Preoccupied with security and ideologically convinced that no useful purpose could be served by entrusting a body dominated by capitalist states with economic and social responsibilities, the USSR was basically uninterested in the UN's having economic and social functions. That attitude carried over to the specialized agencies of the UN system, most of which the Soviet Union did not join or even try to influence significantly in their formative stages.[17]

So the USSR basically left the field to the United States and the other market economy countries.

If the USSR was less influential in shaping the UN system than perhaps it might have been—except in the field of peace and security and voting arrangements—the Third World was barely heard from at all. There was no Third World, of course, in the 1940s. Most of the states that in later years were to mount such a persistent challenge to the economic order established at the close of World War II were not present at the creation. They were still colonies and it was not yet clear that the war and the attendant humiliation visited upon the British, French, Dutch, and other colonial powers would lead so quickly to the end of colonialism and to the proliferation of new states. More than half of the states represented at San Francisco, the UN's original members, belong today to the Group of 77, but in 1945 there was little consciousness of the prospective importance of the economic and social mandate. Just as there was no vocal bloc of developing countries, so there was no development doctrine, no alternative norms and rules with which to challenge the economic regimes that were taking shape under Western, and especially U.S., leadership.

When voices were raised at San Francisco against the deals that had been struck at Yalta and Dumbarton Oaks and elsewhere by the Americans, the British, and the Russians, they were the voices of "small" states, not the underdeveloped states. The conflict was large versus small, not North versus South, as evidenced by the fact that countries such as Australia and New Zealand were among the leaders of the small state contingent. In any event most of the small states' fire was directed at provisions having to do with security and voting rather than economic matters. Needless to say, dissenting voices were even more muted at Bretton Woods.

It was the United States, relatively unscathed by the war and even economically strengthened by its assumption of the "arsenal of democracy" role, that took the lead in erecting both the security and the economic regimes that were to prevent a recurrence of the disasters of the 1930s and 1940s. The system that emerged, especially in matters of finance, trade, and economic cooperation generally, was very much the one favored by the United States. Robert Cox summarizes it this way:

The whole complex of institutions outside of the security field reflected a single, consistent, and dominant view of the world in

which economic liberalism was perceived to be the generator of
material well-being, rising productivity the solvent of social ills,
and pluralism both a social and political good in itself and a condition for the attainment of economic liberalism and higher productivity. . . . There was a high degree of coherence between the
form of international institutions, the norms they embodied, and
the US leadership that provided the key guarantee to the system.
The general acceptance of the values upon which the nonsecurity
system was premised meant that issues dealt with through these
institutions could be considered "technical." They posed problems of means rather than of ends.[18]

As we know, both U.S. hegemony and functionalism were to be
challenged in the years to come, but in the middle and late 1940s
they were the salient characteristics of the UN system. Yet somewhat
paradoxically in the United Nations itself, as opposed to the UN
system, U.S. hegemony was on display only in a loose, permissive
fashion. Although the Charter empowered the UN to do very little,
the provision of equal voting rights in the General Assembly,
strongly supported by the United States, had the effect of leaving
the door ajar, if not open, to future challenges. And functionalism
was compromised by the broad sweep of the Charter and the obviously political character of the new institution.

Much has been written about the importance of hegemonic powers in the creation of strong and reliable regimes. According to one
definition, "hegemony may be conceived as the national capability
to advance long-range views of world order . . . by working with
the preponderant resources available to the hegemon for the success
of institutions charged with that task."[19] The United States had such
a vision in the 1940s and it did bring its resources to bear in creating
and then in sustaining the nexus of regimes that constituted the
second try at world order. Although the regimes and institutions
that were created at that time were the ones favored by the United
States, the hegemonic power did not close the door to change. As
Stephen Krasner has pointed out, hegemonic powers, because their
material dominance is so complete, may feel no need to create regimes that strengthen or reinforce the existing distribution of power;
they will be satisfied to have those regimes reflect their preferences.[20] The United States was also surely motivated by a desire
to win legitimacy for the norms and rules it favored. It believed it
could do so by treating all states as sovereign equals and, except

for the Security Council, distributing votes equally in the United Nations, something it could not afford to do in the Bretton Woods institutions.

So while the United States in the 1940s orchestrated the creation of a network of institutions that reflected its preference for a liberal international economic order, it also supported (1) an Economic and Social Council (ECOSOC) without guarantees that major industrial powers or states of greatest economic importance would be members, (2) egalitarian voting in those UN organs that would deal with economic and social issues—that is, the General Assembly and ECOSOC, and (3) an open-ended authorization for the UN to create new institutions, hold conferences, draft conventions, and otherwise modify the institutional landscape for multilateral cooperation in the economic and social fields. This posture was partly a reflection of confidence in American influence, partly an acknowledgment of the fact that key decisions would be reached in other institutions more firmly under Western control, and partly a bid for broad support or, as Krasner suggests, an attempt to legitimate U.S. hegemony. The inevitable corollary of this relaxation of hegemonic control was a toothless UN, a UN whose decisions would depend for their authority on the consent of member states. Or so it seemed in 1945.

The United Nations was thus both the organization that the United States wanted and an organization that developing Third World countries would later be able to dominate. In time, as U.S. hegemony weakened and as developing countries became more numerous and more assertive, UN rules and procedures were exploited by Third World states bent on changing the principles and norms on which the liberal international economic order rested. But that development was still many years in the future when the UN and the specialized agencies began life in the 1940s.

The second distinguishing feature of the United Nations system was functionalism, a division of labor among UN system agencies so that each had responsibility for a particular policy area. The component institutions of the UN system were conceived as technical, not political, bodies. They were not to debate and decide on the shape of the international economic order as a whole; that had been decided. They were created to permit representatives with specialized competence to address essentially technical issues within specialized agencies. For purposes of economic cooperation the most important of these agencies were the International Monetary Fund (IMF) and the World Bank; the International Trade Organi-

zation (ITO) was to have joined them as one of the institutional cen-
terpieces of the economic order, but the ITO was stillborn and the
General Agreement on Tariffs and Trade (GATT) took its place, although the GATT was of course less an international organization
than an agreement to negotiate trade liberalization. Beyond this trio
of institutions were a host of other specialized agencies whose titles
indicated their sectoral roles.

The creation of these specialized bodies followed functionalist
logic. Functionalists, after all, had argued that technicians and experts were practical and task-oriented, unlike politicians and diplomats, whose loyalty was to the sovereign state and hence to the
pursuit of power and status; the best that the latter could do was to
keep states from each other's throats, a negative goal, whereas the
former, by indirection, could build a peace "that would suffuse the
world with a fertile mingling of a common endeavor and achievement."[21]

Functionalism was thus a formula for insulating technical issues
from extraneous considerations, and, as Sidney Weintraub reminds
us, it "permits progress in one area, say trade, even while there is
conflict in other areas, particularly in political relations."[22] Although
the government of the United States and other advocates of a UN
system were certainly not endorsing all aspects of functionalist theory, the attention paid to economic and social issues and the array
of agencies created to deal with them constituted a significant functionalist experiment.

If functionalism was the rule governing the division of labor
within the emerging UN system, the United Nations itself was the
exception. All of the other institutions, with the possible exception
of UNESCO, were more or less sectorally specific and could be expected to be what their generic name implied: specialized agencies.
The UN, however, more than any other global organization, was (and
is) a multipurpose institution, the antithesis of the functionalist approach. Alone among global organizations the UN's purposes include
both peace and security *and* economic and social cooperation. The
latter is the province of functionalism, whose mission it is "to make
peace possible by organizing particular layers of social life in accordance with their particular requirements, breaking down the ar-
tificialities of the zoning arrangements associated with the principle
of sovereignty."[23] The former is the jealously guarded preserve of
the sovereign state and its diplomatic and military officials, whose
approach to peace the functionalists had sought to discredit.

Even within the field of economic and social cooperation the UN's mandate was more general and diffuse than that of other UN system agencies, and by virtue of that generality was to be a standing invitation to challenge the functionalist division of labor that the United States so obviously preferred. Neither the United States nor any of the other major actors who participated in the drafting of the Charter intended that the United Nations should be an important decisionmaking forum for economic policy. Evidence that the UN's role was to be marginal is abundant. It can be found in the general and residual character of the UN's economic mandate. It can be found even more tellingly in the absence of authority to adopt binding resolutions; the critical Charter language is soft and tentative—"may discuss," "may make recommendations," "shall initiate studies," "shall promote solutions," and so on, language that permits all kinds of activity but that stops far short of investing the General Assembly or ECOSOC with the kind of authority possessed by the Security Council on the one hand and the IMF and the World Bank on the other.

The UN's marginal role is also confirmed by the egalitarian character of those UN organs that are concerned with economic issues, so much at variance with the distribution of economic power at the time the Charter was drafted and with the reflection of that reality in the IMF and the World Bank.[24] As Stephen Zamora has observed, "international economic organizations are reflections of the economic order, determined by—not determining—economic realities."[25] Consistent with that thesis, there was at the time the UN system was established in the 1940s a rough correlation between an organization's authority and the resources it disposed of on the one hand and control over that organization's decision processes on the other. When the institution possessed substantial monitoring or regulatory authority (the IMF) or was responsible for distributing large sums of money (the World Bank), the support of the most economically powerful and influential members was assured by giving them effective control. Where the institution's decisions were primarily rcommendatory or symbolic in character (the UN General Assembly and ECOSOC), egalitarian or majoritarian decisionmaking was acceptable. As Zamora phrases it, "where states are most likely to surrender some autonomy to the international organization, one finds the highest incidence of voting safeguards to protect their interests."[26]

What all of this meant was that the United Nations was to have

a very limited role in the liberal international economic order and
that it would not authoritatively allocate values when it did play a
role. The functionally more specific institutions had the greater role,
and in the case of the Bretton Woods institutions did possess the
authority to allocate values and were effectively under the control
of the Western market economy states. On the other hand the UN
was not an entirely negligible element in the emerging system. With
the creation of ECOSOC the framers of the Charter guaranteed that
the UN would be much more actively involved in this sector than
the League had been. They miscalculated, of course, when in Article
7 they declared ECOSOC to be a principal organ; whatever its formal
status, ECOSOC is not and never has been a principal organ in the
sense that the Security Council has been, and it has had to take a
subordinate position in economic matters to both the General Assembly and, since its creation in 1964, UNCTAD. But ECOSOC's designation as a principal organ gave economic issues a legitimacy and
a prominence on the UN's agenda that they otherwise might not
have enjoyed. The door was open from the beginning for member
states to push the UN into a more ambitious role vis à vis the international economy, although the specifics of the Charter, the diffusion of responsibility among a number of specialized agencies,
and the realities of economic power and influence made it difficult
for the UN to play that more ambitious role effectively.

Several factors, beyond the symbolic designation of ECOSOC as a
principal organ, not only facilitated the emergence of economic cooperation and development as a UN priority but also provided leverage for those who wished UN decisions to derive their authority
from majority votes. First, there is the generality of those Charter
provisions pertaining to the UN's role in economic and social matters.
Although they do not contain a grant of authority that would enable
either the General Assembly or ECOSOC to compel states to do anything, neither do they proscribe areas of activity. They constitute,
in effect, authorization for the UN to promote a variety of broad economic and social objectives, to tackle any subject that concerns the
majority, including, by inference, the most comprehensive issue
of all—the acceptability of the international economic order as a
whole. Writing about the responsibility of the Council, but in terms
equally applicable to the General Assembly, Walter Sharp observed
that "the Charter confers upon it a series of functions which, taken
together, were presumably intended to provide the basis for a general policy forum and quasi-legislative role."[27] Just what is meant

by the phrase "quasi-legislative" is not entirely clear; indeed, it is still the subject of debate in the politics of value allocation within the United Nations. But it is demonstrably true that the UN has become a general policy forum for international economic issues, and that if its resolutions are not of the rule-creating variety, they are important instruments for setting agendas, shaping values, and conferring or denying legitimacy. UN resolutions have come to be perceived by supporters and critics alike as potentially more consequential than mere expressions of majority preference.

A second factor pushing the UN toward a more ambitious role in international economic affairs has been the decisionmaking procedures of the relevant organs. The one-state–one-vote system and majority rule may have been a natural concomitant of the doctrine of sovereign equality, the hegemon's way of legitimating its dominant position in the international economic order, or a harmless concession to the weak in forums without authority. But UN decisionmaking procedures encourage majority-mindedness. Whatever the rationale, the consequences of the Charter's voting provisions have included agenda setting according to the shifting preferences of the majority, a pattern of interest aggregation in which building winning coalitions has become more important than intergroup compromise, and a growing conviction that resolutions reflecting the will of large and sustained UN majorities are appropriate instruments for the progressive development of international law.

The Charter also contains at least three other provisions that have helped to shape the debate over the UN's role in the economic sector and the politics of value allocation in that sector. They are the provisions that permit the Assembly and the Council to establish new institutions,[28] authorize the Assembly to approve the UN's budget and apportion expenses among the members,[29] and enable the Assembly to establish the regulations according to which the staff will be appointed.[30] In each of these cases decisions derive their authority from majority (or qualified majority) votes, not from the consent of the members. In these areas, therefore, decision power is centralized. It may be argued that these provisions pertain only to housekeeping functions—that creating subsidiary organs and managing the budget and the bureaucracy are quite different matters from determining the norms and rules that will govern international economic relations among sovereign states. The UN can survive (and has survived) without the authority to *decide* matters in the latter area; it is difficult to imagine even a minimal UN with a decentralized unit veto system where housekeeping functions are concerned, although provisions giving more control, especially over budget decisions, to states making the greatest contributions to the budget are conceivable.[31]

But it would be a mistake to pretend that these functions are of little consequence. On the contrary they have made it possible for the UN majority to give its interest in economic development tangible and forceful expression, and they have helped to guarantee that in the struggle at the UN over the authoritative allocation of values the Third World enjoys some advantages. It will be useful to examine some of the important benchmarks in that forty-year struggle over the allocation of values in the field of economic cooperation and development.

The Challenge from the Third World

During the early years of the UN's existence, when the members were for the first time exploring the meaning and possible uses of the Charter's often vague and imprecise language in concrete situations, the economic mandate received less attention than the provisions concerning peace and security. The storm clouds of the Cold War were gathering, and it is not surprising that the UN's major efforts were concerned with the interpretation and applicability of Chapters VI and VII, dealing with peaceful settlement of disputes and action with respect to threats to the peace, breaches of the peace, and acts of aggression, as well as with clarification of Charter provisions on voting, especially in the case of the Security Council. It was in these areas that the struggle over the nature and scope of UN authority was first joined. The UN was busy developing rules of procedure and a repertory of practice for all of its organs, of course, but the principal focus of those efforts was not on ECOSOC and the noteworthy controversies they generated fell outside of the economic sector. Nor were economic issues a prime catalyst for benchmark developments in the early evolution of the General Assembly or the Secretariat.

While the UN was preoccupied with such issues as the Soviet presence in Iran, the termination of Dutch rule in Indonesia, post-partition conflict between India and Pakistan, the territorial integrity of Greece, unification of Korea, and the creation of the state of Israel—all issues that put the Security Council in the spotlight—the major economic issues of the day were addressed outside of the UN.

Reconstruction in the aftermath of the war was handled by the World Bank before it became identified with Third World development and through the Marshall Plan; the UN itself was not involved in postwar efforts to create effective monetary and trade regimes, both of which were anchored in other institutions. Thus the dominant issues of the UN's early years were either addressed elsewhere or were not primarily economic in character.

However, during this period the UN's limited role in the maintenance of the international economic order took shape, ECOSOC's modus operandi was developed, and a rather considerable body of subsidiary machinery for the economic and social sectors was created. And it was at this time, even before the major expansion of UN membership, that there appeared the first tentative challenges to the prevailing view that the UN's role in economic and social affairs should be limited. ECOSOC and the secretariat that serviced it quickly became associated with that minimalist Western view, and this fact, together with the Council's small size (and hence its allegedly unrepresentative character), soon led to disenchantment with the Council on the part of many UN members and to a decline in its role relative to that of the General Assembly (as well as to demands for the creation of other, more responsive forums). Although the Council was never a technical or an expert body, its raison d'être as stated in the Charter was considerably more specific than the Assembly's, and it was also much smaller, lending some credence to the view that the influence of functionalism, while compromised, might still be felt in the UN. That hope, never very realistic, collapsed with the decline of ECOSOC and the assumption of primary responsibility for economic and social issues by forums that better suited the needs of an emerging Third World majority.

Two other developments of the UN's first few years might be cited as examples of struggle over the allocation of values. While neither involved the sharp conflict over the UN's role in economic matters that was to become so pronounced in the 1960s and 1970s, both anticipated the North-South dichotomy of later years. Both also involved the creation of new institutions, which, as we have noted, lies within the authority of the UN majority and hence represents an exception to the general rule that UN decisions depend for their authority upon the consent of member states.

One of these developments was the creation of regional economic commissions. Initially ECOSOC rejected the idea of regional commissions (the Charter speaks only of functional commissions), only

to be reversed by the General Assembly.[32] Then, after an Economic
Commission for Europe had been created, "the Asian and Latin
American states engaged in some effective log-rolling which led to
the creation of commissions for each of those regions over the opposition of Western European and North American members. Thus,
by March of 1948 the UN had created three regional economic commissions, had laid the foundation for honoring the claims of other
regions, and had broadened the mission of these commissions from
reconstruction to economic development."[33] The developing country members, at a time when development consciousness and doctrine were quite embryonic, had formed a coalition and won a round
in what would become an ongoing struggle over the allocation of
values.

     The second of these early developments concerned the creation
of institutions to serve as channels for development assistance. The
first of these institutions was the Expanded Program of Technical
Assistance (EPTA), a U.S. initiative that evolved in time into the
United Nations Development Program (UNDP).[34] The launching of
EPTA was an important event because it marked the entry of the UN
into the development game in a significant way, opening an era in
which the UN system would play an ever more active role in development assistance—an era in which the poorer states would press
for more aid, and for more of it to be delivered through multilateral
channels, and in which the more affluent states would cooperate in
this modest redistributive effort so long as the nature and volume
of aid were discretionary with the donors.

     In addition to EPTA's importance as a harbinger of efforts to use
the UN as a fulcrum for redistribution of wealth and skills, this program also helped turn the UN into an operational organization. EPTA
drew the United Nations out of the offices and conference rooms
and corridors of headquarters buildings in New York and Geneva
and elsewhere and took them out into the field. This shirt-sleeve
diplomacy was for a while the UN's major contribution to the development process. It opened up new channels of funding for the
UN, its revenues coming from voluntarily pledged contributions that
would ultimately rival the assessed budgets of the UN and the specialized agencies in size.[35] But most importantly, EPTA sowed the
seeds of expectation among developing countries regarding the UN's
proper role in development: it was to be an activist organization,
not merely a talk shop or a think tank.

     EPTA, like the regional commissions, was a product of Charter-granted authority to create new institutions; it was widely supported, by developing and developed countries alike, so no issue arose as to whether the UN had authority to allocate values. That was not the case with the proposed Special United Nations Fund for Economic Development, whose legislative history reveals in sharp outline the politics of value allocation in this important sector. SUNFED, as this fund was dubbed, was an early warning sign of the Third World's desire to use the UN to effect regime changes. Developing countries wanted more development assistance than EPTA provided; they were also dissatisfied with the World Bank, which was moving only slowly into the field of development lending—and then on hard terms—and they had an understandable preference for multilateral over bilateral aid, with its stated and implied obligations for the recipients. In effect they wanted an international development authority more amenable to their influence than the available alternatives. SUNFED was to be that institution.

Although the developing countries were unsuccessful in their bid for SUNFED, settling instead for a much smaller Special Fund for preinvestment projects,[36] the battle over the fund was symptomatic of a growing polarization of the UN membership over the proper role of the UN in the field of international economic cooperation and development. The Special Fund resulted from a U.S. initiative, but that initiative represented the grudging concession of the United States to the exertion of majority pressures over time. This issue foreshadowed later efforts by the Group of 77 to locate control over resource transfer issues in egalitarian or majoritarian forums, and it revealed the determination of the United States and other developed countries to keep the UN out of those areas and to insist on effective control over resource transfers. The politics of value allocation in economic matters that would become so familiar by the 1970s were already on view in the 1950s, even before the Group of 77 was formed and the class struggle of the poor countries versus the rich was joined in earnest.

But in spite of divisions on specific issues, there emerged fairly early within the United Nations a consensus that economic issues were an important part of its agenda and that it should have a special vocation for development. EPTA, the Special Fund, and the regional commissions for Latin America, Asia and the Far East, and later Africa are all evidence of this consensus. The emergence of the UN as an institution with some responsibility for development *within the framework of the liberal international economic order* was not notably controversial—that is, it enjoyed broad support as long as the UN was not used to challenge the established regimes and the institutions associated with them. Development offered an opportunity for the UN to become identified with an issue of increasing salience that was not the central focus of the activity of any of the regimes or agencies that had been created during the second try at world order. Neither the trade nor the money regime was primarily (or, many would subsequently argue, even secondarily) concerned with development, a situation that would become the cause of considerable Third World frustration in the years to come. The World Bank was, to be sure, a development institution, but no attempt had been made to create a coherent development regime; once past the era of postwar reconstruction, the bank became a principal lender for development purposes, but it never became the centerpiece of a development regime in the sense that its sister institution, the IMF, did in the area of monetary affairs. The field was thus open for the United Nations, and the North as well as the South supported its assumption of a prominent role in development.

By 1960, a watershed year that saw the admission of seventeen new states (all of them but Cyprus from the African continent), the UN had staked out an important if still limited role in system maintenance. It had been the setting for so many pronouncements, commanding such broad support, about the importance of development that it is hard to escape the conclusion that long before the adoption of the NIEO resolutions in 1974—and even before the creation of UNCTAD in 1964—the UN had made the economic condition of the so-called underdeveloped Third World countries a central issue in any assessment of the state of the international economic order. The United Nations may not have legitimated the claim that development is a right or created an obligation for developed states to come to the assistance of developing states. But something close to consensus on these matters emerged relatively early in the UN's history and has persisted ever since. The issue long ago ceased to be *whether* something should be done about development, but *what*. With few exceptions decisions still depended for their authority on the consent of the members; the United States and other economic powers could still "veto" measures not to their liking. Nonetheless, UN decisions concerning development did acquire a certain patina of legitimacy. On Finkelstein's spectrum of the politics of value allocation (outlined in chapter 1), there was some movement from decentralized toward centralized decisionmaking, the result of the ability of persistent majorities to set the agenda and define the terms of the debate, to launch programs and create the environment for provocative staff work (for example, the Economic Commission for Latin America under its distinguished first Executive Secretary, Raoul Prebisch), and otherwise to make it difficult for the economically powerful states to dismiss Third World arguments.

The decade of the 1960s witnessed the intensification of the politics of value allocation. In part this was the result of the membership explosion at the United Nations. UN membership had grown relatively slowly at first because of the deadlock between the Soviet Union and the United States over the admission of new states and the slow pace of African decolonization. Although roughly 60 percent of the membership on the eve of the 15th General Assembly in 1960 became members of the Group of 77, developing countries had not then coalesced into the pressure group that would later figure so prominently in the North-South dialogue. Then the dam burst. Twenty-nine states were admitted between the beginning of the decade and the convening of the United Nations Conference on Trade and Development in Geneva in 1964, and all of them were developing countries.

Moreover, the profile of the UN's developing country membership also changed dramatically. No longer were the older (and arguably more Western) Latin American states numerically dominant. The African bloc quickly gained numerical precedence. Increasingly the developing countries were small in population, heavily dependent on only a very few crops for export earnings, and victims of years of colonial rule that had rarely placed their economic well-being above the interests of the metropolitan powers. The task of defining a development agenda for this large and diverse group of states became increasingly complex. Both the strategy and the pace that had characterized earlier UN efforts in the development field were called into question, and debate about these issues, never narrowly technical, became ever more politicized.

The intensification of the politics of value allocation at the United Nations also owed something to frustration with the "failure" of the aid approach to development. No one was proposing to terminate EPTA or the Special Fund (they were to be consolidated into the United Nations Development Program in 1965), but these high-water marks of UN development efforts in the 1950s were obviously not a sufficient response given the magnitude of the problem. Frustration with World Bank lending practices had led to the establishment of the International Development Association (IDA) in 1960 to provide loans on concessional terms to developing countries that could not service conventional loans. But frustration with the aid approach went beyond the size and terms of loans and grants. Third World economists such as Raoul Prebisch had begun to focus attention on other explanations for the chronic difficulties of developing countries, and these analyses led inexorably to demands for changes in the philosophies of institutions such as the GATT and the IMF, and, failing that, to a much more active role for a much more authoritative United Nations.

As the developing countries embraced the thesis that the causes of underdevelopment were structural, confrontation within the UN between developed and developing countries intensified and confrontation between the UN and the more specialized economic institutions intensified with it. The UN's role, as originally conceived, came under increasingly intense fire and the majority began actively to seek ways to work its will without waiting for the more intransigent members of the organization to give their consent. The struggle over authoritative allocation of values in the economic sphere began in earnest in the 1960s.

The heightened sense of urgency was signaled by the General Assembly's declaration that the 1960s would be the United Nations Development Decade.[37] This declaration was to economic development what the Declaration on Colonialism was to self-determination: a strong, unequivocal assertion by a newly strengthened, self-conscious Third World majority that the pace of change was unacceptably slow and would henceforth be challenged more systematically through the United Nations. This declaration was not, of course, binding in character; the targets set in the program for the Development Decade could not be achieved through coercion. Moreover, some of the goals for this, as for subsequent development decades,[38] were clearly overly ambitious—for example, the goals for minimal annual growth rates in gross national product for developing countries and for minimum resource transfers from developed to developing countries.[39] But these goals clearly bespoke an institutional commitment to development that was both substantial and substantially specific. They constituted successful efforts by the Third World majority to substitute specific performance criteria for general propositions about development, and particularly to ratchet up the level of obligation of developed countries toward the less developed, less fortunate states in the system.

Acquiescence in development decade strategies by some developed countries was sometimes reluctant and accompanied by reservations; subsequent performance has frequently been poor.[40] But no one argues that these declarations (we are now well into the Third Development Decade) are unimportant simply because they are nonbinding or because many of their goals have not been obtained. In the politics of international economic cooperation and development all parties understand that these declarations help to confirm the legitimacy of the Third World's agenda and set standards against which the responsiveness of the developed market economy countries can be measured.

The resolution establishing the First Development Decade was not only a symbolic decision; it was also programmatic,[41] a clear indication that the UN was shifting its priorities, preparing to devote relatively more time and energy and money to development issues. Unlike the security field, where—with the exception of sustained attention to disarmament—the organization's priorities are largely governed by the eruption of specific threats to the peace, the United Nations can make programmatic commitments in the economic sphere in a noncrisis atmosphere, choosing quite deliberately to emphasize certain issues and, at least in a relative sense, to deemphasize others. If members cannot be compelled to modify their policies, the UN can at least juggle the agenda and use such resources as it has to promote causes favored by the majority. The evolution of the UN's role as an international economic organization can be traced through a series of major programmatic decisions, each of which has either been a turning point of sorts for the organization or an attempt at dramatic escalation of its role in international economic affairs. The international development strategies that accompanied each of the development decades were such decisions. The creation of UNCTAD was another—arguably the most important in the organization's history.

The UN has, over the years, created many institutions. Some of these were intended to fill in missing pieces in the mosaic of institutions in the field of economic and social affairs; the regional commissions and technical assistance bodies (EPTA, the Special Fund, and later the UNDP) fall into this category. Others have been created to replace failed institutions or to provide competition for institutions in which the majority of members have lost confidence. UNCTAD is the pre-eminent example of such an institution.

In fact, UNCTAD was a challenge both to the GATT and to ECOSOC.

The complaint against the former focused on the norms and rules of the trade regime, as well as on the virtual exclusion of the developing countries from the GATT decisionmaking process; the complaint against the latter was more general, reflecting disappointment in the Council's unwillingness to take a more active role in challenging orthodox views about economic development and, as noted earlier, in the failure of efforts to enlarge the Council's membership to make it more representative.[42] UNCTAD was very much a product of the rapid growth in UN membership that occurred in the early 1960s. It was the suddenly much larger and more assertive group of developing countries, coalescing into the Group of 77 during the United Nations Conference on Trade and Development in Geneva in 1964, that wanted an alternative to the GATT and ECOSOC. UNCTAD was to be that alternative.

Because the creation of subsidiary organs and allocation to them of a share of the UN's budget are not dependent on the consent of member states, but can be accomplished by majority decision, the United States and other like-minded Western countries were unable in the climate of the early 1960s to block the decision to make UNCTAD a permanent body. They acquiesced in that decision after extracting a commitment to a proviso wherein action by the majority would be deferred during a cooling-off or reconciliation period.[43] But UNCTAD was born in controversy and has remained a forum characterized by confrontation between North and South. This was inevitable given the premise on which it was founded: that it should provide some measure of countervailing power to the now numerous and increasingly frustrated developing countries, with its Secretariat quite openly serving as staff and think tank for the Group of 77.

Like the General Assembly, which has increasingly become its rival, UNCTAD has no compellent authority, but it has been able to command attention for proposals generated by a development-oriented staff and to bring many more states more actively into the development dialogue. And it has, in cases such as the Generalized System of Preferences, been able to change the terms of the debate and to catalyze action by other institutions (in this case the GATT) and by developed country governments. UNCTAD has become a platform and a wedge for system change, the source of ideas that, if carried to their logical conclusion and implemented, would overturn existing regimes and create others. It has thrown the custodians and beneficiaries of the existing economic order onto the defensive.

They can no longer view the UN as a modest component in a network of organizations committed to system maintenance; the United Nations is now the preferred forum for advocates of system transformation. In its very creation UNCTAD provided an instance in which values—in this case attention, status, legitimacy—were authoritatively allocated by the UN through centralized majority decision. It has subsequently been a principal arena for the ongoing struggle between North and South over the authoritative allocation of values.

The United Nations Industrial Development Organization (UNIDO) soon joined UNCTAD as an expression of the majority's frustration with the slow progress in development being achieved through the efforts of other UN system institutions.[44] Although it never achieved the notoriety or respect accorded UNCTAD, UNIDO has shared with that body a reputation as a forum with a pronounced tilt toward the Third World. By the end of the 1960s the institutional arrangements of the 1940s, while still recognizable, had been twisted in ways that were more favorable to the Third World and more frustrating to the hegemonic power. The UN itself had become a network of subsidiary bodies that embraced the structuralist analysis of underdevelopment, "arguing that the international market structure perpetuates backwardness and dependency in the South and encourages dominance by the North."[45] In effect the UN was now challenging the specialized international economic institutions; functionalism was under fire.

In the politics of value allocation, the developing countries held an additional card that they did not hesitate to play—the authority of the General Assembly to establish the regulations according to which staff are appointed, that is, ultimate control over the patterns of staffing for the United Nations. According to the Charter merit was to be the primary consideration in recruitment for the international secretariat, with geographical distribution an important second criterion. As new (and typically developing) countries entered the UN, they frequently found that appointment of their nationals to secretariat posts was effectively blocked by the presence of large numbers of career appointees from Western states. In time this problem led to great pressure for giving priority to geographic distribution in making appointments, until the Charter's priorities had been reversed. Whether merit was sacrificed in the process of meeting country quotas (or bringing countries into their desirable range) can be debated. What is beyond doubt is that the UN Secretariat became in time substantially more critical of the liberal international economic order and not only sympathetic to alternative development strategies but the source of those strategies as well.

The United Nations, like most of the specialized agencies, has from its inception been concerned with the generation of data and its dissemination; but it has never been only a transmission belt, assembling neutral data and passing it along. The evolution of the organization's role in international economic and social affairs has been marked by the publication of reports that are analytical, that make assumptions not necessarily shared by all, and that go on to draw conclusions that have in some cases been controversial. UNCTAD, in particular, has used its research function to challenge conventional wisdom and create a Third World position on a number of issues, demonstrating that UN staff work can shape and steer debate.

The UN's role as a source of knowledge has made the composition of the Secretariat an important consideration for all UN members. Even if the international civil service were truly neutral, which in important respects it certainly is not, the views of staff members do reflect nationality, background, and experience. It is not surprising that the UN Secretariat that handled economic matters in the organization's early years approached its tasks in a manner that did not seriously challenge the doctrines of the liberal international economic order. The changing composition of the Secretariat in New York has inevitably produced somewhat different knowledge; UNCTAD was created precisely because the members have wanted a different perspective and the knowledge it would produce. And so, through the placement of developing country nationals in the Secretariat and the creation of Secretariat units with the avowed purpose of serving developing country interests, the UN's majority has been able to change the terms of the debate and favor the aspirants over the defenders of the status quo.

Nor is "knowledge" the only value at stake in the politics of UN staffing. Status is another. This was never more in evidence than during the debate in the 1970s over creation of the new post of Director General for International Economic Cooperation and Development as part of a major UN restructuring effort.[46] With Kurt Waldheim, an Austrian, holding the office of Secretary-General at the time, it was clear that the Director-General, then being touted as the number two person in the UN Secretariat, had to come from the Third World. It was not clear then, and it is not clear now, that creation of this post would contribute much to restructuring or that it would help appreciably to hasten development. But its value as a status symbol was well understood, with the result that the post was created and initially filled by a Ghanaian, Kenneth Dadzie— the high-water mark of an otherwise disappointing attempt to restructure the United Nations for economic and social activities.[47]

By the time the campaign for a New International Economic Order was launched in the early 1970s the struggle to extend the authority of the United Nations was already a principal feature of UN politics. Most UN decisions still depended for their authority on the consent of member states. But under mounting pressure from developing Third World states, utilizing such tools as Charter and circumstance afforded them, the UN had become at least modestly more authoritative; majorities were able to impose their will in some areas— agenda setting, budget making, staffing—and to gain ultimate, if grudging, acceptance of some of their ideas and institutions after a period of struggle in what Lawrence Finkelstein has termed "the intermediate zone."[48] By the early 1970s the elements of the NIEO agenda had largely been formulated and the UN positioned to play the leading role in creating a new order.

The NIEO and Stalemate at the UN

Prior to the adoption of the NIEO resolutions in 1974, the UN challenge to the liberal international economic order had been piecemeal and unfocused. But events conspired in that year to produce the Declaration and Program of Action on the Establishment of a New International Economic Order. The first and perhaps most important explanation for the timing of the NIEO lies in the breakdown of existing regimes and the decline in U.S. hegemony. As Ernst Haas has argued, international regimes flourish when hegemonic states define and operate and pay for them, and decline when hegemons change their minds.[49] By the 1970s the United States was no longer able or willing (or both) to continue playing the leadership role that it had assumed at Bretton Woods and San Francisco. Richard Nixon brought the old order, or at least the Bretton Woods regime, tumbling down when in 1971 he announced his New Economic Policy, declaring that the dollar would no longer be convertible into gold and that the United States would impose a 10 percent surcharge on dutiable goods. The decline of U.S. hegemony had, of course, been apparent for some time, and the postwar trade

and monetary regimes had been experiencing troubles independently of pressures from the Third World. Nonetheless, the collapse
came in the early 1970s, coinciding with other events that stimulated
action on behalf of a new order.

Although the UN was, as we have noted, marginal to the existing
order, it had come to play an increasingly important role as a forum
for criticizing the inequities of that order and for emphasizing the
urgency of development in ways that so-called old order institutions
had failed to do. Yet the United States had by the early 1970s turned
away from the UN, too, abandoning any pretense of hegemonic
leadership for the organization it had done more than any other
state to shape in the 1940s. The U.S. demand in 1972 that its assessment be reduced to 25 percent was symptomatic of declining
leadership and support.[50] The American disenchantment with the
UN was not then due primarily to economic considerations, but the
result was the same: to yield control of the agenda and the direction
of the UN to others, who turned out to be the relatively radical Third
World members.[51] (It was Algeria, as chair of the Nonaligned Movement, that played such a key role in planning the 6th Special Session
of the UN General Assembly and launching the NIEO.)

A second explanation for the NIEO is the obvious one: frustration
on the part of Third World states with the milder and more fragmented efforts to achieve more tangible progress toward development. By 1974 the Group of 77's numbers had climbed to the 100
level; most of that now-decisive majority of the membership in the
UN were making painfully slow progress according to all recognized
indicators and many believed that they were losing ground relative
to the more economically advantaged developed countries. The
quadrennial conferences of UNCTAD in 1968 and 1972 had disappointing results. This negative trend was punctuated just prior to
1974 by a food crisis. The Soviet Union purchased some 1,000 million bushels of food grain, virtually wiping out reserves in the United
States at a time when drought was decimating harvests in Africa
and Asia and sending prices soaring.

The themes that comprise the NIEO had been percolating for a
while in the UNCTAD Secretariat and had earlier been given expression in the Lusaka Declaration issued at the 1970 Nonaligned Summit. The event that more than any other turned talk into action in
1973–74 was the oil crisis of 1973. When the Yom Kippur War broke
out, the Arab oil-producing states restricted production and ship-
ments of oil to Israel's Western supporters, and within three months

the Organization of Petroleum Exporting Countries (OPEC) quad-rupled the price of oil. These actions, and the economic distress and disarray that followed in the West, convinced the developing countries that the time was ripe to press vigorously for dramatic changes in the international economic order. The custodians of the existing order seemed to be on the ropes, and with the OPEC states in the vanguard, the developing countries set out to wring conces-sions from the developed countries. The oil crisis may not have triggered the demand for the NIEO, but it had a lot to do with the aggressive and confident tone with which the campaign for a new order was launched.

Finally it is just barely possible that the UN's commitment to a system-transforming role could have been deferred or qualified had the United States been ready to assume leadership in the debate on the Third World's agenda at the time of the 6th Special Session. Unfortunately the United States had not only surrendered its he-gemonic role and lost its enthusiasm for the UN, it was simply in-attentive at the time; its President was almost totally preoccupied with the Watergate affair and his chief vicar for foreign policy was essentially uninterested in the Third World and development is-sues.[52]

The result of all these circumstances was that the UN General Assembly adopted the NIEO resolutions and did so by consensus. Whatever the United States and other members might say subse-quently about that decision, it had the effect of converting the NIEO from a Third World agenda into a United Nations agenda. When the agreements reached at the 7th Special Session one year later are added to the consensus decisions of the 6th Special Session, the result can be described as the transformation of "demands" into "negotiated demands." However imperfect the agreement, the UN appeared to have answered the question of what to do, leaving open for further discussion and debate the details, the question of how to do it.[53] Although the appearance of agreement was obviously il-lusory, as the often-bitter confrontations between the Group of 77 and the industrialized Western powers over the ensuing decade make clear, the UN had been enlisted in a campaign aimed at system transformation.

The NIEO is more of a political manifesto than an economic one, and therein lies both its challenge to the liberal international eco-nomic order and its importance to our inquiry into the politics of value allocation. That the NIEO is first and foremost a political man-

ifesto seems to be widely accepted. Stephen Krasner observes that
the NIEO "is basically a political rather than an economic challenge
because it aims at control, not just at wealth."[54] Sidney Weintraub
concurs, asserting that "the central issue in the NIEO relates to the
process of international decision-making."[55]

Although the NIEO Program of Action is vague on specifics, it is
unmistakably clear that in the new order the decentralized unit veto
system would give way in many areas to centralized majority decisions. Inevitably one of the principal objectives of the Group of
77 is reform of voting in the IMF and the World Bank so as to accord
developing countries greater representation and weight in decisionmaking in those institutions. Even more important is the effort
to build Third World control into new multilateral institutions advocated by the NIEO. Whereas it is admittedly difficult to effect such
a reversal of control in long-established institutions, new institutions
such as the International Seabed Authority, the Common Fund for
Commodities, and the International Fund for Agricultural Development have provided opportunities to apply Mohammed Bedjaoui's dictum that " 'membership' must eclipse the 'leadership' of
dominant oligarchies" in structuring a new order."[56] In no one of
these new institutions has the General Assembly-UNCTAD model of
egalitarian decisionmaking been adopted; the realities of economic
power could not be wholly suspended, especially since the new
institutions were to have significant authority. But control over these
institutions was a central and vigorously contested issue in each set
of negotiations and the formula ultimately agreed upon represented
in each case a departure from the World Bank-IMF model and increased Third World prospects for control.[57] The economic benefits
that would result from creation of these new institutions were pro-
spectively great, but political considerations, uppermost in the
minds of the Group of 77 and endorsed by the UN, assumed an even
greater importance.

Just as the UN's Third World majority has demanded that old order
institutions become more egalitarian and that new order institutions
adopt egalitarian or majoritarian decision modes, so does the majority seek a more authoritative voice for the United Nations. Struggle over the UN's authority is not a new phenomenon, but the pressure to treat repeated decisions by overwhelming UN majorities as
having the force of law were never greater than during the conflict
over the NIEO. Algerian Ambassador Bedjaoui stated the case succinctly when he argued that the Third World now possesses a "right

to the creation of law [in the more political and egalitarian UN system forums] thanks to the strength of its numbers."[58] This is not the United Nations of the founders; it is a United Nations not only committed to the creation of a new order but manipulated by its majority in such a way as to prefigure that new order.

Efforts to treat UN decisions as more authoritative also challenge the functional division of labor that has characterized the UN system's role in the existing international order. Over the years the UN's programmatic decisions in the economic sphere, together with its pronouncements on development issues and its establishment of alternative forums such as UNCTAD and UNIDO, have brought the UN into increasing conflict with other institutions, notably the GATT and the IMF. The NIEO is a culmination of this trend, a pointed attack on a norm that was central to the system that emerged after World War II: the depoliticization of economic issues (or a division of labor that would prevent their politicization).

This early norm has been challenged in two ways. The first and most important for our purposes has been the persistent effort to make the UN more than the nominal center of the United Nations system, a sometime agent of coordination. This is not simply a matter of the adoption by the General Assembly or UNCTAD of resolutions criticizing the prevailing philosophy of the GATT or promoting a Special Drawing Rights–aid link within the IMF. To borrow phraseology once heard in the corridors of the U.S. Department of State, it was an attempt to convert the UN from the soft center of the UN system into a hard center, to give the UN a right to oversee the policies and activities of other institutions and to bring them into line with UN-developed development doctrine. It was just such an attempt to strengthen the hand of the UN relative to the specialized agencies that brought the 11th Special Session of the General Assembly to such a dismal conclusion in 1980 and effectively derailed "global negotiations" on a New International Economic Order.[59] The great majority of UN members were bent on using the UN conference on global negotiations to effect fundamental reforms in the structure of the IMF. Rejecting an appeal to join in a consensus resolution on the global negotiations, U.S. Ambassador Donald McHenry stated his government's objection to any language that could be construed "as permitting the United Nations Conference on global negotiations to renegotiate agreements reached in the specialized agencies without any further involvement of those agencies. We are concerned that such an approach would do far more than adversely affect the functioning of the specialized agencies: it might result in an adversary relationship where cooperation is essential."[60]

McHenry's comments express succinctly (if politely) the logic of the old order: the specialized agencies, with their professional approach to technical problems, should be left alone to deal with their respective sectors of international economic relations; the UN, a confrontational political institution, should stay out. That view of the UN system and the UN's role within it is very much a minority view today. The second challenge to this norm is the reverse of the first, and consists of politicization of the specialized agencies. Although this challenge has not yet seriously affected the World Bank and the IMF, where collegiality in decisionmaking has not given way to confrontation in the UN manner, it has penetrated other specialized agencies along with the UN-based group system, blurring the lines of distinction between technical and political issues. The struggle over the allocation of values has visibly eroded, though it has not yet undermined, the functionalist norm.

The politics of value allocation is also illustrated by another phenomenon: the gradual abandonment of any pretense that the global organization exists to provide benefits for all of its members and the increasingly open pursuit of policies that manifestly serve the interests of some and ignore those of others. In effect UN politics are viewed by a great many of the members as a zero-sum exercise, when the contract entered into at San Francisco was clearly predicated on the assumption that everyone would benefit from the creation of such an institution. A positive-sum United Nations is not and never was an organization from which all states benefit equally. But peace and security were presumably collective goods, and later when the UN became involved in development activities, both developed and developing countries had to be convinced that the effort would contribute to the well-being of all, even if some benefited more than others.

This norm of universality of benefits has probably always been honored as much in the breach as in the observance, but in the economic sphere that norm seemed to hold until the creation of UNCTAD. ECOSOC and the New York Secretariat may have been vulnerable to the criticism that they were too slow to respond to legitimate Third World concerns; but UNCTAD made no pretense of trying to serve all of the members, and its Secretariat has in fact served as a staff for the Group of 77. But the presumption that the

UN serves all of its members has been challenged in other ways as well, most conspicuously by the NIEO itself. This agenda was not presented by the South as a set of proposals that, if enacted, would benefit developing and developed countries alike, but as measures the latter were obligated to take to help the former.[61] As Western wags said in criticism of the Charter of Economic Rights and Duties of States, it was all developing state rights and developed state duties.

Another area in which universality of benefits has been a casualty is the use of assessments. The presumption has been that assessments should be used to finance activities beneficial to all members. Although "violations" have been comparatively minor and the sums involved modest, some practices do suggest a disposition on the part of the majority—and in budgetary matters the majority decides—to abandon this norm; among them are UN funding of exclusive meetings and travel costs for limited groups of states, usually from the Third World, and providing financial assistance to national liberation movements over bitter opposition by major contributors to the UN budget. A more important development, related to UN pressure to increase resource transfers to developing countries, has been the trend to use regularly assessed budgets of UN system agencies for technical assistance purposes. Such a use of funds is not a new phenomenon, but it has become a significant issue recently because of the increased volume of assessed funds being shifted to a purpose that the developed states believe should be supported by voluntary contributions (primarily through the UNDP) and because it increases development assistance at the expense of universally beneficial activities.[62]

In virtually every area of international economic activity the NIEO constitutes a fundamental challenge to the existing system. It is a call for global management, whereas the norm has for the most part been a decentralized system in which market forces govern. It is an assault on the decentralized unit veto system of value allocation. It is an attempt to wrest control of international economic decisionmaking from defenders of the liberal economic order and to place it in the hands of developing country majorities and the multilateral institutions that they control or may be expected to control in the new order. But these efforts have largely failed; the negotiations between North and South have been stalemated for several years and the NIEO is moribund. Even the achievements of a decade of bargaining, such as the Common Fund for Commodities and the

Law of the Sea Treaty with its Seabed Authority, look less and less significant with the passing of time. In the struggle that characterizes the politics of value allocation in the United Nations it would appear that the Third World coalition has pushed the cause of an authoritative, majoritarian UN as far as the realities of economic and political power will permit, and that regime change of the magnitude contemplated in the NIEO still requires the consent of important states that are not yet prepared to grant that consent.

Conclusion: The Status of the Struggle Over Authority

For forty years one of the recurring features of UN politics has been the conflict between those who wanted decisions of the organization to derive their authority from member state consent and those who wanted that authority to flow from majority votes. While most states have found themselves on both sides of this conflict at different times, a fairly predictable and stable pattern emerged over the years. It saw the developing Third World states promoting changes in the international economic order *and* trying to stretch the Charter so that the United Nations, acting through its majority, might effect those changes. It further saw some of the developed Western states, the United States almost invariably foremost among them, defending the existing order and resisting the notion that the UN majority could authoritatively allocate values.

In this conflict most of the advantages lay with those who favored the unit veto system, who insisted upon consent; the language of the Charter supported them, as did the logic of functionalism and the existence of other more potent forums to deal with the issues raised by the UN's majority. But their principal advantage was their economic power. On the other hand the advocates of centralized majority decisions enjoyed some advantages, too: their numbers and their persistence, several Charter "loopholes," the generally acknowledged role of the UN as a global policy forum and platform for airing grievances, and the reluctance of the Western states, whether born of conviction or conscience, to close the door on compromise.

This struggle at the UN over the authoritative allocation of values has produced some net movement toward centralized majority decisions. Although most of this movement has come in the end with at least the tacit consent of the minority, it is no exaggeration to say that the majority has prevailed. Development has been moved to or near the top of the list of UN priorities; structural explanations for underdevelopment, while not universally accepted in all of their particulars, have achieved credibility; standards against which to measure developed country responsiveness to developing country distress have been adopted and have affected the behavior of many states; development assistance programs such as the UNDP have become an acceptable, even venerable, part of the UN complex; ECOSOC has been enlarged to better reflect Third World interests, although those interests are now even better served by UNCTAD; budgets have been skewed to accommodate developing country priorities and secretariats have acquired a pronounced Third World caste; UN initiatives have contributed directly or indirectly to modifications in rules of existing regimes (trade preferences for developing countries, compensatory financing, concessional lending) and to negotiations, some completed and others in progress, leading to new or significantly altered regimes (ocean mining, technology transfer, commodities).

In some respects this is an impressive list. But the really major changes sought by the majority have not been realized. The UN has not become a development authority. There is no New International Economic Order, or even much tangible progress toward one. In the final analysis the decentralized unit veto system still prevails when the stakes are really high. Centralized majority decisions are tolerated when the perceived costs to the minority of refusing to accept them are too high. The United States, for example, can live with UNCTAD—with the allocation of funds in what is, after all, a very modest budget—and with a Secretariat that may be biased but that does not possess a fraction of the power of the secretariats of the international financial institutions. It is not yet ready to treat the UN as it has UNESCO. It does not believe, however, that it can live with loss of control over large resource transfers or with centralized management (especially by unpredictable Third World majorities) of important segments of the international economy. Together with like-minded Western states, it has made clear that while the boundary between UN decisions requiring member consent and UN decisions deriving authority from majority votes is flexible, such a boundary still exists and its location will ultimately be determined by the Western market economy states.

There is evidence in the demise of the NIEO and in recent U.S. policy that the movement toward centralized majority decisions has gone about as far as it can go. The Third World coalition may have retreated temporarily from some forms of confrontation, but in view of the size and importance of its unfinished agenda, it will almost certainly be back to challenge the status quo. This is a prescription for continuing struggle within the UN over authoritative allocation of values.

Notes

1. Harlan Cleveland, "The Mutation of World Institutions," in *Global Planning and Resource Management*, ed. Antony J. Dolman (New York: Pergamon Press, 1980), 81.

2. The UN's high water mark may well have been the creation in 1956 of the UN Emergency Force, which ushered in a brief period of time during which the UN accomplished more than most had dared to hope and when it displayed a not insignificant capacity for creative adaptation and task expansion.

3. See Chapter 1 by Lawrence S. Finkelstein in this volume, 5.

4. Ibid., 6.

5. For a discussion on this point, and indeed of the changing role of the UN in this field, see Ernst Haas, "Regime Decay: Conflict Management and International Organizations, 1945–1981," *International Organization* 37, 2 (Spring 1983): 189–235.

6. UN Charter, Chapter I, Article 1,3.

7. UN Charter, Chapter IX, Article 55.

8. Jane Rosen, "How the Third World Runs the U.N.," *The New York Times Magazine* (December 16, 1979): 36.

9. These are the Declaration and Programme of Action on the Establishment of a New International Economic Order (General Assembly Resolutions 3201(S-VI) and 3202(S-VI), respectively); the Charter of Economic Rights and Duties of States (General Assembly Resolution 3281(XXIX)); and Development and International Economic Cooperation (General Assembly Resolution 3362(S-VII)).

10. Without making any attempt to factor in costs for overall policymaking, direction and coordination, for conference services, for administration, management and general services, for public information, or for legal activities, the figures for the 1980–81 biennium were approximately $415 million and $73 million.

11. Relevant data may be found in annual reports of the Secretary-General entitled *List of Staff of the United Nations Secretariat* (ST/ADM/R. . .).

12. See Christine Sylvester, "UN Elites: Perspectives on Peace," *Journal of Peace Research* 17, 4 (1980): 305–24. See also Thomas M. Franck, John P. Renninger, and Vladislav B. Tikhomirov, *Diplomats' Views on the United Nations System: An Attitude Survey*, UNITAR (United Nations Institute for Training and Research) Policy and Effectiveness Study, no. 7 (New York: UNITAR, 1982).

13. There is, of course, a large and growing body of sources on the two principal expressions of Third World solidarity, the Nonaligned Movement and the Group of 77. Among the more useful of recent works are Richard L. Jackson, *The Non-Aligned, the UN, and the Superpowers* (New York: Praeger, 1983); Robert Mortimer, *The Third World Coalition in International Politics* (New York: Praeger, 1980); and Karl Sau-

vant, "The Non-Aligned Movement and the Group of 77," *The Non-Aligned World* 1 (January–March 1983).

14. Mohammed Bedjaoui, *Towards a New International Economic Order* (New York: Holmes and Meier, 1979), 78.

15. The declaration on a New International Economic Order places this language in the text of the resolution rather than in the preamble, and is a veritable compendium of such charges. For example, Paragraph 1 of the resolution states, inter alia, that "the remaining vestiges of alien and colonial domination, foreign occupation, racial discrimination, *apartheid* and neo-colonialism in all its forms continue to be among the greatest obstacles to the full emancipation and progress of developing countries and all the peoples involved. . . . The gap between the developed and developing countries continues to widen in a system which was established at a time when most of the developing countries did not even exist as independent States and which perpetuates inequality."

16. League of Nations Document A.23.1939, *The Development of International Cooperation in Economic and Social Affairs: Report of the Special Committee* (Geneva 1939).

17. To this day the USSR has not joined the IMF, the World Bank, the FAO, or the GATT. Nor has it yet joined the International Fund for Agricultural Development. On the other hand it did reverse itself and become a member of the ILO in 1954.

18. Robert Cox, "Problems of Global Management," in *The US, the UN, and the Management of Global Change*, ed. Toby Trister Gati (New York: New York University Press, 1983), 69–70.

19. Haas, "Regime Decay," 229.

20. Stephen D. Krasner, *Structural Conflict: The Third World against Global Liberalism* (Berkeley, Calif.: University of California Press, 1985), 77, and other writings by this author.

21. David Mitrany, *A Working Peace System* (Chicago: Quadrangle, 1966), 63.

22. Sidney Weintraub, "US Participation in International Organizations: Looking Ahead," in *The US, the UN, and the Management of Global Change*, ed. Toby Trister Gati (New York: New York University Press, 1983), 187.

23. Inis L. Claude, Jr., *Swords into Plowshares*, 3rd ed. (New York: Random House, 1964), 348.

24. The GATT, of course, also reflects economic realities, but is such a very different kind of organization, employing such a very different decision mode, that it is difficult to contrast with organizations that decide by voting or consensus.

25. Stephen Zamora, "Voting in International Economic Organizations," *American Journal of International Law* 74 (1980): 608.

26. Ibid., 589.

27. Walter R. Sharp, *The United Nations Economic and Social Council* (New York: Columbia University Press, 1969), 5.

28. UN Charter, Articles 22 and 68.

29. UN Charter, Article 17.

30. UN Charter, Article 101.

31. It remains to be seen whether the decision to employ consensus on budget questions, adopted at the 41st General Assembly in the face of a budgetary crisis created by U.S. refusal to pay its full assessment, will work in practice *or* satisfy the U.S. government.

32. Robert W. Gregg, "Program Decentralization through the Regional Economic Commissions," in UN *Administration of Economic and Social Programs*, ed. Gerard J. Mangone (New York: Columbia University Press, 1966), 235.

33. Robert W. Gregg, "The UN Regional Economic Commissions and Integration in the Underdeveloped Regions," in *International Regionalism*, ed. Joseph S. Nye (Boston: Little, Brown, 1968), 305–06.

34. EPTA was created by ECOSOC Resolution 222(IX), 1949. It was merged with the Special Fund (General Assembly Resolution 1240(XIII), 1958) into the UNDP in General Assembly Resolution 2029(XX), 1965.

35. UNDP pledges for the calendar year 1982 were $665 million. For the United Nations assessments for 1982 totaled $721 million. The assessed budgets for FAO ($200 million), UNESCO ($199 million), WHO ($247 million), and all of the other specialized agencies were substantially less.

36. See General Assembly Resolution 1240(XIII), 1958.

37. See General Assembly Resolution 1710(XVI), 1961.

38. See General Assembly Resolutions 2626(XXV), 1970, and 35/36, 1981.

39. The most conspicuously inflated goal has been the call for developed countries to transfer 1 percent of their GNP (.7 percent to be in the form of official governmental development assistance) to developing countries.

40. See, for example, Karl P. Sauvant, ed., *Changing Priorities on the International Agenda* (New York: Pergamon Press, 1981), appendix C, table 3.34, p. 264, which shows net official development assistance to developing countries and multilateral agencies as a percentage of GNP by Development Assistance Committee countries for the period 1961 through 1977. The average was .31, and for key states such as the United States, the Federal Republic of Germany, and Japan it was even less.

41. For a typology of decisions, see Robert Cox and Harold K. Jacobson, *The Anatomy of Influence* (New Haven, Conn.: Yale University Press, 1974).

42. ECOSOC was finally enlarged twice by Charter amendment to Article 61, first from 18 to 27 in accordance with General Assembly Resolution 1991B(XVIII), 1963, which came into effect in 1965, and from 27 to 54 in accordance with Resolution 2847(XXVI), 1971, which came into effect in 1973.

43. See General Assembly Resolution 1995(XIX), 1964. It is worth noting that while UNCTAD has resorted to consensus, it has never invoked the conciliation period.

44. General Assembly Resolution 2089(XX), 1965.

45. Joan Edelman Spero, *The Politics of International Economic Relations*, 2nd ed. (New York: St. Martin's Press, 1981), 140.

46. France, for example, vigorously opposed creation of this new post because it was assumed that it would eclipse in importance the post of Under Secretary-General for Economic and Social Affairs, traditionally held by a Frenchman.

47. See UN Doc. A/32/34, 1978, the definitive report of the Ad Hoc Committee on the Restructuring of the Economic and Social Sectors of the United Nations System, and *A New United Nations Structure for Global Cooperation* (UN Sales no. E.75.II.A.7, 1975), the report of a group of experts that laid the foundation for restructuring.

48. See chapter 1 above, 5.

49. Ernst Haas, "Why Collaborate? Issue Linkage and International Regimes," *World Politics* 32, 3 (April 1980), 387.

50. For a discussion of declining U.S. willingness to support the United Nations, see Robert F. Meagher, "United States Financing of the United Nations," in *The*

US, the UN, and the Management of Global Change, ed. Toby Trister Gati (New York: New York University Press, 1983), 101–28.

51. The story of U.S. abdication of leadership and its consequences for the UN is the theme of a number of essays in *The US, the UN, and the Management of Global Change*, ed. Toby Trister Gati (New York: New York University Press, 1983).

52. The story of an inattentive U.S. government is succinctly chronicled by Robert K. Olson in *U.S. Foreign Policy and the New International Economic Order* (Boulder, Colo.: Westview Press, 1981), ch. 1.

53. This point is developed in Branislav Gosovic and John G. Ruggie, "On the Creation of a New International Economic Order: Issue Linkage and the Seventh Special Session of the UN General Assembly," *International Organization* 30, 2 (Spring 1976).

54. Stephen D. Krasner, "The United Nations and Political Conflict between the North and the South," in *The US, the UN, and the Management of Global Change*, ed. Toby Trister Gati (New York: New York University Press, 1983), 218 ff.

55. Sidney Weintraub, "The Role of the United Nations in Economic Negotiations," in *The Changing United Nations*, ed. David A. Kay (New York: The Academy of Political Science, 1977), 96.

56. Bedjaoui, *Towards a New International Economic Order*, 141.

57. The most interesting formula was the one adopted for the IFAD, in which each of three groups of states—developed, developing, and OPEC—holds one third of the votes, and each decided for itself how to distribute those votes—that is, equally, according to financial contribution, or in some combination. The International Seabed Authority constitutes the greatest departure from the World Bank/IMF model (if and when it comes into being), inasmuch as the authority is to have very considerable power, whereas the system of representation in the council of the authority does not accurately reflect economic interests or financial contributions.

58. Bedjaoui, *Towards a New International Economic Order*, 142.

59. For a discussion of the 11th Special Session, see John P. Renninger with James Zech, *The 11th Special Session and the Future of Global Negotiations*, UNITAR Policy and Effectiveness Study, no. 5 (New York: UNITAR, 1981).

60. Quoted in Renninger and Zech, ibid., 17.

61. This frequently voiced criticism is part of Mahbub ul Haq's indictment of the South in "Negotiating the Future," *Foreign Affairs* 59, 2 (Winter 1980–81): 398–417.

62. A combination of UNDP's near financial collapse in 1975 and LDC pressure to increase the resources available to developing countries led in the 1970s to such earmarking of more of the regularly assessed budgets for technical cooperation purposes. FAO and WHO, for example, effected savings by reducing the size of headquarters staffs and diverted these monies to technical cooperation. These and similar decisions have more than once brought the U.S. Congress to the brink of a decision to withhold funds from UN organizations. See Meagher, "United States Financing."

5

The Deterioration of the GATT Framework

in International Trade Relations

Ronald I. Meltzer

●

In November 1982 trade ministers from around the world gathered under the auspices of the General Agreement on Tariffs and Trade (GATT) for the first time in almost a decade to deal with a growing crisis in international trade relations. Recognizing that the international trading system had become "seriously endangered" by frequent disputes over divergent trade practices, spiraling domestic pressures toward protectionist policies, and the inability of the existing GATT framework to manage current relations or keep up with emerging trade problems, these trade ministers sought to reform and strengthen the system of rules and institutional capabilities that had once been able to regulate the conduct of international trade and promote the goals of the Bretton Woods economic order. However, by all accounts, this high-level conference produced very modest results. Indeed, its deliberations were overtaken by the very same factors and conflicts that troubled the overall trading system. Moreover, since that time, the GATT framework has continued to falter amid increased strains and breakdowns in international trade relations.[1]

The deterioration of the GATT framework is important in assessing multilateral diplomacy and the performance of international economic institutions in this policy area. GATT's problems are tied to various factors: the operation of the institution itself, the manner in which trade relations and policymaking have been transformed, and changing systemic conditions. This chapter examines the character and development of the GATT framework and discusses its subsequent deterioration. It also indicates key areas in which the GATT framework needs revision and concludes with some observations about different approaches to and constraints on GATT reform.

Development of the GATT Framework

Since 1947 the General Agreement on Tariffs and Trade has been an important institutional pillar of the Bretton Woods economic order. However, despite its role in promoting trade expansion and liberalization, GATT never attained the stature, authority, or institutional development of companion multilateral bodies created after World War II—the International Monetary Fund and the World Bank. GATT's relative ambiguity and weakness as an international economic institution were tied to its peculiar legacy. Intended as a temporary device pending the establishment of a full-fledged International Trade Organization (ITO), GATT eventually became the permanent replacement for an ITO that was not launched because of conflicts between "perfectionists and protectionists" designing a new global structure to regulate international trade relations.[2] Evolving from this very uncertain beginning, then, GATT developed largely in an ad hoc and periodic manner. GATT's authority and jurisdiction were bolstered by various rounds of trade negotiations and the growing multilateral requirements of managing trade relations. However, it still functioned in the shadow of unresolved questions about government sovereignty in commercial policymaking.

Over time the GATT framework did develop basic elements needed to institute a viable system of international trade regulation: an arena to discuss and review different policies and trends; a capacity to formulate rules to guide behavior and adapt to changing conditions; and a means to resolve formally and informally trade disputes arising among its members.[3] As Gardner Patterson has noted, these functions are critical to the fundamental purpose of multilateral commercial arrangements—the creation of stability and predictability in the trading environment.[4] However, in each instance, these functions were subject to many provisions allowing governments to avoid international commitments and standards in the face of domestic constraint or exigency.

As Finlayson and Zacher have indicated, the GATT framework has been guided by several key substantive and procedural norms. These principles have been important in formulating and implementing rules in the international trading system. One vital substantive norm is *nondiscrimination,* the agreement to adopt universally applied trade barriers by means of unconditional most-favored nation (MFN) treatment among GATT members. Although often cited as the cornerstone of the GATT system, this norm was limited by many exceptions when it was first instituted. Its erosion has continued more broadly as international trade relations expanded and changed during the post-World War II period. For example, by 1980 only 65 percent of GATT trade took place on the basis of MFN tariff treatment—a drop from about 90 percent in 1955.[5]

Another important substantive norm is *trade liberalization,* the commitment to seek a progressive reduction in international trade barriers. This norm has held varying degrees of strength in the GATT trading system, as seen in the different rounds of trade negotiations conducted during the past several decades. The GATT framework, however, remains highly differentiated in its levels of protection—both in terms of sectors involved and countries directly affected.

Other substantive norms include *reciprocity,* the expectation that trade concessions will be mutually exchanged, and *safeguarding,* the ability of members to waive rules in times of economic hardship or domestic exigency. These principles reflect the weight and importance of domestic policy considerations within the GATT framework. They also express perhaps most clearly the political sensitivities of GATT—both in terms of power relationships among trading nations and the constraints that individual governments face at home. Whereas the reciprocity norm insures that the major trading nations can control the tempo and direction of international trade liberalization and regulation, safeguarding gives governments leeway to respond to domestic political pressures without having to reject or withdraw entirely from the GATT framework.

A final substantive norm is the *special treatment of developing countries' trade* in order to promote their development. This notion has gained increased attention within the GATT framework. Developing countries have grown in numbers and importance in the international trading system, and they have sought to create alternative rules and institutional arrangements for managing North-South trade relations. Special treatment for development, however, has held "stepchild" status in the GATT framework. In large part this is because the primary supporters of special treatment—the developing

countries—have less power in controlling international trade relations, and its intended effects are seen as either temporary or
threatening to the realization of other basic GATT objectives.

The GATT framework also has established principles regarding
the nature of decisionmaking, institutional functioning, and the
participation of members. However, the two basic norms—*multilateralism* and *the protection of major countries' interests*—reflect
inconsistent principles of decisionmaking and GATT's overall lack
of effective institutional development. The organizational machinery
and decisionmaking activities of GATT historically have developed
along two separate tracks: those associated with the ongoing affairs
of GATT, such as the annual sessions of the Contracting Parties, the
Council, and subsidiary committees working on various trade practices and issues; and those associated with periodic rounds of multilateral trade negotiations. Although in aspects of both the ongoing
GATT activities and the periodic rounds of negotiations the norm of
multilateralism has gained increased currency and effect, the decisionmaking procedures and participation guidelines of the GATT
framework still largely serve to protect major countries' interests.[6]

The weak institutional development and procedural norms of the
GATT framework derive from its origins. For many years GATT operated without any decisionmaking bodies, since it was seen more
as an agreement among members than as an organization. It was
1970 before the annual sessions of the Contracting Parties were
supplemented with a Council to undertake intersessional planning
and review. Efforts to enhance the decisionmaking capabilities of
GATT led to the creation of the Consultative Group of 18 (CG-18) in
1975, as the need for high-level consultation on an ongoing basis
grew increasingly apparent amidst disputes over divergent trade
practices, the demands of multilateral management and negotiations,
and growing protectionist pressures.

Although the CG-18 became a permanent GATT body in 1979, its
ineffectiveness as a steering body led to yet another effort at collective leadership—the establishment of the so-called "quadrilateral
group" in 1983. This group has been the venue for consultations
among U.S., European Community, Japanese, and Canadian trade
officials, and more recently with representatives from the developing countries. However, the group's uncertain institutional
standing within GATT, along with other political difficulties associated with restricted-member groupings in multilateral bodies, raise
questions about the effectiveness of the quadrilateral group as an

ongoing decisionmaking body within GATT. Further clouding the institutional development of GATT are the various codes of conduct negotiated at the Tokyo Round. Each code has its own set of rule-making and rule-implementation procedures, along with measures for dispute settlement. This element of procedural decentralization has caused further uncertainties and complications in the functioning of GATT machinery.[7]

GATT's institutional performance also has been hampered by the fact that its Secretariat is relatively small and has very confined powers. It has been unable to play an effective role in monitoring the policies of GATT members and in taking initiatives to deal with emerging problems. These incapacities significantly limit the multilateral management functions of GATT. The Secretariat's overall constraints and position in the GATT framework are perhaps best demonstrated by the muted role that the Director-General has played as an executive head. Historically, this office has been given no direct institutional mandate or authority for managing international trade relations. Instead, the Director-General's position and influence have been a consequence for the most part of how he is regarded by key governments at any given time.[8]

GATT's political processes and foundation have been based upon several factors that converged to strengthen its role in international trade relations after World War II. Perhaps most important to GATT's political standing were the strong support and leadership that the United States gave to the GATT framework. As the dominant international economic and political power, the United States was in a position to prod other states to abide by GATT rules and support its activities. The U.S. also could tolerate any short-term costs and asymmetries in ongoing trade relations for the purpose of engendering overall compliance with GATT's evolving framework. In large part U.S. sponsorship flowed from the close correspondence between the normative approach adopted within GATT and American preferences for ordering international trade relations. Indeed, as Raymond Vernon has pointed out, GATT's orientation to the conduct of international trade, particularly concerning the transactional roles of government, was distinctly American in outlook. Over time, however, the GATT framework diverged increasingly from the policymaking directions pursued by other trading nations. This factor, coupled with changing power relations among GATT members, has made it more and more difficult to conclude trade agreements.[9]

A second factor important to the political foundation of GATT was the high level of consensus initially found among trading nations concerning the need for a multilateral framework to provide for trade expansion and liberalization. In part this consensus was related to the willingness of most Western nations to accept the hegemonic position of the United States after World War II. However, this consensus also reflected a strong shared reaction to the "beggar-thy-neighbor" experiences of the 1930s and a widely held belief that multilateral trade negotiations conducted under GATT provisions would be mutually beneficial. This positive view of GATT was tied to the fact that much of what was being proposed and acted upon could be accomplished in a relatively painless manner, given the high initial levels of protection that GATT sought to reduce.

A third factor contributing to the positive views of contracting parties toward the GATT framework was the extensive leeway built into GATT provisions, which allowed countries considerable discretion as to how engaged they became in GATT regulatory activities. In effect this gave members an avenue to avoid multilateral control and supervision when they found it politically expedient or necessary—enabling them to follow what Finkelstein calls a strategy of "opting out."[10] Such discretion works in several ways. It applies when countries resort to escape clause or exception provisions in existing GATT agreements; it also applies in the rule-making processes, which are based upon consensus of all the major parties. Even when GATT rules are broken or subject to disputes among members, governments still retain significant discretion concerning how they might reconcile their differences, or even disregard GATT as a basis for dealing with the trade matter.

Decisionmaking in GATT occurs in a decentralized arena where consensus among the major parties is essential for reaching agreements. Historically the process of GATT trade negotiations reflected the interests of large trading nations, along with smaller countries with significant stakes in particular products. Generally countries with exporting interests tended to initiate GATT action on specific policies; importing countries usually sought to control the scope of any eventual GATT agreements. For the most part GATT's ability to achieve needed consensus or avoid the debilitating effects of a unit veto system was aided by the disproportionate power of the United States in the international trading system. As the dominant trader the United States could strengthen GATT's imprimatur simply by conforming to GATT principles itself. At the same time it could press for GATT objectives in dealings with other nations and afford to look the other way or offer compensatory benefits when others needed to depart from GATT prescriptions. In many respects, then, the GATT framework and its political underpinnings were tied to U.S. participation in the trading system, and GATT affairs tended to follow the rhythm of U.S. trade policymaking. This pattern could be seen clearly in the initiation of various multilateral trade negotiations, which were inspired and made possible by U.S. trade legislation. It also could be seen in the types of policy issues and priorities that GATT addressed. As the Curzons have noted GATT's agenda since the 1950s largely has entailed a process of challenge and response between the United States and other members over persistent and emerging trade problems.[11]

GATT's political order has undergone significant change since the late 1960s, as the capacity of the United States to remain the dominant trading nation receded and its willingness to carry the costs of leadership diminished. By the time of the Kennedy Round (1964) the United States began to resist other nations' receiving disproportionate benefits in various GATT negotiations. Perhaps more importantly, U.S. officials also grew increasingly tolerant of policy departures from GATT standards at home. Indeed, by 1980 some 30 percent of the total U.S. industrial output was traded outside the terms and authority of GATT. This development, combined with the fact that GATT principles held less and less sway over the trade practices of other groups of countries, produced a situation in the 1980s whereby a large proportion of world trade was conducted substantially at variance with the prevailing GATT framework.[12]

In this changed environment the process of consensus decision-making became more complicated and subject to impasse-by-veto. In earlier periods the problems of a decentralized system of consent were eased by the dominant position of the United States, particularly since consensus was built upon interactions on an item-by-item basis among principal suppliers. However, with the establishment of the European Community and the replacement of previous item-specific procedures with linear negotiations, the United States was no longer in a singular position to initiate and command resolution on trade policy matters. Changing realities of power sharing in GATT created greater difficulties in reaching multilateral agreements. In part this is because members' political power and participation in GATT are not only a function of their shares of world trade, but also a byproduct of their domestic struggles between protectionist and free trade forces at home. Increasingly both the United

States and the European Community (EC) faced built-in constraints on their participation in GATT, given the growing protectionist bent and involvement of Congress in U.S. trade policymaking and the rigidities of EC decisionmaking.

This type of power-sharing in a unit-veto system led the major trading nations to seek informal consultations or extra-GATT agreements among themselves. However, developments such as the resort to quadrilateral group discussions have made smaller nations increasingly concerned that GATT affairs could become little more than the byproducts of faits accomplis reached within the closed-off confines of the "Big Four."[13]

Over the years different countries and observers have approached the GATT framework from two basic perspectives, each carrying different implications concerning the identity and role of this international institution. The first perspective sees GATT as the exercise and embodiment of *rule diplomacy,* that is, the establishment of rules governing state behavior, along with institutional means to insure compliance and resolve disputes. The second approach views GATT as the product of *power diplomacy,* that is, its activities and authority are conditioned by the power, goals, and interactions of its major members. The fact that different countries have adopted both "legalist" and "pragmatist" approaches to GATT during different periods has added to its overall institutional ambiguity. It has also contributed to ongoing trade disputes, since each approach connotes different standards and expectations for GATT's capacity to regulate international trade relations. As Harald Malmgren noted, many complaints voiced about GATT's broken rules, lack of enforcement, or organizational ineffectiveness stem from conflicting perspectives about such legalist and pragmatist strains within GATT.[14]

Domestic policy preferences and decisionmaking authority also shape GATT rule-making activities. This can be seen, for example, in the GATT's position vis-à-vis the regulation of domestic policies. GATT makes virtually no effort to harmonize government interventions in the marketplace. Instead rule making is limited to what members can and cannot do when adversely affected by the domestic policies of others, such as in the case of countervailing duties against subsidies or compensation for lost concessions. This limit in GATT's rule-making activities is intended to accommodate the different domestic structures of its members, even though it considerably weakens GATT's regulatory capabilities in the international trading system.

Another area in which GATT defers to government preference and authority relates to the overall character of a country's economy, especially the extent to which it is market-based or subject to high levels of government intervention and planning. GATT's main thrust is to insure that whatever policies governments adopt concerning their economies, they do so in a manner that does not discriminate against imports or unfairly favor exports. Clearly, there is a strong GATT orientation toward market-based economic decisionmaking and efficiency, largely reflecting American views. However, there are many exceptions provided within the GATT framework for government policies that depart from these liberal economic principles, such as in the cases of protecting health standards, infant industries, or national security. Moreover, countries are free to withdraw from particular trade obligations that may require them to adopt free market policies by offering other concessions to members. GATT distinctions are made between market and nonmarket economies in the determination of rights and obligations, but these have more to do with the autonomy of particular countries' economic agents than with any system of ownership or overall level of government intervention prescribed by GATT.

A third limit of the GATT framework involves the regulation of private activities affecting international trade relations. GATT does not attempt to prohibit restrictive business practices, dumping, or other trade-distorting private activities. Instead it is confined to regulating the responses of members to these practices, such as in the case of antidumping rules. Similarly, GATT does not provide for continuing and secure access to the supplies of its members. Quantitative restrictions are prohibited as a discriminatory device. However, the GATT framework contains sufficient exceptions for export controls to allow almost any restriction on foreign access to domestic supplies.

Finally, the GATT framework is very limited concerning foreign policy considerations in the international trading system. The basic thrust of GATT rules is to discourage discrimination among trading nations and therefore curtail the manipulation of trade as a foreign policy instrument. However, the GATT framework contains many provisions that give members a virtually free hand when foreign policy considerations interact with ongoing trade relations. This can be seen, for example, in the rules dealing with the accession of new members to GATT, in national security and emergency exceptions, and in its customs union provisions permitting the formation of regional communities. In a related area GATT also does not oblige members to adopt particular preferential policies toward developing countries. Although GATT contains enabling provisions for special treatment, there is no specific GATT definition or requirement for the designation of "developing countries" eligible for preferences. The particular content and scope of preferential trade arrangements remain primarily matters of national policy discretion.

As seen, the GATT framework is directed as much toward domestic political considerations as toward international economic relations. Its system of rules and obligations allows governments sufficient leeway to respond to domestic policymaking needs. It also offers governments a framework of international constraints and rewards that can be helpful in their relationships with domestic groups affected by the conduct of trade relations. This can be seen in the manner in which GATT agreements become part of the domestic legal order of its contracting parties, a process that helps to protect governments from unwanted and counterproductive claims by private interests. It also is evident in the pattern of reciprocal trade liberalization, which is structured to build domestic constituencies for government compliance with the GATT framework. This function—the provision of international constraints and rewards that governments can draw upon in their dealings with domestic groups—was intended to create a firm basis for GATT's evolving effectiveness.[15] However, changes in the character of international trade relations and the erosion of underlying consensus about trade goals over the past decade have weakened this vital function and source of institutional influence.

Table 5.1 summarizes the principal features of the GATT framework touched on thus far in this chapter.

The Deterioration of the GATT Framework

As noted, GATT's capacity to manage international trade relations and regulate the conduct of commercial policymaking deteriorated significantly by the early 1980s. This breakdown in the GATT framework had various dimensions: a return to sectoralism and bilateralism in many areas of trade policymaking; a growth of trade disputes among major trading nations; and increasing "policy-induced uncertainty" in the international trading environment. Over the past decade governments had repeatedly reaffirmed their commitment to GATT principles and rules, yet just as consistently opted to seek

Table 5.1 Summary Characterization of the GATT Framework

Major Norms

Substantive norms include nondiscrimination, trade liberalization, reciprocity, safeguarding, and special treatment for LDC trade.

Procedural norms include multilateralism and the protection of major countries' interests.

Overall strength of the substantive norms is subject to many provisions permitting government exception. Therefore the effects of substantive norms are highly differentiated.

The protection of major countries' interests has been the prevailing norm of member participation and decisionmaking.

Institutional Make-Up

Convoluted and fragmented institutional machinery involving ongoing GATT affairs, periodic rounds of negotiation, and individual agreements or codes incorporated into GATT.

Confined roles and authority for the Secretariat and Director-General (primarily exhortative and analytical).

Uncertain decisionmaking processes.

Political Order

Earlier development based upon the U.S. role as hegemonic power; greater power sharing now exists among the Big Four, but the United States and European Community retain strong influence over GATT activities.

Agreements are reached through process of consensus, but are subject to impasse as a result of the decentralized unit veto system.

Significant leeway for government discretion in following opting out policies, enabling members to specify how engaged they will become in GATT's rule-making and governance activities.

Political influence shaped by members' shares of world trade and their respective domestic struggles between protectionist and free trade forces.

Major Functions

International functions: discussing and reviewing international trade relations, formulating rules to govern the conduct of trade and behavior of governments, and resolving trade disputes arising among members.

Domestic function: assisting governments through a framework

Table 5.1 Continued

of constraints and rewards in their dealings with domestic groups over trade policymaking.

Major Limits to the Scope of GATT
The regulation and harmonization of domestic policies affecting trade relations.
   The regulation of private sector activities.
   Prescriptions about the level of intervention in or nature of national markets.
   The regulation of export controls.
   The interaction of foreign policy considerations with international trade relations.
   The general ability of governments to claim sanctioned exceptions or withdraw unilaterally from obligations by means of offering other concessions.

exemptions and departures from prevailing GATT standards. In the face of resultant trade problems different governments and trade groups called for more direct action to strengthen the GATT framework, arguing that "words were no longer enough."[16]

The 1982 GATT ministerial meeting sought to deal with this "unmistakable deterioration in the climate of trade relations."[17] However, in the absence of an ongoing GATT capacity to carry out effective preparation and policy coordination, the urgent convening of this ministerial meeting created as many difficulties as it did opportunities for reaching needed agreements. In the end, the conference portrayed how brittle and ineffective GATT had become.[18]

GATT's deterioration can best be understood by using different levels of explanation. First, the deterioration of the GATT framework can be approached from the standpoint of the *functioning of the institution*. At this level of analysis factors such as the confined and uncertain roles of the Secretariat, weak decisionmaking and consultative processes, a tendency toward impasse-by-unit-veto, and ineffective dispute settlement procedures were all important in GATT's eventual inability to manage and regulate trade relations.

Second, the deterioration of the GATT framework can be explained from the standpoint of *changes occurring in this policy area*. At this level of explanation it is critical to understand the transformation of trade relations and policymaking since earlier days of GATT. Perhaps most important here are the extent to which trade policies have become integrated with domestic economic policies in general and the extent to which GATT therefore must deal not only with trade practices as such, but also increasingly with the trade effects of other economic policies. In addition it is important to focus on the amount of sectoral differentiation in trade policymaking, that is, the degree to which various international market structures and levels of adjustment within sectors have created different patterns of liberalization and protection within overall trade relations.[19]

Third, the deterioration of the GATT framework can be approached from a more *systemic* perspective. This level of analysis deals more with the overall trading environment and basic changes occurring in international economic relations. Important factors in this area would include the apparent loss of confidence among industrialized countries in their ability to compete and accept open market access, changing power relations among trading nations and the declining ability of the United States to enforce the regime, the extent of structural change and resistance to adjustment in the world economy, and the declining use and viability of the market price system for international economic decisionmaking.[20]

GATT's high point of performance occurred during the 1950s and 1960s. This was evidenced by the willingness of members to resort to GATT machinery in resolving trade problems, by the extent of overall consensus and compliance vis-à-vis GATT rules and standards, and by the impressive tariff-reducing results of successive multilateral trade negotiations held during this period. However, GATT's capacity to maintain this hold over international trade deteriorated through a long-term process of erosion—piecemeal circumvention, noncompliance, and ineffectiveness that combined over time to make the GATT framework become little more than a "collection of loopholes bound by a few principles."[21]

As C. Fred Bergsten indicated, this process of erosion reflects a momentum theory of trade policymaking, which likens the course of international trade relations to riding a bicycle. This view posits that unless governments can actively move forward in liberalizing and managing world trade, the trading system will slide back into conflict or topple under the weight of domestic pressures.[22] Thus the corrosive effects of continuing government departures from and avoidance of the GATT framework were significant. Not only did this process of erosion limit GATT's capacity to manage existing trade relations, but it also reduced members' willingness to go forward with new commitments to strengthen GATT's rules and governance— in effect creating a vicious cycle of deterioration.

Over time GATT's deterioration created major areas of deficiency in the international trading system. These gaps in GATT rules and functioning stem both from an accumulation of unresolved problems and an inability to respond effectively to emerging trade developments. One major deficiency involves the decline of nondiscrimination as a principle for organizing international trade relations. The steady adoption of different regional arrangements, special treatment policies for developing countries, and selective bilateral approaches to import relief has meant that the principle of equal treatment has become as much the exception as the rule. This trend toward discriminatory trade arrangements has caused an increase in trade disputes and patterns of fragmentation within the trading system.

A second major area of deficiency involves trade-distorting practices and nontariff barriers (NTBs). As tariff barriers were progressively reduced over the past several decades, various nontariff measures became more and more important to the international trading system. They have become the principal means to which governments now resort in restricting or distorting international trade. As a result a complex system of "administered protection" now pervades the conduct of trade relations. The Tokyo Round codes of conduct dealing with subsidies, procurement, and other types of NTBs sought to develop new multilateral rules and procedures in this area. However, their interpretation and implementation have caused continuing problems and conflicts among GATT members. The importance and politicization of unfair trade claims in recent years are only one illustration of the persistent difficulties that NTBs pose to the conduct of international trade relations.

A third major area of deficiency relates to the exclusion of whole industries and segments of world trade from GATT rules and negotiations. Beginning with temperate zone agricultural products in the 1950s, the list of major exceptions grew to include textiles, ships, steel, and automobiles. Other industries and segments of world trade not effectively covered by GATT involve international energy products and countertrade (barter) arrangements. Obviously, these exclusions significantly dilute the regulatory capacity of GATT and further disaggregate international trade relations into separate clusters of transactions, each containing different rules and obligations. Moreover, these large-scale exemptions set into motion pressures for the creation of additional sectoral regimes as other industries confront competitive changes and seek similar treatment.

A fourth major deficiency has to do with the position and participation of developing countries in international trade relations. For the most part developing countries have remained outside the rule-making activities and jurisdiction of GATT. Preferential trade arrangements and other exemptions from GATT obligations have placed developing countries on a separate plane in the trading system. Although some developing countries have gained from such special treatment policies, overall this preferential status has resulted in reduced participation in GATT and highly skewed benefits. As developing countries seek to upgrade their involvement in the trading system the continuation of this special status raises a host of problems concerning differentiated rights and obligations. This dynamic can be seen, for example, in recent attempts to deal with the "graduation" of newly industrialized countries (NICs) in the trading system.

A fifth major deficiency relates to structural change in international economic relations. For the most part the GATT framework has ineffectively handled or been inattentive to changing patterns of production and competitiveness in the world economy. These structural changes have become increasingly important factors in the conduct of commercial diplomacy and in efforts to promote economic expansion. As indicated by the continued disagreements over international safeguarding or disputes concerning national industrial policies GATT rules and governance have not been able to keep up with these changing conditions in the world economy and with the effects of government resistance to structural adjustment.

A final area of deficiency deals with the processes of multilateral decisionmaking and consultation in international trade relations. Over the years established international procedures for reaching agreement on trade matters and resolving trade disputes have proved ineffective or fallen into disuse. Indeed, the greatest disregard for such multilateral processes has occurred among the major trading nations. Countries such as the United States and members of the European Community have consistently preferred to decide unilaterally when they will use or not use GATT processes of consultation and dispute settlement. As a result the major trading nations have been instrumental in producing a framework of trade relations that has moved increasingly away from fixed and objective international criteria for behavior to one that is more dependent on administrative discretion by governments. This trend not only heightens the prospects for discriminatory practices and disputes among member countries, but it places smaller nations in a much more vulnerable position in the international trading system.[23]

Strengthening the GATT Framework

As noted, the 1982 ministerial meeting failed to strengthen GATT's hold over international trade relations and resolve major problems troubling the trading system. According to a report of the Trade Policy Research Centre, this ministerial meeting clearly demonstrated the limits of multilateral commercial diplomacy.[24] Indeed, as Jeffrey Schott noted, serious questions now loom regarding GATT's capacity to act as an arena for making major changes in international trade relations.[25]

Despite past difficulties, a number of different steps could be taken to strengthen GATT's hold over international trade relations. These include: (1) improving existing rules and procedures, (2) extending the framework to cover new trade developments and additional countries, and (3) making needed links between the GATT framework and other economic policy domains.

Improving Existing Rules and Procedures

Much of the current strain and breakdown in international trade relations relates to basic GATT rules concerning nondiscrimination, liberalization, transparency, and multilateralism. These traditional principles of GATT are not so much outmoded in today's trading system as they are weakly formulated or ineffectively applied. To strengthen these general rules of GATT greater focus and international agreement are needed in several key policy areas. For example the Tokyo Round codes concerning subsidies and procurement became increasingly problematic in their interpretation and implementation. Improving these codes to make them clearer and more enforceable would represent a significant step toward providing for greater transparency and nondiscrimination in the trading system. Similarly, international safeguarding provisions need to be strengthened as a basis for guiding national policymaking on import relief and competitive adjustment. Agreement on safeguarding would help considerably in bolstering the authority and salience of GATT general rules. Graduation is another area needing clarification and agreement. Progress in this issue likewise would be important in making the general principles of GATT more applicable to the newly industrializing countries and in providing for greater rule consistency within the GATT framework.

Strengthening GATT's general rules also would allow for greater flexibility of government action in trade policymaking, while still maintaining the overall integrity of the GATT framework. For example many countries, including the United States, have pursued bilateral trade initiatives. If the general rules were strengthened, these efforts could be patterned to serve the overall framework, rather than be inconsistent with GATT. In this manner trade policymaking could be approached much like nuclear nonproliferation— that is, rather than wait until everyone agrees before action is possible, selective agreements could be pursued to maximize the number of countries in compliance and minimize threats to the system.[26]

Improving the force and salience of existing general rules would go far in stemming the process of erosion degrading the GATT framework. However, better GATT rule making in these areas is dependent upon improving its institutional capabilities, especially with regard to international surveillance, decisionmaking, and dispute settlement procedures. Several key institutional reforms are required. First, GATT rule-making activities suffer from the lack of effective international monitoring capabilities. Adequate surveillance would provide for advance notification of pending national trade practices and for assessment of their impacts. This type of institutional reform would be critical in insuring greater transparency and multilateralism in the trade system. Such international monitoring would also be vital to maintaining the integrity of GATT general rules in light of new developments or changes in trade policymaking. The Secretariat could play an important role in such surveillance, providing the "system-tending" capacity that has been so glaringly absent in current GATT operations.

Second, the GATT framework needs an ongoing steering body and negotiating forum to maintain the consistency and strength of its rule system. Current weaknesses in GATT's decisionmaking and consultative processes account for much of the reason why its rules are either overlooked or ineffective, a pattern that has shifted an increasing amount of trade relations outside the GATT framework. Reform of GATT policymaking could be carried out within a resuscitated CG-18 or a new GATT standing committee. Whatever the particular body chosen, it would be important to have the Secretariat and Director-General support its activities by possessing a stronger mandate to raise agenda items for policy discussion. Moreover, this function of continuing policy review and negotiation would be strengthened by making ministerial meetings more regularized and frequent, much like the annual sessions of the World Bank and the IMF. Such high-level involvement would provide for greater governance and discipline within GATT's rule-making activities.[27]

Third, the GATT framework needs improved dispute settlement procedures to insure that GATT rules are carried out effectively and that differences among members do not undermine GATT's rule system. Current processes allow too many opportunities for delay, political intimidation, and circumvention. Moreover, GATT's existing dispute settlement procedures have been complicated by the individual provisions of the Tokyo Round codes, which introduce possible problems of forum shopping and jurisdictional dispute in resolving members' differences. GATT rules dealing with nondiscrimination, transparency, and multilateralism would be strengthened considerably by more centralized dispute settlement machinery and procedures that would be based upon the operation of regularized panels of experts. The Director-General and the Secretariat could play an important supportive role in this area by monitoring government responses to trade disputes to insure that members do not seek resolutions that result in injury to third parties or in a weakening of GATT's rules.[28]

Extending the GATT Framework

Many strains and breakdowns in the current trading system derive from GATT's inability to address emerging areas of trade relations or particular groups of countries' interests. Extending the rules and governance of the GATT framework in these two directions would strengthen its ability to manage changing international economic relations and provide for greater consensus in the trading system. Over the past two decades international trade relations have been strained by domestic and international developments that have not been anticipated or effectively included in the GATT framework. For example GATT has not kept up with trade in international services, with high-technology transactions, with the impacts and requirements of international investments, or with other areas of trade policymaking that currently trouble commercial diplomacy, such as the international counterfeiting of goods.

As Robert Hormats noted, GATT consequently has become irrelevant to many major trade policy issues: "GATT too often is left asking the wrong questions. Rather than ask if an action is legal under the existing articles, it should be asking what types of practices are now distorting trade or impeding necessary adjustments and expansion in trade relations."[29] GATT's limited scope has meant that its regulatory and policymaking activities have been often bypassed, both reflecting and reinforcing the tendency of governments to go outside of GATT to conduct their commercial diplomacy. Dealing with these matters more effectively means not only that GATT's agenda should be expanded, but also that its orientation to trade regulation should be modified to focus more on the trade effects of different government actions and not simply on the trade policies of different governments.

GATT's extension should also be directed toward those countries not effectively represented in its framework. The most significant shortcoming in this regard is GATT's inadequacy in accommodating the developing countries and their participation in North-South trade relations. Existing provisions dealing with special treatment, safeguarding, or graduation do not adequately reflect the changing interests, capabilities, and importance of developing countries in the trading system. Currently these measures are among the most problematic areas of GATT rule making. They either are insufficiently formulated to command necessary compliance, or are at odds with the prevailing thrust of other provisions in the GATT framework. In general, then, GATT has done little to place North-South trade relations on a stable, mutually benefiting basis—one in which each group of countries is regarded as having legitimate interests that can be served by GATT rules and governance. Key issues in emerging international trade relations—structural change, the growing competitive differentiation of various sectors in the trading system, and the changing status of members as trading nations—all involve developing countries. This makes North-South trade relations one of the most important and dynamic areas of future commercial activity. The continued partial and uncertain participation of developing countries in the GATT framework clearly weakens its capacity to manage prospective international trade relations.

Making Links with Other Economic Policies

The current GATT framework has tended to approach international trade issues in a manner that compartmentalizes trade relations from other areas of economic policymaking. This perspective has proved increasingly inadequate in addressing important developments in the international trading system. International economic interdependence and subsequent interconnections among different economic policy instruments have meant that GATT can no longer be inattentive to the trade effects of other areas of economic policymaking. Nor can it achieve its own goal of an equitable and expanding trading system without focusing on other domestic and international economic developments. The need to forge greater policy coordination and review across different economic sectors has become increasingly compelling. This can be seen, for example, when one considers the salience of misaligned exchange rates or global debt pressures for the trade performance of affected countries. The logic and importance of making such links apply similarly to other interconnections, such as those in industrial policy, economic development programs, and trade adjustment assistance.

Making such links is not a new problem for GATT. Its original articles provided for reviewing such matters as a country's balance of payments position when considering a member's rights and obligations in particular trading realms. However, the degree of policy interdependence in current international economic relations makes the forging of such links more and more imperative. Better institutional relations and synchronization of meetings between GATT and other international bodies, such as the IMF, World Bank, and UNCTAD, would help develop the data requirements and policy coordination mechanisms needed for improving the GATT framework in this regard. Strengthening the international monitoring capabilities of GATT would also be an important step toward meeting this need.[30]

Conclusion

As noted, the GATT framework was intended to perform several important functions in the management and regulation of international trade relations. Internationally it provided for the discussion and review of trade matters, the formulation of rules to govern members' behavior, and the resolution of trade disputes among its participants. Domestically GATT offered a framework of constraints and rewards that could strengthen the hands of governments in their dealings with particularistic interests. Over time GATT's capacity to perform these functions has deteriorated significantly as a result of its own institutional weaknesses, transformations that have occurred in the conduct of trade and commercial policymaking, and changes in systemic conditions supporting the GATT framework. As one observer commented, the central question now facing GATT deals not so much with matters of legalism versus pragmatism, as it does with the dangers of "agnosticism."[31]

Strengthening GATT involves a major undertaking of institutional reform and political commitment by members to reinvigorate GATT rules and governance in light of changing circumstances in international trade relations. However, current domestic and international conditions throughout most of the world hardly build confidence for grandiose multilateral initiatives. Indeed, the process of erosion behind GATT's deterioration has produced a vicious cycle that militates against such GATT reforms. Clearly, there has yet to be any emergence of the necessary political will, converging self-interest, and coalition formation that would enable members to pursue a reinvigoration of GATT. Nonetheless, many countries now recognize that the existing crisis in international trade relations must be addressed.

Improving the GATT framework involves a number of different possible actions. In effect three basic approaches can be identified in efforts to strengthen GATT's hold over international trade relations. Each approach suggests different degrees of multilateral involvement and institutional change. The first approach deals with what W. Max Corden has called "complex rules."[32] It seeks to extend GATT rule-making activities to as many new areas of trade relations as possible. The United States has shown strong interest in pursuing this course, as indicated in its efforts to have services, high-technology matters, and investment requirements added to the list of trade matters subject to GATT governance.

However, many issues are raised by adopting this approach, most particularly the problems of enforcement and the tendency to introduce new GATT rules without taking the necessary steps to insure overall coherence within the GATT framework. GATT's rule system already is characterized by a plurality of different subsystems and by a marked divergence between stated rules and actual practice. The difficulties associated with the interpretation and enforcement of the Tokyo Round codes of conduct illustrate the types of ensuing pitfalls and political strains that this approach can produce. In addition, as Richard Cooper has noted, some areas of international trade relations might be left worse off in terms of overall protection and conflict with the negotiation of new multilateral agreements than if such regulation were not imposed.[33]

A second approach to GATT reform involves "decentralized arrangements and agreements." It seeks to attain greater consensus and progress in international trade relations by encouraging efforts to achieve these objectives wherever possible, even if they are reached through special arrangements or limited member agreements. For example arguing that the "old multilateralism" can no longer be maintained in the current environment, Camps and Diebold see "differentiated rule-systems" and "selective actions" as the most viable way to strengthen GATT's hold over international trade relations. Selective trade arrangements have become more and more prevalent in the current trading environment. The key tasks, then, would be to bring these types of decentralized agreements within the context of GATT and to insure that they have positive effects—that is, that they do not injure nonmember parties or undermine other GATT principles.[34]

Although essentially pragmatic in orientation, this approach raises many practical problems of its own, especially regarding the monitoring and enforcement of such decentralized elements within the GATT framework. It also could cause political strains relating to the differential status of countries, raising in addition problems concerning the processes by which excluded nations could enter into existing selective agreements. Since such arrangements necessarily involve particular sectors, these agreements could create political pressures for other industries and countries to seek their own types of special treatment. Thus, rather than provide the basis for building toward a stronger overall system, this approach could precipitate a further unraveling of multilateralism. Moreover, at some point, GATT would run the risk of becoming little more than a regulatory holding company having no real identity and force of its own.

A final approach found in efforts to reform GATT involves "prescribed simplicity." It seeks to devise and enforce a limited number of general rules to guide the conduct of international trade. Rather than preserve the existing collection of rules and principles, which contains many different loopholes, exceptions, and areas of discretion, GATT's hold over international trade relations could be strengthened by setting priorities for the trading system and stipulating a limited number of clear-cut guidelines for behavior. For example these could include the abolition of discriminatory trade practices, the prohibition of quantitative restrictions, or the requirement that all trade practices conform to transparency standards.

A number of problems are raised, however, by this course of prescribed simplicity. While it may clear away much of the abused or ineffective provisions of the existing GATT framework, this approach could lead to a multilateral trading system that is based on rule making by lowest common denominator. Moreover, there is no real assurance that these key priorities of the trading system can be enforced any more effectively than could past provisions. Indeed, redefinitions of basic principles of GATT can and have in practice produced counterproductive results. An example in the present trading environment involves disputes about how the United States may seek to reinterpret the notion of reciprocity to enforce its claims about unfair trade policies of competitor countries.[35] This approach also raises issues concerning the ability of these simple prescriptions to accommodate the changing complexities of international commerce. One could easily envision trading circumstances in which the application of these rules would be called into question, leading to a situation where trade disputes would arise or adjustments be sought among different countries. This could produce a slippery slope of possible exceptions and special provisions that would be hard to restrain—a development that would significantly undermine a basic justification for prescribed simplicity.

Whatever the particular path or combination of steps pursued to reform GATT, its institutional capabilities will need to be strengthened, especially in the areas of international surveillance, ongoing policy review and negotiation, and dispute settlement. As seen, these types of activities are vital for maintaining multilateralism amid the changing demands and patterns of international trade relations. Thus GATT's capacity to function more as an agreement among members than as an international institution has reached its effective limits. The relative progress that GATT makes in managing international trade relations in the future will be based largely on its eventual ability to assume and effectively carry out these critical organizational tasks.

The current state of GATT affairs confirms a characterization of the world trade body that Gerard and Virginia Curzon made more than a decade ago. Arguing that GATT was much like a "bag" into which members placed agreements and ongoing concerns in international trade relations, they noted that GATT needs to spend as much time mending holes in its cloth as it does adding to its contents. They also suggested that "since the fabric that went into the making of the bag was never strong in the first place, . . . the great question is whether the bag will not one day split open."[36]

After several false starts and extensive deliberations, the launching of a new GATT round of multilateral trade negotiations was announced on September 20, 1986, at Punta del Este, Uruguay. This set of trade negotiations is to proceed over a four-year period and cover a comprehensive agenda. In addition to the substantive areas of trade relations dealing with a wide range of products and transactions, significant emphasis within the negotiations is devoted to strengthening the role and functioning of the GATT framework. For example the Ministerial Declaration on the Uruguay Round stated that these negotiations will aim to "strengthen the role of GATT, improve the multilateral trading system based on the principles and rules of the GATT and bring about a wider coverage of world trade under agreed, effective and enforceable multilateral discipline."[37] More specifically, on the issue of GATT reform, negotiations would focus on establishing new arrangements "(i) to enhance the surveillance in the GATT to enable regular monitoring of trade policies and practices of contracting parties and their impact on the functioning of the multilateral trading system; (ii) to improve the overall effectiveness and decision-making of the GATT as an institution, *inter alia*, through involvement of Ministers; and (iii) to increase the contribution of the GATT to achieving greater coherence in global economic policy-making through strengthening its relationship with other international organizations responsible for monetary and financial matters."[38]

If effective agreements can be reached on such arrangements as a result of this new trade round, then significant progress will have been made in resuscitating the GATT framework in international trade relations. However, such efforts to strengthen GATT's institutional seams at this juncture remain hampered by its weakened political foundation. GATT's political order no longer contains the types of supports usually associated with the effective functioning of international institutions. These include the presence of state leadership capable of creating and enforcing a suitable regime; a strong, active executive head able to mobilize authority and commitment in the organization; or a high level of consensus among its members to ease and guide the establishment of multilateral governance. Until one or more of these elements of its political underpinnings can be strengthened, it will be hard to reverse the present course of GATT's deterioration.

Notes

1. See Miriam Camps and William Diebold, Jr., *The New Multilateralism: Can the World Trading System Be Saved?* (New York: Council on Foreign Relations, 1983), 13; *In the Kingdom of the Blind*, Special Report no. 3, (London: Trade Policy Research Centre, 1983), 9–13; and *Trade Policy in the 1980s*, ed. William R. Cline (Washington, D.C.: Institute for International Economics, 1983), 9–53, for further discussion along these lines.

2. See William Diebold, *The End of the ITO*, Essays in International Finance, no. 16 (Princeton, N.J.: Princeton University, 1952); R. Michael Gadbow, "The Outlook for GATT as an Institution," papers from a research and study panel on Managing Trade Relations in the 1980s, American Society of International Law, Washington, D.C., 1982, pp. 1–2; and Jock A. Finlayson and Mark W. Zacher, "The GATT and the Regulation of Trade Barriers: Regime Dynamics and Functions," *International Organization* 35 (Autumn 1981): 562.

3. See John H. Jackson, "GATT Machinery and the 44kyo Round Agreements," in *Trade Policy in the 1980s*, ed. William R. Cline (Washington, D.C.: Institute for International Economics), 160–61.

4. See Harald Malmgren, "Threats to the Multilateral System," in *Trade Policy in the 1980s*, ed. William R. Cline (Washington, D.C.: Institute for International Economics, 1983), 198; and Charles Lipson, "The Transformation of Trade," *International Organization* 36 (Spring 1982): 426–27.

5. The following discussion on GATT norms draws from Finlayson and Zacher, "The GATT," 567–69.

6. See Ibid., 584–93. See also comments of Gardner Patterson, "Roundtable on the Future of the International Trading System," Joint Economic Committee, U.S. Congress, Washington, April 26, 1984.

7. For further discussion see Gadbow, "The Outlook for GATT," 12–16; and William E. Brock, "Trade and Debt: The Vital Linkage," *Foreign Affairs* 62 (Summer 1984): 1046, 1049.

8. See Jackson, "GATT Machinery," 162–63.

9. See Raymond Vernon, "Old Rules and New Players: GATT in the World Trading System," May 11, 1983 paper (mimeo.), Harvard University Center for International Affairs, pp. 2, 9–21.

10. See Finkelstein in this volume: 23–25, 454–55.

11. See Gerard Curzon and Virginia Curzon, "GATT: Traders' Club," in *The Anatomy of Influence*, ed. Robert W. Cox and Harold K. Jacobson (New Haven, Conn.: Yale University Press, 1973), 313–16.

12. See Vernon, "Old Rules," pp. 11, 37. As noted, almost one-half of total trade flows occurred outside of MFN treatment.

13. See C. Fred Bergsten and William H. Cline, *Trade Policy in the 1980s*, Policy Analyses in International Economics, no. 3, (Washington, D.C.: Institute for International Economics, November 1982), 20.

14. See Malmgren, "Threats to the Multilateral System," 193.

15. The preceding discussion draws upon conversations with international trade officials and from an unpublished GATT staff note on the "Scope and Function of the GATT Legal System," March 15, 1984.

16. See *In the Kingdom of the Blind*, 5–6, 76–77.

17. See *GATT* Activities in 1982 (Geneva: General Agreement on Tariffs and Trade, 1983), 8–26, for the GATT Ministerial Declaration, November 29, 1982.

18. See Gadbow, "The Outlook for GATT," 7, for further discussion of this point, and Camps and Diebold, *The New Multilateralism*, 13, for discussion about the failure of this ministerial meeting. Its shortcomings included an inability to deal with: the implementation of the Tokyo Round agreements; safeguarding; U.S. proposals to extend the scope of GATT to cover services, high-technology trade, and investment practices; problems of less-developed countries; and the prolonged stalemate of agricultural trade.

19. See Lipson, "The Transformation of Trade," 421 and 453 for further discussion of this factor in GATT's decline as a regime.

20. See *In the Kingdom of the Blind*, 59–62, for further discussion of such systemic factors. See also *International Trade 1982/83*, (Geneva: General Agreement on Tariffs and Trade, 1983), 21.

21. See *In the Kingdom of the Blind*, 111, for this quoted characterization.

22. See the comments of C. Fred Bergsten at the "Roundtable on the Future of the International Trading System," Joint Economic Committee, U.S. Congress, Washington, D.C., April 26, 1984.

23. Malmgren, "Threats to the Multilateral System," 198. This overall discussion of GATT's deficiencies draws upon Camps and Diebold, *The New Multilateralism*, 14–15, and *In the Kingdom of the Blind*, 112–14.

24. See *In the Kingdom of the Blind*, 9–10.

25. See Jeffrey Schott, "The GATT Ministerial: A Post-Mortem," in *The Contemporary International Economy*, 2nd ed., ed. John Adams (New York: St. Martin's Press, 1985), 89–92. See also *In the Kingdom of the Blind*, 13, and Camps and Diebold, *The New Multilateralism*, 18–19.

26. This analogy was made by Robert Hormats in the Joint Economic Committee Roundtable.

27. For further discussion along these lines, see Camps and Diebold, *The New Multilateralism*, 57, 60–61; Gadbow, "The Outlook for GATT," 13–15; and the remarks of Gardner Patterson at the Joint Economic Committee Roundtable.

28. For further discussion of dispute settlement processes, see Jackson, "GATT Machinery," 181–86 and Gadbow, "The Outlook for GATT," 17–20.

29. Comments of Robert Hormats at the Joint Economic Committee Roundtable.

30. This discussion of areas needing improvement draws upon Camps and Diebold, *The New Multilateralism*, 19–69; Joint Economic Committee Roundtable; and *In the Kingdom of the Blind*, 108–11.

31. See Guy de Lacharrière, "The Legal Framework for International Trade," unpublished paper for GATT study group, March 15, 1984, p. 23.

32. See comments of W. Max Corden, "Toward a Policy Synthesis: Panel Discussion," in *Trade Policy in the 1980s*, ed. William R. Cline, (Washington, D.C.: Institute for International Economics, 1983), 745, dealing with different approaches to reform.

33. See comments of Richard Cooper, in *Trade Policy in the 1980s*, ed. William R. Cline, 738.

34. See Camps and Diebold, *The New Multilateralism,* 49–56.

35. See comments of Jagdish Bhagwati, "Towards a Policy Synthesis: Panel Discussion," in *Trade Policy in the 1980s,* ed. William R. Cline (Washington, D.C.: Institute for International Economics, 1983), 731–33, for reference to "aggressive reciprocity" being sought in proposed U.S. trade policies.

36. Curzon, "GATT," 304.

37. See "Ministerial Declaration on the Uruguay Round," *Journal of World Trade Law* 20, 5 (September–October 1986), 584.

38. Ibid., 589.

6

Value Allocation and North-South Conflict in the Third United Nations Law of the Sea Conference

Robert L. Friedheim

●

On April 30, 1982, delegates to the Third United Nations Conference on the Law of the Sea (UNCLOS III) voted 130 to 4 (with 17 abstentions) to adopt a Convention on the Law of the Sea. It had been under negotiation since 1967 when Dr. Arvid Pardo, then ambassador of Malta, introduced the subject of ocean resource management to the First Committee of the UN General Assembly. On December 6, 1982, the Convention was signed in Jamaica, where an International Seabed Authority, to be created by the treaty, is to be located. The Convention will go into effect when 60 percent of the 117 adhering states have ratified it. As of September 1986, 32 states have ratified the Convention. However, the United States and a number of other developed states have neither signed nor ratified it, nor are many of them likely to do so in the foreseeable future.

The Third United Nations Law of the Sea Conference represents the longest continuous and most technically demanding set of large-scale negotiations ever attempted. Its participants spanned the entire membership of the United Nations and beyond, and the issues covered nearly the entire range of topics concerning ocean use.[1]

In many respects UNCLOS III would seem to provide the perfect case for demonstrating Finkelstein's thesis (see chapter 1) that in recent years, behavior in the United Nations system can be characterized as being Eastonian, or "concerned with the authoritative allocation of values for the society." Certainly many of the themes that run through Finkelstein's analysis can be seen in the long history of UNCLOS III. The decisions were "political" decisions in the Eastonian sense: there was a tendency toward more centralized majority decisions, indeed it was hoped that decisions would be by "consensus" (though they had to settle for "near consensus"); the process was an adaptation for conferences of the General Assembly process of "parliamentary diplomacy"; behavior concentrated in the "intermediate zone," although with a tilt toward the centralized majority pole; many of the values the participants sought to foster were intended to change the rules of what is legitimate internationally (the "legitimation of symbols"); and finally, the greatest struggle at the conference concerned "the struggle to assert and to resist the extension of authority of the international agencies."[2]

A critic could demur and claim that the assertion that UNCLOS III helps prove Finkelstein's thesis is problematic. After all, the majoritarian process was constitutionally set. UNCLOS III was a plenipotentiary conference and was therefore authorized to make decisions and not merely pass resolutions. States sent their delegates voluntarily. Moreover, they voluntarily agreed to make decisions using a requisite majority, with each participating state having but one vote. Thus decisions were to be made for that overworked and underspecified group called "international society" by a centralized majority. States could exercise a unit veto only by choosing not to sign or ratify the treaty.

All of the above is true but irrelevant. All politics are "political" in the Eastonian sense. The United Nations since its beginning can be analyzed using an Eastonian framework, perhaps to test the degree of change, if any, in what structural realists perceive as an anarchic order, and to see if it has been moving toward a hierarchical order.[3] In an anarchic order, or unit veto system, the participants are allocating values in a decentralized fashion. Scholars have never agreed on whether the United Nations has always been a weak central authoritative system—a primitive hierarchical system—or merely an arena for collaboration by the separate nation-states who deem it in their interests to cooperate on specific issues.[4] Some values have always been allocated in the UN system. The questions are whether these values were allocated authoritatively and whether the authority of the United Nations has been increasing over time, perhaps leading eventually to a strong hierarchical system.

What is important about Finkelstein's use of the Eastonian framework is that it allows him to test the relative changes in the process of UN politics over time. There has been a clear trend toward more majoritarian decisions. But is this a successful attempt to develop a hierarchical world order or mere tolerance of a weak majority by a strong minority in a system that remains essentially anarchic?

There certainly has been a clear desire expressed by a developing states majority to have the "world community" make more decisions centrally, and, on more issues salient to themselves. The unanswered question is where this will lead. At the moment, and probably for the foreseeable future, affairs will remain in the "intermediate zone,"[5] as they were at UNCLOS III. Unfortunately an intermediate zone is a very murky place. For UNCLOS III the intermediate zone was a place where the majority that supposedly controlled decisions did not fully control the conference outcome— even if they controlled the process. This theme runs throughout this chapter.

In using an Eastonian framework we must exercise great care. Although Easton did not ignore the moral or ethical content of the concept "value,"[6] it is easy to overlook those attributes in the desire to use the authoritative allocation of values as an operational concept. Value is what is to be allocated. Although it is necessary for some analysis to define value—as Finkelstein has done (chapter 1): "whatever is sought by the relevant actors"—this chapter will also concentrate on the substance of what the actors sought at UNCLOS III. The conference was a clash of values, that is, of moral principles relating to the way in which the various actors perceived that the world system should be organized. What was being negotiated were notions of ultimate ends and instrumental ends emphasized by the regime nature of the negotiation, such as advanced coordination, predictability, impersonal binding nature, and so on.[7]

UNCLOS III was an arena for a clash of values between North and South. Frequently delegates from the states of the North spoke as if they had no ideology or values,[8] but they had no difficulty in pushing their interests and espousing the need of all for rules— advanced coordination, and so on—in their own interest.

Statesmen representing developing states made it clear from the beginning of the negotiation that they were espousing a New International Economic Order (NIEO) as a framework for the overall negotiations. They made no secret of their desire to transform the Grotian system of international law for the oceans into one with a different underlying notion of justice.

Although North-South rhetoric could be heard in all aspects of

the negotiation, its greatest impact was on the debate on the fate
of deep ocean mining. It was at the heart of the struggle for Part
XI (deep ocean mining) of the Convention; therefore, this analysis
will concentrate there. Before doing so, it should be pointed out
that there were two other general thrusts to the negotiation: a struggle over high seas rights and over the enclosure of near-shore waters.
NIEO rhetoric was heard in these struggles as well. On high seas
rights NIEO rhetoric quickly proved hollow and was dismissed, but
in the debate on enclosure such rhetoric was useful to a different
alignment of forces (the coastal states) for justifying a land grab.

Background: Why UNCLOS III?

A shared sense of unresolved problems provoked the convocation
of a Third United Nations Law of the Sea Conference. The regime
for the management of ocean space was in flux. When Arvid Pardo
made his four-and-a-half-hour speech in 1967 he exposed a set of
issues that various states thought should be taken up at that time.
But, while the moment was ripe for entering into negotiations, it
was not necessarily ripe for settlement. Most major parties wanted
negotiations for quite different and often opposing reasons. This
was not an ideal circumstance for an attempt at regime creation or
modification.

   Most of the developed states had a variety of reasons for wanting
negotiations on ocean issues. In the United States, for example, the
impetus for reopening negotiations on ocean issues was clear. The
United States and the Soviet Union had been discussing ways to
"perfect" the results of the treaties promulgated by the First (1958)
and Second (1960) Law of the Sea Conferences. In particular the
superpowers wished to resolve the question of the delimitation of
the territorial sea and the continental shelf. Efforts in 1958 and 1960
to delimit the territorial sea had failed. But in the meantime the
ocean capability of the USSR had increased and its ocean interests
changed. It was now—along with the United States—more interested in preserving the ocean status quo through formal acceptance
of key features of the doctrine of freedom of the seas.[9]

   This approach suited a number of internal U.S. interest groups,
most of whom felt that it was "now or never." That is, the twentieth
century trend toward expansion of national jurisdiction by creation
of, at best, functional zones or, at worst, sovereign zones, was obvious. The newly independent nations that had emerged—espe-

cially after 1955—were eager to protect their own resources and this accelerated the trend. Many interest groups who preferred the status quo feared what had been called "creeping jurisdiction." These groups shared the concern that if relatively narrow bands of national jurisdiction were not recognized within the foreseeable future, it would become impossible to prevent Balkanization of the oceans—carving them up into national lakes. This helped create an odd coalition—the U.S. Departments of State and Defense with American political and religious liberals. All wished to prevent further nationalization of the oceans.[10] A third group of allies included a sizeable number of professional international lawyers, who saw the trends in ocean space as leading to a law of "exclusion" rather than a law of "inclusion."[11]

A very different motivation influenced some of the newer users of the ocean in the private sectors of developed states, particularly those who were actual or potential exploiters of nonliving resources from ocean space. For them legal uncertainty about where they could exploit and with what rights was most important. Uncertainty over the extent of national jurisdiction created uncertainty among bankers whose support was necessary to provide capital to prospective ocean exploiters. For the most part advisers from the oil industry, accustomed to working under U.S. law (the Truman Proclamation and the Outer Continental Shelf Lands Act), preferred a definitive boundary delimitation, but one established well offshore. The nascent manganese nodule industry, hoping to exploit ores found on deep seabeds that were often thousands of miles from shore, was more internationally minded. Exploiters were willing to pay for the privilege of being given legal title to the resource by paying royalties and purchasing licenses. But both groups were aware that the certainty they sought could be gained only in one of two ways—a unilateral claim by the United States backed by a willingness to use force to enforce rights, or consent of the "international community." They were willing to try the latter.

What united all of these groups in their willingness to negotiate was a fear that confusion would result if a number of coastal states continued to act unilaterally. The desire to avoid the Tower of Babel of unilateral claims united most ocean users and gave momentum to the negotiations. Naturally, the ocean users preferred an arena in which they exercised some control or that was at least neutral. Thus they felt considerable trepidation about including all of the issues in a single universal negotiation associated with the United

Nations. But when the "separate packets" proposal failed, they participated vigorously in the alternative.

When Arvid Pardo called for a Common Heritage of Mankind status for the ocean, not many developing states knew very much about the problems of ocean space or had strong opinions about what the solutions to those problems should be. However, they did complain emphatically about the inequalities many experienced under the traditional rules of international law—ocean law included. They sought a new conceptual framework. By the time the formal conference convened for its first substantive session in 1974, the New International Economic Order (NIEO) was the rallying cry of the developing countries, the NIEO having been declared at the 6th Special Session of the General Assembly in the same year. Since Pardo's idea of the Common Heritage of Mankind sounded egalitarian, the developing states interpreted it to have an NIEO content. Among the Third World participants, however, was a minority that was strongly motivated to stage a universal negotiation with ocean subjects on the agenda. In particular the states of the west coast of Latin America—Chile, Ecuador, and Peru—espoused a 200-mile territorial sea, and other Latin American states were developing the notion of the "patrimonial sea."[12] Under the guise of sovereignty these countries could and did make 200-mile claims of varying exclusiveness, but they could not get many other states—particularly developed ocean-using states—to recognize those claims. In particular the U.S. government disputed their authority to deny American fishermen or merchant vessels the rights of fishing and free transit in the outer 197 miles of the zones claimed by these countries. In the mid-1960s these states, members of the Group of 77, perceived the possibility that a universal conference could be useful in their effort to get ocean users from developed countries to recognize their claims.

The fact that the control of deep sea manganese nodules could provide a test case for the New International Economic Order probably did not strike many of the Group of 77 as a major reason for going to the universal bargaining table in the mid 1960s, because little was known about the resource at that time. But delegates from the Group of 77 learned quickly in meetings of the Ad Hoc and Permanent Seabed Committees of the General Assembly, which were charged with preparing the conference. Although seabed minerals quickly became the dominant North-South issue in the conference after 1974, the question of extended jurisdiction over resources within 200 miles was equal with it as a question that affected the NIEO, especially during the early years of UNCLOS III. The fact that the developing nations "persuaded" developed nations—including the United States and the USSR—to endorse the idea of an exclusive economic zone in 1973–74 has led observers to overlook the importance of extended jurisdiction as a North-South issue.

It is important to recognize that most major parties assumed that they could reach their objectives only with the consent of others. None believed that the status quo was an attractive alternative. To be sure, the status quo of unilateral behavior was a possible fallback, and most participants recognized that if they pushed their opponents too far at UNCLOS, there remained the unilateral alternative. However, it was not the preferred one.

Without some widely accepted arrangement for managing the use of ocean space, chaos rather than anarchy would result, making the cost of using the oceans very high indeed. Thus states participating in UNCLOS III recognized that what was needed was a regime or, to be more precise, a reformed regime of rules that would be useful in the management of ocean uses under contemporary conditions. The purpose of the UNCLOS III Conference, therefore, was to engage in regime transformation.[13] Actors' expectations have converged around the principles, norms, rules, and decisionmaking procedures of ocean use since, perhaps, the Laws of Whisby, or at least since Hugh DeGroot (Hugo Grotius) published his *Mare Liberum* in 1608. All participants understood that the purpose of UNCLOS III was, as Young put it, to develop a "negotiated order."[14] UNCLOS III was very explicitly constitutional in that the affected parties voluntarily participated in deciding the future rules of the oceans. What most wanted were rules—rules that were predictable, that would encourage reciprocity,[15] and that expressed values of which the participants approved. This mixing of instrumental with normative considerations is what makes "political" negotiations especially difficult.[16]

Structure of the Negotiations

If the essential nature of negotiation is joint decisionmaking by participants with mixed motives[17] who are trying to anticipate each other's moves (a process characterized by Young as an "outguessing regress")[18] then multiplying significantly the number of parties the negotiator must anticipate creates staggering problems of bargaining management. Even at the most superficial level, if we assume that one of the participants in UNCLOS wishes to understand his own position and those of each of the other participating nation-states on the 320 articles of the UNCLOS treaty and the 118 articles of the six annexes to the treaty, the resultant decision matrix would have 66,138 cells. The "real world," with many large-scale sessions, smaller committees, informal bargaining groups, and inter- and intracoalition meetings is much more complex. Naturally, no one delegate understands it all. Indeed, in complex situations it is possible to muddle through. But in the case of UNCLOS III it took fifteen years from Pardo's speech to convention signature.[19]

"Parliamentary diplomacy," a term invented by Philip Jessup and elucidated by Dean Rusk,[20] has evolved over the forty-year history of the United Nations system. Some recent commentators have implied that the new developments, some of which are discussed below, are independent of parliamentary diplomacy, which supposedly is concerned exclusively with a unit veto system. Rather, I contend, these developments are evolutionary adaptations to changes in the system, which is still structurally parliamentary at its core.

The literature describing behavior in multilateral organizations is voluminous, but remarkably few works deal explicity with multilateral negotiations within large organizations.[21] A number of special characteristics (also found in other UN organs with "parliamentary" attributes) dominate our case: (1) large numbers of participants; (2) numerous agenda items; (3) the technical nature of many of the issues; (4) a skewing of real world power or influence among the negotiating states; (5) the assumption of sovereign equality; and (6) the continuity of the bargaining arena over time.

Parliamentary diplomacy is parliamentary in structure. In order to reduce the confusion that would result if all the participants were to try to negotiate simultaneously on a large number of issues, there must be organizations, leadership, rules of procedure, and rules for formal decisionmaking. All of the major trappings of a domestic legislature are present: formal debate, committees of the whole, substantive committees, working parties, informal negotiating groups, and posts of honor, such as a president, vice presidents, committee chairpersons, and members of general or drafting committees. These honorary posts are the objects of vigorous competition, not only because of the prestige and honor that such appointments bring, but because those who hold such posts are assumed to have a disproportionate role in effecting outcomes. UNCLOS is no exception. The first President of the conference, Hamilton Shirley Amerasinghe of Sri Lanka, seized the moment to develop the procedures by which the first draft of the treaty—the Single Negotiating Text—would be assembled. His successor, Tommy Koh of Singapore, tried to weave his way through the complexities of the final negotiations to achieve a consensus outcome. The chairpersons for the main committees were largely responsible for the general character of the texts that were produced by their committees.

Many participants or observers believe that a different person in a key position at a critical point in time might have effected a different outcome.[22] It should be noted, however, that major posts in UNCLOS are assigned using a formula similar to that used in the General Assembly—that is, seats are distributed to major permanent regional geographic groups. This practice resulted in limited representation of developed states in major posts, although they were represented on general and drafting committees. Except for Ambassador Yankov of Bulgaria (chairman of the Third Committee, which is considered by many to have dealt with lesser issues), all major posts were held by representatives of Third World states— the presidency by an Asian, the First Committee by an African, and the Second Committee by a Latin American.

Formal equal representation of nation-states created two other characteristics of UNCLOS as a bargaining arena: formal debate and formal decisionmaking. Formal debate gave states and groups the opportunity to put their positions on record; it was often used for this purpose. This had the usual consequence of casting opening positions in concrete, making movement from these initial positions difficult, particularly in the case of stances announced as representative of the views of bargaining-groups.[23] Speeches also took an inordinate amount of time, thus reducing the time available for direct interactions of interested parties.

Another consequence of parliamentary organization was a set of formal rules concerning decisionmaking. Decisions in the formal sense had to be made by vote. Since the usual two-thirds present and voting formula, if invoked, would most likely have led to an automatic majority for any position espoused by the Group of 77 on issues of importance to that group, it was assumed that the conference would fail early if the formal rules were invoked routinely. At the first substantive session in Caracas in 1974, a modified two-thirds rule was adopted for the conference. If it had been used, it would have made no difference in the usual two-thirds present and voting formula unless there had been massive abstentions.[24] More important was a gentleman's agreement on voting and cooling off procedures before a vote was invoked. The situation was cooled off for nine years, and only a final overall vote on the package was called in 1982. It was assumed from the beginning that a viable treaty would result only if it emerged as part of a consensus or, at worst, a near consensus. How to arrange it and what represented "near consensus" was left to conference interactions over time.

The notion of working toward a "package" outcome as the only viable way of conducting the negotiations was also widely shared early among the assembled negotiators. Most of the experienced participants understood that if the usual rules of procedure were invoked (vote first on the amendment to the amendment, then the amended article, then the section, and finally the treaty as a whole), there was a substantial probability of failure.[25] They feared that if the delegations split into a large number of small common interest groups, the set of group preferences would be intransitive (Arrow's Paradox) or, conversely, if larger groups (such as the Group of 77) remained disciplined, there would be a majoritarian outcome unacceptable to a significant minority.

A package outcome implies a number of attributes. First, the agenda issues are "interrelated"[26] and therefore a large number of issues may be decided simultaneously. Early in the negotiations the United States, claiming to foresee technical difficulties in dealing with so many issues simultaneously, proposed to split the issues into separate packets. The Group of 77 would have no part of it. Its members correctly understood that a large agenda would help create a willingness among states to accept tradeoffs. Thus the second attribute was the notion that a package would be a mixed bag, with enough favorable outcomes on issues of importance to the vast majority of participants so that they would be willing to accept an overall outcome that included less than favorable results on issues of presumed lesser importance to themselves. This proved difficult to arrange: (1) for many delegations, the necessary tradeoffs were unpalatable to strong domestic interests; (2) the sheer size of the package and the technical complexity of the issues made the sorting-out process long and cumbersome; and (3) the inclusion of favorable outcomes on all or most issues of importance to all major states and groups was not possible. Some parties had to give way not only on unimportant issues but on important issues as well.

Although the formal decision rules of parliamentary diplomacy are based on the notion of equality of participants, the actual rule of decision presupposes inequality. But measuring the degree of inequality accepted by members of the conference and thereby stating a precise decision rule is extremely difficult. What is obvious is that most major states expected that they would not be treated as mere equals. Although they were aware of the formal one-state–one-vote rule, they expected that their influence would be roughly commensurate with their own feelings of prowess in the international economic-political system. Hence, they insisted upon a consensus or near consensus decision rule.

On the other hand states that viewed themselves as more than mere equals were aware that the major weapon of the majority (often composed mostly, but usually not exclusively, of developing states) was their numbers if the formal decision process was invoked. Therefore, the major states were constrained to accept more non-optimal outcomes within a parliamentary diplomatic setting than they would in the absence of the threat of being outvoted. Because what they sought from UNCLOS III was a set of rules that had broad acquiescence (even if universality was too much to expect), they were aware that they had to operate within a system that would be likely to help gain the consent of the vast majority to a set of rules.

Conversely, the majority were constrained to accept less than they might have formally achieved if they merely voted for what was optimal for them. They were aware that in a system more chaotic than the existing system, they were less able to cope with chaos than the powerful few. Although the rules may have been "unjust," they were rules, and they helped make the response of the powerful more predictable. Nevertheless, the awareness of bargaining asymmetry haunted the negotiations. As it turned out the developing states could afford to be unyielding on issues that had high ideological salience but little real world importance to themselves, especially seabed mining. However, all understood that the underlying theme of parliamentary diplomatic interactions is numbers versus real world capability.

Consensus or near-consensus can be achieved in a parliamentary diplomatic setting only by the formation of coalitions. Much of the activity in parliamentary diplomacy is the formation and maintenance of such coalitions. In the case of UNCLOS these coalitions came in a bewildering variety.[27] It is difficult to sort out the process. On the one hand existing coalition theory does not help much; on the other hand most observers of the details of the negotiations have described the interaction at UNCLOS as if they were sui generis.

I do not subscribe to the sui generis explanation. However, theories based on size of winning coalitions were not helpful in this context.[28] More helpful were the notions of "ideological similarity" or "minimization of policy distance" of Axelrod and De Swaan.[29] In addition other groups formed that were based upon shared common interests rather than shared common ideas. Both are important in understanding the bargaining in UNCLOS III.

As in the General Assembly common ideas or values bound various groups together. We can trace the cohesiveness of these groups on a number of major issues at the conference as well as the stability or movement of their positions over time.[30] On most major issues, as defined here, the Group of 77 and its regional component groups—Asia, Africa, and Latin America—were held together by ideology and a sense of common identity, and were quite cohesive. Usually when movement was involved they moved in a coherent direction.[31]

In universal bargaining the fear of being overwhelmed if isolated has led to the formation of groups that coalesced to protect their less widely shared interests. These special groups at UNCLOS III included a coastal states group, the landlocked and geographically disadvantaged states (LL/GDS), the territorial group, the margineers (a group of broad-shelf states), the straits states group, the group of archipelago states, the median line group, the equitable principle group, island states, the group of fourteen maritime states, and various secret groups and "mafias." Two inside observers, Ambassador Jayakumar and President Koh, believe that the coalitions that were more broadly based ideologically or geographically were not as influential in UNCLOS as were the special interest groups that sprang up for UNCLOS bargaining only. However, they do admit that the Group of 77 "did take a united stand on Committee I [deep seabed minerals] matters."[32]

Interactions across group lines were critically important in building the grand coalition necessary to get a consensus document adopted. The steps in building broader coalitions took up many of the sessions of UNCLOS bargaining. Much of the interaction on building large coalitions took place in informal private negotiating groups, such as the Evanson Group of Juridical Experts, the Private Group on Straits cochaired by the United Kingdom and Fiji, the Nandan Group of the rights of the LL/GDS in the economic zone, and others. Much bargaining was also done bilaterally, as well as in secret negotiating sessions within and among groups. The key steps in parliamentary diplomacy are the interactions among the representatives of the special interest groups, the ideologically and geographically broad-based coalitions, the representatives of the "key" states, and the formal and informal leaders that attempted to build the maximum winning coalition in support of *the* package.

Observers have pointed out a number of other important attributes that resulted from the size and complexity of UNCLOS. First, a number of states, particularly smaller developing states, had difficulty understanding the legal, scientific, and engineering complexities of a variety of issues. Related to this is the tendency of many developing countries to fear complex issues because of their lack of technical expertise at home.[33] More of the delegations from the developing countries were composed of political generalists than was the case with delegations from the developed countries.

A third characteristic related to the problem of complexity was the large amount of variability in the number of issues on the agenda in which states had important interests. A number of small states were either not interested at all in certain issues or were intensely interested in other issues. For larger countries, particularly developed ones, the problem was quite the opposite. They were interested in finding favorable outcomes on most issues on the agenda. For them the problem was often making internal trade-offs among interests that were roughly equal in salience. Even when decisions were made it was difficult to make them stick. If ever a demonstration were needed that the state is not a unitary actor, the behavior of a number of major developed states at UNCLOS would serve nicely—particularly the United States. Internal struggles and bargaining took up much of the time of the U.S. delegation. Often these internal quarrels were well known to foreign delegations, which made it easy for other delegations to understand the United States' difficulties and to manipulate its position.

Another related characteristic was the difficulty in establishing the "national interest" on most of the major issues, making it commensurately difficult to establish opening positions, fallback positions, and settlement points. These were questions of both what and how much. Developing states often had difficulties because too few issues were salient. On the less salient issues, particularly during the early negotiations, the range in statements on what was in their national interests was very large.

For developed states the problem was different and relates to the benefits associated with internal tradeoffs. On many issues it can be quickly established that a particular position has a potential benefit to one party, while the opposite would have little or no benefit. Decisions in these situations are obvious.

The real difficulty arises on issues in which the opposing poles represent one type of benefit versus another, rather than no benefit. For example, at the beginning of UNCLOS, the United States had to make a choice on the basic jurisdiction question. It could have espoused as its national interest the principle of a 200-meter depth of water to delimit national jurisdiction on the seabed, thereby ending "creeping jurisdiction," and protecting movement and other rights in the area beyond. Or the United States could have espoused extended resource jurisdiction by accepting a 200-mile exclusive economic zone. If possible, both would have been desirable. The United States would have liked to have as much near-shore resource jurisdiction as it wished and as many distant-water rights as its citizens could use. But at a universal bargaining conference, it was forced into a trade-off. Not only was this decision the source of a fierce internal battle, but it was also a source of confusion to others when the United States, at the Caracas session in early 1974, did a 180-degree turn on this issue. Indeed, although the extension of resource jurisdiction was ardently espoused by the coastal state members of the Group of 77 (especially Latin Americans), the chief beneficiary (by comparative standards) was the United States. As a way of specifying its rights, about a year after it rejected the UNCLOS treaty, the United States adopted a 200-mile economic zone over waters adjacent to the continental United States, Alaska, Hawaii, and the Commonwealth of Puerto Rico, the Commonwealth of the Northern Marianas, and the Trust Territory of the Pacific Islands. This presidential proclamation enclosed 6 million square nautical miles of ocean space—the largest ocean resource area under the national jurisdiction of any country in the world.[34]

Two other observations specially drawn from the particular characteristics of UNCLOS may not affect other parliamentary diplomatic negotiations. First, UNCLOS was a plenipotentiary conference that was expected to produce a definite outcome. Because the outcome was to be a treaty rather than, say, a nonbinding resolution of the General Assembly, it was assumed that whoever was in control of the conference process would gain greater than normal leverage. Second, UNCLOS III was very poorly prepared. The previous comprehensive UN Law of the Sea Conference (UNCLOS I) had been aided by a draft convention prepared by the International Law Commission. Not only was no such draft prepared by experts for the subsequent multiissue conference (UNCLOS III), there was no agenda to guide the preparatory work of the Seabed Committee, merely a list of issues. The learning process was long and arduous, but the lack of formal preparation was deliberate. It effectively reduced the importance of the technical aspects of the work of the conference and emphasized the political or allocation aspects. This, too, was a choice forced by the developing state majority in the United Nations.

The Process of Bargaining in UNCLOS III

As befitting a negotiation that went on for more than fifteen years and resulted in a treaty with 320 articles and 8 annexes, UNCLOS III had a most complex process of encounters. It went through numerous stages in which there was a recognizable principal type of encounter, but within these stages other means of interaction were often used simultaneously. The general stages are shown in table 6.1.[35]

In stage 1, there was little concern among the parties for movement toward an outcome. The issues were new and technically demanding, and many of the participants needed time not only to become acquainted with them but also to determine where they should stand. Debating and recording what various states thought their positions should be were the basic functions of the process of interaction.

Stage 1 of the Law of the Sea negotiations was a search for a framework for agreement. On the issues assigned to Committees II (high seas and enclosure issues) and III (environmental and science issues), the frameworks were found, but not without years of effort toward their refinement. Alas, the framework for resolution of Committee I issues, the quintessential North-South deep seabed resources issues that could have been managed under free market principles, NIEO principles, or perhaps some blend, was not found. The parties came close, according to some observers,[36] but not close enough for the Reagan administration. The United States objected to the facts that (1) potential exploiters would not be treated on a first-come–first-served basis; (2) "the Enterprise," a rival international agency (to private enterprises or state corporations), would

Table 6.1 Stages of the LOS Negotiations

Stage	Process	Outcome
1. 1967–70	Stating basic orientations; exploring others' positions; looking for coalition partners	Better understanding of issues and alignments
2. 1970–73	First statement of formal proposals; firming up of coalitions	Realization of basic trade-offs necessary for a treaty
3. 1973–74	Formal negotiations; beginning of informal negotiating groups' drafts showing patterns of agreement on some issues	Announcement of basic trade-offs being accepted
4. 1975–80	Formal drafts of committee chairmen; informal single negotiating text, revised single negotiating text; informal composite negotiating text, etc.	Basic outline of the full treaty; resolution of many issues in disagreement by refinement of language, drafting improvements
5. 1981–82	Crisis: United States reviews draft after a year and insists upon major revisions; compromises offered but not enough; United States calls the question	Treaty adopted with most industrial countries either abstaining or opposing

be created that could also exploit the resources; (3) production controls and mandatory technology transfers were featured; and (4) there was the possibility that within twenty years after implementation, new private and/or national rights could be eliminated. In any case much of the damage may have begun in stage 1 because of the tendency of a number of states to put themselves on record on the basis of general ideological principles rather than on a specific assessment of their national needs—often before the facts of the situation became clear. For the most part these principles were free market and NIEO. Although there was little unity on these archetypical positions, they became the poles around which the various camps gathered later in the negotiation. Afterward further complications arose because in stage 1 much nonsense was put on record that vastly exaggerated the nature of the resource in dispute, making it difficult to evaluate whether or not the game was worth the candle. Since the economic rents are likely to be small for a number of years, the candle was not worth very much in the short run to either the developing or the developed states. But through all of the phases of the negotiation the game on this issue became a search for mutually agreeable referents, a search for the "principles of justice on which both parties [could] agree."[37] It was largely a search for acceptable symbols.

In the first two stages it became obvious that the only method by which a successful outcome could be reached (one that represented consensus or near consensus) was adoption of a package. It was apparent that all of the major groups would have to have positive outcomes within the package on issues of high salience to themselves if the package had any chance of being adopted. Thus by the time of the first full conference session at Caracas in 1974, the shape of the package was understood and the trade-offs were announced, even though formal treaty language had not yet been worked out. Both of the superpowers had expressed their willingness to accept extensions of national resource jurisdiction to 200 miles in return for the establishment of a relatively moderate 12-mile territorial sea and a formal affirmation of rights of movement through straits and archipelagos. Almost implicitly, opposition to narrow territorial seas and rights of movement melted away. It is difficult to say precisely whether or not statements by the United States and the Soviet Union that acceptable territorial sea limits and rights of movement were fundamental to their participation in a package outcome were perceived by others as a threat or as a signal that on these issues it would be profitless to push hard. The statements were a fairly obvious signal that the superpowers had to be willing to accept a trade-off elsewhere. As mentioned previously it was difficult to arrange trade-offs only on lower salience issues in return for favorable outcomes on higher salience issues. By 1975 the trade-offs were alleged to be part of the fundamental package. According to Edward Miles, radicals among the Group of 77 claimed that a NIEO-type solution on deep sea minerals should be demanded from the United States as the price for its preferred solution on straits transit.[38] There is no evidence that the United States ever made such a commitment, even in the earlier years of the conference when U.S. administrations were generally receptive to the idea of a comprehensive treaty to resolve overall ocean management problems. After the Reagan administration was installed in Washington in 1981, such a commitment would never have been considered, much less made.

Getting to the next stage of developing a single proposal that could be modified into a formal agreement presented one of the most difficult problems in the UNCLOS process. Essentially, a solution was found in stage 4 with the development of the Informal Single Negotiating Text and its subsequent modifications, which were eventually refined into a treaty.

Even though the general shape of the agreed-to trade-offs and the outline of the package issues on which there was general agreement were known, it would have been difficult to hammer these out in face-to-face bilateral meetings or even in meetings of the informal negotiating groups, although some of the individual issues or subsets of related issues were worked out by these means. Rather, in a very parliamentary manner, the task of assembling the text was entrusted to the three committee chairmen. They were expected to reflect the understandings reached on those issues on which there was general agreement and to suggest on their own where they thought consensus might lie on issues on which general agreement had not been reached. Even Ambassadors Koh and Jayakumar were somewhat nonplussed that the delegates were willing to entrust this task to persons, whatever their personal reputations for integrity, who "were themselves representatives of states having clear national interests."[39] They speculated that perhaps most delegations were frustrated at the slowness of progress toward agreement in the previous stage. In any case the chairmen's texts were to be negotiating—not negotiated—texts. But in fact they became a guide for the remainder of the negotiations. If a state did not agree with a chairman's formulation of the issue, it could not simply ignore his text; instead, the text became the base point for further negotiations.

Stage 4, which encompassed the several iterations of the negotiating text, was primarily a process of refinement.[40] Refinement in the general process of negotiation means working toward making marginal improvements on a general outcome that the parties essentially have decided upon. It presupposes the acceptance by the parties, willingly or unwillingly, of a conceptual framework.

The day-to-day activities of the negotiator, after the conceptual framework has been formulated, are aimed at incrementally improving his principals' utility.[41] He pushes and probes to get a bit more than he gives. He seeks to sharpen or to make vague the language describing what is agreed to. He tries to increase or decrease the exceptions to the general rule that supposedly all parties will accept. He seeks a different way to express the agreement being negotiated to make the language more palatable to his principals. He seeks a face-saving gesture or tries to arrange a side payment (a payoff on a different item for a concession on the agenda item).

The process and consequences of working to make incremental improvements differ significantly, depending upon whether the general principle is agreed to willingly or unwillingly. If it is agreed to willingly, then the task of the negotiator is essentially technical— to perfect the document to which all parties are likely to agree. The outcome should be at, or somewhere near, the classic 50 percent solution. What conflict is present is largely personal or professional; it does matter whose formula proves acceptable.

The process and consequences are quite different if the underlying framework is still under dispute. Any negotiator in the position of trying to make incremental improvements to a conceptual framework with which he or his state disagrees, but cannot alter fundamentally, has one or two (or both) purposes in mind. The first is to make sufficient incremental improvements to make the agreement minimally acceptable to his masters. The second is to undermine the general principle in the detailed provisions. He can do this by working for piecemeal improvements, changes in language, a multiplication of detailed provisions that allow his principal(s) an escape hatch, time limits to provisions, conditional requirements, and so on. In this latter purpose a negotiator will often have difficulty demonstrating to skeptics in his own government that he is really "protecting the national interest." In operating at the margin or trying to improve a client's welfare by increments the negotiator risks having clients judge that they may be better off with the status quo.

In stage 4 of the UNCLOS negotiations it seems that many of the occurrences when NIEO-related issues were being resolved were incremental negotiations of the above-mentioned type, where negotiators from the developed states tried to make the provisions under negotiation initially acceptable or to undermine them. There were three subtypes, each with hard-fought interactions occurring over a relatively narrow range of possible outcomes. In the most critical type the conceptual framework remained in dispute, even though it was clear that, if put to a vote, a majority—indeed a substantial majority—would have voted for a particular version of the framework. Many of the key points in the First Committee that were viewed as essentially North-South issues were of this nature.

North-South Bargaining in UNCLOS III

Although most observers have conceded a strong North-South dimension in some parts of UNCLOS III, they are skeptical about how central the considerations of North-South or NIEO elements have been to the overall treaty. Although the degree of North-South polarization has varied among issues, themes characteristic of the debate can be found through the negotiations.

An earlier study demonstrated (1) a strong North-South dimension to the issues relating to creation of an International Seabed Authority and the Enterprise to manage deep ocean mineral resource exploitation; (2) less, but quite visible, North-South polarization concerning most issues dealing with the extension of national jurisdiction to 200 nautical miles;[42] (3) substantial North-South polarization concerning control or freedom of ocean science in the economic zone;[43] and (4) less polarization relating to matters of ocean pollution. There is no reason to change these assessments as a result of later events in the bargaining history between the Single Negotiating Texts of 1975 and the treaty of 1982. To a substantial degree, UNCLOS III was one of the most important North-South confrontations of our time.

In contrast many observers point to the roles played by the varied special interest groups in influencing the outcome of UNCLOS III. For them this was a demonstration of the fact that states devoted greatest attention to protecting their own special interest(s), regardless of "ideological distance." This view seems defective because many of the participants frequently experienced what Axelrod called "overlapping cleavages."[44] They participated simultaneously in several of the major ideology-based and interest-based groups. The drives of each group reinforced each other. For example members of the Coastal States group were motivated to extend national jurisdiction off their shores, including coastal states that dominated the Group of 77. Being poor and suspicious of the designs of developed states on their coastal resources, they specifically insisted on pushing the developed states away from their shores. Therefore,

being coastal overlapped to a considerable degree with being poor.
Being rich and coastal, however, caused what Axelrod called "cross-
cutting cleavages" for countries such as the United States, which
had difficulty in reconciling its distant water interests and its coastal
interests.[45]

The data used for the analysis of the different tactics of incremental movement on three North-South issues were derived from
a Law of the Sea (LOS) project I directed from 1969–75 (as well as
from a reasonably complete collection of information for the remainder of the conference).[46] In order to be able to deal with mixed
motive problems we had to create a set of conflict issue "variables."
Figure 6.1 shows one of them, the central North-South issue of the
conference.

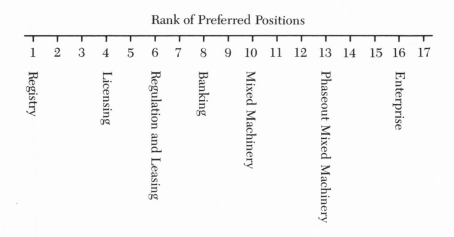

Figure 6.1 Minerals Management System, Article 153

We discovered an array of issues and ordered them on the basis of a dimension—in this case from the least to most central authority structure for the management of deep ocean minerals. These issues were first scaled ordinally and then, in an attempt to replicate the perceived world of the negotiator, were transformed into an interval scale.[47] Conflict issues are thus developed in one-dimensional space. Many of the issues later became articles in the UNCLOS III treaty.

Data indicating where states or groups of states stood on the issues were derived by performing a thematic content analysis of the ocean debates between 1967 and 1975 in the First Committee of the General Assembly, the Ad Hoc and Permanent Seabed Committees, and the Law of the Sea Conference. Since not all states spoke on all issues, we had to estimate the "missing data" with a regressional model. Using data and estimates we were able to develop national profiles of states on the issues by calculating their preferred positions.

In order to understand the negotiations, we had to develop decision models. If we assumed that states would be "forced" at any given time to decide, we could reasonably further assume that the median of their preferred positions would show the central tendency of the collective opinion. Moreover, distribution, if strongly single peaked, would show if there is consensus or movement toward consensus. Because we were able to divide the data into time periods, we could show change over time for individual states or groups. We also had a measure of the discipline shown by the groups, obtained by calculating the mean and standard deviation of the preferred position of their members. We can also display on the same spectrum the opening positions of the states and the fallbacks, as well as the outcome of various draft texts and the final treaty on the conflict issue in question.

The LOS forecasting project also developed more sophisticated tools. A model built on the individual issues model calculates the probable package and trade-off outcomes. Figure 6.2 shows the same critical issue—the nature of a deep sea minerals management system—that we used as an example of scaling in figure 6.1.

The potential positions ranged from a registry system only (the Soviet opening position), which would put the least restrictions on states' access to the minerals of the international commons, all the way to the other end of the spectrum, where no access by national or private entities would be allowed. If the policy position represented at rank 16 came to fruition, the deep sea would be a monopoly

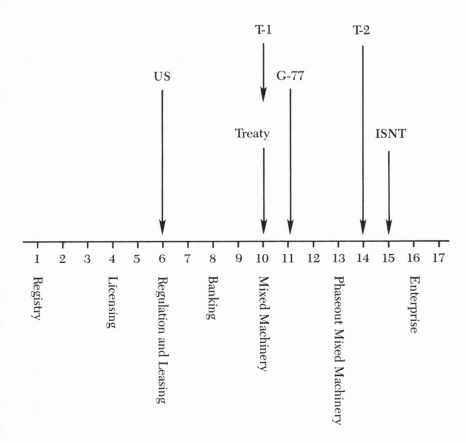

Figure 6.2 Minerals Management Issue, Article 153

zone for the exclusive exploitation by the Enterprise. Although the
United States opened the negotiations with a pure licensing proposal
(rank 4), it quickly moved to a position that would have allowed an
international seabed agency to regulate mining as well as grant licenses to private enterprises or national government agencies (rank
6). It was obvious even early in the negotiations that mere licensing
alone (the U.S. maximum preferred position) was not negotiable. But
licensing plus regulation might be, the U.S. delegation thought, and
it was close enough to what the United States wanted to characterize
the fallback position as a "preferred position." On the other side,
the preferred position of the Group of 77 was rank 11 (the mean of
the positions of its members).[48] Thus the spread between the states
that advocated private access and those searching for what they

claimed was a more equitable solution was five ranks, a substantial policy distance. To measure change we divided our content analysis data into two time periods: 1967–73 (T-1) and 1974–75 (T-2). As figure 6.2 shows the median or central tendency for T-1 was at rank 10, or a dual system. This demonstrates that if the Group of 77 had a specific plan at the time, it was close to a winning position. But the distribution was relatively flat across the spectrum and the standard deviation was rather high (2.85), indicating lack of unity as they searched for a common position. But as members explored the types of measures they wished to impose—measures they thought would exemplify a new international economic order—they became more extreme. In 1974–75 the Group of 77 mean moved to 14.7 (with a standard deviation of 0.18, demonstrating great unity) and the median of all states consequently moved to rank 14. The developing nations were increasing the substantive distance between themselves and their opponents. The first version of the negotiating text, the Informal Single Negotiating Text, was judged to fall out at rank 15, reflecting approximately where the overwhelming majority preferred to be.

In the meantime the United States made further incremental adjustments and moved toward its opponents by introducing the banking proposal (rank 8). While the negotiations were not stalemated, they proceeded slowly. It was only after March 1981, when the Reagan administration insisted on reviewing U.S. participation in the negotiations, that the leadership of the conference was able to persuade the more radical members of the Group of 77 to accept significant modifications of the demand for an immediate imposition of a NIEO system. A genuine mixed system would be created by including pioneer status (a guarantee that the first-generation claimants of a "pioneer" country would be granted a license to mine), an assured seat for the United States on the Seabed Authority's Council, and the operation of the dual system, in which two areas for exploitation would be nominated, with one granted to the national claimant and one "banked" away for the Enterprise. The question of converting the system to an exclusive monopoly of the Enterprise, a favorite NIEO idea, was shelved—perhaps permanently, perhaps temporarily. That subject can be raised at a review conference twenty years after the first commercial production commences. The relatively rapid movement in the last sessions toward a compromise treaty provision (a fallback of 5 ranks to a dual system at rank 10, as shown on figure 6.2) engineered by the conference leadership and accepted by the Group of 77, was also not enough. The Reagan administration was also moving, but away from the developing states, perhaps to a position less forthcoming than the United States' opening position. The shell of the NIEO concept is still embodied in treaty provisions, but agreement proved elusive.

Refinement of issues of importance to North and South also occurred in other ways. The second typical pattern was to establish an NIEO framework and to stick rather firmly to it, forcing the developed states to accept it. What made this framework minimally acceptable to the developed states was developing states' acceptance of some exceptions to the general rule. What was negotiable by incremental tactics narrows in this second case. As we can see in figure 6.3 this happened on the issue of conducting scientific research in the economic zone.

The positions range from freedom of scientific research (rank 1) to complete and unfettered coastal control of the right to conduct scientific work in the economic zone (ranks 15–16). In the 1967–73 time period science was looked upon widely as a benefit to mankind, and the freedom of science was ardently supported by both the United States (1.5) and the Soviet Union (2.4). Since the median in that time period (T-1) was at 5, it seems that most states would have preferred some restrictions—although modest—on gathering data in the coastal zone. But the beginning of a shift toward control of science could be seen. What was emerging was the feeling that knowledge in the hands of the developed states might be a potential threat to the resource control of the developing states. In particular the radicals among the Latin American group (rank 8.9 in T-2) and, to a lesser extent among the coastal African states (rank 7.5), were helping to move the Group of 77 toward further control measures. These groups were by no means united on the issue at that time, but by 1974–75 (T-2), opinion had moved solidly to a consent regime (rank 12) that made relatively few concessions to the preferences of the developed states. Not only had the median increased drastically, but the distribution shows a single peak (support) with a small flat tail (opposition). In other words a substantial majority had formed, although not a consensus. Moreover, the Group of 77 and all its major components now were solidly in the consent camp (rank 12). If we gauged preferences correctly, control of science became a cornerstone of the NIEO approach. Although some marginal improvement was necessary to gain consensus, there was little reason for the Group of 77 to move far. We judged that they moved to rank

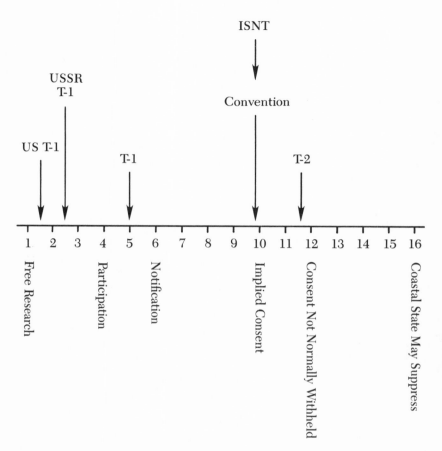

Figure 6.3 Ocean Science in the EEZ, Articles 246, 248, and 252

10 on the consent regime by accepting some limitations. One such concession was a required six-month lead time for permit requests (Article 248 of the treaty); if a reply is not received after six months, the consent of the coastal state is assumed (Article 252). Although the scientific community bitterly protested that its interests were being traded off,[49] most of the developed states accepted this slight compromise by the Group of 77 as a protection of their minimal national interests and they accepted consent as part of the package deal. The national salience of the scientists' preferred outcome on this issue was not high. Scientists have been heard to lament that they cast few votes. The U.S. negotiators prior to the Reagan administration team judged that the improvements made by incremental bargaining were sufficient to make the science provision minimally acceptable.

The third pattern in the process of refining the negotiating texts into a draft treaty shows a confident majority seemingly unwilling to move in order to make a key portion of the text acceptable to a recalcitrant minority. However, the majority was willing to juggle the technical details of its winning formula. The bargaining range in this case of incremental adjustment was the narrowest of the three cases under examination.

Among the important features of the arrangements to manage deep ocean mineral resources were the measures taken to protect the economies of the major land producers of the constituent minerals from competition from ocean producers of the same minerals. The favored method was production controls. As we can see in figure 6.4, there was never any question of what type of provision would be placed in the various drafts.

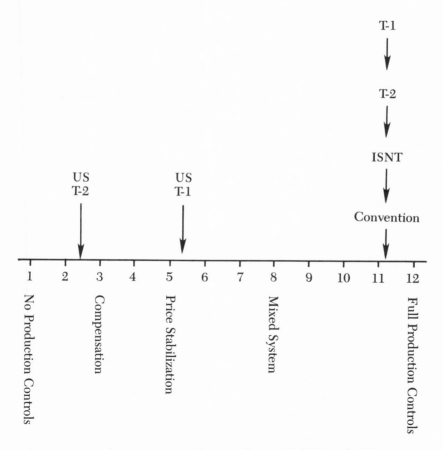

Figure 6.4 Production Controls, Articles 150(e)(g) and 151

From the beginning, there was no question of what the majority wanted. During the first period (T-1) when, on many other issues, most states were feeling their way (as shown by the high standard deviations on group positions) they were certain on production controls. Not only was the median at rank 12, but the Group of 77 as a whole was also at rank 12. All of the constituent subgroups (Latin America, Africa, and Asia) were at approximately rank 12, and only Asia had a standard deviation of more than 1.0 (1.4). There was no change in the pattern at T-2. As in T-1 the United States, the European Economic Community, and other groups representing the developed countries opposed the imposition of production controls on the nascent ocean mining industry. Indeed, U.S. opposition to production controls seems to have grown. Our data show a U.S. retreat from price stabilization schemes at ranks 5–6 in T-1 to support for compensation-only schemes shown at rank 2.4 in T-2. This finding was a good tip-off to the actual position the United States took after it reviewed its continued participation in the negotiations. But the stability of the developing states' position was also a signal that they did not consider this item renegotiable. Despite the fact that the U.S. should have had little real hope for success, when it published its "Green Book" of preferred revisions of the draft treaty, its redraft of Article 151 allowed only for adjustment assistance or compensation during a fifteen-year period.[50] As figure 6.4 shows the informal negotiating text and the treaty showed production control measures written into the documents. However, the formula for calculating the allowed levels of production did change over time. The composite negotiating text specifies that production for the first seven years should not exceed the "projected cumulative growth . . . of the world nickel demand." Thereafter, output should not exceed 60 percent of cumulative growth. The rate of increase is to be calculated for a twenty-year period by the least-squares method.[51] The treaty provides for production controls to be enforced during a twenty-five year interim period. They are to be based upon the sum of the trend line values for annual nickel consumption and 60 percent of the difference between the trend line values for nickel consumption. The rate is to be calculated by the linear regression of the logarithms of actual nickel consumption.[52] Perhaps there is a significant difference between the two texts, but it is one only an econometrician could appreciate. A valiant effort was made to find a technical fix. If found, that technical fix might have involved a marginal improvement sufficient to mask the lack of agreement on a conceptual framework. In any case critics of the U.S. position claim that the quota is so generous that it would not inhibit the pioneer producers, therefore making an objectionable framework meaningless, at least for the first generation of miners.[53] Moreover, given what the developing countries may have learned about the "real" world of ocean mining, perhaps the framework itself will melt away over time. Obviously, the United States and other mineral producers were not willing to take the risk that Third World perceptions would change favorably toward their interests. They wanted immediate guarantees of access under significantly better conditions.[54] But the majority forming the near consensus saw no reason to make any changes other than technical ones.

As we have seen by the manner in which the major issues were assembled into a package, it was assumed through much of the long, arduous negotiations that the outcome should provide a balance of benefits to all of the major parties. Only if all major states and groups were satisfied would the resulting treaty be widely adopted and ratified, the stated goal of negotiators willing to operate under a consensus or near consensus rule. Concessions were sought on that basis. By 1974 the basic outline of a treaty had emerged. At Caracas the developed states—East as well as West—openly traded off coastal control over living and nonliving resources (in the guise of a 200-mile exclusive economic zone) and the acceptance of a modified rather than a classic archipelago concept[55] for a formal ratification and perhaps strengthening of transit rights through straits and archipelagic waters and acceptance of a 12-nautical-mile territorial sea. Once the basic shift had taken place, many developed coastal states moved to the coastal camp with a vengeance. They soon became supporters of the claims of coastal states with extensive seabeds to a right to control out to at least 350 nautical miles, 60 miles beyond the foot of the slope or 100 nautical miles beyond 2,500 meters' depth of water (Article 76 of the UNCLOS III Convention). A number of developing states also claimed that the developed states should have been forced to throw in support for an NIEO-influenced deep seabed regime in return for navigation rights. This became the major sticking point in reaching agreement and is the basis for the current argument as to whether nonsignatories are eligible for treaty benefits, such as establishment of 200-mile exclusive economic zones (EEZs) or a right of transit passage through straits used for international navigation, as long as they remain outside the treaty.[56]

The lineup of states supporting the emerging package was remarkably robust over time. Based on data gathered in T-2 (1974–75), we ran many iterations of our packaging model. The model compares one set of packages of preferred outcomes (we used seventeen) with another set of packages of preferred outcomes. What forced states to "make a choice" in the model was not only how close a state's preferences are to one of the two packages posited in the model, but how salient each of the issues in each package is to each deciding state.

In most of the runs that reflected known real packages or that were incremental modifications of real packages, the lineups consistently were in the range of 115–120 states on one side and 20–34 states on the other. (We had 149 states participating by 1975; more joined later.) The vote taken in 1982—seven years after the last data were gathered—was quite similar, showing a winning majority of 130 for, 4 against, and 17 abstaining. The opposition and abstention votes were recorded by the same states that the model showed clustered together—the United States, the Soviet Union, and the other industrial states of the communist bloc and European Economic Community, with the other negative voters, Israel and Turkey, folded or clustered nearby.

The problem during the last seven years of the UNCLOS III negotiations was obviously to satisfy the last remaining twenty to thirty-five states that their essential interests would be taken care of in the treaty. If we were to plot the preferred positions of states on most issues within the overall package, we would see that on most issues there would be a single peaked distribution with a tail. The tail, of course, would be composed of the twenty to thirty-five mostly developed states that were disturbed by the NIEO features of the draft treaty. There was never any possibility that those twenty to thirty-five objectors could have reversed the trends established throughout the history of the negotiations. The developed nations could only hold out as stubbornly as possible in the hope that the majority wanted a consensus treaty badly enough to modify some important features of the widely preferred package. This is essentially what went on in the bargaining efforts during much of the long period of perfecting and polishing the negotiating texts into a draft treaty.

To achieve further redistribution of benefits would have required acquiescence to the U.S. effort to coerce the majority with a threat of noncooperation. Clearly, when it withdrew from the negotiations

in 1981, the United States signaled that it demanded very fundamental concessions from the majority. The only way to achieve such
concessions was by a gesture as dramatic as the one attempted. In
other words the United States made it clear that it was not interested
in incremental improvements. If the United States wanted to achieve
a moral victory—a justification of its unswerving loyalty to capitalist
principles—it succeeded. If what it really hoped to do was achieve
a tactical victory by forcing the majority to make fundamental
changes in the treaty, its effort was a miserable failure.

Did the UNCLOS Treaty Allocate Values?

In the most formal sense UNCLOS III was a success. After fifteen
years of total work and nine years of official conference deliberations, a long, complex treaty was produced. It spanned a broad range
of ocean use problems and promulgated a number of policy measures that will have a fundamental impact on the way in which the
oceans will be used and managed for a number of generations to
come. Thus the treaty (or perhaps the outcome measured by the
issues on which there was broad agreement) also may be judged a
success in terms of the degree to which it transformed the previous
status quo.

Ocean management after UNCLOS III is already very different than
it was before the convocation of the conference. The most notable
change was the broad acceptance of the trend toward expanded national jurisdiction—or enclosure, if you will. Most coastal states are
already enforcing their versions of a 200-mile zone. Many are already
exercising much tighter control of fishing, minerals exploitation,
science, and pollution activities. The right to make these management decisions in the 200-mile zone is now less frequently challenged by states whose citizens have been affected adversely. Perhaps there will be a broad acceptance of a uniform territorial sea
of 12 miles and straits states will accept the right of transit passage,
thereby reducing the number of ocean issues that might threaten
peace. In any case, on a broad range of issues covered by UNCLOS
III, there will be no going back.

The answer to the question of whether the treaty will alter the
way in which the states of the world attempt to gain access to and
manage the process of exploiting deep ocean mineral resources must
await the outcome of the ratification processes. Japan and France
were the only major industrial countries to vote for the treaty draft,

and France was the only non-Eastern-bloc developed state to adhere to the treaty when it was first opened to signature in December 1982. The interesting question will be whether the industrial North, other than the United States (at least during the Reagan administration), will ultimately accept in extended signature and ratification stages the imposition of a management system they deemed unacceptable.

It should be obvious that the delegates to UNCLOS III did successfully allocate some values. Moreover, the process appeared to be very Eastonian, and indeed more majoritarian than in the earlier two UN Law of the Sea Conferences of 1958 and 1960.[57] The Convention that was produced was signed by most states, and I believe that it will one day come into force. But regardless of whether it comes into force, the delegates at UNCLOS III did create a legal regime for the oceans. It is an imperfect regime, and some of the participants probably did successfully "nullify" the application of some of the provisions to themselves. Nevertheless, most of the regime is being applied, and indeed defended, by the officials of the very U.S. administration that refused to sign the treaty. Oran Young reminds us that compliance does not have to be perfect for a regime to survive or prosper as social convention.[58] But was UNCLOS III an example of an increasingly more centralized system in which more values are allocated, and that may eventually, because of success on oceans and other issues, become the classic Eastonian government, capable of allocating most public values and having a monopoly on the legitimate use of force? Those claiming so can point to the fact that a treaty emerged after fifteen years of hard bargaining.

Opponents of the view that UNCLOS III has moved us closer to a hierarchical order can point to the self-help argument. That is, states at UNCLOS III agreed to enforce what the largest and most important states wanted in their self-interest. It seems to me that this argument is particularly cogent if we examine *what* values were allocated.

The UNCLOS III Convention lays out a "mixed" system. It has elements of traditional Grotian values in the open ocean sections, national enclosure in near-shore waters, and a form of NIEO-influenced central enclosure on deep seabed minerals. Nevertheless, despite the noisy circus it became, UNCLOS III produced a much more traditional document than first estimated by most observers. It is my contention that the developed states did very well in terms of allocating their values at UNCLOS III. They helped themselves. The parts of the new regime that will probably prove to be enforce-

able will reflect the interests of the developed states. They probably
will be successful in nullifying the values of the developing states
on the deep seabed issue.

Let us look in more detail at the three sets of major themes that
ran through the conference. The first theme is a reaffirmation of
movement rights in straits, archipelagoes, economic zones, and territorial seas. Although each of the specific rights to move freely has
been altered—expanded in a few cases and slightly restricted in
others—nevertheless there has been no substantial alteration of the
rights of major blue water naval and merchant marine states to move
at will. The threat of the developing states to substitute a non-Gro-
tian approach in developing new ocean use proved to be hollow.
The world community shared an interest in the preservation of traditional movement rights of the law of the sea. As a result the threat
to these rights at UNCLOS was tactical in nature. Because of the sensitivity of the superpowers on this theme, it was a useful ploy to
seem to threaten these movements in order to get the superpowers
to the bargaining arena. But virtually all of the participants understood that this issue was not really negotiable, because the major
ocean users would never have agreed to severe restrictions, and that
while no one before U.S. Secretary of the Navy John Lehman had
threatened to shoot his way through the straits, the capability to do
so was available and therefore the implied threat was credible.[59]

The second theme that is embodied in the treaty is a reaffirmation
of the trend toward the enclosure of ocean space. In the twentieth
century it has become obvious that underlying assumptions of the
freedom of the seas are no longer valid as they relate to ocean resources. We can overutilize the resources and we can damage the
ecosystem. We might have enclosed the oceans centrally (turned
over allocation and management of ocean resources to an international agency in all areas of the ocean beyond a narrow band of
national jurisdiction), as Pardo suggested in his original formulation
of the Common Heritage of Mankind, but that was never probable.
Coastal states had the advantage of possessing government structures that could easily extend their jurisdictional reach. Moreover,
it is the coastal states that have had to face the problems brought
by heavier patterns of near-shore use. UNCLOS III consolidates the
hold of the members of our decentralized world political system.
Both those I have called elsewhere the functional and normative
nationalists should be pleased.[60] While the Latin American "terri-
torialists" and "patrimonialists" will also be pleased, the big winners

will be the major developed coastal states, which not only acquired millions of square miles of "territory" with a stroke of the pen but which also have the technology to exploit the oil, gas, mineral, and seafood resources they have theoretically acquired.

The final theme that runs through the UNCLOS III draft treaty is the need for international equity. To achieve this developing states insisted that the framework and rules for deep seabed minerals exploitation be based upon a NIEO framework. On this issue the developing states stood firm, and since they controlled the process they could dominate the formal outcome. I believe that the negotiations over the fate of manganese nodules on the sea floor had more to do with whether the developed states could be persuaded or coerced into accepting a different approach to North-South economic relations than they did with whether the new seabed mining industry needed to be managed. At the end the developing states compromised—significantly, I believe. They modified some of the rules, but retained the NIEO framework. Nevertheless, although the developing states dominated the process, in my opinion they failed. Although it is often important to them to repeat the themes associated with the NIEO—and that alone may keep the pot boiling for a while—they are not likely to succeed in extending authority to a new international agency that will succeed in making authoritative decisions on seabed resources. There are too many avoidance mechanisms available to industrialized countries.

In sum UNCLOS III was Eastonian in process. Values were allocated, but the new regime of the oceans did not (1) make any fundamental alteration in the world political system, (2) sharply curtail developed state superiority in ocean use through curtailed access to valuable ocean areas, or (3) force the developed states to acquiesce in a new conceptual framework on the ocean or the world ocean order. The future is likely to be like the past.

Did the Third United Nations Conference on the Law of the Sea provide an authoritative precedent for the future use of parliamentary diplomacy as a mechanism for authoritatively allocating values? Overall, more states had reasons to be satisfied with the results than might have first appeared in the crisis atmosphere of the conference's termination. Nevertheless, what was accomplished was accomplished at a considerable cost in time and effort. It seems to me that many states—especially the developed ones—will be extremely reluctant to get involved in another large-scale multilateral conference in the foreseeable future. But if universal consent, or at least the acquiescence of most of the world community, is needed for the effective functioning of a regime, there are few alternatives to a universal conference in which all of the pressures push in the intermediate zone toward centralized majority decisions.

Notes

In preparation of this chapter I borrowed some materials I used in "The Third United Nations Law of the Sea Conference: North-South Bargaining on Ocean Issues," in *Positive Sum: Improving North-South Negotiations*, ed. I. William Zartman (New Brunswick, N.J.: Transaction Books, 1987).

1. Robert L. Friedheim and Robert E. Bowen, "Neglected Issues at the Third United Nations Law of the Sea Conference," in *Law of the Sea: Neglected Issues*, ed. J.K. Gamble (Honolulu: Law of the Sea Institute, 1979), 2–39.

2. David Easton, *The Political System: An Inquiry* (New York: Knopf, 1953), 125–41.

3. Kenneth N. Waltz, *Theory of International Politics* (Reading, Mass.: Addison-Wesley, 1979), 88–93.

4. John Gerard Ruggie, "Continuity and Transformation in the World Polity: Toward a Neorealist Synthesis," in *Neorealism and Its Critics*, ed. Robert O. Keohane (New York: Columbia University Press, 1986), 139.

5. This is similar to a point made by Stephen D. Krasner. Krasner claims that "Plan B" of the Third World is "to enhance their influence in international organizations that can alter the economic regime." "North-South Economic Relations: The Quest for Economic Well-Being and Political Autonomy," in *Eagle Entangled: U.S. Foreign Policy in a Complex World*, ed. K.A. Oye, D. Rothchild, and R.J. Lieber (New York, London: Longman, 1979), 124.

6. Easton, *The Political System*, 220–23.

7. Friedrich Kratochwil, "The Force of Prescriptions," *International Organization* 38, 4 (Autumn 1984): 691–97.

8. This was particularly true of U.S. delegates. For an explanation of this phenomenon see Daniel Boorstin, "How Belief in the Existence of an American Theory Has Made Theory Superfluous," *The Genius of American Politics*, chapter 1 (Chicago: University of Chicago Press, 1953).

9. Robert L. Friedheim and Mary E. Jehn, "The Soviet Position at the Third U.N. Law of the Sea Conference," *Soviet Naval Policy: Objectives and Constraints*, ed. M. McGwire, K. Booth, and J. McDonnell (New York: Praeger, 1975), 341–62. For an interesting evaluation of U.S.-USSR collaboration at UNCLOS III that shows how cooperation collapsed, see Bernard H. Oxman, *From Cooperation to Conflict: The Soviet Union and the United States at the Third U.N. Conference on the Law of the Sea* (Seattle: Washington Sea Grant, 1984).

10. Robert L. Friedheim, *Understanding the Debate on Ocean Resources*, Monograph Series on World Affairs, 6,3 (Denver, Colo.: University of Denver, 1968–69).

11. Myres S. McDougal & William T. Burke, *The Public Order of the Oceans* (New Haven, Conn.: Yale University Press, 1962).

12. For a description of the "patrimonialist" group see Anne L. Hollick, *U.S. Foreign Policy and the Law of the Sea* (Princeton, N.J.: Princeton University Press, 1981), 252–53.

13. Oran R. Young, "Regime Dynamics: The Rise and Fall of International Regimes," *International Organization*, 36, 2 (Spring 1982): 290.

14. Young, "Regime Dynamics," 283.

15. Robert Axelrod, *The Evolution of Cooperation* (New York: Basic Books, 1984), 173–74.

16. I. William Zartman, "Negotiations: Theory and Reality," *Journal of International Affairs* 9, 1 (1975): 71.

17. I. William Zartman, *The 50% Solution* (Garden City, N.Y.: Doubleday, 1976), 9.

18. Oran R. Young, *Bargaining: Formal Theories of Negotiation* (Urbana, Ill.: University of Illinois Press, 1975), 13.

19. Kratochwil, "The Force of Prescriptions," 696, indicated that there were only two options for surmounting the difficulties of large-scale multilateral negotiations: (1) reduction of the number of participants, and (2) reduction in the set of available alternatives. UNCLOS III demonstrated a third: muddling through an extensive agenda by a large number of participants over a prolonged period of time. On muddling through see Francis W. Hoole, "Muddling-Through, Modeling-Through, Comprehensive-Integrating and Unitary-Rational-Actor Policy-Making Processes," in *Making Ocean Policy*, ed. F.W. Hoole, R.L. Friedheim, and T.M. Hennessey (Boulder, Colo.: Westview Press, 1981) 145–61.

20. Philip Jessup, "Parliamentary Diplomacy," *Recueil des Cours* 89 (1956): 181–320; "International Negotiations under Parliamentary Procedure," Lectures on International Law and the United Nations (Ann Arbor, Mich.: University of Michigan Law School, 1957); Dean Rusk, "Parliamentary Diplomacy—Debate vs. Negotiation," *World Affairs Interpreter* 26 (Summer 1955): 101–12.

21. For example Midgaard and Underdahl cite more from the coalition literature than from works on parliamentary diplomacy. Knut Midgaard and Arild Underdahl, "Multiparty Conferences," *Negotiation: Social-Psychological Perspectives*, ed. D. Druckman (Beverley Hills, Calif.: Sage, 1977), 334.

22. Leigh S. Ratiner, "The Law of the Sea: A Crossroads for American Foreign Policy," *Foreign Affairs* 70, 5 (Summer 1982): 1006–21; and S. Jayakumar and T.T. Koh, "The Negotiating Process of the Third United Nations Law of the Sea Conference," unpublished, first preliminary draft, March 1980.

23. This phenomenon has been characterized by Gidon Gottlieb as "parity diplomacy." "Global Bargaining: The Legal and Diplomatic Framework," in *Law-Making in the Global Community*, ed. Nicholas G. Onuf (Durham, N.C.: Carolina Academic Press, 1982), 109–10.

24. Joseph B. Kadane, "Analysis of Voting Rule Possibilities of Law of the Sea," Memorandum 9013-74, Center for Naval Analyses, June 18, 1974.

25. Kenneth J. Arrow, *Social Choice and Individual Values*, 2nd ed. (New Haven, Conn.: Yale University Press, 1963), 203; and Robert Abrams, *Foundations of Political Analysis: An Introduction to the Theory of Collective Choice* (New York: Columbia University Press, 1980), 28–39.

26. The term is that of Jayakumar and Koh.

27. See Jayakumar and Koh, "The Negotiating Process"; Edward Miles, "The Structure and Effects of the Decision Process in the Seabed Committee and the Third United Nations Conference on the Law of the Sea," *International Organization* 31, 2 (Spring 1977): 159–234; and Barry Buzan, "Informal Negotiating Groups and UNCLOS III," *Marine Policy* 4, 3 (July 1980): 183–204.

28. For a review of coalition theory see Robert Abrams, "Foundations of Political Analysis," and Eric C. Browne, "Coalition Theories: A Logical and Empirical Critique," *Sage Professional Papers* 4, (1973).

29. Robert Axelrod, *Conflict of Interest* (Chicago: Markham, 1970), 168–87; Abram De Swaan, *Coalition Theories and Cabinet Formation* (San Francisco: Jossey-Bass, 1970).

30. See, in particular: Robert L. Friedheim and William Durch, "The International Seabed Resources Agency Negotiations and the New International Economic Order," *International Organization* 31, 2 (Spring 1977): 343–84.

31. Peter Willetts, *The Non-Aligned Movement* (New York: Nichols, 1978), 22–29; and Richard L. Jackson *The Non-Aligned, the UN and the Superpowers* (New York: Praeger, 1983), 236, cited in chapter 1.

32. Jayakumar and Koh "The Negotiating Process," 52.

33. Robert L. Friedheim, "The 'Satisfied' and 'Dissatisfied' States Negotiate International Law; A Case Study," *World Politics* 18 (October 1965): 20–41.

34. For the 200-mile zone proclamation and its interpretation, see: "Exclusive Economic Zone of the United States of America: A Proclamation by the President of the United States of America," *Fact Sheet: United States Ocean Policy*, Office of the Press Secretary, The White House, Washington, D.C., March 10, 1983.

35. For an attempt to show general stages of negotiations that are compatible with this case, see: I. William Zartman and Maureen R. Berman, *The Practical Negotiator* (New Haven, Conn.: Yale University Press, 1982), ch. 3–5.

36. Elliot Richardson has written a number of articles indicating how close he thought agreement had come under his leadership. See, for example, "Sea Bed Mining and the Law of the Sea," *Department of State Bulletin*, 80, 60–64.

37. Zartman, "Negotiations," 71.

38. Miles, "The Structure and Effects," 211.

39. Jayakumar and Koh, "The Negotiating Process," 103.

40. To keep the discussion manageable, only the first of these, the Integrated Single Negotiating Text (ISNT), will be discussed.

41. I. William Zartman points out that a substantial school of bargaining analysts have concentrated on the incremental aspect of negotiation, including John Cross, Otomar Bartos, Frederik Zeuthen, John Nash, Glenn Snyder, and Paul Diesing. I. William Zartman, "Explaining North-South Negotiations: Approaches and Questions," March 17, 1982, unpublished. See also *Positive Sum: Improving North-South Negotiations*, ed. I. William Zartman (New Brunswick, N.J.: Transaction Books, 1987), 7–8.

42. Friedheim and Durch, "The International Seabed Resource Agency," 343–84.

43. Robert L. Friedheim and Joseph B. Kadane, "Ocean Science in the UN Political Arena," *Journal of Maritime Law and Commerce* 3, 3 (April 1972): 473–502.

44. Axelrod, *Conflict of Interest*, 160–63.

45. The major exception was Canada, a state that is rich and coastal and did not act cross-pressured; rather, it was an ardent proponent of the expansion of national jurisdiction. Canada's overlapping cleavage was that it is rich but had no distant water interests.

46. For an exposition of the forecasting methods developed in the LOS Project, see Robert L. Friedheim, Karen G. Goudreau, and William J. Durch, *Forecasting Outcomes of Multilateral Negotiations: Methodology, Techniques, and Models*, CRC

291, vol. I, Center for Naval Analyses, January 1977; Karen G. Goudreau, William J. Durch, *Forecasting Outcomes of Multilateral Negotiations: Methodology and Code Book*, CRC 291, vol. II, Center for Naval Analyses, January 1977; Karen G. Goudreau, *Forecasting Outcomes of Multilateral Negotiations: Computer Programs, Guide for Users*, CRC 290, vol. I, Center for Naval Analyses, January 1977; Karen G. Goudreau, *Forecasting Outcomes of Multilateral Negotiations: Computer Programs, Guide for Programmers*, CRC 290, vol. II, Center for Naval Analyses, January 1977.

47. Since the project was commissioned by the U.S. government the initial scaling was done by project members and refined by members of the U.S. delegation to UNCLOS III. An interval scale was chosen to meet their needs. After some experimentation members of the project determined that an interval scale provided approximately the same level of precision in forecasts as an ordinal scale. This matter is explicated in the publications listed in note 46.

48. The opening positions and the medians displayed were derived from the data of the forecasting project. The placement of the ISNT and the Convention on the scale are the personal estimates of the author.

49. Warren S. Wooster, "Ocean Research under Foreign Jurisdiction," *Science* 212 (May 1981): 754–55; David A. Ross and John A. Knauss, "How the Law of the Sea Treaty Will Affect U.S. Marine Science," *Science* 217 (September 1982): 1003–08.

50. The U.S. Proposals for Amendment to the Draft Convention of the Law of the Sea (The Green Book).

51. Article 150, 1 (g)B(i), Composite Single Negotiating Text (A/CONF. 62/WP. 10/Corr. 1), 15 July 1977.

52. Article 151, 2(b)(i)(ii)(iii), Draft Convention on the Law of the Sea (A/CONF. 62/L. 78), August 1981.

53. Richardson, "Seabed Mining," 62; Ronald S. Katz, "Are There Workable Principles for Managing the Resources of the Deep Seabed?" Ocean Studies Symposium, Asilomar Conference Center, November 1982; Jennifer S. Whittaker, "Outside the Mainstream," *Atlantic* (October 1982): 22.

54. F.G. Adams claimed, based upon a model of future seabed mining efforts, that seabed mining would convert producer net benefit into consumer net benefit. For developed market economies that are both producers and consumers, the net transfer is positive. But for developing producer countries the transfer would result in a loss of $1½ billion per year. Cited in Per Magnus Wijkman, "UNCLOS and the Redistribution of Ocean Wealth," *Journal of World Trade Law* 16, 1 (January–February 1982): 40.

55. The traditional archipelago concept long supported by Indonesia and the Philippines would allow the drawing of a line around the outermost point of the outermost islands. The territorial sea would use that line as its baseline and all would become internal waters. The modified archipelago concept that was drafted by the UNCLOS III delegates gives the archipelagic state all economic rights within a line drawn around the island group and some other attributes of sovereignty, but also gives ships a right of transit through the sealanes of archipelagic waters.

56. Hugo Caminos and Michael Molitor, "Progressive Development of International Law and the Package Deal," *American Journal of International Law* 79, 4 (October 1985): 871–90.

57. Friedheim, "The 'Satisfied' and 'Dissatisfied,' " 20–41.

58. Oran Young, "Regime dynamics," 278.

59. Mary McGrory, "Sailing the Sea Treaty Shoals without the Lighthouse of Facts," *Washington Post* (July 22, 1982): John Lehman, "Letter to the Editor," *Washington Post* (July 30, 1982).

60. Friedheim, "Understanding the Debate," 2–27.

7

The United Nations and Ecosystem Issues:

Institutionalizing the Global Interest

Donald J. Puchala

●

In a remarkably candid interview with a group of Western intellectuals in December 1986, Soviet leader Mikhail Gorbachev acknowledged that there are "human needs *above* the tasks of the proletariat." "Translated out of Leninese," interviewers Heidi and Alvin Toffler told readers, "this means that certain global crises— environmental problems, for example—cannot simply be solved by exhorting workers to overthrow capitalism or its vestiges." Even in Gorbachev's thinking, there were issues of global concern that transcended the communist preoccupation with the class struggle— problems that would not be resolved if socialism triumphed over capitalism, or that would not disappear no matter which superpower emerged ascendant from the Cold War struggle. For the Tofflers there was "a bombshell buried in this idea."[1]

Perhaps there was some moment in the fact that in 1986 a superpower leader could harbor and articulate a modicum of globalist vision, because, generally speaking, the 1980s have not been years of imaginative world leadership emanating from Moscow and Washington. Although it has not been much heralded in the superpower capitals, the globalist vision, or what this chapter later calls the "global problematique," was not new in the 1980s. Scientists have long recognized that there are a number of ominous, interconnected problems affecting the relationship between the earth's resources and the human condition. These experts' proddings in the 1960s, some subsequent bold strokes at international leadership (mostly on the part of smaller countries), and some blatant real world examples of the true delicacy of man-planet balances all propelled ecosystem issues into the diplomacy of the 1970s. During this decade concerns with the human ecology significantly influenced the agenda of the United Nations and the content of its policies.

At age forty the UN was deeply involved in problems of the global ecosystem. How ecosystem problems got onto the UN agenda, how and how well they were handled once they were there, how and how appropriately the UN has been institutionally modified to deal with its new ecosystem concerns, and how the international community has been affected by the UN's ecosystem dealings are all taken up here. The thesis of this chapter is that there was a discernible cluster of happenings and conditions that together contributed to some rather remarkable international organizational growth between 1969 and 1981. Many of the factors that contributed to general international organizational dynamism at that time directly affected United Nations involvement in, decisionmaking about, and impacts on ecosystem problems. Examining the UN, its ecosystem dealings, and the political-economic contexts of the 1970s therefore yields insights into how, when, and why international organizations grow.

As noted, *ecosystem* issues concern the planetary balance between human life and the natural environment that sustains it. In the research that underlies this analysis, ecosystem issues were operationally defined to include problems of rapid population growth, food scarcity, and matters concerning the quality of the human environment, such as air and water pollution, deforestation, and desertification, as well as the impacts of perverse settlement patterns. Admittedly, these matters of population, food, and the environment, although very broad in their substance and implications, do not exhaust the inventory of interrelated elements that influence the biosphere's balance. Nor do they cover the full range of UN concerns with the ecosystem. Questions of energy and the oceans, for example, are obviously left out of this analysis, and a more elaborate treatment of ecosystem concerns would surely have to take these additional issue areas into account. Still, in terms of their variety, development through time, politics, and implications, the issues analyzed here are reasonably representative of the UN's ecosystem activities.

Analytically, it is very difficult to discuss ecosystem issues and their treatment in the United Nations without introducing the somewhat unconventional notion that the UN is an international decisionmaking institution that formulates and attempts to implement *policies*. Such policies are the products of decisions taken by the UN's deliberative organs, either by vote or acclaimed consensus. Policies can be variously thought of as defining either the goals and action preferences of the organization, the convergent wills of its member governments, or the interests of the "international community" that is increasingly referred to in UN documents.[2] Marvin Soroos calls such policies "global policies," and says that they are "the products of the international community as a whole." Most global policies, Soroos indicates, "are set forth in treaties or resolutions, which are adopted either in the regular meetings of the central organs of the United Nations, in the affiliated specialized agencies, or in ad hoc conferences convened to focus world attention on a particular problem of widespread concern."[3]

This chapter adopts Soroos's convention of calling UN policies global policies. Whether the policies represent the interests of an international community or even whether there is such an entity are not directly relevant to this analysis. What is important is that by the resolutions they adopted during the 1970s United Nations members decided that the world organization should become more deeply involved in problems of population, food, and the environment and that it should deal with these problems in collectively agreed and prescribed ways.

Increasing UN Involvement in Ecosystem Issues

In 1979 Secretary-General Javier Pérez de Cuéllar devoted his foreword to the *United Nations Yearbook* to reflecting on the passing decade. The 1970s were a "turbulent decade," the Secretary-General wrote, but "while dealing with the world's acute crises, the Organization also found time for novel and far-reaching initiatives . . . to deal with such basic human concerns as . . . environment, food (and) water."[4] In light of what happened during the 1970s Pérez de Cuéllar was undoubtedly right. Compared to the UN's very modest efforts in the areas of food and population between 1946 and 1969, and in light of the fact that for practical purposes prior to the late 1960s the UN was not involved in environment questions at all, the rapidity and depth of UN movement into ecosystem problems in the 1970s were rather remarkable. United Nations expansion in the ecosystem area was multifaceted. Attention to and emphasis on man-resource balances heightened throughout the UN system, and particularly within the policymaking nexus that links the General Assembly, the Economic and Social Council (ECOSOC), the specialized agencies, the regional economic commissions, the Secretary-General, and the Secretariat's departments.

Increasing organizational attention to ecosystem matters is easily documented in a variety of ways. For one thing, the intensifying ecosystem interests of UN deliberative bodies heightened their needs for information and thus prompted requests for a proliferating series of reports from the Secretariat via the Secretary-General, the executive heads of the specialized agencies, the regional commissions, and special consultative groups.[5] In addition ECOSOC and General Assembly resolutions addressed to ecosystem issues greatly increased in number during the 1970s. Many of these were prompted by preparations for and follow-ups after the several world conferences on the environment (1972), food (1974), population (1974), human settlements (1976), desertification (1977), water (1977), agrarian reform and rural development (1979), and new and renewable sources of energy (1981). The conferences themselves obviously also indicated the UN's shifting emphasis and attention; they consumed vast amounts of staff time, comparably substantial amounts of national delegates' time, and sizable amounts of money as well.[6] Increased attention to ecosystem matters was also in evidence in major UN planning documents. Whereas the *International Development Strategy for the First United Nations Development Decade* (1950–60) contained only twenty-four words about ecosystem issues, the strategy for the Third Development Decade (1970–80) alloted more than three thousand words, or nearly a fifth of its total content, to these matters.

Even more revealing of the expansion of ecosystem concerns within the United Nations in the 1970s were substantive changes in the definitions of issues and in the scope of UN deliberations. In the area of population, for example, the UN's perennial and increasingly routine discussions about ways to improve the gathering of demographic statistics were supplanted, quite dramatically, in the late 1960s by intense debates about rapid population growth and fertility control.[7] These opened the way to the organization's active participation in family management programs around the world.[8] Similarly, in the food area, the UN's traditional preoccupations with agricultural trade and multilateral aid and its early cursory attention to the world's perceived "protein gap" expanded in the early 1970s into concerns about world hunger as a crisis phenomenon, mechanisms for assuring world food security, provisions for vulnerable groups, emphasis on rural modernization in developing countries, more equitable distribution of food nationally and internationally, and wider and more efficient and effective dissemination of the results of agricultural research.[9] In the environment field the United Nations started virtually from scratch in the late 1960s and discovered more or less willy-nilly that approaching problems of the biosphere impelled international organizational involvement in questions of pollution, desertification, deforestation, the climate, water and soil resources, minerals, the oceans, and human settlements. By the middle of the 1970s the UN was in fact involved in all of these questions, as well as in the interrelationships among them. Problems of the natural environment, which failed to generate even one agenda item for General Assembly consideration in 1967, were generating dozens by 1975.

The 1970s, stretching the chronology a bit at beginning and end, were also years of enthusiastic UN institution building and policymaking in ecosystem areas. These two sets of developments went hand in hand. UN policymaking in ecosystem issue areas focused primarily on the creation of international regimes—that is, on the articulation of principles, norms, rules, and decisionmaking procedures to guide international and national action.[10] The regimes, once adopted, frequently required new institutions for implementation and monitoring. In turn the institutions required the legitimation and policy guidance contained in the regimes. Tenets of the various ecosystem regimes are embodied in the declarations and plans of action produced by the different UN world conferences as well as in documents like the *Declaration and Programme of Action on the Establishment of a New International Economic Order*, and the *International Development Strategy for the Third United Nations Development Decade* that resulted from key debates and planning experiences.[11] Notably, all of the declarations and action plans were endorsed by the ECOSOC and the General Assembly and solemnized in resolutions that were usually adopted without voting. They all rallied large majority support, and recorded national objections usually represented disagreements with specific items rather than opposition to general principles or programmatic thrusts.[12] By these acts it became the policy of the United Nations to promote internationally, concertedly, and with vigor a managed and balanced human ecosystem. The United Nations manifestly rejected a "no growth" strategy for dealing with increasing strains on the earth's resources, and while not endorsing it explicitly, it appears to have opted instead for an overall policy favoring "organic growth."[13] This welcomes continuing growth as long as it is globally orchestrated to contain entropic forces.

With regard to population matters it became UN policy to stem the overly rapid growth of the world's population by assisting in the employment of whatever means peoples deem practical and morally appropriate, including modern methods of contraception.[14] Similarly, the food policy of the UN affirms that the quantity and quality of the world's food supplies must be enhanced, that much of this enhancement must follow from agrarian reform and rural development in Third World countries, that foodstuffs must be more equitably distributed both between and within countries, that markets alone cannot facilitate this distribution, that world food security is a responsibility of the entire international community, and that problems of food scarcity and rapid population growth are directly interrelated and must be treated as such.[15] In the realm of environmental policy the main tenets of the UN-endorsed regime hold that the resources of the earth must be safeguarded for both present and future generations, that the capacity of the earth to produce renewable resources must be equally safeguarded, that the discharge of toxic substances into the environment must be contained, that the perversities of unplanned urbanization must be combatted, that the results of mass poverty endanger the human environment as much as the results of wasteful affluence, and that problems of the environment, population, food, and resources are interconnected and must be treated as such.[16] Where time horizons have been written into United Nations ecosystem policies, 2000 is the usual year of denouement.

Together the action plans in the ecosystem issue areas that were negotiated by UN member states during the 1970s set down and affirm a number of broad theses that most governments acknowledged during the different world conferences and in the diplomacy that surrounded the drafting and passage of numerous ECOSOC and General Assembly Resolutions. These theses affirm five points.

1. A world ecosystem image of interrelated social, economic, and demographic phenomena is accurate, and that (a) conditions in the

ecosystem have been deteriorating, (b) stemming further deterioration should be a matter of priority, (c) primary responsibility for combatting adverse ecosystem developments rests with individual countries, but (d) concerted action at the international level will also be required to meet and deal with ecosystem problems.

2. Protecting and enhancing the quality of human life should be the primary aim of international activities addressed to improving the ecosystem, and in this sense priority must be given to problems that most jeopardize human welfare and to places where living conditions are the poorest.

3. Issues of economic underdevelopment and problems of the global ecosystem are interrelated. Overly rapid population growth, malnutrition, inadequate sources of fuel and energy, and unhealthy urban and rural environments both cause and exacerbate underdevelopment. At the same time economic underdevelopment exacerbates and perpetuates its perverse environmental causes.

4. International aid should be provided to poor countries grappling with problems of food, population, environment, and energy, and it is the responsibility of the more affluent countries to provide this aid either directly or through multilateral channels.

5. International organizations, UN bodies in particular, have legitimate and important roles to play in addressing problems of the human ecosystem.

International institutionalization in ecosystem program areas also burgeoned during the 1970s. Most dramatically, almost the entire institutional framework for UN activities in the environment field was created after the Stockholm Conference on the Human Environment in 1972. It continued to grow throughout the decade. Similarly, the World Food Conference led to the creation of the World Food Council (WFC), the International Fund for Agricultural Development (IFAD), a world food reserve, a revamping of the World Food Programme, an expansion of the UN-sponsored international agricultural research network, and the creation of several other new action-oriented and coordinating bodies. The Conference on Human Settlements in 1976 led to the establishment of the Commission on Human Settlements and its Secretariat in Nairobi, the United Nations Centre for Human Settlements (HABITAT). The Conferences on Desertification and Water in 1977 and on New and Renewable Sources of Energy in 1981 led to the creation of new UN-administered development funds. Table 7.1 summarizes these major UN Institutional developments in ecosystem areas.

Table 7.1 UN Institutionalization in the Ecosystem Area

Population

1965 ECOSOC endorses expanded program of action in population area; Secretary-General establishes Trust Fund for voluntary contributions to UN population programs.

1969 United Nations Fund for Population Activities (UNFPA) becomes an organ of General Assembly managed by Administrator of the United Nations Development Programme.

1970 Scope of UNFPA programs substantially broadened.

1973 Network of Demographic Training Institutes expanded.

Food

1974 World Food Council

1974 Global Agricultural Information and Early Warning System

1974 Intergovernmental Committee on World Food Programme receives expanded mandate and becomes Committee on Food Aid Policies and Programmes.

1974 Consultative Group on Food Production and Investment in Developing Countries

1975 International Emergency Grain Reserve

1976 International Fund for Agricultural Development

1978 International Emergency Food Reserve becomes permanent.

Environment

1972 United Nations Environmental Programme (UNEP)
Governing Council of the United Nations Environment Programme
Environment Secretariat
The Environment Fund
Environment Coordination Board
Earthwatch

1973 United Nations Sudano-Sahelian Office (UNSO)

1974 Habitat and Human Settlements Foundation

1977 Commission on Human Settlements
UN Centre for Human Settlements (HABITAT)

1977 Sudano-Sahelian Office of UNEP

1979 Trust Fund for Endangered Species

1979 Fund for Water Development

1979 Special Account for Implementation of Plan of Action on Desertification

Not only were the UN ecosystem institutions expanding in number during the 1970s, but their mandates and programs were also growing as more ambitious tasks were assigned to them by their governing boards and the General Assembly. The expansion of tasks was reflected in increasing expenditures on personnel and programs such as those shown in table 7.2. The index numbers in the table exhibit trends in the expenditures of the United Nations Fund for Population Activities (UNFPA), and United Nations Development Program (UNDP) assistance to the Food and Agriculture Organization (FAO) for the decade of 1970s, as well as the annual outlays of the United Nations Environment Programme (UNEP) Environmental Fund from its first year of operations in 1973 to the end of the decade.[17] All of the indexes in table 7.2 are adjusted for the inflation of 1970 dollars.

Table 7.2 Representative Trends in UN Expenditures on Ecosystem Programs, 1970–1980

Year	UNFPA	UNDP Allocations to FAO	UNEP Environmental Fund
1970	100	100	—[a]
1971	209	158	—[a]
1972	281	176	—[a]
1973	622	162	100
1974	765	146	114
1975	882	220	389
1976	935	192	462
1977	881	146	645
1978	1176	188	675
1979	1626	221	792
1980	1740	292	772

a. Funding began in 1973.

Index numbers represent percentage changes between base periods and index years in constant 1970 dollars.

Sources: *United Nations Yearbook* for respective years; General Assembly, *Official Records: Thirty-Seventh Session*, supplement no. 5F (A/37/5/Add. 6), 4; United Nations Fund for Population Activities, *Financial Report, 1975–1980;* United Nations, *Financial Report and Accounts, 1970–1973;* OECD *Economic Outlook* 34 (December 1983): 161.

Table 7.2 shows that UN expenditures in ecosystem areas were expanding quite rapidly during the 1970s. Allocations to population activities through the UNFPA, for example, attained levels by 1980 that were roughly seventeen times greater than in 1970. In 1980 the UNFPA disbursed nearly $142 million for programs in ninety-five countries. Table 7.2 also shows that UNDP support for FAO agricultural development projects was nearly three times in 1980 what it had been in 1970, though this index fluctuated during the decade. It should also be noted, however, that after the World Food Conference in 1974 there were major expansions in other UN food and agricultural programs, such as the World Food Programme, the International Fund for Agricultural Development, World Bank agricultural projects, and FAO activities. Maurice Williams and Thomas Stephens have calculated that total UN expenditures on agriculture increased from $1.7 billion in 1974 to $5.2 billion in 1982.[18] Likewise, UNEP funding took off between 1974 and 1975, expanded very rapidly through the mid-1970s, and leveled off near the end of the decade. By 1980 UNEP was spending about $27 million a year on its operations, or roughly seven and one-half times its real dollar outlays in 1973.

The UN and the Ecosystem:
The Dynamics of Task Expansion

To students of international organization the United Nations' programmatic expansion, its policymaking, and its regime- and institution-building experiences in the ecosystem area have to be intriguing. For one thing such instances of bold initiative and rapid international institutional growth occur only very rarely, and they usually do not happen in established, conservative, intergovernmental organizations with universal membership, normally decentralized decisionmaking, and questionable legitimacy. Yet during the 1970s member states of the United Nations allowed the organization to venture into problem areas where it had never operated, and to broaden consideration and action greatly in areas where there was some precedent. They also allowed the organization to enhance its own capacities substantially and to add new units that would preserve and protect the new prerogatives. What was equally important was that member states financed all of this organizational growth. With regard to the UNFPA, at least, there were years when contributions surpassed budgeted needs.[19]

The UN's ecosystem initiatives during the 1970s, furthermore, appear somewhat anomalous when they are set in the decade's political-ideological context. The mid-1970s were, after all, years of intense North-South conflict within and without the United Nations. For example, 1974 saw the convening of the 6th Special Session of the General Assembly, with its vitriolic debates, ideological polarizations, and thoroughly fragmenting results.[20] Prior to the 1970s analysts of the UN had concluded that East-West antagonisms rendered the world organization helpless in dealing with most political and security questions. After the 6th Special Session and the *Declaration and Action Plan on the Establishment of a New International Economic Order* many felt that the intense North-South differences would also keep the organization from dealing meaningfully with most economic and social questions. There was considerable truth in this, but, interestingly, not with regard to ecosystem issues.

Initiative and Action within the United Nations

To explain why the United Nations was able to move so impressively into ecosystem areas, it is helpful to understand exactly how this movement was accomplished. Within the UN two primary driving forces operated during the 1970s to create and sustain the momentum that moved ecosystem activities along. First, a political leadership emerged and lent dynamism to moving from new ideas to new policies. Second, much of what was accomplished by way of regime- and institution-building resulted from unusual diplomacy conducted before and during the rather spectacular series of ecosystem conferences of the 1970s. These global events were important thresholds to international organizational expansion.

Constitutionally speaking, all direction and legitimation for UN activity in social and economic affairs emanates from resolutions of the General Assembly. In this regard the tip of the iceberg of ecosystem initiative is traceable to particular activities or sequences of events that resulted in the adoption of key resolutions. General Assembly Resolution 2211(XXI), for example, opened the way to United Nations involvement in family planning; 3180(XXVIII) convened the World Food Conference; 2997(XXVII) established the United Nations Environment Programme; 3327(XXIX) created the Habitat and Human Settlements Foundation; and many more resolutions moved the UN ever deeper into ecosystem concerns. As a rule the Economic and

Social Council first considers the issues that later become the subjects of General Assembly resolutions. Sometimes, therefore, the key moves behind new UN initiatives are those taken to attract the ECO-SOC's attention or endorsement. For instance the sequence of events that led to the Stockholm Conference on the Human Environment can be traced to a Swedish initiative taken at an ECOSOC session in May 1968.[21] Similarly, ECOSOC sessions between 1971 and 1973 pointed the UN toward the Mar del Plata Water Conference, which was endorsed by the General Assembly in 1975.[22]

What is significant about the initiating resolutions in the ecosystem area is that nearly all of them were sponsored by the same group of countries, or, more accurately, the same groups of countries. Sweden, the Netherlands, and Canada were almost always among the sponsors of ECOSOC and General Assembly Resolutions that called for world conferences, new institutions, or new programs in ecosystem areas. In taking these initiatives the three countries were frequently joined by Australia and New Zealand, and always by a more-or-less sizable group of nonaligned countries that invariably included the Philippines and usually Argentina, Mexico, India, Indonesia, and Egypt. From among the socialist countries, only Yugoslavia appeared with any regularity among the sponsors of ecosystem initiatives. On funding initiatives, and particularly those launched during the later years of the decade, like the Special Account to Implement the Action Plan to Combat Desertification, the principal sponsors were usually large groups of developing countries, or sometimes simply the chairman of the Nonaligned Movement acting on behalf of the Group of 77.[23] The United States was very active and quite successful during the late 1960s and early 1970s in promoting UN involvement in population matters. Washington was also occasionally among the sponsors of other ecosystem initiatives, as when Secretary of State Kissinger called for a World Food Conference in 1974, though the United States exercised much less leadership in the latter half of the 1970s than in the earlier years. The Soviet Union was never among the initiators.

United Nations officials were also active promoters of new ecosystem programs, successive Secretaries-General most of all.[24] But the initiatives of the member states were most significant, and on the key ecosystem resolutions the leadership of the North-South coalition of small states was crucial. Though it borders on the obvious, it should be underlined that unless the member states exercise political leadership, not very much happens in the UN. Or, putting it slightly differently, for anything to happen in the UN, at least some member states must enthusiastically want it to happen, and they must be willing and able to exercise the necessary leadership to move resolutions through UN deliberative bodies. It appeared to be the case with the ecosystem initiatives that it was more important for the leaders to be politically acceptable than necessarily materially powerful. The northern European–moderate Third World combination that frequently led on ecosystem issues turned out to be very credible. Resolutions sponsored by this group invariably attracted substantial support from all caucusing groups. Such was not the case, for example, with resolutions exclusively sponsored by the Group of 77; the United States, West Germany, and other large Northern countries usually either abstained or opposed them. Besides exercising the creative imagination that placed new issues and approaches on the United Nations agenda, members of the leadership coalitions also typically supervised the preparation of texts and acted as advocates in the ECOSOC, the Second Committee, and the General Assembly. They enthusiastically lobbied and frequently brokered crucial compromises. For assembling and cementing many of the leadership coalitions, the Swedes probably deserve a lion's share of the credit.[25] The leadership groups were the political motors that propelled the UN into ecosystem areas. Their importance cannot be overestimated.

The ecosystem conferences of the 1970s also had a great deal to do with the formulation of global ecosystem policies and the creation of new UN programs. The UN-sponsored world conferences that took place in rapid succession from 1972 to 1981 were unwieldy, costly, probably overly demanding, and inefficient in their consumption of UN professional time and resources; moreover, they were often overly politicized and sometimes tyrannical and insensitive to minority views.[26] But they were dramatically effective in placing ecosystem issues before the international community. They compelled governments to face perplexing problems and to arrive at positions, and they also captured and focused high-level attention, compiled and disseminated information, and established and strengthened professional and political networks in ecosystem issue areas.[27] In addition they greatly abetted the efforts of groups that were pressing ecosystem concerns at national levels.

From conception, to authorization, to preparation, to culmination, the conferences were regime-building undertakings. They produced the declarations and plans of action that embodied and legitimated the globalistic perceptions and prescriptions that are the main tenets of the UN's ecosystem regimes. Such global policymaking might have been accomplished in less spectacular ways. Still, there was something in the style and tempo of the conference processes—the isolated settings, highly mobilized expectations, immovable deadlines, compressed duration for debate and interaction, imperatives for tangible product, premium on agreement, aura of "globalness," and publicity—that catalyzed regime-building and often raised rather than lowered common denominators in international bargaining. In creating the World Food Council, the International Fund for Agricultural Development, the emergency grain reserve, and the early warning system, for example, the 1974 World Food Conference gave the United Nations many more instruments for dealing with global food problems than any member state going into the conference could have expected. Assessing the World Food Conference, James P. Grant, President of the Oversees Development Council, said that the event "may come to be seen as comparable in significance to the Bretton Woods meeting that established the International Monetary Fund and the World Bank."[28] More modestly, Thomas G. Weiss and Robert Jordan ended an evaluative chapter in their fine study of the Food Conference by concluding that:

> This meeting accomplished well what a global, ad hoc conference can by providing a framework within which governments discuss problems and propose responses. Various governmental bureaucracies were pushed to consider issues and iron-out positions on them that such bureaucrats might prefer to postpone or ignore. The delegations at the World Food Conference have indeed sketched the basic outlines of a viable global policy for food and an institutional mechanism to oversee its implementation.[29]

The ecosystem conferences had very definite global policy consequences. Mobilized by the sense of urgency that the conferences inspired, the General Assembly quickly turned the conferees' recommendations into UN resolutions, and these, as noted, became the launching pads for steadily deepening UN involvement in ecosystem issues. The political leadership discussed above created the conferences and the conferences mobilized the international support that created the new regimes and institutions.

Changing Perspectives outside the United Nations

In a broader, and perhaps more revealing, perspective, it can be argued that the expansion of United Nations concerns and activities in ecosystem areas had at least as much to do with developments outside the organization as with processes within. As noted previously most of the recommendations of the world conferences, as well as most of the resolutions on ecosystem issues considered by the ECOSOC and the General Assembly, were adopted by consensus. Those that were actually voted were usually passed without dissent. Some of the larger Organization for Economic Cooperation and Development (OECD) countries often abstained on resolutions that called for increased funding for the United Nations, though they did not always do this, and occasionally the United States would vote against a resolution that contained over zealous Third World phraseology. But consensus was usually reached.

Cynically, it could be argued that the consensus registered on ecosystem issues within the UN was fictitious. What appeared to be expressions of agreement were really gestures of indifference, or obligation-free affirmations of high-sounding principles that could never be practically implemented. Or perhaps they were cheap endorsements of activities that could not be expected to amount to much anyway. Or, it might simply have been that the international ecosystem agreements emerged because their terms were sufficiently ambiguous to offend no one.

The cynics may be right. But the burden of proof is on them, since most of the evidence that can be gleaned from developments and circumstances surrounding the UN's thrust into the ecosystem area suggests that the principal reason for UN expansion was that there was a great deal of international support behind it from many quarters. The principal explanation for this support is that elites around the world were prepared to endorse and facilitate collective action because it accorded with an emergent Weltanschauung they could accept. It also responded to real problems they could recognize.

The deepest origins of the UN's expansion into ecosystem concerns were in the realm of ideas. Two courses of intellectual development, both originating in the 1960s, profoundly affected potentialities for later United Nations activities. One was the specification of what John Gerard Ruggie calls "the global problematique," a holistic appreciation of man-planet interdependencies.[30] The other intellectual course was the rethinking of Third World development goals, wherein achieving higher qualities of life came to be set ahead of attaining quantitative economic growth.

As a result of the work of the Club of Rome and similar world-modeling projects, plus the reviews and debates that followed the publication of *The Limits to Growth* and its sequels, critiques, and companion pieces, Western intellectuals pieced together a rather ominous picture of what was happening to the human ecosystem as a result of mutually reinforcing secular trends in increasing population, industrialization, and pollution.[31] Although some elements of this picture may not have been new to some people, the total display was new—and discomfiting—to almost everyone who took it at all seriously. Population-resource balances were observed to be going awry and conventional ways of restoring them by relying on new technologies were at least questionable and possibly even self-defeating inasmuch as certain technologies were in themselves environmentally destructive. Techniques for increasing agricultural yields through the intensive use of fertilizers and insecticides, for example, have the effect of easing food shortages in the short run while polluting water and upsetting biosystems in the longer run.

This perceived pattern of interconnected negative impacts on the man-planet relationship was "the global problematique." "What distinguishes the processes and problems that go to make up the so-called global problematique from a simple inventory of disparate pressing concerns," Ruggie argues, "is that they are systematically related to one another at both ends of the cause-effect chain."[32] These interrelated processes and problems are also, according to Ruggie,

> global in character [in] that they occur in many places, affect many people, take place in areas beyond or across national jurisdiction, pose the danger of future world conflict, offend universal moral standards, threaten the physical survival of humankind, emanate from the same underlying structure, and require action at the global level.[33]

The credibility of the global problematique was rather shockingly enhanced in the early 1970s by the world food crisis, caused partly by desertification in Sahelian Africa, partly by failures in overexploited world fisheries, partly by perverse weather, and mostly by inappropriate food distribution systems.[34] Furthermore, the food crisis overlapped the oil crisis. The latter, of course, was a man-made distortion of the man-resource balance, and it was shortlived. But it greatly heightened the world's anxieties about the finiteness of natural resources, and the global problematique thus became even more believable.

Assumptions about the fragility, complexity, and holistic character of humankind's relationship with its physical environment, and the conclusion that the environment was deteriorating and that humankind was therefore also in jeopardy, together created an intellectual framework within which ecosystem issues could be considered within the UN. It should be underlined that this problematique was new in the early 1970s; it could play no part in UN deliberations before the 1970s because it did not exist. But, once formulated, it played a crucially important UN part because it offered a way of reasoning through ecosystem issues that was not premised on previously established Northern, Southern, Eastern, or Western positions. It was not therefore immediately (or at least not wholly) divisive along standard political-ideological lines. In addition it offered opportunity and rationale for stipulating a level of social reality that transcended nation-states—that is, there was out there (as Chairman Gorbachev acknowledged in the quotation that opened this chapter) a single, interdependent world society that was being commonly threatened by ecosystem failure, and only policies and actions framed and taken at the level of this world society could adequately combat the threat. This vision prompted the conceptual invention of the international community that appears so frequently in UN documents drafted during the 1970s. It further made it conceptually possible to attribute interests to the international community and to seek to formulate policies on its behalf.[35] What was most important politically was that the symbolism of the global problematique could be and was used effectively by leading coalitions and UN officials to build international support for ecosystem initiatives.

Despite the appeal of the global problematique, it is not clear exactly how many Third World elites were persuaded by it, at least initially. Third World support for UN attention to and programmatic involvement in ecosystem issue areas evolved slowly, and, for some, like the Brazilians, official positions shifted over time from opposition to support. Early UN attempts to move into family planning and other population management programs were greeted with suspicion from several Third World governments. Their spokesmen alleged that population control was targeted at the Third World and that it was a Northern device for slowing development or preventing the accretion of Asian, African, and Latin American power.[36] Similarly, early calls for cleaning up the environment, stemming industrial pollution, and conserving natural resources were also suspect in the Third World. Such practices were seen as luxuries that

only the rich could afford, and to engage in them would mean either
slowing development or incurring costs that those already rich did
not have to contend with on their way up.[37] Many Third World governments were also initially reluctant to acknowledge deteriorating
agricultural situations, or to link solving food problems with moving
toward agrarian reform and rural modernization.[38]

The Third World's initial reticence regarding ecosystem matters
changed, however. The record shows that in the 1970s an impressive
number of Third World governments were regularly among the
sponsors of initiatives that involved the UN in ecosystem matters.
Furthermore, the entire Group of 77 in the 1970s usually acclaimed
the resolutions that expanded UN programs in population, food, and
the environment. On the part of some governments this shift from
suspicion to support was unquestionably an opportunistic grab for
whatever kind of technical and capital assistance they could squeeze
out of the industrialized countries. For these governments the UN
was to be the great redistributor of the world's wealth, and their
support went to all UN programs, ecosystem ones included, that
promised funded projects for poorer countries.

Many other Third World governments, however, were more sincere in their warming toward ecosystem concerns. Evidence suggests that this was the result of a redefinition of the goals of development that occurred in the early 1970s and that was reflected
in statements such as the "Founex Report" (1971), the 1973 appraisal
of the Second Development Decade, the "Cocoyoc Declaration"
(1974), the *Declaration and Programme of Action on the Establishment of a New International Economic Order* and the *International Development Strategy for the Third United Nations Development Decade*.[39] For almost three decades most Third World
elites had embraced development aspirations that pictured the less
developed South ultimately coming to look like the industrialized
West, statistically anyway. They therefore measured the distance
to their goals in terms of GNP, GNP per capita, annual industrial output, and the like.[40] Development was seen as primarily economic;
it was a phenomenon of financial, commercial, and labor force ag-
gregates and it was quantitatively assessable in terms of conventional economic indicators devised in the West.

The 1970s, however, saw Third World elites shifting to embrace
a more qualitatively-oriented developmentalism, where "the ultimate objective of development must be to bring about sustained
improvement in the well-being of the individual and bestow benefits

on all."[41] Economic growth had not become irrelevant to development in the new thinking; it was still a prerequisite. But, in the eyes of many Third World elites, economic growth was no longer either the definition or the measure of development. The quality of individuals' lives was the new criterion. When this became the case, from the early 1970s onward, Third World elites could look at ecosystem issues in a new light. Solving problems of the deteriorating ecosystem was no longer either antithetical or tangential to development, but instead the very essence of it. Social and economic development and a protected and enhanced ecosystem went hand-in-hand. Each was cause and effect of the other. "During the last decade, new perceptions have emerged," agreed the delegates gathered in Nairobi for the tenth anniversary of the Stockholm Conference:

> The need for environmental management and assessment, the intimate and complex interrelationship between environment, development, population and resources and the strain on the environment generated, particularly in urban areas, by increasing population have become widely recognized. A comprehensive and regionally integrated approach that emphasizes this interrelationship can lead to environmentally sound and sustainable socioeconomic development.[42]

In the context of this new developmentalism, the Group of 77 could rally behind the ecosystem initiatives of the 1970s. They did.

There were other, more practical, reasons the United Nations was able to expand its ecosystem concerns and programs in the 1970s. For one thing, the superpowers did not greatly obstruct the organization or the leadership coalitions that were launching the ecosystem initiatives. The United States was occasionally supportive, as on population matters and for a time on food problems as well. But Washington was mostly passive except when handed the bills. During the period of East-West détente, which ran almost to the end of the 1970s, neither superpower was making very great efforts to fight the Cold War at the UN, so they refrained from sidetracking debates by trying to make ecosystem issues into East-West contests. The Soviet Union tried occasionally to do this, but when the effort to set the South against the West failed, Moscow appeared to lapse into a relatively benign indifference toward ecosystem matters at the UN.

Another more positive reason for the UN's rapid and extensive

movement into ecosystem issues was that UN officials had a good
deal to do with preserving momentum by keeping open the path-
ways that led from ideas to policies. They researched, wrote, and
issued reports in timely fashion that kept governments' attention
focused. Notable among these were the Secretariat's report on
problems of the human environment, the FAO's assessments of the
international food situation issued at the opening of the World Food
Conference, the Secretary-General's report to the World Population
Conference, and the Secretariat's report on interrelationships among
population, resources, environment, and development.[43] UN officials
also engaged in considerable and continual behind-the-scenes urging, and by imposing schedules, calling meetings, and the like, they
kept the diplomatic processes going and administratively orchestrated the global conferences. Either by good judgment or sheer
serendipity, the UN also placed strong and imaginative directors at
the UNFPA, FAO, UNDP, UNEP, and other key ecosystem agencies in
the 1970s. In sum what made the UN system move, and what moved
it into ecosystem problems were (1) talented and committed political
leaders among the member states, (2) appropriate diplomatic contexts like the global conferences, (3) agreement-seeking instead of
confrontational modes of intergovernmental interaction, (4) important intellectual and ideological developments outside the UN that
greatly facilitated global policymaking within, (5) relatively unob-
structive superpower behavior, and (6) committed and capable international civil servants.

The Impacts of International Policies
on Ecosystem Issues

Even harsh critics of the United Nations will often concede that
the globalism the organization promotes is benign.[44] There is nothing ominous or mischievous about bringing governments together
and encouraging them to cooperate to promote enhancing the quality
of individuals' lives throughout the world. But the crucial question
is whether such efforts are actually being made, and the extent to
which they are or were influenced by UN policies and programs.
What has come from the UN's expansion into ecosystem issue areas?

There is no question that efforts are being made in many parts
of the world to stem overly rapid population growth, overcome hunger and malnutrition, clean up the environment, develop new and
renewable energy sources, and generally contain and reverse the

negative interaction patterns revealed in the global problematique. Compared to the level of such efforts twenty years ago, today's actions are impressive in terms of commitment, sophistication, and invested resources. Furthermore, in some areas actual accomplishments are being made toward establishing a better balance between humanity's demands and the earth's carrying capacity. It is true that the energy situation remains precarious, despite the glut on the oil market, particularly in the area of household fuels in the Third World. In addition, problems of deforestation, soil erosion, and desertification are increasing in severity, again particularly in the Third World.[45] Yet, on the more promising side, population growth rates are dropping—not everywhere, but in many places nonetheless. Food supplies and nutritional quality are increasing—again obviously not everywhere, since famine conditions prevail in Sahelian Africa. But in many places, like India and elsewhere in South and Southeast Asia, food production is outpacing population growth and food distribution is being better managed.[46] Today many rivers and freshwater lakes, especially in Northern countries, are cleaner (though increasingly acidic), drinking water and sanitation are improved in some Third World countries, the Mediterranean Sea is probably less polluted, air quality is better over many metropolitan areas in Northern countries, and the earth's ozone layer is somewhat better protected. Naturally, no one would argue that the race against the limits of the earth's carrying capacity has been won, that environmental catastrophe in the future has been definitely avoided, or that efforts to avert this dreadful future have been anywhere near adequate.[47] Still, the prognosis is not nearly as bleak as it would have been if countermeasures had not been taken in many places in the world in recent years.

But did the UN have very much to do with this? What kind of action did the ecosystem action plans produce, and how meaningful has all of this been in practical terms?

First, the UN has had some notable failures. Combating desertification, for example, has not gotten much beyond the high-sounding rhetoric of the 1977 Desertification Conference, nor has the World Soils Policy made much headway.[48] UN programs to promote agrarian reform are not registering very much progress, programs concerned with new and renewable energy sources have moved very slowly and without notable impact, and policies to stem population growth are still not in place in several African, Asian, and Latin American countries that apparently need them the most.[49] Apart from a few exceptions like the Mediterranean cleanup effort—which is moving apace—most UN-sponsored ecosystem projects that require regional cooperation are not doing very well, mainly because regional neighbors are reluctant to cooperate. Relatively little has been done, for example, in the Persian Gulf area, even though a UN fund exists to support cooperative efforts against pollution. Moreover, few of the UN's ecosystem efforts, except perhaps the population programs, have generated enough enthusiasm and commitment among governments to keep needed resources flowing into UN programs in expanding amounts in the 1980s.[50] The 1980s have brought new budgetary austerities within and without the UN, extraordinary non-responsiveness from Washington, new and disruptive East-West dueling, and altered international organizational priorities because of the debt crisis. All of this has caused a slackening in the tempo of all UN programs, ecosystem ones included.

It is also true that distracting politicization has affected UN ecosystem programs in much the same way that it has affected most of the UN's other functional activities. The consensus that produced the ecosystem policies has often been lost during ideologically charged debates over implementation. Deliberating bodies with Third World majorities have tended to overwhelm and antagonize First World governments with excessive demands for resources— for example, the environmental issue concerning the "remnants of war," in which First World countries were handed the bill for cleaning up Third World battlefields.[51] So, too, have debates about population policy, food, and environmental affairs been frequently diverted toward questions of Palestinian liberation and apartheid in South Africa. Such tactics have been distinctly unhelpful in promoting the implementation of ecosystem action plans.

Abstractly, it could be argued that while international policy processes during the 1970s placed enhanced power, prerogative, wealth, and rectitude at the disposal of the United Nations so that it could initiate action against ecosystem imbalances, these have not proven fully sufficient to sustain a global assault. Whatever power was shifted to international agencies has not been enough to overcome the indifference of some governments to ecosystem problems, or to blunt the resistance of others to collective international action. Whatever wealth was placed at the UN's disposal has not been nearly enough to make major inroads against the problems caused by man-planet imbalances. Whatever rectitude has accrued to globalism has not been enough to keep fully alive the kind of momentum that initially propelled UN action in support of accepted principles.[52]

With all of this said, however, several observations on the positive side deserve to be underlined. First, the activities of the United Nations in ecosystem issue areas have had the definite effect of raising international consciousness concerning problems of population, food, and the environment, and of mobilizing people and resources for problem-solving efforts. It is unlikely that the world would have been as informed and aroused about population-resource imbalances, hunger, and environmental deterioration in the 1970s, or that governments would have been as predisposed to act remedially, if the United Nations did not convene its topical world conferences, display its analyses, and promote its action plans. As Jordan and Weiss noted in the passage cited earlier, the conferences had the effect of shaking bureaucracies around the world because preparation for and participation in the conferences forced officials to confront problems and issues that many might otherwise have chosen to ignore. Third World delegates returned from the conferences shaken in their convictions that resource transfers from the North were all that were required to stem deteriorating qualities of life in the South. First World delegates returned shaken in their convictions that the wealthy countries could be indefinitely insulated from the general deterioration of the global ecosystem. In addition the publicity that the UN generated for ecosystem causes, and the auras of importance and legitimacy that the conferences and surrounding debates and resolutions created, all fortified and encouraged activists to press their national governments on ecosystem issues. Hunger lobbies, for example, were notably abetted by the World Food Conference and its follow-up, and after the Stockholm Conference national environmental lobbies formed where none had existed before.[53]

Second, as already noted, the UN, through those coalitions of member states that took the initiative, promoted regime-building in ecosystem issue areas during the 1970s. These efforts were largely successful. The global problematique is accepted by many governments today; its assumptions underpin their national positions on questions pertaining to the global ecosystem; and the interpretations and prescriptions regarding ecosystem problems that are embodied in the major UN resolutions today engender little dissent. While all of this might be considered only symbolic, and thus of little practical consequence, the fact that the international community has closed on the definition of a range of problems and on the form of preferred solutions should not go unrecognized. This represents accomplishment because two decades ago there was no general acknowledgment that the world faced a population problem, a food problem, or a pollution problem, and there certainly was no agreement that dealing with such problems required transferring resources among countries, focusing on the qualitative well-being of individuals, creating new international organizations, or enhancing the capabilities of existing ones. Historically, regime building has been a necessary prerequisite to subsequent convergent or collective international behavior.[54] Activities at the UN during the 1970s, therefore, satisfied the normative prerequisites for continuing collective action in ecosystem issue areas.

Third, the UN's impacts have not been only symbolic, since its programs have been directly, indirectly, and altogether very practically combating the problems of the global ecosystem. Generally speaking, there have been two main thrusts to UN ecosystem programs—monitoring and assisting. First, United Nations agencies have been assigned by member states the task of monitoring global ecosystem conditions and periodically reporting their findings to the international community. It has thus become the UN's responsibility to determine and describe the extensiveness of problems in the man-planet relationship, to note and report improvements or deteriorations in ecosystem conditions, and, perhaps most importantly, to offer early warning of impending ecosystem disasters. Extensive and effective monitoring operations are in place in the UN population, food, and environment agencies. Experts associated with the UN Secretariat, the Population Commission, and the regional economic commissions constantly study all aspects of global demography, and the UN's periodic assessments and population projections are accepted as authoritative around the world. Similarly, FAO experts monitor plantings, harvests, herds, fisheries, and forests around the world. UN researchers also keep track of food flows through the international system, via trade and aid, and of food distributions and nutritional conditions within countries. The UN has in place a global early warning system to anticipate dramatic abnormalities in food production and distribution that could cause disasters. It also has a World Food Council that analyzes and anticipates developments in the world food situation and recommends global food policies. Through the Global Environmental Monitoring System (GEMS) UNEP coordinates the worldwide monitoring of renewable natural resources, pollution, and climate. Relatedly, through the International Environmental Referral System (INFOT-ERRA) UNEP is able to link globally those who have questions about environmental degradation to those who might have answers. Plentiful, high-quality information is a prerequisite to effective problem solving. The United Nations has been providing ecosystem information in increasing volume during the last fifteen years. The information is frequently used by national governments in their policymaking, and it is essential to global policymaking. Even critics of the United Nations have complimented the quality of its monitoring activities.[55]

By far the greatest number of UN-sponsored projects in ecosystem management have been directed toward enhancing countries' capacities for dealing with their own problems. The 1974 *United Nations Yearbook* summary of technical assistance in the population field is typical of the goals of UN technical assistance generally. They are: "To help developing countries to achieve self-sufficiency . . . in formulating and executing . . . policies related to national development planning, by promoting the establishment of and strengthening national institutions to deal with these issues."[56]

Technical assistance is an unglamorous aspect of UN programming, but it cumulatively strengthens governments' problem-solving capacities. A great deal of this kind of investment in human and institutional resources has taken place in the area of ecosystem problem solving. During the last fifteen years hundreds of national ministries and agencies have been advised by UN technical assistants, and thousands of technicians and administrators have been trained at UN-sponsored seminars, in UN-operated training centers distributed throughout the world and through UN-awarded fellowships. Through UN population programs, for example, thousands of Third World technicians have been instructed in demography so that they can begin to determine the nature of demographic changes in their countries and thus generate the knowledge that might inform population policies. The People's Republic of China, with its enormous population and challenging demographic planning tasks, has recently been a major recipient of such technical assistance from the UN. Throughout the Third World UN technical assistance has also helped to establish family planning programs and the administrative superstructures necessary for their effective operation. In 1980 the UNFPA supported 125 demographic and family planning projects; it sent 77 experts to 44 countries, awarded 328 fellowships for study at the 7 UN regional population training centers, held 2 major international technical conferences and dozens of international and interagency seminars.[57] The direct result of UN technical assistance is that many governments are more capable of dealing with population problems now than they were ten or twenty years ago. The indirect effect is that many governments are more capably dealing with population problems now.

The results of UN technical assistance in the area of food and agriculture have been even more notable.[58] The FAO is the UN's major vehicle for the dissemination of agronomic information and the transfer of agricultural technology, and this organization has also evolved into a leading agricultural development agency. Here, too, the UN's emphasis has been on providing assistance and information that have the ultimate effect of making national governments more technically competent and peoples more self-reliant. In 1980, for example, the FAO implemented more than 1,900 technical assistance projects in some 70 countries, ranging in substance from seed improvement to fishery development, forest and woodlot management, remote sensing, and nuclear applications in agriculture. That same year the FAO trained thousands of Third World agricultural administrators in matters pertaining to fertilizer use, the prevention of diseases in animals, setting and enforcing food standards, and dozens of other technical and policy arenas.[59] 1980 found the World Food Programme spending $380 million on "food for development" projects (while also launching 62 emergency food relief operations in 26 countries).[60] Through the IFAD and the World Bank the UN has also recently been allocating hundreds of millions of dollars yearly to improving the lot of small farmers in the poorer countries. During the 1970s the UN-supported system of agricultural institutes contributed to the Green Revolution by helping innovations in the development of strains of wheat, rice, maize, and other grains that can produce high yields in Third World climates. If we consider the UN's record of technical assistance to agriculture, and bear in mind that UN-sponsored research created the Green Revolution, and if we then observe the improved state of global food security, it is difficult to argue that UN programs have not made inroads against hunger.[61]

UN technical assistance in the area of the environment has been more modest, partly because UNEP's resources have been much more modest than either the UNFPA's or the FAO's and partly because the United Nations Environment Programme was assigned a "catalyzing" rather than an implementing mission. UNEP's task has been to alert other UN agencies and international organizations to the environmental implications of their operations. As a result major portions of the annual disbursements from UNEP's Environment Fund are allocated to other UN agencies, such as the World Health Organization, the FAO, and the World Meteorological Organization, to assist them in adding environmental dimensions to their programs. UNEP's other catalytic task is to promote environmental consciousness and policy activities in member states and in regional groupings. To these ends it dispatches technical experts, conducts international seminars, and encourages collaborative projects. The Regional Seas Programme, for example, invites littoral states to join in collective protective and cleanup activities in regional bodies of water. Among the several regional seas projects initiated the cleanup effort in the Mediterranean has made most progress and is serving as a model. To encourage national efforts against environmental degradation, the UNEP in 1980 assigned 101 experts to projects in 9 countries and conducted 79 international seminars on problems ranging from the pollution of mangrove ecosystems to waste water technology and techniques of remote sensing. The UNEP Governing Council has recently been urging the United Nations Environment Programme to move directly and deeply into extending technical assistance.[62]

UN activities in ecosystem issue areas have also had the important effects of either creating or strengthening international scientific, transgovernmental, and other transnational elite networks. Sizable parts of the program budgets of most UN agencies operating in ecosystem areas are annually spent on bringing together experts and administrators for consultation, education, and deliberation on common problems. Such networking has contributed to better analysis and understanding of ecosystem problems—as, for example, through UN-sponsored expert seminars on desertification, freshwater resources, fisheries and the migratory behavior of fish, soil erosion, toxic materials, and scores of other matters. UN-encouraged networking has also linked experts around the world in ways that facilitate continuing collaboration and the sharing of knowledge. Innovations and problem-solving algorithms thus move much more expeditiously among countries than would be the case in the absence of the networks. In particular, UN networking had a good deal to do with integrating the international agronomic and demographic research communities and it has contributed notably to the effectiveness of the GEMS and IFOTERRA systems.

In the broadest sense the United Nations has transferred the global problematique from the realm of intellectual discourse into the field of international relations. This was an important accomplishment. For governments, and more particularly for individual delegates, participation in UN ecosystem affairs has forced an intellectual confrontation between globalistic and nationalistic perspectives on practical and pressing problems. Largely as a result of the UN's movement into ecosystem issues in the 1970s there is now a legitimate alternative to traditional thinking about matters of population, food, and the natural environment in terms of narrow, national self-interest. The global problematique establishes a compelling rationale for holistic thinking and collective action on the part of the international community. Now that this alternative is acknowledged by many governments there is a greater chance that it will be more frequently selected as the international community's response to problems of the threatened ecosystem.

Notes

1. Heidi Toffler and Alvin Toffler, *Christian Science Monitor* (January 5, 1987): 14.

2. See, for example, *International Development Strategy for the Third United Nations Development Decade* (New York: United Nations Department of Public Information, 1981). In this most recent plan for world development, the "international community" is acknowledged to have identity, interests, obligations, and policy preferences, and all of these are accorded considerable legitimacy.

3. Marvin S. Soroos, *Beyond Sovereignty: The Challenge of Global Policy* (Columbia, S.C.: University of South Carolina Press, 1986), 20.

4. "Foreword," *United Nations Yearbook, 1979* (New York: United Nations, 1982).

5. See, for example, *Population Growth and Economic Development*, Note by the Secretary-General, A/6104 and Corr. 1, 1965; *Problems of the Human Environment*, Report of the Secretary-General, E/4667, 1969; *Appraisal of Prospective Food Deficits and Food Aid Needs*, Addendum to the Report of the Director-General of FAO, prepared in response to General Assembly Resolution 2462(XXIII), E/5050/ Add.1, 1973; *Interrelationships of Population, Resources, Environment and Development*, Report of the Secretary-General, E/1979/75, 1979.

6. Thomas G. Weiss and Robert S. Jordan, *The World Food Conference and Global Problem Solving* (New York: Praeger, in cooperation with UNITAR [the United Nations Institute for Training and Research], 1976), 155–66; Mohammad A. Qadeer, "The Futility of World Conferences," *International Development Review* 19, 1 (1977): 13–15.

7. *United Nations Yearbook, 1954, 272–73; United Nations Yearbook, 1965, 387–92; World Population Conference, 1965.* Report of the Secretary-General. A/6101, 1965; *United Nations Yearbook, 1974, 552; Population Plan of Action, E/Conf/60/ .19.* See also Richard N. Gardner, "Toward a World Population Program," in *The*

Global Partnership: International Agencies and Economic Development, ed. Richard N. Gardner and Max F. Millikan (New York: Praeger, 1968), 332–61; Charlotte G. Patton, "The United Nations and the Politics of Population," unpublished doctoral dissertation, Columbia University, 1984.

8. Patton, "The United Nations," ch. IV–VI.

9. General Assembly Resolution 2319(XXII); General Assembly Resolution 3344(XXIX); *International Development Strategy for the Third United Nations Development Decade*, Paragraphs 81–95.

10. Stephen D. Krasner, ed., *International Regimes* (Ithaca, N.Y.: Cornell University Press, 1983), 2; and especially Oran Young, "Regime Dynamics: The Rise and Fall of International Regimes," 93–114.

11. General Assembly Resolution 2626(XXV); *Report of the United Nations Conference on the Human Environment, Stockholm, Sweden, 5–16 June 1972*, U.N.P. Sales no. E.73.II.a.14; General Assembly Resolutions 2996(XXVII), 32/172, 32/158, 3201(S-VI), and 3202(S-VI); *Report of the United Nations World Population Conference, Bucharest, 19–30 August 1974*, U.N.P. Sales no. E.75.XIII.3; *Report of the World Conference on Agrarian Reform and Rural Development, Rome, 12–20 July 1979* (WCARRD/REP); *World Food Conference Programme of Action*, E/Conf/65/20, 1974; *Report of Habitat: United Nations Conference on Human Settlements, Vancouver, Canada, 31 May–11 June, 1976*, U.N.P. Sales no. E.76.IV.7; *International Development Strategy for the Third United Nations Development Decade*.

12. The U.S. government, however, systematically objected to passages in the plans of action that affirmed or implied endorsement of the NIEO. The United States also tended to object to creating (and thus financing) new agencies in the UN system, and in this Washington was sometimes joined by London, Paris, Bonn, and other OECD governments.

13. *Report of the United Nations Conference on the Human Environment* (see the Secretary-General's opening remarks to the conference); see also, *United Nations Yearbook, 1972*, 319. For a discussion of the concept of "organic growth" see Mihajlo Mesarovic and Eduard Pestel, *Mankind at the Turning Point: The Second Report to the Club of Rome* (New York: New American Library, 1974), 1–9.

14. *International Development Strategy for the Third United Nations Development Decade*, Paragraph 166.

15. *Universal Declaration on the Eradication of Hunger and Malnutrition*, E/Conf/65/20, Paragraph 12. See also, Resolutions no. I, II, IX, XVIII, and XIX adopted by the World Food Conference, E/Conf/65/20.

16. *Report of the United Nations Conference on the Human Environment*; General Assembly Resolution 3345(XXIX); *Report of Habitat*.

17. UNEP's financing accrues mainly from the Fund of the United Nations Environmental Programme, a voluntarily subscribed fund, plus a modest biennial allocation from the United Nations Regular Budget.

18. Maurice J. Williams and Thomas W. Stephens, "Resource Flows through the Multilateral System for Food and Agriculture," *FOOD POLICY* 19, 4 (November 1984): 355.

19. *United Nations Yearbook, 1970*, 462.

20. Branislav Gosovic and John Gerard Ruggie, "On the Creation of a New International Economic Order: Issue Linkage and the Seventh Special Session of the

UN General Assembly," *International Organization* 30, 2 (Spring 1976): 314; See also, A/PV.2229, 2230, and 2231.

21. *United Nations Yearbook, 1968*, 476.

22. General Assembly Resolutions 1572 D(L), 1971; 1673 E(LII), 1972; and 1761 A-G(LIV), 1973.

23. See, for example, General Assembly Resolutions 34/184 and 34/190.

24. See note 5, above.

25. Patton carefully describes the efforts of Sweden's Ulla Lindstrom. See Patton, "The United Nations," ch. II and III.

26. Qadeer, "The Futility."

27. Weiss and Jordan, "The World Food Conference," 75–80, 156–67.

28. Ibid., 80.

29. Ibid., 80.

30. John Gerard Ruggie, "On the Problem of 'The Global Problematique': What Roles for International Organizations?" *Alternatives* 5 (May 1980): 517–50. See also Ervin Laslo, "Global Goals and the Crisis of Political Will," *Journal of International Affairs* 31, 2 (Fall–Winter 1977): 199–214.

31. Donnella H. Meadows, et al., *The Limits to Growth: A Report for the Club of Rome's Project on the Predicament of Mankind* (Washington, D.C.: Potomac Associates, 1972); Dennis L. Meadows, et al., *Dynamics of Growth in a Finite World* (Cambridge, Mass.: Wright-Allen Press, 1974); Carlos Mallamann, "The Bariloche Model," in *Problems of World Modeling: Political and Social Implications*, ed. Karl W. Deutsch, et al. (Cambridge, Mass.: Ballinger, 1977), 33–46.

32. Ruggie, "On the Problem," 526.

33. Ibid., 520.

34. Raymond Hopkins and Donald Puchala, "Perspectives on the International Relations of Food," pp. 3–40; and Cheryl Christensen, "World Hunger: A Structural Approach," pp. 171–200, in *The Global Political Economy of Food*, ed. R. Hopkins and D. Puchala (Madison, Wis.: University of Wisconsin Press, 1978).

35. See note 2, above.

36. Krishna Roy, "Population Policy from the Southern Perspective," in *Beyond Dependency: The Developing World Speaks Out*, ed. Guy F. Erb and Valerina Kallab (Washington, D.C.: Overseas Development Council, 1975), 95–119; *Issues Before the 35th General Assembly of the United Nations* (New York: United Nations Association of the United States of America, 1980), 121.

37. *Issues before the 35th General Assembly of the United Nations*, 102; Tim E.J. Campbell, "The Political Meaning of Stockholm: Third World Participation in the Environment Conference Process," *Stanford Journal of International Studies* 8 (1973): 138–53; Richard N. Gardner, "The Role of the UN in Environmental Problems," *International Organization* 26, 2 (1973): 237–54.

38. Laurence Hewes, *Rural Development: World Frontiers* (Ames, Ia.: Iowa State University Press, 1974), 58–81.

39. General Assembly Resolutions 3201(S-VI) and 3202(S-VI); "The Cocoyoc Declaration," Annex A-2 in *Beyond Dependency: The Developing World Speaks Out*, ed. Guy F. Erb and Valerina Kallab (Washington, D.C.: Overseas Development Council, 1975), 170–82; "Founex Report on Development and Environment," *International Conciliation* 586 (1972): 1–36. *Issues before the 36th General Assembly*

of the United Nations (New York: United Nations Association of the United States of America, 1981), 106–07.

40. Ruggie, "On the Problem," 524–25.

41. General Assembly Resolution 2626(XXV), Paragraph 7.

42. "Nairobi Declaration," *UN* Chronicle (July 1982), 92.

43. See note 5, above.

44. Burton Y. Pines, ed., *A World without the UN* (Washington, D.C.: The Heritage Foundation, 1984), xviii. Critics who advocate U.S. withdrawal from the United Nations nonetheless recognize the importance of multilateral cooperation in various issue areas, including those concerning the ecosystem.

45. Erik P. Eckholm, *Losing Ground: Environmental Stress and World Food Prospects* (New York: W.W. Norton, 1976); Lester Brown with Erik P. Eckholm, *By Bread Alone* (New York: Praeger, 1974), 45–57; Nicholas Guppy, "Tropical Deforestation: A Global View," *Foreign Affairs*, 62, 4 (Spring 1984): 928–64.

46. Barbara Insel, "A World Awash with Grain," *Foreign Affairs* 63, 4 (Spring 1985): 892–911.

47. Erik Eckholm, for example, is particularly pessimistic. See, *Down to Earth: A Report Prepared in Commemoration of the Tenth Anniversary of the Historic Stockholm Conference on the Human Environment* (New York: W.W. Norton, 1982), passim.

48. *Issues before the 39th General Assembly of the United Nations* (New York: United Nations Association of the United States of America, 1984), 100–01.

49. Eckholm, *Down to Earth*, 36–48.

50. In 1985, for example, the U.S. government, under pressure from anti-abortion groups, drastically cut its contributions to the United Nations Fund for Population Activities.

51. *Issues before the 38th General Assembly of the United Nations* (New York: United Nations Association of the United States of America, 1983), 103.

52. Soroos, *Beyond Sovereignty*, 370–74.

53. Ruggie, "On the Problem," 537–39; see also, UNEP/GC.10/3, p.1; *Issues before the 37th General Assembly of the United Nations*, 106; United Nations Association of the United States of America, *Government Agencies with Environmental Responsibilities in Developing Countries* (New York: Center for International Environmental Information, United Nations Association, 1980); Jeffrey H. Leonhard and David Morrell, "Emergence of Environmental Concern in Developing Countries: A Political Perspective," *Stanford Journal of International Law*, 17, 2 (1981): 281–313; Thomas G. Weiss and Robert S. Jordan, "The World Food Conference," 131–38.

54. Joseph M. Jones, *The United Nations at Work: Developing Land, Forests, Oceans and People* (Oxford, England: Pergamon Press, 1965), 118 ff.; United Nations Environment Programme, *Report of the Governing Council*, 9th Session, May 13–26, 1981 (A/36/25), 42–43.

55. Georges Fauriol, *The Food and Agriculture Organization: A Flawed Strategy in the War against Hunger* (Washington, D.C.: The Heritage Foundation, 1984), 41–44.

56. *United Nations Yearbook, 1974,* 552.

57. *United Nations Yearbook, 1980,* 792 ff.

58. Raymond Hopkins and Donald Puchala, *Global Food Interdependence: Challenge to American Foreign Policy* (New York: Columbia University Press, 1980), 134–45.

59. *United Nations Yearbook, 1980,* 1265–71.

60. Ibid., 685–702.

61. Lester Brown, *Seeds of Change: The Green Revolution and Development in the 1970s* (New York: Praeger, 1970); Lester Brown, *By Bread Alone,* 133–46.

62. A/36/25, p. 61.

8

The Politics of Efficacy: The United Nations and Human Rights

David P. Forsythe

●

A marked change occurred in the treatment of human rights at the United Nations between 1945 and 1985. On the foundation of a few vague references to human rights in the Charter there evolved an International Bill of Rights (the 1948 Universal Declaration, plus two basic Covenants in 1966) indicating numerous obligations of increasing salience. This core of global rules was supplemented by a series of particular human rights instruments, some with special control mechanisms. Moreover, whereas once the subject of human rights seemed idealistic and abstract, by the 1980s there was growing attention to specific countries and patterns of behavior through an increasing array of organs. The subject of human rights did not fade away as did military measures to maintain peace and security under the Security Council. Rather, it emerged more and more as part of high politics—one of the subjects to which member states give great attention, if not always for the same (much less high-minded) reasons.

This sea change in the treatment of human rights at the United Nations resulted from many factors: the consequences of states' foreign policies, some of which were intended and others not; the assertiveness of nongovernmental organizations; the mostly quiet but nevertheless persistent influence of persons in the Secretariat; the sometimes surprising independence of individuals on uninstructed bodies; perhaps even a shift in what passes for world public opinion.

There is a considerable debate, however, over the significance of this change. It seems clear enough that institutional and procedural changes at the United Nations in the field of human rights have been striking. It also seems clear that there is some legal significance—both theoretical and practical—to the changes that have occurred. At least it can be said that states have accepted a number of new legal obligations and that the record includes numerous cases that can be used as precedents should actors choose to do so in pursuit of human rights values. Ambivalence begins to set in, however, when one tackles the subject of the practical significance of these changes for the condition of human rights beyond UN meeting rooms. On this subject there is considerable disagreement, including a debate on what constitutes progress in human rights and how to discern it. There is also debate over whether events at the United Nations constitute a global regime on human rights.

This central notion of significance is frequently discussed in terms of the UN's movement from promotion to protection—that is, from negotiating norms to supervising their implementation. This is not incorrect. One can go further. In the area of human rights the UN has moved from an early deference to state consent to an increasing use of majority decision to override state consent. Somewhat paradoxically, negotiations involving promotion are still largely characterized by the lowest common denominator approach, or the attempt to gain the largest number of adherences by removing provisions objected to by an important minority. Yet, once on the books, the rules are increasingly supervised by a process of majority voting that overrides minority objection. Whether such majority voting is effective in securing the application of the rule desired by the majority remains an open question. In the short run the evidence many times is clearly negative; the state or states targeted by the majority do not change their policies immediately. Some states do make changes, and some states may make changes when they are so targeted over a long time—for example, South Africa.

In the pages that follow attention is given first to the more striking institutional and procedural changes at the United Nations concerning human rights. Then some of the reasons these changes have occurred are discussed. These first two sections present evidence that should help correct a widespread misunderstanding about the UN and human rights. Next the difficult subject of the significance of the changes is tackled. In so doing something can be said about what can realistically be expected from the United Nations on human rights issues, and thus something about what the UN has achieved against that standard of expectation. If the conclusion manifests ambivalence—both optimism and pessimism about the UN and human rights—perhaps this is understandable in a complex and uncertain world.

An Overview

There are a variety of views on the historical evolution of the United Nations and human rights.[1] Most observers agree that there were three stages, each lasting about a decade. From 1945–47 to 1954 human rights diplomacy at the UN focused primarily on promotion or on the drafting of norms—the elaboration of the Charter provisions on the subject. From about 1954 to around 1967 optimists say that human rights diplomacy turned to indirect protection or promotion efforts through the holding of seminars and the publication of various studies on human rights problems in general, without the naming of countries or specific patterns of behavior. Pessimists see this period as one of inaction, despite a supposed UN action plan on human rights. This view has some merit, although numerous persons at the UN were active on several human rights matters. The Eisenhower administration, however, traded away much activity on human rights at the UN in return for the demise of the movement in Congress for a Bricker amendment to the U.S. Constitution that would have limited Executive authority in foreign affairs.[2]

A third period clearly started around 1967 when the United Nations began selective specific protection or the targeting of specific countries like South Africa and Israel for human rights consideration. These targets had long been attacked by other states in the General Assembly. After 1967 other parts of the UN system began to deal with human rights specifics in these and other states. At some point these efforts at protection became almost global, especially after the two major Covenants—or treaties—on human rights came into legal force. Countries were not guaranteed freedom from some type of UN supervision of their rights record.

Given that the definition of most historical eras is partly arbitrary, I will speak simply of before and after the mid-1960s. This simple bifurcation allows one to note clearly the change that has taken place at the UN on human rights. Before the 1960s there was a certain timidity on the part of member states toward the human rights issue and almost all expectations were low about utilizing the United Nations to act on human rights questions.[3] The superpowers and Great Powers were not terribly interested in international human rights at the start of the San Francisco Conference, although the United States and several nongovernmental organizations (NGOs) acted to get Article 55 placed in the Charter.

This timid climate of opinion continued during the early years of the United Nations, although specific debates and finger pointing occurred. The UN Commission on Human Rights, an instructed body reporting to the Economic and Social Council (ECOSOC), issued a self-denying ordinance in 1947 holding that it had no authority to hear specific complaints about human rights violations addressed to the UN. The commission functioned basically as a research and drafting organ. As part of the action—or inaction—plan of the 1950s, states were asked to report voluntarily on their rights policies. Reports were generally self-serving and not subjected to careful review. When the commission's uninstructed Sub-Commission on Prevention of Discrimination and Protection of Minorities had a rapporteur who became assertive and tried to push an analytic summary drawn from state reports, the subcommission buried the project. Western states sought the termination of the commission's subgroups, ironically succeeding concerning the one on freedom of information. The one on discrimination and minorities was barely saved by other coalitions.[4] The one on women continued as a separate commission. Sporadic resolutions on particular subjects like forced labor did not change the dominant pattern of this early period, a pattern marked more by lip service to human rights than by specific protection efforts.

It is well known that during this early period before the mid-1960s, the Universal Declaration of Human Rights was adopted in 1948 and the two major Covenants were negotiated (one on Civil and Political, the other on Economic, Social, and Cultural Rights). These instruments, as will be shown later, came to have considerable salience legally and politically. However necessary this drafting was, in this first period it was accompanied by considerable foot dragging. Even Eleanor Roosevelt repeatedly defended the idea of a declaration that was not intended to be legally binding against the pressures of some for a binding instrument.[5] The Covenants, while substantially completed by 1954, were not approved by the General Assembly and opened for signature until 1966, and did not reach the number of adherences required for entry into legal force until 1976. It seemed that most states were not anxious to accept specific and binding obligations concerning general human rights, and they did not want the UN Commission on Human Rights or other organs of the UN system to be assertive in the cause of human rights.

Prior to the mid-1960s, however, a number of other human rights instruments were developed. Concern with labor rights and slavery carried over from the time of the League of Nations. New legal instruments were created concerning refugees, genocide, women's political rights, the rights of the child. Toward the end of this first period treaties were drafted on the prevention of educational and racial discrimination. It was as if states could not avoid drafting documents proclaiming high-minded goals, even if their specific policies fell short of the standards they were approving. Many states failed to submit required reports to the Committee on the Elimination of Racial Discrimination (CERD) after adhering to the treaty.[6]

In the second twenty years of the United Nations, and despite the definitely mixed if not depressing record of the first twenty, the situation changed markedly. Efforts increasingly moved from the general and the abstract to the specific and the concrete, although some drafting efforts continued—for example, on a special instrument concerning torture. That is, promotion was accompanied by protection. The UN accepted the principle of the permissibility of individual petitions and created several mechanisms to deal with them. Increasingly UN bodies used publicity as a means of pressure against specific states. Targets were not limited to South Africa and Israel—or even Chile. Increasingly across the UN system there was a fragile but persistent movement toward improved supervision of states' policies on human rights. More and more human rights treaties came into legal force, and various agencies tried to see that they were implemented. A brief synopsis of the major UN organs on human rights will highlight the process and perhaps provide new information to some readers.

The Human Rights Committee

The UN Covenant on Civil and Political Rights came into legal force for adhering states in 1976. Since then the number of parties has grown to about seventy-five states. These elect an eighteen-member committee of uninstructed persons to review state reports and to hear individual petitions from persons whose states have accepted an optional protocol permitting such action (about thirty in number at the time of writing). The committee does not take instructions from UN bodies, but it reports to the General Assembly and interacts with the UN Secretariat. By most accounts since 1978 the committee has been energetic and assertive, seeking to make the review process as rigorous as possible but staying within the bounds of a generally cooperative attitude toward states.[7]

In 1980 there arose an important discussion about the authority of the committee in the light of Article 40, paragraph 4 in the civil-political Covenant. This reads: "The Committee shall study the reports submitted by the States Parties to the present Covenant. It shall transmit its reports, and such general comments as it may consider appropriate, to the States Parties. The Committee may also transmit to the Economic and Social Council these comments along with the copies of the reports it has received from States Parties to the present Covenant."

A majority of the thirteen Committee members participating in the debate wanted to give considerable scope to the word "study" and not be deterred from vigorous action by the word "general." This majority was made up of Third World as well as Western personalities. Clear support for an active Human Rights Committee came from the members from Ecuador, Jordan, Tunisia, and Senegal, as well as West Germany and Norway. The members from Eastern Europe—especially from the USSR, East Germany, and Romania—were a distinct minority. Eventually a compromise statement was reached: "general comments" would be addressed to state parties; the committee could comment on the implementation of the Covenant; protection of human rights—not just promotion—was a proper subject for the committee; the committee could take up the subject of "the implementation of the obligation to guarantee the rights set forth in the Covenant;" the committee might later consider further what duties it would undertake; the Secretariat would be asked to make an "analysis" of states' reports and the pattern of questions by members. Subsequently other comments by members indicated that many would continue to push for a serious review process and that an attempt would be made to be systematic in order to establish patterns over time.[8] If this compromise seemed in the short run a concession to the East Europeans, it contained ample language to legitimize expansive and assertive action by the Western and Third World members. Since 1980 "general comments" have been used to interpret the Covenant in a specific way.

In 1981 the committee publicly criticized Uruguay for its treatment of certain individuals. The committee in effect rejected a report from Chile and criticized the inadequacies of several other reports. The committee also requested the Secretariat to put pressure on Zaire for its failure to file a report on time. Many states have been questioned closely about their reports and policies; frequently additional information is requested and provided. Aside from the Soviet Union and its close allies, the nature of questioning does not usually follow ideological alignments. At one point in 1983 the member from Yugoslavia seemed very tough on the subject of Nicaragua's treatment of Miskito Indians. At another point the member from West Germany was exceedingly tough in addressing the presenter of the report from France. The member from Tunisia led the effort to put pressure on Zaire.[9]

The Human Rights Committee has not functioned for very long. Its authority, procedures, and impact are still in flux. It seems clear thus far that the majority on the committee, irrespective of turnover, intends to have as much impact as it can generate. National laws in Sweden and Senegal have been changed, apparently as a result of committee questioning.

The Human Rights Sub-Commission

Over time the United Nations Sub-Commission on Prevention of Discrimination and Protection of Minorities has become an uninstructed body on human rights in general, functioning under the Charter under whatever mandates might be received from its parent commission, the ECOSOC, or the General Assembly and under whatever initiatives it might seize for itself.[10] On the one hand its membership has not been that different from its instructed parent, which elects its twenty-six members. In 1982, according to the index of Freedom House, ten members came from "Free," seven from "Partly Free," and nine from "Not Free" nations.[11] Many individuals have served as instructed representatives of states in other bodies and also as supposed uninstructed members of the subcommission. This is a prevalent personnel pattern not limited to Eastern European delegations, one that reappears in the Human Rights Committee as well. On the other hand the members of the subcommission have been so assertive at times that its superior bodies have found it "necessary" to suppress its activity, ignore its projects, change its mandates, or change its membership. It has been more willing than its superiors to use public pressure on states. It has sought to do as much as it can on a number of particular problems like detained or disappeared persons. It has tried a variety of procedures to improve its efficacy, such as working groups that meet before its regular session to address particular problems. The working group on slavery has been notable in this regard. It is the UN body of first recourse for private communications under important resolutions that are noted below, and it has performed that review with seriousness of purpose since 1972. At times it has attempted direct, public, and specific protection—for example, the sending of a telegram to the government of Malawi concerning a violation of human rights.

At one time there was some fear that the expansion of the subcommission's membership—and thus an increase in Third World members—would dilute or slant its activity. This does not appear to have happened. In the 1980s members from Eastern Europe, joined by the one from Pakistan, tried to have established the principle that the subcommission would act only by consensus. This would have given a blocking role to a minority that might wish to curtail the persistently assertive subcommission. This move was rejected, with a number of Third World members lining up with Western members.[12] The subjects taken up by the Human Rights Sub-Commission, the states criticized, and the resolutions passed do not show a simple East-West or North-South bias. At the time of writing the subcommission seemed as serious and assertive as in the past—and as seriously circumscribed.

The Commission on Human Rights

The United Nations Commission on Human Rights is an instructed body elected by ECOSOC and now comprising forty-three states. Using the rating system of Freedom House, one finds that in 1982 the commission was made up of seventeen states classified as "Not Free," ten as "Partly Free," and sixteen as "Free."[13] If 63 percent of states making up a human rights body show major deficiencies in their own records concerning civil and political rights, one might reasonably expect that body to be less than enthusiastic in its activity—at least on those rights. This assumption, however, is not completely substantiated by the facts.

If one looks at the decade of the commission after the drafting of the Covenants and later after two expansions of its membership it can be said that doctrinal disputes over the relationship of socio-

economic and civil-political rights—and over which had priority—
gave way to an increasing focus on the protection of specific civil
and political rights.[14] During the 1980s

> the West has become increasingly successful at enlisting majority
> support for new implementation measures to protect civil and po-
> litical rights. In 1980 the Commission for the first time indirectly
> condemned an Eastern bloc ally by passing a resolution calling
> for withdrawal of foreign forces from Kampuchea. In the following
> two sessions, the Commission denounced foreign intervention in
> Afghanistan. The West also narrowly succeeded in getting Com-
> mission action on Poland and Iran in 1982. [There were also]
> several important Western-sponsored resolutions adopted by
> consensus—involving the appointment of special rapporteurs on
> mass exoduses and summary or arbitrary executions, and studies
> on the role of the individual in international law.[15]

The key to these and other developments within the commission
has been the role of Third World states that are truly nonaligned.
They have voted their concern for self-determination in Kampuchea
and Afghanistan, and they have also voted for economic rights and
against racial discrimination.[16] Some Third World states like Senegal
have been vigorous and balanced in their attention to human rights
violations. It seems evident that a number of Third World states are
genuinely interested in human rights, even civil and political rights.
Daniel Patrick Moynihan noted that one of the merits of framing
issues in terms of human rights, rather than democracy pure and
simple, was that a state did not have to be a democracy to pursue
the subject with some real interest.[17] Of course some Third World
states, of various ideological stripes, have sought to limit the activity
of the commission. For example, Pakistan, India, and Ethiopia have
all taken restrictive positions in commission debates at one time or
another. And any state may seek to block attention to its own
transgressions.

Yet, in the final analysis, it has been Third World support for
Western positions, and vice versa, that has allowed the commission
to do as much as it has. Since 1978 the commission has been publishing a "Black List" of states that have been the subject of private
complaints as noted confidentially by the subcommission. Over time
this list has shown considerable balance.[18] To be sure, this Black
List is a very weak form of pressure; specifics are not provided. A
working group of the commission has been focusing in a balanced

way on states in which persons "disappear" by forceful action.[19] A summary statement about the Commission on Human Rights seems accurate:

Representatives continue to assert the principle of non-intervention when it suits their national interest, but in practice most members of the Commission have supported some initiatives to protect the human rights of citizens against violation by their own governments. . . . the Commission has systematically reviewed confidential communications alleging violations by members. . . . the Commission has expanded its concern for violations far beyond the early narrow focus on South Africa and Israel and has reviewed allegations involving over thirty states. Members and NGOs now disregard the former taboo against attacking states by name in public debate and make sweeping public indictments. After thirty years, the Commission has become the world's first intergovernmental body that regularly challenges sovereign nations to explain abusive treatment of their own citizens.[20]

ECOSOC

The Economic and Social Council receives the reports of the Commission on Human Rights, as well as state reports under the UN Covenant on Economic, Social, and Cultural Rights—a treaty now in legal force in about eighty states. In this part of the United Nations system there does not at first glance seem to be striking change in the treatment of human rights. The conventional wisdom has been that on human rights ECOSOC functions as a post office, carrying mandates from one body to another.[21] A recent analysis by an insider argued that ECOSOC was still giving "very superficial scrutiny" to state reports on socioeconomic rights and had failed to develop or borrow standards by which to evaluate violations.[22] Yet several further points can be noted, even if the ECOSOC votes on human rights discussed below reflect decisions already made in the Commission on Human Rights.

In the late 1960s Third World states pushed for specific attention to human rights violations by South Africa and Israel in many parts of the United Nations system, including ECOSOC. That body, stimulated by reports not only from the Commission on Human Rights but also from the UN Special Committee on Decolonization, passed E/RES/1235 in 1967. This resolution—originally intended only for

situations of racism, colonialism, and alien domination, but amended
by the West to include other human rights violations—authorized
ECOSOC's suborgans to deal with specifics revealing a pattern of
gross violations of human rights. The following year an effort to
close the barn door failed; ECOSOC again refused to limit the scope
of Resolution 1235 to only some violations of human rights, and
thus the Commission on Human Rights and its subcommission were
authorized to take up specific patterns with full publicity.[23]

Three years after the passage of Resolution 1235, ECOSOC adopted
E/RES/1503, which permitted its suborgans to deal with private
communications alleging violations of human rights. This resolution
permitted NGOs as well as individuals—anyone with direct and reliable knowledge—to lodge an allegation confidentially with the
Secretariat, which then passed a sanitized version to the Human
Rights Sub-Commission for possible future action.

The result of these two resolutions in ECOSOC was to make possible the expanded activity of the Human Rights Commission and
Sub-Commission noted above. Specifics could be pursued and private information could be formally utilized. There was both a public
and a confidential process, although the two did not always remain
distinct. The point worth stressing is that certain Third World and
Western states succeeded in getting authorized more serious attention to human rights. An effort by the East Europeans and other
Third World states to keep the process limited to the international
pariahs was not successful. The margin of success for the majority
was very small on both resolutions. The key to the majority, in addition to Western states, was certain Third World states that sought
a balanced approach to human rights protection.[24]

General Assembly

Much has already been written about the General Assembly and
its standing committees on human rights. A widespread impression,
supported to be sure by considerable evidence, is that the Assembly
has "politicized" human rights by employing double or otherwise
unfair or unacceptable standards. Israel is publicly and harshly criticized by a special committee made up of three states that do not
even have formal diplomatic relations with the Jewish state. Yet the
Soviet Union's gulag is never formally condemned by the UN bodies
discussed here. The litany about the tyranny of the majority in the
General Assembly is too well known to require restatement. Con-

siderable attention has also been given to the view that the majority
has tried to erase serious attention to civil and political rights by
elevating social and economic rights to a place of exclusive priority.[25]

In the present chapter there is space only to suggest a counter
thesis and to give one example as evidence. Much is wrong with
the General Assembly's treatment of human rights. Politics controls:
equity suffers. Increasingly, however, one sees—at least in the Third
Committee on Social and Humanitarian Affairs—an improved balance in the treatment of human rights, produced by the same West-
ern-Third World coalition found in other organs. Take the following
example.

In 1982 the Third Committee held yet another doctrinal debate
about the priority of rights. As the representatives of both New Zealand and Senegal noted, the debate was about the balance between
individual and collective rights. An Irish resolution emphasized the
former, a Cuban the latter. The crux of the matter came down to
whether each resolution could be adopted without distorting
amendments, thus signifying that each type of right had importance.
The Cuban resolution was voted upon first and adopted by 104–1–
24 (the single negative vote was cast by the United States, the ab-
stainers were mostly Western). The Irish resolution was also finally
adopted 75–30–22. Voting with the West in the majority were 46
nonaligned states.[26] A similar alignment carried the day on paragraph
12 of the Irish resolution, which authorized a study of the mandate
of a possible High Commissioner for Human Rights.

As on any vote in any political body, there is no one simple reason
explaining a coalition. The list of those voting for the Irish resolution
does not reflect a club of the pure on civil and political rights—
witness the inclusion of Paraguay. Despite the fact that the Cuban
resolution was assured passage and the Irish was not, the end result
was that individual civil and political rights received equal formal
endorsement. This was made possible by the number of Third World
states that were not prepared to endorse a one-sided approach to
human rights—at least in principle.

Security Council

The Security Council has not been generally linked to the protection
of human rights. This is not correct. Indeed, on the two occasions
when the Council reached a "decision" concerning enforcement
action in relation to the Charter's Chapter VII, the real issue at stake

was human rights. The decision in the 1960s to consider Ian Smith's Unilateral Declaration of Independence in Rhodesia as a threat to peace meriting mandatory economic sanctions was a decision designed to implement the right to self-determination for the majority in what was to become Zimbabwe. That right is the first right listed in each of the two general UN Covenants on human rights. The decision in the 1970s to consider arms traffic with South Africa a threat to the peace requiring a mandatory ban on such traffic was an indirect approach to the subject of apartheid as a gross violation of internationally recognized human rights, and perhaps as a violation of self-determination as well. Especially with regard to South Africa and Namibia, the Council has called upon states to implement the principles contained in the Universal Declaration of Human Rights. As a member of the Secretariat has observed, in these actions the Council "treated respect for the basic provisions of the Declaration as a legal obligation of States as well as of their nationals."[27]

The Reasons

It can be easily seen from the incomplete synopsis above that on human rights the United Nations is not what it was. What are the underlying reasons for this change? At least five sets of factors contributed to this modification.

States' Foreign Policies

A view achieving some popularity in the 1980s is that events unfold at the United Nations according to a struggle between the United States and the rest of the world.[28] It follows, then, that on human rights questions any progress must be because of the quality of the diplomacy of the United States–led West. This view is overstated, although it is correct in one sense.

The Soviet bloc, joined by some Third World states, has been consistently hostile to international civil-political rights and to any meaningful UN review process. The Soviet interpretation of human rights under Marxísm, one that is inhospitable to the prima facie meaning of UN instruments, is stated openly. "The political freedoms—freedom of the press, of expression, of assembly—are interpreted from class positions as conditions of the consolidation of the working people and the spread of socialist ideology which rules out the 'freedom' of anti-socialist propaganda, the freedom to or-

ganize counter-revolutionary forces against the fundamentals of socialism."[29] Thus the individual has the right to say and do what the
party-state decrees is progressive for socialism. That being so, the
Soviet-led socialist bloc will try to avoid real supervision of its rights
policies by a nonsocialist review body.

The Soviet Union has been consistent in opposing real international standards and supervision. In 1947 it opposed having the UN
Commission on Human Rights made up of uninstructed individuals.
In 1948 it first tried to postpone and then finally abstained on the
vote on the Universal Declaration. In the 1980s it argued that the
UN Human Rights Committee should have no real control over
states' interpretation of the civil-political Covenant. The member
of that committee from East Germany even argued that the committee had no right to take any action whatsoever when a state failed
even to submit a required report.[30] On issue after issue during the
first forty years of the United Nations, the Soviet Union and its allies,
joined occasionally by such non-Marxist authoritarian states as Pakistan and the Philippines, tried to suppress attention to international
civil-political rights and to vitiate real UN supervision of rights policies. The Soviet Union deviated from this orientation only when
it had the opportunity to make difficulty for a strategic adversary—
for example, supporting intrusive UN supervision of the rights situation in Pinochet's Chile.

That the Soviets and their shifting bedfellows on human rights
have not always, or even fundamentally, triumphed at the United
Nations is because of two factors. First, other states have displayed
an equally persistent interest in a different interpretation, especially
of civil and political rights (as well as a real interest in socioeconomic
rights), and have fought for a genuine review process at the UN. One
thinks primarily of the Scandinavian states, but also at times of the
United States, the rest of the Western coalition, and some Third
World States.

Second, a self-serving interpretation equal to that of the Soviets
by some U.S. administrations has offset the Soviet position and, in
a dialectical process, caused a number of states to seek a compromise
leading to a certain type of progress. If the Soviet Union consistently
displayed a double standard in favor of socialist states, so the United
States at times manifested a double standard in favor of authoritarian
and capitalistic states aligned with it. When a rapporteur for the
Human Rights Sub-Commission authored a report criticizing economic relations supporting the governing junta in Chile after 1973,

the United States helped suppress it.[31] When resolutions were introduced in various UN organs criticizing the gross violations of human rights in El Salvador and Guatemala, the United States voted against.[32] At one point the United States voted against a commission study on the right to food,[33] and it is well known that the United States was the only government to vote against World Health Organization voluntary guidelines designed to protect mothers and infants from questionable marketing practices by the Nestlé Corporation. It was obvious that the Reagan administration liked to publicly castigate leftist governments, such as Cuba's, while remaining silent about mass political murder by governments of the right, such as Argentina's. Ambassador Jeane Kirkpatrick had written approvingly of such double standards.[34] Thus a U.S. double standard, an American self-serving bias, could be and was observed at the United Nations.[35] This provided a counterpoint to the Soviet position.

In sum, because some states were genuinely interested in a cosmopolitan human rights program and because some states sought a compromise between the self-serving positions of the superpowers, states' foreign policies contributed mightily to alteration of the United Nations' record on human rights. State hypocrisy, narrow self-interest, and blatant double standards, along with more cosmopolitan forces, combined to produce a certain progress over time.[36]

Nongovernmental Organizations

One of the main reasons the United Nations record on human rights is different in the 1980s from the earlier days is the activity of nongovernmental international organizations. Groups such as Amnesty International, the International Commission of Jurists, the International League for Human Rights, and others have been creative and energetic in keeping the pressure on states to acknowledge and then implement international human rights standards.

It was NGO information that started various UN organs down the path of a slow but eventually interesting treatment of human rights violations in Equatorial Guinea in the 1970s. Confidential NGO information was provided to the Human Rights Sub-Commission and eventually the commission sent a rapporteur for an in-country visit, which led to a public report critical not only of the fallen regime but of the sitting one as well. NGO pressure after the passage of E/RES/1235 quickly broadened the Human Rights Sub-Commission's focus beyond Israel and South Africa; information was submitted on Greece under military rule and also on Haiti. NGOs successfully pushed for passage of E/RES/1503 permitting confidential communiques, again of broad scope. They kept the pressure on states to do something about the growing problem of torture and they pushed successfully for a special group on disappeared persons. NGO reports are used openly by the Committee of Experts under the Racial Discrimination Convention. In the Commission on Human Rights their information is referred to formally by Secretariat reports. In the Human Rights Committee it is now acknowledged that members can informally use NGO reports as a basis for questioning the accuracy of state reports.[37]

Nongovernmental organizations have been so active on human rights at the United Nations that various states have threatened to curtail their activity—sometimes succeeding, but more often failing. The Soviet Union, for example, tried unsuccessfully to exclude NGO reports from ECOSOC and its suborgans.[38] Other threats against NGOs have been made—by Argentina and Iran, for example—such as to deny a group consultative status, but these have not been carried out. The very fact that NGOs are attacked by states suggests that these groups are taken seriously by states. Several observers believe that NGO activity is essential for continued efforts at protecting human rights.[39]

Secretariat

Members of the Secretariat have contributed to the changing United Nations record on human rights, from the Secretary-General down through the Directors (now Assistant Secretary-General) for Human Rights to the Secretariat officials who service the various human rights working groups. The five Secretaries-General have been supportive of human rights to varying degrees. On a number of occasions the Secretary-General has used his good offices for quiet diplomacy designed to correct some human rights problem.[40] Publicly they have endorsed the cause, as when Pérez de Cuéllar said in his 1983 annual report, "In the common quest to realize the ideals and objectives of the Charter, we must never lose sight of the quality of the world we are seeking to build and of the ultimate raison d'être for all our objectivities: the individual human being."[41]

The head of the Human Rights Division (now Centre) in the Secretariat has always been a Westerner: John P. Humphrey of Canada, Marc Schreiber of Belgium, Theo van Boven of the Netherlands,

Kurt Herndl of Austria, and Jan Marteson of Sweden. Van Boven was perhaps the most assertive, so much so that he was dismissed by Pérez de Cuéllar after conflicts with certain states like the Soviet Union and Argentina under military rule, which was diplomatically supported by the United States.[42] Humphrey was highly active in a somewhat more diplomatic way, playing a key role in the drafting of the Universal Declaration, suggesting ideas to states that then pursued them through the United Nations system, and strongly defending civil and political rights as traditionally understood by the West.[43] Schreiber was perhaps less dynamic than van Boven or Humphrey, although these things are difficult to prove given the possibility of extensive quiet diplomacy. Herndl held his position for only a short time and made little impact, perhaps keeping a low profile after the dismissal of his predecessor. Marteson is also Director of the Geneva office of the UN, which may diminish the time he devotes to human rights activities.

Uninstructed Individuals

Individuals on the Human Rights Sub-Commission and the Human Rights Committee especially must be given credit for contributing to increased efforts at specific protection. Mention should also be made of other uninstructed bodies not given adequate attention in this chapter because of lack of space: the Committee of Experts under the Racial Discrimination Convention, the Commission on Women, the Commission on Discrimination Against Women, the Committee of Experts and the Freedom of Association Commission of the International Labor Organization, and the office of the UN High Commissioner for Refugees (UNHCR). The UNHCR is perhaps the uninstructed agency given the highest marks for its human rights work and merits extended analysis (see chapter 9 by Leon Gordenker in this volume). On all these bodies there have been individuals keenly interested in the protection of human rights. They have generated some influence, impossible to measure in the aggregate. A number of these persons have come from the Third World.

World Public Opinion

One can certainly overstate the importance of the hoary idea of world public opinion. And it is certainly unwise to attribute much importance to something that cannot be precisely identified or clearly discerned in impact. Even so, I think it prudent to note what other scholars have observed. "National political leaders have to reckon with the possibility, and on occasion the reality, that powerful voices in their own societies will echo the words of the General Assembly, as they have done on issues of colonialism, human rights . . . and humanitarian assistance."[44] If this is what is meant by world public opinion, then there is probably a process at work that bears noting— and merits more research attention in the future.

It seems highly probable, but not proven in all cases, that various public groups draw some of the inspiration and legitimacy for their human rights activity from United Nations resolutions, declarations, and conventions. Various groups in Eastern Europe refer to these documents as well as to others, such as the Helsinki Accord. The various human rights groups in Argentina did the same, in addition to relying on human rights instruments under the Organization of Amerian States. Obviously there is some overlap between what is called "world public opinion" and the impact of nongovernmental organizations. Yet some groups and private citizens do not act directly on the United Nations system but are active at home in demanding that their governments abide by global—that is, United Nations—standards on human rights. In that sense there is something that passes for world public opinion—weak and uneven in distribution, but extant and possibly even growing. There is at least fragmentary evidence that even in closed societies governments are asked by some of their citizens to observe the human rights standards endorsed at the United Nations.

In the United Nations political process concerning human rights, coalitions frequently form to protect a particular right in a specific situation; these are made up of interested state delegates, uninstructed individuals, members of the Secretariat, and concerned officials of NGOs. They exchange information and coordinate tactics. Sometimes world public opinion is represented by large or important states or NGOs. Sometimes world public opinion operates indirectly as a background condition; participants in the UN system are aware of demonstrations or riots or other actions by individuals not really represented in UN decisions—for example, Chileans demanding democratic rights.

The Significance

The significance of United Nations activity on human rights can be discussed in terms of immediate and long-term effects. The immediate impact is usually slight, for the United Nations was not—

and is not in the 1980s—used primarily to bring about direct protection. Efforts of this genre exist from time to time: telegrams to Malawi; public reports about specific individuals in Uruguay; public debates about specific policies, states, and persons; special reports about Equatorial Guinea. These efforts of direct protection will continue; states and individuals and groups will press the United Nations to take short-term action on particular problems.

There is not much evidence, however, that such protection activity by the UN bodies discussed in this chapter has had much impact on target states, at least in the short run. In some cases this negative and public approach has backfired, as in the 1970s when Pinochet used United Nations pressure about human rights violations in Chile to produce a national plebiscite endorsing his military regime. In these situations in which change in human rights clearly occurs— for example, in South Africa in the mid-1980s—it is difficult to attribute change directly to the UN, since so many other variables are present. Furthermore, when a ruling group is determined to violate human rights consciously, it is doubtful that any international arrangement short of armed intervention will bring an end to these violations in the short run—witness Greece under the colonels, Argentina under the junta, and so on. Nevertheless, the cumulative effect of UN activity may contribute to progress over time, and it is provocative to consider "glasnost," or increasing openness, in the Soviet Union in this regard.

This last observation leads to the general point that the bulk of United Nations activity on human rights is not designed to produce short-term change. The Human Rights Committee's main activity is to produce a record of *patterns* over time drawn from states' reports and members' questions. Under E/RES/1503 confidential communications and the Human Rights Sub-Commission's analysis are supposed to deal with patterns of gross violations of human rights. The Commission on Human Rights' publication of a Black List about states, even though it is devoid of specifics, is designed to focus on certain states *over time*. Moreover, what would be required for successful direct protection? The authority to command states to abandon practices that violate protected rights? The ability to enforce such a command? Overwhelming political pressure directed to human rights violations to the exclusion of other interests? No United Nations human rights body has such authority and power. Only the Security Council comes close, and even its power to enforce is tenuous, as seen in the history of economic sanctions on Rhodesia.

Those most familiar with the United Nations and human rights understand that the organization does not normally utilize its authority and power for direct protection.[45] As a general rule only states and a few international agencies have the capacity to attempt direct protection: the European Court and Commission on Human Rights, the Inter-American Commission on Human Rights, the International Committee of the Red Cross, the United Nations High Commissioner for Refugees.[46] The United Nations' primary raison d'être in the human rights field is long-term.

The long-term effects of the United Nations on human rights can be viewed in two ways. One can say that the sum total of UN activity is supposed to socialize or educate actors into changing their views and policies over time toward a cosmopolitan human rights standard as defined by United Nations instruments. Or one can say that the sum total of UN activity is to dispense or withhold a stamp of legitimacy on member states according to their human rights record.

A version of the latter view has gained some currency in American circles in the 1970s and 1980s. Ambassadors Moynihan and Kirkpatrick, among others, have charged that the United Nations is a dangerous place where a majority attempts to delegitimize the Western democracies while legitimizing its own violations of civil and political rights in the name of economic development.[47] This chapter demonstrates that the Moynihan-Kirkpatrick thesis is essentially correct when applied to the Soviet bloc and some Third World states, but that it is not accurate as a description of the overall UN record on human rights.

It does seem correct to highlight the socialization process and the dispensing of legitimacy, which are two sides of the same coin, as the main activity of the United Nations in the human rights area. It can be persuasively argued that in some cases—for example, Somoza's Nicaragua, the Shah's Iran, perhaps Marcos' Philippines— the ruling regime lost its legitimacy in the eyes of important actors because of human rights violations. UN definitions of human rights, along with other international standards and actors, probably contributed to the process.[48]

The preceding examples might suggest that primarily non-Marxist authoritarian states have the most to fear from attention to international standards of human rights. Certainly the major democratic states have shown periodic discomfort about their close alignments with human rights violators. Yet it also seems true that Marxist states have problems of legitimacy and do not fare well when international sources of legitimacy are denied. Those who rule Poland have not been helped by persistent condemnation by the International Labor Organization, not to mention sporadic censure by the UN Commission on Human Rights. And there are a number of specialists on the Soviet Union who believe that achieving international legitimacy is still a pressing problem and priority for the Soviet Union itself,[49] not to mention Nicaragua under the Sandinistas.

United Nations activity on human rights is most important for this long-term socialization process in which legitimacy is given or withheld because of the state's human rights performance. Any number of states are in need of the United Nations' stamp of approval, or in need of avoiding its disapproval, although all have other sources of legitimacy such as their own traditions, performance, and internal procedures. United Nations impact is further attenuated because its human rights endeavors are poorly coordinated.

At some point the long-term effects of the UN must become short-term if the organization is to show real impact on states and individuals. Socialization and manipulation of legitimacy must change specific behavior, must lead to direct protection by some actor, if the United Nations is to have real significance for human rights. In a few situations this linkage can be demonstrated. In the case of *Filartiga vs. Peña-Irala* in the United States, a federal court held torture to be prohibited by customary international law, using United Nations instruments and actions as part of its legal reasoning.[50] This case opened the possibility of specific prosecution for torturers of any nationality who appear in the jurisdiction of the United States. Other courts in the United States have also used UN instruments and activity on human rights as part of their decisions.[51] Other countries also show some influence from UN instruments in their legal and administrative decisions.[52] Politically it is clear that various groups and individuals refer to events at the United Nations to justify their existence and activity, and it is highly likely that in situations like that in the southern cone of South America in the 1980s the United Nations—along with other bodies—had a real if indirect impact on human rights and even the structure of national politics.

Therefore a smattering of evidence suggests that UN activity on human rights over time can have some real impact in changing behavior by contributing to direct protection by national authorities. Other evidence suggests that in other situations United Nations activity has very little, if any, impact.[53]

Conclusion

We do not lack for criticism of the United Nations when it comes to human rights. Already noted was the Kirkpatrick-Moynihan thesis, as well as the argument that socioeconomic matters are being used to exclude attention to civil and political rights. Ernst Haas writes that UN efforts to implement human rights standards "do not work."[54] Richard Ullman concludes that "the UN human rights machinery has become so politicized as to be almost completely ineffective for either monitoring or for enforcement."[55] Moses Moskowitz reminds us that UN standards on human rights remain vague and their supervision weak.[56]

There are facts to support these views, some of which have not been emphasized either for lack of space or because this conventional wisdom is widely known. The United Nations review system is neither so streamlined nor so authoritative as that under the European Convention on Human Rights.[57] United Nations core procedures are less developed and less effective than those used by the ILO.[58] Some UN bodies have been less dynamic than the Inter-American Commission on Human Rights.[59] Information from nongovernmental organizations is more formally employed in some European international regimes.[60] After all, even the League of Nations permitted individual petitions and accorded nongovernmental organizations a good deal of formal status on human rights.[61]

And yet there is a second view. Antonio Cassese remarked that much criticism of the United Nations is "largely unfounded."[62] In the same vein Louis Henkin argued that "disappointment may reflect unwarranted expectations."[63] Both of these authors speak to the point stressed by John Gerard Ruggie: United Nations activity and "international human rights instruments are designed not to provide human rights or to enforce human rights provisions, but to nudge states into permitting their vindication."[64] Or, in Henkin's words, "For the most part, human rights can only be promoted indirectly" by the United Nations.[65]

This chapter has shown in some detail that the second view can be supported by considerable evidence, even if the first view remains correct in its own way. That is, even if there has been inequitable treatment of human rights in the General Assembly, and even if there has been a lack of sustained success in direct protection efforts, there has also been a marked and improved record of treating human rights in the other organs of the United Nations system—

and even at times in ECOSOC and the General Assembly's Third Committee. This improved record holds the promise of a more equitable dispensation of legitimacy from the United Nations, although that goal has not yet been reached. Indeed, the process of socialization in pursuit of a cosmopolitan understanding of human rights could be undone by concerted state attack.

A formal human rights regime is associated with the United Nations, despite the fact that expectations of important parties do not converge in this issue area. For example, the Soviet Union does not accept an international standard on civil and political rights, as shown in this chapter, and the Reagan administration does not accept the existence of socioeconomic rights, as analyzed elsewhere.[66] Yet a core coalition of states drawn from the industrialized democracies and from the truly nonaligned Third World has repeatedly converged to maintain the United Nations human rights regime and to try to embarrass states that violate its rules.[67] The various mechanisms of the regime remain somewhat chaotic, since not all supervising bodies or decisionmaking organs act in concert. Warts and all, there is, in the last analysis a "tutelage regime" associated with the United Nations that seeks to improve human rights policies by states.[68] The Peña case, among other things, shows clearly that this indirect protection can eventually have discernible effect.

Professor Ruggie tells us that United Nations activity on human rights "to some extent" alters day-to-day politics, but that human rights activity still occurs in a fundamentally inhospitable environment.[69] Secretary-General Pérez de Cuéllar says in his 1983 annual report that there has been progress in human rights at the international level, but that "gross violations of human rights . . . are taking place in many parts of the world."[70] Both are correct, as to some extent are the pessimists (Haas, Ullman, et al.) and the optimists (Henkin, Cassese, et al.). That is why there are reasons to be ambivalent about the United Nations and human rights.

Notes

This chapter is a revision of my previously published study, "The United Nations and Human Rights 1945–1985," *Political Science Quarterly*, Summer 1985.

1. Howard Tolley, Jr., *The United Nations Commission on Human Rights* (Boulder, Colo.: Westview Press, 1987); Theo C. van Boven, "United Nations and Human Rights: a Critical Appraisal," in *U.N. Law/Fundamental Rights*, ed. Antonio Cassese (Alphen aan den Rijn: Sijthoff & Noordhoff, 1979), 119–36; *The International Dimensions of Human Rights*, ed. Karel Vasak, vols. 1–2 (Paris: UNESCO, 1982).

2. James Frederick Green, an advisor to Mrs. Roosevelt, confirms that the "Action Plan" was a diplomatic device to deflect criticism away from the U.S. policy shift. Interview, Atlanta, 1984. See also, Robert E. Asher et al., *The United Nations and Promotion of the General Welfare* (Washington, D.C.: Brookings Institution, 1957), 699–705.

3. M. E. Tardu, "United Nations Response to Gross Violations of Human Rights: the 1503 Procedure," *Santa Clara Law Review* 20,3 (Summer 1980): 559; and Van Boven, "United Nations and Human Rights," 122. For a good overview of the early climate of opinion at the UN, see Leon Gordenker, "Development of the U.N. System," in *The U.S., the U.N., and the Management of Global Change*, ed. Toby Trister Gati (New York: New York University Press, 1983), 11–21.

4. The fight to save the subcommission was led by Chile, Mexico, and the Philippines. The Soviet bloc gave its support. Those voting to keep alive the subcommission were: Afghanistan, Argentina, Burma, Byelorussia, Chile, Colombia, Czechoslovakia, Denmark, Dominican Republic, Ecuador, Egypt, Ethiopia, Haiti, Indonesia, Iran, Iraq, Liberia, Mexico, Pakistan, Paraguay, Peru, Philippines, Poland, Saudi Arabia, Syria, Ukraine, Soviet Union, Uruguay, Venezuela, Yemen, and Yugoslavia. *United Nations Yearbook, 1951* (New York: United Nations, 1954).

5. A/C.3/SR.89, September 30, 1948. See further A. Glenn Mower, Jr., *The United States, the United Nations, and Human Rights: The Eleanor Roosevelt and Jimmy Carter Eras* (Westport, Conn.: Greenwood Press, 1979).

6. Thomas Buergenthal, "Implementing the Racial Convention," *Texas International Law Journal* 12, 2 and 3 (Spring–Summer 1977): 187–222. While this convention came into legal force in 1969 and now has over 120 adherences, it was not until 1982 that ten states permitted individual petitions and thus brought that part of the treaty into legal force.

7. Dana D. Fischer, "Reporting under the Covenant on Civil and Political Rights: The First Five Years of the Human Rights Committee," *American Journal of International Law* 76,1 (January 1982): 142–53. Under Article 41 states may declare that the committee is authorized to receive complaints from other states. Too much can be made of this. The history of other instruments—that is, the European Convention on Human Rights—shows that states are reluctant to make such legal claims. Similar political claims can already be made in the General Assembly or Commission on Human Rights.

8. CCPR/C/SR.201, March 24, 1980. CCPR/C/SR.231, July 24, 1980. CCPR/C/SR.232, July 23, 1980. CCPR/C/SR.253, October 28, 1980. CCPR/C/SR.260, November 4, 1980.

9. *United Nations Chronicle* 20,1 (January 1983): 105; *United Nations Chronicle* 20,7 (July 1983): 92–95; *United Nations Chronicle* 20,10 (November 1983): 57–64.

10. See further Tolley, *The United Nations Commission on Human Rights*.

11. "Free" countries were Belgium, Costa Rica, France, Greece, India, Nigeria, Norway, Peru, the United Kingdom, and the United States. "Partly Free" were Bangladesh, Egypt, Mexico, Morocco, Panama, Sudan, and Zambia. "Not Free" were Argentina, Ethiopia, Ghana, Iraq, Pakistan, Romania, Syria, the Soviet Union, and Yugoslavia. There is much controversy about the accuracy of this index.

12. *Human Rights Internet Reporter* 9,1 and 2 (September–November 1983): 58–59.

13. "Free": Australia, Canada, Costa Rica, Cyprus (Greek sector), France, West Germany, Greece, Italy, the Netherlands, the United Kingdom, Denmark, Fiji, India,

Japan, Peru, and the United States. "Partly Free": Panama, Philippines, Uganda, Uruguay, Zimbabwe, Brazil, Gambia, Mexico, Senegal, and Zambia. "Not Free": Algeria, Bulgaria, Ethiopia, Jordan, Rwanda, Syria, Zaire, Argentina, Byelorussia, China, Cuba, Ghana, Pakistan, Poland, Togo, the Soviet Union, and Yugoslavia. Again, this index is controversial.

14. Philip Alston, "The Alleged Demise of Political Human Rights at the U.N.: A Reply to Donnelly," *International Organization* 37,3 (Summer 1983): 537–46; van Boven, "United Nations and Human Rights," 90.

15. Tolley, *The United Nations Commission on Human Rights.*

16. Ibid.

17. Daniel Patrick Moynihan, *A Dangerous Place* (Boston: Little, Brown, 1978), 281.

18. Through the Spring of 1984 the following states had been targeted: Albania, Argentina, Benin, Bolivia, Burma, Chile, Equatorial Guinea, Ethiopia, Greece, Indonesia, Iran, Malawi, Nicaragua, Paraguay, South Korea (not a UN member), South Africa, Uganda, Uruguay, and the Soviet Union.

19. Through the Spring of 1982 the following states had been targeted: Argentina, Bolivia, Brazil, Chile, Cyprus, El Salvador, Ethiopia, Guatemala, Guinea, Honduras, Indonesia, Iran, Lesotho, Mexico, Nicaragua, Philippines, Sri Lanka, Uganda, Uruguay, Zaire, South Africa, and Namibia. Interestingly, the Working Group was made up of three "Not Free" states (Ghana, Pakistan, and Yugoslavia) and two "Free" ones (Costa Rica and the United Kingdom).

20. Tolley, *The United Nations Commission on Human Rights.*

21. James Frederick Green, "Changing Approaches to Human Rights: The United Nations, 1954 and 1974," *Texas International Law Journal* 12,2 and 3 (Spring–Summer 1979), 223.

22. Alston, "The Alleged Demise." See also his "The United Nations' Specialized Agencies and Implementation of the International Covenant on Economic, Social and Cultural Rights," *Columbia Journal of Transnational Law* 18,1 (1979): 79–118.

23. Tardu, "United Nations Response."

24. Ibid.

25. Jack Donnelly, "Recent Trends in U.N. Human Rights Activity: Description and Polemic," *International Organization* 35,4 (Autumn 1981): 633–55.

26. Bahamas, Barbados, Botswana, Burma, Chad, Colombia, Costa Rica, Cyprus, Democratic Kampuchea (represented by the Pol Pot faction), Djibouti, Dominican Republic, Ecuador, Egypt, El Salvador, Fiji, Gabon, Guatemala, Ivory Coast, Jamaica, Kenya, Lesotho, Liberia, Malawi, Mali, Mexico, Morocco, Nepal, Niger, Papua New Guinea, Paraguay, Peru, Philippines, Senegal, Sierra Leone, Singapore, Somalia, Sri Lanka, Sudan, Tanzania, Thailand, Trinidad and Tobago, Upper Volta, Uruguay, Venezuela, Zambia, and Zimbabwe. Voting with the East Europeans in the minority were Afghanistan, Algeria, Angola, Argentina (under military rule), Congo, Cuba, Democratic Yemen, Laos, Libya, Madagascar, Mongolia, Pakistan, Syria, Vietnam. Other states abstained, including Ethiopia and Nicaragua. A/C.3/37/SR.60, December 1982, 7, 17–19.

27. Egon Schwelb and Philip Alston, "The Principal Institutions and Other Bodies Founded under the Charter," in *The International Dimensions of Human Rights*, vols. 1–2, ed. Karel Vasak (Paris: UNESCO, 1982), 262.

28. Richard Bernstein, "The United Nations vs. The United States," *New York Times Magazine* (January 22, 1984), 18ff. On human rights see esp. 25–26.

29. Vladimir Kartashkin, "The Socialist Countries and Human Rights," in *The International Dimensions of Human Rights*, vols. 1–2, ed. Karel Vasak (Paris: UNESCO, 1982), 633.

30. CCPR/C/SR.201, March 24, 1980, 4–5.

31. Tolley, *The United Nations Commission on Human Rights*.

32. *United Nations Chronicle* 20,6 (June 1983): 28.

33. *United Nations Chronicle* 21,7 (July 1983): 80.

34. *Dictatorships and Double Standards* (Washington, D.C.: American Enterprise Institute, 1982).

35. If the U.S. double standard was particularly pronounced during the Reagan administration, in fairness it should be noted that in 1974 Rita Hauser, a former representative to the UN commission, testified in Congress that the United States frequently used a double standard at the UN. U.S. House of Representatives, Committee on Foreign Affairs, "Human Rights in the World Community: A Call to Leadership," *Report of the Sub-Committee on International Organizations* (Washington, D.C.: U.S. Government Printing Office, 1974), 10,11. See also Tolley, *The United Nations Commission on Human Rights*.

36. On the subject of how state hypocrisy can lead to beneficial change, see Louis Henkin, "The United Nations and Human Rights," *International Organization* 19,3 (Summer 1965): 514.

37. The literature on NGOs has grown voluminously. Particularly enlightening for this essay were: Virginia Leary, "A New Role for Non-Governmental Organizations in Human Rights," in *U.N. Law/Fundamental Rights*, ed. Antonio Cassese (Alphen aan den Rijn: Sijthoff & Noordhoff, 1979), 197–210; Nigel S. Rodley, "The Development of United Nations Activities in the Field of Human Rights and the Role of Non-Governmental Organizations," in *The U.S., the U.N., and the Management of Global Change*, ed. Toby Trister Gati (New York: New York University Press, 1983), 263–82; and Chiang Pei-Leng, *Non-Governmental Organizations at the United Nations: Identity, Role, and Function* (New York: Praeger, 1981).

38. Philip Alston, "UNESCO Procedures for Dealing with Human Rights Violations," *Santa Clara Law Review* 20,3 (Summer 1980): 669.

39. For example, David P. Forsythe, *Human Rights and World Politics* (Lincoln, Neb.: University of Nebraska Press, 1983).

40. B. G. Ramcharan, "The Good Offices of the United Nations Secretary-General in the Field of Human Rights," *American Journal of International Law* 76,1 (January 1982): 130–41.

41. *United Nations Chronicle* 20,9 (October 1983): 78.

42. Other reasons may have contributed to his dismissal. Some of his candid views are found in his book, *People Matter: Views on International Human Rights Policy* (Amsterdam: Meulenhoff, 1982).

43. John P. Humphrey, *Human Rights and the United Nations: The Great Adventure* (Dobbs Ferry, N.Y.: Transnational Publishers, 1983). Excerpts published as "The Memoirs of John P. Humphrey," *Human Rights Quarterly* 5,4 (November 1983).

44. Gordenker, "Development of the U.N. System," 33.

45. See especially John Gerard Ruggie, "Human Rights and the Future International Community," *Daedalus* 112,4 (Fall 1983): 93–110; and N. G. Onuf and V. Spike Peterson, "Human Rights and International Regimes," *Journal of International Affairs* 37,2 (Winter 1984): 329ff. See also Henkin, "The United Nations and Human Rights"; Tardu, "United Nations Response"; and an unpublished paper, Helge Ole

Bergesen, "The Power to Embarrass: The U.N. Human Rights Regime between Realism and Utopia," paper for the International Political Science Association World Congress, August 1982.

46. Direct protection has never been defined legally or analytically. It may be a phenomenon known when seen but resistant to precise definition. All international regimes or agencies that seek direct protection activities depend to some extent on state cooperation. This dependence does not denigrate direct protection. See Onuf and Peterson, "Human Rights." The key is that a human rights actor trying direct protection seeks immediate and specific change either by command—for example, the European Court of Human Rights, or by diplomatic action—for example, the European and Inter-American Commissions, or by administrative action (perhaps combined with diplomacy)—for example, the International Committee of the Red Cross and UNHCR.

47. Moynihan, *A Dangerous Place*, 11 and passim; Jeane Kirkpatrick, *The Reagan Phenomenon* (Washington, D.C.: The American Enterprise Institute, 1983).

48. Moynihan talks of the UN as a repository of "ideological authority," *A Dangerous Place*, 12. For a discussion of international human rights as a new standard of legitimacy with the potential to transcend debates over democratic capitalism versus authoritarian Marxism, see Forsythe, *Human Rights*, ch. 6.

49. Seweryn Bialer, "The Soviets May Actually Want a New Cold War," Commentary, *The Washington Post* (national weekly ed.) (February 6, 1984): 21.

50. U.S. Court of Appeals, 2nd Circuit, June 30, 1980, no. 79-6090. 630 F. 2d 876. A synopsis can be found in *The American Journal of International Law* 75,1 (January 1981), 149–53.

51. This has been especially true on refugee and immigration matters. See Gilburt D. Loescher and John A. Scanlan, "The Global Refugee Problem: U.S. and World Response," *The Annals* 467 (May 1983). More generally see James C. Tuttle, ed., *International Human Rights Law and Practice* (Philadelphia: American Bar Association, 1978).

52. See especially Louis Henkin, ed., *The International Bill of Rights: The Covenant on Civil and Political Rights* (New York: Columbia University Press, 1981), ch. 13.

53. In an important study Ernst Haas shows that ILO activity on behalf of freedom of association failed to alter the policies of a number of states, especially those in Eastern Europe: *Human Rights and International Action* (Stanford, Calif.: Stanford University Press, 1970).

54. Ernst Haas, "Human Rights: To Act or Not to Act?," in *Eagle Entangled*, ed. Kenneth A. Oye et al. (New York: Longman, 1979), 188.

55. Richard Ullman, "Human Rights: Toward International Action," in *Enhancing Global Human Rights*, ed. Jorge I. Dominguez, et al. (New York: McGraw-Hill, 1979), 10.

56. Moses Moskowitz, "Implementing Human Rights: Present Status and Future Prospects," in *Human Rights: Thirty Years after the Universal Declaration*, ed. B. G. Ramcharan (The Hague: Martinus Nijhoff, 1979), 109–30.

57. Michael O'Boyle, "Practice and Procedure under the European Convention on Human Rights," *Santa Clara Law Review* 20,3 (Summer 1980), 697–732.

58. Ernest A. Landy, "The Implementation Procedures of the International Labor Organization," in *Santa Clara Law Review* 20,3 (Summer 1980), 633–63; and Haas, *Human Rights and International Action*.

59. Lawrence J. LeBlanc, *The OAS and the Protection of Human Rights* (The Hague: Martinus Nijhoff, 1977).

60. The review process, especially under the European Social Charter, makes extensive and formal use of NGO information. See further A. H. Robertson, *Human Rights in the World*, 2nd ed. (New York: St. Martin's Press, 1982), 197–211.

61. Chiang Pei-Leng, *Non-Governmental Organizations*, ch. 2.

62. Antonio Cassese, "Progressive Transnational Promotion of Human Rights," in *Human Rights: Thirty Years after the Universal Declaration*, ed. B. G. Ramcharan (The Hague: Martinus Nijhoff, 1979), 249.

63. Henkin, "The United Nations and Human Rights," 507.

64. Ruggie, "Human Rights," 106.

65. "The United Nations and Human Rights," 514.

66. David P. Forsythe, "Socioeconomic Human Rights: The United Nations, the United States, and Beyond," *Human Rights Quarterly* 4,4 (Fall 1982): 433–49.

67. On the role of the UN in embarrassing states see esp. Bergesen, "The Power to Embarrass," and Ruggie, "Human Rights."

68. See especially Onuf and Petersen, "Human Rights."

69. Ruggie, "Human Rights," 107.

70. *United Nations Chronicle* 20,9 (October 1983): 78.

9

The United Nations and Refugees

Leon Gordenker

●

For a decade or more, the UN High Commissioner for Refugees has supervised programs affecting eight million men, women, and children the international community treats as refugees.[1] Its budgets have come to as much as $500 million per year during that time. Expenditures totaled more than $459 million in 1985 and were projected at nearly $378 million for 1986.[2] While the total number of assisted refugees stays roughly constant, new people enter the ranks while others find permanent asylum or escape refugee status in other ways. All have experienced the needs of the homeless, the absence of normal national protection, and the threat of persecution in their homelands.

From a humanitarian point of view, supplying the material needs of refugees and protecting their legal rights are highly meritorious activities. From that point of view, it would be reassuring if the United Nations could respond actively and continuously wherever there were human need. But it cannot always do so. What explains its capacity to assist refugees and how are decisions made? To what extent is the UNHCR the real decision-maker for assistance to refugees and how authoritative are its processes? What are its politics?

Spokesmen for UNHCR (UNHCR refers to the office or institution; High Commissioner refers to the executive head of UNHCR), beginning with the High Commissioner himself, tend to regard questions about the politics of the organization as a trifle impolite. Its work, according to the standard treatment, has to do with humanitarian assistance and not with politics.[3] It impartially seeks to give succor to refugees. Its decisionmaking thus has to do with humanitarian needs, not with political goals. Yet this same organization forms an integral part of the UN system, which promotes particular choices among values of many sorts, including the maintenance of international peace. This requires a decisional process and the specification of allocations of values, by any definition a political activity. Furthermore, refugees as the United Nations narrowly defines them[4] and forced migrants generally grow out of acts of commission or omission by governments, that is, out of political decisions. This chapter will concentrate on the political aspects of UNHCR in order to analyze the most elaborate established mechanism at the international level for dealing with refugees.[5]

UNHCR in the Formal UN System

Although the UNHCR has a substantial budget for a UN agency, raises its own funds, and treats directly with governments, it is legally a creature of the UN General Assembly to which it reports through the Economic and Social Council. A resolution of the General Assembly, the Statute of UNHCR, sets out the formal mandate.[6] The Statute has been readopted for periods varying from three to five years. The High Commissioner of UNHCR is nominated by the Secretary-General of the United Nations and is then elected by the General Assembly. His annual reports are discussed in the Third Committee of the General Assembly, which also deals with human rights, and he takes part with other grandees of the UN system in the Administrative Committee on Coordination.

The High Commissioner functions within an institutional framework that follows the conventional UN pattern. His version of a full-membership policy organ is the Executive Committee, which meets annually. It is served by the UNHCR staff, simultaneously the High Commissioner's secretariat and a formal part of the UN Secretariat. This Executive Committee, to which members are appointed by the General Assembly, is open to any UN member that wants to participate. It receives detailed reports on the UNHCR program and it has subcommittees to survey specialized parts of the work, including protection and administration.

Yet this formal structure is no simple carbon copy of the UN structure. UNHCR is not an organization of sovereigns, but a dependency of an intergovernmental organization. Its constitution is not a treaty ratified by its membership. The budget is made up almost entirely

of voluntary contributions by governments, not of obligatory assessments.[7] The Executive Committee, however persuasive it may
be, is advisory. As for the UNHCR staff, specialization has promoted
its autonomy, but it remains formally a part of the UN Secretariat.[8]

In one crucial respect, UNHCR relies on an independent legal basis, which gives it the authority to approach governments regarding
the treatment of refugees. The UN General Assembly reacted to the
complex postwar issues of human displacement first by replacing
the UN Relief and Rehabilitation Administration (UNRRA) with the
narrower-gauge, temporary International Refugee Organization (IRO)
to which it gave the task of emptying the European refugee camps.[9]
As IRO's mandate ran out in the late 1940s, the General Assembly
ordered the drafting of a new Convention on Refugees, which came
into force in 1951. This multilateral treaty explicitly obligates its
adherents to treat refugees in a humane and responsible manner.
This standard for treatment of refugees is a mandate for the High
Commissioner through the statute of his office. The General Assembly also charged UNHCR with supervising the convention, which
obliges adhering governments to cooperate with the High Commissioner and to furnish reports on their application of the treaty.
At the time of drafting, the convention was strictly limited to the
protection of asylum seekers in Europe whose troubles were caused
by events before January 1, 1951.[10] Sixteen years later the General
Assembly recommended a protocol that lifted the geographical and
time limitations; it came into force the same year.[11] Both the convention and protocol, however, impose legal obligations only on
governments. It is no constitution for UNHCR; rather, it gives the
office the capacity to request information and to approach adhering
governments about the application of the treaty.[12]

Public Policy and Legislation in UNHCR

The functions of UNHCR have in fact greatly expanded since the
office came into existence in 1951. Originally, no massive flow of
refugees was expected. Those who did appear would need primarily
legal protection, ensured under the convention. The High Commissioner would keep an eye on this with the help of a very small
office, including only some fifty professionals for a worldwide field.
He would have no standing right to appeal to governments for money, no operational function, and little assurance of heading a permanent institution. The mandate for UNHCR was limited to three

years. As the postwar camps were, for the most part, cleared and only a handful of residual refugees and displaced persons remained dependent on the kind of care offered by the predecessor organizations, UNHCR could concentrate on legal protection, including travel documents, and on promoting accessions to the convention.[13]

In hindsight, this conception of refugee affairs is astonishing in the inaccuracy of its forecasting and in its perhaps disingenuous expectations of governmental behavior. Refugees had been a poignant part of the contemporary international scene during this century. The Czarist pogroms, the Bolshevik Revolution and its aftermath, Nazi Germany, and Fascist Spain and Italy all produced their own streams of desperate asylum seekers between the world wars. The end of the Second World War brought to light huge forced migrations of labor and accordingly mass refusals by displaced persons to return to what they considered intolerable repression. In addition, a new brand of asylum seekers streamed out of Soviet-dominated eastern Europe. After all that, how could serious statesmen have anticipated that refugee policy could be as limited as the UN action suggested?

International refugee policy always involved the sensitivities of immigration policy, which governments jealously guard as their own business. It also involved broader political aims, including the "Cold War." It appears that the United States also sought to collect intelligence and recruit political warfare operatives of various sorts from among refugees. The Soviet Union tried to reduce American chances to get more intelligence data and reacted to refugees as persons who were automatically anti-Communist and enemies of the Soviet state but nonetheless subject to its authority.[14] Thus, explanations for the design of the UNHCR mandate can be extracted from the foreign policies and the activities of interest groups in leading countries.

In 1950 the United States promoted international, limited refugee policy. Along with Western European governments, it gave special importance to the key concept, *non-refoulement,* in the convention. (The term means that a refugee may not be returned to his place of departure if he would be endangered or subjected to persecution.) It furthermore supported the proposition in the UN Universal Declaration of Human Rights that everyone had a right to leave his country (although no one ever proposed a general right of immigration). The Soviet Union, on the other hand, insisted that the movement of people was the business of the state and that it had the right to demand the forcible return of its nationals to their homeland if they did not want to come home of their own accord. This difference in policy colored the handling of refugee issues from the end of the Second World War. The Soviet group has never accepted international responsibility for refugee matters. In general, Western European countries supported the principle of international programs, while the rest of the world showed a mixture of attitudes ranging from sporadic or selective interest to outright indifference.[15] Interest in international assistance to refugees remains unevenly distributed, as the fact that only some 90 UN members have adhered to the convention and protocol testifies.

Expansion of the Mandate

Although the tiny office for refugees could not appeal to governments for financing, the first High Commissioner, G. J. van Heuven Goedhart of the Netherlands, contrived to bring in a grant from the Ford Foundation to broaden a program of preparing some refugees still receiving assistance for permanent resettlement. Before his unexpected death, he generally sought to expand the work of the office, lobbied a reluctant General Assembly into setting up an ill-supported emergency fund, and took pleasure in the award of the Nobel Peace Prize to the office.

His successor, the Swiss diplomat, August R. Lindt, took office in the midst of the Hungarian revolution of 1956. That event marked an important turning point in the way refugees issues were approached in the UN system. Led by the acting High Commissioner, UNHCR immediately gave emergency funds to Austria. On taking office in 1957 Lindt responded efficiently and actively to a call by the General Assembly to aid the people streaming out of Hungary, mainly to Austria but also to Yugoslavia. During 1957 UNHCR coordinated all emergency measures in Austria, worked closely with the United States and the Intergovernmental Committee on European Migration in sending the migrants on to permanent resettlement and made clear to governments its wish to accept responsibility. Lindt took pains to justify these actions under his mandate from the General Assembly, whose recommendations already had in effect sanctioned a much more active role for the modest organization. Thus, the General Assembly and the High Commissioner effectively allocated resources and set the policies for their use, illustrating the political coloration of the process of international aid for refugees. Financial contributions flowed in from the developed countries of Europe, North America, and Oceania. Voluntary agencies helped raise funds and were engaged in every phase of the operation from the emergency reception of refugees to their eventual integration into new homes. The General Assembly rejected Soviet bloc moves to force repatriation of the fleeing people and eventually heard the Hungarian representative cautiously express gratitude for what had been done for his people. UNHCR did help repatriate those who wanted voluntarily to return.

Growth of Flexibility

The steady expansion of UNHCR's scope of activities was accomplished in part by using a formula, entitled "good offices," under which UNHCR cared for refugees stranded in Shanghai, obviously outside of its geographical limits at that time.[16] This formula was later used in the Algerian conflict and eventually was expressed in the notion that persons in "refugee-like situations" could in exceptional circumstances be given help even if they were not outside their own countries. It allowed UNHCR to deal with refugees from the communal strife on Cyprus. The concepts of good offices and refugee-like situations made it easier to cover mass exoduses, such as that in Bangladesh and later in Southeast Asia, around Indochina, the Horn of Africa, and on the Afghanistan-Pakistan border. In such large-scale emergency situations, UNHCR obviously could not urge or join in careful investigations of individual claims for asylum on the basis of well-founded fear of persecution. Consequently, it took the position that a *prima facie* claim of rights to refugee treatment could be accepted in such situations of mass exodus. The sorting out could come later. All these developments were endorsed explicitly or implicitly by the UN General Assembly, which never formally rewrote the statute of UNHCR. Furthermore, in dealing with refugees from Indochina in Thailand, UNHCR stepped around the limitation in its statute on conducting operations[17] by directly managing a principal refugee camp.

At the same time, UNHCR did not include all possible forced migrations in its purview. It largely withheld attention from the migrations from Cuba until the exodus from the port of Mariel in 1979 and the accompanying flow of asylum seekers from Haiti, as well as from Central America, led to complaints that the United States was abusing the rights of some who landed on its coasts.[18] It has had no part in the departure of Jews from the Soviet Union, although the United States treats them as refugees. It also experienced a significant failure in trying to get acceptance of a draft convention on the right of territorial asylum, based on a declaration by the General Assembly, at a plenipotentiary conference in 1977.[19] Despite this failure, in terms of organizational expansion and ability to define the boundaries of its activities and to maintain its identity and autonomy, UNHCR has flourished while other parts of the UN system have languished.

Constraining Factors

Despite its expansion of functions, UNHCR acts, or abstains, within a framework of constraints. Some of these have a structural character, while others relate primarily to which policies are adopted and how they are executed.[20]

The activity of UNHCR promotes the welfare and safety of individuals who qualify for assistance and protection as refugees. Yet it has no authority over either the General Assembly or the UN member states. UNHCR may recognize that an individual is a refugee and request a government to issue internationally recognized travel documents to that person, but the ultimate protection of the rights of such a person, his admission to asylum, the physical receipt of a travel document, or his permission to return to his point of departure depend on national authorities. Although UNHCR may plead the case of individuals or groups, it hardly has a formal share in national decisional processes. It can only call attention to the legal obligations undertaken by governments that have adhered to the convention. Legally and in fact, it is powerless to change the course of a stubborn government (or its ignorant official) that intends to violate treaty commitments to protect and aid refugees or to ignore the policies of the United Nations with regard to refugees. The expansion of the UNHCR's mandate, moreover, may have a mandatory quality with regard to the organization itself, but seen by national governments, it rests on recommendations. Such recommendations are supposed to be taken seriously by UN members, but in actuality they frequently are brushed aside, even by governments that have voted in favor of them. UNHCR requires in fact and law the consent of the government controlling the territory where its program is to be carried out. It does not have the simple capacity to send its own representative to a trouble spot without consent of a host government.

Furthermore, UNHCR acts under a mandate that discourages operations. With rare exceptions, it must rely on other organizations to execute programs of material assistance and to finish the refugee process by resettlement or repatriation. In all cases the government on whose territory refugees are sheltered formally consents to such activities and more often than not serves as the executing agent for the program sponsored by UNHCR. When voluntary agencies or other intergovernmental institutions are engaged to carry out a UNHCR program, the host government retains the last word. Thus, UNHCR activities are constrained by a tension between the duty to protect qualifying individuals with humanitarian needs and the legal, administrative, and political fact that as an organization it cannot supplant the governments that support it or benefit from its services.

In addition, the legal definition of a refugee tends to constrain UNHCR activities.[21] It was deliberately framed in the UN General Assembly to limit the number of persons it might cover. It was not designed to cover people who depart from a country that denies human rights generally but rather those who flee specific actions that comprise what is popularly thought of as political persecution. Because the definition, aside from those instances where the General Assembly has recommended its ad hoc extension, applies to no one who has not entered another country, it precludes early intervention by UNHCR into cases of persecution. At the same time the phrase "well-founded" in connection with a fear of persecution leads to the need to have some agent of a national government endorse the perception that a refugee has of his own peril. It emphasizes the needs of individuals, rather than large groups of asylum seekers. Finally, asylum seekers are sometimes turned back at the border without scrupulous examination of claims to refugee status. In such circumstances *refoulement* may have taken place before anyone else has reacted or probably even become aware of what has happened. In other instances UNHCR learns of faulty procedures or allegedly illegal decisions and can react in a timely way. Nevertheless, such reactions remain in the realm of persuasion, not command.

As a result, UNHCR must temper its zeal with caution and good timing if it expects to produce the results foreseen in its statute; it has little incentive to inveigh against destructive or illegal acts of governments in regard to refugees. Even over a longer term, after the immediate need for action on behalf of refugees, UNHCR uses the instrument of publicity with great caution. The High Commissioner only very rarely specifically refers to failures by a particular government to act according to the UN standard. The possibility that he will use publicity does, however, signify that he has some ability to put pressure on a government.

Refugees entail expenses for governments and budgetary demands for UNHCR. Under the Convention refugees must generally be granted the same rights as nationals in their country of asylum. As time is needed for refugees to adjust to new surroundings and become self-sufficient, social welfare costs can be substantial. UNHCR can assist governments with such costs. Moreover, whenever refugees must be held in camps until they can return to their homelands or can be resettled, either in countries of first asylum or elsewhere, UNHCR can be called upon to assist. The involvement of UNHCR offers the High Commissioner another opportunity to influence governmental policy.

With the exception of an emergency fund of $10 million, the High Commissioner must appeal to governments to contribute to new enterprises on an emergency basis (see table 9.1). Later the expenditures can be incorporated in the annual budget recommended to the General Assembly, but even this is voluntarily contributed by governments. Thus, material assistance, including projects for self-sufficiency, is limited to what governments give. Most of the governments that make substantial contributions can be found in the usual list of relatively rich countries that are identified by membership in the Organization for Economic Cooperation and Development.[22] In view of the multiple demands made on these countries for contributions to international programs ranging from development to the gatherings of the most obscure international institutions, funds for refugees do not automatically flow. In fact, compared to original expectations or the pre-1970s budgets, UNHCR has attracted financing for programs of a relatively large scale. Since the very large budgets of the early 1980s, when the multiple crises in the Horn of Africa, Afghanistan, and Southeast Asia called forth unprecedented simultaneous refugee programs, the principal donor countries, led by the United States, have given the administration of UNHCR ever-closer attention. This took the form in part of the creation of an administrative subcommittee of the Executive Committee and of unusually intense consultations between UNHCR and donor representatives in Geneva.

Controversy inheres in refugee situations. No government known so far displays pleasure that its nationals flee in fear and must publicly be given relief by an international institution. Governments of origin sometimes deny that there is reason for flight and some-

Table 9.1 UNHCR Expenditures 1965–85 in thousands of U.S. dollars[1]

Year	Total
1965	4,811
1966	5,733
1967	6,200
1968	7,041
1969	8,651
1970	8,308
1971	9,427
1972	24,087
1973	24,456
1974	34,826
1975	69,006
1976	92,862
1977	111,436
1978	134,681
1979	269,995
1980	496,956
1981	474,256.5
1982	406,959
1983	397,664
1984	444,200
1985	457,849

1. Expenditures on general and special programs combined. General programs contain anticipated items; special programs contain unexpected or as yet unintegrated items.
Source: UNHCR "General Information Paper" (mimeographed), July 1986.

times denounce as accessories to subversion those who shelter migrants.[23] Receiving countries, especially those that suffer the impact of mass exoduses or want to maintain good relationships with originating countries, also often find themselves in controversy. Sheltering refugees involves not only financial costs but also social disturbance, as the neighborhoods of refugee camps everywhere demonstrate. On another level, UNHCR and other international agencies and voluntary bodies assisting refugees require reactions from host governments, especially when they direct large programs. The presence of refugees, moreover, frequently causes friction between hosts and countries of origin, which are invariably sensitive to any signs of guerilla movements or other political organization among the migrants.[24]

Aside from the organizational vulnerabilities already noted, UNHCR shows special sensitivity to attacks based on alleged political partiality. It seeks to ward them off in advance by emphasizing its humanitarian goals. Beyond that, it carefully paves the way to an annual endorsement by its Executive Committee and the General Assembly so as to reiterate its organizational legitimacy. A substantial group of its officials in the Geneva headquarters prepare for such decisions, serve as secretariat personnel in meetings and represent the organization in meetings of other agencies that have an interest in refugee affairs. Senior officials have explicit duties concerned with money-raising and other governmental relationships, including preparations for intergovernmental meetings. The High Commissioner himself, as well as his most senior officials, spend a great deal of time explaining the work of their agency to governmental representatives. Officials in field offices in various capitals are expected to keep fully informed and carry on friendly relations with their host governments. These functions serve to build protective organizational walls to counter the corrosive effects of the controversial atmosphere. Nevertheless, the expectation of controversy around its activities colors UNHCR reactions and makes organizational maintenance a constraint on policy.

The Political Process in UNHCR

Demands made on UNHCR for services, maintenance of the organization, and the constraints on action compete and coincide in complex ways. This competition and coincidence is adjusted in a political process that in many ways resembles that of other UN organs but also displays unique qualities. The political process results in decisions as to the allocation of material resources and other benefits to governments and to refugees, the distribution of values to the individuals connected with the process (such as international civil servants), and the opportunity for governments and other organizations to advance goals outside the framework of help to refugees. The decisionmaking process helps UNHCR exercise its authority, allocate values, and defend its own position.

Political Groups and Coalitions

The familiar one-state, one-vote pattern of organization in the supervisory structure of UNHCR permits an observer to infer the existence of voting groups.[25] These form around policy issues. The groups sometimes function as coalitions, in which the partners have somewhat different approaches but hold similar opinions on policies of the United Nations regarding refugees. These policies cover and may even go beyond UNHCR's functions.

In the General Assembly, the Soviet group sometimes attacks specific UNHCR programs and supports none of them. The Western European and connected countries, including the United States, generally offer strong support to the resolutions approving the work of UNHCR. As they are the principal donors, this constitutes an influential, usually decisive group. Some of the developing countries, especially those affected by refugees, show interest in the resolutions on UNHCR. The same may be said for all that have adhered to the Convention. Generally speaking, these divisions involve no striking confrontational activity. Nevertheless, the repeated resolutions by the General Assembly,[26] singling out specific African countries, such as Sudan, Ethiopia, and Somalia, for special attention suggest a degree of dissatisfaction with UNHCR's policies toward that continent. Spokesmen for African governments have commented on the great difference in expenditure per capita on refugees in Africa and those in Southeast Asia who are resettled in advanced countries. The African countries seek a greater share of the support offered by UNHCR. In that sense they are critical of, but not opposed to, the general policies of the High Commissioner. Some developed-country members of the General Assembly show a keen interest in preventing refugee flows. This has led the General Assembly to adopt a West German-sponsored resolution on causes of refugees and to approve efforts by the Commission on Human Rights to deal with mass exoduses of people.[27]

Deliberations in the General Assembly make it clear that a decisive fraction of UN members takes a favorable view of treatment of refugee affairs in the United Nations and thus by UNHCR. These positions may be divided into those that support refugee activities on the basis of human rights or other ideological considerations, those directly affected by refugee flows, and those opposed. Similar divisions no doubt exist in the Economic and Social Council, but for many years it has adopted the practice of sending the High Commissioner's report to the General Assembly without debate.

The voices opposed to the UNHCR activities in principle are not heard in the UNHCR Executive Committee because those governments are not represented. The governmental representatives there either support UNHCR in principle or have direct contact with its activities.[28] Some governments are represented by observers and are not full members. Some governments that address the Executive Committee have not adhered to the Convention. The discussions here show differences of approach similar to those in the General Assembly, but the subject matter is more technical, more concrete, and treated in a more informed way. In the Executive Committee, senior officers of UNHCR aside from the High Commissioner also join in the meetings and are even more active in the subcommittees. The Executive Committee meetings make clear that the highly developed donor countries give particular importance to good administration and organization in UNHCR. They caucus before the meetings[29] and also will have met with the High Commissioner and senior officials. The African members have also shown particular interest in the "fair shares" argument, relating to the difference in per capita support given refugees in Africa and those elsewhere, and in anything that touches on apartheid in South Africa. The "fair shares" argument also has surfaced in relation to the geographical distribution of staff appointments.

The suggestions that UNHCR programs are unfairly distributed result primarily from the differences in refugee incidents and handling in Southeast Asia and Africa. Partly because they cannot do otherwise and partly because of traditional practices, the African governments have almost always followed the policy of admitting people who claim asylum. Africa has offered the main examples of what refugee officials call "spontaneous settlement," by which is meant self-rescue and adaptation. In Southeast Asia, where governments have flatly declined to offer chances for resettlement or self-sufficient asylum,[30] much more expensive camp arrangements and preparation for departure to third countries have become the rule. The differences in per capita expenditure, therefore, are striking. In addition, African representatives have coalesced around proposals to provide development assistance in connection with refugee self-sufficiency and resettlement. This coalescence appears to be based more on the accident that several African countries have given shelter to large groups of refugees than on African regional solidarity.

An important difference between Executive Committee proceedings and the superior General Assembly organs can be seen in the presence of thirty or more representatives of voluntary organizations in the former.[31] Along with representatives of other intergovernmental organizations, they are given opportunities to address the

Committee, some represented by the International Confederation of Voluntary Agencies (ICVA) and others on their own. The Red Cross movement, for example, represents its own position. Some of the organizations represented, such as the African National Congress of South Africa, aim primarily at political change. Formal status makes it easier for these organizations to go beyond official meetings and to operate easily in the lobbies in the familiar manner of interest groups. The importance of these occasions can be read in the fact that voluntary organization representatives from Asia, Africa, and North America attend Executive Committee meetings. They constitute an integral part of the network of informed individuals who keep informed on and help operate refugee services. Moreover, the delegates of some voluntary organizations usually have far more direct experience with refugees and their difficulties than do the largely diplomatic personnel sent by governments from their missions in Geneva to Executive Committee meetings.

The representatives of voluntary agencies meet frequently with UNHCR officials, either because of their involvement in field operations or because a policy issue has arisen. UNHCR includes a specialized office for dealing with voluntary agencies, some of which themselves use an ICVA committee to seek a common position. These contacts result in constant exchange of information through bureaucratic channels. It may be assumed that the continual discussions have some influence on policy decisions.

During the last decade, as the UNHCR program expanded and refugee situations involved intense political controversy, discussions in the Executive Committee have increasingly included critical tones.[32] The Committee became much less a claque for UNHCR and more representative of national policies and of various groupings of voluntary organizations. The Executive Committee was not polarized, but it would be misleading to overlook tendencies to form groups around certain issues. These include priorities, budget, the efficiency of UNHCR, and the comparative costs of programs. Decisions as to which programs should have priority depend in part on their geopolitical background. The influential attention of the United States, along with some of its allies, has concentrated on those incidents where the Soviet Union is directly or indirectly involved. Other governments, such as those in Africa and Latin America, are likely to give special treatment to incidents in their own areas. Some governments also must be sensitive to domestic opinion. Dutch[33] and Scandinavian groups, for instance, strongly support

humanitarian, as distinguished from geopolitical, approaches to refugees, and in the Executive Committee the representatives of their
governments can be counted on to strive to prioritize programs based
on the need for assistance; at the same time, they do not nonchalantly
offer places for resettlement. Consequently, it would be misleading
simply to assume that political divisions based on military alliances
external to the United Nations determine discussions in the Executive Committee. They appear to have much stronger salience
in discussions in the General Assembly than at the lower, more
technical level of Geneva.

Executive Leadership

The constitutional foundations of UNHCR strongly encourage the
development of executive leadership, in contrast to relying on national initiatives and deliberations among governments in United
Nations organs. The High Commissioner is a single individual, not
a committee or the representative of a government. He was at first
given only a small staff but a mandate with wide implications and
narrow powers. He was in effect instructed to persuade governments
to accede to the Convention and thus behave in accordance with
an internationally approved standard. This standard was supposed
to govern the High Commissioner's behavior. Until 1958 the UN
member governments did not even have a supervisory body in place
at the Geneva headquarters level. It was only then that a minor
supervisory body, connected with a fund that has since disappeared,
was turned into the Executive Committee with functions at first
limited to the program of assistance.

Van Heuven Goedhart, the first High Commissioner, passionately
believed in the importance of his office and sought at once to increase its influence. His successors without exception thought it
important to try positively to lead governments to act in a humanitarian manner toward refugees. All of the High Commissioners actively sought diplomatic opportunities to persuade governments of
the importance of the office. The following are some examples. Van
Heuven Goedhart successfully sought to give his office more prominence in public opinion, especially among groups interested in
humanitarian affairs, and to increase the financial base for his work.
August Lindt made the most of the Hungarian refugee emergency
and successfully extended assistance to refugees, some of whom
did not conform to the narrow definition in the Statute and Con-

vention. Felix Schnyder presided over the drafting of the 1967 Protocol that in effect gave global scope to his office. Sadruddin Aga Khan actively promoted a role for his office in giving relief to displaced Cypriots, was able to convince Ethiopia that programs in Sudan for Eritrean refugees constituted no threat, and engaged the office in the complex Bangladesh affair. Poul Hartling, the High Commissioner until 1986, directed the vast expansion of the program in the Horn of Africa, Southeast Asia, and Pakistan, sought great attention to engaging refugees in the economic development of their host lands, and tried to organize the office in Geneva to cope more efficiently with the new, larger programs. Jean-Pierre Hocké, the present High Commissioner, emphasizes tighter management and close involvement with operations. During the first four administrations the network of branch offices expanded and the representation on the Executive Committee grew.

Leadership by UNHCR takes on several guises. These include diplomatic, legal, programmatic, and public relations. All of these functions, which are common to all executive heads of international agencies,[34] tend to blend with each other in actuality. They depend in considerable part on the possession of information that either does not come into the hands of every government or else is not collated with special attention to refugees. The emphases on one or another functional line, however, reflect the specialized character of UNHCR, the approaches of the High Commissioners and the political environment of the moment.

Diplomatic Functions

UNHCR's diplomatic functions[35] affect national governments individually in their capitals and collectively in UN organs. High Commissioners travel a great deal and spend weeks away from Geneva. Some of this travel takes the High Commissioner to the field programs supported by his office. Hartling, for instance, visited Southeast Asia in 1984, where he went to Bangkok and Hanoi, capitals of countries still deeply involved with the unresolved refugee issues of Indochina. He also visited parts of Latin America and Africa. Such visits provide opportunities for discussions with governments, for clearing away misunderstandings, and for opening new relationships. If the High Commissioner seeks reelection to a new five-year term, his conversations may result in support in the General Assembly. Visits offer direct mutual access to information between high officials in governments and the High Commissioner and his staff. Such visits are carefully prepared by headquarters and field staffs.

Some of the field officers in the UNHCR structure have continuing diplomatic functions. They carefully follow the development of national policies with regard to refugees and, necessarily, immigration. They consult officials and ministers in an effort to keep national policies consistent with legal obligations and the views of UNHCR. They furnish information and arguments to voluntary agencies and mass media. They report on developments and their conclusions to Geneva. Some of these reports contain specific recommendations as to the way UNHCR should react to developments in their territories. In addition, the UNHCR field offices routinely attempt to protect the legal rights of asylum seekers and recognized refugees. This entails representation with regard to individual cases and means also that field officers have direct contact with refugees. They may also provide financial support for refugees who are without other means. In a few instances, UNHCR representatives join national administrative decision makers, either as observers or as full partners, in determining the status of individual refugees. In case of abuses, UNHCR representatives may take the initiative locally to urge corrections and may also call on special help from their headquarters. Sometimes this results in pressure from Geneva on government representatives there or in other instances the visit of higher ranking officials to the spot.

If a flow of refugees, or their situation, suggests an emergency, the UNHCR field officials gather information, keep their headquarters informed, and put before their host government the services available from their organization. They may actively urge the government to make a request for UNHCR services and even frame the request. They may seek to enlist the help of their colleagues in headquarters or of the High Commissioner himself. These activities usually take place under a mantle of discretion consistent with the UNHCR doctrine that governments request services and that the international organization does not forecast refugee incidents. Whatever the diplomatic fictions, UNHCR must steer a course between pressure that would be resented by a host government and the possible accusation of inaction in case of a developing emergency. UNHCR has, for example, been criticized for reacting too slowly and with insufficient vigor in Thailand and Somalia where local officers discreetly put the case for outside help to the government.[36] In both instances, according to the critics, governmental reactions came so late as to cause unnecessary suffering because UNHCR acted with insufficient vigor. In both these cases large programs were approved by the concerned governments only after extraordinary (and poignant) publicity in the mass media of the usual developed donor countries.

The mass exoduses of refugees that have caught so much public attention during the last decade have raised questions within the ranks of UNHCR as to the vigorousness with which the High Commissioner should attempt to lead. Some officials in the middle ranks have privately criticized what they think of as a lack of enterprise. At the same time mass exoduses such as those during the formative months of Bangladesh or from hunger in Cambodia or Ethiopia tend to raise issues that go beyond UNHCR's usual role. In Africa and in Southeast Asia the UN Secretary-General has sometimes taken the lead, while UNHCR functioned as one of the concerned parties. At the same time the Secretary-General's staff has neither the experience nor the connections that those specialized in dealing with refugees have as part of their institutional being. These developments suggest that the High Commissioner may need, in some instances, to consider whether he will attempt to take the initiative among his colleagues in other UN organizations.

Legal Functions

UNHCR's legal functions can be separated into two categories. The first of these seeks to extend law by promotion of accessions to the Convention and by elaboration of international rules concerning refugees. The promotion of accessions uses primarily diplomatic methods, such as urging by the High Commissioner and enlisting the support of governments interested in extending the rules. No flamboyant campaigns are likely in this realm. The High Commissioner also may propose changes in existing rules, as in the outstanding case of the 1967 Protocol and the unsuccessful attempt to create a multinational treaty on the rights of asylum. A continuing campaign of legal seminars and education produces slow results in which a causal process is difficult to discern. Furthermore, legal experts from the UNHCR attend meetings of other organizations that attempt to create rules affecting refugees. In this connection UNHCR had a leading role in the creation of an African refugee regime that provides protection to a larger fraction of forced migrants than does the Convention.

The other legal function has to do with the rights of individuals and groups of refugees. UNHCR is charged with an active role in protecting these rights. The means are, as is apparent from the earlier discussion, primarily diplomatic. The usual practice of the office is to make such efforts in a guarded and secret manner. Officials explain that publicity, or even scholarly research on the part of experts, would jeopardize lives. It is therefore nearly impossible to estimate accurately how often leadership by UNHCR succeeds in protecting the threatened refugees. Reports made to the Executive Committee and through it to the General Assembly describe this activity in such generalized terms that even geographical locations are vague.[37] The organization has sometimes been criticized for timidity in this realm. It is certain that it does not always succeed in convincing governments of its point of view, as was the case when it argued in favor of refugee status for Haitian and Salvadoran asylum seekers in the United States.

Operations and Influence

Although UNHCR shuns an operational role, which it defines as directly managing and supervising social and material assistance to refugees, it nevertheless provides financing for large-scale refugee operations. In the world of international institutions an annual budget of some $400 million is reckoned as substantial indeed. It implies, moreover, that the governments of the places where it is spent will feel at least some impact. In countries with large refugee populations that impact can reach important levels as food and supplies are imported and other goods and services are purchased on local markets. In Thailand, for instance, the government requires that rice and other food be purchased locally. As 200,000 or more people may receive daily rations, the economic effect is considerable.

UNHCR's support of programs to assist refugees opens opportunities for it to persuade and influence governments, other international agencies, and voluntary groups. It also retains an important residual power to cut off assistance already offered. That UNHCR's programs lead to a certain influence follows from the form of its relations with governments and with supervisory organs. Once a government makes a formal request for aid, it is likely that UNHCR will already have, on the basis of preparatory discussions, some proposals on exactly what should be done and by whom. As noted above, the government is usually the agent and in many instances

UNHCR and the government agree that certain voluntary agencies should be brought into the program. UNHCR specifies and seeks agreement on standards for the operation. Its officials will observe the execution of the programs and try to ensure that they conform to the agreed standard. They come to possess information in quantity and in quality of specialization that few governments have.

UNHCR's watchdog role guarantees that the agency will be a factor in decisions made by the executing agents for the programs. This is not to say that UNHCR eagerly seeks to threaten or punish. It can usually rely on some officials in the national realm who want the programs they helped set up to succeed. UNHCR officials thus can work with allies who know that utter failure would have unpleasant results for the refugees, the officials involved, and for UNHCR, whose wish to protect itself would increase pressure. Furthermore, UNHCR can provide technical advice on projects that may attract more outside help and at the same time cope with the effects of the presence of refugees. It also provides a ready-made means to approach other international agencies whose help would be useful.

The influence that UNHCR may exert on governments needing aid for refugees should not, however, be overestimated. UNHCR's mandate is to help refugees, not to set governments on the proper course. Governments working with UNHCR to assist refugees know perfectly well that they ultimately control the programs and never prove infinitely malleable. Nor do their concerns with internal security, local politics, possible threats to the governing group, economic factors, domestic prejudices, and social values disappear simply because UNHCR appears in the middle of a foggy situation. Clean lines of responsibility can hardly be drawn in such symbiotic relationships.

Large-scale programs of assistance also affect the internal decisionmaking structures of UNHCR. In accordance with bureaucratic lore, an organizational entity that waxes tends to outshine those that it surpasses. Large scale programs require both more time and personnel in the field and at headquarters. Control and surveillance functions must grow apace with size. Eventually questions arise as to exactly what is happening. Meanwhile, the growth of the assistance function gives the bureau in charge increasing prestige in the organization generally. Its field operatives make it an increasingly significant source of information. This work now puts a heavy overprint on the entire budget. The scale of its expenditures and wide distribution of its programs increase difficulties with management and thereby call forth more elaborate organization and attention from the senior official ranks. This is the scenario UNHCR experienced as it grew. In consequence, UNHCR organized an internal research program and a personnel training venture in 1980. Soon thereafter, it established an emergency unit, which for the first time attempted to anticipate how the office would have to react during emergencies and to encourage some standardization of procedures to cope with crises. A consultant was engaged to survey the organization with a view to improving management, although no vigorous changes followed. The accession of Hocké to the leadership of UNHCR, with strong backing from the United States, signaled an even stronger emphasis on management. The new High Commissioner reorganized the office. A significant appointment was his deputy, an experienced American who had been a senior official in the Bureau of Refugee Affairs of the Department of State and was known to have a strong interest in administrative matters. These developments represent a shift from predominant concerns with legal protection of rights of refugees to a deepening commitment to deliver material assistance and related services.

Voluntary Agencies, Networks, and Opinion

The political process in UNHCR includes a large network of voluntary agencies, experts, and civil servants dealing with refugee affairs around the world. This relationship emerges, in part, out of the need by those interested in or charged with the care of refugees to exchange information. This exchange is inherent in the function, undertaken by some voluntary agencies with humanitarian goals, of a pressure group. The exchange process in turn helps maintain a network of refugee specialists and organizations.

The shared humanitarian goals of a group of transnational private organizations, many of them linked to churches but a few directed primarily to refugees, are a principal reason for the formation of a network of refugee specialists. These specialists are divided among those who work principally at influencing opinion generally, those who furnish the liaison among organizations, and those who have operational responsibilities. From its beginning, UNHCR strove to develop public support and therefore immediately came into contact with organizations or their suborganizations that sought to influence opinion. These included groups seeking to promote human rights generally as well as some which concentrated on forced migrants of certain ethnic backgrounds, such as Jews from Eastern Europe or Hungarians. The functionaries of such organizations became consumers of information furnished by UNHCR and in turn furnished information. They also took part in meetings at various levels, either as representatives or as observers. They made up an informal lobby.

Some of their colleagues in their own organizations and others had from the end of the Second World War worked in refugee camps or had duties in resettling forced migrants. They had "hands on" experience of operations. In the time of UNRRA and IRO they operated on the basis of contracts with the international institutions. This pattern of contract operations took on new life with the exodus from Hungary and now is a standard pattern by which voluntary organizations assist refugees. Some of the staff members of these organizations shift to and from national governmental bureaucracies and international secretariats. They come to know the key officials in UNHCR and sometimes work in that organization. They constitute part of the stock of experienced officials who can be brought into the field in a large-scale emergency.

The world of voluntary organizations includes almost endless variations of outlook. The complexity resulting from the interplay of organizational aims and the importance of their operational capacities and, to a lesser extent, their own financial resources have led UNHCR to maintain an office for direct liaison with them. In their turn, they have created forms of cooperation, carried out by formally appointed individuals and in informal ways. The people engaged in this cooperation, which extends horizontally across organizations and into national civil services and vertically into governments and international agencies, make up the part of the network that deals mainly with liaison. Related to this liaison section, as well as to other parts of the network, is a growing group of international and domestic lawyers and academic specialists with direct knowledge of refugee affairs.

Because this network as a whole touches every part of the handling of refugees from early information in the field to the ultimate resettlement or repatriation, it is an important source of information to UNHCR and to governments. As it manages much of the actual operations concerning refugees, it is also in a position to bring forward standards and goals that may differ from UNHCR's. This creates and encourages a constant dialogue with the international officials and with governmental representatives. It simultaneously offers both possible support and opposition to UNHCR and at least marginally shapes the development of the international approach to refugee affairs.

Beyond that specific network, UNHCR reaches out to a broader, undefined public with publications; speeches by officials at seminars, universities, and other meetings; films; photographs; film strips; posters; and interviews for journalists and other related services. Some of this material feeds back into the voluntary agency components of the refugee network, while some finds its way to corners of the infinitely varied general public in many countries. Although such activities parade under the name of public information, they obviously help to some degree to promote knowledge and nurture positive opinions about UNHCR and counter those that are negative.

Conclusions

Although the structure of UNHCR differs somewhat from the usual model of international institutions, it comprehends a political process that in grand lines resembles that of other agencies. Yet it also includes particularities of considerable importance to its continued maintenance as an organization. These particularities also help to explain the long-term growth of what was perhaps too lightly considered a temporary or at least very restricted organization.

UNHCR has rarely directly served as a forum for the East-West debate so characteristic of much of the UN system. From the majority of governments, however, UNHCR gets its annual endorsement without much negative comment. Because policymaking in UNHCR itself takes place without East-West competition and because the Palestinian refugees are the responsibility of another agency, the organization escapes the currently popular accusation of "politicization."

The very opposition in principle of the Soviet group to UNHCR may give the organization some special protection. It is favored by the rich polities, themselves the main places of third party settlement of refugees and the headquarters of the most active voluntary agencies. The network of refugee specialists is rooted in these non-Communist countries. The most important of them, the United States, has repeatedly framed its immigration policy to make the admission of refugees from countries controlled by Communist governments, especially in Europe and Southeast Asia, relatively easy. It can then both support UNHCR programs and maintain the customary opposition to Communist governments. Other important donor countries, such as the Netherlands, the Scandinavian lands, and France, may emphasize humanitarian aims in their approach to UNHCR; these goals do not conflict with geopolitical undertakings in the North Atlantic Treaty Organization and elsewhere.

As a vehicle for dealing with the humanitarian issues posed by refugee flows, UNHCR offers governments several advantages. They can avoid the direct responsibility for operating assistance programs by supporting UNHCR as the source of financing and supervision for programs organized outside their own administration. They can also usually keep clear of unpleasant direct representations to other governments with regard to violations of the rights of refugees. UNHCR can undertake the main burden in this realm. In a sense the governments spread the risks of dealing with refugees by cooperating in UNHCR. At the same time, they do not have to undertake limitless programs with regard to refugees. Their own prestige and financial participation in UNHCR programs guarantee considerable influence in the policy process and therefore an ability to set limits. They also make their own decisions on the level of financial contributions. Beyond that, the fundamental legal limitations on UNHCR activities set some boundaries. Cooperation in UNHCR does not prevent governments from carrying on their bilateral programs for refugees, as some of the main donors do.

Recognition of these advantages to national governments should not be taken as a cynical dismissal of humanitarian approaches with regard to refugees. The existence of an extended network of refugee specialists and organizations ensures that many governments cannot gratuitously disregard humanitarian aims in framing their policies. Furthermore, political leaders may also give great importance to humanitarian causes out of a personal ethical sense or because of religious faith. National policies do not inherently reject benefiting other people in difficulties. In the case of refugees, important governments have made precisely such aims one of their priorities. It is all the easier to do so if that priority fits with national security and immigration policies. In countries directly affected by the presence of refugees, the governments have an obvious interest in what UNHCR can offer. Even the bitterest complaints of governments that think they are short-changed in distribution of benefits to refugees do not strike out against the organization.

Because UNHCR has proved either useful or not harmful to many governments, it has had a rather comfortable basis for development. Executive leadership in UNHCR can rest on a foundation of international legal commitments and of expertness and information that are not otherwise easily available to governments. In addition, its

relationship with the work of voluntary agencies and the participation of members of its secretariat in the network of refugee specialists helps it to frame tenable policies. It is consistent with its
valuable stock of experience and information that its programs
should expand rapidly in times of crisis. UNHCR does develop friction
with governments, either of the countries giving asylum or those
functioning mainly as financial donors, but it has been able to limit
its effects by diplomatic activity, responsiveness to some criticism,
and terminating particular programs as rapidly as possible. It has
adroitly defined its role as humanitarian in a political universe. Its
performance obviously supports the claim that it has directed benefits to large numbers of people. In the obviousness of these benefits
UNHCR has an advantage available to only a few international institutions. Most of them produce almost exclusively recommendations and studies for execution by national governments. The results
are visible only after programs are handled by many bureaucratic
intermediaries. Even then the results may lack concrete qualities
and direct impact on the lives of both the intended beneficiaries
and the communities around them. UNHCR's political process may
resemble those of sister organizations in the international realm,
but its results often do not. That difference serves partly to explain
both the establishment and survival of what was planned as a minor
enterprise.

Notes

The author gratefully acknowledges the support of the Center of International Studies,
Princeton University.

1. Refugees constitute a limited category of human sufferers from man-made disasters. For historical, legal, and political reasons the United Nations and other international institutions concentrate on those forced to migrate who flee from readily
visible proximate causes, such as political, racial, or social persecution. According
to this usage, refugees would not have included, for example, those who fled Ireland
during the potato famine, although if they had stayed there, they would have faced
hardship and even death. The term, "economic refugee," probably has little de-
scriptive value.

2. UN Document A/AC.96/657, August 5, 1985, p. 35.

3. "UNHCR's work must always transcend the narrowly political and, instead, be
guided by internationally accepted humanitarian principles and considerations. To
say that we are non-political is not in the least to say that we are politically insensitive.
I am well aware that we must balance, in harmony, national and regional perceptions
and concerns with ideals and actions that are universally valid." Statement by the
High Commissioner (Sadruddin Aga Khan) before the Third Committee of the UN
General Assembly, November 13, 1978, quoted in *World Refugee Crisis: The In-*

ternational Community's Response, report to the Committee on the Judiciary, United States Senate, by the Congressional Research Service, 96th Congress, First Session (Washington, U.S. Government Printing Office, 1979), p. 281.

"The High Commission for Refugees whose work 'shall be of an entirely non-political character [quoted from UNHCR Statute],' has systematically avoided engaging in analyses of, let alone controversies on, the causes of refugee problems which obviously are to be found in the internal conditions of the states of origin." Gilbert Jaeger, "Refugee Asylum: Policy and Legislative Developments," *International Migration Review* 15, 1–2 (Spring-Summer 1981): 59. Mr. Jaeger is a retired UNHCR Director of Protection with decades of experience in refugee policy.

In her detailed history of UNHCR until 1972, Holborn concludes that the agency conforms to David Mitrany's description of a functional institution and thus is not political. Louise W. Holborn, *Refugees: A Problem of Our Time,* 2 vols. (Metuchen, N.J.: Scarecrow Press, 1975), 1428.

Cf. Leon Gordenker, "Organizational Expansion and Limits in International Services for Refugees," *International Migration Review,* 15, 1–2 (Spring-Summer 1981): 77–78.

4. The basic definition as stated in the UN Convention on Refugees, adopted on July 28, 1951, is: "the term 'refugee' shall apply to any person who . . . owing to a well-founded fear of being persecuted for reasons of race, religion, nationality, membership of a particular social group or political opinion, is outside the country of his nationality and is unable or, owing to such fear, is unwilling to avail himself of the protection of that country; or who, not having a nationality and being outside the country of his former habitual residence as a result of such events, is unable or, owing to such fear, is unwilling to return to it." *UN Treaty Series,* vol. 189, no. 2545,137.

5. The chapter does not deal with the special mechanism for caring for refugees from Palestine, centered in the UN Relief and Works Agency for Palestine Refugees. Protection, assistance, and the long-term future of Palestinian refugees all connect directly with an eventual settlement of the disputes between Israel and its neighbors. In this respect, the handling of the Palestinians differs from that in refugee situations that are not as specifically defined and not linked from the outset to a political settlement. UNHCR deals with the latter sort. The UN definition of the Palestinian refugees is even more limited than the Convention definition employed by UNHCR, because in UNRWA only people of one specific origin are assisted. For a recent examination of the UNRWA refugees, see David P. Forsythe, "The Palestinian Question: Dealing with a Long-Term Refugee Situation," *The Annals of the American Academy of Political and Social Science* 467 (May 1983): 89.

6. UN General Assembly Resolution 428 (V), December 14, 1950.

7. Continuing an old practice, a minor appropriation is made annually by the UN General Assembly as part of the organization's administrative budget. As this appropriation has been held steady over the years, its significance has declined with inflation and growing UNHCR expenditures. The appropriation by the General Assembly is dwarfed by annual voluntary contributions, the overwhelming majority of which come from governments.

8. UN Staff Rules are applied by UNHCR. The general personnel procedures of the UN Secretariat also apply, but as UNHCR functionaries quickly point out, their work differs from that of the rest of the UN Secretariat. Personnel decisions of crucial importance are made in Geneva, not New York. UNHCR personnel show little eagerness to be brought further under New York's umbrella. Interviews by author.

9. For a brief account, see Holborn, *Refugees*, 57–64. Holborn wrote the standard treatment of IRO in *The International Refugee Organization, Its History and Work, 1946–52* (Oxford University Press, 1956). A comprehensive treatment of UNRRA is George Woodbridge, *The History of UNRRA*, 3 vols. (New York: Columbia University Press, 1950).

10. Holborn, *Refugees*, 65–84, recounts the UN deliberations. The convention came into force on April 22, 1954.

11. UN *Treaty Series*, vol. 606, no. 8791, 267. See Holborn, *Refugees*, 117–82 for historical background.

12. Guy S. Goodwin-Gill, *The Refugee in International Law* (Oxford: Clarendon Press, 1985), 133–36. This study also contains a useful bibliography drawn from the vast legal literature on refugees.

13. Holborn, *Refugees*, 62–63.

14. G. D. Loescher and John Scanlan, *Calculated Kindness: Refugees and the Half-Opened Door: 1945 to the Present* (New York: Free Press, 1986), chap. 3.

15. Holborn, *Refugees*, 62–63.

16. Goodwin-Gill, *Refugee in International Law*, 7–11.

17. Holborn, *Refugees*, 88. Paragraph 8 of the statute empowers the High Commissioner to persuade others to do the actual work of caring for refugees. "*Whenever possible, UNHCR seeks to implement material assistance programmes through an operational partner, rather than directly.* There are a number of reasons for this policy, the origins of which are reflected in the Statute of UNHCR." *Handbook for Emergencies* (Geneva: UN High Commissioner for Refugees, 1982), 24. On Southeast Asia, see William Shawcross, *The Quality of Mercy* (New York: Simon & Schuster, 1984), 176.

18. Loescher and Scanlan, *Calculated Kindness*, chap. 11; Goodwin-Gill, *Refugee in International Law*, 62; and Naomi Flink Zucker, "The Haitians Versus the United States: The Courts as a Last Resort," *The Annals of the American Academy of Political and Social Science* 467 (May 1983): 156.

19. UNHCR put a great deal of effort into the drafting of a convention guaranteeing refugees the right of asylum but was unable to persuade enough of the conferring governments to support the idea. If applied, the convention would have greatly reduced the range of decisions left to national governments about who could have asylum and under what circumstances. The conference to approve the draft ended in failure. See Holborn, *Refugees*, 228–34, for the background of this draft. For a recent statement on asylum, see Gilbert Jaeger, "Refugee Asylum: Policy and Legislative Development," *International Migration Review* 15, 1–2 (Spring-Summer 1981): 52–61; and Goodwin-Gill, *Refugee in International Law*, 109–11.

20. Gordenker, "Organizational Expansion." See Goodwin-Gill, *Refugees in International Law*, 129–36, for legal treatment of this point. For a detailed analysis of the actions of and constraints on UNHCR and other organizations dealing with refugees, see Gordenker, *Refugees in International Politics* (London: Croom Helm, 1987), esp. chaps. 2, 3, and 5.

21. See note 4, above, for text.

22. The donors that contributed more than $2 million for 1985 were as follows (in $U.S.): United States, 126,674,391; Intergovernmental organizations, 53,493,101; Japan, 47,021,317; German Federal Republic, 30,198,441; United Kingdom, 18,075,057; Nongovernmental organizations and other donors, 16,323,553; Denmark, 14,280,794; Sweden, 13,200,535; Norway, 12,350,537; Canada, 12,324,824; Switzerland, 10,168,019; Netherlands, 9,745,089; Italy, 5,875,821; Australia, 5,851,864;

France, 4,670,404; Saudi Arabia, 4,104,293; Belgium, 3,178,402; and Finland, 2,669,729. In addition, sixty-two other governments offered sums between $500,000 and $1.1 million. Source: UN General Assembly, Official Records: 41st Session, Supplement No. 12, *Report of the United Nations High Commission for Refugees*, A/41/12, 37–39.

23. For a clear example, see Barry Wain, *The Refused: The Agony of the Indochina Refugees* (New York: Simon and Schuster, 1981), 144–46.

24. The Somali ethnic refugees from Ethiopia generate repeated accusations and armed attacks from Ethiopia on border areas, including refugee camps, because the authorities in Addis Ababa believe that guerrillas entering Ogaden province are based in camps or at least supplied from them. The situation of the Afghanistan refugees on the border of the Northwest Frontier province of Pakistan is similar.

25. This section relies on direct observation and interviews in Geneva and other offices of UNHCR.

26. For example, UN General Assembly Resolutions 35/181, 35/182, and 35/183.

27. Respectively UN General Assembly Resolution 35/124 and UN Document E/CN.4/1503.

28. At the October 1986 meeting the following were represented as members: Algeria, Argentina, Australia, Austria, Belgium, Brazil, Canada, China, Colombia, Denmark, Finland, France, Federal Republic of Germany, Greece, Holy See, Iran, Israel, Italy, Japan, Lebanon, Lesotho, Madagascar, Morocco, [UN Council for] Namibia, Netherlands, Nicaragua, Nigeria, Norway, Sudan, Sweden, Switzerland, Tanzania, Thailand, Tunisia, Turkey, Uganda, United Kingdom, United States, Venezuela, and Yugoslavia.

The observers included Angola, Belize, Bolivia, Botswana, Burundi, Cameroon, Chile, Congo, Costa Rica, Cuba, Cyprus, Djibouti, Ecuador, Egypt, Ethiopia, Guatemala, Honduras, India, Indonesia, Iraq, Ireland, Kampuchea, Libya, Luxembourg, Malaysia, Mexico, Mozambique, New Zealand, Pakistan, Peru, Philippines, Portugal, Rwanda, Senegal, Somalia, Spain, Swaziland, Syria, Uruguay, Viet Nam, [North] Yemen, [South] Yemen and Zambia. UN General Assembly, Official Records: 40th Session, Supplement No. 12A, *Addendum to the Report of the United Nations High Commissioner for Refugees*, 1–2.

It is evident that some countries most affected by refugees take part only as observers and that the relevance of some representation seems difficult to establish. Some governments that are allies of the Soviet Union are represented at the meetings, as are those that make a point of nonaligned foreign policies.

29. The principal developed countries that donate the majority of contributions to voluntary budgets of UN agencies meet as the Geneva Group. The United States is the most important single member of this group, but its contributions now generally comprise only a minority of the funds put at the disposal of the agencies dealing with refugees, including UNHCR. The High Commissioner also meets informally several times a year with the Geneva representatives of the Executive Committee membership. Similar meetings are also held with voluntary agencies.

30. "In one six-week period, 40,000 boat people arrived off the tiny island of Pilau Bidong off the Malaysian coast. No one knew how many more had died in the attempt ... The governments of first asylum were expressing more and more impatience. The prime minister of Malaysia warned in January [1979] that no more would be allowed to land. The Thai Prime Minister ... warned that no refugees from either Vietnam or Cambodia would be allowed to enter Thailand, as 'we have too many

already.' " Shawcross, *The Quality of Mercy*, 83. The only possible "deal" in these circumstances was to promise governments that actual first asylum would be no asylum at all. Refugees in Southeast Asia flow out; if they do not, then their successors might be subjected to *refoulement* as the governments concerned were not obligated to avoid it. Cf. discussion of local pressure in Wain, *The Refused*, chap. 6.

31. At the October 1985 meeting, eighty-eight nongovernmental organizations sent observers. These included ICVA, which itself represents some of the voluntary groups present and others not represented. In addition, representatives of fourteen other offices or organizations in the UN system and of five other intergovernmental organizations, all of which are in touch with nongovernmental organizations, also were represented. United Nations, General Assembly, Official Records: 40th Session, Supplement No. 12 A, *Addendum to the Report of the United Nations High Commissioner for Refugees*, 2–3.

32. This refers to discussion of specific programmatic developments. Some interventions in the Executive Committee involve broad political approaches to inherently controversial situations, such as South Africa or the Western Sahara. The passionate speeches on such issues have been heard so often that they have hardly more than ritual significance.

33. Details of the Dutch reaction are discussed in J. A. Hoeksma, *Tussen Vrees en Vervolging* (Assen, Netherlands: Van Gorcum, 1982), 251–55.

34. Robert W. Cox, "The Executive Head: An Essay on Leadership in International Organizations," *International Organization* 23 (Spring 1969): 251–55.

35. This section relies on interviews and observation by the author in Geneva.

36. Shawcross, *The Quality of Mercy*, 34–36; Wain, *The Refused*, 263–65; and author's interviews and observation in Geneva and Mogadishu.

37. The following is an example of the language employed by UNHCR in publicly discussing protection:

26. There has been a growing trend for States to view asylum as involving only the grant of temporary admission. On an increasing scale, States, while admitting refugees, have pursued restrictive policies with regard to the granting of a durable solution within their own borders. In almost all parts of the world, UNHCR was confronted with requests for the resettlement of refugees who had been admitted temporarily to countries of asylum pending the finding of a durable solution elsewhere.

27. Problems relating to the identification of the State responsible for examining an asylum request acquired a certain prominence during the reporting period. This problem arises when an asylum-seeker has passed through one or more countries before arriving in the State where he or she wishes to submit an asylum request. In such situations, the authorities may refuse to consider an application on various grounds, including the fact that protection was, or could have been, obtained elsewhere. When this occurs, the asylum-seeker is frequently turned away and becomes what has been called a refugee in orbit.

UN General Assembly, Official Records: 38th Session, Supplement No. 12, *Report of the High Commissioner for Refugees*, 7.

The latter passage refers, among other things, to the widely reported difficulties that Tamil ethnics have encountered in Sri Lanka, Eritreans in Ethiopia, and Afghanistanis in Western Europe. The first paragraph has to do, among other things, with the Cambodians in Thailand.

10

The Role of the International Atomic

Energy Agency in the International

Politics of Atomic Energy

Christer Jönsson and Staffan Bolin

•

One basic question guiding this series of inquiries into the UN system forty years after is whether the constituent organizations have evolved from mere forums for multilateral diplomacy toward genuinely political bodies authoritatively allocating values, from a highly decentralized toward a more centralized decision mode. Hence the purpose of this chapter is to delineate the specific premises and patterns of the political process in the International Atomic Energy Agency (IAEA) and, on the basis of our findings, to speculate about the general prerequisites for the political role of international organizations.

International organizations obviously display different "mixes" between the old decentralized decision mode emphasizing state sovereignty and the new political processes presupposing more centralized decisionmaking within the international bodies themselves (see Finkelstein's introduction). Where an international organization falls on that spectrum depends on that organization's relationship with national governments. The interface between states and international organizations is typically administered by members of international secretariats, on the one hand, and government bureaucrats, on the other. The bureaucratization of decisionmaking in international organizations has been noted[1] and Harold Jacobson[2] has characterized international organizations as "meta-bureaucracies." In assessing the political role of international organizations, it therefore makes sense to focus on the interplay of national and international bureaucrats. This is the main perspective we shall adopt in studying IAEA's role in the international politics of atomic energy. In addition to traditional documentary material our study draws on interviews with some forty senior civil servants in the IAEA secretariat and with Swedish officials in charge of atomic-energy matters.

Background

IAEA owes its origin to President Eisenhower's famous "Atoms for Peace" speech of December 8, 1953, in which he proposed that governments with a nuclear capability diminish their stockpiles of fissionable military materials by making joint contributions to a pool administered by an international agency under the aegis of the UN. This fissionable material was to be distributed for use in national civilian programs, in particular "to provide abundant electric energy to the power-starved areas of the world." The proposed agency would be responsible for the impounding, storage, and protection of the contributed materials and for their distribution and peaceful uses.[3]

If the peaceful usefulness of atomic energy was becoming increasingly obvious at the time of Eisenhower's speech, so were the potential dangers of a nuclear holocaust. The virtual U.S. nuclear monopoly and the "Secrecy Regime"[4] had crumbled with the Soviet nuclear explosion of 1949 and more or less collapsed with the Soviet thermonuclear explosion of August 1953. Pandora's box was opened and its contents had to be dealt with. Yet this was not a "traditional" disarmament problem. First, there was the problem of magnitude. The potential danger of nuclear weapons was unprecedented; any nuclear-arms agreement had to be verifiable, since the smallest possibility of noncompliance by any one party would constitute an intolerable risk for other parties. A nation caught with its guard down in the nuclear age would face a far greater danger from a "cheating" adversary than had resulted from the Axis powers' noncompliance with international disarmament agreements of the interwar period.

Second, there was the problem of alternative use. Nuclear power was not only a destructive force but also had great potential as an energy source. In the 1950s it was regarded as the energy source of the future with almost euphoric enthusiasm.[5] The two were inseparable; there were "no two atomic energies."[6] Out of this dilemma grew demands for some kind of international control of all aspects of atomic energy. The question was how to control, and preferably prohibit, the production of nuclear weapons while at the same time helping individual countries to profit from the peaceful uses of atomic energy.

The American Atoms for Peace initiative was an effort to reconcile military and commercial interests. Nuclear cooperation was to be conditioned on explicit assurances and guarantees against the diversion of nuclear assistance to military purposes. However, the grand scheme of an internationally safeguarded pool of nuclear fuel did not survive long in the Cold War climate. Distrust prevailed, not only between the United States and the Soviet Union but between all the "great powers" of World War II.[7] The immediate Soviet reaction to the Atoms for Peace program was negative. The entire concept of international cooperation in the peaceful uses of nuclear energy was rejected until nuclear disarmament was achieved, and the Soviet Union refused to participate in discussions about an international atomic energy agency. Yet in a dramatic reversal of policy the USSR in late 1954 agreed to discuss the issue of an international agency separate from disarmament, and its behavior in the subsequent negotiations was unusually cooperative.[8]

The United States and the Soviet Union were initially at odds over controls and safeguards. The Soviet Union sided with the Third World countries in objecting to international safeguards, stressing the need to observe the sovereign rights of states.[9] This disagreement reflected different practices in their bilateral nuclear transfers. Whereas all U.S. exports of nuclear materials were conditioned on safeguards, the USSR failed to apply safeguards to its early transfers to China and East European countries.[10]

However, in late 1956 the Soviet Union accepted a compromise on safeguards that paved the way for the establishment of IAEA in 1958.[11] The role of the new organization fell short of that envisaged in Eisenhower's Atoms for Peace address. Gone was the original conception of IAEA as a custodian and sole transfer agent for fissionable materials. The new organization was merely to arrange and supervise transactions among its members.

IAEA's Functions

The statutes of IAEA delineate the organization's objectives: "The Agency shall seek to accelerate and enlarge the contribution of atomic energy to peace, health and prosperity throughout the world. It shall ensure, so far as it is able, that assistance provided by it or at its request or under its supervision or control is not used in such a way as to further any military purpose" (Article II). Thus, the agency was put in the rather unusual position (at least for an international organization) of promoting a universal value while at the same time charged with preventing "misuse" of this universal value by individual nations. IAEA's dual role is not unproblematic, as the borderline between peaceful and nonpeaceful uses of nuclear power is blurred. India, for example, has consistently claimed that its nuclear explosion in 1974 was a "peaceful" one. And up to 1982 IAEA's Department of Technical Operations had a "Unit for Peaceful Nuclear Explosions Services." The most comprehensive attempt to define what really constitutes nuclear arms proliferation was made in 1968 when the Treaty on the Nonproliferation of Nuclear Weapons (NPT) was signed. IAEA had then been operative for more than a decade.

The NPT commits nonnuclear weapon states (NNWS) not to manufacture, accept the transfer of, or otherwise acquire nuclear weapons and requires them to accept IAEA safeguards on their peaceful nuclear activities, whether imported or indigenous. Owing to the persistent Soviet opposition to inspection, the NPT does not prescribe safeguards on the peaceful nuclear activities of the nuclear weapon states (NWS).

Subsequent developments in the international nuclear market—growing competition among an increasing number of exporting countries, export not only of power reactors but the full range of nuclear fuel cycle facilities—have challenged the conception of nonproliferation on which the NPT rested. The prevalent assumption has been that nuclear weapons development would always require long and costly programs and would most probably involve clandestine diversions of fissionable materials. The NPT safeguards system is geared to detect and deter such developments. However, as the Indian case demonstrated, the easiest and cheapest way to acquire a bomb is via a small plutonium-producing reactor and an unsophisticated, pilot-scale reprocessing facility dedicated to a weapons program.[12] In addition, the spread of enrichment and reprocessing facilities has opened up the prospect of a complete and sudden reversal of a nuclear program from a peaceful to a military project.

IAEA acts as promoter in the atomic energy field on basically two different levels—a "high-technology" and a "low-technology" level. The latter concerns such areas as the use of radiation and radioactive isotopes in industry, medicine, farming, etc. The agency's own technical assistance program, mainly geared to the Third World, deals almost exclusively with "low technology." IAEA is the world's largest publisher of literature in this field and runs its own laboratories.

In the "high-technology" field, which concerns nuclear power plants and the nuclear fuel cycle from uranium mining to nuclear waste disposal, IAEA's role is more elusive. The agency constitutes what one respondent called "the international nuclear power club."[13] The "club" serves as a meeting place and clearinghouse for the exchange of information concerning most aspects of nuclear energy. The agency arranges, or helps to arrange, some three hundred meetings, conferences, and seminars annually on such topics as nuclear waste management, nuclear plant safety and performance, etc.[14] This aspect of the agency chiefly caters to those IAEA members that belong to the "nuclear power club"—which is less than one-fourth of all IAEA members.[15] For example, Sweden— a small country with heavy involvement in the nuclear power industry—in 1981 sent a total of 124 delegates to 60 IAEA-sponsored conferences, specialist meetings, technical committees, and the like.[16]

If IAEA's only task were to promote the peaceful uses of atomic energy for "peace, health and prosperity throughout the world," it would be similar to other specialized agencies of the UN family. But IAEA has been given an additional responsibility: the agency is the guardian of the NPT, mandated to ensure that the treaty is implemented. Every NNWS signatory to the NPT must also sign a safeguard agreement with IAEA that entitles the agency to make safeguard inspections of all nuclear facilities of that nation. These inspections are to be carried out in such a way as to insure that no fissionable material can be diverted to possible military use without detection.

IAEA's right to inspect NPT signatory nations is in itself unique. No other international organization of the UN family has been given such far-reaching rights of access to sovereign nations. In the words of the present IAEA Director General, Hans Blix, "this is the first instance in history of sovereign States inviting an impartial international organization to audit their accounts and carry out inventories and other inspections on their own territory."[17]

Why have sovereign nations acquiesced in endowing an inter-

national organization with such authority? The potential danger of
unbridled nuclear-arms proliferation is so immense—especially
since "the technology of making nuclear weapons is becoming
steadily more widely known, thus eroding the barriers of horizontal
proliferation"[18]—that all international cooperation and trade in the
atomic energy field would be next to impossible without some kind
of NPT regime. If, for example, Sweden had refused to sign the NPT
and to place its nuclear plants under IAEA safeguards, it would
probably have been impossible for Sweden to import nuclear fuel
for its twelve nuclear power reactors—thus making them a very un-
economical investment. The nuclear industry is well aware of this,
and in some countries it has even exerted pressure on its own government to accept IAEA safeguards, fearing that normal trade in fissionable material would otherwise be endangered.

For example, the nuclear industries of West Germany, Italy, and
Belgium allegedly supported IAEA—against their own governments—in IAEA's attempts in the late 1970s to replace the internal
safeguard inspection routines of the Euratom countries with a system
based on IAEA standards and executed by a joint team of IAEA and
Euratom inspectors. This support was of great importance for IAEA
and for the entire NPT regime at the time. Failure to incorporate
Euratom into the IAEA safeguard system would probably have entailed the withdrawal of Eastern bloc support of the NPT regime and
would have made it extremely difficult for IAEA to reach workable
safeguard agreements with other countries, such as Japan, that were
determined not to get a "worse" or stricter agreement than the
Euratom countries.[19]

Thus, in a sense, the promotion and control of the uses of nuclear
power go hand in hand. Assured peacefulness makes promotion
possible. One high IAEA official called the agency's safeguard activities the "political backbone of IAEA."[20] Yet carrying out IAEA
safeguards is an intrusion, both in the running of nuclear power
plants and other kinds of nuclear installations, and in the political
sovereignty of a country. In a way, safeguards are like taxes—we
all agree they are necessary, but personally we would like to pay
as little as possible. Similarly, a state always wants effective safeguards in as many other countries as possible—especially hostile
neighbors—but doesn't mind leniency toward itself. And nuclear
power companies know that they must comply with safeguard regulations in order to stay in business, but the less burdensome the
inspection routines, the better.

The dilemma created by the ambiguous attitudes on the part of safeguard "clients" is compounded by the practical problems of designing a "foolproof" safeguard system and the grave international and intraorganizational complications in case of a questionable system of verification. A kind of enforced consensus among member states governs IAEA decisionmaking, but in implementing decisions the agency has to deal with the states individually, and then the spirit of consensus might not prevail. Yet the agency claims that it has a good record thus far concerning safeguards. An estimated 98 percent of all nuclear installations in the nonnuclear weapon states (NNWS) of the world are under IAEA safeguards at the present time,[21] and "no country has yet breached an IAEA safeguard agreement."[22]

Safeguards cannot prevent a violation of obligations—the diversion of fissile material—any more than bank or company audits can prevent a misappropriation of funds. All they can do is expose infringements or arouse suspicions—in effect, sound the alarm. The inspectors are not police officers with physical powers of prevention. All they can do is report. If they should be denied admittance, they can only report the fact. But this has never yet happened. Nor has the IAEA yet identified any diversion of fissile material, and this, we hope and believe, is because nothing of the kind has occurred in any safeguarded nuclear programme.[23]

Passing a judgment on IAEA's positive role in promoting atomic energy is perhaps more difficult. Its technical assistance program is small, amounting to $31 million in 1984, but enjoys a very good reputation.[24] This can be illustrated by the fact that IAEA receives far more applications for development projects from member states than can be financed through the regular budget. But since IAEA in many cases is the only international organization that has the means to implement many of the projects not funded through the regular IAEA budget, about one-third of the $31 million assistance budget is financed by other international development organizations (mainly UNDP and FAO) as well as several national development organizations.[25]

IAEA's Decisionmaking Structure

How does IAEA's decisionmaking structure compare with that of other UN agencies? First, it should be noted that IAEA is only loosely associated with the United Nations. The agency's relations with the

UN Security Council and General Assembly are usually represented by dotted lines in organizational charts of the UN family.

The agency's statutes make only oblique references to the UN. IAEA shall "conduct its activities in accordance with the purposes and principles of the United Nations to promote peace and international cooperation" (Article III B1). More concretely, the agency shall "submit reports on its activities annually to the General Assembly of the United Nations and, when appropriate, to the Security Council" (Article III B4); and all cases of noncompliance with safeguard regulations must be reported to the General Assembly and the Security Council (Article XII C). In all other areas—including budget and financing, employment of personnel, intraorganizational priorities, etc.—the decisionmaking authority rests with the agency's own bodies, the General Conference (GC) and the Board of Governors (BOG).

Formal Decisionmaking Structure

The Board of Governors is considered the more important of the two main decisionmaking bodies. One observer claims that the BOG "predominates over the General Conference and the secretariat to a greater degree than is true of similar organs in most international organizations."[26] The General Conference, which meets regularly only once a year, consists of representatives of all member states. They approve the budget, the Annual Report, new board members, etc. Meeting for about five days annually, the General Conference, in the words of one experienced delegate, "is a forum for general statements and approval."[27]

The Board of Governors is a smaller body; at present thirty-four persons are assigned as governors, each representing one member state. The board has a unique—and complicated—set of rules governing its composition, the purpose of which is to guarantee representation for the most advanced nuclear nations, without forgoing the traditional demand for a wide geographical distribution of seats in the governing body.

Although they are formally elected by the General Conference, "the nine members most advanced in the technology of atomic energy" are designated for membership by the outgoing board (IAEA Statutes, Article VI A1). These seats on the board are in effect permanent, since the status of "most advanced" is awarded to countries on a more or less permanent basis. For example, Sweden has tried to replace Italy as a "most advanced country" on the BOG. Despite the obvious fact that Sweden is indeed a more advanced nuclear nation than Italy, IAEA has not turned over the permanent seat to Sweden.

An additional twenty-two seats are distributed among the member states, divided into eight different regions. If a region is not represented among the nine permanent members, the most advanced nuclear nation of the region is given an additional "permanent" seat on the board. Thus, the board today has twelve rather than nine permanent members, representing the most advanced nuclear nations around the world, and 22 other members, geographically distributed and elected for a term of two years.[28]

This complex election system serves several purposes. It guarantees permanent seats to the most advanced nuclear nations, which are also the largest contributors to the IAEA budget, thus giving them both voting power and "staying power" or "power of continuity." Yet they have no veto power. In most matters, the board decides by majority vote. On budgetary questions, amendments to the statutes, and appointment of the Director General, decisions require two-thirds majority.

Member States and Groupings

The elected members other than the "most advanced" comprise a formal majority of the Board of Governors. Many of them have little interest in the agency except in the field of technical assistance. Yet thus far the potential leverage of this majority has not been exploited. One reason is the strong consensual attitude among the permanent members of the board, which is hard to break. Very few formal votes are taken on the board; most decisions are taken by consensus.[29] This is in itself a rather unusual phenomenon in the decisionmaking body of an international organization with all the major powers represented and with no veto as bargaining chip. As a matter of fact, the traditional East-West rivalry, which tends to permeate international organizations, has been almost totally absent in the work of the BOG since the early 1960s.[30] The fact that all board meetings are closed to the public has contributed to the more substantial and less rhetorical character of the proceedings. The need to master intricate technical questions and language has also been conducive to keeping rhetoric-prone diplomats at bay and to diminishing media interest in the proceedings. This relatively low media interest in IAEA, in turn, contributes to keeping rhetoric-prone diplomats at bay.

However, one problem that worries several outside and inside observers alike concerns the rising demands of the less developed countries (LDCs), usually referred to as the Group of 77. They have little interest in the NPT but emphasize questions relating to technology transfer. Many LDCs regard nuclear energy as a kind of "development status symbol," as proof of technical independence and a symbolic step into the future. Also, the Group of 77 includes four prominent member states with more or less outspoken ambitions to produce nuclear weapons: Argentina, Brazil, India, and Pakistan.[31]

When capable of agreeing among themselves, the Group of 77 controls a blocking vote in the BOG, but so far their attitude has mainly been "fundamentally ambivalent: they desire the IAEA to safeguard their neighbors' activities, but not their own."[32]

Another aspect of the growing significance of North-South issues in the BOG is the contagion of what members of the IAEA secretariat call the "UN disease," that is political filibustering within the organization, directed more toward home audiences than toward resolving issues. According to one high IAEA official, one of the reasons for this is the tendency, especially among the Group of 77, to appoint new governors to the BOG of a more general diplomatic background and with less technical acumen in the atomic energy field than their predecessors.[33] This is sometimes labeled the "UNIDO problem" by IAEA officials. UNIDO (United Nations Industrial Development Organization) is a relatively new organization that has grown considerably in the past decade. Located in Vienna, UNIDO is together with IAEA the main tenant of the new Vienna International Center on the Danube. Many LDCs have a relatively greater interest in UNIDO than in IAEA, as the scope of UNIDO is broader and more oriented toward development technologies. In efforts at diplomatic cost-saving, many LDCs have accredited the same individual diplomats to both UNIDO and IAEA. But in the view of many IAEA officials UNIDO is a place of lofty aims and no action, of much discussion and few accomplishments; it is populated by politicians and diplomats "infected with the UN disease" who are difficult to socialize into the low-key, consensual approach still prevailing in IAEA's Board of Governors.[34]

The Secretariat

The BOG works in close collaboration with the agency's secretariat. The size of the IAEA secretariat can be described as "medium," compared to other intergovernmental organizations (IGOs) within the UN family. The "Preliminary Manning Table for 1983" lists 631 persons in the "professional" category and 817 in the "general service" category.[35] The corresponding figures for ILO, FAO, WHO, and UNESCO, to mention a few examples, are two to three times greater.[36] The IAEA secretariat is divided into five departments, plus the office of the Director General. These are the Departments of Administration, Safeguards, Technical Co-operation, Nuclear Energy and Safety, and Research and Isotopes. Of these, the Department of Safeguards is the largest with almost 40 percent of all the employees in the "professional" category.[37]

As in most IGOs, the Director General (DG) has quite a strong position. The first DG of IAEA was an American, W. Sterling Cole. The second, and one of the most durable leaders of an IGO ever, was Dr. Sigvard Eklund, a Swedish nuclear scientist. He headed the IAEA secretariat for twenty years, from 1961 to 1981. He was replaced by another Swede, Dr. Hans Blix, a lawyer, diplomat, and former foreign minister. But the one man most responsible for the present shape of the agency is, without question, Dr. Eklund. Within the agency he is remembered for his great skill in two very important areas: in the recruitment of competent persons to the secretariat and in working closely together with the BOG to create the foundation for the political consensus needed to run the agency in an efficient manner.

The recruitment policies of IAEA are somewhat unorthodox. Since the foundation of the League of Nations, it has been the policy of Western nations to staff international organizations with civil servants, employed on a permanent basis. The idea of an independent career service has been regarded as a way to enhance the "objectiveness" and "impartiality" and thus the effectiveness of IGOs.[38] This has been opposed mainly by the Soviet Union and its allies, which have favored fixed-term contracts for all international civil servants. Arguing that no "international persons" exist, they have advocated that all members of an IGO have full authority to appoint and dismiss "their quota" of secretariat staff—a staff that would ultimately be representatives of their respective nations *as well as* international civil servants. Many Third World countries are also in favor of fixed-term contracts, both for the above-mentioned reasons and because many of them cannot afford to spare much-needed skilled personnel for the remainder of their careers.

But the prevalent assumption is that international civil servants with fixed-term contracts would be severely hampered by divided loyalties and would also have to spend a disproportionate portion of their contracted time in learning their job. Advocates of a career civil service argue that considerations of efficiency, continuity, experience, and cost point to keeping the share of fixed-term appointments at a minimum.[39] Dag Hammarskjöld commented on this in 1961: "To have 'more than a third' of the secretariat staff in the 'fixed-term category' would be likely to impose serious strains on its ability to function as a body dedicated exclusively to international responsibilities."[40] IAEA has the highest percentage of fixed-term contracts of all the international organizations in the UN family. In 1975 it was estimated at 82.2 percent, as compared to 34.4 percent for the UN itself.[41] The few permanent-contract employees in IAEA are mainly "holdovers" from the early days of the organization. Today, no permanent contracts are offered; all contracts in the "professional" category are on a fixed-term basis. The average employment span for a "professional" staff member in a technical department is only about five years.[42] Still, the organization is able to function without too much strain. What, then, are the reasons behind this policy of rapid turnover?

First, it should be emphasized that this policy has great support within the secretariat—at least among the forty-odd members we interviewed in 1981. They claim that the policy is necessary since IAEA is basically a technical organization that "needs a technically competent staff."[43] And since the field of atomic energy is developing very rapidly, there must be a continual influx of new people in order not to fall behind.

But this is not the whole truth. The highly qualified people that IAEA needs constitute a rare commodity in their respective home countries. A government or a company does not like to see an "investment" such as a qualified nuclear scientist or engineer disappear permanently into an international organization. And since all applicants to professional posts in IAEA are "cleared" with their home governments before they are employed (as is the case in almost all IGOs), the member states have virtual veto power in this respect. This normally means that if an international organization offers such a post on a permanent basis, national governments may not allow it to employ "the best" candidate. The organization may have to choose from persons expendable to their home governments. But if the post is on a fixed-term basis, the organization may get top candidates—if they can offer something in return.

In IAEA's case the agency can offer the *individual* a couple of years in Vienna, a good salary, and collaboration with other qualified professionals from all over the world. For *national governments* (or private companies) IAEA can offer insights into, and an informal channel of influence within, the agency as well as a degree of scientific cross-fertilization. In view of the political and economic values at stake, member countries cannot ignore the IAEA secretariat. The agency benefits from getting qualified applicants to secretariat positions; it can also limit the consequences of any errors in judgment by automatically getting rid of less competent or otherwise unwanted employees.

Fixed-term contracts can of course be renewed, once or several times. A secretariat cannot work without some kind of continuity in its administration. IAEA has stressed this need for continuity and experience at two administrative levels: the very top and the "top of the bottom." Until 1981 the very top consisted of Dr. Eklund and his personal staff and advisors, a group of about ten persons, all handpicked by Eklund, and most with long experience in or of the agency. The "top of the bottom" consists mainly of Section Heads, a group of some twenty-five persons who have made their career within the organization. Their formal superiors, chiefly the five Deputy Directors General (DDG) and the Directors (Division Heads), are changed regularly (with few exceptions). These posts are considered more "political," have great "status," and are distributed strictly in accordance with geopolitical considerations. The DDG in charge of the Department of Administration holds an "American" post, while one particular directorship in the Department of Safeguards is a "Japanese" post, and the DDG in charge of the Department of Technical Cooperation must come from a Third World country, etc.

These high positions are filled with qualified and competent persons, but since they do not stay long—only around five years—they have to rely to a great extent on their section heads, many of whom have more than twenty years' experience in the organization. One DDG, only nine months into his term, commented on this and "complained" that everything in his department seemed to "function almost too smoothly," and that his function was that of a "signature machine" rather than a leader.[44]

As is true of other IGOs, IAEA's Statutes prescribe that staff members be recruited "on as wide a geographical basis as possible." At the same time, "the paramount consideration in the recruitment and the employment of the staff . . . shall be to secure employees of the highest standards of efficiency, technical competence, and integrity"

(Article VII D). These goals, shared by most IGOs, are not always compatible. The fact that a secretariat post is reserved for a specific nationality does not mean that *anyone* of that nationality would do. According to his closest associates, Dr. Eklund was willing to take political and geographical considerations into account when appointing staff members, but he always demanded that even "earmarked" positions be filled by qualified and competent persons.[45] He could do this much because of his insistence on fixed-term contracts only, thus consciously violating what amounts to near dogma among IGO experts. In doing this, he imperiled the impartiality of the secretariat and opened it to political pressures, but he also supplemented the carrot, with which many executive heads of international organizations run their secretariats, with a very useful stick. There are no "honor posts" in the IAEA secretariat, no sinecures for persons with the right connections.

IAEA has been able to benefit from the fixed-term employment policy in an indirect way as well. Every year some one hundred staff members of the "professional" category leave IAEA and resume their careers "back home." These persons are sometimes called "graduates" from the agency, and the interchange results in what is known as an "alumni effect"[46] or "in-and-outer process."[47] This creates an international network of scientists, technicians, and administrators working in the atomic energy field. This network is extremely valuable to IAEA. It helps the agency to recruit competent personnel. It is instrumental in implementing safeguard inspection routines, etc. Maurice Strong has put it thus:

> In my view, international organizations must in essence be masters of process. Their business is the creation and management of the networks around particular issues that concern the international system. The in-and-outer provides a key element in the functioning of these networks and systems. These in-and-outers may be of various kinds: . . . all are part of a re-circulation process making nationally sensitive people out of international public servants and internationally sensitive people out of national servants.[48]

IAEA in the International Atomic Energy Network

A social network may be loosely defined as "a patterned set of relationships among actors or groups in a social space"[49] or a "structure of recurrent transactions."[50] Participants in networks are typically not organizations in their entirety but rather certain role occupants in the constituent organizations. The interface between organizations consists primarily of "boundary-role" occupants, linking an organization to its environment through either information processing or external representation.[51]

Boundary-role occupants may be found at various levels of national organizational structures. In international organizations they are typically found within the secretariat. Boundary roles do not necessarily follow formal positions, and boundary-role occupants constitute only fractions of national units and international secretariats.

Students of interorganizational networks have pointed to the centrality of so-called linking-pin organizations in such networks. "Linking-pin organizations that have extensive and overlapping ties to different parts of a network play the key role in integrating a population of organizations. Having ties to more than one action-set or subsystem, linking-pin organizations are the nodes through which a network is loosely joined."[52]

In the following we shall argue that IAEA constitutes a linking-pin organization in the international atomic energy network, performing an important broker function. Boundary-role occupants in the IAEA secretariat and IAEA "alumni" in national administrative units play key roles in this network.

The establishment of an international network of civil servants, scientists, and technicians in the atomic energy field has been facilitated by the fact that the field in itself is a specialized and rather homogeneous one. The alumni effect—along with the extensive contacts established by safeguard inspectors in their line of duty and through the abundance of IAEA conferences, seminars, and the like—has been instrumental in forging a close-knit network.

In order to be efficient, this network must be kept informal, if not hidden. The IAEA secretariat and its "alumni" cannot bypass the traditional diplomatic channels and routines, since all formal exchange with member states must follow these paths. Many nations are extremely sensitive about network "interference" in their exclusive sphere of national sovereignty. Boundary-role occupants in the network must always keep in mind who the final decisionmakers are and downplay their own influence.

This constitutes a dilemma for an outside observer. He has to look beyond the manifestations of formal decisionmaking to the actions taken, and the influence exerted, by the informal network. But since this influence is usually veiled in a properly arranged post factum, it is very difficult to acquire "hard data" establishing network influence in specific cases. However, in more general terms, the pattern is more discernible. About one-fourth of all the high-level IAEA officials we interviewed claimed that they spent "a very large part"—over 30 percent—of their working hours "keeping in touch" with national civil servants in different member countries.

The rationale for these consultations (as the IAEA officials prefer to call them) is said to be the smooth operation of the organization, not any conspiracies. They claim that this is a necessary procedure and one that is well accepted in national administrative systems, though hampered at the international level by diplomatic routines. One official in the Department of Safeguards, responsible for safeguard inspection routines in a large Western nation, said he was in almost daily (informal) contact with his official national counterpart. In these contacts they worked out inspection schedules, procedural questions, etc., and when they had reached an agreement, this was routinely confirmed by their respective decisionmaking authorities. Another IAEA official in the Department of Technical Operations argued that the network was extremely useful to him when considering applicants for vacant posts in his department. It was instrumental in keeping the quality of the professional staff on a high level.

In the Department of Administration and in the Office of the Director General, some high officials claimed that more than half their working hours were spent in informal "consultations" with national representatives on all questions that were to be settled by the Board of Governors and the General Conference. An indirect indication of the effectiveness and usefulness of this consultation process is the fact that the decisionmaking system of IAEA operates in such a smooth way.

Decisionmaking is a reflection of power. In an international organization power is spread thinly. According to organization theory, "organizations with dispersed bases of power are immobilized unless there exists an effective inner circle."[53] In most types of organizations this "inner circle" can be found in coalitions within their decisionmaking systems, and decisions are reached through the establishment of "working majorities." These organizations usually work within well-defined limits of authority and have instruments for implementation normally not found in international organizations, where majority decisions are hard to enforce and hence of limited value.

We thus have to look elsewhere for an "effective inner circle" that can "mobilize" the organization into action. The only body that can fulfill this role is the secretariat. Members of the secretariat must assume the chief responsibility in making the political decisionmaking machinery work. They must be the "brokers of consensus." The top management of IAEA is cognizant of this, and the major share of their time is devoted to such boundary-role functions rather than to purely administrative tasks. This "consultation process," as they prefer to label it, is greatly facilitated by information received through the network outlined above.[54] Acting on this information and on the official positions of the member states, the secretariat works out solutions to decisionmaking problems prior to the formal meetings. Issues that cannot be settled this way are usually just tabled in order to give the "consultation process" more time.[55]

By probing not only the present position of the parties involved but also their flexibility, a good broker simplifies the formation of consensus in an international decisionmaking body (see figure 10.1). One prerequisite for this brokerage to work is that the member states share an interest in reaching agreements at all. There must be a prior consensus regarding the domain of the organization.[56] Without such prior consensus, an international service organization cannot produce much service.

Figure 10.1 Interaction Patterns among 12 States

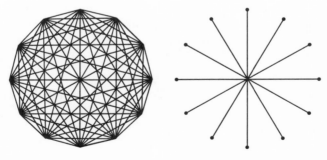

12 states in a multilateral bargaining situation without "broker"

12 states in a bargaining situation with an IGO acting as "broker"

Figure 10.1 Interaction Patterns among Twelve States

Consensus formation in an IGO is a very delicate and difficult
matter. The member states usually have divergent views as to what
should be done and how. All international conflicts are reflected,
and often amplified, in IGOs. Many IGOs become paralyzed and are
reduced to rhetorical platforms for member states. Even IGOs with
functional and delimited purposes are immobilized because of this
atmosphere of confrontation. In part, this is due to the fact that many
times the formal decisionmakers, that is, the national delegates to
the decisionmaking body, are not the ones who are directly concerned with the functional purpose of that organization.

IAEA has so far avoided the worst pitfalls of discord and dissension.
Compared with many other IGOs, it has been relatively free of East-
West polarization, and the North-South conflict has not yet proved
decisive. The major area of political discord within the organization
is the Middle East. Here East and West as well as North and South
clash concerning the status of Israel, especially after the Israeli attack
on nuclear installations in Iraq. Without doubt, the situation in the
Middle East represents an indirect political threat to the organization. In view of the rumored stockpiles of nuclear weapons in the
area, it could easily develop into a serious direct threat as well,
since the credibility of the organization as well as the entire NPT
regime rests on the impossibility of using nuclear arms in regional
conflicts.

The Chernobyl accident did not prove a threat to the organization.
On the contrary, a year later it looks as though it actually strengthened IAEA, insofar as it has become even more obvious among nations that international safety standards for nuclear power plants
must be set through an international organization. Less than a year
after the Chernobyl accident an international Convention on Early
Notification of a Nuclear Accident and a Convention on Assistance
in the Case of Nuclear Accident or Radiological Emergency were
adopted by the IAEA General Conference.[57]

On the whole, the organization supplies a variety of services to
the member states that they ultimately regard as positive, be it safeguards, exchange of information, or technical assistance. At the same
time, the multifaceted issue-area of atomic energy displays high
"stakes salience" (see Finkelstein's introduction). Yet, contrary to
the widespread notion that salience correlates positively with decentralized decisionmaking in IGOs, the secretariat has been allowed
to assume a leading role in the procurement of consensus in the
Board of Governors and a linking-pin position in an informal international network.

In our opinion, one important reason behind the relative success of IAEA, as compared with other specialized agencies of the UN family, can be found in its personnel policy. The practice of employing secretariat members on fixed-term contracts has entailed a high level of professionalism within the secretariat and, as a positive side effect, an extensive global information network of former employees. This has placed the secretariat in a strong position vis-a-vis the decisionmaking bodies, mainly the Board of Governors. As a result, the "political" side of the organization works remarkably smoothly. A spirit of consensus (one interviewee called it the "Spirit of Vienna"), which has not been imposed through veto rules, permeates the organization.

Notes

1. R. W. Cox and H. K. Jacobson, eds., *The Anatomy of Influence: Decision Making in International Organization* (New Haven: Yale University Press, 1973), 424–25.

2. H. K. Jacobson, *Networks of Interdependence* (New York: Alfred A. Knopf, 1979), 141.

3. H. L. Neiburg, *Nuclear Secrecy and Foreign Policy* (Washington, D.C.: Public Affairs Press, 1964), 80–81; C. K. Ebinger, "International Politics of Nuclear Energy," *Washington Papers*, No. 57 (Beverly Hills: Sage, 1978), 12; R. T. Mabry, "The Present International Nuclear Regime," in *International Cooperation in Nuclear Energy*, ed. J. A. Yager, (Washington, D.C.: Brookings Institution, 1981), 149.

4. C. Jönsson, *Superpower: Comparing American and Soviet Foreign Policy* (London: Frances Pinter and New York: St. Martin's Press, 1984), 199.

5. B. Goldschmidt, *The Atomic Complex: A Worldwide Political History of Nuclear Energy* (LaGrange Park, Ill.: American Nuclear Society, 1982), 253.

6. Ernst Bergmann, quoted in SIPRI, *Postures for Non-Proliferation* (London: Taylor & Francis, 1979), 2.

7. Goldschmidt, *The Atomic Complex*, 254.

8. J. L. Nogee, *Soviet Policy Towards International Control of Atomic Energy* (Notre Dame: University of Notre Dame Press, 1961), 224–27.

9. Ibid., 226–27.

10. G. Duffy, "Soviet Nuclear Exports," *International Security* 3 (Summer 1978): 84.

11. Nogee, *Soviet Policy*, 227.

12. Ebinger, "International Politics," 43; T. Greenwood et al., *Nuclear Proliferation: Motivations, Capabilities, and Strategies for Control* (New York: McGraw-Hill, 1977), 33.

13. Interview, Swedish resident diplomat in Vienna, 1981.

14. Interview, IAEA official, 1981.

15. L. G. Epel et al., "IAEA Efforts to Improve Nuclear Power Plant Operational Safety" IAEA *Bulletin*, September 1983.

16. Industridepartementet, "Sveriges deltagande: IAEA" (Stockholm: internal memo, 1982).

17. H. Blix, "Safeguards and Non-Proliferation," IAEA *Bulletin* 27 (Summer 1985): 6.

18. H. Blix, "The Relevance of the IAEA," IAEA *Bulletin* Supplement, 1982, 4.

19. Interview, IAEA official, 1981.

20. Interview, 1981.

21. Blix, "The Relevance of the IAEA," 5.

22. W. Walker and M. Lonnroth, *Nuclear Power Struggles* (London: George Allen and Unwin, 1983), 122.

23. Blix, "Safeguards and Non-Proliferation," 5–6.

24. C. V. Ocon, "IAEA Technical Co-operation and the NPT," IAEA *Bulletin* 27 (Summer 1985): 10.

25. Ibid.

26. L. Scheinman, "IAEA: An Atomic Condominium," in *The Anatomy of Influence,* ed. Cox and Jacobson.

27. Interview, 1981.

28. At present, the "permanent" members are: Australia, Brazil, Canada, Egypt, France, Federal Republic of Germany, India, Italy, Japan, USSR, United Kingdom, and the United States. The eight regions are: North America, Latin America, Western Europe, Eastern Europe, Africa, the Middle East and South Asia, Southeast Asia and the Pacific, and the Far East.

29. L. Scheinman, "IAEA"; Interview, IAEA officials, 1981.

30. Interviews, IAEA officials, 1981.

31. Walker and Lonnroth, *Nuclear Power Struggles,* 124. Interview, IAEA official, 1981.

32. Ibid.

33. Interview, 1981.

34. Interview, IAEA official, 1981.

35. IAEA, *Programme for 1981–1986 and Budget for 1981* (Vienna: IAEA GC(XXIV)/630,1984).

36. N. A. Graham and R. S. Jordan, eds., *The International Civil Service: Changing Role and Concepts* (New York: Pergamon, 1980), 50.

37. IAEA, *Programme for 1981–1986.*

38. Graham and Jordan, *International Civil Service,* 17.

39. T. Meron, *The United Nations Secretariat* (Lexington, Mass.: Lexington Books, 1977), 103–17.

40. Quoted in H. Reymond, "The Staffing of the United Nations Secretariat," *International Organization* 21 (1967): 767.

41. Graham and Jordan, *International Civil Service,* 84.

42. Interview, IAEA official, 1981.

43. Interview, IAEA official, 1981.

44. Interview, IAEA official, 1981.

45. Interviews, IAEA officials, 1981.

46. Jacobson, *Networks of Interdependence,* 98.

47. M. Strong, "Comments," in *The International Executive: Papers from a Princeton University Conference,* April 26–29, 1977, ed. L. Gordenker (Princeton: Center of International Studies, 1978).

48. Ibid., 35.

49. S. B. Bacharach and E. J. Lawler, *Power and Politics in Organizations* (San Francisco: Jossey-Bass, 1980), 205.

50. H. Aldrich, "The Origins and Persistence of Social Networks: A Comment," in *Social Structure and Network Analysis,* ed. P. V. Marsden and N. Lin (Beverly Hills and London: Sage, 1982), 283.

51. L. L. Roos and F. A. Starke, "Organizational Roles," in *Handbook of Organizational Design,* vol. 1, ed. P. C. Nystrom and W. H. Starbuck (New York: Oxford University Press, 1981), 302.

52. H. Aldrich and D. A. Whetten, "Organization-Sets, Action-Sets, and Networks: Making the Most of Simplicity," in *Handbook,* ed. Nystrom and Starbuck, 390.

53. J. D. Thompson, *Organizations in Action* (New York: McGraw-Hill, 1967), 14.

54. Interviews, IAEA officials, 1981.

55. Interview, IAEA official, 1981.

56. Thompson, *Organization,* 28.

57. The texts of the conventions can be found in the IAEA *Bulletin* 28, 4 (Winter 1986): 52–58.

11

Three Times Forty:

The ITU in a Time of Change

George A. Codding, Jr.

●

No discussion of the evolution of modern international organization would be complete without the inclusion of the International Telecommunication Union (ITU). The ITU is the oldest of the modern-day international organizations, having come into being in Paris in 1865. The ITU, along with the Universal Postal Union, was one of the more important models available to the architects of the League of Nations, and the founders of the UN early on asked the ITU to become affiliated with the new world peacekeeping body. If international organizations are indeed in a process of change, that change should be reflected in the 120 years of history of the International Telecommunication Union.

Changing Structure and Functions

Functional Evolution

According to the ITU's own terminology, telecommunication involves "any transmission, emission or reception of signs, signals, writing, images and sounds or intelligence of any nature by wire, radio, optical or other electromagnetic systems."[1] In short, the ITU is the UN specialized agency primarily involved in the instantaneous transport of information, by almost any means, from one point in the world to another.

Telecommunication has three major characteristics that tend to shape its structure and the manner in which it functions. First, tele-communication is an essential element in the life of the modern nation-state. Telecommunication is the lifeblood of commerce, it is a necessity for the military, and is important in almost every other aspect of modern life. Second, international cooperation is necessary in order to take full advantage of telecommunications. Standards must be adopted if a country is to be a part of the international telecommunication network, and rules must be adhered to in order to protect one country's radio communication from harmful inter-ference by another. And third, telecommunication technology and the uses to which it is put are in a state of constant change and evolution.

The electromagnetic telegraph, which made its appearance in the first half of the nineteenth century, was one of the first developments in rapid and reliable means of communication since the invention of the diligence in England in 1784. Governments quickly recog-nized its value and soon began to create domestic telegraph net-works as adjuncts to their domestic postal services (with the major exception of the isolated United States, where the operation of the telegraph was turned over to the private sector). It was soon found expedient to link the telegraph lines of different European coun-tries.[2] However, with no means of coordinating their arrangements, the European telegraph system quickly became a hodgepodge of differing technical standards and administrative procedures with a complicated and confusing rate structure.

It was this situation that led the European states of the time to convene a conference in Paris in 1865 to draw up an International Telegraph Convention and appended Telegraph Regulations, to standardize and rationalize the emerging European telegraph net-work, and to create the International Telegraph Union, the pred-ecessor of the International Telecommunication Union. The Tel-egraph Union was intended to be the vehicle for reviewing and revising the rules and regulations governing the operation of the new international telegraph network as changes occurred.

The 1865 convention provided only for periodic conferences of representatives of member telegraph administrations in which each country was given one vote and decisions were made by a majority. The second telegraph conference in 1868, however, added an in-ternational bureau, a primitive form of secretariat to be provided by the Swiss government, to help in the preparation of conferences, and to carry out other administrative duties. This remained the structure of the International Telegraph Union well into the 1920s.

The International Telegraph Union rapidly increased in membership as more and more states followed the lead of the Europeans in creating domestic telegraph networks and connecting them to the growing international network.

When the telephone became operational in the early 1880s, it was considered by many as a supplement to the telegraph and postal services rather than an important new means of communication. Consequently, most countries were slow in providing telephone services except in cities. The international expansion of the telephone was further inhibited by the language barrier and the fact that there existed no method for transmitting telephone calls over long distances of water. As a consequence, until the 1920s about all that was done by the International Telegraph Union was to request member administrations to use compatible equipment and procedures and to establish a time unit for charges in the international service.

The 1925 Paris Conference of the International Telegraph Union saw the first serious attempt to bring about a European telephone network. By that time, however, the European post and telegraph administrations had adopted such a variety of equipment and procedures that it was believed it would take more time to establish the necessary rules and regulations than was available at that conference. Instead, the delegates decided to give the task to a semi-independent group of volunteer experts, both governmental and nongovernmental, named the International Consultative Committee on Telephone (CCIF).[3] The same conference, almost as an afterthought, and in order not to embarrass those whose primary interest was the telegraph, also created an International Consultative Committee on Telegraph (CCIT) to carry out interconference research on matters concerning the international telegraph network. As a result of the work of the CCIF, the international telephone service was finally given its own set of regulations in 1932.

The original title of the CCIF was the *Comité consultatif international des communications telephoniques à grande distance* and only later abbreviated to *Comité consultatif international telephoniques*.[4] The CCIF and the CCIT were combined in 1956 to create the present International Consultative Committee on Telegraph and Telephone (CCITT).

Radio, when it came into practical application around the turn of the century, was introduced rapidly throughout the developed world because it provided the first means of effective communication with ships at sea, both military and commercial. There was a problem, however. The United States had refused to become a member of the International Telegraph Union because her telegraph and telephone services were operated by private enterprise rather than by the government as was the case in most of the countries that were members of the International Telegraph Union. Because of the fear that adding radio communication to the competence of the Telegraph Union would preclude the participation of the United States, radio was turned over to a separate, informal group of countries referred to by many at the time as the International Radiotelegraph Union. Starting in 1903 this new group, which included the United States, organized its own conference structure, adopted its own set of rules and regulations, and created its own international consultative committee. Rather than create a separate secretariat, however, this new body made an arrangement to have the International Bureau of the Telegraph Union handle its administrative duties.

Radio also demanded a new response from the international community. To create an international telegraph or telephone network, all that was needed were rules that would result in a commonality of equipment, administrative procedures, and, to a certain extent, tariffs. Radio communication, however, also required protection from harmful interference. At first, this was done by the simple expedient of requesting administrations to inform the International Bureau of the International Telegraph Union of frequencies they were using that had long-distance propagation characteristics for the information of other administrations. This, added to a rule adopted later by the Radiotelegraph Union that radio stations of one administration should not cause harmful interference to those of other administrations, resulted in the creation of an international right to interference-free operation of radio stations based on the principle of prior usage.[5]

After World War I it became increasingly apparent that all three types of communications were parts of a whole and thus it was no longer rational to treat them separately in two different international organizations. In addition, in most countries all three were regulated by the same governmental entity. The details of the merger that created the International Telecommunication Union were worked out at the Thirteenth International Telegraph Conference and the Fourth International Radiotelegraph Conference meeting simultaneously in Madrid in 1932. A single convention containing the major elements of the older telegraph and radio conventions was created to which were attached telegraph, telephone and radio regulations.[6]

At the invitation of the United States three International Telecommunication Union conferences were held in Atlantic City in 1947 to take into account the developments in telecommunications that had taken place during the war years (especially as concerned radio): a plenipotentiary conference, a general administrative radio conference, and a special administrative conference devoted to high frequency broadcasting. These conferences made significant changes in the manner in which the ITU operated. Of major importance was bringing the ITU into relationship with the new United Nations organization. In addition to the reciprocal right to be represented at each other's meetings and an exchange of information, this included the right to participate in certain UN activities such as the UN technical assistance program, since 1965 the United Nations Development Program (UNDP).

The ITU structure was also modernized. An Administrative Council was created to act as a liaison with the United Nations and to supervise the ITU's work. In order to make it more like other UN agencies that were in the process of being created and to reduce the influence of the Swiss government, which was still providing the ITU's International Bureau, an international secretariat was created headed by an elected Secretary-General.

The actions of the 1947 Atlantic City Conferences that had the most potential to change the ITU's functions were the decision to establish a new international list of radio frequency use "engineered" to satisfy all the actual and potential radio frequency requirements of all the members of the ITU and the creation of an elected International Frequency Registration Board (IFRB) to oversee changes that administrations might wish to make in the list. In the words of one observer, the Bureau's potential authority over the list was seen "as something of a cross between the Federal Communications Commission and the International Court of Justice."[7]

Although the International Frequency Registration Board survived in a modified form, as will be described later, it was found impossible to create the new international frequency list. The failure of the ITU to create the list has been attributed to several factors, including a lack of the necessary tools to carry out such a tremendous task and the submission of highly exaggerated requirements on the part of the members of the ITU. It has also been attributed to a decision by the USSR, made around the beginning of the Cold War period, that such a list would be an unwarranted invasion of its sovereign rights.

The International Telecommunication Union enlarged the scope of its activities as a result of the beginning of the space age in the late 1950s and early 1960s. In addition to the fact that communications are essential to their operation, satellites themselves turned out to be ideal instruments for communication over long distances, especially those that were placed into geostationary orbit. When there were only a few geostationary communication satellites in orbit, the ITU's role was limited to the recording of requests from administrations for satellite systems, including orbital locations and the appropriate frequencies for their use, in a manner similar to what the ITU did for frequencies for terrestrial communication.[8]

The most recent stage in the development of the functions of the International Telecommunication Union coincides with the marriage of the computer and telecommunications. Computers provide a sophisticated method for the processing and transmission of large amounts of information. Consequently, the ITU has been forced to take into account the introduction of computers into domestic and international telecommunication systems and to coordinate its efforts with those of other international organizations, such as the International Organization for Standardization, that were already involved in setting computer standards.[9] The impact that the merger of computers with telecommunications will have for the future of the International Telecommunication Union is only beginning to be explored.

Structure

A fairly complicated structure has evolved to carry out the functions that have been described above. At the summit is the plenipotentiary conference, the supreme organ of the ITU with the power to revise the ITU's basic treaty, the International Telecommunication Convention. It is composed of delegations from member states and is supposed to meet once every five years.[10] The plenipotentiary determines the general policies of the Union, establishes the basis for the Union's budget, and examines the Union's accounts. In addition, the plenipotentiary conference elects the Secretary-General, the Deputy Secretary-General, the Directors of the CCIR and CCITT, the members of the IFRB, and the states that send representatives to serve on the Administrative Council.[11]

Administrative conferences of the ITU are of two types, world and regional. World administrative conferences have the power to revise the Radio Regulations, the Telegraph Regulations, and the Telephone Regulations either partially or completely and to consider any other matter of a "worldwide character within the competence of the conference." Regional administrative conferences deal with "specific telecommunication questions of a regional character."[12]

The Administrative Council meets once a year at the Union's headquarters in Geneva and is composed of forty-one representatives of member states chosen "with due regard to the need for equitable distribution of seats on the Council among all regions of the world."[13] The Council acts as the agent of the Plenipotentiary Conference in the interval between plenipotentiary conferences and is charged with facilitating the implementation by the members of the ITU of the provisions of the Convention, the service regulations, and the decisions of ITU conferences; the determination of the ITU's policy of technical assistance, including the promotion "of international cooperation for the provision of technical cooperation to the developing countries by every means at its disposal"; ensuring the efficient coordination of the work of the Union; and exercising financial control over the ITU's permanent organs.[14]

The International Consultative Committees study technical and operating questions (including tariff questions for the CCITT) and issue recommendations. The CCIR deals with radiocommunication and the CCITT with all other types of telecommunication. Both bodies are headed by Directors and carry out their tasks by means of study groups, world and regional plan committees, and plenary assemblies that meet every four years. The Directors of the CCIs have traditionally been elected by the plenary assemblies of the appropriate consultative committee for terms ranging from six to eight years. As a result of a decision by the 1983 Nairobi Plenipotentiary, however, starting with the next plenipotentiary the Directors will be elected by the plenipotentiary conference for a term equal to the interval between plenipotentiaries.

The International Frequency Registration Board (IFRB) is made up of five individuals elected by the Plenipotentiary Conference.[15] The major function of the IFRB is to effect an orderly recording and registration of frequency assignments and positions assigned to geostationary satellites in order to ensure formal international recognition and protection thereof. The IFRB also provides advice to member administrations concerning the most efficient use of radio frequencies and geostationary satellite orbits and provides technical assistance in the form of preparations for radio conferences.

The rules of procedure for ITU conferences and meetings provide that each delegation of a member of the Union is entitled to one vote and that the majority shall prevail in all decisions, with the exception of the admission of new members.[16]

The ITU also has a secretariat, but a secretariat in four parts. The major component is the General Secretariat, which has the status of a permanent organ of the ITU and which is headed by a Secretary-General who is assisted by a Deputy Secretary-General. At the end of 1985 there were 408 permanent and 118 nonpermanent employees of the General Secretariat. There are also specialized secretariats assigned to the CCITT, the CCIR, and the IFRB. The sizes of these secretariats in 1985 were 46 for the CCITT, 29 for the CCIR, and 139 for the IFRB.[17] Although the individuals in the specialized secretariats are under the direction of their appropriate Directors as concerns duties, they fall under the general supervision of the Secretary-General as concerns their salary and general status as employees.

Because of the federal nature of the ITU, there has been some conflict in the past over the authority and functions of the permanent organs. In order to overcome this problem, the ITU is equipped with a Coordination Committee made up of the Secretary General, Deputy Secretary-General, the two Directors of the International Consultative Committees, and the Chairman and the Vice-Chairman of the IFRB. The purpose of the Coordination Committee is to "advise and give the Secretary-General practical assistance on all administrative, financial and technical cooperation matters affecting more than one permanent organ, and on external relations and public information."[18]

Over the years the voting procedures of the Coordination Committee have been the cause of a great deal of discussion. At present, the Committee is requested by the Convention to "endeavour to reach conclusions unanimously," but the Secretary-General is authorized to make decisions on his own responsibility if he deems the matter in question is urgent and cannot await the next session of the Administrative Council. If he should do so, the Secretary-General must "promptly" report the matter in writing to all of the members of the Administrative Council, including his reasons for taking the action along with the views of any other member of the Coordination Committee who wishes to have his views on the matter on record.

The ITU's financial arrangements reflect an earlier time when international cooperation was the exception rather than the rule. The ITU convention establishes nineteen different classes of contribution to the expenses of the ITU, ranging from 40 units down to one-eighth of a unit. Members are free to choose their class of contribution, with the exception that the one-eighth unit is reserved for the least developed countries as determined by the United Nations or the ITU's own Administrative Council. The Plenipotentiary Conference establishes a budget ceiling that applies until the next Plenipotentiary. The Administrative Council establishes the annual budget based on these limits and members pay their annual contributory shares in advance.[19]

Actors

As might be expected, ITU rulemaking conferences are dominated by representatives of member governments with national telecommunication administrations providing the bulk of the delegates. Usually, there is also a strong contingent from foreign offices. Smaller countries often use individuals from their local diplomatic missions as delegates and, in those countries where it is important, the private telecommunication sector is often represented. The mix of delegates is also affected by the simplicity or complexity of the domestic telecommunication policymaking structure. The delegation of the Netherlands to the 1982 Plenipotentiary, for example, was made up of nine members from the Dutch Post, Telephone and Telegraph bureau (PTT) and two individuals from the Dutch embassy staff in Nairobi. The United States delegation, however, was made up of eight individuals from the private sector (including three from American Telephone and Telegraph), seven from the Department of State, six from the Federal Telecommunication Commission, three from the National Telecommunications and Information Administration, and one each from the Department of Commerce, the United States Senate Commerce Committee, the White House, NASA, the United States Information Agency, and the U.S. diplomatic mission in Geneva.[20]

The delegations of all member states are equal in ITU conferences and meetings, but as usual some are more equal than others. In a study done on the 1979 World Administrative Radio Conference, the most recent general radio conference, it was revealed that only 58 of the 140 delegations were considered to have had any influence whatsoever in the proceedings of the conference. Western, developed nations were the top three (France, the United States, and the United Kingdom) in influence and developed nations made up 13 out of the first 25.[21] (See table 11.1.)

The perspective of the delegates to ITU conferences toward the role of telecommunications has changed considerably over the years, a change that has coincided with developments in the national administrations that control most of the world's communications, the PTTs. For many years the telephone and telegraph were considered to be supplements to post offices rather than services in their own right. The pro-postal service orientation of the PTTs was reflected in the delegations that were sent to ITU conferences, and as a result the development of telecommunication systems tended to suffer. In recent years telecommunications have been given at

Table 11.1 Influence Ranking of Delegations to the 1979 WARC

1.	France	10		Spain	4
	U.S.A.	10		Switzerland	4
3.	U.K.	9	23.	Argentina	3
4.	Algeria	7		Greece	3
	Australia	7		Italy	3
	Canada	7		Jamaica	3
	Germany (F.R.)	7		Mexico	3
	India	7		Nigeria	3
	Iran	7		Papua/N.G.	3
	USSR	7		Yugoslavia	3
11.	Brazil	5	31.	Botswana	2
	Cameroon	5		Denmark	2
	Netherlands	5		Ivory Coast	2
	Sweden	5		Jordan	2
15.	China	4		Malawi	2
	Cuba	4		Senegal	2
	Iraq	4		Syria	2
	Japan	4		Sudan	2
	Kenya	4			
	Norway	4		All others one or less.	

Source: George A. Codding, Jr., "Influence in International Conference: WARC 79," *International Organization* 35, 4 (Autumn 1981): 722.

least equal billing to the post office in most administrations, and in others telecommunications have been elevated to cabinet status, with a corresponding change in the makeup of delegations and their attitude regarding the role that telecommunications should play.

Private operating agencies in the field of telecommunications have a critical role to play in the ITU's work. Most importantly, if they have the approval of their governments, private operating agencies may participate as full members of the international consultative committees, which do much of the research on new technologies and issue recommendations concerning how those technologies should be applied. This can include acting as the representative of a member administration in study group meetings or serving as the chairman of a CCI study group. In 1976, for instance, employees of the American Telegraph and Telephone Company alone provided the chairs for three of the CCITT's eighteen study groups. One other study group was chaired by an employee of the American company, General Telephone and Electronics.[22]

The origin of this practice was the desire of the organizers of the international telephone consultative committee to secure the participation of the major operating agencies in those few countries where the supplying of telephone services was not a government monopoly at that time, especially the United States. Over the years the number of private operating agencies affiliated with the two committees has steadily increased. As of the end of 1985, for instance, there were sixty-three private operating agencies affiliated with the CCITT and fifty-three with the CCIR.[23]

The ITU convention also permits "scientific or industrial organizations, which are engaged in the study of telecommunication problems or manufacture of equipment intended for telecommunication service," to participate in meetings of the CCI study groups in an advisory capacity if their governments approve.[24] In 1985 thirty-six such agencies were affiliated with the CCIR and 160 with the CCITT.[25]

The importance of the nongovernmental participants in the work of the CCIs should not be minimized. In 1985 the CCITT had fifteen active study groups. The average number of representatives of government administrations in these study groups was twenty-six. The number of representatives of recognized private operating agencies was sixteen and of scientific or industrial organizations twenty-five. Nongovernment representatives were the majority in thirteen of the fifteen study groups.[26]

If the present tendency toward deregulation of the telecommunication industry in various parts of the world should continue,[27] the involvement of the private sector in the work of the ITU consultative committees can only be expected to increase in the future.

The ITU also permits representatives of international organizations to play a role in its activities. The United Nations has the right to send observers to all ITU conferences. The UN Specialized Agencies, the International Atomic Energy Agency, and regional international telecommunication organizations may send observers to ITU plenipotentiary and administrative conferences if invited. Observer status can also be granted to other international organizations that request it. In addition, any international organization or regional international telecommunication organization that coordinates its work with the ITU and has "related activities" may be admitted to participate in the work of the international consultative committees in an advisory capacity.[28]

Because telecommunications are important to almost all international organizations, there is always a good turnout at ITU conferences. The UN agencies that can usually be expected to send representatives to ITU conferences include the UN, UNESCO, ICAO, UPU, WMO, ILO, and WHO. Others include the IMO, the IMF, the World Bank, and the IAEA. The public international agencies in the UN group are less inclined to participate in the work of the CCIs, but the same is not true of other international organizations. In 1982, for instance, fourteen non-UN international organizations took part in the CCIR's Fifteenth Plenary Assembly and in 1984 ten participated in the CCITT's Eighth Plenary Assembly.[29]

The Decisionmaking Process

The complexity of the organizational structure of the ITU is reflected in the variety of its decisionmaking processes.

Rule Making

One of the characteristics of the ITU that strikes the observer is its heavy reliance on the treaty-making method for creating or modifying the rules that govern the ITU and regulate international telecommunications. The ITU, for instance, held on an average one major treaty-making conference a year in the 1970s and the first half of the 1980s. Plenipotentiaries account for three of these conferences, telegraph and telephone administrative conferences for two, and the remainder all concern radio or satellite communication. A formal treaty-making conference is an expensive undertaking and an excellent opportunity for mischief-making on the part of dissatisfied delegations.

On a number of occasions the ITU has investigated ways of cutting down on the number of such conferences. Two of the recent efforts are worthy of note, the attempt to create an ITU constitution and the substitution of international consultative committee recommendations for the formal rules and regulations created by conferences.

A desire to reduce expenses, together with an uneasiness on the part of some of the older members of the ITU as to the intentions of some of the newer members, led the 1965 Montreux Plenipotentiary to investigate the possibility of creating a constitution out of the more basic and permanent provisions of the Convention. The constitution would then be reviewed at less frequent intervals and would require more than a simple majority for change or modification as had been the case in the past. The Convention, containing only the remaining, more transitory, articles, would be reviewed at more frequent, less formal conferences where decisions could be made by a simple majority vote.

Because of time constraints, the Montreux Plenipotentiary created a special study group to draw up proposals for presentation to the next plenipotentiary conference. This group worked from 1967 to 1969 and presented a plan to the 1973 Malaga-Torremolinos Plenipotentiary. By 1973, however, the developing countries had become the majority in the ITU and were having second thoughts about creating a situation in which a minority of members would have a substantive veto over any future change they might want to make in the structure or functions of the ITU. A proposal to create an ITU constitution was decisively defeated in 1973, and although the subject was raised again in Nairobi in 1982, it received little support.[30]

The ITU was more successful in reducing the use of treaties for making the more specific rules governing telecommunications. At one time there were four sets of regulations appended to the Telecommunication Convention, the Radio Regulations, the Additional Radio Regulations, the Telegraph Regulations, and the Telephone Regulations; each took the form of a legal treaty.[31]

The major tasks of the consultative committees were to study technical, operational, and tariff problems and to suggest solutions to members of the ITU in the form of nonbinding recommendations.

It was anticipated that the more seminal of these recommendations would be transformed into binding regulations by incorporation into the appropriate regulations at the next suitable administrative conference. Because of the high quality of the output of the consultative committees, the urgency of resolving the problems that were being considered, and the fact that most of the major users were involved in the creation of the recommendations, it was discovered that most of these recommendations were put into effect by member administrations almost immediately after being issued, without waiting for the appropriate conference.

The 1958 Administrative Telegraph and Telephone Conference decided that the conference/treaty method was too slow to keep up with the rapid changes in telegraph and telephone technology, and too expensive, and requested that the CCITT investigate the possibility of substituting CCITT recommendations for the vast majority of the regulatory treaty obligations. The results of the CCITT investigation were presented to the 1973 World Administrative Telegraph and Telephone Conference, which proceeded to initiate the necessary changes. The resulting Telegraph and Telephone Regulations contain only a few general rules concerning the need for cooperation among member administrations and the need to keep up with new technological advances. The operative clause in both of the new streamlined Telegraph and Telephone Regulations reads: "In implementing the principles of the Regulations, Administrations (or recognized private operating agencies) should comply with the C.C.I.T.T. Recommendations, including any Instructions forming part of those Recommendations, on any matters not covered by the Regulations."[32]

This change in the ITU's decisionmaking process seems to have met with the approval of the members of the ITU. The first call for a new telegraph and telephone administrative conference, to deal with new technologies, was not made until the 1982 plenipotentiary and is scheduled for 1988, fifteen years after the decision to substitute recommendations for treaty provisions was made.[33] In addition, suggestions have been forthcoming that a similar procedure be adopted for most of the Radio Regulations.[34]

Rights-Vesting in the ITU

The closest the ITU comes to acting like a government is in relation to the radio frequency spectrum and more recently the geostationary satellite orbit. The very nature of radio communications requires the absence of harmful interference from other radio services and other radio stations. As a result, the ITU has long been involved in establishing the rules that tend to protect radio stations from unwanted interference.

The first step, which dates back to the beginning of international collaboration on radio communication matters, involves the allocation of discrete portions of the radio frequency spectrum to specific types of radio services such as broadcasting, fixed, maritime mobile, aeronautical mobile, and the like.[35] At some time quite early in the ITU's history, member administrations began notifying the ITU secretariat of the specific frequencies in the service bands that they were assigning to individual radio stations. The list that resulted was quickly used as a guide by administrations authorizing new stations, which in effect vested in the first station a right to operate without harmful interference from stations that were later placed into operation.

The IFRB is the monitor of the present-day list, known as the Master Frequency Register. Administrations notify the IFRB of frequencies that they desire to use. If the IFRB finds the notifications to be in accordance with the provisions of the Radio Regulations, and not likely to cause harmful interference to previous assignments, the notified frequency is registered in the Master Frequency Register and from that time on has the right to operate without harmful interference from others. This rights-vesting procedure soon became known as "first-come, first-served" and tended to satisfy the needs of the members of the ITU as long as there were enough frequencies to meet everyone's requirements.[36]

When members of the ITU became convinced that certain portions of the radio frequency spectrum were in danger of becoming overcrowded, thus making it difficult for new entrants to obtain the necessary frequencies, the ITU turned to a new system of rights-vesting. This system, which became known as the a priori rights-vesting system, involves allotting specific portions of the service allocations to member states, to be assigned to their radio stations as they see fit. The details of the plan, including the duration of the agreement, are included in a formal treaty that is then ratified by the parties involved. The first use of this new rights-vesting system took place in the 1920s and dealt with broadcasting stations in the European region.

Soon after World War II the United States advocated that the a priori system be adopted for the major portion of the then usable radio frequency spectrum. According to the U.S. plan, a series of ITU conferences should be held to establish allotment plans that would meet the needs of all members through modern "engineering" techniques. For a number of reasons, including exaggerated requirements and a feeling on the part of the Soviet bloc of nations that the plans would adversely affect their communications, it was possible to develop plans only for a few radio services below 4 MHz and for the aeronautical and maritime services between 4 and 27 MHz. In 1959 the attempt to draw up a priori plans for other services was summarily abandoned.[37]

This left the ITU with two rights-vesting systems, the first-come, first-served system for the major portion of the radio frequency system and the a priori system for the remainder.[38]

The ITU also adopted a modified first-come, first-served plan for satellite communication purposes in 1971. This plan provided for advance notification of satellite services, coordination among affected administrations, and registration of orbital positions and associated radio frequencies. At the same time, however, at the instigation of the developing countries, the 1971 World Administrative Radio Conference for Space Telecommunications passed a resolution to the effect that administrations should not be given any permanent priority in the use of orbit-frequency resources and that a conference should be scheduled to work out a comprehensive plan for the new broadcasting-satellite service. Many of the developing nations had become worried that all of the better orbital positions and radio frequencies would soon be occupied by the more developed nations and the common user organizations under their control, making it difficult or even impossible for the developing countries to reap the benefits of satellite communication when they are in a position to take advantage of it.

At the 1983 ITU Plenipotentiary, the developing countries obtained an addition to the ITU Convention of a clause recognizing the right of all countries to "equitable access" to the geostationary orbit and the appropriate radio frequencies and, at the 1974 World Maritime Administrative Radio Conference, a formal allotment plan was adopted for the terrestrial maritime service.

The developing country majority was successful in having the 1979 World Administrative Radio Conference pass resolutions to the effect that the geostationary satellite orbits are considered to be "limited natural resources" and that a conference should be held to "guarantee in practice for all countries equitable access to the geostationary satellite orbit and the frequency bands allocated to space services."[39]

This subject will be dealt with again when we review some of the North-South political problems that have beset the ITU in recent years.

Regional Arrangements in the ITU

The ITU has always relied to a certain extent on regional solutions to problems, especially concerning radio communication. For example, it was discovered very early that signals from radio stations using low and medium frequencies did not adversely affect radio stations using low and medium frequencies in other parts of the world. It was thus found practical to authorize different uses for the low and medium portions of the radio frequency spectrum in different areas of the world, depending on the particular needs of the countries involved. Different regional approaches to radio frequency management could also be permitted in the same portions of the radio frequency spectrum, as evidenced in the decision of the European PTTs to create the first frequency allotment plan for European broadcasting stations in the 1920s.[40]

The most recent use of the regional approach to problem-solving occurred at the ITU's 1977 space conference when a serious dispute arose over the timing of a decision to create a formal allotment plan for the geostationary satellite broadcasting service and the appropriateness of the criteria to be used in formulating that plan. In order to solve the dispute it was decided to permit the countries of Regions 1 and 3 to continue to draw up an allotment plan while authorizing the dissatisfied countries of Region 2 (the Americas) to hold their own conference to draw up an allotment plan at a later date.[41]

The regional approach has also been used in ITU elections. In electing the forty-one countries that send individuals to sit on the Administrative Council, for example, the world is first divided into five regions: Region A (the Americas), Region B (Western Europe), Region C (Eastern Europe and Northern Asia), Region D (Africa), and Region E (Asia and Australasia). The delegates from each region then caucus to choose their candidates. Finally, an election takes place in which all delegations are allowed to vote on all of the regional lists of candidates. The election for the five-man IFRB is similar. Although candidates are grouped by regions and all delegations vote for all five regional lists, any member of the ITU may nominate candidates for any of the lists.[42]

Role of the Secretary-General

As is the case in most international organizations, the Secretary-General is the individual most closely associated with his agency.[43] While delegates to conferences and meetings come and go, the Secretary-General is almost always available to greet important visitors, to answer inquiries about the ITU and its activities, and to make speeches concerning the ITU on appropriate occasions. The Secretary-General is highly involved in official ITU conferences and meetings. His name is on numerous reports and documents that greet the delegates when they arrive at the conference site; he initiates and orchestrates the negotiations for the choosing of conference officials, gives one of the main opening and closing addresses, and is always at the side of the conference chairman to give advice and counsel. His duties also include sending regular reports to administrations and supervising publication of the well-known *Telecommunication Journal,* which often carries an editorial under his name.

The Secretary-General of the ITU has gained additional visibility in recent years. One reason has been the ITU's heavy reliance on conference diplomacy since it was reorganized in 1947. Another is the relatively long term of the last Secretary-General. Mohammed Mili was elected Deputy Secretary-General by the Montreux Plenipotentiary Conference in 1965 and was chosen by the Administrative Council to assume the position of Secretary-General on the death of Secretary-General Manohar Sarwate in 1966. Mili was elected Secretary-General in his own right by the Malaga-Torremolinos Plenipotentiary in 1973 and served in that position until he was unseated by Richard Butler in 1982.

The third reason for this development involves boundaries. The ITU is not the only international organization with an interest in communications. UNESCO, for instance, has always been interested in the international flow of information, and its financial resources have always been significantly greater than those of the ITU. For this reason, there has always been a danger of an overlap of the activities of the ITU and UNESCO. This danger has tended to increase as UNESCO has become involved in what is known as the New World

Information and Communication Order. And, as mentioned earlier, computer technology has recently demonstrated its usefulness in modern telecommunications, resulting in closer contact between the ITU and other international agencies, such as the International Organization for Standardization (ISO),[44] which had previously been involved in setting computer standards. There are still some differences of opinion as to the proper boundaries between the ITU and UNESCO; as a result, both Mili and Butler have made it a point to defend the ITU's interests before almost any gathering that provides a convenient forum.

All of this, of course, has tended to build the constituency of the Secretary-General and thus increase his influence in ITU affairs.

Politics in the ITU

In view of the importance of telecommunication to commerce and government, it is not surprising that the ITU should be affected by the international political climate. Some of the disputes that have occurred have little or nothing to do with the work of the ITU in telecommunications while others involve it directly.

In the former category we can include the decision of Napoleon III to hold the first conference of the International Telegraph Union in Paris in order to support his attempt to re-create the imperial glories of France and to increase his own standing in the eyes of the French people and the refusal of the United States to invite the Soviet Union to attend the 1927 Washington Radiotelegraph Conference because the United States did not recognize the Soviet Union or like its political leanings.

It would also include the frequent verbal conflicts during the Cold War over membership in the ITU. As a general rule, the USSR was the advocate of "universality," arguing for the admission of the Balkan countries to membership and later in the period, East Germany, North Korea, and Communist China. The United States, on the other hand, advocated keeping "politics" out of the ITU by leaving such matters to the United Nations to decide.

The most recent manifestation of such politics in the ITU would be the exclusion of South Africa from ITU conferences and meetings since the 1965 plenipotentiary and the acrimonious debate at the 1982 plenipotentiary over the possible exclusion of Israel.[45]

Of more importance to the outcome of the ITU's work would be the successful attempt in the late nineteenth and early twentieth centuries on the part of the colonial powers to obtain additional votes in ITU conferences for their various colonial possessions. By 1925 France had eight votes in International Telegraph Union meetings, one for herself and one for each of the following: French Indochina, French Somaliland, Madagascar, Morocco, New Caledonia, Senegal, and Syria. Even the United States received an additional vote for its territories as a whole when the United States became a member of the International Telecommunication Union in 1934.[46]

The more recent North-South controversy has been clearly reflected in the ITU. Almost every conference and meeting held under ITU auspices since 1965 has seen a major clash between the two groups, especially as concerns aid to the developing countries to create efficient domestic telecommunication systems. The developing nations have been successful in passing resolutions in conferences and in making additions to the ITU Convention emphasizing the need for development assistance in telecommunications, despite a reluctance on the part of the developed countries. They have also been successful in passing directives requiring the ITU's permanent organs to give more attention to the needs of the developing countries.[47]

The developing countries have been less successful in obtaining development assistance directly from the ITU. A proposal was made at the 1973 Plenipotentiary, for instance, to create a Special Fund for Technical Cooperation to assist developing countries with urgent telecommunication problems and to be financed from the regular ITU operations budget.[48] The opposition of a number of developed countries, including several from the Soviet bloc, resulted in the elimination of the provision that the new fund should be financed from the regular budget on the grounds that there were other agencies in the UN system that provide development assistance. The developing countries, however, were able to obtain reluctant agreement to creating a fund, but only on the basis that it would be financed from voluntary contributions. The fund came to naught, however, because of the reluctance of most of the developed countries to make contributions.

The 1982 Plenipotentiary replaced the 1973 Special Fund with a slightly altered Special Voluntary Program for Technical Cooperation and established an Independent Commission for World-Wide Telecommunications Development to examine "the totality of existing and possible future relationships between countries in the field of telecommunications involving technical cooperation and a transfer of resources in order to identify the most successful methods of such transfer."[49] The Commission officially released its report on January 22, 1985. Among other things, it recommended a massive increase in the flow of resources into telecommunication development assistance.[50] It is still too early to determine what will be the practical effect of these latest initiatives, but if past developments are any indication substantial help to the developing countries will be a long time in arriving.

The two groups have also been divided on the subject of the proper structure of the ITU, as has been discussed above. The third world has fought hard, and usually successfully, to make changes in the ITU's structure that tend to take important decisions out of the hands of the older developed nation majority. These include increasing the size of the Administrative Council, taking the election of the Directors of the CCIs away from the plenary assemblies of the CCIR and CCITT and giving it to the plenipotentiary conference, refusing to permit the creation of an ITU constitution, and eliminating votes for colonies. They also include setting limits on the length of terms of elected officials, favored by the South and disliked by the North.

The most difficult political issue presently facing the ITU concerns the geostationary orbit and the appropriate radio frequencies. The developing world has become convinced that telecommunications are essential to their development. As stated in the Maitland Report: "Our study of the role [that efficient telecommunications systems] can play has persuaded us that telecommunications can increase the efficiency of economic, commercial and administrative activities, improve the effectiveness of social and economic benefits of the process of development more equitably throughout a community and a nation."[51] It is also convinced that satellite communications are especially appropriate for their needs and that the resources, orbit, and frequencies necessary to have satellite communication will become scarce in the not too distant future.

This has led the developing nations to use their voting power to require the ITU to explore methods for attaining equitable access to the space resources. As a general rule the developing countries have supported the use of formal a priori allotment plans for establishing rights to portions of the frequency allocation table and the geostationary orbit where there is evidence of scarcity, while the developed countries, especially the United States, usually support the flexibility of the older first-come, first-served rights-vesting mechanism.

The first tangible result of this strategy was the allotment plan for geostationary orbits and associated frequencies adopted by the 1977 ITU Broadcasting-Satellite Conference for the broadcasting-satellite service. The plan that was adopted, however, did not apply to the entire world as had been expected but only to regions 1 and 3 (all of the world except for the Americas) because the United States was successful in convincing the other countries of its region to postpone drawing up their plan. The United States felt that it was too early to predict the requirements of administrations accurately in 1977 because of technical innovations that were soon to take place. The allotment plan for the Americas was finally drawn up in 1983 at the Region 2 Satellite-Broadcasting Conference using slightly different technical parameters than those that were used in 1977.[52]

The second was the decision of the ITU to hold an Administrative Radio Conference in two parts (1985 and 1988) that would plan the geostationary satellite orbit and the frequency bands allocated to space services in such a manner as to guarantee equitable access to all member countries. While the United States was a reluctant participant in the creation of an a priori allotment plan for the broadcasting satellite service, there is evidence that an attempt to create such a plan for other services could lead to a decision on the part of the United States to achieve its national objectives alone or in another international forum.[53]

Suffice it to say at this point that politics has always been involved in the work of the ITU, and it seems likely that it will be involved as much if not more in the future.

Conclusions

The major conclusion that can be drawn from this brief review of the 120 years of ITU history is that while the ITU has changed, the changes that have occurred have not been fundamental. The ITU retains a highly decentralized process of decisionmaking, relying heavily on the consent of the nation-state members. The reasons are not hard to discover. In the first place, the ITU is a prisoner of its own history. Its manner of functioning was designed at a time when international cooperation on nonpolitical matters was in a very primitive state. The formal diplomatic treaty, requiring ratification before it is binding, was the only instrument for arranging international concerns that was available in the early years of the ITU's predecessor. Consequently, the formal treaty has remained an important tool for regulating international telecommunications. Another reason for the lack of any fundamental changes is the high salience of the subject matter with which the ITU is concerned. Because of its importance in almost every aspect of national life, member countries have been very reluctant to give up their freedom to use telecommunications in any way they see fit beyond those constraints imposed by the technology itself. The more decentralized decisionmaking process gives member countries the feeling that they will not be forced to lend their support to a decision that may be contrary to their national interests.

The prospects for change in the future are dim at best. The two sides in the present international political struggle are deeply suspicious of each other's demands on the ITU. As long as that suspicion remains, it will be difficult if not impossible to obtain agreement on almost any request for a change in the manner in which the ITU operates. On the one hand, the developing countries will consider any proposal that emanates from the opposition as an attempt to keep them from enjoying their newly achieved power in ITU conferences and meetings. The developed countries, on the other hand, will consider proposals from the new majority as attempts to diminish the power of the developed country minority in ITU affairs even further.

Change may therefore depend on the technology of telecommunications, which is in the process of rapid and fundamental change. On several occasions in the past, members of the ITU with different political inclinations have put aside their differences in order to create the conditions that were necessary to enable all of the parties involved to reap the benefits of a new technology. It is not beyond the realm of imagination to envision a day when countries will once again see cooperation as the only road to mutual benefit.

Notes

1. See ITU, *International Telecommunication Convention, Nairobi 1982* (Geneva, 1982), annex 2, para. 2015.

2. The details of the history of the ITU that follows are mainly from the following two publications, unless otherwise indicated: George A. Codding, Jr., and Anthony M. Rutkowski, *The International Telecommunication Union in a Changing World*

(Dedham, Mass.: Artech House, 1982); and George A. Codding, Jr., *The International Telecommunication Union: An Experiment in International Cooperation* (Leiden: E. J. Brill, 1952). (Reprinted in 1972 by Arno Press.)

3. In point of fact, the CCIF had been created two years earlier by a group of representatives of European telephone administrations who were worried about the absence of standards that would be needed if the telephone were to cross national boundaries. See Codding and Rutkowski, *International Communication*, 83–84.

4. The original acronym CCI was changed to CCIF by the Madrid International Telegraph Conference in 1932.

5. See also below, pp. 337–40.

6. All members of the new organization were required to ratify the Convention, the basic treaty, and to agree to be bound by at least one of the appended regulations.

7. See Harold K. Jacobson, "The International Telecommunication Union: ITU's Structure and Functions," *Global Communications in the Space Age: Toward a New ITU* (New York: The John and Mary Markle Foundation and the Twentieth Century Fund, 1973), 49.

8. See ITU, *Radio Regulations, Edition of 1982* (Geneva, 1982), Article 11.

9. See, for instance, ITU, VIIIth Plenary Assembly, Malaga-Torremolinos, 1984, Resolution No. 7, Collaboration with the International Organization for Standardization (ISO) and the International Electrotechnical Commission (IEC).

10. The ITU has held six plenipotentiary conferences since the end of World War II: Atlantic City, 1947; Buenos Aires, 1952; Geneva, 1959; Montreux, 1965; Malaga-Torremolinos, 1973; and Nairobi, 1982. The Nairobi Plenipotentiary set the interval between plenipotentiaries at five years. The next plenipotentiary is set for 1989, five years after the 1982 Convention came into effect.

11. For specifics of the ITU's structure, see *International Telecommunication Convention, Nairobi, 1982*, Articles 5–12.

12. Ibid., Article 7.

13. Ibid., Article 8, 1. (1).

14. Ibid., Article 8, 4. (4).

15. Ibid., Article 10.

16. An applicant that is not a member of the UN must obtain a two-thirds majority to be admitted to membership in the ITU. For the rules and procedures governing ITU conferences and meetings, see ibid., Article 77.

17. See ITU, *Report on the Activities of the International Telecommunication Union in 1985* (Geneva, 1986), 142.

18. *International Telecommunication Convention, Nairobi, 1982*, Article 12.

19. For many years no sanctions were applied to member countries that failed to make their annual contribution to the expenses of the ITU. The 1973 Plenipotentiary changed that situation by adding a provision to the Convention whereby members in arrears in an amount equal to two years of contributions shall lose their right to vote in ITU conferences and meetings.

20. See ITU, Plenipotentiary Conference, Nairobi, 1982, List of Participants, October 20, 1982, and Supplement No. 1, October 28, 1982.

21. See George A. Codding, Jr., "Influence in International Conferences," *International Organization* 35, 4 (Autumn, 1981):715–24.

22. See CCITT, Sixth Plenary Assembly, Geneva, September 27–October 8, 1976, *Orange Book*, vol. I (Geneva, 1977), 217–21.

23. See ITU, Administrative Council, 41st Session, Geneva, June 1986, Doc. No.

6442-E (CA 41–28), April 22, 1986, 6. 4/3. In addition, if they have the approval of their government, private operating agencies may apply for permission to attend administrative conferences in an advisory capacity.

24. *International Telecommunication Convention, Nairobi, 1982*, Article 68, 4 (1).

25. See *Report on the Activities of the International Telecommunication Union in 1985*, 104, and ITU, CCIR, XVIth Plenary Assembly, Dubrovnik, 1986, Doc. Plen./ 1-E, 48–49. Unless they receive an exemption, both the recognized private operating agencies and the scientific or industrial organizations must make a financial contribution to the consultative committee with which they are affiliated.

26. See *Report on the Activities of the International Telecommunication Union in 1985*, 117.

27. See, for instance, "International Competition and Deregulation: Impossible, Improbable or Imminent," in The Federal Communications Bar Association and the International Law Institute of Georgetown University, *New Developments in International Telecommunication Policy* (Washington, D.C., 1983), 171–236.

28. See *International Telecommunication Convention, Nairobi, 1982*, Articles 60, 61, and 68.

29. See CCIR, *Recommendations and Reports of the CCIR, 1982, XVth Plenary Assembly, Geneva, 1982*, vol. 14-1, 26–27 and CCITT, VIIIth Plenary Assembly, Malaga-Torremolinos, October 8–19, 1984, *Red Book*, vol. 1, 279.

30. See Codding and Rutkowski, *International Telecommunication*, 204.

31. The Additional Radio Regulations contained provisions dealing with tariff questions in which the United States refused to be involved. By putting them in a separate treaty, the United States could approve the Radio Regulations without the necessity of making reservations to the tariff articles. The Additional Radio Regulations were abolished in 1979 and the provisions that were considered still valid were transferred to the Radio Regulations.

32. See ITU, *Telegraph Regulations, Telephone Regulations* (Geneva, 1973), Article 1.

33. The 1988 World Administrative Telegraph and Telephone Conference was added to the ITU's schedule of conferences in order "to revise existing administrative regulations with a view to making them applicable to new services (Teletext, Telefax, data transmission, etc.)." See ITU, Plenipotentiary Conference, Nairobi, 1982, Document No. 329-E, October 30, 1982, 1.

34. See Anthony M. Rutkowski, "Deformalizing the International Radio Regulations," *Telecommunications Policy* 7, 4 (December, 1983): 309–25.

35. Leive actually refers to this as the ITU's legislative process. See David M. Leive, *International Telecommunications and International Law: The Regulation of the Radio Spectrum* (Leyden: A. W. Sijthoff, 1970), 19.

36. For the modern version of this procedure, see *Radio Regulations, Edition of 1982*, Article 12.

37. As we will see later, the United States has reversed its position as concerns communication by geostationary satellites and now argues vigorously for the retention of the first-come, first-served system for this means of communication.

38. See Codding and Rutkowski, *International Telecommunication*, 31–35.

39. See *Radio Regulations, Edition of 1982*, Resolution No. 3.

40. In 1947 the ITU divided the world into three general regions for the purposes of radio frequency management: Region 1 (Europe, Russia, and Africa), Region 2 (the Americas), and Region 3 (Asia and Oceania).

41. See *Radio Regulations, Edition of 1982*, Appendix 30 and U.S. Department of State, *Report of the United States Delegation to the ITU Region 2 Administrative Radio Conference on the Broadcasting Satellite Service, Geneva, Switzerland, June 13–July 17, 1983* (Washington, D. C., October 31, 1983).

42. See ITU, Plenipotentiary Conference, Nairobi, 1982, Doc. No. DT/4A-E, August 15, 1982, Procedures for the Election of the Members of the Administrative Council, and Doc. No. DT/4C-E, August 15, 1982, Procedures for the Election of Members of the IFRB.

43. The ITU has had seven Secretaries-General since the post was created in 1947: (1) Franz von Ernst (Switzerland), 1948–49; (2) Leon Mulatier (France), 1950–53; (3) Marco Aurelio Andrada (Argentina), 1954–58; (4) Gerald C. Gross (United States), 1958–65; (5) Manhour Balaji Sarwarte (India), 1966; (6) Mohamed Mili (Tunisia), 1966–82; and (7) Richard E. Butler (Australia), 1982 to present.

44. Formerly the International Standardization Organization.

45. For an account of the Israel issue see U.S. Secretary of State, *Report of the United States Delegation to the Plenipotentiary Conference of the International Telecommunication Union, Nairobi, Kenya, September 28–November 6, 1982* (Washington, D.C., 1982), 4–6.

46. The practice was not completely ended until 1973.

47. For a further discussion concerning politics in the work of the ITU, see the author's "Politicization of the International Telecommunication Union: Nairobi and After," in *Policy Research and Telecommunications: Proceedings from the Eleventh Annual Telecommunications Policy Research Conference*, ed. Vincent Mosco (Norwood, N.J.: Ablex Publishing Corporation, 1984), 435–47.

48. See ITU, *International Telecommunication Convention, Malaga-Torremolinos, 1973* (Geneva, 1974), Resolution No. 21.

49. See *International Telecommunication Convention, Nairobi, 1982*, Resolution No. 20.

50. See ITU, *The Missing Link*, Report of the Independent Commission for World-Wide Telecommunications Development (Geneva, 1985).

51. Ibid., 10–11.

52. See *Radio Regulations, Edition of 1982*, Appendix 30 and U.S. General Accounting Office, *U.S. Objectives Generally Achieved At Broadcasting Satellite International Conference—Improvements Can Help in Future Conferences* (Washington, D.C., August 2, 1984).

53. See U.S. Federal Communications Commission, An Inquiry Relating to Preparation for an International Telecommunication Union World Administrative Radio Conference on the Use of the Geostationary-Satellite Orbit and the Planning of the Space Services Utilizing It, *Third Notice of Inquiry* (Washington, D.C., October 7, 1983) and *Fourth Notice of Inquiry* (Washington, D.C., May 10, 1984).

12

The Political Roles of

Recent World Bank Presidents

Michael G. Schechter

●

Structure and Goals of the World Bank Group

The World Bank Group consists of three legally separate institutions, the International Bank for Reconstruction and Development (IBRD), the International Finance Corporation (IFC), and the International Development Association (IDA), all of which share a single President and a common goal: "helping to raise standards of living of the people in the developing countries by channelling financial resources from developed countries to the developing world."[1] The IBRD and IDA also share the same officers, directors, and staff. Control of both institutions is exercised through a Board of Governors, consisting of one governor and one alternate appointed by each of the member states.[2] Most of the Board's functions, however, have been delegated to twenty-one full-time executive directors, five of whom are appointed by the largest stockholders (the United States, Japan, West Germany, France, and the United Kingdom). The remaining executive directors are elected by the other member states. The IFC's organizational structure is separate but similar. Actually the first task of the IBRD, as agreed to at the Bretton Woods Conference of July 1944 at which it was established, was to assist with the reconstruction of Europe. Accordingly, most of the IBRD's initial loans, after its Articles of Agreement (i.e., its constitution) had obtained the requisite number of ratifications on December 27, 1945, were made to countries in Western Europe. But the IBRD's role in that region and indeed in postwar reconstruction was soon dwarfed by that of the massive Marshall Plan instituted by the United States. Thus the IBRD soon turned to the other task implied by its title: aiding in the development of its less-developed member states. In the development arena, the IBRD's main objectives are to stimulate, support, and provide from its own resources flows of capital into worthwhile projects and programs.

But the IBRD quickly encountered a major obstacle in achieving these ends: it was prohibited by its own constitution from investing in countries without a government guarantee. And many governments in developing countries were unwilling to guarantee loans to private firms either for ideological reasons or because of fears of being accused of favoritism. While this did not prohibit IBRD from making loans to nationalized industries, at least in the first ten years of its history, it seemed to show some hostility toward public enterprises.

One of the ways by which the IBRD overcame this difficulty was the creation in 1956 of the IFC. The IFC's objectives are providing capital for private enterprises, encouraging the development of local capital markets, and promoting foreign private investment in developing countries. Significantly, the IFC does not require government guarantees.[3]

The final institution in the World Bank Group, the IDA, was established in September 1960 and began operations two years later. Its purpose is also to provide development assistance, but exclusively to very poor countries—mainly those with an annual per capita gross national product of less than $731 (in 1982 dollars)—and on easier terms than those of the IBRD and IFC. This is possible because contributions from the association's richer members are the chief source of IDA funds rather than private loans, a funding source that necessarily leads to lending at near commercial rates and emphasis upon projects' rates of return rather than the needs of recipient countries.

Given that the World Bank Group only came to fruition in the early 1960s with massive growth[4] and a reorientation in Bank lending in terms of geographical regions, sectors, and projects, this study of World Bank Group Presidents begins then.

Sources of Political Influence

The following discussion of the political roles of recent World Bank Presidents combines the various approaches noted in Robert Cox's classic study of executive heads, namely legal-constitutional, sys-

temic, moral, and individualistic.[5] For example, drawing attention
to the ambiguities of the World Bank's Articles of Agreement and
the specific provisions of the Bretton Woods Agreements Act adopted by the U.S. Congress shows that the president of the World Bank
was intended to be the chief officer "responsible for the organization, appointment and dismissal of the officers and staff, subject to the general control of the Executive Directors";[6] that in re-
cruiting the staff the President is not limited by geographical quotas,
as are heads of most other United Nations agencies, and he (and
his staff) are charged with being international civil servants, with
allegiance only to the World Bank.[7] Obviously such provisions,
when considered in tandem, offer each President considerable latitude in terms of the size, quality, and biases of the bank's staff.

More important, however, and certainly something that a simple
legal-constitutional approach would not suggest, is that by being
able to exert considerable influence over the choice of their successors, most recent World Bank Presidents have been able to extend
and prolong their influence.

In addition, perhaps because the IBRD is not dependent on funds
from member governments for its budget, it "can reflect the objectives, ambitions, personality, and prejudice of its president,"[8] and
the traditionally American administrative style of the Bank has assured that the top executive "dominates the organization and encounters few internal checks and balances."[9] Thus each recent
World Bank President has found it quite easy to put his own administrative cachet on the organization, either through dominating
the Governing Board or by delivering public addresses that set a
tone both for the organization and for the global development community at large. Indeed one of the themes that will emerge from
this study is the increasing personalization of the World Bank,
which, while peaking in McNamara's administration, continues to
this day. More specifically, World Bank Presidents are able to influence significantly the sorts of guidelines that are applied to loan
applications as well as the overall growth pattern of the IBRD's outstanding loans and the IDA's credits. In part this is because the
President, working with his Senior Vice Presidents, has the ability
to enlarge the bank's sources of funds through the choice of alternative and additional capital markets. Bank Presidents are also able
to influence the amount and type of research performed in the bank
by the world's largest body of developmental economists. Indeed,
the global respect for that body of researchers further reinforces the

World Bank President's potential political influence, by insuring that Bank initiatives will be taken seriously on intellectual grounds as well as because they come with an implicit link to funding.

Limits on the World Bank Presidents' Political Influence

Each of these sources of potential influence, of course, also implies a possible limit on presidential authority. For example attention needs to be given to the degree to which World Bank Presidents are subservient to American interest groups and agencies on at least some sorts of issues and dependent on the perceptions of those controlling the capital market as well as the votes of the American delegation, always the preeminent power in the organization. Likewise, attention has to be devoted to the ability of World Bank Presidents to readjust the Bank's mission, organizational ideology, and image in accordance with systemic changes, most notably the increase in "third world" power, changes in the global business cycle and the reemergence of a "cold war." Even such mundane matters as the health and working styles of World Bank Presidents can inhibit political influence as much as provide a foundation for it.

Nature of Political Roles of Recent World Bank Presidents

George Woods

On January 1, 1963, George Woods became the third President of the World Bank. The situation he faced had been well described by his predecessor, Eugene Black, in his valedictory speech a year earlier. Then, Black suggested that the World Bank was approaching a peak in its career. Bankable projects were running out because most potential borrowers had enough debt to carry. Therefore, Black—who had been crucial in winning Congressional and U.S. Presidential support for the establishment of the International Development Association a year earlier[10]—prophesied that the IDA "soft loan" business would have to be increased in order to fill the gap.[11] More specifically, Black urged his successor to find new resources for the "technically sound," but "unbankable projects" in the developing countries.[12] Thus the major tasks confronting Woods were taken to be the same as Black's primary goals, that is, obtaining a big transfusion of capital to the International Development Association and further pushing private investment in economic development projects.[13]

Woods was expected to be particularly adept in the area of private investment given his professional background. Prior to assuming the World Bank's Presidency, Woods had chaired the investment body—First Boston Corporation—that was the principal underwriter of World Bank bonds. Moreover, experience in investment banking suggested that he was "willing to stick his neck out to expedite the transformation of the Bank into a development financing agency."[14] In addition, he was known as a skilled financial troubleshooter (particularly during the Anglo-Egyptian settlement after the Suez crisis) and had served as a principal advisor in the World Bank's relations with private capital markets, especially in their dealings with developing countries. Moreover, he was a long-time friend and business associate of Black's.[15] Indeed, Black had played a visible role in the selection of Woods as his successor.[16] Not surprisingly, then, commentators observed that "his appointment evidently assures continuity of policy, with little departure from the strict but necessary standards that Mr. Black has laid down for the Bank's business."[17] Moreover, with a view toward his extensive and successful business career, and his possession of the conservative Republican credentials presumed to be necessary to enjoy the esteem of the private financial community, it was generally agreed that "if experience spells success, Woods has it."[18]

However, some were less pleased, ironically for many of the same reasons. Indeed, the "main criticism" of Woods was that he was too much like Black at a time when the World Bank was facing new challenges that called for new approaches.[19] There were questions about his age, sixty-one at the time of assumption of office in an organization where retirement at the age of sixty-five was expected.[20] How effective an administrator could he be? There were those who believed that after thirteen years of "benevolent dictatorship under Black" the World Bank needed some administrative overhauling if it were to function effectively. Others questioned the new President's ability to work effectively with the U.S. Congress, given that he had withdrawn his nomination in 1961 to be the head of the Agency for International Development (AID) because of Congressional opposition.[21] Some even asked whether his previous work with the First Boston Corporation might not be a handicap, fearing the First Boston would give up its vital role as the major underwriter of World Bank bonds to avoid the appearance of a conflict of interest.[22]

In part, the critics appear to have had the better crystal balls. Within seven months of taking office, Woods underwent major surgery: "Frustrated and often suffering from nervous exhaustion during the latter half of his tenure, he became progressively irascible and undiplomatic."[23]

Consequently, relations with the staff and Executive Board were "markedly less harmonious" than during Black's tenure. He "hectored" the Bank's board of directors into approving loans for India and Pakistan.[24] Likewise, he "offended member governments" by his tactics in putting into practice his view that the Bank's president should take the lead in negotiations. For example his style of negotiations in trying to secure a second replenishment of funds for the International Development Association—first dealing with the United States (whose contributions to the Bank's budget were by far the largest and whose concern with its ongoing balance-of-payments deficit was growing almost daily) and then, much later, with America's previously uninformed European allies—was characterized this way by *The Economist:* "Mr. Woods apparently believes in multilateral giving but bilateral asking."[25] Not surprisingly, he got a mere 40 percent of what he had requested.[26] Prominent among those who were not forthcoming was Woods's old nemesis, the U.S. Congress.

But neither Woods's supporters nor his critics, nor Black himself for that matter, appear to have accurately anticipated Woods's willingness to experiment.[27] Indeed the early soothsayers were probably surprised at how hard Woods worked to transform Black's Bank into Woods's Bank.[28]

Almost immediately, Woods raised serious questions about his predecessor's observation that the Bank's lending had peaked. As Woods himself put it at the time, in a clear allusion to his predecessor's remarks, "from where I sit the prospect is not for a downtrend in the Bank's operations."[29] Woods achieved a dramatic turnabout at least in perceptions by working on the premise that it was the dearth of well-prepared projects that had been the main constraint on the volume of Bank lending and not any debt limitations.[30] Accordingly, he built up the Bank's economics staff, increased the number of non-Americans among the principal officers, and tried to instill informality into the Bank. This last step was intended to stimulate creativity as well as expertise in project design.[31]

Moreover, as the Canadian Bank Governor at the time put it, Woods's leadership facilitated "an interesting raising of the Bank's hemline of bankability." The Bank extended grace periods for borrowers. Colombia, for example, received a thirty-five year loan in February 1964.[32] The Bank itself began siphoning off funds to IDA to help supplement its base, even though Woods had earlier opposed such an activity and had promised the financial community that there would be no such connection between IDA and Bank funds.[33] Woods's ability, with the encouragement of the United States and West Germany, to transfer a portion of the Bank's surplus to the IDA, demonstrates his growing independence from his nonstate constituents (i.e., the world's financial community), especially when supported by his major state constituents. Obviously, the Bank, and particularly Woods, was growing in political power in the international system.

More specifically, Woods felt that the Bank could do much more with its skills and resources to help developing countries than it had previously, particularly in the educational, agricultural, and industrial sectors.[34] The Bank's movement into agriculture and education and the evolution of an incestuous relationship between the Bank and IDA paralleled the paradigmatic change that was occurring in the development field. A kind of confluence of intellectual catharsis among the members of the foundation world (especially the Ford Foundation), UN specialized agencies, and the Kennedy Administration occurred at this particular point in time: all saw the challenges of the newly independent, developing countries and recognized the seemingly limited applicability of models of the past for rapid economic development and political modernization.[35]

Woods was particularly influential in this regard. "He was a precursor of important things to come" including his opening "the door for the expansion of [Bank] activities in the rural sector."[36] With the assistance of his recently enlarged economics staff, which itself was closely allied with the members of the Kennedy administration, Woods imaginatively "reaped the benefits of Black's cautious first steps" toward nontraditional funding and eagerly sped the transformation of the Bank into something more nearly resembling a development financing agency. "[C]ourageous, and either unaware of, or contemptuous of the adage that 'discretion is the better part of valor,' Woods pressed forward." He sought to put in place a broad-based program in agriculture, including assistance with storage and marketing, agricultural credits, institutions, and techniques to help the family farmer. But he did not try to accomplish this alone. He developed new and stronger relations between the Bank and other international agencies and encouraged the establishment of consultative groups to facilitate the coordination of external assistance. For example, funding consortia for India and Pakistan were initiated during his Presidency.[37] In addition, he looked to the Food and Agriculture Organization (FAO) for leadership. Indeed, in spite of considerable opposition from the Bank staff, he worked out an accord with the FAO in 1964 that included a kind of division of labor, identifying the Bank's role more as a financial patron and the FAO as the technical assistance agent, responsible for identifying, preparing, and presumably carrying out agricultural projects.[38] This sort of arrangement worked as long as Woods remained at the Bank's helm, although, interestingly, the FAO was never "able" to recruit personnel for all of the posts authorized for the joint project and, at times, had difficulty raising its 25 percent of the shared budget.[39]

Even in the much more traditional (for the Bank) industrial sector, Woods's innovations were evident. It was his goal to make industrial financing available on a much more flexible basis than it had been in the past. He sought to assist less-developed countries in diversifying their economies. Accordingly, the Bank began to permit the financing of local currency expenditures, a somewhat radical departure from the past.[40] Woods also modified the Bank's policy against lending for industrial projects in the public sector, presumably because of his desire to stimulate the production of chemical fertilizers, which in many states was done by the public sector. On the other hand, not until 1968, on the eve of his departure from the Bank, did Woods relax restrictions against lending to publicly controlled development corporations.[41]

Woods's most lasting contribution, however, might be seen in the area of social sector financing, and particularly the dramatic move of the Bank into financing for education. At the time of his assumption of the Presidency, Woods had found that the Bank's management had come to accept the notion that education was an important aspect of development and that the Bank Group (really meaning the International Development Association) ought to play a role in the financing of education. In this instance, however, as in many others, the management was "ahead of many members of the staff of the Bank."[42] In addition, the Executive Directors of several countries, like Valery Giscard d'Estaing of France, raised questions about the movement into "non-economic projects."[43] In spite of this, Woods quickly moved in this direction. He was able to use the $750 million recently pledged to the IDA for three years, as well as to build on the support of the increasingly important West Germans, whose Executive Director seemed particularly receptive to an expansion of IDA's activities.[44] Accordingly, Woods moved swiftly to establish an Educational Projects Division, which has been portrayed as an institutional manifestation of his success in reorienting the Bank Group.[45] It was this department that was to be responsible for evaluating applications for education loans and for deciding whether a loan or a credit would be granted.

There were clear limits, however, to the Bank's entrance into the educational field. The Bank concentrated on projects in the modern sector[46] and was biased toward upper division schooling,[47] technical education, and vocational training for industry, commerce, and agriculture.[48] Not surprisingly, such a set of priorities fit well with Woods's view of the role of any sort of development assistance.

> Whatever else is said about the needs of the developing countries of Asia, Africa and Latin America, the criterion that really counts when it comes to engineering an escape from poverty is productivity.

> To get more output from a given input should be the motto of all those engaged in "foreign aid"—or development finance, as I would rather call it . . . when a few years ago the Bank began to address itself to the huge problem of education for development, we approached the subject from the point of view of increasing productivity.[49]

Accordingly, the Bank's criteria for approving loans even in the education field continued to have an "overtly narrow economic orientation."[50] Woods himself later noted that the terms of these early educational loans were usually determined by the creditworthiness of the country and not the value and/or need for the project.[51] Accordingly, Woods was able to maintain the faith of the moneylenders as well as the support of the American political community, while he subtly, but significantly, altered and expanded the Bank's mission and ideology into one involving a more complex understanding of the meaning and sources of development.

Another interesting insight into Woods's activities as executive head is provided by noting his conscious choice to work *with* the United Nations Educational, Scientific and Cultural Organization

(UNESCO) as the Bank moved into the education field. He did this rather than pursue the "normal" expansion route desired by "most people at the Bank," that is, hiring necessary experts and proceeding with the same degree of independence as the Bank had in fields like electric power and transportation. Woods overruled his staff on this issue because of his recognition of "the nature of the decision taken by the international community when it established a series of functional agencies."[52] Accordingly, Woods is often credited with making the Bank a more integral part of the UN system.[53]

Thus the Bank's entry into the educational field under Woods evidences a considerable growth in the political power both of the Bank and its executive head. Woods was able to alter the Bank's orientation significantly and, in conjunction with two sympathetic and equally vigorous UNESCO executive heads, to begin to establish the institutional mechanisms for working toward the alleviation of illiteracy in less-developed countries (LDCs). At the same time, the Bank and its executive head came to be recognized as significant voices in the world of economic development theorizing and pros-elytizing. Perhaps most noteworthy in this regard was Woods's widely quoted January 1966 article in *Foreign Affairs* and his call in 1967 for a "grand assize" of the development effort by interna-tionally respected figures, a call that ultimately resulted in the fa-mous Pearson Report.[54]

Also of note in terms of Woods's approach to the job of executive head was his attempt to build relations between the Bank and church organizations as part of his overall effort to educate and enlarge the constituency in support of development activities.[55] As Ernst Haas most clearly articulated, generalizing from the case of labor unions, an executive head's ability to identify and build a constituency both among member countries and within relevant and potentially pow-erful nongovernmental constituents is an essential characteristic that distinguishes the languid executive head from the innovative lead-er.[56] In Woods' case, of course, questions can be raised about the differences between the potential influence of church organizations in the international economic or even educational fields and that of labor organizations in the social and employment sectors.

Several further acts demonstrate the increased political power and savvy of the World Bank Presidency under Woods. During the five years before Robert McNamara became Bank President, Woods sharply reduced the proportion of principal officers in the Bank and IDA who were U.S. citizens. The figures of 55 percent going to 40 percent are generally accepted.[57] Significantly, the Young Professionals' program—initiated by Woods in 1963—had a much lower percentage of Americans during Woods's years in office than during McNamara's: 8.2 percent versus 14.2 percent for 1969–74 and 17.1 percent for 1975–77.[58] The consequence of this was expected to be greater sympathy for LDCs' attitudes by the Bank's staff. Woods thus administratively maneuvered to accommodate the Bank to international systemic changes, most obviously decolonization and the growing importance of "third world" states in international economics. Second, under Woods's administration, the historically heavy concentration of IBRD aid to South Asia began to decline. Under Black 18.5 percent of IBRD loans had gone to India; 5.3 percent went to that country under Woods.[59] This was another accommodation to international systemic changes, that is, the growing relative importance (at least numerically) of independent states in Africa. Third, it is worth noting that much credit has been given to Woods in selecting his successor. Although there is some controversy about the timing of President Johnson's decision to recommend McNamara as the United States' "first, second and third" choice for the Bank Presidency, several things are clear about that appointment, Woods's instrumental role being one of them.[60]

Thus, as even this cursory review of Woods' activities suggests, recent World Bank Presidents have become critical political actors as development theory changed and as the Bank has become more intimately involved in the funding of social sector projects, such as those in education. Woods's success in this regard has been explained in terms of his subtle reorientation of the Bank's ideology, in a way that appeared to meet the demands of LDCs, yet failed to antagonize the omnipotent Americans.

Robert Strange McNamara

The context surrounding Robert S. McNamara's inauguration on March 1, 1968, as the fourth President of the World Bank Group was somewhat ominous. Less-developed countries were suffering from increasingly severe problems in acquiring the funds needed for even servicing their debts. The first development decade was coming to a close, with a widely shared realization that it had failed to achieve many of its essential goals. There was a general disappointment among LDCs with the results of the United Nations Conference on Trade and Development (UNCTAD) II as contrasted to the euphoria surrounding that organization's first conference. The developed countries, suffering from aid fatigue, evidenced little interest in continuing, much less increasing, their foreign aid commitments.[61] The United States' leadership role in North-South relations was clearly on the decline. There was a general sense of despair and a leadership vacuum. The latter included international institutions. No organizations or organizational leaders seemed to be preeminent or particularly innovative in the development field.[62] Moreover, it was a time when overlap and competition between intergovernmental organizations seemed at something of a peak, with no single organization predominating. To some, McNamara's appointment only seemed to compound this ominous situation. Those included people who thought the World Bank Group Presidency was merely a convenient place for U.S. President Johnson to "retire" a tired and increasingly dissatisfied and disaffected bureaucrat.[63]

McNamara's professional background differed from that of all of his predecessors. To a large degree that was intentional, at least in Woods's mind. McNamara was the first Bank President to come from a nonbanking background. He had been an assistant professor at Harvard Business School during the 1940s before joining Ford Motor Company, of which he became president in 1960. From 1961 to 1968 he was U.S. Secretary of Defense. He left the Defense Department with the reputation as the man who had tamed the Joint Chiefs of Staff and who had exercised the firmest civilian leadership there ever. Moreover, he was credited with introducing rigor into the U.S. defense decisionmaking process. Whereas his association with the controversial Vietnam war complicated his takeover at the Bank, his academic and work experiences in the managerial field were precisely what Woods had had in mind when he helped select his successor. Woods felt that the Bank was in need of a managerial expert. No longer was there need for the executive head to be drawn from the ranks of Wall Street.[64] That had been done frequently enough in the past to have won their faith and allegiance, to say nothing of the credibility garnered as a result of the creditworthiness of the Bank and its tradition of at least speaking only of economic criteria for loans.[65] McNamara himself thinks it was a big advantage not to have been a commercial banker, in part because the commercial banking function was the "least important aspect of his job."[66]

Evidence that McNamara was not only going to manage the Bank well came quickly. In the education field, for example, it took the form of a very positive response to René Maheu's letter to the Bank in which the UNESCO Director-General had called upon the Bank to go along with UNESCO in broadening its concept of education, one which would include primary as well as out-of-school education.[67] More generally, in his first speech before the joint annual meetings of the International Monetary Fund and the World Bank, McNamara outlined a very bold five-year program, including a proposal that the Bank double its overall lending. That meant that in the period 1969–73 McNamara expected the Bank Group to lend nearly as much as it had lent in its entire twenty-two year history. At least one observer understood this massive expansion of Bank resources and commitments as one which:

> specifically excluded looking into the availability of money for aid; it looks instead upon absorptive capacity of poor countries on the assumption that money is no object. Mr. McNamara's clear intention is to prove to himself that the third world can accept a massive increase in aid without running into excessive inflation or into debt servicing problems, and then to use these findings as ammunition to justify a large increase in activities in the World Bank.

Accordingly, McNamara again manifested his reputation as a classic "Kennedy activist": one who believed in the "exercise of power."[68]

In addition to his call for a massive expansion of Bank activities, McNamara boldly declared on September 30, 1968, that the Bank would also be shifting its lending emphasis geographically and sectorally. Accordingly, in the first five years of the McNamara Presidency, lending to Latin America doubled, while that to Africa tripled. "But it was his proposed shifts in sectoral emphasis that most surprised many listening to McNamara. World Bank lending for education would triple. For agriculture it would quadruple." The focus was particularly on rural poverty.[69] Then he dropped his bombshell: a new initiative in the area of population control.[70] His particular personal commitment to achieving progress on this last issue was manifest the following year when he chose to give a speech solely on population control at the University of Notre Dame in hopes of generating maximum interest and attention, including a front page story in the *New York Times*.[71] In each of these instances, McNamara as dramatically as is imaginable demonstrated the political nature and clout of the World Bank Presidency.

The sources of McNamara's September speech are revealing. In part they were clearly a reflection of his own vision of the Bank. As he bluntly stated: "I have always regarded the World Bank as something more than a Bank, a Development Agency."[72] That assertion, not surprisingly, "was not well received by many conventional bankers present."[73] Nor would they be amused by his related quip: "If I had wanted to run a bank, I would have been a banker."[74] Perhaps in an attempt to calm some of the aroused bankers, McNamara liked to point out that Black and Woods were really the first to make the point that the World Bank was more than a bank; that is, it was more than a mere lender of funds. Certainly its extensive technical assistance projects and its assistance to less-developed countries in developing sound projects were proper nonbanking functions for which the World Bank was well known.[75] But McNamara had little to fear on this score. A permissive economic climate had been established by the Bank's record in its earlier economic program that clearly had met the economic standards set for it.[76] The political mood was also increasingly sympathetic to redistributionist policies. Together they provided a receptive setting for McNamara's boldness.

More specifically, McNamara saw the Bank as having three roles. "One the narrow one of being a major source of funds." Secondly, it was to be an advisor to less-developed countries. Indeed, McNamara has recently suggested that all of the nonbanking functions had one real purpose in mind: to be able to assist "third world" countries in pursuing the right macroeconomic policies. But, he quickly added, that's "damned difficult to do," owing at least in part to domestic political opposition. Thus the Bank's shift in priorities and even its adoption of particular projects that appealed to the tastes of "third world" elites resulted from the Bank's and particularly McNamara's vision of the best way to influence "third world" finance ministries. Since it appeared that the Bank could not loan money for righting macroeconomic policies, it had to loan money for what policymakers sought and then use the access accorded it to make suggestions as to how to stabilize their economies and get the countries growing.[77] Finally, McNamara thought of the Bank as a focal point for discussion of key development issues and of the policies required to deal with them.[78] "Though clearly aware of the sensitivity involved, McNamara felt a strong responsibility to use the presidency of the World Bank as a unique podium from which to say candidly to the world those things which he felt needed saying on the subject of development."[79]

In this way, McNamara thought of himself as a conscience of both the rich and the poor, the developed and the developing.[80] As often as he called on less-developed countries to make tough and courageous decisions, he issued similar pleas to the governments of developed countries.[81] His message to the developed countries, especially to the United States, was, however, the subject of some controversy. Was McNamara's only concern for multilateral aid its importance in developing and maintaining a global economic market for the United States, or was that merely rhetoric to win the support of members of the U.S. Congress?[82] Was he sincerely committed to redistribution of wealth in the world either for moral or some other reasons? There is some evidence to suggest that his commitment to multilateral aid emanated from a belief that only aid could prevent revolution in the Third World.[83] Perhaps this was a lesson he derived from his frustrating involvement with the Vietnam war.[84]

In some of his subsequent speeches, McNamara came to embrace something approaching a basic needs approach aimed at improving the well-being of the lower 40 percent of the population of LDCs through increased productivity and improved income distribution.[85] Such speeches, however, only came after McNamara had seen much of the globe and had come to realize that the Bank's earlier capital investment projects had had little effect on rural areas. McNamara's insight was sustained by many of the "third world" personnel he had brought into the Bank's upper echelon of decisionmaking.[86] Indeed, it appears that McNamara came to question the entire "trickle-down" approach to development. In part, this was because he saw too much abuse of power by those responsible for redistributing wealth.[87]

The consequences of McNamara's speeches are also interesting, particularly as they relate to his attempt to maintain and expand the Bank's constituency. This was especially important in McNamara's capacity as IDA President where he had to satisfy donor governments. For example, while urging the Group of 77 (a large coalition of developing countries) to sign the multilateral trade negotiations (MTN) of the General Agreements on Tariffs and Trade (GATT), McNamara simultaneously expressed his concern about growing protectionism in the developed countries.[88] Accordingly, Escott Reid noted that "Today too many influential people in too many member countries of the Bank think that the Bank is somebody else's bank."[89] Mason and Asher concluded, that, more than any of his predecessors, McNamara was able to cultivate strength from among the low-income as well as the Bank's richer member governments.[90]

Indeed McNamara's least successful tightrope walking may have been within his own country. For there he found himself with a unique nemesis—Vietnam—as well as an obvious advantage. He entered office with a clear understanding of American Presidential policy preferences and priorities. In fact Woods had specifically wanted a successor who was familiar with Lyndon Johnson's thinking.[91]

But that knowledge was a wasting asset given the rapidity with which Johnson was replaced by Richard Nixon. From then on, it would be the application of McNamara's general knowledge of the process of American government, knowing how to "work the system," which would explain his success or failure in cultivating the support of the Bank's most important client. He was usually successful, avoiding Congress where the Bank's critics were most numerous except when absolutely essential and then playing "games" with the committees: "He says he can't talk to a committee chairman and then meets with a freshman congressman to convince him the World Bank is wonderful."[92] When he failed, it was often due to the ability of Congressional critics to garner support based on McNamara's Vietnam past. One critic, Representative Bill Young, a Republican from Florida, thought he was attacking McNamara unmercifully when he suggested that "McNamara considered himself an internationalist, a citizen of the world, immune from U.S. rules."[93] Such a characterization would likely have seemed a compliment to McNamara and certainly captures the essence of the Bank's Articles of Agreements' understanding of an international civil servant.

To a significant degree, however, McNamara's success resulted from his promulgation of a revised ideology for the Bank, one which built on the findings of the Bank's expanded research branch.[94] For example, Chenery's analysis seemed to prove empirically that growth and equity could be achieved simultaneously.[95] Superficial critics of McNamara suggest that "the legacy of the McNamara era in the World Bank had been to raise third-world expectations beyond any reasonable hope of realization; to subtly redirect the need for long-term structural reform in these countries to a short-run need for balance-of-payments help, and to add to the burdens of an illiquid international debt."[96] Such criticism is clearly unfair to McNamara. He did try to get increased Bank resources to meet the expectations that he engendered *and* that prime ministers and finance ministers brought with them, and he continually harped on the message that international aid could not suffice without domestic structural reform. But this criticism does hit on one very important point: the Bank, during the McNamara period as well as at all other times throughout its history, was not supportive of programs requiring significant structural changes. Given the nature of the constituency with which it had to work, it could not be. The major donor countries were convinced of the desirability of peaceful change, rather than the revolutionary change that significant structural changes might encourage.[97]

An additional insight into the difficulties of McNamara's accommodation to systemic changes, particularly the massive increase in the number of newly independent states joining the Bank, comes from Richard Cooper's discussion of the GATT. Cooper observes that the attempt to achieve universalism can weaken an organization's effectiveness because its principles or procedures, almost of necessity, are distorted to accommodate the diverse circumstances of an enlarged membership.[98] In the case of "McNamara's Bank" the rapid expansion into the "third world" necessitated a movement into social sectors. They were politically more contentious and less susceptible to the systematic, quantitative evaluation with which the Bank had considerable experience and expertise than were other sectoral programs.

A somewhat more direct criticism of McNamara comes from within the Bank itself. Vice President and Treasurer Eugene H. Rotberg has noted that the Bank's image did not reflect the Bank's basic conservatism because McNamara had been more interested in talking about world poverty than about the Bank's complex operations.[99] Likewise, Weberman observed that "many bankers came to believe . . . that McNamara put the Bank's social obligations ahead of sound loans and the prospect of repayment."[100] Accordingly, the Bank taken over by McNamara's successor suffered from criticisms of widely different ideological perspectives: conservatives, centered in the United States, who were disturbed by the Bank's apparent anti-poverty image; and those of the left, centered in the "third world," who were disturbed by the Bank's seeming belief that significant progress could be made in the absence of major structural changes, either domestically (i.e., within developing countries) or internationally (i.e., in terms of the economic and political relations between rich and poor states).[101] Perhaps this was simply the logical consequence of the Bank's increased size, visibility, and involvement in politically sensitive social sectors.

Thus, whereas Woods' reorientation of the Bank's activities and ideology was both subtle and narrowly defined, deferring to the power and biases of the United States and other Western powers and of his staff, to say nothing of his own personal predilections, McNamara's much more dramatic action took on some of the appearances of a moral crusade, reflecting both his personal beliefs and the evolution of an increasingly powerful and economically desperate "third world." While it is unclear whether McNamara converted all of his staff to his goal of social reform or if he merely silenced and bypassed them, it is clear that his actions greatly expanded the economic and political activities of the Bank. Thus even more thoroughly than under his predecessors, the Bank became closely identified with its President, with the names McNamara and the World Bank becoming almost indistinguishable in the minds both of the Bank's critics and of its supporters. While McNamara's *public* comments remained focused on the economic rationales for the Bank's activities, none could again mistake the Bank for an apolitical actor, and none could fail to recognize that the preference of the Bank's President and staff for development strategies had come to carry a great deal of weight in the world of the 1970s, when the Bank's image was that of an agent of social reform, within limits, rather than a central bank.

Alden Winthrop Clausen

The appointment of A. W. (Tom) Clausen as McNamara's successor came as something of a surprise, in terms of its timing and of who was actually named. It is not that Clausen lacked the traditional background of a World Bank president. On the contrary, he was cut from the mold of Black and Woods: since 1970 President and Chief Executive Officer of the globe's largest bank, the Bank of America, the Bank that initiated and had the most extensive cofinancing arrangements with the World Bank; on a first name basis with the heads of all the major banks abroad; well known and admired in central banks around the world.[102] But what was odd was that it was not really the Board, or even the previous Bank President who had suggested, much less pushed, for Clausen. He was appointed by former President Carter, with the approval of then Republican Presidential candidate Ronald Reagan.[103] He had been reportedly sounded out by the Carter administration several times before about becoming the Secretary of the Treasury, but he supposedly said that he felt that he could be more "influential and helpful in the

private sector." Others suggest that he did not particularly care for
Carter and that he considered himself a conservative Republican.[104]
What is clear is that Carter was looking for someone with credibility
within the private banking community and particularly someone
with acceptable credentials to the U.S. Congress so that the latest
long impasse over IDA funding might be overcome. In choosing
Clausen, he appeared to get just such a person.[105] Indeed the appointment was described as "music to the ears" of Republicans such
as Jerry Lewis and Bill Young, who along with Clarence Young and
Senator Jesse Helms had "waged an unrelenting battle in and outside the United States Congress to bring what they see as profligate
and unprincipled multilateral development institutions to heel."[106]
That is, his nomination was greeted with enthusiasm by some of
the same members of the U.S. Congress who had most opposed
Robert McNamara.

At the same time, Clausen's appointment "delighted" the Bank's
staff, who were cheered by the decision to appoint a highly reputed
commercial banker instead of a social reformer. And the enthusiasm
seemed quite genuine. For if the staff really knew enough about
Clausen to be relieved at his tendency to arrive in the office late,
unlike McNamara, they would also have known that he was a work-
aholic, had a photographic memory, was a master of organizational
detail,[107] and was a perfectionist who admitted to having a "tendency
to make all decisions" himself.[108]

While the Clausen appointment was clearly politically motivated,
he also appeared to have had the attributes to make him an ideal
World Bank President for the 1980s. His reputation was that of a
competent banker who had worked to change the Bank of America's
image. "I'm tired of the biggest financial institution in the world
being thought of as a regional bank," he was quoted as saying.
Whatever the sources of success in that instance,[109] the image was
changed at the Bank of America and the World Bank's image needed
reshaping. Likewise, the success of the California bank under Clausen's leadership was credited to two vital skills, which were needed
by any international organization head in the 1980s: "an ability to
shape new and concrete goals for his mammoth organization and
the dogged thoroughness to carry through on those goals."[110] More
specifically, under his leadership the Bank of America had come to
be known for the quality of its management.[111]

The context confronting Clausen when he became Bank President
on July 1, 1981, was as inauspicious as that confronting his pre-

decessor thirteen years earlier but different. For example, there was the aforementioned impasse with the U.S. Congress over the American financial commitment to IDA. Here Clausen was expected to be particularly effective given the motives behind his initial appointment. Secondly, Clausen was charged with working out a more effective division of labor between the Bank and its sister institution, the International Monetary Fund (IMF). Over the years that division, like those among many of the UN's specialized agencies, had become fuzzy. Clausen seemed ready to step less on the IMF's toes (for example, not to loan to countries with sustained balance of payments difficulties). Third, Clausen was forced to address the issue of precisely what sort of role the "third world" was to play in its quest for greater influence within multilateral development institutions such as the World Bank. Fourth, Clausen was expected to be involved in assessing various alternative development strategies for the 1980s.[112] Finally, Clausen was expected to play a role in dealing with the financial problem of the 1980s: the international debt question.

And indeed, even though his period in office was relatively short, Clausen had a substantial impact on most of the items on this wide-ranging and explicitly political agenda. The area in which he had the least impact, contributing to theories of development, was probably a matter of choice. Given the context in which he was operating—massive debt problems confronting a significant number of developing countries in the world—Clausen took the position that research should be applied and, wherever possible, directly tied to particular projects. As he graphically put it, when the man with the meat ax is at your door, you don't have time to think in the long term, much as that might be desirable. It should be added that Clausen resented the view of many academics that such applied or tactical research was neither significant nor likely to make a lasting contribution to the study of alternative development strategies. Moreover, it was not that Clausen disagreed with McNamara's basic premise—he too saw the World Bank as more than merely a bank— but rather that the context was different and consequently his priorities were different.[113]

His first priority was to improve the image of the Bank in those constituencies where it was "not as great . . . as it ought to be,"[114] and in particular to restore the image of the Bank as a source of funds rather than an agent of social reform, as if the two could be separated in practice. This was to be accomplished by a carefully

organized public relations campaign. For example, immediately after Clausen took office he lunched with members of the U.S. House
of Representatives.[115] Subsequently, he carefully and very publicly
pruned the Bank's development projects, particularly those that
were most controversial.[116] Critics, like Mahbub ul Haq who left
the Bank to return to his native Pakistan, feared that such moves
indicated that the Bank lacked a long-term strategy or the means to
develop one. Others viewed the Clausen Bank as being "too cautious" and "too solicitous" of the Reagan Administration.[117] The last
set of critics bolstered their arguments by noting that Clausen spoke
of a "more commercial, hard-nosed approach by the World Bank,"
and even of "tough minded concessional development assistance."[118] He "openly cajoled" poorer countries to take more steps
to put their economies in order, and he bluntly told better-off developing countries (like India) that they would not continue receiving interest-free IDA loans indefinitely.[119] In addition, the Bank
quickly instituted a front-end fee of 1.5 percent for new IBRD loans
and increased the charges on IDA credits. Some of these changes
were merely the inevitable consequences of the increased cost of
borrowing. The long-term market was drying up, especially as the
Swiss and West German markets had become glutted with the
Bank's "paper" and the Bank had been told it had to turn elsewhere.
As a result, it was necessary to turn to the much more expensive
short-term market, especially the American market. But some of the
changes also reflected Clausen's own preferences and beliefs, fash-
ioned by thirty-two years at the Bank of America. All the changes
evidenced his sensitivity to the intimate connection between politics
and economics.

Direct consequences of Clausen's experience at the Bank of
America included his attempt to expand rapidly the World Bank's
cofinancing activities—"I liked it then as a commercial banker; I
like it now as a development banker"—and his changes in the Bank's
management style. In the latter regard he was credited with trying
to decentralize and to depersonalize the Bank's administration. Indeed, it was Clausen's contention that in the past too much attention
had been accorded to the Bank's President (presumably meaning
McNamara). Clausen bluntly asserted that: "I'm a World Bank man.
[You] do your job the best you can for your institution and if the
institution prospers, you'll get your due recognition—be it at Church
or at the grocery store."[120]

Accordingly, in July 1982 the Bank introduced a "fundamental change in the way the interest rate on loans was set," by adjusting it every six months to the costs of the Bank's borrowing on the market. In September of the same year, the Executive Directors authorized the selling of short-term securities to provide the Bank with additional sources of funding.

These changes in the Bank's financial structure and operations clearly reflected Clausen's view that the Bank's prosperity depended upon its ability to cope more effectively with the financial market's volatility.[121] They also represented Clausen's political savvy, that is, his view of what was necessary to alter the Bank's image among its most important financial clients.[122] Indeed, Clausen estimated that some 60 percent of his time was spent trying to correct people's perception of the Bank and of the IDA. Again and again, Clausen tried to hammer home the argument that the "IDA is not an international entitlement program. And the basic issue is not generosity. On the contrary, IDA is a hardheaded investment in international trade, economic growth, and greater global stability and cohesion."[123]

However, in spite of all of his efforts at image-rebuilding and his Republican credentials, Clausen failed to get the Reagan administration to commit the resources he, and most of America's allies, sought from it for the seventh replenishment of the IDA's funds or any commitment at all in terms of an eighth replenishment. Admittedly this was one of Clausen's major frustrations as Bank President.[124] One of Clausen's top aides explained this by the unwillingness of those in the Reagan administration who knew the facts to make the Bank's case to Congress as strongly and effectively as they could. That is, while the Bank's top administrators were resigned to the fact that some members of Congress would never understand the basic facts of Bank and IDA financing and goals, they were perturbed that the Reagan administration did not make the extra effort to educate and convert those who could be made to understand them.[125]

While Clausen did not achieve his aim of solidifying the Bank's right flank, he did much to strengthen its financial base. Of course, Clausen was also helped in this regard by the global recovery from the recession of the late 1970s and early 1980s and the attendant general decline in interest rates. As a consequence the Bank was able to reverse the trend of the first Clausen years and to cut its lending rate and to abolish its front-end fee.[126]

Whereas Clausen's policy alterations and reforms strengthened the Bank's financial status, Clausen's endorsement of the need for "tougher terms for lending" was opposed by many in the developing world. And even some within the Bank were leery.[127] Indeed, opposition to Bank conditionality (i.e., the conditions under which the Bank would make loans to member countries) was so severe that a two-day Governing Board meeting was convened in February 1985 on the subject, and there is some indication that several major borrowers were led to reassess their needs and either put them on "hold" or turn to commercial banks rather than make the painful policy changes upon which Bank loans were coming to be conditioned. Some have suggested that the lending slippage was significant enough to explain why Clausen postponed for six months his call for a general capital increase for the Bank.[128]

Such actions prompted some in the Bank to wonder if Clausen—unlike McNamara—was less willing to fight for his organization's independence.[129] Was he listening too carefully to the politicians in Washington and to his former banking colleagues in the commercial world?[130] Or was this merely an epiphenomenon catalyzed by the IDA funding crisis, that is, toeing the line preferred by the Reagan administration until he got its approval for a funding increase for the IDA? A positive response to the first question and a negative one to the second would not bode too well for the executive head's future in light of the importance of staff support and owing to the inability of Clausen to replicate McNamara's trick of sidestepping staff dissent. In the 1980s executive heads can not merely hire additional personally loyal personnel.[131] Likewise, a more widely accepted view of the Bank as a "doler" out of capitalist ideology as well as capital would likely decrease its popularity among its vital "third world" clients and curtail any hopes Clausen might have had for expanding or even maintaining the Bank's central role in the global development process.[132] Yet a clear and resounding negative response to the first question—especially a failure to listen to the budget-cutting concerns of the U.S. Department of the Treasury and the Office of Management and Budget—was expected to result in Reagan's replacement of Clausen before he was ready to depart his office.[133] While such a recommendation could have been rejected by the Bank's Executive Directors, such an act of defiance was unprecedented in the Bank's history, which includes acquiescence in American Presidents' preferences as to who should run the Bank. Indeed that is exactly what happened: on April 3, 1986, the Executive Directors ratified President Reagan's decision to appoint former U.S. (Republican) Congressman Barber B. Conable to succeed Clausen, effective July 1, 1986, rather than to appoint Clausen to the second term he desired.

Although a definitive discussion of Clausen's Presidency may be premature and any assessment of the reasons for his dismissal (technically his retirement) from office may be incomplete, there is some suggestive evidence on both points. For example, while Clausen's proposals for a Multilateral Investment Agency and a global investment code to help moderate the risks to investors in less-developed countries clearly suggested a commitment to private sector strategies for development,[134] at the same time, both of these proposals suggested reliance on governmental (particularly inter-governmental) institutions rather than the "market." Thus Clausen supported organizational task expansion at the same time that he distanced himself, somewhat, from some of the most conservative voices in Washington. Likewise, U.S. Treasury officials were reportedly quite upset that Clausen had not followed their recommendation to name a Latin American financial expert to an important post at the IFC. Instead, he had named a British subject.[135] More in keeping with the desires of the Reagan administration, and the precedents of previous World Bank presidents for that matter, had been his constant attack on protectionism, which "spreads like a cancer, destroying the vital tissues of global commerce."[136] Less in keeping with the administration's ethos, however, was his constant refrain calling for more multilateral, official development assistance, which "is *not* an issue of charity. It is one of national self-interest in an interdependent world economy. I refuse to believe that it is so complex that rich and powerful nations cannot recognize the political, commercial and security arguments for doing so."[137] Moreover, he connected the need for development assistance with the debt crisis in a way that many members of the Reagan administration might not have found appealing: "The debate about debt has generally drawn attention away from the potentially explosive effects of the recession in the world's poorest countries. They need development aid now."[138] Even more pointedly, Clausen had remarked: "Even though less developed countries (LDCs) provide export markets and investment sites, the developed world does not see the secure link between its future prosperity and the LDCs. The misguided belief grows that less developed countries cannot weather their current indebtedness and that we should not jeopardize our own recovery by becoming any more economically involved than we already are."[139]

Less publicly but potentially much more importantly, the debt crisis had animated Clausen's Bank in the direction of explicit macroeconomic planning in "third world" countries. Done basically under two rubrics—structural adjustment loans[140] and other non-project loans—fully 18 percent of the Bank's funds went into such activities. Thus Clausen's Bank explicitly accomplished the ends that McNamara had set for the Bank but had found politically difficult to achieve, much less to argue for publicly. The likelihood of this happening . . . and the necessary preconditions for it . . . were perhaps best articulated by McNamara: "Developing countries today need far more macroeconomic policy advice than they are receiving. There has been a major shift during the past ten years [i.e., 1971–81] in the willingness of the developing countries to seek and accept the Bank's advice in economic policy. I can think of no service which the Bank could offer with higher leverage."[141] Indeed, the idea of structural adjustment loans had had its origins in the twilight years of the McNamara Bank but came to fruition only under Clausen. Additionally, whereas Clausen and his senior administrators agreed to live with a 10 percent ceiling on macroeconomic planning via structural adjustment loans,[142] they had found other innovative ways to achieve the same ends. Moreover, while the public record has focused on the links between loan recipients and the IMF, there appears to have been much more economic planning and advising going on than appeared in the IMF's letters of intent. Clausen's Bank both worked in concert with the IMF and, at times, found an inevitable overlap in jurisdiction. Indeed, the only element of macroeconomic planning the Bank excluded specifically from its purview was foreign exchange rates.[143]

Thus it appears that in a desperate economic environment, Clausen, donors, and recipients were willing to increase the explicitly political activities of the Bank and, relevantly, limit the headway being made in reestablishing a clear division of labor between the Bank and the IMF. More interestingly, perhaps, whereas the public record seemed to suggest that the IMF had been able to eclipse Clausen's Bank, especially in terms of the debt issue, the complete record seems much less clear. In this connection, it is relevant to note that whereas McNamara's vision for the Bank was as a macroeconomic planner and advisor, Clausen's was that of a financial body that provided economic advice.[144] That understanding of the Bank's proper role, Clausen aides were quick to add, was not fundamentally different from some of the views held at Bretton Woods, where, for example, the El Salvadoran representative had proposed that the Bank be called the "International Financial Institution for Reconstruction and Development," and the great British economist John Maynard Keynes himself had suggested that "the Bank should be called the [International Monetary] Fund and the Fund the Bank."[145]

To a great extent then Clausen appeared to be trying to return the Bank to where it had been before Woods and McNamara had presided over it. That is, he was trying to restore the faith of the American Congress and Wall Street in the Bank by clothing the Bank's inevitable political actions in economic wraps. The restrained, revamped, and less visible research activities of the Bank as well as the reemphasis on Bank management techniques and public relations can be explained in this way. Similar explanations can be provided for the innovative use of Structural Adjustment Loans to influence macroeconomic planning in LDCs. All of these changes, of course, required a liberal interpretation of the Bank's constitutional documents and a commitment to an organizational ideology, closely tied to capitalism, with which most of the Bank's staff remained closely if quietly identified. Still the Bank could never altogether return from where Woods had begun to reorient it subtly: neither Clausen's personal commitment to development nor systemic conditions, especially the enhanced power of the LDCs and the ongoing global debt crisis, would permit that.

Conclusions

Throughout this review of the evolution of the World Bank, it has been demonstrated that Bank Presidents "cannot ignore political considerations despite a formal ban on their doing so" (for example, in terms of preferring to fund countries with one sort of political system rather than another), that the Bank's activities "affect the distribution of influence both within and among international actors, which is to say that such activities have political effects" (especially with the dramatic movement into funding of social sector projects), and that they seek "to get governments to do things they would not otherwise do" (perhaps most explicitly and effectively as a consequence of the "policy dialogues" accompanying Structural Adjustment Loans).[146]

Likewise, it has been shown that each of these three Presidents has performed the tasks of banker, administrative head, diplomat, and development strategist. Differences in emphasis and success in these tasks have been explained particularly by reference to systemic and individualistic factors. For example, Woods's and Clausen's emphasis on and relative success as financial managers have been explained, in part, by their professional training and their personal preferences. But a full understanding of how they spent their time also required reference to systemic conditions. Woods presided at a time before the rapid expansion of a European capital market upon which to draw and Clausen began office in an era of global recession and fears of debt defaults. Accordingly, both had to find much time for activities much more akin to those of commercial bankers. On the other hand, McNamara's Presidency coincided with an era of rapid economic growth in the industrial world and the explosion of political independence and the revolution of rising expectations in the "third world." Accordingly, his years as President—excepting the last perhaps—were among the most dynamic in the Bank's history, with his global influence and independence of internal Bank constraints hard to overestimate.

More unexpected perhaps was the contrast between McNamara and Clausen in terms of their roles in affecting the most sensitive and political of Bank activities, macroeconomic planning in "third world" countries. Here the evidence suggests that systemic conditions, particularly the fear of debt defaults and the lack of significant progress in Sub-Saharan African economic growth during the McNamara years, perhaps more than individualistic factors or staff predilections, led Clausen to charge right into McNamara's highest priority area and, apparently, with some success.

Also largely for systemic (in this instance the emergence of political and economic conservatism in the Bank's most important member country) and individualistic reasons, the most recent past Bank President has been portrayed as stressing the Bank's financial roles rather than its redistributionist effects. Still, even with that reorientation of rhetoric and image, the Bank President remains an important international political figure, a sort of global diplomat, and an influential development strategist. This is the legacy of his predecessors and, accordingly, the mandate for World Bank Presidents now and in the foreseeable future.

Notes

Appreciation is expressed to James Madison College and the Office of the Dean, International Studies and Programs of Michigan State University, for administrative and research support in the preparation of this chapter. Financial support came in the form of a Michigan State University All-University Research Grant. Appreciation is also due to Professor Ron Meltzer of SUNY-Buffalo, two anonymous reviewers, and especially Professor Lawrence Finkelstein of Northern Illinois University for their comments on earlier versions.

1. United Nations, Department of Public Information, *Everyone's United Nations*, 10th ed. (New York: United Nations, 1986), 412.

2. As of June 30, 1985, the IBRD had 148 members, IDA had 133, and the IFC had 128.

3. A. I. MacBean and P. N. Snowden, *International Institutions in Trade and Finance* (London: George Allen & Unwin, 1981), 211–22.

4. The Bank Group now is the largest single source of development assistance for developing countries. In the year ending June 30, 1985, the Group approved $15.3 billion in loans and investments, bringing the total cumulative commitment by the Group to over $150 billion. United Nations, *Everyone's United Nations*, 412.

5. Robert W. Cox, "The Executive Head: An Essay on Leadership in International Organizations," *International Organization* 23 (Spring 1969): 205–30.

6. IBRD, Articles of Agreement, Article V, section 4(e).

7. Edward S. Mason and Robert E. Asher, *The World Bank Since Bretton Woods* (Washington: The Brookings Institution, 1973), 30–31.

8. Ibid., 62, 63.

9. Ibid., 86.

10. James H. Weaver, *The International Development Association: A New Approach to Foreign Aid* (New York: Frederick A. Praeger, 1965), 82, 88.

11. "Mr. Woods Looks for New Business," *Economist* 209 (October 5, 1963): 59.

12. "The New President," *Economist* 205 (October 20, 1962): 293.

13. "What Faces New World Bank Chief," *Business Week*, October 20, 1962, 125.

14. Mason and Asher, *World Bank*, 98.

15. "What Faces," 123. They worked together for Harris, Forbes and Company in the 1920s.

16. Mason and Asher, *World Bank*, 89.

17. "New President," p. 293. This was particularly so as Black had often sought Woods's advice on dealing with developing countries. *Current Biography, 1965*, 467.

18. "What Faces," 123.

19. Ibid.

20. "New President," 293.

21. Opposition to Woods came from liberal Democrats, who continued to chastise him for his involvement in the Dixon-Yates controversy, long after he was cleared of any criminal wrongdoing. *Current Biography 1965*, 467.

22. "What Faces," 124. In fact, during the period of Woods's presidency, there were no long-term dollar security issues sold by the World Bank to First Boston, in part because Woods felt that the World Bank's cash holdings were already too large and in part because of the increasing difficulty, for balance-of-payments reasons, for the World Bank to secure the consent of the U.S. Treasury to sales in the American market. Mason and Asher, *World Bank*, 136.

23. Ibid., 98.

24. Ibid., 88, 99.

25. As quoted in ibid., 409n. See also pp. 99, 409.

26. Ibid., 99.

27. Weaver, *International Development Association*, 218.

28. Mason and Asher, *World Bank*, 98.

29. "Mr. Woods," 59.

30. Aart van de Laar, *The World Bank and the Poor* (Boston: Martinus Nijhoff, 1980), 124. Significantly, the problem of external debt did not become a central preoccupation of the World Bank until later in Woods's tenure. Then, however, it contributed to his ill-fated attempt to raise $1 billion in the IDA's second replenishment. On this point, see Mason and Asher, *World Bank*, 232.

31. Mason and Asher, *World Bank*, 98, 222. Note that van de Laar argues that informality does not lead to creativity because of the lack of research and openness to new ideas. van de Laar, *World Bank*, 232.

32. Mason and Asher, *World Bank*, 100, 407.

33. Weaver, *International Development Association*, 220. Opposition to significant transfers of funds continues to exist, both within the financial community and in parts of the U.S. government. There is an ongoing concern about the solvency of the World Bank and, tied to that, about its possibility of raising funds on bond markets. Such concerns have always seemed out of place, because, in percentage terms, the Bank has never transferred any significant amount of money and the sums transferred have always been drawn from balances remaining after the Bank has met all of its own demands, including insuring that it has more than adequate reserves to meet any possible contingency. In this connection, it is a bit ironic that such arguments continued to be made by those in the Reagan administration who should have approved of such transfers, which actually transfer the burdens of funding the IDA from the rich (especially the budget and debt conscious United States) to the middle-income states (whose proportionate contributions to the Bank are greater than they are to the IDA). Interview with Moeen A. Qureshi, Senior Vice President for Finance of the World Bank, March 22, 1985.

34. Interestingly, however, he has been portrayed as having antagonized India "and other borrowers" over the changes he demanded in their economic plans. One might wonder how much of the Indians' antagonism resulted from that and how much from his attempt to diversify the pool of Bank borrowers, whereby India went from receiving 18.5 percent of the IBRD's loans under Black to 5.5 percent under Woods. On these points, see Mason and Asher, *World Bank*, 99 and van de Laar, *World Bank*, 17.

35. Of Bank personnel, perhaps Paul Rosenstein-Rodan is most notable. J. H. Alder, "The World Bank's Concept of Development—An In-House Domengeschite," in *Development and Planning: Essays in Honour of Paul Rosenstein-Rodan*, ed. Jagdish Bhagwati and Richard S. Eckaus (London: George Allen and Unwin, 1972), 45. Paul Rosenstein-Rodan, in turn, credited many of the members of Kennedy's New Frontier and their imaginative approaches to development assistance. Phone conversation with Rosenstein-Rodan, August 18, 1982. See also Mason and Asher, *World Bank*, 473.

36. Roger Chaufournier, "The Coming of Age," *Finance & Development* 21 (June 1984): 35.

37. Mason and Asher, *World Bank*, 98–99, 697.

38. Ibid, 374.

39. Ibid, 203.

40. Weaver, *International Development Association*, 219.

41. Mason and Asher, *World Bank*, 374.

42. William Diamond and Michael Hoffman, Interviews (taped July 27, 1961), on file at Columbia University, World Bank Oral History Project, 31.

43. "Mr. Woods," 60.

44. Ibid, 59.

45. Mason and Asher, *World Bank*, 224.

46. World Bank, *The Assault on World Poverty: Problems of Rural Development, Education and Health* (Baltimore: The Johns Hopkins University Press, 1975). See also: H. M. Phillips, "The Redeployment of Educational Aid," in *Education and Development Reconsidered: The Bellagio Conference Papers* (New York: Praeger Publishers, 1974), 260–61.

47. During the period 1963–69, no funds were devoted to primary and basic education. External Advisory Panel on Education, *Report of the External Advisory Panel on Education to the World Bank* (Washington: The World Bank, October 31, 1978), 14.

48. George D. Woods, "Sow Education Aid, Reap Economic Growth," *Columbia Journal of World Business* 1 (Summer 1966): 39.

49. Ibid., 37.

50. H. M. Phillips, *Educational Cooperation Between Developed and Developing Countries* (New York: Praeger Publishers, 1976), 54. See also Milagros Fernandez, "The World Bank and the Third World: Reflections of a Sceptic," *Prospects: Quarterly Review of Education* 11, 3 (1981): 298.

51. Woods, "Sow Education," 40.

52. Mason and Asher, *World Bank*, 571.

53. Chaufournier, "Coming of Age," 35.

54. Thus as one of his final formal acts, Woods tried to set in motion a mechanism for enhancing the financial base of the World Bank Group, including its proliferating activities in the social field. Mason and Asher, *World Bank*, 99. See also Harry G. Johnson, "Pearson's 'Grand Assize' Fails: A Bleak Future for Foreign Aid," *Round Table* 237 (January 1970): 17–25; Chaufournier, "Coming of Age," 35.

55. Mason and Asher, *World Bank*, 99.

56. Ernst B. Haas, *Beyond the Nation-State: Functionalism and International Organization* (Stanford: Stanford University Press, 1964), part one.

57. Escott Reid, "McNamara's World Bank," *Foreign Affairs* 51 (July 1973): 808–09.

58. van de Laar, *World Bank*, 101.

59. Ibid., 17.

60. Some suggest that McNamara was sent to the Bank because he had gone "dove" on L. B. J. See, for example, "McNamara: Why Is He Leaving?" *Newsweek* 70 (December 11, 1967): 25–30. Ho Kwon Ping, "End of the McNamara Era . . . But the Vietnam Legacy Continues to Haunt Him," *Far Eastern Economic Review* 109 (September 19, 1980): 106–7. See also Henry L. Trewhitt, *McNamara* (New York: Harper & Row, 1971), 238, 246, 270–74; Lyndon Baines Johnson, *The Vantage Point: Perspectives of the Presidency 1963–1969* (New York: Holt, Rinehart & Winston, 1971), 20.

61. David H. Blake and Robert S. Walters, *The Politics of Global Economic Relations*, 2d ed. (Englewood Cliffs: Prentice-Hall, 1983), 134–40.

62. Raymond F. Mikesell, "The Emergence of the World Bank as a Development Institution," in *Bretton Woods Revisited: Evaluations of the International Monetary Fund and the International Bank for Reconstruction and Development*, ed. A. L.

K. Acheson, J. F. Chant, and M. F. S. Prachowny (Toronto: University of Toronto Press, 1972), 81.

63. "Robert McNamara, Banker," *Economist* 227 (June 8, 1968): 70.

64. Mason and Asher, *World Bank*, 100, 134–35; "The Real Job McNamara is Taking Over," *U.S. News & World Report* 64 (March 4, 1968): 63.

65. The distinction between the appearance of economic motivations and the Bank's real evaluative criteria is made explicit in David A. Baldwin, "The International Bank in Political Perspective," *World Politics* 18 (October, 1965): 68–81.

66. Phone interview with Robert S. McNamara, September 7, 1983.

67. *Report of the Director-General on Actions of the Organization in 1968*, UNESCO, CF 3.69/1.23/A., 193.

68. "Robert McNamara, Banker," 70.

69. By 1980 agriculture and rural development accounted for 40 percent of IDA's loans and 22 percent of those of the Bank, making it the Bank's single largest lending category. Christopher Madison, "The Days of McNamara-Style Expansion at the World Bank May be at an End," *National Journal*, August 15, 1981, 1450.

70. John L. Maddux, *The Development Philosophy of Robert S. McNamara* (Washington: World Bank, June 1981), 10–11.

71. Madison, "Days of McNamara," 1450.

72. Indeed, McNamara remains convinced that thinking of the Bank as a bank is dysfunctional, and he has suggested that it would be desirable to drop the word "bank" from its title. Phone interview with McNamara.

73. William Clark, "Robert McNamara at the World Bank," *Foreign Affairs* 60 (Fall 1981): 169.

74. U.S. Department of the Treasury, *United States Participation in the Multilateral Development Banks in the 1980s* (Washington, D.C.: Department of Treasury, February 1982), 184. This vignette was first cited in a *Barron's* editorial of June 18, 1980.

75. "Interview: Robert S. McNamara," *Banker* 119 (March 1969): 199. McNamara explains the "flack" he got from the Bank's Executive Board on this issue by their confusion of development assistance with "charity." Phone interview with McNamara.

76. Mason and Asher, *World Bank*, 134–35.

77. Phone interview with McNamara.

78. "A Plea for Aid to 800 Million on Margin of Life," *U.S. News & World Report* 89 (December 27, 1980): 39–40.

79. Maddux, *Development Philosophy*, 46.

80. McNamara also thought of the sector policy papers instituted while he was in office as having this goal. Ayres, *Banking on the Poor*, 24–25.

81. Less charitable observers than Maddux have characterized McNamara as a friend of state planning rather than of capitalism: a man whose ambition is to aid the "third world," even at the expense of the "first world . . . income equality rather than economic growth, who at best could be mistaken by believing that income equality and economic growth can be achieved simultaneously, but much more likely someone who uses that rhetoric duplicitly as he ignores critics of intervention and works toward distribution of the world's wealth." "McNamara's Regrets," *Wall Street Journal*, June 25, 1981, 26. "McNamara's L'Envoi," *Wall Street Journal*, October 2, 1980, 33. Robert L. Ayres, "Breaking the Bank," *Foreign Policy* 43 (Summer 1981): 106–7. See also Leonard Silk, "McNamara Warns U.S. of Perils of Reducing Aid to World's Poor," *New York Times*, June 21, 1981, 46.

82. Perhaps significantly, McNamara saw as one of his own failures as Bank President the failure to "inform" industrialized countries of their various narrow interests being served by IBRD acts. Perhaps the verb should be "convinced" instead of "informed." Silk, "McNamara Warns," 46.

83. On this point see Fernandez, "World Bank," 298; Kazuo Takahashi, "A Comparative Analysis of the World Bank Group and the United Nations Development Programme" (Ph.D. diss., Columbia University, 1975), 230, 235, 318.

84. Ho, "End of McNamara Era," 106.

85. See, for example, his Annual Address to the Board of Governors, September 26, 1977.

86. Clark, "Robert McNamara," 169, 172. Moulton particularly credits V. D. Dandekar and Nilakantha Roth. Anthony D. Moulton, "On Concealed Dimensions of Third World Involvement in International Economic Organizations," *International Organization* 32 (Autumn 1978): 1032.

87. Phone interview with McNamara. Moulton provides an interesting vignette in this connection that evidences both McNamara's relatively late turn to a concern with the concept of absolute poverty as well as his openness and willingness to change. Moulton notes that McNamara reportedly threatened to resign if the Agency for International Development recommended that the United States vote against several Indian projects that included expenditures for tractors, which AID felt would have the disastrous effect of displacing labor and consequently exacerbating the stratification effects of the "green revolution." After a study of the labor effects of tractorization, McNamara eliminated expenditures on tractors for agriculture credit projects funded by the Bank. Moulton, "Concealed Dimensions," 1026.

88. See Ho, "Protectionist Roll-Call," 70.

89. Escott Reid, *The Future of the World Bank* (Washington: International Bank for Reconstruction and Development, September 1965), 20.

90. Mason and Asher, *World Bank,* 698.

91. "Real Job," 63.

92. Brophy quoting a "house staffer." Ben Brophy, "The View from Capitol Hill," *Forbes* 125 (May 26, 1980): 128.

93. Ibid.

94. Reid, "McNamara's World Bank," 804.

95. Hollis Chenery, Montek S. Ahlurvalia, C. L. B. Bill, et al., *Redistribution with Growth* (London: Oxford University Press, 1974), xv. Although later analyses have questioned Chenery's conclusions and specifically noted the atypicality of the countries that he used as models—South Korea, Taiwan, and Japan—they came too late to affect McNamara.

96. Warren C. Robinson, "Where the World Bank Failed," *New York Times,* July 3, 1981, A18.

97. For this line of argument, see, for example, Martin Carnoy, "International Institutions and Educational Policy: A Review of Education-Sector Policy," *Prospects: Quarterly Review of Education* 10, 3 (1980).

98. Richard N. Cooper, "Prolegomena to the Choice of an International Monetary System," in *World Politics and International Economics* (Washington: Brookings Institution, 1975), 95n.

99. Madison, "Days of McNamara," 1448. In the same vein see Nathaniel M. McKitterick, "The World Bank and the McNamara Legacy," *National Interest* 1 (Summer 1986): 47–52.

100. Ben Weberman, "A Neat Trick If You Can Do It, Tom," *Forbes* 126 (November 24, 1980): 194.

101. On this point generally see Andres Federman, "Poverty's Strange Bedfellows," *South,* June 1981, 7–12.

102. "It was undoubtedly Clausen's growing international stature, as much as his known skills as an administrator, that prompted the Carter administration to move his name to the top of the list of possible successors to McNamara." Cary Reich, "Unmasking Tom Clausen," *Institutional Investor* 15, 1 (1981): 63.

103. The unorthodox timing of the appointment—prior to the American presidential election—was explained by the desire to respond to European criticism that postponement of the appointment might jeopardize the world's financial markets, especially if the timing made it appear that the appointment was going to be clearly political (e.g., if President Carter were to lose his reelection bid and then appoint a Democrat during his "lame duck" months in office). Further it was speculated that such resentment—if left unresponded to—might result in pressure for a non-American Bank President. John Edwards, "The New Hand at the Bank Till," *Far Eastern Economic Review* 115 (November 14, 1982): 73.

104. Credit has been given to George Shultz for getting candidate Reagan's approval. Lewis James, "Clausen Will Help Those Who Help Themselves," *Euromoney,* December 1980, 30. Reich, "Unmasking," 63–65. *Current Biography 1981,* p. 61.

105. James, "Clausen Will Help," 30.

106. Anthony Rowley, "Clausen and a More Worldly Bank," *Far Eastern Economic Review* 115 (March 26–April 1, 1982): 131.

107. Reich, "Unmasking," 57.

108. Richard I. Immel, "Rousing a Giant: Clausen Bids to Change Regional Image Held by Bank of America," *Wall Street Journal,* March 22, 1979, 33.

109. In part, he changed the Bank of America's image by making it the first American bank to establish a permanent representative in the People's Republic of China.

110. Reich, "Unmasking," 60.

111. "Listening and Responding to Employees' Concerns: Through Six Supportive Programs, Everyone at the Bank of America Has a Voice and a Way to Get Help: An Interview with A. W. Clausen," *Harvard Business Review* 58 (January–February 1980): 101.

112. Edwards, "New Hand," 73.

113. Interview with A. W. Clausen at the World Bank, March 22, 1985.

114. "A Conversation with Mr. Clausen," *Finance & Development* 19 (December 1982): 9.

115. Art Pine, "Clausen Holds World Bank's Course," *Wall Street Journal,* May 13, 1982, 31.

116. Rowley, "Clausen," 132.

117. Pine, "Clausen Holds," 31.

118. Rowley, "Clausen," 131.

119. Pine, "Clausen Holds," 31.

120. "Conversation," 7. Interview with Clausen.

121. Thomas Hoopengardner and Ines Garcia-Thoumi, "The World Bank in a Changing Financial Environment," *Finance & Development* 21 (June 1984): 12.

122. One of the Bank's harshest critics put it somewhat differently: "Close observers of the bank's actions have long known that its chief function is to smooth the way for private foreign investment. But this activity (which is engraved in the bank's

charter) was obscured during the years Robert McNamara was president by a smokescreen of rhetoric about what the bank was doing to help the poor. Now that the most dangerous criticism of the bank's policies is coming from the right rather than the left, its public relations effort has shifted to bragging about what the bank has been doing all along." Cheryl Payer, "Reagan and the World Bank: Cutting Off Your Own Best Friend," *The Nation*, September 11, 1982, 207.

123. A. W. Clausen, "A Concluding Perspective," in *The Future of the World Bank*, ed. Edward R. Fried and Henry D. Owen (Washington: The Brookings Institution, 1982), 76.

124. Interview with Clausen.

125. Interview with Qureshi.

126. Robert Manning, "Embarrassing Riches," *Far Eastern Economic Review*, March 14, 1985, 58.

127. Mohan Ram, "Their Soft Options," *Far Eastern Economic Review* 115 (February 5, 1982): 98–99.

128. Manning, "Embarrassing Riches," 58.

129. One commentator graphically described the situation suggesting a loss of Clausen's independence: "Like a chameleon changing colour to avoid its enemies, the World Bank is undergoing a subtle metamorphosis, shedding what critics discern as its pinkish socialist tint and taking a bluer hue which merges better with the currently more conservative, right wing environment in Washington." Rowley, "Clausen," 131, 136.

130. Ibid., 137.

131. Also relevant is Sewell's somewhat more general observation that the key to successful leadership in the Bank "seemed to be autonomy from member governments." James P. Sewell, UNESCO *and World Politics: Engaging in International Relations* (Princeton University Press, 1975), 283.

132. Rowley, "Clausen," 138.

133. See, for example, Herbert W. Cheshire, "Why Reagan May Dump Clausen," *Business Week*, July 30, 1984, 123.

134. "Conversation," 6–7.

135. Cheshire, "Why Reagan," 123.

136. A. W. Clausen, "Destiny Is a Matter of Choice," *Atlantic Community Quarterly* 21, 3 (1983), 256.

137. Ibid., 258.

138. A. W. Clausen, "Let's Not Panic About Third World Debts," *Harvard Business Review* 61, 6 (1983), 113.

139. Ibid., 106.

140. To date the most successful use of structural-adjustment loans (SALs) has been in South Korea, Thailand and the Philippines. Some feared that the difficulty in garnering contributions for IDA VII would jeopardize the expansion into Sub-Subharan Africa of such loans and their related "policy dialogues." Anthony Rowley, "Banker Without Portfolio," *Far Eastern Economic Review*, September 29, 1983, 66.

141. Robert S. McNamara, "Developing Countries and the World Bank in the 1980s," in *The Future Role of the World Bank*, 68.

142. "The Challenge of Development Today: A Conversation with Ernest Stern, Senior Vice President, Operations, of the World Bank," *Finance & Development* 20 (September 1983): 5.

143. Interview with Qureshi.

144. Interview with Clausen.

145. Interview with Qureshi. See also Selim M. Hassan, *Development Assistance Policies & The Performance of Aid Agencies: Studies in the Performance of DAC, OPEC, the Regional Development Banks and the World Bank Group* (London: The Macmillan Press, 1983), 339.

146. Conclusions that accord with Baldwin's comments about the Bank in his classic study, "International Bank," 68.

13

The Political Role of

the Director-General of UNESCO

Lawrence S. Finkelstein

●

In the United Nations system UNESCO has been in the eye of the political storm. At the end of 1983, after a period of tumult in its relations with the organization, the United States served notice of its intention to withdraw at the end of 1984 if its demands for reform were not met to its satisfaction. Despite frenzied diplomatic activity in the organization during the preceding twelve months, the United States withdrew at the end of 1984. Its example was followed by the United Kingdom. Singapore also withdrew.

In these events, and in the political history of the period leading up to these climaxes, the Director-General (DG) of UNESCO played a central and critical role. Numerous commentaries suggested that the incumbent DG, Amadou-Mahtar M'Bow, was a source of the American animus and a target of the U.S. policy.[1] Although the United States took great pains to deny this when it gave notice of its intent to withdraw,[2] there is every reason to believe that the fact that the Director-General had come to play so important a political role in the organization was itself a key factor in the tensions leading to the American and British withdrawals.

The record of the two years between the American announcement of intention to withdraw and the completion of the British withdrawal points to the centrality of a political struggle between the majority of members—the G-77 and the NAM—and a minority led by the United States over political control of UNESCO. In this struggle, the political power of the Director-General was both an important objective and an important factor.

One way to illuminate the political power exercised by the two most recent Directors-General is to describe the difference between two UNESCO budget decisions taken three decades apart. In November 1952 the second Director-General, Jaime Torres Bodet, resigned because the UNESCO General Conference rejected his preferred two year budget of $21 million.[3] In November 1983 the roles were reversed. The budget ceiling of $374.4 million adopted by the General Conference for the 1984–85 biennium exceeded the "zero growth" budget the United States had fought for. Even that total represented a remarkable political act by Director-General Amadou-Mahtar M'Bow. On his own authority he sought a compromise to satisfy the United States by accepting a Nordic group proposal to trim $10 million from the budget he had earlier proposed and which had been approved by the Executive Board of UNESCO. The United States opposed the compromise and cast the sole vote against it.

The contrast between the two budget actions reflects the change in the intervening years in the role and power of the Director-General. In 1983, as in the two preceding decades, budget increases proposed by the Director-General were adopted against the opposition of the United States, which was the largest contributor. The dominance of the Director-General on the budget issues dates from 1962, the first year of the long tenure of M'Bow's predecessor, René Maheu. That year the United States found itself unable to defeat the budget Maheu proposed. In the end it acceded to a compromise budget greater than the amount it preferred.[4] That was not the only important issue on which the United States did not prevail that year. It had opposed the election of Maheu and lost.[5]

The budget issues are more than simple tests of strength between the United States and other major states on the one hand and the DG on the other. To begin with, these are "political" decisions as the latter are defined in this volume. That is, they are about the authoritative allocation of values, in this case money and the program purposes and levels it supports, for the UNESCO society. The General Conference of UNESCO is authorized to set the budget and assess the members their proportional shares.[6] In this, it is like the UN General Assembly.[7] The initiative in proposing the budget lies with the executive head in both cases.[8] The DG, however, is not a free agent. He has to feel the pulse of the membership and judge what the membership desires, what they will accept, and how they will vote. That does not exclude the possibility that the DG may have a role in influencing what the members want.

That involves both the overall totals of the budget for the fiscal period and the subordinate subheadings for program proposals acceptable to the membership and the budget figures attached to them. In coming to such assessments, however, the two most recent DGs, Maheu and M'Bow, have concluded that their efficacy in UNESCO depended on their being seen to oppose efforts of the big contributors, the United States chief among them, to limit the program directions and the activity levels of UNESCO. Neither DG wanted such limits to be imposed anyway. Thus they were effectively allied with the majorities that shared their interest in growth in UNESCO's program and expenditures. In this more complex way M'Bow's budget prevailed over the opposition of the United States in 1983 with the support of the majority of members, which he could rely on in good part because their interests coincided on the issue of the budget.

For more than two decades, beginning with the incumbency of René Maheu, the DGs of UNESCO have exercised effective political power as that term is employed here, that is, "the ability to dominate or, preferably, to determine the allocation of values at issue in international arenas."[9] In fact, there is reason to believe that the DG is the most influential actor in UNESCO. A former Deputy Director-General who served under M'Bow referred to the "growing power of the post of Director-General, regardless of the incumbent, but especially under present circumstances."[10]

The "circumstances" referred to in that remark have changed since it was made. The main change in circumstances, however, itself results from the fact that the observation was correct, that is, the withdrawal of the United States and Britain resulted in part from their frustration over inability to alter quickly enough the political conditions of the DG's power. One theme of the reform movement since the United States announced its intent to withdraw has been that too much power has passed to the Secretariat, of which the Director-General is the head. That is attributed at least in part to default of the membership, or what Sewell has labeled the failure of the leading powers to "engage" effectively enough in UNESCO.[11] This perception was widely shared among the Organization for Economic Cooperation and Development (OECD) countries comprising the group for mutual consultation, which labeled themselves the "Western Information Group" (WIG).

Their efforts in 1984 and 1985 produced some change but not enough to avert the American and British withdrawals. The respect shown Director-General M'Bow in the letter by Secretary of State Shultz announcing the U.S. intent to withdraw[12] may have been hypocritical but also reflected respect for his power in the organization. That power was rooted in the symbiosis of interest between the DG and the voting majority of less-developed countries (LDCs), the African states prominently among them. Africans' support for their fellow African had implications not only for what was feasible in UNESCO, but for other interests of the United States involving relations with African countries.

Secretary Shultz's carefully respectful tone, therefore, acknowledged, perhaps paradoxically, that the DG's collaboration was necessary if effective reforms were to be accomplished, even reforms affecting the membership bodies, and that no direct assault on him could be expected to succeed. Shultz's later letter announcing that the United States would carry out its intent to withdraw omitted the buttery language. The United States had given up the struggle and thus no longer needed to maintain the fiction in order to preserve the goodwill of a powerful DG.[13]

Recent events supply evidence of the paradox. In what proved a futile effort to avert the U.S. withdrawal, the Executive Board of UNESCO agreed in the fall of 1984 to recommend that there be "zero growth" in UNESCO's budget for the 1986–87 biennium, to be acted on by the General Conference in Sofia the following year. Even after the U.S. withdrew, the guiding bodies of UNESCO acted in 1985 to meet the continuing demands of the Western Information Group members for budget constraint and to avert the threatened withdrawal of Britain and perhaps others. Accordingly, the General Conference adopted essentially a "zero growth" budget, acting on the advice of the Executive Board.

This result could not have been achieved without the DG's willingness to accept it.[14] Had he opposed the compromise, it seems most likely that the agreement of the LDCs to such limitation of UNESCO's budget would not have been forthcoming. Moreover, there is further evidence of the DG's power in the fact that, in order to achieve this outcome, first the United States and then the United Kingdom and others associated with them had to employ the ultimate available leverage—the threat to resign.

This chapter will examine and seek to explain the political role of the DG in UNESCO, which is unusual in the UN system, as will be shown below. It will concentrate on the period covering the tenure of its two most recent Directors-General, René Maheu and Amadou-Mahtar M'Bow, both of them strong personalities and towering figures in the affairs of UNESCO. Both occupied the office for extended periods, Maheu from 1962 until 1974, and M'Bow since then.

The DG's unusual power in UNESCO will be examined under three headings: its sources in UNESCO's historical inspiration and constitutional arrangements, the DG's political role in recent years, and reasons for and limitations on the DG's political role and power.

The Historical and Constitutional Background

If, to paraphrase Harlan Cleveland's observation about the United Nations, the power of UNESCO's Director-General is for the United States and its Western allies a lump in UNESCO's "diplomatic bed,"[15] they put the lump there themselves.

UNESCO was founded in the heady, liberal atmosphere immediately following the end of World War II. The Western democracies were the prime movers. They believed—indeed they inspired—the UNESCO philosophy captured in the famous words of the Preamble to UNESCO's Constitution: "since wars begin in the minds of men, it is in the minds of men that the defenses of peace must be constructed." The liberal inspiration of UNESCO's founders had two effects relevant to the theme of this chapter.

The Sources of Controversy

One source of controversy was the early imprinting on UNESCO of the idea that UNESCO should work for peace in its chosen fields of effort—education, science, culture, and communication (which the United States insisted should be added to the domains of the organization's acronym). The Constitution calls for UNESCO "to contribute to peace and security by promoting collaboration" in its fields "in order to further universal respect for justice, for the rule of law and for the human rights and fundamental freedoms which are affirmed for the peoples of the world."[16]

The breadth and complexity of that mandate in itself ensured that UNESCO would be broader and more complex than any other UN agency except the UN itself and that it would be inordinately difficult to manage. The problem was compounded by the complexity of motives that inspired participation in it. The liberal ethic ensured that UNESCO would be open not only to participation by governments but also to intense involvement by all the sectoral communities concerned with UNESCO's fields of endeavor. The Constitution incorporated unusual provisions ensuring that this would be so.

One such provision stated that, although only governments should be represented in the General Conference, delegates should be chosen after consultation with the National Commissions called for elsewhere in the Constitution or with "educational, scientific and cultural bodies." Another was the provision that members of the Executive Board should serve in their individual capacities, not as representatives of their governments. Thus they could represent the membership as a whole, rather than their own countries.[17] A third was the provision for consultation with "non-governmental international organizations" akin to the authority given the UN Economic and Social Council in the UN Charter. Finally, there was the provision requiring members to set up "National Commissions or National Co-operating Bodies" to associate with UNESCO's work each country's "principal bodies interested in educational, scientific and cultural matters."

Thus it was assured that UNESCO's "fields" would be deeply implicated in UNESCO's affairs and would be drawn into UNESCO's decision processes. Although the provision for individual participation in the Executive Board was replaced by direct representation of governments in that body in an amendment adopted in 1954, the overall pattern has more or less persisted throughout UNESCO's history.

The result was predictable. Representatives of education, science, culture, and communication were bound to seek to direct UNESCO's effort toward service to their disciplines. Conflict inevitably arose over how to allocate UNESCO's resources, which were especially limited in its early years. From the beginning there has been the issue whether UNESCO should advance education, science, culture, and communication as worthwhile in themselves or employ them in the service of peace, human rights, and the other objectives set forth in UNESCO's Constitution.

As to the primary "causes" with which the organization was charged, it was apparent even before UNESCO's membership expanded that these were politically and ideologically controversial matters. As early as 1947, Jacques Maritain, the renowned author and a French delegate to the General Conference that year, called attention to the dilemma that what the founders had believed universally held values were in fact controversial and did not easily lead to universal agreement as to what should be done: "However deeply one may delve, there are no longer common bases for speculative thought. There is no longer a common language for it." The conclusion he drew was that UNESCO should base its action "not on a shared conception of the world" but "on common practical ideas."[18]

Over the years UNESCO has been in existence, interests and priorities have shifted. In part, that has been because the membership grew. One cause of membership growth was the decision of the USSR after the death of Stalin, and of other East European countries in tandem, to join UNESCO (in a few cases, rejoin) and some other agencies of the UN system. Another was the influx of newly independent states as a result of the colonial revolution. New members brought different outlooks and priorities into UNESCO. The Western countries of liberal conviction eventually lost control of UNESCO's political processes and, hence, of the outcomes on issues they considered politically important. This was particularly important to them because of the development of a Third World purpose to employ UNESCO as an instrument to assert international authority affecting such objectives as the New International Economic Order, the New World Information and Communication Order, and the elimination of racism and apartheid.[19] As a result, the issue Maritain had posed in 1947 has been a central point of controversy since the late 1970s. The United States, in particular, has recently opposed as *ultra vires* and contrary to UNESCO's original purposes the very kinds of programs its representatives vigorously advocated in the early years. The East European and most Third World members, and various of UNESCO's professional and intellectual constituents, have been the ones to argue that it is not only appropriate but necessary that UNESCO should continue to perform the role of "intellectual conscience of the United Nations system."[20]

This fundamental schism has been superimposed on the already difficult enough issues of establishing priorities for UNESCO. It has been one of the central recent issues of political conflict in the organization. It has constituted a fundamental obstruction to the ability of the members to agree as to overall guidance to UNESCO. In consequence, it has both provided great opportunity for leadership by the Director-General and placed great responsibility on him. It has, in addition, made it extremely awkward politically for him to ex-

ercise the leadership required of him. The fundamental conflict over
what UNESCO should do and be has generated a need for leadership
from the DG and has simultaneously made it impossible for him to
lead successfully.

The schism on this issue accounts for the effort led by the WIG
members to focus UNESCO on practical tasks, emphasizing assistance
to developing countries in UNESCO's fields, and to direct UNESCO's
attention away from contention over policies affecting global issues
such as peace, racism, human rights, apartheid, and disarmament.
M'Bow has been less than fully helpful in this WIG effort to finesse
these sources of conflict in UNESCO. He has been aligned with those
who have persisted in the view that UNESCO must continue to carry
out the constitutional mission.[21] Because the resulting controversy
risks destroying UNESCO itself, some concessions were made toward
the WIG view in the process of setting program priorities and allocating budgets during the 23rd General Conference in Sofia in
1985. By then, however, the United States had already withdrawn,
and what was done did not prevent Britain from pulling out soon
after the Conference ended.

The extraordinary demand for leadership by the DG, resulting from
the struggles over priorities and, particularly in recent years, the
schism over UNESCO's role, has been one consequence of the liberal
impulse that inspired the founding of UNESCO. That schism has also
meant that the DG has been in a nutcracker from which he could
not easily escape: to satisfy one set of contending forces risked
evoking the wrath of the other side.

The Decision System

A second consequence of that impulse was the liberal imprint on
the constitutional structure of UNESCO, including the unusually important role given the Director-General. As events were to prove,
it was also especially important that the Constitution established a
liberal system for reaching decisions.

First of all, the UNESCO Constitution provides for an open membership system. Any member of the United Nations has the right
to be a UNESCO member.

A second provision is as significant. The UNESCO Constitution
provides for no veto over applications for membership by nonmem-
bers of the UN. Any such state may be admitted by recommendation
of the Executive Board[22] and a two-thirds majority vote of the Gen-

eral Conference. These provisions ensured that the principle of universality—in the sense that any state wishing membership could have it—would prevail in the end in UNESCO. It has been many years since any applicant was denied admission. There has been no constitutional obstacle to the growth that has occurred in the size of the Third World majority in UNESCO. Membership grew from 28 members in 1946 to a peak, before the three recent withdrawals, of 161.

The General Conference is the primary decision body in UNESCO. Like the UN General Assembly and most of the plenary bodies in the UN system, it takes decisions on a one nation-one vote basis. The evident consequence of that has been that the growth in membership, especially the influx of newly independent countries, some of them minuscule, in the 1960s and 1970s deprived the original liberal members of power to block decisions they opposed.

While the norm is that decisions should be taken by consensus rather than by counting votes, consensus decisions are strongly affected by understanding of how votes would line up if they were taken. The result has been severe limitation of the real ability of states in the minority to obstruct unfavorable outcomes by employing the threat to disrupt consensus. There are political disincentives to doing that because in UNESCO "consensus" has become something of an institutional totem and violating it invokes penalties accompanying disapprobation. Besides, the benefits of disrupting consensus are limited because while members in the minority have the capability to do so on matters of great importance to them, they thus risk being outvoted in the end.

In these political circumstances any DG, especially one interested in the possibility of reelection to the post, would find it difficult to avoid thinking it advantageous as a rule to be identified with the preponderance of votes, rather than offend the majority by asserting the presumed neutrality of his office or, even more hazardous to his political health, siding with the minority. M'Bow's views have in any event tended to coincide with those of the Third World countries, which comprise the majority in UNESCO. He has, therefore, had to suffer little personal anguish in seconding the majority's interests on most issues. He has often taken the lead in shaping the organization's position. In terms of the issue as Thomas M. Franck formulated it with respect to the UN Secretary-General, M'Bow has clearly chosen "alignment with the non-aligned" in preference to "non-alignment."[23]

Only extraordinarily, when the survival of the organization itself was at stake, did he intervene to prevent the adoption of measures, such as proposals affecting Israel and the mass media that threatened to precipitate the withdrawal of the United States, which his institutional interest required him to prevent if possible. A measure of his effectiveness in this respect is that no unacceptable event in UNESCO triggered the U.S. and British withdrawals. When they left, it was by predetermination and under their own momentum. While the DG's role was certainly not the only factor in this course of events, his influence was joined with others to prevent actions that might be provocative to the countries threatening to leave.

The General Conference (GC), most would agree, is too large, too unwieldy, too riven with controversy, and is charged with too broad and complex an agenda to be effective in guiding UNESCO's affairs. It is also very expensive, both in its demands on UNESCO's budget, and hence on members' contributions, and in its demands on undermanned delegations and their undermanned governments. That is one reason the GC meets biennially, instead of annually as it originally did.

Controversy dominates when what is involved are the prickly issues of high political salience. By far most of the General Conference's effort is devoted to the more routine business of establishing the organization's direction through the Medium Term Plans and authorizing its action via the biennial Programs and Budgets. These matters, however, call for more expert knowledge than can be adequately available in delegations that stretch thin the resources of even the rich and powerful countries. They call also for more continuity of attention and interest in the preparatory periods between sessions of the GC than even dedicated, well-staffed, and well-managed governments are generally able to maintain. Pierre de Senarclens's synopsis seems right: "The General Conference, given the great variety of views and of interests that arise within it, is unable to give clear and coherent directives to the Secretariat, or to examine its output in any detail."[24] In UNESCO the interstices of governments' agreement are wide.

The Constitution anticipated that a smaller body would be required to plan and to provide continuing oversight and effective preparation for sessions of the GC. The Executive Board was created to perform these functions. Its constitutional authority, however, only ambiguously empowers it to direct the organization's activities between sessions of the GC. Also, its mandate imposes on it the same need to perform its guidance and oversight roles across too broad an agenda that afflicts the GC. It is not equipped to perform its tasks of guidance and oversight with penetration and comprehensiveness. Because UNESCO's mandates are so multifarious, the Executive Board can execute its mandates only superficially and spasmodically. The limitation on the Board's effectiveness, which stems from UNESCO's breadth and complexity, is reinforced by its political structure and performance. Again, Senarclens seemed to have had it right when he wrote that "the Executive Board has lost its importance in decision-making."[25]

The Constitution calls on the Executive Board to prepare the agenda for the GC, examine the program of work for the organization and corresponding budget estimates "submitted to it by the Director-General . . . and shall submit them with such recommendations as it considers desirable to the General Conference." It is responsible for the execution of the program adopted by the Conference. In doing that, it is to "take all necessary measures to ensure the effective and rational execution of the Programme by the Director-General." Constitutionally, thus, the Executive Board shares responsibilities with the DG with respect to preparation of the program and budget and conduct of UNESCO's program. It does not adopt the budget to be proposed to the GC; it is empowered merely to transmit its recommendations on the DG's proposal for a budget. As has been observed above, the DG felt competent on one recent occasion to propose a revised budget figure to the GC after the Executive Board had acted on the previous version. While the language of the Constitution authorizes the Board to hold a tight rein on the DG in carrying out the program, it has not been competent to do that. Given what Senarclens has called "the ever closer links between the director-general and most members of the board" and "the subtle bargaining inherent in such relationships,"[26] there has not been much disposition on the part of most Board members to exercise the powers the Constitution gives them.

Politically, the Board is a smaller GC. The original provision for membership by individuals gave way in 1954 to a purely governmental composition. That is disguised somewhat, but for many years now has not fundamentally been altered, by the injunction to appoint as members "persons competent in the arts, the humanities, the sciences, education and the diffusion of ideas, and qualified by their experience and capacity to fulfil the administrative and executive duties of the Board." Participation in the Board has been marked

by a steady decline in the relevant competence of governments'
representatives, as artists, scientists, and men of letters have given
way to functionaries and diplomats. Most observers outside the U.S.
government and many within it would agree that the United States
has been notably delinquent in trying to appoint individuals of such
qualification to represent it on the Executive Board, going back to
the end of the 1960s.

Growth in the size of the Board has also interfered with its efficacy.
From a body of eighteen individuals at the beginning, the Board
has grown to fifty-one representatives of governments. Not only is
geographical representation the norm, but UNESCO's rules provide
for election to membership in the Board on the basis of "groupings"
for the purpose of elections that are largely "geographic" or "regional," although they are not called that.[27] In effect, regional caucuses nominate their candidates for the number of seats to which
they are entitled and for what amounts to automatic election by the
General Conference.[28]

As in the General Conference, the membership balance has shifted adversely for the original Western members. In 1946 the countries that have formed the Western group for purposes of election
to the Executive Board (Group I in UNESCO's parlance) had ten of
eighteen places, or 56 percent of the membership. In 1984 they still
had ten seats, but the Board had grown to fifty-one and the proportion had fallen to 20 percent. Representation for countries of
Latin America, Asia, and the Middle East and Africa (Groups III,
IV, and V) had grown from six in 1946 or 33 percent of the total to
37 or 72 percent of the total in 1984, before the United States withdrew. The normal decision rule is simple majority. Even when the
Western members vote together, the Western group cannot by itself
block that small category of decisions that require a two-thirds vote.
Consensus procedures are the norm. Once again, however, the voting rules, and beliefs as to outcomes if there were votes, cast their
shadow on the content of what can be agreed on by consensus.

The scope and complexity of UNESCO's functions intervene to
render the Executive Board and its members little better able than
the GC and its members to cope with the demands of decisionmaking. Governments are not disinterested parties and are very prone
to pursue their ideological, material, and otherwise selfish purposes.
The group structure plays an important role in the decision processes
of the Executive Board, with regional representatives often advo-
cating the positions of the caucusing groups that nominated them

and, in effect, elected them. Even those few individuals who are left free by their governments to vote as they see fit are too often ill equipped by experience and training to cope with the complex technicalities of programmatic decisionmaking. Not even the large powers are adequately staffed to be fully informed on the issues that arise. The documentation is complex and voluminous. The draft programs and budgets run to hundreds of pages of often obscure project plans and poorly documented budget estimates. "Transparency" has been an often sought but rarely attained quality of program and budget materials that come before the Executive Board.

The situation, in short, is ready made for a kind of pork barrel politics with the DG in the catbird seat and providing the initiative. The structure of the Executive Board, the nature of its functions, and the character of its politics cry out for executive leadership. The original liberal impetus ensured that the office would have an adequate constitutional basis for providing it.

UNESCO's Constitution names the DG as the primary component of the UNESCO Secretariat. He is intertwined deeply with the other organs in the affairs of the organization and given extensive powers by the Constitution.

He is "appointed" by the General Conference on nomination of the Executive Board. The candidate thus chosen—"prepackaged" seems more fitting—serves for six years and is eligible for "reappointment" by secret procedures and simple majority votes.

The DG is designated "the chief administrative officer of the Organization" and in that capacity appoints the staff. He is given the right to participate without vote in all meetings of the GC and the Executive Board, including even the private meetings the latter is authorized to hold under its Rules of Procedure. He may make oral or written statements to the GC or any of its subordinate bodies with the permission of the presiding officer. He is entitled to make such statements without qualification in the Executive Board and all its organs, including the small steering group called the "Bureau." He is required to prepare for submission to the Board "a draft program of work for the Organization with corresponding budget estimates" and, as has been noted above, it is his document that goes to the GC with the Board's recommendations attached.

The agenda of the General Conference must include the DG's Report giving his perspective on the work of the organization since the preceding Conference (the C/3 document) and items the DG chooses to introduce. Similarly, the Executive Board agenda includes "all questions raised by the Director-General." These provisions make the DG a major actor in UNESCO. Many of them have grown from the original Constitutional powers given the DG and are to be found in the Rules of Procedure of the GC and the Board. Presumably, these rules can be changed; they are, however, deeply imbedded in the practice of UNESCO. The role they have established for the DG has become intrinsic to UNESCO. Changing them would be a difficult political process and one in which any DG would have an intense and active concern. In any event, they are to a large extent implied by the powers given the DG in the Constitution. Those reflect the liberal instincts and bureaucratic norms of the Western founders. For the United States in particular it was second nature to place great reliance on the chief administrative officer of a bureaucracy.[29] This seemed especially appropriate for UNESCO, which was not expected to be a center for political contention but rather a focus for the shared intellectual effort to construct the defenses of peace.

The malaise in UNESCO in the past dozen years stems in good part from the conflicts over UNESCO's nature conducted in the constitutional-political framework described in preceding paragraphs. A close observer said recently that "UNESCO's present day difficulties are caused by birth defects."[30] The defects have been compounded by insufficient attention to remedying them through much of UNESCO's history.

The Scope and Nature of the DG's Political Role

The preceding section has shown that the Constitution gave the DG a central place in the structure and workings of UNESCO. Moreover, it has shown how the scope and complexity of UNESCO's agenda have, in a sense, been compounded by the scope and complexity of participation in UNESCO. Add to these ingredients of organizational "gridlock" the immobilizing effect of the struggle among members over the soul of UNESCO in recent years, and it is apparent that UNESCO depends heavily on leadership by the DG.

This section will delineate the extent and nature of the DG's leadership role. In accordance with the definitions employed in this study, most of what UNESCO, and hence, the Director-General, does is political. That is so because, to a large degree, its decisions and actions are concerned with the authoritative allocation of values as that term is broadly defined for the purposes of this volume (that is, what the actors seek). The values at stake include both those that UNESCO may allocate for its members, or the society without, and those, mainly instrumental ones, it allocates within its own confines.

In UNESCO the DG is an important actor with respect to all kinds of decisions, including the most important and most sensitive ones. That observation applies not only to responsibilities with which the DG is charged by the Constitution and to responsibilities that can be inferred from them, but also to matters that lie within the responsibilities of the other organs composed of members. Some of his role is visible and even spotlighted. Much of it goes on invisibly behind the scenes.

To begin with, no one who has attended a meeting of UNESCO's General Conference or Executive Board can fail to be impressed by the ubiquitous and active involvement of the DG. He and members of the Secretariat are omnipresent. Utilizing to the full the Constitutional powers of participation and the rules based on them that permit Secretariat participation, the DG evidently strongly influences the course of events. He adds his items to those from other sources that comprise the agendas of the governing bodies. The DG's written reports on the work of the organization appear in advance of the General Conferences and give him a biennial opportunity to shape the perceptions of members as to what the issues are, what has been achieved by the organization, and what he believes needs to be done. His introductions to these reports, like those of the UN Secretary-General, allow him to highlight the items and issues he wishes to focus attention on and sometimes to outline the results of his consideration of issues with which he has been charged by previous sessions of the Conference.

Since UNESCO Directors-General have been inveterate travelers, and since the DG's office in Paris has been a magnet for permanent delegates, for visiting cabinet ministers concerned with UNESCO affairs, and for delegations of all descriptions, the DG has ample opportunity to exert his influence concerning issues coming up in the governing bodies. The predictable consequence is that the meetings, records, and resolutions of the governing bodies are peppered with affirmations of appreciation and with endorsements of what the DG reports he has done or says should be done, both by those who are of his outlook and part of his political entourage and those who are more independent but who nevertheless are happy to find opportunities to show their esteem for the figure they may wish to influence on other matters. "I'll scratch your back if you'll scratch mine" is a device not unknown to UNESCO as to other political organizations and the DG is well situated to indulge in the practice.

Most of the important documents on which the governing bodies are asked to act or by which they are informed are prepared by the DG or under his authority. In the commissions and other bodies of the GC and in the Executive Board and its subsidiary bodies, as indeed in all UNESCO-sponsored meetings, the usual arrangement is that the DG or his designee from the Secretariat introduces each agenda item, intervenes frequently in the discussion, and concludes the discussion of each issue and the meeting as a whole with a statement summarizing the discussion and drawing the implications from it. Governments have generally been content to have the DG and the staff perform these roles.

The public role and the private one mix. Much private palaver and much public taking of positions by delegations, the latter obviously considerably influenced by the former, precede the DG's public intercession at the end of the debate to spell out his policy responses to the issues raised, define what he believes to be the limits of the available consensus, and, frequently, delineate what he believes ruled out by the organization's rules, history, and precedents.

In recent times, the issues have often affected directly important interests of his own. That was the case, for example, during the Executive Board meeting in the spring of 1984 when there were critically important discussions of the so-called United States and United Kingdom agenda items growing from the U.S. announcement of its intention to withdraw and the subsequent British letter outlining grievances. The issues spanned at least three of the Cox-Jacobson categories:[31] symbolic issues because one of the things at stake was how UNESCO described its mission and another was UNESCO's role in the struggle over the "acceptability of the goals or ideologies"[32] of the G-77; representational issues because one objective of the WIG was to change the decision rules affecting certain types of UNESCO decisions; programmatic issues were involved in the attempts to limit budget growth and to alter priorities in the direction of more operational, development assistance projects and away from the ideologically divisive intellectual and normative functions.

The DG's responses to the debates on these two items offered mainly procedural concessions to the demands for change in the organization—the institution of four expert working groups to look into problems of program, recruitment procedures and staff management methods, budgeting techniques and presentation of the budget (which had to do with "transparency" and control of allocation), public information, and evaluation methods and techniques. He made it clear that he was in charge and that the groups would report to him. He thus set limits to his willingness to concede. Particularly, he urged, not without some disingenuity as will appear hereinafter, that questions about the rules to govern decisionmaking in UNESCO were for member governments to deal with and not for their servant, the Director-General.

In setting such limits the DG was able to rely on earlier interventions by some members of the Board, some of them no doubt influenced by what they believed to be the DG's preference or by what he had told them privately on that score. "Many of the representatives of member states depend upon the Secretariat, and particularly upon the Director-General, to determine their own positions."[33] He and they were able to base resistance to change on the rules, respect for prior decisions of the governing bodies, and their interpretations of the Constitution. Respect for the DG's views in such matters is reinforced by his role as the main repository of the organization's "institutional memory."

In another case, the struggle over the Mass Media Declaration during the GC in 1978, the issues were both symbolic and rule-creating. (Although UNESCO has no power to set rules, the rule-creating category in the Cox-Jacobson typology covers norms as well.) What was at stake for the DG was the risk that adoption of a resolution unacceptable to the United States, Britain, the Netherlands, the Federal Republic of Germany, and perhaps other Western powers might precipitate their withdrawal from UNESCO. That would have violated the principle of universality in which M'Bow placed great store, deprived UNESCO of the resources of all kinds they contributed, and represented a major defeat to his leadership.

The issue had been one of the first to confront M'Bow when his tenure began in 1974. His diplomacy had averted the crisis that threatened at the GC in Nairobi in 1976. M'Bow's exertion had resulted in the matter being put off until the next General Conference, the one in 1978.[34] Then, his effective role was played out largely behind the scenes and through a trusted intermediary. In a veritable sandstorm of diplomatic activity, the central negotiation was be-

tween the DG and the United States. M'Bow was one pole and the
United States of America was the other in a tense, negotiatory search
for a damage-limiting compromise. In the course of defining the
acceptable, the DG maneuvered to exclude Soviet influence on the
outcome and even denied them effective participation in the negotiation. Through his ability to persuade delegations of the Third
World to accept his definition of what was necessary, he was able
to guide the compromise resolution to passage in the General Conference.[35]

The DG's efforts to salvage the situation in the face of the withdrawal threats continued. In 1980, at the General Conference in
Belgrade, he is credited with having used his influence with African
delegates to help "limit confrontation and ensure a relatively harmonious outcome."[36] Much the same was said of the DG's role during
the 22nd GC in Paris in 1983. Edmund P. Hennelly, chairman of
the U.S. delegation, said that "Director-General M'Bow worked actively behind the scenes to assure a fruitful outcome in Paris. . . .
He mobilized the African delegates in ways that were designed to
assure that the U.S. and the West got a fair hearing at the conference."[37] M'Bow may have hoped to engage the United States in a
secret bilateral exploration of the U.S. requirements to remain in
the organization during the second half of 1984.[38] The United States,
it appears, declined to be drawn into such a bipolar exercise.

The issues concerning the mass media and the U.S. and British
withdrawals saw the DG involved as a political actor, by any definition of that term. The intrusion into UNESCO of hotly contested
issues of high political content has drawn recent Directors-General
willy-nilly into affairs that might be thought the preserve of members. That the executive head of an IGO exercises a good-offices and
intermediary role in the development of agency policy comes as no
surprise. A leading study said: "Executive heads are . . . called upon
to be a bridge between the participant subsystem and the representative subsystem."[39] In UNESCO, however, the DG has sought to
bridge not just the two subsystems but the chasms between groups
of member states comprising the "representative subsystem" as
well. Further, he has served not merely as a bridge, but as a negotiating partner and then as a "whip" to assure the needed support
for the compromises arrived at.

The DG also has a role in affecting "representational decisions."
That is surprising. These are matters that traditionally lie in the
domain of states. That expectation is captured in the observation of

two scholars that: "Executive leaders of international organizations have strong influence over their own bureaucracies, but only weak influence over member organizations and their representatives (General Assembly, Governing Body, etc.)."[40] Cox and Jacobson concluded that significant influence of executive heads is limited to the appointment of Secretariat officials.[41]

The DG's role extends further than that. He is consulted about the distribution of seats among members in UNESCO's organs. He is consulted in negotiations leading to the choice of officers as important as the Chairman of the Executive Board and the President of the General Conference when that body meets in Paris. (When it meets elsewhere, the Presidency falls to the host country.) He plays a role in the choice of states and of some INGOs to be invited to less than universal international conferences convened by UNESCO or under its auspices, even though the formal power to determine the list of invitees is vested in the GC or the Board.[42] In some such cases, he may exercise a controlling voice.

He directly appoints the members of commissions established by UNESCO. Some of these are important, visible, and controversial. For example, the mass media and communications issues preoccupied the GC at Nairobi in 1976. It was the DG who was invited "to hold further broad consultations with experts" looking toward a draft declaration on the mass media.[43] M'Bow proceeded by creating the Commission for the Study of Communication Problems, the "McBride Commission," and appointed Sean McBride as chairman.[44] As he has himself made clear, he chose and appointed the Commission's members. He also set its terms of reference.[45] While he proceeded slowly and cautiously in his handling of these delicate matters, there is no doubt that the actions were visible and the Commission's impact was controversial. While the DG, in this instance, was responding to a request of the GC, he exerted a significant leadership influence in doing so.

The DG's roles in the acute political matters sketched in preceding paragraphs are examples of power devolving on an executive head of an agency because of the difficulty member states have had in dealing effectively and directly with sensitive political issues. In a minor key there is a resemblance to some of the major political roles performed by the UN Secretary-General in the "leave it to Dag" period in the UN. Franck has described this as the "black box" phenomenon in his recent work about the UN.[46] An informed commentator on UNESCO, with experience from the inside, referred to the

DG as being seen, and seeing himself, "as the one main stay against centrifugal disaster."[47]

Much of the intense political controversy in UNESCO is over symbolic issues with little if any direct consequence. The treatment of Israel in UNESCO is an issue that comes to mind. Arab rejectionists sought to attach legitimacy to anti-Israeli symbols through majority decisions. The decisions and resolutions thus adopted during UNESCO's "Israeli period," which peaked in 1976, had no discernible effects that mattered, except for their influence on views about UNESCO generated as by-products of the much-publicized confrontations. UNESCO is not where important decisions are taken about politics in the Middle East, or results achieved.

By this measure the most important decisions taken in UNESCO are those that determine the scale and direction of UNESCO's program. This chapter has already argued that the most important influence on the size of UNESCO's program has been the Director-General. That has been true for more than two decades. Anecdotally, the point is made dramatically by the puzzled and frustrated reaction of then Assistant Secretary of State Harlan Cleveland when, in the early 1960s, he emerged from his first official meeting with the newly appointed DG, René Maheu. Maheu had told Cleveland in no uncertain terms that he did not plan to follow the budget guidelines Cleveland had urged on him.[48] This was a new and unsettling experience for the official charged with administering the participation in international organizations of a great power, the one, moreover, that contributed far more than any other state and that expected commensurate influence over budget decisions. The experience has been recurrent. In recent years the United States has consistently either voted against the budget or abstained in the General Conference.

The DG also predominates in setting the direction to be followed by UNESCO's program. This has been true from the very beginning of UNESCO.[49] In recent UNESCO practice the biennial Program and Budget document translates the broad program objectives outlined in the six-year Medium Term Plan into specific program plans with budget allocations for the biennium.[50] Both involve satisfying government desires expressed in preceding General Conferences, through extensive consultations with member governments by means of the latter's response to lengthy questionnaires, and by tightly scheduled discussions in the Executive Board. Moreover, international nongovernmental organizations associated with

UNESCO are consulted. Considerable influence is exerted through the myriad of fora through which UNESCO conducts much of its program—expert and governmental conferences and meetings of all descriptions—in a variety of consultations with other IGOs, and by UNESCO program staff and experts. All the same, shaping the final product is the DG's task and responsibility. UNESCO's abundant pluralism leaves plenty of scope for executive influence, even discretion. In performing the responsibility, the DG relies heavily on the Secretariat's Bureau of Evaluation and Planning (BEP), which reinforces his centralized control over the process. His real power over the development of the program and budget plans derives from his location in the processes. Only he, or senior staff personnel under his direction, have access to all the sources of influence and to all the views expressed.

The program cycle, set by the governing bodies but shaped to meet the necessities of the staff as well as the scheduling problems of the organs, has the result that what the DG proposes to the General Conference runs only the slightest risk of being substantially modified, either as a result of advice from the Executive Board or of ideas advocated in the GC. There are occasional exceptions, such as the GC decision in 1976 to authorize a congress on the teaching of human rights. Usually, however, the cycle means that if a government wishes to effect changes in what UNESCO does, it has to advance its ideas at the GC preceding the one in which it hopes to have the change take effect, that is ordinarily two years ahead of time. Ideas advanced this way have a good chance of finding their way into the DG's next set of program and budget proposals. That few governments avail themselves of this opportunity reinforces the general point that governments have shown themselves relatively incapable of directing UNESCO. Altogether, the conclusion reached in a Department of State review is not unreasonable: "Neither the General Conference or [sic] the Executive Board of the Organization is capable of action independent of the proposals and agenda formulated and staffed by the Secretariat.[51]

Another basis for the DG's dominance of program is to be found in the fact that a large part of the resources UNESCO spends comes from external sources and is additional to the regular program budget appropriated by the General Conference. In the 1983–84 biennium, for example, it was estimated that 38 percent of the total of about $608 million expected to be available would come from other UN agencies, funds-in-trust and other extrabudgetary sources.[52]

Of course, the source agencies and governments provide the funds in accordance with the program guidelines established by their own policymaking organs. They also approve and supervise the terms for UNESCO's employment of the funds on a project-by-project basis. All the same, UNESCO Secretariat members under the DG's overall direction shape UNESCO's part in the international technical assistance effort. They play the main role in seeking out such funds, negotiating the arrangements with the sources, and relating the projects thus made possible to UNESCO's program. Such externally funded activities may shape future programs brought under UNESCO's regular budget.

The extrabudgetary funds estimated to be available in a forthcoming budget period are, to be sure, included in the budget tables approved by the General Conference. These estimates, however, are poor predictors of what sums will actually become available. There appears to be no further control exerted by the governing bodies over the planning, negotiation, programming, and expenditure of such extrabudgetary revenues. The DG, in effect, has exclusive control in UNESCO over the allocative consequences of the programmatic use of these substantial funds. He both exercises and gains power through the control he thus acquires over a great deal of short-term employment in UNESCO not subject to the hiring standards and procedures established for regular employees. The DG's role in arranging for and managing such extrabudgetary expenditures gives him considerable potential for influencing the course of UNESCO's program.

The DG also directly controls the distribution of other funds that are, in UNESCO's terms, considerable. One of them, the Participation Programme, has been in existence since 1955.[53] It is an arrangement under which members may receive grants from UNESCO up to relatively small fixed limits for the conduct of UNESCO-related activities. These funds come from UNESCO's regular budget. In the 1984–85 biennium, about $14 million was appropriated for this purpose.[54] The DG has authority under broad guidelines approved by the GC to make direct cash appropriations of up to $25 thousand per project.[55] In the 1981–83 triennium, such grants went to more than 160 members.[56]

The DG administers another fund, the Special Account for Increased Aid to Developing Countries.[57] It derives from money loaned to UNESCO by member governments during the period in the mid-1970s when the United States was withholding its dues payments. When the United States paid up, the loaned funds became redundant, but they were allowed to continue to earn interest for UNESCO. These funds are supplemented as a result of Executive Board decisions to transfer to the Special Account some of the income earned from the sale of stamps, medals, and book coupons. As of the end of 1983 the fund had received $8.5 million. The Special Account is treated as a supplement to the Participation Programme, especially for the least-developed countries. It is altogether extra-budgetary and full authority is vested in the DG, with no supervision by the governing bodies, under a decision of the Executive Board in 1979.[58]

Finally, there is the control the DG exercises over UNESCO's internal affairs. Constitutionally, that is his bailiwick, subject to very few external controls. He may, for example, authoritatively allocate the large sums appropriated for nonprogram purposes, as in the budget approved by the GC in 1985 for the 1986–87 biennium: general policy formulation and management (includes General Conference, Executive Board, Directorate, and participation in joint services of the UN) $26.8 million; general activities (includes external relations and public information) $21.2 million; program support services (includes UNESCO library, publications and information, statistics, archives, and documentation) $30.8 million; general administration services (includes offices of the comptroller, personnel, data-processing services) $25.7 million; and common services (includes building management, upkeep and supplies, safety and security services) $26.5 million.[59]

These sums come to some $60 million per year. Of course, the DG is far from having discretionary control over all this money. All the same, the funds are expended on his authority. They include some discretionary freedom for him. Assuming that the internal and external audits required under the organization's "Financial Regulations"[60] are fully effective and beyond reproach, it remains true that the DG exercises considerable allocative authority in spending these large sums.

The DG also appoints UNESCO's staff. That is not an unusual power for the executive head of an IGO. It is, however, an authoritative exercise of allocative power as that concept is employed in this study. As is true of other IGOs, the appointment power is constitutionally vested in the DG. Selection is supposed to be guided by the constitutional injunction to pursue "as the paramount consideration the highest standards of integrity, efficiency and technical

competence" and, subject to that requirement, to appoint "on as
wide a geographical basis as possible." Some limits on his appointment power result from the need he confronts to make appointments
that respond to the pressures governments and delegations exert
on him to find places for their preferred candidates. Several former
insiders have commented critically on the politicizing effect on
professional employment in UNESCO of the interpretation given the
principle of geographical distribution during the administrations of
Maheu and M'Bow.[61] In practice the DG exercises considerable discretion. The Executive Board has established a right to be consulted
on the most senior appointments, those at the directorial level and
above, beginning with grade D-1. Consultation does not mean decision power and, in practice, the consultation usually amounts to
no more than the DG telling the Board what he plans to do. Moreover, even this limited restraint is confined to staff appointments
under the Regular Program, leaving the DG altogether free to make
appointments under extrabudgetary funding.

Hoggart has pointed out how extensive was the exercise of the
DG's personnel power under Maheu. He himself exercised the appointment power down to the level of P-5, the highest professional
grade below the directorial level. He ran the Secretariat with an
iron, even tyrannical, hand.[62]

M'Bow has guarded the appointment power even more assertively
and has directly controlled appointments at even lower levels of
professional staffing. As a result of the recent uproar over bad management in UNESCO, he delegated appointment power at grades up
to the P-4 level, a middle grade in the professional scale, to the
Deputy Director-General and the Assistant Director-General for
General Administration.[63] While this intention was welcomed in
the Executive Board's Temporary Committee considering reform
in 1984,[64] the new practices involve minimal real change, especially
since the DG has absolute control over the tenure of the officials to
whom the power has been passed.

The DG's authority over the staff is virtually absolute. A small
exception may be found in the fact that senior staff members appointed because their governments support them may be able to
call on that support in offsetting the authority the DG seeks to exercise over them.[65] The Staff Regulations, finally, establish only
procedural restraints on the DG's ultimate power to fire staff members, and those are subject to exceptions controlled by the DG.[66]

The existence of the Staff Association provides a degree of counterbalance to the DG's authority, but even that is reduced by M'Bow's action in inspiring creation of a counterorganization of his supporters in the staff.[67]

This section has depicted the range and character of the allocative authority exercised by the Director-General of UNESCO, definitively in most cases and influentially in others, in short, his political power. It has been shown that his political role applies to all aspects of the functioning of UNESCO. The next section will summarize and spell out the sources of that authority and the limitations on it.

The Bases of the DG's Power and the Limits on It

A main, perhaps the main, basis for leadership by an executive head of an IGO is the respect accorded the position as the primary institutional representation of the organization. In even the least-complex IGO, there is multiplicity—of members, of organs, of tasks, of programs. The more complex is the organization, the more multiplex are its components and its emanations and the more difficult it is for the organization to identify itself, or be identified, amid the multiple claims to define its ethos. Only one actor is available to fill this identity vacuum and that is the executive head. Constitutionally neutral, the executive head is in a position to attract the confidences of all and, thus, is enabled to claim their confidence as well. Their relatively extended tenures give them advantages over possible competitors for the role of institutional symbol—presidents and chairs of plenary bodies—and their constant availability makes them the natural voice of the organization. Almost inevitably, it seems, they come to personify their organizations.

UNESCO, it should by now be apparent, is no simple organization. Its multiplicity is notorious. If any organization needs a central identification device, that organization is UNESCO. Its multiple agenda implicates multiple constituencies. Diplomatic egalitarianism—the equal formal weight given to as many as 161 national votes in the General Conference and, perhaps even more important, to as many voices—ensures that direction cannot be imparted by the membership. The regionalization of members' participation facilitates trading, may produce compromises enabling consensus, but is not likely to clarify institutional goals with which all can identify.

In a word, a 161 member intergovernmental organization concerned with education, science, culture, and communication cries out for an identifier. The only candidate for the function is the Director-General. Certainly, Maheu and M'Bow have filled it eagerly. Hoggart said of Maheu that "at his peak he was UNESCO."[68] The same is true of M'Bow, turbulent though his tenure has been.

Because of the complexities described in preceding pages, UNESCO may have depended even more on personification for its identity than have other IGOs. That is because of the difficulty UNESCO has had, in Cox's derivation from Haas, in defining "an ideology which gives clear goals to the organization."[69] No one "ideology" could comprehend the missions of UNESCO in all its fields, particularly if it also had to inspire constructive engagement by all its members. Thus, the closest approximation of a UNESCO "ideology" under Maheu may well have been UNESCO itself under his leadership. Certainly, he stood for and realized a great expansion in its scale and activity. And, as has been said, he personified the organization. In M'Bow's time the predominant theme has been service in the development of the Third World, with attendant subthemes such as "indigenization"[70] and "endogeneity." But, while most if not all members were willing to support such development programs, not all UNESCO's constituencies were enthusiastic about their "disciplines" being put to service instead of being served. The subthemes were sources of contention rather than of ideological unification. And, most of all, the development mission, although pragmatically acceptable, was politically and ideologically contentious because of its inspirational proximity to the movement to assert the new international "orders." If it identified UNESCO, it did not unify it. Politically in UNESCO, the development mission served to forge political ties between the DGs, M'Bow even more than Maheu, and the G-77 majority in the organization.

Herein lay another source of strength for the DG. As long as the major Western members were willing to lie relatively doggo, the DG derived great political influence from his symbiosis of interests with the G-77. For Maheu the shared interest was the growth of UNESCO, particularly its development program. For M'Bow it has been that and the practical and doctrinal dimensions of UNESCO's emphasis on Third World themes. M'Bow's enunciation of the Third World liturgy, especially his identification with the new international "orders," combined with the advantages inherent in his institutional position, have made him the leader of "the G-77 party" in UNESCO.

It is no coincidence that the political power of the DG can be traced to the election of Maheu. That event coincided with the turning point in UNESCO's history, as in the history of the United Nations. The years 1960–62 saw twenty-four newly independent African states become members of UNESCO. During M'Bow's tenure the number of G-77 countries reached 122, before Singapore's withdrawal, of a total membership of 161 at that time. The G-77 thus comprised 76 percent of the total membership.

In this political constellation, both recent DGs have found the political bases of effective leadership in identification with the goals of the G-77: the elimination of racialism and, especially, apartheid; education and science for development; cultural development or, in UNESCO's jargon, "endogeneity"; and the new international orders. For both Maheu and M'Bow political advantage coincided with personal conviction in these respects. M'Bow particularly warmly, in some cases even passionately, believes in these goals. While some of the goals were shared with the developed countries, others, as has been suggested above, were divisive. As political contest over such issues heightened in UNESCO, during M'Bow's term the natural consequence was that his role was, and came to be seen, as partisan. The leader of one party in an organization of multiple parties loses his magnetism for those in the other groupings. In this case, that meant especially that he seemed unneutral to the countries of the WIG.

M'Bow has also benefited from an empathetic relationship with third world representatives and their governments, especially the Africans among them, because of his special cachet as the first African to become the executive head of an IGO in the UN system. As a Muslim, he has had close connections with the Islamic members.

He has benefited also from the sophisticated and long-range strategy of the Warsaw Pact and other Communist bloc members that seek whenever possible to cultivate collaborative relations with the G-77. They prefer, therefore, not to place themselves in opposition to objectives of the latter or to solutions that command their support. Most of the time it is easy for the Soviet Union and its allies to line up with the G-77 and the DG. Since this is their preferred location, little concession has to be made to keep them there. The Russians do not hesitate to state their disagreement when their policy calls for it. That has been true, for example, of the expansionist budgets the DG advanced in full agreement with the G-77. The Russians, however, have shrewdly limited their disagreement to verbal remonstrations and abstentions on the votes, rather than risk more acute confrontations with the DG and his political supporters among the G-77. In other ways M'Bow's conduct in office has not always corresponded with Russian positions. He has sometimes locked horns with them, or other members of the Pact, or subverted their policies in the organization. As has been recounted above, he did the latter in the media crisis during the GC in 1978. All the same, the controlled Russian behavior has buffered the relationship and avoided the sharp decline in cordiality and respect that characterized Western views of M'Bow in recent years.

In his political role the DG has certain assets that deserve to be mentioned. One is the benefit of being the natural "friend in court" to whom members normally turn when, as is often the case, they cannot agree. He benefits also from the well-developed structure of regional groups that enables him to deal with a relatively small number of key leaders of regional groups in testing his ideas and mobilizing the voting support he requires for positions he advocates.

The DG's role as diplomatic leader is reinforced too by control over the UNESCO staff. To begin with the organization cannot meet its members' demands without the performance of their functions by the staff he heads. So long as UNESCO exists as a center for the exchange of ideas and information among its members and as an agency of development, the DG and the Secretariat will be indispensable. Moreover, the DG, because of his domination of the processes of interaction with the members and the governing bodies, is the only one who knows what is going on. He commands unique access also to information about what is going on in the world relevant to UNESCO's roles. Since he sits atop the only UNESCO body whose personnel serve extended terms, that is, the Secretariat, he also is in effect the institutional memory and the interpreter of its history. These kinds of knowledge comprise a formidable source of power.

Both Maheu and M'Bow have derived support also from the Francophone culture that has dominated in UNESCO almost from the beginning. An important component of that is the long-standing practice of equipping the DG with a *cabinet* that is an instrument of central control. In UNESCO it is expected that policy will flow from the top down. This has been an issue in recent efforts to reform UNESCO. Although M'Bow has expressed himself as favoring "decentralization" in the sense of regionalization of UNESCO's program functions to some extent, he has shown less enthusiasm for internal devolution of authority, beyond the limited devolution of power over lower level personnel appointments referred to above. Great changes in the organization in that respect seem unlikely while he remains DG.

One asset available to the DG deserves emphasizing. UNESCO has for many years had its own "foreign office." Since 1975 it has been called the Sector for Cooperation in Development and External Relations (CPX), although there were comparable predecessors called Bureau of Relations with Member States (BMS) and the Bureau of Relations with Member States and International Organizations (RIO).

The purpose of CPX is to stay in close and continuing touch with all UNESCO's constituencies, governmental and nongovernmental, to be informed of their wishes and views, and to be a channel for two-way communication. From this office have come the "assistant whips" who have served as the DG's eyes and ears and as his messengers on political errands during the coalition-forming phases of recent General Conferences. In performing these functions for the DG, CPX's utility was fortified during much of M'Bow's term in office by being responsible also for administering various UNESCO programs of direct assistance to member states and by the global deployment of its personnel on overseas assignments.

The DG's control over personnel, especially appointments, is another source of power. Although, as mentioned earlier, his control suffers from the need to accede to some appointment pressures exerted by governments and their representatives, that coin has another side, that is, the claim he thus gains to the responsiveness of governments when he needs support they are able to give. In addition, a number of senior positions are occupied by individuals who previously represented their governments in the Executive Board. That practice does not necessarily indicate corruption, or even bad personnel management. Indeed, service on the Board may well qualify individuals for superior service to the organization; some are able and dedicated people. Nevertheless, the existence of this practice cannot fail to influence the views of Board members as to whether or not to go along with the DG's preferences in light of the possibility that they may some day be dependent on the DG's benevolence in finding a place in the organization he heads. The ability to appoint personnel may also tilt in his favor the influence of government officials looking toward refuge for themselves should there be political turmoil in their countries, or sponsoring friends or relatives for employment by the organization.

Finally, the power inherent in the control the DG has over allocation of UNESCO funds is self-evident and needs no elaboration here.

All this adds up to a very considerable potential for the exercise of power by able, ambitious, and domineering leaders. Both Maheu and M'Bow have fit that description to a tee. There is little reason to doubt the conclusion reached by a scholar: "no nation-state represented in UNESCO can claim influence to match the Director-General's."[71]

That the DG is powerful in UNESCO there can be no doubt. Is he, however, all-powerful? To that question, the answer is "obviously not." The main counter to the DG's power is that it rests ultimately on the voting support he can command among the members. Yet there is an important tension between the power of votes and the compliance it can command from reluctant sovereign states. Voting strength, it has been pointed out, does not necessarily determine outcomes.[72] Since the real results sought by the G-77 in what is widely thought of as the North-South conflict are controlled by the rich and powerful members, majority votes that are by definition rarely binding even in theory cannot achieve their desired ends without the collaboration of those at whom they are aimed, usually at the minority end of the voting balances. Even where majorities can determine legal obligations, as is the case of the UNESCO budget and its apportionment among members, there is the risk that, as Cox and Jacobson put it, majority decisions against their interests might "diminish the willingness of the most powerful states to support the organization."[73] That is precisely what has occurred in UNESCO.

The ability to deny the cooperation that is the object of majority pressures is a source of counterpower in an IGO. The United States has evidently been the main holder of such counterpower in UNESCO, along with other like-minded countries commanding the kinds of power and resources essential to the results sought by the majorities. During the 1970s the United States pursued relatively limited aims in the organization. It worked to limit what it considered excesses in the rhetoric of General Conference Resolutions on, for example, the NIEO, apartheid, and issues which it considered "politicized," such as Israeli archeological activities in Jerusalem and education in the West Bank, the attacks on the Pinochet government in Chile, and on various alleged misdeeds of the United States itself. On these issues, it was content to use its threat to obstruct consensus as a means of moderating the language negotiated through the Drafting and Negotiating Group (DNG) created at successive General

Conferences starting in 1976 to provide an off-the-record, limited membership forum for negotiations on politically contentious issues. M'Bow helped to give legitimacy to the DNG and also lent his influence to fortifying the resort to consensus procedures that, despite their limitations, helped in balance to strengthen the bargaining power of the minority in the organization.

The United States fought hard for its moderating views in the DNG but, finally, was content to live with the rhetoric that emerged, usually joining in the consensus votes in the GC plenaries, although sometimes registering its reservations.

Three issues, however, were more serious for the United States. They laid the basis for the Reagan administration's decision to withdraw. All three posed for the DG more difficult issues of balancing the conflicting pressures.

One, of course, was the set of issues affecting Israel, most notably in the years leading to the Nairobi GC in 1976. The threats to Israel were all relatively well contained with the DG's politically astute help, as has been recounted above. Israel was given a place in a regional grouping in 1976. The 1974 decision to "withhold assistance from Israel" because of Israel's archeological activity in Jerusalem was contained by forthright Secretariat action to give the GC language a narrow interpretation. The issue of labeling Zionism as racism in accordance with UN General Assembly Resolution 3379 (XXX)[74] arose briefly in 1975, and again in 1978, but vanished not to reappear. The criticism about educational policy on the West Bank remained rhetorical and along with rhetoric on the digs in Jerusalem has continued at a relatively steady level in subsequent General Conferences. However much the Israelis would prefer not to be singled out in this fashion, they have learned to tolerate the discriminatory abuse. It seems appropriate to summarize that the pressure against Israel was contained in UNESCO.

The second critical issue was the complex of media and communications initiatives that occupied center stage through the 1970s and into the 1980s. M'Bow has been a clear partisan of the view that LDCs suffer from imbalance and distortion in the world flow of information and that righting the balance is an important ingredient of successful development in the Third World. To some extent the United States and other Western democracies have gone along with the idea that positive measures should be taken to help strengthen the capabilities of LDCs to participate better in the world's information exchanges. The United States took a lead in UNESCO in establishing the International Program for the Development of Communication (IPDC) in 1980.[75] The Western members have remained alert, however, to the pressures of some members to move toward adoption of norms and, ultimately perhaps, rules that might restrain freedom of journalists and of the media. On such issues the DG has seemed to avoid joining the advocates of change. He continues to reiterate and urge support for UNESCO's constitutional mission of advancing the "free exchange of ideas and knowledge" and to "promote the free flow of ideas by word and image" (Constitution, Preamble and Article 1.2.[a]). As has been noted earlier in this chapter, he was distinctly helpful in keeping the issue under control, essentially from the beginning of his tenure as DG. This issue too, it is reasonable to conclude, was contained in UNESCO.

What was not contained, however, was the emergence of powerful domestic opposition to UNESCO in the United States and other Western countries over these two issues. UNESCO was labeled the enemy by those in the United States and elsewhere who firmly support Israel. They comprise a significant segment of the neoconservative movement that has gained in influence in the United States in recent years, with power reaching into the White House. As important has been the mobilization of hostility by the media in the United States, Britain, and elsewhere as a result of the controversy over the mass media declaration and continuing concern over possible ambitions of some UNESCO members to pursue UNESCO actions that might limit freedom of information. The effective power of these forces in the United States and Britain underlay the decisions of both the United States and Britain to quit UNESCO.

The budget issue has been a third factor contributing to the contretemps, although its real importance was probably less than that of the other two issues. On this issue, although the United States had consistently opposed increases in UNESCO's budgets over a long period, the DG apparently concluded that the United States would be content to achieve some moderation in the level of the budget increases while accepting defeat in its aspirations to achieve even lower levels. This proved correct until the Reagan Administration elevated the issue to the proportions of a crusade for "zero growth." Even the DG's reluctant willingness in the end to lead the organization to the preferred U.S. solution did not prove adequate to stem the tide of political opposition in the United States and other like-minded countries. Widespread publicity given to waste and mismanagement as the source of what was painted as UNESCO's excessive budgetary demands no doubt turned people against UNESCO and deprived UNESCO of effective political support to block the governmental decisions to withdraw.

Thus two important members of UNESCO have removed their relevant resources—money, technical and intellectual assets, and political leverage—from the arena in which UNESCO's majority sought to commandeer them. The loss of about 30 percent of UNESCO's budget has resulted in cutbacks in budgets, programs, and staff. Simultaneously, reports of administrative confusion and recoil against M'Bow's tyrannical administration of UNESCO's internal affairs leading to numerous resignations of staff imply that M'Bow may be losing his grip over the Secretariat.

If G-77 members of UNESCO pursue the interests with which they have been identified in UNESCO in recent years, they must seek to attract the United States and the United Kingdom back into UNESCO. Without the willing collaboration of those two countries, the G-77's goals for UNESCO cannot be realized. Their plight will worsen if other Western countries withdraw henceforward. Hints that such a reevaluation of their position is underway are plentiful. A particularly intriguing one was the report that an Eastern bloc diplomat said that, because the return of the United States was essential for both economic and political reasons, the Soviet Union and its allies would join Western nations in opposing M'Bow's reelection to a third term in 1987.[76]

This chapter began by emphasizing the goal of the Western countries, the United States among them, to alter the institutional conditions of power in UNESCO to offset the disadvantage they have suffered under the one member-one vote decision rules. Such a program would surely have to include arrangements for closer intergovernmental control of the power of the DG of the organization. It seems likely that any negotiation or exploration over the conditions under which the United States and the United Kingdom might be induced to return to UNESCO would have to include this issue. If the analysis to this point has been correct, the majority in the organization might think it necessary to offer concessions in the voting rules and the bases of the DG's authority to create conditions in which the Western countries might again be willing collaborators. For the USSR, reducing the DG's power might seem attractive, in view of the longstanding Soviet doubts about the passage of power to international civil servants.[77]

In short, G-77 willingness to see the DG's powers reduced seems a condition of the return by Britain and the United States. Conceivably, it is a realizable outcome. Third World attachments to M'Bow still exist. The situation is confused. For a while, the air was blue with hints, no doubt inspired by M'Bow himself, that he had not abandoned the possibility of running for a third term.[78] The mood seemed to shift during the Executive Board meeting in October 1986, when M'Bow announced that he did "not intend to ask for a third term."[79] That assertion seems a touch Delphic compared with General Sherman's classic withdrawal from candidacy. Evidences of continuing support emanate from various Third World sources. M'Bow watchers in Paris and elsewhere say "maybe" in virtual unison.

Were he to run again, that would complicate the decisions G-77 members would have to make. They would not only have to agree to constitutional changes to cut back the powers of the DG, but they would have to do so in the face of the resistance that would undoubtedly be mounted by their fellow Third Worlder, Amadou-Mahtar M'Bow.

These circumstances make it seem likely that M'Bow's candidacy for a third term will not finally be encouraged. Another candidate would be less likely to resist the changes, which would comprise part of the package that included the nomination. The sweetener, in this admittedly optimistic scenario, would be hope that more collaboration would be forthcoming from minority members of UNESCO if they were to enjoy a more harmonious relationship with a less powerful Director-General.

Notes

This chapter is a revision of a paper delivered at the annual meeting of International Studies Association/West, Denver, Colorado, October 25, 1984. The chapter has benefited greatly from the criticisms received then and subsequently from Margaret P. Karns, John E. Fobes, Leonard Sussman, James P. Sewell, Stephen P. Marks, Martin David Dubin, Greg Schmidt, and friends in UNESCO whose request for anonymity I respect. They should be held blameless for errors or other flaws that remain.

1. See, for example, Pierre de Senarclens, "Fiasco at UNESCO: The Smashed Mirror of Past Illusions," *Society* 22,6 (September–October 1985), 10; Peter Lengyel, *International Social Science: The UNESCO Experience* (New Brunswick, N.J.: Transaction Books, 1986), 84; Flora Lewis, "A Shoddy Trick," *New York Times*, May 10, 1984; Henry Tanner, "After 10 Years as Director, M'Bow Personifies Power," *International Herald Tribune*, May 9, 1984; Michael J. Berlin, "UN Watch: UNESCO in Transition," *The Interdependent* 11, 6 (November–December 1985), 5; Michael Massing, "UNESCO Under Fire," *Atlantic Monthly*, July 1984; John Cunningham, "Disaffection with

an Ailing Institution," *Manchester Guardian Weekly*, December 15, 1985, 6; Paul Lewis, "Soviet Said to Shift on UNESCO," *New York Times*, November 9, 1985; "UNESCO Head Refuses to Decide on New Term," *New York Times*, November 11, 1985; Paul Lewis, "26 in UNESCO Act to Remove Leader," *New York Times*, March 13, 1986; Paul Lewis, "Western Nations Split Over UNESCO Head's Future," *New York Times*, June 8, 1986.

2. The letter from Secretary of State Shultz to DG M'Bow announcing the U.S. intent to withdraw said: "You, Mr. Director-General, have our esteem, our appreciation, and our pledge of the fullest cooperation to make the year intervening between this letter and the date of our withdrawal as harmonious as possible. We recognize that you will continue to do your best, in the difficult circumstances in which you operate, to make UNESCO activities productive, and relevant to the unmet needs of the world," in *U.S. Withdrawal from UNESCO*, Report of a Staff Study Mission February 10–23, 1984, to the Committee on Foreign Affairs, HR, April 1984, 52–53. This official view was confirmed by Assistant Secretary of State Gregory Newell in an "On the Record Briefing" to explain the U.S. decision. See ibid., 65.

3. James P. Sewell, *UNESCO and World Politics: Engaging in International Relations* (Princeton University Press, 1975), 153–54.

4. See UNESCO General Conference *Records* (hereinafter GC *Records*) 12 Sess., Paris, 1962, 424–25, 434–35.

5. U.S. Del 12 C/8.

6. UNESCO Constitution, Art. IX.

7. UN Charter, Art. 17.

8. In the UN case the Secretary-General's initiative has no specific constitutional basis in the Charter. Presumably, it is derived from his identification in Article 97 as the "chief administrative officer of the Organization." The DG's budget authority is constitutionally stronger. Article V.B.5(a) refers to "budget estimates submitted to it [the Executive Board] by the Director-General" and Article VI.3(b) requires the DG to "prepare for submission to the Board a draft programme of work for the Organization with corresponding budget estimates." Article V limits the Executive Board's role to submitting the DG's estimates to the General Conference "with such recommendations as it considers desirable."

9. Lawrence S. Finkelstein, "Some Aspects of Power Sharing in International Organizations," in *Shared Power: What Is It? How Does It Work? How Can We Make It Work Better?*, ed. John M. Bryson and Robert C. Einsweiler (Lanham, Md.: University Press of America, forthcoming).

10. Address to the 44th Meeting of the United States National Commission for UNESCO, Washington, D.C., December 1, 1980, by John E. Fobes, Chair, 4.

11. For one example among many of this view that the role of the DG had been magnified because the General Conference and Executive Board lacked the ability to guide UNESCO, see Senarclens, "Fiasco at UNESCO," 9–10. For the concept of "engaging" as it has been used by Sewell, see James P. Sewell, *UNESCO and World Politics*. I am grateful to him for calling my attention to the relevance of the concept in the present context in his letter of January 25, 1985.

12. See p. 385 and n. 2 above.

13. See *Assessment of U.S.-UNESCO Relations, 1984*, Report of a Staff Study Mission to Paris-UNESCO to the Committee on Foreign Affairs, HR, January 1985, 77.

14. "Preliminary Report of the Director-General Concerning the Draft Programme

and Budget for 1986–1987," UNESCO Doc. 120 Ex/5, Parts 3 and 4 (Paris, August 27, 1984).

15. See Harlan Cleveland, "The U.S. vs. the U.N.?" *New York Times Magazine*, May 4, 1975.

16. UNESCO Constitution, Article 1, 1.

17. This approach was advocated strongly by the State Department and by members of the U.S. delegation to the founding conference in 1945. See the records of the delegation's proceedings kept by Luther Evans in Luther H. Evans, *The United States & UNESCO* (Dobbs Ferry: Oceana Publications, 1971), 6.

18. Senarclens reminds us of this record in his "Fiasco at UNESCO," 7. See also UNESCO, *UNESCO on the Eve of Its 40th Anniversary*, Prepared under the Direction of Mr. Amadou-Mahtar M'Bow, Director-General of UNESCO (Paris: UNESCO, 1985), 18. (Hereinafter, "On the Eve.")

19. See especially Stephen D. Krasner, *Structural Conflict: The Third World Against Global Liberalism* (Berkeley: University of California Press, 1985).

20. The idea has had wide acceptance in various forms of words. This particular quote is from Senarclens, "Fiasco at UNESCO," p. 7. DG Torres Bodet said it, and Pandit Nehru called UNESCO "the conscience of mankind." See "On the Eve," 18. M'Bow continues to advance this theme.

21. M'Bow has expressed this view frequently. For one example, see his "Reply to the General Policy Debate" during the 22nd session of the General Conference, November 10, 1983, given in Amadou-Mahtar M'Bow, *Hope for the Future* (Paris: UNESCO, 1984), 181.

22. Under the Executive Board's Rules of Procedure, voting on membership recommendations is by simple majority. See *Executive Board Manual: Edition 1984*, rules 45 and 46, p. 20.

23. Thomas M. Franck, *Nation Against Nation: What Happened to the U.N. Dream and What the U.S. Can Do About It* (New York: Oxford University Press, 1985), 131.

24. See Senarclens, "Fiasco at UNESCO," 10.

25. Ibid., 9.

26. Ibid., 10.

27. See *Manual of the General Conference*, 1981 Edition, 67–69.

28. Ibid., 30.

29. An early commentator noted that "chief administrative officer" implied a less limited scope to the Americans than to the British. See Charles S. Ascher, *Program-Making in UNESCO, 1946–1951* (Chicago: Public Administration Service, 1951), 16. For examples of the American view, see Evans, *United States*, 41, 60, 63, 71, 81, 98–100. See also Leon Gordenker, "Development of the UN System," in *The U.S., The UN, and the Management of Global Change*, ed. Toby Trister Gati (New York: New York University Press, 1983), p. 28.

30. Ambassador M. Mourik, "UNESCO: Problems of Politicization in the UN," lecture given December 4, 1985 in a series organized by the Netherlands Association for International Affairs and the Institute of Social Studies in the Hague.

31. See Robert W. Cox, Harold K. Jacobson, eds., *The Anatomy of Influence: Decision Making in International Organization* (New Haven, Conn.: Yale University Press, 1973), 8–12.

32. Ibid., 9.

33. Senarclens, "Fiasco at UNESCO," 9.

34. *Report* of the U.S. Delegation to the 20th General Conference of UNESCO (Paris, 1978), 40.

35. The descriptions of these two affairs rely heavily on the author's observations at the time. See also Lawrence S. Finkelstein, "The United States and Public Policy in UNESCO," Paper prepared for the Annual Convention of the International Studies Association; *Report* of the U.S. Delegation to the 20th General Conference of UNESCO (Paris, 1978); Diary notes of William Attwood, member of the U.S. Delegation to the 20th session of the UNESCO General Conference.

36. "21st UNESCO General Conference: Assessment of Information and Communications Issues" (mimeo, n.d., document distributed to U.S. National Commission for UNESCO, 44th Meeting, Washington, D.C., December 1–3, 1980), 8–9, 10–11.

37. *U.S. Withdrawal from UNESCO,* Hearings before the Subcommittee on Human Rights and International Organizations and on International Operations of the Committee on Foreign Affairs, HR, April 25, 26, and May 2, 1984, 29.

38. Inference drawn by the author from interview with DG M'Bow (Paris, May 29, 1984).

39. *Anatomy of Influence,* 398.

40. Paul R. Saunders and Leon Gordenker, "Executive Leadership and Influence in International Organizations," Prepared for Annual Meeting, International Studies Association, February 22, 1978, Washington, D.C., 22.

41. *Anatomy of Influence,* 379.

42. "Regulations for the General Classification of the Various Categories of Meetings Convened by UNESCO," *Manual of the General Conference,* 1981, 97.

43. GC Res. 4.143, November 29, 1976.

44. *UNESCO 1977–1978: Report of the Director-General on the Activities of the Organization in 1977–1978* (Communicated to Member States and the Executive Board in Accordance with Article VI.3.b. of the Constitution.), Doc. 21 C/3, xiii–xiv; and Amadou-Mahtar M'Bow, "Foreword," in Sean McBride, et al., *Many Voices: One World: Towards a New More Just and More Efficient World Information and Communication Order* (Paris: UNESCO, 1980), xiv–xv.

45. For the list see *Many Voices: One World,* 295.

46. Franck, *Nation Against Nation,* 134–35.

47. Richard Hoggart, *An Idea and Its Servants: UNESCO from Within* (London: Chatto & Windus, 1978), 141.

48. Author's recollection, confirmed in conversation May 12, 1984 with Dean Harlan Cleveland and in conversation, October 23, 1984, with former Assistant Secretary of State Samuel de Palma.

49. See Sewell, *UNESCO and World Politics,* 118.

50. The last Programme and Budget adopted over the dissent of the United States covered the biennium 1984–85. See UNESCO, *Approved Programme and Budget for 1984–1985.* 22 C/5 Approved (the "Green Book"). It was the first of three biennial programs and budgets to implement the current Medium Term Plan. See UNESCO, *Second Medium Term Plan (1984–1989).* 4XC/r Approved.

51. "Executive Summary of the U.S./UNESCO Policy Review," (Appendix 6) in *U.S. Withdrawal from UNESCO,* Report of a Staff Study Mission, February 10–23, 1984, to the Committee on Foreign Affairs, HR, April 1984, 101.

52. U.S. General Accounting Office (GAO), *Improvements Needed in UNESCO's Management, Personnel, Financing and Budgeting Practices,* November 20, 1984, (GAO/NSIAD-85-32), 80.

53. UNESCO, *The Participation Programme of the United Nations Educational, Scientific and Cultural Organization: Why, What, How?* 1978.

54. 22 C/5 Approved, p. 631.

55. GC Res. 15.8.6, November 22, 1983. See also GAO, *Improvements*, 95–98.

56. Ibid., 97.

57. Ibid., 98–102.

58. Decision 4.1.1 III, 107 EX/Decisions, June 15, 1979.

59. "The 1985 General Conference: A Renewed Commitment to UNESCO," Canadian Commission for UNESCO, *Bulletin* 1 (February 1986): 3. The figures are more indicative than exact because, among other things, the budget will have to be reduced by some 5 percent to account for the withdrawal of the United Kingdom and Singapore.

60. See *Manual of the General Conference*, 1981, 77, esp. Arts. 10–12, and 82–85.

61. Hoggart, *An Idea and Its Servant*, 47–51, 153–54; Senarclens, "Fiasco at UNESCO," 11; Letter to the Director-General by Peter Lengyel (former editor, *International Social Science Journal*), May 30, 1984, excerpted widely in the press. See Lengyel, *International Social Science*, fn. 69.

62. Hoggart, *An Idea and Its Servant*, 143–44, 148–49, 152–54.

63. "Rapport Oral du Directeur général sur l'activité de l'organization depuis le 118e session," Doc. 119 Ex/Inf. 3 (prov.), May 9, 1984, 15.

64. *Report of the Temporary Committee of the Executive Board Responsible for Reviewing the Functioning of the Organization*, Doc. 120 Ex/3, October 3, 1984, 16, 72.

65. Such governmental intervention, of course, violates Article 4, 5 of UNESCO's Constitution. For an amusing anecdote about this phenomenon, in the UN rather than UNESCO, see Franck, *Nation Against Nation*, 108–9.

66. UNESCO, *Staff Regulations and Staff Rules*, 1983, esp. Rule 104.1 and Regulation 9.1, 9.1.1, 9.1.2.

67. See Lengyel, *International Social Science*, 90.

68. Hoggart, *An Idea and Its Servant*, 148.

69. Robert W. Cox, "The Executive Head: An Essay on Leadership in International Organization," in *International Organization: Politics and Process*, ed. Leland M. Goodrich and David A. Kay (Madison, Wis.: University of Wisconsin Press, 1973), 163.

70. Lengyel has pointed to the "rare degree of contradiction when an international organization like UNESCO proposes as it does repeatedly in [the second Medium Term Plan] to intervene in a process that can only mature from within the areas concerned." See Lengyel, *International Social Science*, 106–8.

71. James P. Sewell, "Pluralism Rampant," in *The Anatomy of Influence*, 173.

72. Ibid., 419–20.

73. Ibid.

74. See Charles William Maynes, "American Policies in the United Nations," in *U.S. Policy in International Institutions: Defining Reasonable Options in an Unreasonable World*, ed. S. M. Finger and J. R. Harbert (Boulder, Colo.: Westview Press, 1978), 413.

75. "On the Eve," 162.

76. Paul Lewis, "Soviet Said to Shift on UNESCO," *New York Times*, November 9, 1985.

77. For a recent Soviet position about the international civil service in UNESCO, see Lengyel, *International Social Science,* 35.

78. "UNESCO Head Refuses to Decide on New Term," *New York Times,* November 11, 1985; Paul Lewis, "26 in UNESCO Act to Remove Leader," *New York Times,* March 13, 1986.

79. "M'Bow Announces He Will Not Be Candidate for Third Term as UNESCO Director-General," UNESCO News Release, UNESCO/NYO/86-10A, October 7, 1986.

14

"Truly" International Bureaucracies:

Real or Imagined?

Robert S. Jordan

International Administrations were intended to form a nucleus of international forces around which a global community would develop. While no one seriously expected sovereign states to subordinate what they perceived as their national interests to the good of a wider community, theorists reasonably hoped that the international civil service might transcend nationalism.—T. G. Weiss, International Bureaucracy

●

The debate over the nature and functions of international bureaucracies has gone on at least since the founding of the League of Nations, when Lord Hankey (then Sir Maurice Hankey) and Sir Eric Drummond (first Secretary-General of the League of Nations and, later, Lord Perth), both from the United Kingdom, disagreed as to how best to organize the League Secretariat. Even though Sir Eric's announced conception of a politically neutral international secretariat modeled after the British secretariat tradition appeared to prevail over Hankey's proposal to have national delegations in the Secretariat, he had to compromise in individual appointments with that "pure" conception as a result of pressure from member governments.[1] His successor, Joseph Avenol, commented upon leaving office in 1939, perhaps with relief as the organization was buffeted by the ideological and power clashes of Europe in the mid-1930s:

"In this heartbreaking hour, I found ease in the simplest duty: being faithful to my country."[2]

Being faithful to one's country is the prime value of nationalism and is a value to which both of the two major powers in contemporary world politics have held, albeit not without mixed feelings as far as the United States' overall commitment to the Drummond conception is concerned. Nonetheless, even the United States, initially the most forceful exponent of the "pure" concept of an international secretariat composed of nationals of the member-states who were loyal only to the organization in which they served, before too long compromised this principle. The relevant provision is in Article 100 of the United Nations Charter:

> 1. In the performance of their duties the Secretary-General and the staff shall not seek or receive instructions from any government or from any other authority external to the Organization. They shall refrain from any action which might reflect on their position as international officials responsible only to the Organization.
>
> 2. Each member of the United Nations undertakes to respect the exclusively international character of the responsibilities of the Secretary-General and the staff and not to seek to influence them in the discharge of their responsibilities.

In Article 101, the pursuit of "highest standards" in recruitment is paramount over due regard for "geographical distribution." As we shall see later on, this provision was honored more in the breach after decolonization created intense political pressures on the Secretary-General and the Executive Heads of the various United Nations Specialized Agencies to make room in their Secretariats for nationals of the new member-states.

As to Article 100, in 1952 the United States raised the issue of the "national loyalty" of its citizens employed as international civil servants when President Truman issued Executive Order 10422. This order, which appeared to violate paragraph 2 of Article 100, required a full field security investigation not only of all United States nationals to be recruited by the United Nations, but of all United States nationals already working for the organization. Not unexpectedly, this political "means test" aroused strong domestic opposition, which came to a head when an American under investigation who had invoked the Fifth Amendment was dismissed.

The International Court of Justice was asked in 1954 to consider the case, which had first been appealed to the United Nations Administrative Tribunal as a case of wrongful discharge. The Tribunal had ruled in favor of the complainant and had awarded damages, which the Secretary-General, as the administrative head of the Secretariat, was obligated to pay.[3] The General Assembly, at the urging of the United States (i.e., the insistence of Congress), was about to refuse to vote the budgetary appropriation necessary to make the payment. The Court, however, ruled that the General Assembly did not have total budgetary power according to the will of a majority of the member-states, because the Assembly had created the Administrative Tribunal and had enacted the Staff Regulations that empowered the Tribunal to decide on cases concerning personnel management. The Court, in fact, was of the view that the General Assembly, being composed of representatives of member-governments, and acting as a political organ, was not suited to act as a judicial organ. As was said: "the assignment of the budgetary function to the General Assembly cannot be regarded as conferring upon it the right to refuse to give effect to the obligation arising out of an award of the Administrative Tribunal."[4]

The reason this case is cited here is that it demonstrates that virtually from the earliest days of the United Nations, ideological predisposition aside, the member-states have resisted openly the provisions either of Article 100 or of 101. To put it bluntly, along with the lapse of the United States and the outright and consistent rejection by the Soviet Union of Article 100, the progressive de-Westernization of the United Nations—a process that has gone on for at least twenty-five of the United Nations' forty years—has brought with it an open challenge to Article 101. Both situations reflect differing national concepts of bureaucratic responsiveness to political authority.

Why then is it important even to make this point in a chapter of a book discussing the general subject of the "politics of value allocation" as a means of commemorating the fortieth anniversary of the United Nations? The answer is, quite simply, that even in the breach of the principles, there persists the notion that there is an international administrative norm, expressed in Articles 100 and 101, that sets the limits of acceptable bureaucratic behavior for international civil servants. This norm, even though often compromised and openly flouted, stands as an alternative to the primacy of nationalism as the ultimate measure of the international as well as national behavior of the citizen. Somehow, even when the authoritarian regimes of either the Right or the Left insist on political orthodoxy from their nationals serving in, or nominated by, international organizations, one can discover a persisting, almost nagging, tug in the direction of at least nonnationalism, if not devoted political loyalty to the organization in which they serve, on the part of international civil servants.

Can a Value Allocation Be Made Between "High" and "Low" Politics?

Can a distinction be made as between the "high" politics of a state's security considerations (power-politics) and the world's humanitarian needs, perhaps labeled "low" politics?[5] If so, then it follows that those members of an international secretariat engaged in international organizational activities involving the "high" politics of the member-states would be least likely either to be predisposed, or to be given the opportunity, to behave according to the "pure" theory.

Conversely, those members of an international secretariat engaged in "low" politics would be predisposed and able to carry out their official duties without necessary reference to their own state's interests. But as Thomas Weiss put it: "Commitment to the primacy of an individual nation's security aims militates against a consideration of a possible political consensus that would result from satisfying purely non-security, welfare needs."[6] Or, to put it another way: "all peace-keeping interventions are proclaimed as 'non-political' and all assistance activities, no matter how far-ranging and politically significant, are described as 'technical.' "[7] In fact, both are highly political, and the international civil servants, whether members of a United Nations military force or civilian specialists, are engaged in acts of "intervention" in the domestic affairs of one or more member-states. Andrew Scott summed it up thus (and in so doing erased any theoretical distinction between "high" and "low" politics):

> The behavior of even well-established organizations may be indeterminate at times, for an international organization does not have a mind or soul to guide it along a consistent path. There is no General Will determining the actions of the United Nations, for instance. Calling an organization 'international' does nothing to remove its decision-making processes from the political arena. Its decisions will still be produced by a political process, one that reflects the preferences and relative strengths of the nations involved.[8]

In fact, at one time immediately prior to the outbreak of World War II the notion was entertained that two separate, distinct kinds of international organizations would be needed: one devoted to security questions (i.e., dispute settlement) and one devoted to economic and social questions (i.e., welfare and humanitarian). Presumably, by drawing this distinction, the dilemma that persists today would have been avoided. Lord Hankey's conception of a secretariat including national delegations could be seen as applying to the political organ(s) created to deal with "high" politics, and therefore the prime value of national loyalty would be understood and accepted; Sir Eric Drummond's conception of a politically neutral cadre of international civil servants on permanent appointment could be seen as applying to the international bureaucracies created to deal with "low" politics, and thereafter the alternative value of international loyalty would be understood and accepted.

The trouble with this distinction is that it is not supported by the evidence from the League. Drummond took charge of an organization that was almost exclusively created to deal with "high" politics, and the fact that the peacemakers of Versailles neglected to take account of the economic and social consequences of their settlement, and thereafter the ultimate effect on the domestic politics of its member-states, contributed to the League's failure. So we are once again left with the necessity of embracing an all-inclusive notion that *all* activities of international organizations are by definition "political" and hence the duties performed by their bureaucracies must also be considered "political" in nature—subject to conflicting national aspirations and interests.[9] Small wonder, therefore, that the civil servants composing these international bureaucracies are under constant tension as they seek the "international" mandate to guide them in the performance of their duties.

"Loyalty" Is Often in the Eye of the Beholder

Generally speaking, when it comes to peace or conflict issues, there is no single "international bureaucracy" that moves and shapes events. For the United Nations, for example, there is a section of the Secretariat that works under the Under Secretary-General for Political and Security Council Affairs; there is a small number of international civil servants who work directly for the Secretary-General either as part of his "office" or who are directly responsible to him or his chief aides, and there is perhaps some minor element of military forces or observer corps composed of seconded officers and enlisted personnel who are kept carefully on a national string in case conditions turn against the contributing states' interests.[10] But even here, partly because of the Security Council veto, the pressure *not* to do something is often greater when an international crisis occurs, than the pressure to do something.

As regards economic and social activities, Roland Vaubel has observed that "international organizations allow national politicians to get rid of unpleasant chores by letting the world agencies do their dirty work."[11] He cites the changing roles of GATT and the IMF as examples, but it could be equally applied to the UN High Commissioner for Refugees, the UN Environment Program, the UN Fund for Population Activities, etc. He also noted that international meetings and conferences involving multilateral decisionmaking can provide opportunities for the mutual approval of each other's policies, helping to stifle any political objections at home. Or, the mere fact that negotiations are taking place—as, for example, between the United States and the Soviet Union over arms control issues— can stifle domestic or allied discontent without in fact intending anything to come from the negotiations. Thus, international bureaucracies are at times virtual cat's paws of their member-states.

An example of an attempt at national control is provided by Arkady Shevchenko, former Soviet Under Secretary-General for Political and Security Council Affairs, in the memoirs he wrote after his defection:

> I set about establishing in my department order and discipline according to the inflexible Soviet model I was accustomed to. I insisted that all documents, even insignificant ones, be submitted for my clearance and approval, creating bottlenecks at every turn. I demanded that all contacts of my senior staff with other departments of the Secretariat be approved by me. Nothing was too minuscule for my attention. I even attempted to encroach upon the responsibilities and functions of other departments.[12]

Bureaucracies, however, have a way of adapting. As Michael J. Berlin reported: "Westerners who worked under Shevchenko recall that they would habitually prepare two different reports on sensitive subjects. The real one would go directly to the Secretary General, quietly. The second would go through Shevchenko, who, they assumed, would send it to Moscow before forwarding it, possibly in altered form, to the Secretary General."[13]

The Soviet Union is often pointed out as the prime violator of the "pure" concept, but even the United States has been prepared at times to violate aspects of it. This leads to the problem of using the United Nations Secretariat for purposes of national espionage and intelligence-gathering, a subject that has received considerable publicity of late in the American press. Although the tendency of the Soviet Union and the Soviet-bloc states to engage in this practice is well-documented and often deplored, other states are not without sin. After all, when Arkady Shevchenko asked the United States government—presumably in the form of an agent of the Central Intelligence Agency—for political asylum, the response according to Shevchenko was only if he would continue to serve in his high United Nations post as an anti-Soviet American agent. As he put it:

> Johnson broke into my thoughts: "A minute ago you said you wanted to do something worthwhile. Do you think that defecting is the only way you can do this?"
>
> "Well . . . " I hesitated. "By defecting I can contribute a great deal."
>
> "There's no doubt about that," he said. "But think about how much more you could do if you stayed where you are a little while."[14]

Although, as mentioned earlier, the United States is overall a consistent supporter of leaving its nationals and the nationals of other member-states alone in the pursuit of their duties as international civil servants, obviously, exceptions can be assumed to be made. The same cannot be said for many—perhaps most—of the member-states. Is the Soviet Union the only United Nations member to pursue objectives such as the following?

(1) to ensure that the Soviet Union and other Socialist states occupy approximately one-third of the professional positions in the Secretariat.

(2) to ensure that these positions are filled by persons proposed by the government, rather than through direct, or competitive, recruitment by the UN.

(3) to prevent the creation of a career international civil service and to ensure that Soviet citizens be limited to serving a five- (exceptionally eight-) year contract, after which they are to be recycled back home, with some possibility of serving a second term later.

(4) to ensure that Soviet citizens serving in the Secretariat act as representatives, directly serving Soviet interests in the UN and, to some extent, representing UN interests in Soviet circles.

(5) to secure specific, important, and even semi-important posts as the hereditary right of Soviet citizens, to be passed along from one incumbent to the next.[15]

Institutionally, Can We Speak of "Globalism?"

If it is indeed true that form follows function in the evolution of international organizations, can we also say that practice determines values in the definition of the attributes of international bureaucracies? Or, perhaps, as is true of the human condition as such, can a worthy abstract principle (the "pure" concept of the international civil service) be tied to another worthy abstract principle (a "global" concept of some of the basic challenges of mankind), yet have their admittedly imperfect realization achieved through mere mundane means? In other words, can a formally Charter-inspired denationalized cadre of international civil servants, formed into an international bureaucracy (or bureaucracies), focus on global issues, yet work to achieve them in an international political system constrained by the value of nationalism in order to protect the primacy of the national interest?

To overcome, or to bridge, the apparent contradiction, there have been numerous attempts to analyze international organizations and their functions in the abstract, sometimes with interesting results. For example, Robert McLaren observed that it is quite possible to analyze international organizational activities without necessarily calling them such. He notes twelve commonly accepted analytic approaches to the study of the interstate system that share the trait of *not* referring to the United Nations, at least in its institutional sense, although obviously none of them can avoid the "presence" of the United Nations operationally. These are: national interest studies; power theories ("balance of power," the "ingredients" of national power, or capabilities analysis); equilibrium and stability analysis; geopolitical approach; imperialism; nationalism, war and peace; community; market approach (international trade); law and institutions (to regulate the conduct of nation-states); value theory (sources of behavior); and means-end analysis (techniques to achieve objectives).[16]

Explicit, of course, is the assumption that none of these analytic approaches can approximate reality without the implied intrusion of some form of international bureaucracy, whatever the nature. What is interesting, though, is that the variety of ways that states can interact with one another is so complex that abstract models are needed to capture the interaction. Andrew Scott perceived this phenomenon in his discussion of the prevalence of international organizations in the informal as well as formal intervention in states, when he observed: "When institutions do not behave the way they are expected to, men may ultimately have to change their ideas. In the short run, however, a typical human response is the development of fictions that serve to obscure the contradiction between expectation and reality."[17] "Globalism," along with the "pure" concept, in my opinion, is such a necessary fiction to bridge the contradiction between expectation and reality when the performance of international organizations is examined.

Bureaucracies perform functions; international organizations can be designed to prevent as well as to promote national interactions in pursuit of a global goal, depending on fluctuating circumstances.[18] Thus the contradiction between expectation and reality. The veto by one or more of the five Permanent Members in the Security Council as a means to prevent multilateral peacekeeping action is an obvious example of frustrating what otherwise might be a firm majority reflecting the sentiments of the membership as a whole. The expectation was that the veto would be used sparingly, if at all. Similarly, an expectation was aroused early in the life of the United Nations that the Uniting for Peace Resolution would restore peacekeeping effectiveness to the organization by providing that when the Security Council is "unable to act" because of the veto, the issue could be taken to the General Assembly where action could be voted by a majority of the member states. Unfortunately, in practice, such an unobstructed majority found that an effective voting minority could ignore the General Assembly, thus frustrating not only the majority but also the Secretary-General and his staff.

The tension that thus results from the contradiction between expectation and reality can leave the international civil servant either in a condition of impotence, reacting to the natural or imposed inertia of his organization, or paradoxically in a condition of considerable influence, pressing on both his organization and on the organization's member states new, renewed, or altered global responsibilities.[19] We are already familiar with Dag Hammarskjöld's apparent success, after the Suez crisis, in formulating a doctrine of "preventive diplomacy" to justify the United Nations' military and/ or diplomatic intervention in situations that he termed threats to peace. And we are also familiar with the eventual consequences of his applying this doctrine in a situation in which the United Nations itself was seen as a threat to the peace by an important segment of the membership.[20]

More recently, and not in overt conflict situations, the effort taken up by UNCTAD to establish orderly marketing agreements for primary commodities, and the persistent effort by UNESCO to develop a "New World Information Order" are two very controversial examples of aggressive secretariat involvement in initiatives in the pursuit of a goal viewed by a significant segment of the international community as "global" that subsequently have foundered because of the fragmented, nonglobal nature of the international political system. Nonetheless, as one observer commented: "Citizens often are interested when new organizations are in the planning stage, but interest tends to decrease with time. So international bureaucracies can make small decisions that, taken together, have large results."[21]

Specifically, after the round of conferences in the 1970s and early 1980s having to do more or less with a Third World–sponsored "New International Economic Order" (NIEO), there appeared to be emerging a kind of "global agenda" of responsibilities being mandated to the United Nations that tended to transcend the narrow interests of the member-states, or coalitions thereof. However, when it came to staffing the international bureaucracies that were charged with the implementation of various NIEO-mandated responsibilities, the Third World member-states insisted on challenging the Secretary-General's (or Executive Heads') right to recruit without fear or favor when presumably their purposes might have been served by impartial bureaucrats.[22]

Tension developed between the national and the overall institutional interests because of mistrust harbored by the Third World states that the international bureaucracies created or reestablished at the time of the formation of the United Nations presumably did not, after the decolonization of the 1960s, acquire a sufficient commitment to Third World needs, often characterized as "global."

By emphasizing, for example, the principle of geographic distribution over merit in the staffing of the United Nations, and by reinforcing the principle of a national "range" of number and level of appointments, the Third World Group of 77 has helped to create bureaucracies composed of persons who are dependent upon the

political support of their governments not only in many instances
for their initial appointments, but also for their subsequent career
development.[23] As Thomas Franck put it:

> Suspicion of the loyalty to the international system of fixed-term
> employees on short contracts is accentuated because these ap-
> pointments are effectively bestowed by the employee's govern-
> ment rather than by the Secretary-General. Long after Senator
> Joseph McCarthy's demise, and after U.S. loyalty probes had
> waned from the obstreperous to the perfunctory, the socialist
> countries have continued to insist on preselecting those of their
> citizens who may be employed by the UN. In this, they have set
> an example which is happily followed by the new authoritarian
> regimes of the Third World.[24]

How, then, is it possible for such a nationally fragmented international civil service even to contemplate—let alone execute—a
"global agenda" that transcends nationalism?

If we look at the general field of science and technology as an
instance, which is a field commonly thought to embrace key elements that can affect not only the future prospects of the impov-
erished two-thirds of the world but also of mankind as a whole, we
find little evidence of a universalistic approach to the subject. There
have been, of course, through such nongovernmental organizations
(NGOs) as the Club of Rome and the Aspen Institute, attempts to
create a global awareness of the dangers and opportunities posed
by science and technology. There also have been many studies on
discrete issues, such as technology transfer, pollution and environmental degradation, agricultural and nutritional research and experimentation, etc. But out of this, can we find emerging a distinct
form of international bureaucratic behavior in the United Nations
system that can operate at a level beyond, or perhaps in disregard
of, the nation-state?[25] Volker Rittberger would say not likely. In
considering science and technology as an international issue, he
concluded: "A new international order for science and technology
will be a system of limited collective state interventionism based
on an enhanced state responsibility for the steering of scientific and
technological change, *especially in the developing countries.*"[26]
Perhaps Rittberger has put his finger on the true dimension of the
balance between globalism and nationalism when he went on to
observe:

The politicization of development activities and international economic relations, which the United Nations system has no doubt facilitated, serves to compensate the developing countries for the structural weakness in their dealing with the industrially developed countries. By the same token, however, it also exerts a degree of consensus pressure on the developing countries that prevents them from exploiting their numerical majority and keeps the developed countries committed to a policy of working through the United Nations system as suiting their own vital long-term interests.[27]

It is thus no historical accident, if we agree with Rittberger, that all parts of the United Nations have been buffeted in recent years by political disputes often rooted in the member-states' acquisition or consolidation of short-term national gain, which presumably suits their vital long-term interests. But what happens when the short-term national gain of some members appears to be at the expense of the long-term interests of other members? How else can we explain the political disorder of UNESCO in the early 1980s? It might be in the short-term interests of some of the Third World–Socialist bloc majority to advocate the imposition of a "New World Information Order" that would allow governments to suppress the free flow of news by restricting the movement of journalists in their territories, but it also might well be, as the Western industrial democracies claim, that if these means of control were institutionalized internationally, the long-term interests of the global community as a whole would be irretrievably damaged.

Are International Bureaucracies Real or Imagined?

In a physical sense, of course, international bureaucracies are real, but in a fundamental sense perhaps they are imagined, as suggested in the preceding section. The presence of large cadres of persons employed by the United Nations, as has been evident in this chapter, does not necessarily add up to the staffing of bureaucracies of an international organization that is greater than the sum of its nationalistic parts. Therefore, from one perspective—the global—it is imagined. Thus, perhaps a useful bureaucratic political myth is being perpetrated that serves to justify bureaucratic behavior that is at variance much of the time with that myth—or, if you will, with that ethos. Societies are often built on similar mythic situations stemming from an ethos or relying upon it for sustenance. However, we should not condemn this situation as being either at variance with human political or social behavior as such, or even as being wrong in a normative sense.[28] The slogan "We Are the World," which has energized food relief efforts for Africa, is both factually incorrect and symbolically real.

Societies encompass values that often clash; Harold Guetzkow has labeled this, for individuals, the clash of "multiple loyalties."[29] Similarly, just as national societies might erect a hierarchy of values against which the formal and informal forces in the society might measure individual behavior, international society might eventually come to the same thing. Or perhaps we are already arriving at that point. One way to examine this possibility is to measure how the principle of accountability applies to the roles and functions of international bureaucracies.

One of the major activities of international organizations, and therefore a responsibility of their bureaucracies, is monitoring specified conditions in member-states. The United Nations performs this role in a variety of ways. For example, as a result of the global ad hoc conferences referred to earlier, international secretariats were established or were mandated (if already in existence) to determine the nature and extent of the follow-up of the resolutions passed at the conferences. Some of these resolutions were directed to member-states.

Surveys and questionnaires are often used, but increasingly, in addition, information gathered by nongovernmental organizations (both national and international) have figured in the accumulation of the kind of accurate and relatively nonpoliticized information against which national or international actions could be measured. This has been especially evident, for example, in fields as seemingly diverse as environmental protection or degradation, the role of women, and disarmament. A code of conduct for measuring the activities of multinational corporations, especially in Third World states, could be laid alongside the Universal Declaration of Human Rights or the NIEO's Charter of Economic Rights and Duties of States, or various "Programs" or "Plans" of action.[30] If these kinds of norm-producing activities have any true merit—other than their rhetorical utility in attacking or defending the status quo—then there must be some credibility attached to the agencies that are charged with collecting and measuring the data that provide the political decisionmaking body with the capacity to assess the accountability of the member-states to their collective commitment(s).

However, unfortunately, the integrity of the particular international bureaucracy can and sometimes does become a political issue. This is certainly one aspect of the current dispute over the effectiveness of UNESCO, as it was over the ILO, and perhaps also to a lesser extent the International Fund for Agricultural Development (IFAD), which the United States initially nurtured and for a time seemed to be rejecting.[31] There is no doubt that the UNCTAD and IMF secretariats have been both praised and deplored as being one-sided in their approach to their responsibilities.[32] This does not necessarily mean that the bureaucracies of these organizations were entirely—or even minimally—at fault. As pointed out earlier in this chapter, international bureaucracies can be used as "whipping-boys" for what might appear to be politically inspired monitoring by governing boards or committees composed of national representatives, or by UN-sponsored conferences. This is why, rightly or wrongly, fairly or unfairly, these bureaucracies can be drawn almost willy-nilly into the politics of monitoring.

There is a view, however, that "advocacy" international secretariats perform more useful roles than international secretariats that try to avoid political controversy (if that is ever possible). Perhaps the range of international organizational activities involving the United Nations—pluralism if you will—simply defies any attempt to establish a common code of conduct or behavior for international civil servants. If the particular mandate for the secretariat unit is highly controversial politically, such as those of the special units concerned with Palestinians or with South Africans, then the civil servants involved are inevitably also going to be politically controversial. The political fates of Trygve Lie and Dag Hammarskjöld, caught between the superpowers, are not all that unique in the annals of international administration.

In the case of the International Civil Service Commission, merely getting a common definition of basic terms relating to the recruitment and career development of international civil servants in the United Nations system has proven overwhelmingly difficult. If we take into account the points made above, then the attempts by the Commission and its staff to establish a "common system" have been doomed from the start, and, moreover, the Commission should view itself fortunate if its efforts succeed even partially if at all![33] This problem is a good example of the contradiction between "neutral" facts and their collection and application in a political environment that is anything but neutral.

Therefore, a "real" or "pure" international bureaucracy, in the sense of being politically neutral, must be viewed as imaginary in many if not most of the various agencies of the United Nations system. The reality more closely approximates the highly politicized bureaucracies of most of the member-states. Just as it is often true that the national bureaucracies are viewed as bearing the responsibility of ensuring the continuation in power of the dominant political party or perhaps military faction, and not as ready to serve any other parties or factions that may be standing in the wings, it may equally be more "real" that, at best, international bureaucracies inevitably are intended to preserve the current political mandates of their organizations and thus inevitably are vulnerable to accusations of political partiality (as well as laziness, corruption, etc.) by those elements of the membership opposed to the status quo.[34]

Why, then, continue to promote an image, or imaginary or mythical standard of conduct, for international civil servants when the reality is often otherwise? Obviously, in the example of accountability through monitoring that we have chosen, the only explanation is that the principle (or value) of accountability as a justifiable mandate for an international bureaucracy can best be achieved by preserving this image. Otherwise, accountability, in its meaning of measuring the actual performance in a certain sector of international and/or national life becomes itself a hopeless captive of political contention and can only lead to more international political confusion and recrimination and thus diminish any hope for a reasonable alternative "global" allocation of values. As Arkady Shevchenko put it: "The Secretariat not only has problems common to any large bureaucracy but suffers from some special headaches all its own. The big ones are conflicting loyalties, different administrative traditions, and lack of a cohesive executive comparable to that of national governmental institutions. For instance, just making yourself understood in the context of UN procedure was not always easy: in my department there were about 150 officers of nearly fifty different nationalities."[35]

Put another way, to admit the reality that international civil servants carry around with them in the performance of their official duties multiple loyalties, rather than a single loyalty to the organization, raises the troublesome dilemma of distinguishing between those

multiple loyalties in a highly pluralistic global international political
environment that are acceptable and those that are not.

The Political Environment of the United Nations
and Task Performance

The quality or effectiveness of the bureaucracy of any international
organization—and especially those bureaucracies composing the
United Nations system—is perceived according to the expectations
that the member-states held when the bureaucracy was created. But
it is also obvious that the circumstances, national and international,
that prevailed when the creation of the new bureaucracy was considered have likely changed over time. Specifically, the tremendous
changes that have taken place in the political, economic, and physical environment of the global arena since the United Nations'
founding inevitably have been reflected in the relations within states
as well as in the relations among these states. This is why Andrew
Scott has stressed the notion of "intervention" when speaking of
the national state—in contrast to what was once called the "impermeability" of the territorial state a mere quarter-century ago.[36]

No wonder, then, that the turbulence of global and national
changes has also affected the international civil services of the bureaucracies of the United Nations and their task performance, producing new conditions under which their activities and effectiveness
are mandated and measured.[37] As pointed out earlier, it has been
a characteristic of practically every international bureaucracy that
the initial enthusiasm associated with its creation starts to diminish
within a relatively short time, and when this process sets in, its task
performance begins to suffer. For the United Nations this enthusiasm was inspired at first by the vista of a world without devastating,
catastrophic war; then by the idea of self-government for colonial
peoples and territories accompanied by economic and social improvement and revolutionary changes in science and technology;
and finally, by a worldwide (although primarily Western-encour-
aged) concern over human rights. Under these circumstances, it was
hardly to be expected that the international civil service—the mid-
wife, if you will, of much of these changes in expectations if not in
accomplishments—would remain unchanged from its original
"pure" concept.

But also, at the outset, national foreign policy goals were very much on the minds of the statesmen who laid the ground rules of the United Nations. In 1985 as one of the few surviving signers of the United Nations Charter, the late Dr. Carlos Romulo, commented at a ceremony celebrating the signing of the Charter forty years earlier in San Francisco: "The ink was obsolete before it was dry."[38] From statements at the time of its birth, however, the United Nations was clearly seen as a potential instrument of national policy, and indeed, national interests have never been very far from any explanation of bureaucratic behavior in the United Nations, as has been discussed from a variety of approaches in this chapter. It is largely for this reason that the task performance of the United Nations' bureaucracies has often begun to lag as time passes.[39]

One important cause for the apparent decline in the quality of task performance is that member-states use international organizations to shore up or to supplement their national capabilities and resources militarily, economically, or politically. They become apprehensive, however, over time, about the perceived gradual loss or dilution of their national prerogatives and tend to blame this on the international bureaucracies themselves. This has been true both for the more advanced industrial states (the Group of 24) and the Third World states (the Group of 77).

This attribution of blame is closely accompanied by a sense of disappointment that the hoped-for utilization of the United Nations bureaucracies for the promotion of their foreign policy goals either did not materialize or became increasingly difficult and frustrating. The latter is one reason for the growing American disenchantment with the United Nations as a whole, and this has, overall, had a negative impact on the task performance of the international civil service.[40] Closely related to this point is the fact that many member-states, and even the citizens of these member-states, perceive that the distribution of benefits received through the United Nations and the economic, social, and political costs incurred are inequitable.[41] In most cases this perception probably reflects reality, and this is undermining and may even destroy any hope for improving the task performance of the bureaucracies. But what else can we expect when the world is confronted with huge disparities in wealth and consumption?

One consequence has been an increasing trend toward resorting to unilateral or bilateral intergovernmental relations that bypass the United Nations decisionmaking and implementation process as laid out in the various constituent treaties and other instrumentalities.

An example discussed in this chapter is the irritability and hostility aroused in participating member-states when the international bureaucracy tries to uphold the principle of accountability through monitoring. It is easier to blame (and perhaps kill) the messenger who brings bad or embarrassing news than to blame the news itself.[42]

Another consequence is, therefore, waning enthusiasm for the notion of political and economic world organization in general. In the minds of most people, the nation-state remains the focus of their loyalty and support: the nation-state retains the highest level of legitimacy, and obtaining or retaining this level often requires engaging in protracted domestic conflict and violence that defeats the "globalism" of many of the United Nations' activities—hampering severely the effectiveness as well as the perceived legitimacy of especially the functional, technical, or humanitarian bureaucracies. Nationalism is held up as a virtue, both morally and instrumentally.

Conclusion

Secretary-General Pérez de Cuéllar, addressing the budgetary crisis and its effect on the UN's bureaucracy in his annual Report for 1986, observed:

> While the underlying causes of the budgetary problems of the United Nations are political, the structural and administrative efficiency of the United Nations is also unquestionably an important factor. . . . Unless there is some parallel consolidation and rationalization of the intergovernmental machinery and a clearer sense of priority in mandated programmes, reduction of Secretariat staff cannot but have an adverse effect on the services expected by intergovernmental bodies and the membership as a whole. . . . The present year has demonstrated anew and in very stark terms, however, that the overriding element in the financial, as well as political, viability of the United Nations is compliance by Member States with the provisions of the Charter.[43]

Put in other terms, the international civil service, caught between "global" responsibilities and "national" constraints on policy decisionmaking and policy implementation, can only muddle along, performing in an imperfect way according to admittedly imperfect criteria of accomplishment. But not to the extent that the member-states can either afford to eliminate them altogether (and thus snuff out entirely the "pure" concept of Sir Eric Drummond) or to reinforce their subordination to national control (which would represent the triumph of Lord Hankey).

Notes

1. See, for example, Robert S. Jordan, "The Influence of the British Secretariat Tradition on the Formation of the League of Nations," in *International Administration: Its Evolution and Contemporary Applications*, ed. Robert S. Jordan (New York and London: Oxford University Press, 1971). For a discussion of a "middle way" between the juxtaposition of "national vis-à-vis international" in regard to international secretariats, see Martin Dubin, "Transgovernmental processes in the League of Nations," *International Organization* 37, 1 (Summer 1983).

2. Letter from Avenol to Sir Anthony Eden of January 6, 1941, quoted by Stephen M. Schwebel, *The Secretary-General of the United Nations* (Cambridge: Harvard University Press, 1952), 21. Cited also in Thomas George Weiss, *International Bureaucracy* (Lexington, Mass.: Lexington Books, 1975), 61.

3. There is, of course, a *bona fide* question as to whether a person who might be defined legally (or politically) as a security risk could automatically be presumed disloyal. These points are discussed more fully in Thomas Franck, *Nation Against Nation: What Happened to the UN Dream and What the U.S. Can Do About It* (New York: Oxford University Press, 1985), chap. 6.

4. Ibid., 100. Professor Franck goes on to comment: "In other words, the Court recognized the rights of international civil servants to carry out their administrative duties with appropriate independence and integrity, as against attempts by member states to use the power of the purse to punish them. It is not insignificant that the U.S. judge was one of the four dissenting in the first opinion, and one of the three dissenting in the second" (p. 100).

5. For a discussion of these terms, see Edward L. Morse, "The Politics of Interdependence," *International Organization* 23, 2 (Spring 1969): 311–26; and "Transnational Economic Processes," *International Organization* 25, 3 (Summer 1971): 373–97.

6. Weiss, *International Bureaucracy*, 6–7. For a discussion of changing concepts of the international civil service, see *The International Civil Service: Changing Role and Concepts*, ed. Norman A. Graham and Robert S. Jordan (New York: Pergamon Press, 1980), esp. chaps. 1 and 5.

7. Andrew M. Scott, *The Revolution in Statecraft: Intervention in an Age of Interdependence* (Durham, N.C.: Duke Press Policy Studies Paperbacks, 1982), 152.

8. Ibid., 153.

9. Drummond did not see staff neutrality limited according to high and low politics because the mandate of the League to get into "low" politics came only after the onset of the depression, culminating tragically too late in the Bruce Report of 1939, which fell victim along with the League to World War II. Some scholars would maintain that the distinction between political and nonpolitical activities of IGOs is not drawn by a line between high and low. In my view, as global resource problems of production and distribution bear more and more heavily on the economic and military stability of rich and poor nations alike, high and low politics are blending

together, thus also ensuring their multilateral manifestations in intensely political environments.

10. There is a large literature dealing with United Nations peacekeeping or dispute settlement activities that need not be listed here. One essay that could be noted is Larry L. Fabian, "International Administration of Peace-keeping Operations," in *International Administration.*

11. Lindley H. Clark, Jr., "Are World Agencies Really Helpful?" *Wall Street Journal,* June 10, 1985, 1.

12. Arkady Shevchenko, *Breaking with Moscow* (New York: Alfred A. Knopf, 1985), 223. He went on to observe, however: "The primary tasks of the Secretariat are administrative, but there is at all levels room for intelligent exercise of initiative and influence" (p. 224).

13. Michael J. Berlin, "The UN Spy Game: Everybody Plays," *Interdependent* 11, 1 (January–February 1985): 1. As is well-known, to get around this problem, the Secretary-General can have both a "kitchen cabinet" of dedicated and experienced senior civil servants to assist him in his dispute-settlement and peacekeeping responsibilities, and an informal network of non-United Nations "eminent persons" who may or may not hold high positions in their governments on whom he can call. For a discussion of how Dag Hammarskjöld used formal and informal, national and international channels, see *Dag Hammarskjöld Revisited: The UN Secretary-General as a Force in World Politics* ed. Robert S. Jordan (Durham, N.C.: Carolina Academic Press, 1983).

14. Shevchenko, *Breaking with Moscow,* 10. Some doubt has been raised over the authenticity of this and other portions of this book. See, for example, Edward Jay Epstein, "The Spy Who Came In To Be Sold," *New Republic,* July 15 and 22, 1985.

15. Cited by Franck, *Nation Against Nation,* 105–6.

16. See Robert I. McLaren, *Civil Servants and Public Policy: A Comparative Study of International Secretariats* (Waterloo, Ontario, Canada: Wilfred Laurier University Press, 1980), esp. chap. 2.

17. Scott, *Revolution in Statecraft,* 152.

18. Lindley Clark, along with many other persons such as former United Nations Ambassador Jeane Kirkpatrick, has pointed out that: "The conventional argument is that the world is steadily becoming more interdependent, so nations must get together more to 'cooperate.' In some cases, however, cooperation can make matters worse" (Clark, "Are World Agencies Really Helpful?").

19. The best-known study of the uses of influence in international organizations is *The Anatomy of Influence: Decision Making in International Organization,* ed. Robert W. Cox and Harold K. Jacobson (New Haven and London: Yale University Press, 1973). For a general background discussion of the growth, diversification, and proliferation of international organizations, see Werner J. Feld and Robert S. Jordan, *International Organizations: A Comparative Approach* (New York: Praeger, 1983).

20. See Jordan, *Dag Hammarskjöld.*

21. Clark, "Are World Agencies Really Helpful?."

22. See former Assistant Secretary-General James Jonah's criticism in his unpublished paper, "Independence and Integrity of the International Civil Service: The Role of Executive Heads and the Role of States," cited in Franck, *Nation Against*

Nation, 287. Although the Third World Group of 77 has maintained a high degree of homogeneity in regard to NIEO-related concerns, it is also fragmented into regional subblocs whose interests are not always the same.

23. See Graham and Jordan, *International Civil Service*, and Franck, *Nation Against Nation*, for further elaboration on this point.

24. Franck, *Nation Against Nation*, 107.

25. The increasing role of nongovernmental organizations, both national and international, should not be overlooked. Andrew Scott discusses this growing form of intervention (*Revolution in Statecraft*), as do Feld and Jordan (International Organizations). See also Robert S. Jordan, *Interest-Group Politics in Global Conferencing: An Assessment of the Contemporary Role of Nongovernmental Organizations in International Organizations*, Occasional Paper of the Section on International and Comparative Administration, American Society for Public Administration, Second Series, No. 5, 1984. There are many areas of international concern where NGOs are taking a major, if not leading role, such as conventional disarmament, famine relief, refugee resettlement and/or rehabilitation, population control. The persons who staff these organizations are indeed a form of international civil servant that perhaps conforms more closely to the "pure" concept.

26. Volker Rittberger, ed., *Science and Technology in a Changing International Order* (Boulder, Colo.: Westview Press, 1982), 39 (emphasis added). See also Robert S. Jordan, "International Scientific and Professional Associations and the International System," in *Knowledge and Power in a Global Society*, ed. William M. Evan (Beverly Hills, Calif.: Sage Publications, 1981).

27. Rittberger, *Science and Technology*.

28. See, for example, *The Concept of International Organization*, ed. Georges Abi-Saab (Paris: UNESCO, 1981), esp. chap. 7, which discusses how conceptions of power have changed according to theories of power and social-economic structures. The classic reference is Talcott Parsons, *The Structure of Social Action* (New York: McGraw-Hill, 1937). Also useful is Neil Smelser, *Theory of Collective Behavior* (New York: The Free Press, 1962).

29. Harold Guetzkow, *Multiple Loyalties: Theoretical Approach to a Problem in International Organization* (Princeton University Press for the Center for Research on World Political Institutions, 1955).

30. A good discussion of the nature and implications of the New International Economic Order, but by no means the only one, can be found in *The Emerging International Economic Order: Dynamic Processes, Constraints, and Opportunities*, ed. Harold K. Jacobson and Dusan Sidjanski (Beverly Hills, Calif.: Sage Publications, 1982).

31. For a discussion of the issues, see Robert S. Jordan, "Boycott Diplomacy: The U.S., the UN and UNESCO," *Public Administration Review* (July–August 1984). For views from internationally respected humanitarian NGOs, such as Bread for the World and Lutheran World Relief, as to why the United States should continue to support IFAD strongly, see *New York Times*, June 4, 1985, A28. Also "IFAD's Jazairy: How Investing in the Rural Poor Pays Off," *Interdependent* 11, 1 (January–February 1985).

32. A short assessment of UNCTAD from the angle of task performance can be found in Feld and Jordan, *International Organizations*, 113–15.

33. One of the few external analyses of the Common System and the International Civil Service Commission is John P. Renninger, "Can the Common System be Maintained and Improved? The Role of the International Civil Service Commission,"

a paper prepared for the Annual Convention of the International Studies Association, Atlanta, March 27–31, 1984. An expanded version of the paper can be found in John P. Renninger, *Can the Common System Be Maintained: The Role of the International Civil Service Commission* (New York: UNITAR Policy and Efficacy Studies, 1985).

34. For a discussion of this point, see Robert S. Jordan, "What Has Happened to Our International Civil Service? The Case of the United Nations," *Public Administration Review*, April–May 1981.

35. Shevchenko, *Breaking with Moscow*, 224.

36. Some of these points are made in Feld and Jordan, *International Organizations*, 293–96. Also Scott, *Revolution in Statecraft*, 141. Of course, the advent in the 1950s of the nuclear-tipped ICBM rendered the territorial state vulnerable in a security sense, as authors such as John Herz and Bernard Brodie pointed out early on, leading in the 1960s to the doctrine of Mutual Assured Destruction (MAD) as the ultimate deterrent-defense.

37. It might be helpful to distinguish three possible uses of the term "bureaucracy." First, there is what one could term the constitutional usage, focusing on the legal machinery of public administration. Second, the term can be used in the political science sense that distinguishes certain general organizational characteristics, such as leadership or decisionmaking. Last, there is the sociological definition employed by Max Weber that refers to a general type of organizational structure and to the effects of specialization. All three uses have been included in this chapter.

38. Quoted in Elaine Sciolino, "San Francisco Looks Backs [sic] to UN Birth," *New York Times*, June 25, 1985, A9. Romulo was referring specifically to the fact that the delegates to the San Francisco Conference were kept ignorant of the atomic bomb, which was dropped only weeks after the Charter was signed. This event, of course, changed forever the way the world was to exist politically.

39. The point is underscored as far as the United States is concerned, for it has become commonplace for both major domestic political parties, and some of the Ambassadors appointed by the President to represent the United States in the various agencies and activities of the United Nations, to campaign *against* the United Nations, thus weakening perhaps irresponsibly its credibility in the eyes of the American public.

40. In a *New York Times*, CBS News, and *International Herald Tribune* poll taken on the eve of the fortieth anniversary of the signing of the United Nations Charter, some 42 percent of Americans polled said the United States had too little influence in the United Nations (*New York Times*, June 26, 1985, A8).

41. The poll referred to in note 40 was followed up with interviews with Americans that revealed considerable ignorance about the United Nations, its mandate, and activities. Some Americans thought the United States, which pays one-fourth of the United Nations budget, contributed double that. Others said the United Nations gave member countries military aid. (Ibid.)

42. An example of a member-state attempting to control the news is given by Arkady Shevchenko, in his memoirs: "Like all other Soviets in the Secretariat who had orders to 'use or manipulate,' I was required to exercise every effort to prevent inclusion of anything detrimental to Soviet interests in Secretariat reports or studies, whether true or not. On the other hand, I was to see that materials or conclusions favorable to the Soviet Union were included, also irrespective of the truth" (*Breaking with Moscow*, 225).

43. UNGA Doc., Forty-First Session, Supplement No. 1 (A.41/1), 6–7.

15

Comparative Politics in the UN System

Lawrence S. Finkelstein

●

This volume views the United Nations as a political system, that is, one which is concerned with the authoritative allocation of values for its society. Making that assumption does not eliminate reasonable controversy about the nature of politics in the system. Indeed, the theoretical framework of chapter 1 speculated that there is a complex "mix" in the politics of value allocation. It hypothesized a spectrum from predominantly decentralized unit veto diplomacy to centralized majority decisions, by way of an important intermediate zone characterized by struggle over authoritative allocation. The central issue is whether there has been discernible movement toward centralized authority as the theoretical framework hypothesized. The framework called for comparative investigation of the hypothesis, looking at functional and institutional similarities and differences among and within agencies in the system. Attention would have to be given the actors, the issues, the processes, and the consequences of UN system politics.

One paradox needs to be addressed at the outset. The international system, including the international organizations in the system, is generally assumed to lack hierarchy and to rest on the sovereign independence of states that cannot be bound to do what they do not agree to do. How then can UN agencies be said to allocate values with authority? The assertion that they do that is evidently implausible. Moreover, doubt is reinforced by the failure to build consensus among states that comprise the system, confrontation along North-South lines and the continuation of East-West tension, and the invigorated assertion of the national over the collective interest. It seems reasonable to conclude that these trends have reduced rather than increased the ability of the agencies to reach viable decisions about allocating values, much less to ensure that any such decisions are carried out. In this view, the international system has apparently been regressing from authority rather than progressing toward it.

One element of the paradox is immediately apparent. The preceding paragraph argues that the direction of change in the international system has been toward decentralization rather than centralization. Yet, all must agree that there has been great growth in the "domain" of international organizations. Both the range and volume of international organization activity have increased substantially since World War II. If proof were needed, ample evidence is supplied in preceding chapters. Puchala describes the emergence of the ecosystem as a virtually new item on the international agenda, incorporating a concept of community interest and midwifed by the international agencies centered on the UN. Likewise, economic development of less-developed countries has erupted as a major focus of international organization interest under the propulsion of changing systemic and political circumstances. Gregg argues that it has become the superordinate item on the UN system agenda and also describes the change as something of a revolution in the UN's priorities. Forsythe examines the extension of the original UN Charter mandate to "promote" human rights to encompass the "protection" of such rights as well and notes the spread of points of protection in the system. In the case of refugees, Gordenker chronicles the extension of the original function of the UN High Commissioner for Refugees (UNHCR) from protecting the rights of refugees in Europe to doing so in widening geographic circles and providing direct relief and humane assistance as well. Meltzer shows that the functions of the General Agreement on Tariffs and Trade (GATT) have stretched beyond regulation of tariff barriers to cover nontariff obstructions as well. Schechter's chapter underscores the World Bank's growth in scale and in the range of functions for which it provides financial support. Not surprisingly, technology has driven the creation and expansion of international agencies' functions as shown in Codding's chapter on the International Telecommunications Union (ITU), Jönsson and Bolin's on the International Atomic Energy Agency (IAEA), and Friedheim's on the UN Law of the Sea Conference (UNCLOS).

Even with respect to the peace and security functions of the United Nations itself, there has been an extension of the definition of what that involves which was not, and could not have been, anticipated when the UN was founded. This has occurred even though, as James and Gregg show, the originally contemplated peace and security "domain" of the UN has probably shrunk rather than expanded.

Growth by UN agencies has involved a variety of programmatic and operational functions. A different kind of growth has been the emergence of an emphasis on rule creation as a primary function. Regulation in this way was considered the function of some agencies from their beginnings. That was especially so for agencies concerned with what can be considered technological agendas, such as the ITU and IAEA, but also others such as GATT, the World Health Organization (WHO), and the International Labor Organization (ILO). The extent of the emphasis on this task, however, has been surprising. An important part of the extension of the range of UN system activities has been the growth in the number of issues and agencies caught up in the regulatory, rule-creating effort.

The paradox is thus complete. If "authority" is understood to include the constitutive bases for dealing with issues legitimately, it has grown extensively in the UN system. That conclusion says nothing about how the agencies deal with the issues that are thus legitimately before them. It says nothing about the consequences of whatever the agencies do. It says only that they are now legitimately entitled to be concerned with more issues, in more ways, than used to be true. Without doubt, the years since the UN was founded have seen remarkable incursions of such authority upon what had previously been the exclusive domain of sovereign states. Issues now routinely considered appropriate for consideration and action by UN agencies used to be dealt with by states alone or, if they entered into international affairs, by states in direct diplomatic relations with each other, usually one on one, but sometimes multilaterally. There has been substantial centralization in international organizations of constitutional authority to deal with international issues.[1] Moreover, the aspiration to make rules about the issues thus legitimately on the agenda inescapably involves effort to allocate values among the actors involved in the issues, especially the states. As has been hypothesized in chapter 1, and as has been shown in a number of the other chapters, that often results in issues moving from the decentralized, unit veto end toward the centralized, majority decision end of the spectrum.

Thus, the UN system has acquired authority to deal with many kinds of issues. As the theoretical framework hypothesized, and as the case studies in the volume show, it has other kinds of authority as well. As Robert Friedheim points out, it has always been political in the Eastonian sense that it has always allocated "some values."[2] The theoretical framework hypothesized, and the case studies show, that the range and significance of the values allocated have swelled with the burgeoning of the authority to consider and act on issues.

Saying that does not resolve the central question of the study. Values can be, indeed they are, allocated by international organizations in "traditional" ways, with the consent of the relevant actors and without being imposed on them. International organizations in this sense are instruments of diplomacy that serve to clarify issues, facilitate exchange of knowledge about what is at stake, develop common understandings, and encourage agreement. The authority of the allocative decisions is the authority of consent or agreement. It may be described as the politics of sovereign consent. It may be expressed in voting or decisions by consensus.

This category, however, merges with its opposite, the politics of majority decision, the "centralized decisionmaking" of the hypothesis, when the weight of majority actions is employed to induce the consent of originally reluctant minorities. Apartheid is a case of minority resistance being worn down by majority pressure, except, of course, for South Africa itself. The extreme case, of course, is the attempt by impatient majorities to compel compliance—to allocate values by voting down the still resistant minorities. Can such actions be deemed authoritative?

Some Important Distinctions

To begin with, the case studies reported in preceding chapters have helped to focus on and to clarify some distinctions the theoretical framework left obscure.

Authority

It makes considerable difference how authority is conceived. One meaning is "directives," that is, an agency ordering a state to do something that it then has to do. Alan James relies on that definition in his chapter on the UN's role in peace and security. The only persuasive conclusion is that the UN has very little of that kind of authority. Members have in general complied with the constitutionally authoritative decisions of the agencies to assess members' contributions to agencies' budgets. Recent limitations enacted by the U.S. Congress, however, raise new questions about the efficacy of this authority given the UN by Article 17 of the UN Charter, even though many judge U.S. nonpayment of what it has been assessed as clearly unlawful. The powers of compulsion given the UN Security Council have clearly atrophied. Judged by this standard, the movement has been away from centralization and toward decentralization.

That is not, however, the only meaning authority can have. Robert Riggs' chapter on the politics of law emphasizes that the UN agencies have authority over their internal affairs in ways that do not "order" states to do anything but that nevertheless compel compliance. Citing Philip Jessup, Riggs calls this a lawmaking power. Under this kind of authority, UN agencies set agendas; determine rules and procedures to be followed in reaching decisions beyond what is specified in the constitutional instruments; create subordinate organs, commissions, committees, inquiry missions, and panels of various kinds and fix their terms of reference; organize international conferences and decide where they meet; establish the principles and guidelines to be followed in employing secretariat members; choose executive heads; elect members of organs and subsidiary bodies and name officers of plenary and other bodies; and alter constitutional instruments.

The importance of decisions made under such authority is evident. Much of the growth in the functions of the agencies has been accomplished this way, as appears in the chapters by Gregg, Puchala, Forsythe, Gordenker, and Codding. In this brief treatment, one specific instance merits underscoring. The power to create a subordinate body was employed by the UN General Assembly to create the United Nations Conference on Trade and Development (UNCTAD). As Gregg demonstrates conclusively, that was not only an important incident in the struggle over authoritative power in the UN system but it has also had major allocative consequences. In addition, the agencies have complete authority, limited only by political processes, to allocate the resources available to them, whether assessed or contributed voluntarily.

This kind of authority is significant. Much of it is instrumental to members' pursuit of their ends. Much of it directly affects the ends, as is true of funds sought for program purposes, memberships and offices of various kinds that convey status, and principles that are valued in themselves. Much affects both ends and means.

Authority may also mean the determination of conclusions that, although they cannot compel states to obey, nevertheless definitively decide issues of importance to them. A majority, however large, cannot compel a state to be bound by a treaty. It can, however, authoritatively determine the content of the treaty. Robert Friedheim's chapter on UNCLOS is precisely about that and other chapters are full of instances of such determinative decisions. More broadly, the agencies definitively set the terms of reference for consideration of the issues on their agendas and for action about them, beginning with the consequential agenda setting decisions they make. Minimally, the agencies can definitively foreclose options for states. Further, they can ascribe and deny legitimacy to general practices and to the particular behaviors of individual states, as is shown in the chapters by Forsythe, Puchala, Codding, Gordenker, and Jönsson and Bolin.

Thus, giving a broader meaning to the idea of authority leads to very different conclusions about the nature and extent of authoritative allocation of values in the UN system than result from the narrower conception. Authority inheres in a broad range of decisions that are not directly compulsory, many of which do not even purport to impose duties on states, but which nevertheless constrain them.

Effect versus Output

Because the UN system lacks hierarchy and the power to compel directly, there often is a gap between what is decided by UN agencies and quickly visible consequences in the "real world" and in the behavior of the states that compose it. In such cases, judging by the extent to which what the UN says is actually done leads to the conclusion that what is said is not important. That is often correct. John Fobes' unpublished paper[3] and the chapters by Robert Riggs and Alan James emphasize the limits on UN ability to produce consequences. The conclusion is, however, often erroneous. For one thing, argument over what is to be said often serves as a means of political warfare among opposing factions.[4] Furthermore, members struggle mightily and expend considerable resources to obtain leverage to influence such verbal outcomes. Such outcomes, in the terminology of this study, dispose values sought by the actors. No one denies that they are political, in this or any other sense.

This conclusion that what is decided by UN organs can be important even when visible consequences do not soon ensue is reinforced by the recent avowal by U.S. officials, including the Secretary of State and the UN Ambassador, that the United States does take the rhetoric seriously. Minimally, they pay it the respect of vigorous criticism. They couple the criticism, however, with overt acknowledgment that, in Secretary Shultz's words, "the United Nations has a unique influence on global perceptions. The United Nations defines, for much of the world, what issues are and are not important and of global concern."[5] Beyond that, the Secretary might have noted that many UN verbal outcomes—resolutions, declarations, draft treaties, and conventions—set policy even when they do not directly change the behavior of members they are intended to affect.

A few examples will support this point. Israel has not withdrawn from the "occupied territories" and peace in the Middle East has not resulted from the adoption by the Security Council of the famous Resolution 242 following the Six Day War of 1967. Yet, that resolution, adopted finally without dissent, has effectively set the policy on the issue that guides the UN, is paid at least lip service by most interested states, and is inescapably an important part of the setting for the policies they are free to pursue. In this case, while the conclusions have not been "carried out," they have had real effects that might, perhaps, be thought of as indirect or second order effects.

Another example is to be found in Donald Puchala's chapter on ecosystem issues, which describes the "global policymaking" on ecosystem issues that took place in the UN beginning in the late 1960s. He attributed the following effects to ecosystem policies: established principles for collective action, set objectives, prescribed and legitimized courses of action, assigned tasks to member states and international agencies, and set guidelines for pooling and allocating international resources.[6] Except for instructions agencies gave themselves, none of this was mandatory for anyone. Yet, Puchala concludes that the UN processes created a set of regimes that, together, amounted to a UN policy "to pursue internationally, concertedly and with vigor a managed and balanced human ecosystem."[7] He points out that while the policies have been unevenly and inadequately carried out by the states whose action is essential for success, they have authorized actions by the UN agencies themselves that have made a difference.[8]

In the sphere of human rights, Forsythe shows how struggle occurs in the UN system over the dispensation of legitimacy. Even though states may be, charitably viewed, sluggish in giving full ef-

fect to the standards developed in the UN over the years, the standards are, nonetheless, the basis for worldwide governmental and
private pressures to improve compliance. Robert Gregg describes
how authority itself has been an object of political struggle with
respect to the international economic order. The debates and political processes not only were intended to alter the rules of the
international economic game but were also seen as establishing the
right to do that and as laying the basis for further extensions of such
authority in the future. The outputs of international organizations
thus include policies intended to change the external world and the
behaviors of actors, even when the compliance of the latter leaves
something to be desired.

They may also directly change the decision processes. Resolutions
that do not bind states do fix policies for agencies. They set directions of future policy implementation vis-à-vis members and decide
what the agencies may and may not consider legitimate in the conduct of members. They also, it deserves to be emphasized, comprise
the constitutive bases of agency programs. They set directions and
limitations for agencies' information programs. They may result in
budget expenditures.

In sum, the case studies of this volume support the notion that it
is important, in considering the politics of the UN agencies, to attend
to their "output" and not only to their efficacy in the short term.
The former are important values at stake in the allocative processes.

Unit Vetoes

The theoretical framework equated the idea of a "unit veto" system
with decentralization dominated by state sovereignty. It failed,
however, to be sufficiently clear about whether that means the ability to block action by others or the ability to protect oneself against
being bound to act. The distinction is important. Both kinds of veto
operate in the UN system. It is necessary to be specific about which
kind is involved in individual instances.

The term comes from Morton Kaplan's seminal work, *System and
Process in International Politics*. By defining a unit veto system as
a "standoff" system,[9] Kaplan implied that a veto may be employed
to block action when actors have the ability to threaten sufficient
harm to other actors to persuade them they cannot afford to act as
they wish. He was concerned with force and the threat of force in
the international system. In this study, its use has been broadened

so that it deals with decisionmaking concerning a broad range of issues, to which force is rarely relevant. The "harm" actors generally pose each other in the UN system is the ability to deny the benefits of decision to those who wish to decide. Like Kaplan's "harm," it is negative—denial of benefit. Unlike Kaplan's threat to destroy, it is ordinarily not active but consists of passive negation.

The capacities to deny the benefits of decision are unevenly distributed in the international system and are distributed differently by issues. The use of the term in this study may thus differ from Kaplan's usage because he postulated that all actors had such capacity in his hypothetical system. To give one example, the USSR was not able in the years 1960–64 to block the majority in the General Assembly from taking decisions governing the United Nations Operation in the Congo (ONUC). It had no veto enabling it to prevent the UN Force being used contrary to its interests. It was, however, able to protect itself against participating in the action by refusing to pay the assessed contributions for the force. In the circumstances, it exercised the self-protection veto, but not the blocking veto. The United States in recent years has found itself in a comparable position, unable to block some UN actions favoring the PLO but able to withhold payment of that portion of the budget devoted to this and other purposes of which it disapproves. Sometimes states lose in this way not as a matter of unavoidable necessity but by choice. An example is the agreement of permanent members of the Security Council that their failure to vote for a substantive measure counts as an abstention and not as a "veto" under Article 27/3 of the Charter.[10] That is a form of "opting out," protecting oneself against participation while permitting those who wish to do so to proceed.

The sovereign ability not to be bound or to refuse to participate is available to all members of the UN agencies. They can, and frequently do, veto being obliged to do what others decide. Whether they are able to exercise the other kind of veto—the ability to block action—depends on whether, singly or with others of like mind, they control the benefits sought by advocates of the decision and, if they do, on whether they wish to go so far as to obstruct the will of the majority. Often, the mandated procedures for deciding (the rule of majority in many UN bodies, for example) deny individual members or small minorities the capacity to block majority decisions. In such cases, the resistant members may show their refusal to comply by voting against the measure, abstaining, or entering a "reservation." They may refuse to sign the "Final Acts" of UN conferences or to sign or ratify treaties prepared under UN auspices. The

general effect of their doing so depends on how important to the
purpose at hand are the assets they control relevant to the benefits
being sought by advocates of the actions being taken.

The distinctions drawn in preceding paragraphs are important
because, while many blocking vetos are exercised, many more
"opting out" actions are taken. The UN High Commissioner for Refugees (UNHCR), for example, as Gordenker points out, involves non-
participation by the Soviet group. The Russians and their allies oppose UNHCR, do not participate in it or contribute to its voluntary
funding, but refrain from exercising obstructive influence from
within. Codding's chapter on ITU illuminates the provisions in ITU
instruments and the practices that enable members to avoid being
bound by decisions that majorities are thus enabled to take. Friedheim's chapter on UNCLOS III can be interpreted to imply that it
remains uncertain whether United States refusal to ratify the convention will comprise a blocking veto, or a veto protecting its own
right not to participate in the seabed regime. Meltzer's chapter on
GATT emphasizes the loopholes that enable general rules to be
adopted by allowing individual states not to be bound by them,
although not always without compensating obligations.

The veto exercised to evade obligation when a state cannot or
does not wish to block action by others, one form of which has been
described as "opting out," is an important component of many decisions that are taken by UN agencies. It thus enables rules to be
adopted and programs to be undertaken. The distinction between
the two ways of thinking about vetoes is a significant one. One is
obstructive. The other can be and often is enabling.

Processes and Procedures

The case studies also illuminate the need to go beyond "substance"
to processes and procedures if UN politics is to be understood. That
is not an original idea. A great deal of scholarship in recent years
has applied a magnifying glass to the ways in which UN agencies
work in producing what have here been termed "outcomes" and
effects—the "hows" and "whys" as well as the "whats" of international organization behavior. This has been notably true of research on North-South encounters, especially over the NIEO. Eminent scholars have emphasized the importance of process. Ernst
Haas has said that "What matters is process."[11] In the words of Sewell and Zartman, "process dominates—even if it does not determine—outcomes."[12] If the policies and effects of UN agencies' be-

havior comprise the woof of their politics, their processes and procedures are the warp.

The lesson that outcomes take on political meaning when they are examined in the light of the processes that produced them is reinforced by the case studies. Robert Friedheim's interest in applying aspects of decision theory to the UNCLOS negotiations led him into fruitful exploration of the complexities of forming national positions, bargaining in and among groups, the role of leadership and of personalities, and the institutional influences of a "parliamentary" setting, as well as of the processual unfolding of the results over time. His concern for processes and procedures unmistakably enriches understanding of the treaty that resulted. Similarly, other chapters call attention to such factors. Interest group pressures and bargaining figure in the chapters by Gregg, Puchala, Gordenker, Forsythe, Codding, and Jönsson and Bolin. The influence of nongovernmental actors emerges in several chapters, notably Gordenker's on UNHCR, Forsythe's on human rights, Codding's on ITU, and Puchala's on ecosystem issues. Several stress the role of the agencies in policy-forming nexuses with nongovernmental groups and collaborating sectors of governments and individuals from both the latter. Such an interest in "networks," whether called that or not, is to be found in the chapters by Jönsson and Bolin, Puchala, and Gordenker.[13] The important roles of executives and staffs are highlighted in most of the chapters and two of them, Schechter's on recent Presidents of the World Bank and Finkelstein's on the Director-General of UNESCO, focus on the executive heads.[14] Voting rules and decision procedures are important in the analyses by James, Meltzer, Gordenker, Forsythe, Jönsson and Bolin, and Finkelstein.

Frequently, the significance of the outputs of international agencies, including policies and external effects, depends on their procedural and processual roots. In this collection, that point is well confirmed in several chapters. Even when that is not evidently the case, however, it seems almost a solipsism to say that understanding politics requires attention to how it occurs as well as to what it produces.

Explaining Centralization

Centralization, it has already been said, is occurring in the UN system if that means the growth in the range of issues the agencies have authority to deal with, the diminution in the number of issues that remain within the exclusive jurisdiction of sovereign states, the expansion in the number of bodies of various descriptions that populate the system, and the numbers of meetings, programs, activities, and people involved. The growth and diversification of membership in IGOs has been termed "a multiplying entanglement."[15] By this quantitative measure, centralization in the UN has been occurring as the term has been used in this study.[16]

A corollary of this growth has been the growth in agenda setting at the center. This itself is a considerable centralization of allocation authority. It transfers the power to decide what remains exclusively within the jurisdiction of states. Members long ago lost the ability to shield from UN intervention the relations with their colonies that they had thought protected by the domestic jurisdiction clause, Article 2/7, and other provisions of the Charter on which they had relied.[17] Incrementally, as Forsythe says, states have lost assurance of immunity from UN surveillance of their domestic human rights practices.[18] The long established rule that immigration policy was a matter of sole concern to sovereign states has given way, as Gordenker shows, to definition and attempted application of international standards by UNHCR. Gregg's paper is about the establishment of the practice of discussing and, more, seeking to set rules about the international distribution of economic benefit. Much of this centralization of agenda-setting power represents the agreement of states that international problems require international responses through the UN. Much of it, however, represents the imposition of jurisdiction against resistance, as in individual cases involving colonies or of human rights violations.

Agenda setting is authoritative allocation as this study defines it. It is also instrumental to allocating the values at stake in the agenda items. The rest of this concluding chapter is about the latter. What determines the degree of centralization or of decentralization? It is important to recall that the answer to the question depends to a great extent on what the question means, as explained in the section on "Some Important Distinctions" above. Chapter 1 hypothesized that centralization would reflect functional differences and salience of issues.

Functional Differences

The term "functional" means both the topics dealt with by international agencies and the roles they play or tasks they perform.[19] It is tempting to conclude that centralization correlates with either or both of these definitions of functions as independent variables. A common view, for example, holds that sovereignty is defended most vigorously and international authority is least developed when the issue is national security, the use of force, and other matters of what is often termed "high politics." The opposite side of that coin is that "technical" issues involving "low politics" matters such as trade, health, education, and social welfare lend themselves most readily to centralized management. Similarly, it might be postulated that centralization will proceed furthest when what is involved is performance by a UN agency of a role that least impinges on states' control of their destinies. It might be expected that the "symbolic" category of the Cox-Jacobson typology would correlate with the greatest centralization of UN allocative authority and that "rule creation" and "rule supervision" would involve the least. Thus, one might expect a matrix looking like the one in figure 15.1.

That simple scheme does not work, except for such trivial conclusions as: "operational" roles do not involve allocation (as Cox and Jacobson say in their typology) and, therefore, they can be highly centralized;[20] and, when members agree readily on the performance of some essential function, such as international provision of information that can only be supplied internationally, it does not matter

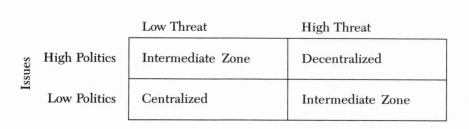

Roles

		Low Threat	High Threat
Issues	High Politics	Intermediate Zone	Decentralized
	Low Politics	Centralized	Intermediate Zone

Figure 15.1

whether the decision is thought of as "unit veto" or centralized, although the function is thereafter centrally performed.

One reason it does not work is that the approach of this study defines broadly the values over which actors compete. In a way, it defies the inherited wisdom that only war and military force really matter. For the inherited pyramid of state values with health, social welfare, culture, and other "low" issues at the bottom and war and force at the apex, this approach may be said to substitute a number of pyramids, each representing a sphere of state interest. It acknowledges that what is important to governments depends on their perceptions of what matters rather than on an objective hierarchy that differentiates "high" from "low" political issues.

Values are arranged within the pyramids. This study argues that the pyramids incorporate instrumental as well as goal values.

It does not follow that the pyramids must be totally discrete or isolated from each other. Gregg argues that, for the LDC majority, the issues interact in relation to conceptions of a revised international order that subsumes values at stake in international economic cooperation and development, racial and "neocolonial" issues, and even war and peace. If this is correct, Gregg has limned a new "high politics" of the future replacing the old "high politics" of realist theory—if not a single different pyramid, at least a predominant pyramid, subsuming lesser ones and towering over those it does not subsume. Even accepting Gregg's thesis, the LDCs are not the entire community, nor are they the most powerful in many relevant ways. That leaves room for other emphases and priorities than theirs. The image of multiple, parallel pyramids will serve. The factors determining centralization and decentralization must be sought within each pyramid, not excluding the possibility that their walls may be porous, permitting issue linkage, the politics of crosscutting alliances, and, sometimes, the necessity to set priorities among pyramids.

This study's broad definition of values implies interest in authoritative allocation of values of different kinds: the overarching ends of states implicated in the principles and rules of the international order; the foreign policy objectives of states intended to serve those ends in various international "issue areas"; the effects or consequences of United Nations agencies' decisions; the decisions themselves whether comprising policies or other forms of "output"; the rules and procedures by which other values are to be allocated; and representational objectives as ends and means toward ends. This is, admittedly, an expansive view of politics. It is thus evident that centralization and decentralization may result from the allocation of different values sought within any of what have been labeled pyramids. Particularly, the approach allows for distance in the degrees of centralization and decentralization between the processes of politics in the United Nations system and the products of that politics.

The approach thus has not generated simple correlations between functions and centralization. Indeed, it emphasized the search for diversity within agencies performing various functions. The phenomenon of salience makes such diversity more probable. It will be dealt with in the next subsection of the chapter.

Given the limits on what can be done in this chapter, a few examples will have to suffice to give a hint of the complexities involved. Of all the chapters in this volume, Alan James's on peace and security is the most "realist." Starting from a definition of authority that depends on compulsion, he concludes that the UN does not have such authority. The UN's activities in this sphere are of the "unit veto" kind. The record bears out his conclusion that what may have been the UN's greatest success, the peacekeeping force introduced in the Middle East in 1956 (UNEF), depended on the will of the states involved to have it. James labels it one of several "face-saving" operations of the UN. The same was true of the other "face-saving" operations he refers to. When Egyptian consent was withdrawn in 1967, so was UNEF. Unit veto politics determined the decision to create the "face-saving" forces and also determined their effectiveness when, in some such cases and in others such as the case of the UN Peacekeeping Force in Cyprus (UNFICYP), the mission became what James terms "fire watching," that is, to preserve a precarious peace as long as the parties want it that way. Even here, however, James finds that the unit veto quality of the politics may be affected by the UN's being linked to the preservation of the peace when the parties may be disposed to deviate from it and by the UN's ability to say things that might be politically consequential to an offender, or potential offender, at least at the margins.

When the UN mission becomes what James calls "finger pointing," the situation changes. Here, there is the possibility that a majority will take over and decide the rhetoric of the organization against the will of minority states. In the Korean case in the early 1950s the Security Council legitimized military action against the offender. In that case the UN decisions did not cause North Korea to end its aggression against South Korea or prevent China from entering the war. Nevertheless, they had real consequences beyond the choice of the targets at which to point the fingers and the determination that their behavior was not legitimate. The decisions were also the basis for the conduct of the UN war against North Korea and China and for national decisions to participate in it. In the case of the United States, the UN decisions served as an acceptable alternative to the Congressional Declaration of War, required under the Constitution. James is unmistakably correct in denying that the UN has had compulsory authority. It has, however, dispensed other kinds of legitimacy with real consequences in various degrees and in the Korean and other "finger-pointing" cases has done so against resistance. The decision of the United States, for example, to reinstitute the chrome embargo against Southern Rhodesia (Zimbabwe) was at least consistent with the Security Council's act in ordering it done. The U.S. decision overrode significant domestic resistance and had to overturn a Congressional legislative barrier. The United States, still a superpower if a declining hegemon, could not be coerced but found it in its interest to comply with UN authority. It did what it had not really wanted to do.

Thus, in this "issue area" of presumed highest politics, UN decisions sometimes authoritatively establish bases of legitimacy that produce direct consequences in the "real world" behavior of even powerful states. In cases of what James has called "finger pointing," the UN has gone beyond the original expectations of the Charter to pull Rhodesia's Unilateral Declaration of Independence (UDI) and South African apartheid under the umbrella of "threats to the peace" to permit application of sanctions in support of the campaigns to delegitimize those behaviors and to end them. The decisions about legitimacy and about sanctions were taken by the Security Council as authoritative actions. So were the General Assembly's and Security Council's actions revoking the South African mandate over Namibia. The 1976 resolution on Namibia has been described as "the standard by which any Namibian settlement must be judged, as all parties to the conflict have at some point accepted its provisions."[21]

Preceding paragraphs have been concerned with the outward authority of the UN in peace and security matters. Looking inward to the UN processes, space permits reference only to the extraordinary development of the role of the Secretary-General in conducting UN affairs in the peace and security issue area. Dag Hammarskjöld was political and military commander-in-chief of two major peacekeeping operations. His authority, it was said in chapter 1, was found "in the interstices of agreement among the powers." Franck has made the same point by referring to "the black box" phenomenon, in which the members provide "inputs" of such limited specificity that it is left to the Secretary-General to convert them into the UN's "outputs." Franck says that, as a result, "The Secretary-General has found not only voice but also muscle." He is the UN's leading actor in conducting good-offices missions and in constructing the institutions of peacekeeping.[22] The explanation is the disappointment of hopes about the role to be played by UN members through the Security Council. All the same, the result is an extraordinary centralization of roles and authority in the peace and security field in the office of the Secretary-General.

Thus, it appears that while the UN has not effectively exercised compulsory authority as the Charter empowered the Security Council to do, it has exhibited the capability to act in a number of ways that fit the study's definition of "centralization." Some of them have been consequential in the "real world."

Let us move to the other end of the presumed spectrum from "high" to "low" politics. George Codding shows that effective authority with respect to the highly valued radio frequencies and spaces in the geostationary satellite orbit is exercised by an elected body of individuals, the International Frequency Registration Board (IFRB). It monitors and, in effect, authenticates rights to these important facilities. Moreover, regulations of technical, operational, and tariff issues are in effect promulgated by international consultative committees. These are headed by Directors elected by the membership for relatively long terms of office and include representatives of private operating organizations in the field of telecommunications, such as AT&T. Study groups set up by the commissions are strongly influenced by such nongovernmental participation. It appears to be a system in which governments cede co-participation to private interests. At the same time, however, the ITU has been the setting for a developing North-South controversy, relying, to some extent, on voting powers over access to the limited facilities for communication and over technical assistance to LDCs. In this respect, ITU is an adjunct to the contest over authority and how it should be exercised and over the rules of the system that has been going forward in UNCTAD, the UN General Assembly, and other bodies in the system. Moreover, intensely political issues of representation have intruded in ITU as elsewhere. Codding's overall summation emphasizes the high salience of telecommunications to member states as the basis for what remains essentially a unit veto system, despite the elements of centralization referred to above.

There is little support here for the hypothesis that centralization will coincide with the lack of salience to be found at the "low" end of the political spectrum. The politics differs depending on what is involved. Members with a great deal at stake depend on unit veto processes to protect themselves against basic rule changes that might constrain their use of the telecommunications on which they depend. The Northern countries have sought to reinforce their unit veto powers as a bulwark against the majoritarian tendencies that have emerged in recent years. All the same, within the basic system of rules even those with most at stake have seemed willing to allow not insignificant regulations to be established in what seems a very centralized way.

GATT as described by Meltzer has similarities to the ITU, especially in the dependence of members on their defenses against being bound to outcomes that harm their economic interests. In GATT the protective veto prevails in the shape of opting out opportunities. Unanimity is not required for new rules to be adopted, and, therefore, there is formally no blocking veto.

GATT differs from ITU, however, and from other agencies as well, in the sparseness of its institutional structure. It may almost be termed a nonorganization in a unit veto system. Meltzer has said it is suffering "deterioration." While it has extended its rule-making role to incorporate nontariff barriers, it has also been undergoing a considerable diminution in its relevance.[23] Whereas protective unit vetos appear to have been a helpful buffer in the case of the ITU, in GATT resort to the loopholes seems to be destroying the integrity of the structure. In all, GATT seems to be a case of what has always been an emphasis on protective unit vetoes decentralizing toward disintegration. If its utility is to be preserved, even strengthened, Meltzer sees it necessary that GATT extend its domain, strengthen the existing rule structure, and build up its institutional capabilities. Whether these unlikely advances can be achieved may depend on whether the unifying fear of the disaster that would accompany unrestrained competition for national advantage—the resurgence of the "beggar thy neighbor" spectre of the 1930s—can be revived. The perception that a solution is necessary may, thus, overcome the incentive to compete over stakes of high salience. The "solution" sketched by Meltzer in the GATT case would be greater centralization. A recent study puts it this way: "GATT must be made to work and members to comply because the alternative is unthinkable."[24]

Such a "present imperative"[25] recurrently appears in UNHCR when refugee crises erupt. That may explain its ability to balance highly centralized executive leadership with essentially decentralized dependence on supporters who endorse policy decisions and provide needed funds and on host countries reluctant to complicate their problems by taking responsibilities for refugees in need of everything. The system works in part because of the existence of UN policy enjoying sufficient general support. That policy authoritatively legitimizes specified rights of refugees. It provides the basis for monitoring by the UNHCR staff, discreet diplomatic pressures, and financial help to induce compliance by host states. UNHCR indisputably mixes centralized and decentralized political processes in a manner that seems to work.

Robert Gregg's chapter on economic coordination and development is not about an organization at all, but about a political process. The same can be said of Robert Friedheim's chapter about UNCLOS, except that the latter is necessarily more concerned with the influence of institutional arrangements in the extended conference, which is the centerpiece of Friedheim's story.[26] The two studies are remarkably parallel in a number of ways. Both describe extended efforts to arrive at global rules in their domains, in the economic case almost entirely through new "legislation" and in the law of the sea case through a combination of codification and "legislation." In both cases, a central feature was the struggle to assert the philosophy to dominate the international order—in one case, replacement of the philosophy of economic liberalism by the structuralist explanation of underdevelopment and, in the other case, the substitution of the "common heritage of mankind" for the Grotian principle of freedom as applied to the seabed. In both cases, one of the important values at stake was authority itself, with the LDC majorities intent on establishing decision structures and procedures from which they would benefit.

Indeed, the two negotiations were linked, primarily through the infusion of the aspirations of the UN system's NIEO party into the seabed portion of the law of the sea negotiations. Both negotiations involved from the outset an intimate interaction between majoritarian and unit veto processes. In both cases, the aspiration of the LDC majority to achieve the rules they desired had to be bounded by the possibility of defection of the states that commanded the assets needed if the LDCs were actually to benefit from the rules they sought.[27] Conversely, the minority's perception of the objectives attainable had to take into account the necessity to command the majorities required to adopt rules. In the UNCLOS case that involved achieving "near consensus."[28] Both studies conclude that the majoritarian surge, which altered the terms of the international debate and succeeded in gaining some of the aims of the majority, has run aground on the shoals of unit veto politics. Stabilization rather than further centralization seems the order of the day.

These examples should be enough to demonstrate that, in the conceptual framework of this study, politics in UN agencies is very mixed. Centralized and decentralized modes and outcomes coexist. There is no clear progression along a spectrum. It is hard to discern a direct connection between function and the character of politics practiced.

Salience

The framework chapter introduced issue salience as an explanation of centralization. The idea was that the more salient are the stakes to actors with power to obstruct the less likely are centralized processes, and vice versa.[29] That simple and apparently cogent hypothesis, however, encountered the complicating idea that determination to solve a problem might sometimes dominate the salience of the stakes to the actors and enable a centralized outcome. That idea has recently been labeled "a present imperative," described as impelling the actors to seek resolution of the issues by policy action and showing them how to do it.[30]

Salience is a difficult concept to grapple with.[31] Here, it means the intensity of the importance to members of the stakes involved in decisions and actions of UN agencies. If this means national security, presumably the stakes have deep and wide import not only for the member's delegation to the agency, but for the government it represents and for the society of the country.[32] But, as Mansbach and Vasquez have well put it, while "actors do strive to enhance security . . . they are not so much interested in surviving as in surviving well."[33] That implies that issues of high salience to members may arise in all the "pyramids" representing sectors of state interest. That in turn opens the possibility that some stakes may be salient to interested domestic sectors within members and not necessarily to the members viewed as unitary entities. Thus, understanding the role of salience as it affects centralization in UN agencies may require probing into the processes of domestic bargaining as the international negotiating situation emerges and unfolds and as the sectoral interest may encounter considerations affecting other sectoral interests or some notions of the overall national interest.

Moreover, salience is difficult to pin down empirically. It gets enmeshed in the natural instinct of negotiators to achieve the best outcome they can for their clients and to claim salience of the issue as a means of doing so. Determining the negotiator's real "bottom line" or "final offer" is notoriously difficult. In this sense, even what the president or prime minister says about salience may be part of a bargaining tactic. Thus, there is a high risk that salience will be inferred from the negotiating behavior of the actors or, in the context of this study, from the degree of centralization or decentralization of the processes or outcomes being examined. The analytical logic risks being self-confirming.

Finally, salience is not static. The hypothesis set forth in the theoretical framework on the basis of the recent experience in UNESCO, that salience may be a function of change of government as much as of national interest, is confirmed in the UNCLOS history. In that case, a new administration in Washington swiftly elevated to very high salience the application of the freedom of the seas principle to the resources of the seabed, to which previous administrations had assigned much lower salience. That salience may also respond to the evolving negotiating circumstances is shown in Friedheim's exposition of how the G-77 learned that it could attach to the NIEO principles a much higher salience than had been given them at the outset of the extended UNCLOS III negotiations.

In all of this there is reason to entertain doubt that the hypotheses about salience will prove very helpful instruments for understanding centralization and decentralization in the UN system. That belated wisdom is reinforced by the sparseness of the attention paid directly to them in the preceding chapters. There are some clues, however, that may be worth a few sentences.

First, there is enough evidence to support a strong presumption that the theoretical framework was correct in speculating that the perceived need for a solution can dominate the competitive impulses of stakes salience. Thus, centralization becomes preferable to, or at least less undesirable than, defense of the stakes by unit veto. Friedheim emphasizes the importance to a variety of states, and even of relevant private interests and segments of governments, of the establishment of rules to avoid chaos in the use of the seas. That forced agreement that there should be negotiations, which were the only feasible way to achieve the desired rules. In turn, the prospect and reality of negotiations forced domestic accommodations of sectoral interests in national positions that made possible the complicated package bargaining processes that produced the treaty. Meltzer points out that small states feel vulnerable in an unregulated trade system and prefer centralized regulation.[34] The importance of dealing with the problem of the tension between nuclear threat and nuclear promise accounts for the creation of IAEA. That objective dominated the conflict between autonomy, which was more salient to those without nuclear weapons, and regulation to avoid proliferation, which was more salient to those with. The need for rules to permit orderly use of telecommunications explains the extension of ITU's functions and authority in the face of the highly salient desire of states for autonomous development of their own capacities. Reference has already been made to the "present imperative" to relieve suffering, which has enabled UNHCR to mount or support operations to cope with new waves of refugees in the face of various reluctances of apparently high salience to those affected. The evidence supports the presumption of the theoretical framework that "the high salience of a value to an actor does not necessarily correctly predict the acceptability of a centralized versus a decentralized procedure or outcome."[35]

One feature of such centralization, as Riggs well shows, is that once agreement is reached that problems have to be dealt with, it follows that those charged with the responsibility, in some cases new organizations such as IAEA and UNHCR, must be endowed with the capacity necessary to perform the task. That includes authority. In such cases, the salience of the stakes has been dominated by the centralizing decisions. It has not died. It may revive to ensure a continuing struggle over authority. As Meltzer says of the GATT experience, permanent domination by the agreement to cooperate is not assured. The ratio between the "present imperative" and stakes salience may change as a result of changing circumstances such as economic malaise in Europe or Japan's ascendancy as a world trader or changing assessments of salience. Examples of the latter are the Reagan administration's conclusion that what UNESCO was doing had become so salient it could not be tolerated, and Nasser's decision to ask that UNEF be withdrawn.

Robert Gregg's exposition of the politics of allocation of rules and

authority to govern economic cooperation and development reveals
an unanticipated dynamic that may not have been an aberration.
He describes how the economic agenda grew in salience to both
the developed and less-developed countries, both absolutely and
in relation to the other agendas of the UN system. As this occurred,
the faction seeking rule change intensified its pursuit of majority
authority as the means to attain its ends. Salience generated a preference for centralization on the part of the majority. For the minority,
the effect was the opposite. As salience grew for the developed
countries, so did commitment to unit veto processes. This seems to
have been a split outcome, in which salience produced, not either
centralization or decentralization, but a contest between them. The
same thing was true in the UNCLOS context and in ITU. That this is
so should not really be surprising. It is another way of saying that
majorities will seek to establish majority procedures and minorities
to resist them, the more so as their interest in the object of that
authority increases.

A third presumption about salience seems justified by the case
studies. Mansbach and Vasquez advanced the somewhat surprising
hypothesis that the less concrete the issue, the more salient it will
be to the actors. Concrete issues are least salient, symbolic issues
more so, and "transcendent" stakes are the most salient of all.[36] The
case studies generally support this theory. The friction between aspirations for centralization and unit veto assertions, in other words,
the struggle over authority, has been most acute when the issues
have been the overarching principles—liberal principles versus
structural ones in the economic domain, free enterprise versus the
common heritage in the law of the seabed case, and equity versus
free enterprise in the telecommunications arena. In the case of human rights, the contest has been less symmetrical. It pitted the liberal principles of civil and political freedom on the one hand against
the narrower self-interests of oppressive regimes on the other. The
contest over authority has been no less acute in this domain, thus
casting a shadow of doubt over the cogency of the hypothesis.

Salience, thus, seems very relevant to understanding centralization. Its effect, however, is not simple or unidirectional. Theory
has to take account of the volatility of salience, or at least its mut-
ability. It also has to make room for the likelihood that all the actors
will rarely balance "present imperative" and issue salience the same
way at the same time. Therefore, it is likely that differences in salience to the actors will contribute to struggles over authority. In

such struggles, salience itself is only one of the variables affecting
the outcomes.

Allocative Processes

This study is about allocative processes that either authoritatively
dispose of the values at stake, including legitimacy and authority,
or involve conflict over doing so. The latter sometimes do not lead
to allocative outcomes. As the chapter by Gregg makes clear, the
NIEO-related processes did not achieve either the endorsement of
most of the new rules or the changes in authority structures sought
by the G-77. When the value sought requires change in the behavior
of states in the "real world," the allocative efforts often fall short
of authority. It remains to be seen, for example, whether the UNCLOS
negotiations will produce for the LDCs the benefits of seabed resources they professed to be demanding. Most are doubtful that
they will, among them Robert Friedheim in his case study, in part
because of doubts as to the economic benefits of seabed exploitation
in the short term. That has given rise to the speculation, referred
to above, that the LDCs were not really after material benefits of
that kind anyway and were using the seabed issue as a means of
advancing their real interest in the endorsement of new, transcendent norms of distributive equity. In that respect, Friedheim argues,
they did better, although the outcome was a bargained one that fell
short of meeting their aspirations. In the terms of this study, such
norms are valued as ends in themselves but are also desired because
they can serve instrumentally as platforms for further efforts to alter
the world's distribution of material wealth, social benefit, and status
recognition. The efforts to give effect to rules and establish authority
over states' treatment of people within their boundaries and their
behavior affecting the ecosystem are under way, but are far from
conclusive, as is shown in the chapters by Forsythe and Puchala.

These processes go forward in a mixed and complex system, even
when the issue domains are regarded as separated from each other
as this chapter has done. On the one hand, with no sovereign authority to order compliance, the authority sought and exercised is
necessarily ambiguous, involving constant interplay among the only
sovereigns, the member states. On the other hand, as Friedheim
has emphasized in his chapter, and as appears in a number of the
others, the institutions are parliamentary, at least in form. But they
differ from parliaments in national systems in important ways. They

rest on narrower and less certain bases of consensus than is true of most national parliaments. Moreover, they cannot command the compliance of the constituency. They differ also in that the constituency consists of insiders, that is, the states that are the members. The parliamentary bodies are thus trying to allocate values authoritatively among themselves rather than decide allocations for others. The premium, thus, has to be on persuasion—convincing each other of what has to be done and inducing each other then to do it. Real consensus among states is the primary objective of the international organization exercise, the kind that generates follow-through, that is, doing what has been agreed should be done. Recent scholarship emphasizing this as the main function and rationale for international organizations is entirely correct.[37] (That slides over another use of the institutions, to gain political leverage with respect to conflictual relations outside the organization, such as scoring propaganda victories over Cold War adversaries, or trying to delegitimize Israel.)

Much of the authority emphasized in this study is central to the development of effective consensus. Apart from program allocations, which share benefits directly among recipients, and a few relatively less important allocative roles, authoritative allocation in the UN system is a means members employ to influence each other's understandings of what their options are with respect to the issues on which action is sought. Much of the output of UN agencies—the agendas, the mission and committee reports, the draft conventions, the resolutions, the declarations, and the action programs—is intended to shape the debate, point future directions, narrow the options of the opposition, bring pressures to bear, and, ultimately, induce consensus. In this sense, the allocation politics of the UN system is an inseparable part of the consensus formation that is the system's primary purpose.

Different though they are, the parliamentary bodies in the UN system share characteristics with national parliaments. Friedheim emphasizes this in his study: "parliamentary diplomacy is parliamentary in structure . . . all of the major trappings of a domestic legislature are present: formal debate, working parties, informal negotiating groups, and posts of honor such as a president."[38] Not only the trappings, but also the practices are there. The UN bodies seek to set rules, adopt nonbinding expressions of majority or general opinion,[39] allocate resources, authorize programs, and monitor performance under the rules. They also employ the same means to do these things: voting, interest aggregation, lobbying, arm twisting, "side payments," pork barrels, horse trading, filibusters, and many of the other legislative techniques employed in domestic parliaments.

This section will now turn to some of the most salient features of the allocative processes in this strange parliamentary system.

Rules, Norms, and Legitimacy

The case studies amply bear out the speculation of the theoretical framework about the uses to which nonbinding adoption of norms in various forms are put in the effort to affect the real world by the adoption of rules. Riggs' chapter refers to the fact that some agencies have constitutional authority to adopt binding rules or regulations that may take effect in some circumstances without ratification by all. Most agencies do not have such authority. Since the heterogeneity of the membership insures that they will rarely agree on new rules that all can quickly accept, protracted negotiations are frequent. When the disagreements are narrow, resolution can be reached by bargaining, in which isolated disagreements are identified, narrowed through explanation and expert analysis, and eliminated through mutual concessions. Agreement becomes preferable to continued resistance, just as in domestic bargaining situations. Roughly, this was the case in GATT negotiations in successive "rounds" of tariff-cutting negotiations. These negotiations were facilitated as Meltzer points out by the supportive hegemonial influence of the United States, which was able in the halcyon times to absorb many of the costs of enabling agreement to be reached. Friedheim describes the role of the negotiator seeking incremental improvements in the outcome when the underlying principle is acceptable.[40]

The development of UN ecosystem policies and institutions in the 1970s followed a roughly parallel path as described in Donald Puchala's chapter. In this case, there were special favoring circumstances. The whole field was relatively new so that few entrenched interests had to be overcome. The institutions were new and thus more than usually able to innovate and initiate. The enterprise profited from, indeed may well have been spurred by, the development of convincing analyses of the problem, ideas about what should be done, transcendent principles on which all could readily agree, from outside the UN institutional structure. The emergence and, hence the availability, of relevant ideas played a critical role in precipitating the agreements that were reached that ecological threats were global and real, that they were connected with each other, and that, in consequence, global responses were essential and possible. In this case, the ideas served to facilitate and promote agreement, unlike the situation with respect to the Law of the Sea and the world economy in which, as has been shown, there was conflict to establish dominance of one set of ideas over another. Another recent study emphasizes the significant role of "intellectual breakthrough" in facilitating regime formation, contrasting "the acceptance of Keynesianism as the new economic orthodoxy" making possible the Bretton Woods agreement in 1944 with the lack of such international agreement in the cases of the NIEO and UNCLOS.[41] Puchala points out the important role played by nonbinding instruments in developing the set of United Nations policies referred to earlier in this chapter. The General Assembly was employed as the means of authorizing the series of extraordinary conferences that provided the venues for the diplomacy that led to the agreements. None of these, incidentally, took the form of a treaty. All were hortatory statements intended to evoke the voluntary support and then the compliance of member states. Puchala shows how the enunciation of norms in this fashion gradually, really rapidly as these things often go, attracted the support of countries that had originally been opposed. As Puchala emphasizes, action by states falls far short of fulfilling the demands of the international instruments adopted. The normative bases for continued efforts to induce compliance have, however, been laid in the processes Puchala has described.

When, as is often the case, differences are not narrow and relatively easily bridgeable, the role of norm adoption by groups of states that can command the voting outcomes under the relevant rules is less to induce agreement than to compel it. Both the Gregg and Friedheim studies describe just such a process. Relatively cohesive voting blocs, large enough to determine parliamentary outcomes, sought to employ their voting power to put the stamp of legitimacy on the preferred outcomes. This tactic sought to narrow the options available to the minority and to use the leverage of legitimacy to press the opposition to abandon resistance and, finally, to accept the preferred norms as rules with binding effect. That it failed in the NIEO negotiations and may have failed in the seabed case does not change the fact that this was what was intended. In a nuanced and careful argument, Robert Riggs concludes that the legitimacy attaching to formal adoption of a resolution, by whatever majority

and however often reiterated, does not make it law. He acknowledges, however, that the practice fits into an ongoing process by
which states may be persuaded to accept the principles as binding.
"Denying the legislative competence of the Assembly," he writes,
"still leaves a place for Assembly declaration within the existing
law-making processes of the international system."[42] This fact is at
the center of the politics of legitimizing norms in the UN agencies.
A study by the United Nations Institute for Training and Research
suggests that the nonbinding instruments of the NIEO have had some
real consequences in the laws of members.[43]

Interest Aggregation

That voting is the principal means of deciding in the UN agencies,
of course, highlights the anachronistic character of parliamentary
institutions composed of states in a system of sovereignty. Yet, even
when the UN organs choose to proceed by other devices than voting,
by consensus proceedings, for example, which have assumed increasing prominence in recent years, the processes are always conditioned by awareness of how the votes would line up if votes should
be taken. Friedheim vividly describes the conditioning effect on
the expectations of UNCLOS III members of their awareness of the
dynamic interaction between the ability of the majority to win if
votes should be taken and the unit vetos in the hands of key major
states without whose participation the rules being sought would
lack real effect.[44]

In the UNCLOS case interests were very fragmented vis-à-vis the
complex agenda. If the voting dilemma were to be resolved, consensus or near consensus had to be sought. The primary means was
the concept of the "package" outcome.[45] This would encourage bargaining trade-offs across the issues, the balancing of benefits for all,
and the formation of coalitions across the issue lines adding up to
the near consensus necessary if voting crises were to be avoided.
In fact, only one vote was taken in the entire nine-year conference
and that was the formal vote to endorse the bargained outcome.[46]
Even so, the emergence of polarization on North-South lines over
the seabed issues underlined the voting strength of the South and
led the South to harden its positions and, as time passed, to increase
the distance between its demands and what the United States had
shown willingness to accept.

The NIEO negotiations, as Gregg described them, were simpler.

There was no "present imperative" such as had pressed on the UN-CLOS participants to agree. The possibilities for a package approach to permit trade-offs were more limited, especially as the G-77 developed cohesion over the issues, largely symbolic and philosophical, which enabled them to maintain voting pressure against the minority. The latter had no blocking veto. They could, however, employ protective vetos to withhold endorsement of the conclusions adopted by the majority, thus casting a shadow over their legitimacy. They could also withhold the resources on which material fulfilment of the G-77 aspirations would depend. Gregg emphasizes how, despite the standoff that eventuated, representing the effective balance between voting power on the one hand and relevant real capacity on the other, the predominant tendency over most of the period was the centralizing effect of the majority's ability to control the issues, set the terms of the debate, and provide the momentum of successive acts of majority legitimization of the conclusions it could not get the minority to agree to.

Human rights present another picture. Forsythe's study emphasizes the formation of coalitions to give some balance to efforts to monitor violations of human rights standards as a result of the willingness of some nonaligned countries moved by concern for human rights to join with liberal Western countries. Similarly, Donald Puchala emphasizes the importance of coalitions among Western and moderate nonaligned countries in providing leadership, which led to the wide support of the policy conclusions on the ecology adopted in the 1970s.

Only one author, Friedheim, dealt with the issue raised by Gidon Gottlieb's theory that a new form of decision process, which Gottlieb termed "parity diplomacy" or "equality between groups of states," is replacing the one nation-one vote practice of parliamentary diplomacy and, by implication, decisions by majorities.[47] Friedheim's analysis of the UNCLOS negotiation gives considerable weight to the role of groups, all of which, in effect, had to be satisfied and receive a fair share of the benefits to be allocated by the proposed treaty. This did not, however, prevent the reversion to majority versus minority dynamics over the seabed issues in the later years. In UNESCO groups are formally recognized and operate through representatives in decision bodies such as the Executive Board. In practice group participation in consensus is necessary on important issues, giving groups what amounts to a blocking veto.

Several of the chapters emphasized the central role of leadership in forging agreements prerequisite to decision. In GATT the "Big Four" have become a focal point, although not without stimulating concern among others about the risk that they may generate outcomes not acceptable to all. Gordenker, Puchala, and Friedheim called attention to the existence of relatively stable small groups of states, or their representatives, serving as spearheads in generating convergence on the issues. In the complex setting of UNCLOS III, the role of individuals serving as chairmen was especially critical in producing the draft texts that became the object of further negotiations to narrow remaining differences and produce agreement. John Fobes has called attention to the role of executive heads as catalysts of consensus.[48] Finkelstein's chapter on the Director-General of UNESCO goes further in identifying the Director-General as the leader of a majority party in the organization and a major determinant of the policies that could be adopted. Michael Schechter's study calls attention to the leading role of the Presidents of the World Bank in shaping its policies.

In all, the case studies highlight the complexity and variety of interest aggregation processes in the UN system. Despite the statements by some of the authors that they discern centralizing tendencies implicit in the assertion of majority dominance in many cases, it is hard to be certain that the conclusion is generalizable. Even introducing once again the distinction between effects and outputs does not eliminate uncertainty because it appears that various kinds of vetos apply even to the latter. When it comes to the translation of policies into compliant behaviors of states, diplomacy and persuasion still dominate.

It is, however, striking that the generally evident practices, notably reliance on voting as the decision mode, even when votes are not actually taken, the extreme importance of leadership in helping to find the bases of decision, and the widespread role of the executive heads in doing that, while they do not themselves prove that there is a centralizing tendency, do suggest that there is. And it bears noting that these practices parallel what occurs in national parliaments, which, there can be no doubt, are institutions of central decisionmaking.

The Role of Nongovernmental Actors

The case studies reflect the widespread growth of the role and influence of nongovernmental organizations in the decision processes of UN agencies, except for GATT and the peace and security organs. In all the other cases, NGOs are involved and important in varying degrees. Forsythe and Gordenker in effect consider them indispensable as sources of information and expertise necessary for decisions and, in the case of human rights, for monitoring of adherence to the standards. In a number of cases, including GATT, NGOs participate in shaping domestic positions that directly affect the international negotiations.

One aspect of nongovernmental involvement deserves special attention. That is what Jönsson and Bolin call "networking." Agencies' executive heads and staffs, or sectors of staffs, form intimate communication and influence relations with functionally indicated sectors of member governments and interested private groups. In a case reported in an earlier work of Jönsson, such processes enabled an executive head to bring about a change in the policy of the U.S. government.[49] Closely related is the phenomenon of what Jönsson and Bolin, in their chapter, call the "in and outer," the qualified personnel who move back and forth between service in UN agencies, in this case IAEA, member governments and NGOs. They are part of the pattern of liaison among relevant national and international agencies that contributes to policymaking.

Executive Heads and Staffs

Executive heads and staffs should be treated separately but will be lumped together for the sake of brevity and on the not altogether accurate assumption that staffs are directed by their superiors.

They can be centralizing factors in three ways: (1) as exemplars of the ideal of international service, (2) by performing policymaking roles as nonnational servants of their agencies, and (3) as program executors similarly engaged in the direct allocation of values.

The epitome of the concept of centralization as it has been employed in this study is the employee of an international agency bound to the service of all the members that comprise it, denationalized as it were in the performance of duty. The case studies present us with opposing tendencies. Gordenker, Jönsson and Bolin, and Codding emphasize the professionalism and international independence of the heads and staffs of the agencies they write about. Forsythe lauds the commitment of staff personnel to the cause of human rights and emphasizes the indispensability of their roles in the monitoring of human rights practices and advancement of their observance. Gregg, on the other hand, describes the importance of partisan staff, aligned as it were with the LDC faction in the UN agencies, in supporting, even making possible, the policies of part of the UN membership directed against other UN members. He sees this as an aspect of the broader development that he regrets, "the gradual abandonment of any pretense that the global organization exists to provide benefits for all of its members."[50] Finkelstein's chapter on UNESCO emphasizes the Director-General's alignment with the nonaligned. It thus parallels Gregg's conclusion.

Jordan is of this view. His chapter is about the corruption of the concept of international loyalty and responsibility of UN civil servants. United States' loyalty probes and clearance requirements infringed on the principle of internationality.[51] The Soviet Union has been the worst offender. It has from the beginning disregarded the guidelines of Article 100 of the Charter and has treated its nationals in the Secretariat as its agents and employees. The recent Shevchenko revelation added little to what has been known in this respect. Newly independent countries, as John Fobes has pointed out, have "traditions with less clear distinctions among different types of political positions and *influences*"[52] than informed the ideal of the international servant. As the new countries have taken their places in the UN agencies, they have claimed their share of places in the staffs. As Jordan shows, the result has been a further corruption of the ideal.

Not much need be said about the contributions of executive heads to policymaking. In some cases, the World Bank and UNHCR for example, the executive heads are institutionally expected to be the primary policymakers. In UNESCO the history of strong leadership by two successive Directors-General, both of whom have served long terms, in conditions of relative inattention by members has resulted in a leading policy role for the Director-General. The role of the UN Secretary-General as the leading figure in many peacekeeping activities has been alluded to earlier and need not be repeated here. In a good many ways the Secretary-General *is* the UN in many eyes. Of the agencies studied, only the ITU does not seem heavily dependent on the executive head as a contributor to policy. GATT provides perverse evidence about the importance of executive leadership. The fact that it has not had a strong executive head may be an explanation of why it has been faltering.

Executive heads and staffs play major roles, even indispensable ones, in program administration. They are part of complete feedback loops in which they have significance both in shaping the program decisions and in administering the resulting programs. It is hard to know how much of what they do is no more than administering guidelines clearly set forth in policy. Probably, a great deal of discretion exists and the staffs thus make judgments that are allocative. When what is allocated is not limited to material benefits, such as UNDP grants, but extends to justice and equity as is true of staff in the fields of human rights and refugees, the allocative functions take on special significance.

Conclusions

The expansive concept of politics employed in this study casts an unusual light on politics in the United Nations system. By defining values broadly to mean anything the actors seek, it extends politics defined as the authoritative allocation of values into all the nooks and crannies of the UN system in which what goes on is not narrowly confined to carrying out clearly established policy guidelines leaving no room for discretion. What has here been termed "expansive," some might think imperialist. The question is whether it is useful.

Finally, of course, the reader has to judge. The author believes the approach is useful. Together with the other expansive definitions set out in this study, this broad conceptualization enables us to discriminate among several aspects of politics in the UN system—results or effects, outputs including policies, and processes and procedures. It thus enables us to escape from the limiting approach that considers politics in terms only of directed consequences and concludes too readily, therefore, that UN politics is inconsequential. This study argues that, apart from the fact that some effects are produced in the real world and in the behavior of states, UN politics is consequential because the values it allocates are important in themselves and may establish the bases for consequences that develop over time.

The discrimination made possible by this approach helps also to unveil the full complexity of the politics of the system. The studies in this volume do little more than begin to do that. Yet, they reveal that many significant values are allocated in centralized ways even though the politics produces few results that directly require members to act. At the same time, the ability of resistant states to withhold compliance on which fulfillment of majority purposes depends constitutes an effective veto. The resort to this device in recent years

has been intended to check the trend toward centralization as well
as to protect the particular minority interests threatened by majority
claims to authority.

Overall, however, the studies support the conclusion that there
has been movement, uneven to be sure, toward centralized authority
in the system. That contradicts the widely held belief that, since
the UN cannot compel, it has no authority. This study suggests that
is a misleading conclusion. It may lie at the bottom of much mis-
apprehension about the UN. It does not help to design wise and
effective policies to guide our relations with the UN system.

At the level of procedure and process, the UN often decides by
majority principles common to parliamentary institutions. If majorities can command value allocations against the resistance of minorities, that is centralization of authority. It occurs with great frequency. The executives of the agencies make many allocative
judgments directly themselves and are important participants in the
decisionmaking of many of the membership organs. The executives
represent the totality of the memberships of their organizations,
comparable one might say, to the President of the United States
who is the only national official (the Vice-President excepted) who
represents all the people of the country.

At the level of outcomes, which include policies, decisions of the
system accept or reject the policies, ideas, and proposals of member-
states. Definitive decisions are made which, even though they do
not coerce states to obey them, nevertheless channel the behavior
of states and of the organizations themselves. Some such decisions
prove effective over time. Security Council Resolution 242 following
the 1967 war in the Middle East is one such document. Some take
on the qualities of law. General Assembly Resolution 1514 is such
a document. It effectively declared colonialism illegal. Robert
Friedheim's chapter concludes that UNCLOS had demonstrable effects on the regime of the seas without reference to the state of
ratification. Robert Gregg shows that NIEO has had direct consequences, a view borne out by a carefully prepared study for UNITAR.
The UNCLOS conclusions, incidentally, are judged by Friedheim to
be decentralizing rather than centralizing in their effect, because
they legitimize enclosure of vast expanses of the oceans that used
to be thought open to all under the doctrine of freedom of the seas.
In the field of human rights, the policies include those set forth in
the Covenants on Human Rights, which are binding for those states
that have ratified, other treaties similarly binding, and a great body

of nonbinding instruments. Together, they constitute a human rights code overwhelmingly compatible with Western liberal beliefs about human rights. This body of laws and principles lays the base for increasing protection of the rights under it against the oppressors of the world. Progress is already being made in that campaign.

That the UN system is becoming centralized is not cause for alarm. It does not mean that sovereign states are being displaced or swept aside. It does not mean that world government is upon us. It does mean that the world's states have been finding new ways to conduct the business they have to conduct internationally. Centralized authority in the UN is a means of conducting international relations, not a substitute for them. Adapting to that understanding of UN politics may be the key to accommodating better to what there has been a tendency to regard as alien and threatening.[53] It may turn out on examination to bear much resemblance to how we have comfortably conducted our affairs at home all along.

Notes

This chapter is a revision of a paper presented at the 1985 Annual Meeting of the American Political Science Association, New Orleans, August 29–September 1, 1985. The author wishes to express special gratitude for extensive critical comments received from M. J. Peterson and for constructive comments received also from Harold K. Jacobson, Martin David Dubin, Edward Thomas Rowe, David Forsythe, and Ronald I. Meltzer.

1. For a fuller development of this theme, see Lawrence S. Finkelstein, "Some Aspects of Power Sharing in International Organizations," in *Shared Power: What is It? How Does It Work? How Can We Make It Work Better?* ed. John M. Bryson and Robert C. Einsweiler (Lanham, Md.: University Press of America, forthcoming). For a relevant analysis of the phenomenal growth in the number of intergovernmental organizations, see Harold K. Jacobson, William Reisinger, and Todd Mathers, "National Entanglements in International Governmental Organizations," *American Political Science Review* 80, 1 (March 1986).

2. Friedheim, above, p. 176.

3. John E. Fobes, "Interaction of Administration and Politics in the UN System," draft paper presented at the 26th Annual Convention, International Studies Association, Washington, D.C., March 1985.

4. See, for example, Maurice Tugwell, "The United Nations as the World's Safety Valve," in *A World Without a UN: What Would Happen if the United Nations Shut Down,* ed. Burton Yale Pines (The Heritage Foundation, 1984), 157–58: "The rhetoric in the General Assembly that some view as useful in venting steam through the 'world's safety valve' is in fact often a form of political warfare . . . it poisons the atmosphere."

5. Secretary Shultz, "The United Nations After Forty Years: Idealism and Realism," Address before the United Nations Association of San Francisco, the San Francisco

Chamber of Commerce, and the World Affairs Council of Northern California, San Francisco, California, June 26, 1985 (*State Department Bulletin* 85,2101 (August 1985), 20.

6. Puchala, chap. 7 above.

7. Ibid., pp. 218–19.

8. Ibid., pp. 237–40. See also the chapter by Gordenker on UNHCR, and Karen A. Mingst, "WHO and National Policy: Webs of Influence," prepared for presentation at the Annual Meeting of the International Studies Association, Atlanta, Georgia, March 27–31, 1984, 10–11.

9. Morton A. Kaplan, *System and Process in International Politics* (New York: John Wiley and Sons, 1957), 50–51.

10. The word "veto" does not appear in the Charter. A substantive decision by the Security Council, according to the Charter, requires the "concurring votes" of the five permanent members. The convention that an abstention by a permanent member does not invalidate a decision is an informal amendment to the Charter, achieved by consensus in practice.

11. Ernst B. Haas, "Words Can Hurt You: Who Said What to Whom About Regimes," in "International Regimes," ed. Steven D. Krasner, *International Organization* 36, 2 (Spring 1982): 241.

12. John W. Sewell and I. William Zartman, "Global Negotiations: Path to the Future or Dead End Street," in *Power, Passions and Purpose: Prospects for North-South Negotiations*, ed. Jagdish Bhagwati and John Gerard Ruggie (Cambridge, Mass.: MIT Press, 1984), 83. See also Robert L. Rothstein, "Regime-Creation by a Coalition of the Weak: Lessons from the NIEO and the Integrated Program for Commodities," *International Studies Quarterly* 28, 3 (September 1984): 310.

13. See also Karen A. Mingst, "The Multilateral Development Banks: Dominance and Dependency in United States Foreign Policy," prepared for delivery at the 1983 Annual Meeting of the American Political Science Association, The Palmer House, September 1–4, 1983, 20; Helge Ole Bergesen, "Norms Count, but Power Decides," paper prepared for the 25th Annual Convention of the International Studies Association, Atlanta, March 27–31, 1984, 11. Onuf described a "network" of lawyers in referring to the "tight community" of members of the International Law Commission and foreign office legal personnel. See Nicholas Greenwood Onuf, "International Codification: Interpreting the Last Half-Century," in *International Law: A Contemporary Perspective* (Studies on a Just World Order, No. 2), ed. Richard Falk, Friedrich Kratochwil, and Saul H. Mendlovitz (Boulder, Colo.: Westwood Press, 1985), 274–75.

14. See also Nathaniel M. McKittrick, "The World Bank & McNamara's Legacy," *The National Interest* 4 (Summer 1986); and Kendall A. Stiles, "A Glimpse Inside the IMF: Some Observations on Staffing, Power and Debt Negotiations in the International Monetary Fund," Paper prepared for delivery at the 1985 Annual Convention of the International Studies Association, Washington, D.C. March 5–9, 1985.

15. Jacobson et al., "National Entanglements."

16. Although no attempt has been made to arrive at ratios of relative growth, comparing that of the UN agencies with non-UN international agencies, bilateral diplomatic relations, or national governments, it is possible that, relatively, there has been decentralization in the sense that, even though allocative authority has grown in the UN system, it has grown more in national governments and in bilateral relations. Moreover, the accrual of allocative powers by international organizations no doubt

involves considerable dispersion among UN and other international bodies. See Finkelstein, "Shared Power."

17. Franck has this right. See Thomas M. Franck, *Nation Against Nation: What Happened to the U.N. Dream and What the U.S. Can Do About It* (New York: Oxford University Press, 1985), 188.

18. Forsythe, p. 248.

19. Finkelstein, chap. 1 above, p. 7.

20. Robert W. Cox and Harold K. Jacobson, eds., *The Anatomy of Influence in International Organization* (New Haven, Conn.: Yale University Press, 1973), 11. That is not the same as saying that all implementation of programs is "operational." Much program implementation is "programmatic" and has to resolve undecided issues of principle, set guidelines, and allocate resources among subprograms or projects and among recipients. Even so, it is predominantly centralized and predominantly carried out by agency staffs. See Fobes, "Interaction of Administration and Politics," 5.

21. Donald J. Puchala, ed., *Issues Before the 39th General Assembly of the United Nations: 1984–1985* (New York: United Nations Association of the United States of America, 1984), 29.

22. Franck, *Nation Against Nation*, 134, 135. In general, the chapter from which these citations come, "Filling the Void: Action by the Secretary-General in the Face of Inaction by Everyone Else" (chap. 8), is an excellent survey of the development, the utility, and the hazards of the Secretary-General's role going back to the Palestine case in 1948.

23. See also Javed Ansari, *The Political Economy of International Economic Organization* (Boulder, Colo.: Rienner, 1986), 57.

24. Robert Henriques Girling, *Multinational Institutions and the Third World: Management, Debt, and Trade Conflicts in the International Economic Order* (New York: Praeger, 1985), 137–38.

25. Kenneth A. Dahlberg et al., *Environment and the Global Arena: Actors, Values, Policies and Futures* (Durham, N.C.: Duke University Press, 1985), xvi.

26. But see Robert W. Gregg, "Negotiating a New International Economic Order: The Issue of Venue," in *The Future of International Organization*, ed. Rudiger Jütte and Annemarie Grosse-Jütte (New York: St. Martin's Press, 1981).

27. Although Gregg seems to demonstrate that the LDC majority paid insufficient attention to this relationship. That certainty is the conclusion of other scholars, notably Robert L. Rothstein. See also Gregg's argument elsewhere about the law of the sea that, since the benefits to be attained were not substantial, certain or imminent, the LDCs did not have to pay much attention to the states that would control access to the seabed. Therefore, in their own terms, they were justified in pursuing a strategy of ramming through the legitimacy of the new order they preferred. Gregg, "Negotiating a New International Economic Order," 64.

28. Friedheim above, pp. 176 and 184.

29. Finkelstein, chap. 1 above, pp. 8–12; Cox and Jacobson, *The Anatomy of Influence*, 420–23; and Richard W. Mansbach and John A. Vasquez, *In Search of Theory*, 102–13.

30. Dahlberg, *Environment and the Global Arena*, xvi–xvii.

31. Mansbach and Vasquez have shown how complex it is, in *In Search of Theory*, 102–103.

32. Although national security is not uncontroversial and may be an "ambiguous symbol," as is apparent in the daily headlines and as we have been told by scholars since Arnold Wolfers' famous article. See Arnold Wolfers, "National Security as an Ambiguous Symbol," *Political Science Quarterly* 67, 4 (December 1952).

33. Mansbach and Vasquez, *In Search of Theory*, 104.

34. In a letter to the author, September 23, 1985.

35. Finkelstein, chap. 1 above, p. 12.

36. Mansbach and Vasquez, *In Search of Theory*, 104. The hypothesis does not imply proof of the framework hypothesis that "high issue salience may correlate with high centralization of agency decisionmaking and action." Finkelstein, chap. 1 above, p. 12. It does, however, define salience for the purpose.

37. See, for example, Robert O. Keohane, *After Hegemony: Cooperation and Discord in the World Political Economy* (Princeton University Press, 1984).

38. Freidheim above, p. 182.

39. Just like Concurrent Resolutions of the U.S. Congress. See Lawrence S. Finkelstein, "The Politics of National Governments and International Intergovernmental Organizations: Are They Comparable?" Paper prepared for presentation at the Annual Meeting of the International Studies Association, Mexico City, April 1983.

40. Friedheim above, p. 193–94.

41. Ansari, *Political Economy*, 48–49.

42. Riggs above, pp. 53–59. The quoted passage is on p. 58.

43. "Progressive Development of the Principles and Norms of International Law Relating to the New International Economic Order: Analytical Papers and Analysis of Texts of Relevant Instruments," UNITAR/DS/5, August 15, 1982.

44. Friedheim above, p. 185. Karen Mingst made a similar point about the influence of the potential for voting in the multilateral development agencies in which formal votes are rare. See Mingst, "The Multinational Development Banks," 6.

45. The omnibus or package resolution to permit interissue bargaining and interest aggregation has also characterized UNESCO General Conference proceedings, beginning in the mid-1960s. See Lawrence S. Finkelstein, "The United States and Public Policy in UNESCO," prepared for the Annual Convention of the International Studies Association, Philadelphia, March 18, 1981, 11.

46. Friedheim, p. 184.

47. Gidon Gottlieb, "Global Bargaining: The Legal and Diplomatic Framework," in *Law-Making in the Global Community*, ed. Nicholas G. Onuf (Durham, N.C.: Carolina Academic Press, 1982), 109–10.

48. Fobes, "Interaction of Administration and Politics."

49. Christer Jönsson, "Interorganization Theory and International Organization: An Analytical Framework and a Case Study," *International Studies Quarterly* 30, 1 (March 1986).

50. Gregg above, p. 140.

51. Franck has recently emphasized this. See Franck, *Nation Against Nation*, 100–103.

52. Fobes, "Interaction of Administration and Politics," 6.

53. Richard Williams agrees. See "U.S. Multilateral Diplomacy at the United Nations," *Washington Quarterly* 9, 1 (Summer 1986): 5–18. See also "Required Reading: When Diplomats Fail," *New York Times*, July 24, 1986, B8.

Names Index

Index

●

Contributors

●

Lawrence S. Finkelstein, the volume editor, is Professor of Political Science at Northern Illinois University and a former vice president of the Carnegie Endowment for International Peace, deputy assistant secretary of defense, acting dean of the graduate school at Brandeis University, and secretary of the Harvard University Center for International Affairs. He was a member and chairman of the board of editors of the journal *International Organization* and has been chair of the International Organization Section of the International Studies Association. His current research focuses on the politics of international organization on U.S. relations with UNESCO.

Staffan Bolin is a Ph.D. candidate at the department of political science, University of Lund, Sweden, working on a dissertation about the international politics of atomic energy.

George A. Codding, Jr., is a Professor of Political Science at the University of Colorado where he serves on the board of directors of the Center for International Relations, Center for Space Law and Policy, and Master of Science in Telecommunications Program. He is the author of *The International Telecommunication Union: An Experiment in International Cooperation; Broadcasting Without Barriers; The Federal Government of Switzerland; The Universal Postal Union;* and coauthor with Anthony M. Rutkowski of *The International Telecommunication Union in a Time of Change.*

David P. Forsythe is Professor of Political Science at the University of Nebraska where he writes on international human rights and humanitarian affairs. His latest book is *Making Morality: Congress, Human Rights and Foreign Policy* (1988), winner of the Dauer Prize.

Robert L. Friedheim is a Professor of International Relations and Director of the Sea Grant Program at the University of Southern California, Los Angeles. He has written extensively about law of the sea issues.

Leon Gordenker is Professor at the Graduate Institute of International Studies, Geneva. He was for many years professor of politics at Princeton University and a research associate at the Center of International Studies. His publications include *The UN Secretary-General and the Maintenance of Peace; The United Nations in International Politics; International Aid and National Decisions;* and, most recently, *Refugees in International Politics.*

Robert W. Gregg is Professor of International Relations, School of International Service, American University. He is a former chairman of the political science department at Syracuse University and a former dean of the School of International Service at American University; he has also served as a special assistant to the assistant secretary of state for international organization affairs. He has written on international administration, international drug control, the UN's regional economic commissions, the New International Economic Order, and other issues of multilateral cooperation. Themes addressed in this essay were first developed during a Ford Foundation fellowship when he was based at the United Nations Institute for Training and Research.

Alan M. James has been Professor and Head of the Department of International Relations at the University of Keele, Staffordshire, since 1974. Before that he taught at the London School of Economics. He has been a Rockefeller Research fellow at the Institute for War and Peace Studies at Columbia University. He has also been a visiting professor at the School of International Studies, Jawarhalal Nehru University, New Delhi, and at the Department of International Relations at the University of Ife, Nigeria. He was chairman of the British International Studies Association for four years. He has published voluminously about United Nations and other peacekeeping, including *The Politics of Peacekeeping* (1969) under the auspices of the International Institute for Strategic Studies. He is at work on a new study on the same subject for the International Institute. His most recent book is *Sovereign Statehood* (1986).

Christer Jönsson is Research Fellow with the Swedish Council for Research in the Humanities and Social Sciences at the Department of Political Science, University of Lund. He is the author of *Soviet Bargaining Behavior* (1979), *Superpower: Comparing American and Soviet Policy* (1984), and *International Aviation and the Politics of Regime Change* (1987) as well as several articles in edited volumes and journals.

Robert S. Jordan is Professor of Political Science at the University of New Orleans. His chapter for this volume was written while he was distinguished visiting professor at the Naval War College, Newport, Rhode Island, in 1984–86. (Responsibility for the chapter rests with the author, and not the Naval War College.) He was director of research of the United Nations Institute for Training and Research and is a past chairman of the International Organization Section of the International Studies Association. His most recent books include: co-author with Werner Feld, *International Organizations: A Comparative Approach* (1983); editor and contributor, *Dag Hammarskjöld Revisited: The UN Secretary-General as a Force in World Politics* (1983) and *The United States and Multilateral Resource Management* (1985); coauthor with Werner Feld, *Europe in the Balance: The Changing Context of European International Politics* (1985); and *Generals in International Politics: NATO's Supreme Allied Commander, Europe (1987)*.

Ronald I. Meltzer is Professor of Political Science at the State University of New York in Buffalo. His recent publications have been about structural reform in the UN system and issues of international trade.

Donald J. Puchala is the Charles L. Jacobson Professor of Public Affairs at the University of South Carolina and director of the University's Institute of International Studies. He is coauthor (with Raymond Hopkins) of *Global Food Interdependence* (1980) and was for five years editor of *Issues Before the United Nations General Assembly*.

Robert E. Riggs is Professor of Law in the J. Reuben Clark Law School of Brigham Young University. He has in progress, with Jack Plano, a revision of their text, *Forging World Order;* he also has coauthored with I. Jostein Mykletun, *Beyond Functionalism: Attitudes Toward International Organization in Norway and the United States* (1979).

Michael G. Schechter is Assistant Dean of International Studies and Programs and Professor of International Relations at Michigan State University. He has been chairperson of the International Relations Field of James Madison College at MSU. A former intergovernmental organization editor of the *Political Handbook of the World,* he has recently published (with Karen Mingst) "Assessing Intergovernmental Impact: Problems and Prospects" and *Assessing the Impact of Intergovernmental Economic Organization: The Case of the World Bank and Nonformal Education.*